A Place Where Success Was Expected

FINAL EDITION

**David Hartmann commissioned by
Greensboro City Schools 1927**

*"The true status of a School can be measured
by the success of its students."*
James Benson Dudley

DR. JO EVANS LYNN, Ed.D.

Copyright © 2023 Jo Evans Lynn

All rights reserved. No part of this book may be reproduced or transmitted in any form or by any means, graphic, electronic, or mechanical, including photocopying, recording, taping, or by information storage retrieval system, without the permission, in writing, from the publisher except in the case of brief quotations embodied in critical articles and reviews.

Published by This 1 Matters Foundation, Greensboro, North Carolina 27406

Notice: The information in this book is true and complete to the best of our knowledge. In some cases, it is an anthology of news articles, biographies, and obituaries of graduates, teachers, and administrators of James B. Dudley High School. It is offered without guarantee on the part of the author, the Publishers, or the first-person resources. The author, Publishers, and first-person resources disclaim all liability in connection with the use of this book.

Cover Design: "A Collage of Success" by Jo Evans Lynn.

ISBN

Dedication

This book is dedicated to every past, present and future student, teacher, and administrator of James Benson Dudley High School; our storied past has set the stage for an even more glorious future.

Acknowledgements

Special thanks to David Moore (Class of 1962) for not only encouraging me to write this book but also for the use of his Dudley High School memorabilia, without which it would have been impossible for me to do such a thorough job. I also want to acknowledge all the help that I received from Chapelle Morgan Davis (Class of 1965) in documenting her father's tenure as Dudley's band director. Carolyn Walden Munchus (Class of 1962) was particularly useful in assisting me in the documentation of Mrs. Richmond's tenure as the music teacher and choir director, Dudley's Christmas programs, other Dudley Music Department Programs, and the Visual Arts Department. Davetta Florance-Bristow (Class of 1960) also helped fill in some gaps in my research on every cultural art, the Panther's Claw Newspaper, and other student organizations at Dudley 1935-2005. I also want to thank Mr. Samuel Penn Pass (Class of 1970) for sending me pictures and information about Mrs. Penn, who was both a band director and music teacher at Dudley. Cassandra Feaster Hamilton (Class of 1965) located rare pages from the Dudley Cheer Book. Mr. Paul Gilmer's excellent research and compilation of the military service of the Class of 1965 was very helpful in completing the chapter on military service. Linda Glasgow (Class of 1963) supplied pictures and commentary about Dudley's Practical Nursing Program, which helped certify dozens of Practical Nurses through 1963. Mr. Rufus Williams (Class of 1965) offered some additions to the military section and help me finally decide on a title for the book. Special thanks to Lt. Col. Clifton Girard Johnson (Class of 1969) for his contributions to the military section and for contributing the selection that he wrote about his brother Lt. Col. Wendell "Sheik" Johnson and details about their military service and pictures. Virginia Griffin (Class of 1960) and Naaman Griffin III (Class of 1988) contributed extensive assistance in updating the book. Eddie Favors (Class of 1953) also supplied a photo and names for the 1951 undefeated State Champion Football Team and additional insight about the Dudley Scholar-Athletes of the 1950s. Joseph Craig Cotton contributed the biographical sketch about his father, Harold Charles Cotton, Sr. John Wynn supplied valuable information about the businesses in Warnersville where he grew up. The research that Veda Patterson suggested that I conduct about Roy H. Lake led not only to the inclusion of an except about Lake but also to a more in-depth analysis of James Parsons, Warmouth T. Gibbs, Jr., and the B-1 Navy Band. Joyce Spruill and Sonja Gail Cobb were also helpful in updating the information about the Women's Track and Field teams at Dudley.

Many others supplied valuable bits and pieces of this book that I want to thank all the alumni, teachers, and class historians who gave me access to their James B. Dudley High School memorabilia. Special thanks to the members of the Committee to Save-Dudley, the Classes of 1950, 1951, 1952, 1953, 1957, 1958, 1959, 1960, 1962,1963, 1964, 1965, 1966, 1967,1968, 1969, 1970, 1971, 1972,1973, 1977, 1978, 1982, 1983, 1988, 1989, 1990, 1992, 1993, 1994, 1996, 1997, 2001, 2002, 2003, 2004, 2005, 2015, 2021, and 2023 your insights, memories, and pictures helped make this book historically-actuate.

Foreword

This book aims not to simply relate historical facts; any researcher or historian could do that. Instead, the goal is to paint a picture of the lives and education of more than five generations of African Americans in Greensboro, North Carolina. I do this using a writer's voice that is a unique combination of narrative and analytical writing. As my paintbrushes, I invoke the words and insights of some of the people who lived, went to school, worked, and taught in the communities in and around James B. Dudley High School. The picture is "colored" by the experiences and emotions of growing up, working, and living as a Colored person in the South.

I was meticulous about double and triple-checking facts and dates. Whenever possible, I used eyewitness accounts or the accounts as told to close relatives or interviewers. My sources often came from newspaper clippings taken from the Future Outlook (A weekly newspaper published and distributed in the Colored Community (1941-1947, 1949, 1952, and 1958-1972). I also used The Carolina Peacemaker (1967-present) and The Panther's Claw, Dudley High School's student newspaper (1935-2005). The Greensboro News (1890) and Greensboro Record (1890)-Daily newspapers- during the period from 1909-1985- Greensboro had a morning newspaper, the Greensboro Daily News, and an evening newspaper, the Greensboro Record. Dudley High School Yearbooks (1957-2015) and the Price School Strap Book, 1922-1984 were valuable resources.

Unfortunately, many clippings were found in personal strap books and often did not include the dates or bylines. I used the content of the articles (names and events) to fix times and dates as closely as possible. If I was involved or was relatively close to the situation, I used my recollections. When my memories of an event or situation were very different from those of other informants, I went back and researched several additional sources. Sometimes I was right. Sometimes the other sources were correct. Sometimes we were both right, but specific details were a little "off." For example, I seemed to remember that Franklin McCain had graduated from Dudley, while one of my informants was confident that he had never attended Dudley. I was wrong. He did not graduate from Dudley. My informant was also wrong. He attended Dudley during his sophomore and junior years of high school until his family moved back to Washington, D.C.

There were also some "facts" that varied depending on the source and the age of the informant. When I attended Dudley, the name on my diploma and other official documents was James Benson Dudley Senior High School. I assumed that the term "Senior" was about the fact that it was a high school for the upper grades rather than a junior high school for grades 7-9. However, during my research, I learned that some of Dudley's earlier graduates resented the term "Senior" because of what they perceived as a reference to the all-white Greensboro Senior High School. Since I feel that including or deleting the word in no way alters James Benson Dudley High School's legacy, I do not use the term "Senior" in the school's

Dr. Jo Evans Lynn, Ed.D.

name. In other cases where the "facts" varied, I used the closest "first-person" resource available. When some of the facts conflicted with those presented in a printed text with quotes by Dr. Tarpley, other Dudley staff members, parents, and students, the events found in this book reflect their words and point of view rather than those "other" outside sources.

In one case, when one of my most respected sources, Dr. John A. Tarpley, appeared to contradict other known sources, additional research was required. In an article (Jenkins, 1979), when asked about high school education for Colored people in Greensboro when he arrived in 1922, Tarpley is quoted as saying, "There weren't too many accredited high schools of any kind in North Carolina at the time. Most of them were run just according to someone's notion. But they didn't have a high school anywhere in Guilford County for black folks." Since Palmer Memorial Institute, which had a high school department was open (1902) and an interview in 2007 with Mother Alberta Boyd verified a high school department at Bennett Seminary in the late 1870s, I needed to determine why Dr. Tarpley believed that neither program existed by 1922. I did not think that this was a significant issue when I wrote the first edition of the book; however, others have used Dr. Tarpley's claim to discredit the entire First Edition. I will explain my findings in a later chapter.

Although I am a seasoned researcher and am thoroughly aware of the restraints and requirements of objectivity in relating historical facts, I do not claim that the contents of this book are an impartial representation of the feelings and emotions that evolved from living and attending school in the South during the 1940s, the 1950s and 1960s. As a life-long resident of Greensboro, North Carolina, a student of three of the schools in Dudley's school district (Washington Street School, Bluford Elementary School, and Lincoln Junior High School), a 1967 graduate of James B. Dudley High School, I have a unique perspective. My experience as a teacher at Grimsley Senior High School (10 years), a teacher at Dudley High School (8 years), and a teacher and parent at Page High School (1 year as a teacher and all three of my children graduated from there) adds depth to my perspective.

I am too close to certain events to pretend to be impartial. In relating certain information, when I am using my unique perspective of a particular event or time in history, I will make this clear by using the first-person narrative.

This book is more than an attempt to present the cold, hard facts of African Americans' education in the city of Greensboro and black communities in Guilford County, North Carolina. Still, it is intended to help others see that period of history through our eyes and hearts. Our ancestors, siblings, classmates, and I lived much of the history related here, and it has "made" all of us. The segregated schools and racism of our time did not "scar" us. It tempered us and bonded us into people with a unique joint history and culture. I am unabashedly proud of the people and their accomplishments related in this book. We are Dudley, still here and proud of it! Please continue reading starting with **The Authors Notes** on page **536** so that you understand my passion for setting our history in print forever!

Changelings

Jo Ann Evans Lynn

Three things remain.
Undaunted.
Unchanged.
Through slavery
And Jim Crow
Though the fear, pain,
Hatred, and violence
Could have lynched them right out
Of us,
But it didn't.
They couldn't.
For we knew then
What we still know.
All that we were -Nubian princesses and kings,
All that we are - Changelings in a changing land,
All that we will be -Still here and finally free,
Is in us,
And ever will be.

Dr. Jo Evans Lynn, Ed.D.

Table of Contents

Preface 1

Chapter One: We Have Come: The Anti-bellum Period 5

Chapter Two: Our new Day Begun: Post Civil War Education . 10

Chapter Three: From Behind the Mask 33

Chapter Four: Striving On, A High School Is Built 50

The Man for Whom the School Was Named 51

An Educational Institution Evolves 54

Chapter Five: A Place Where Success Was Expected 60

Chapter Six: Academically Speaking 65

Chapter Seven: Petition, Again and Again, Until 80

Chapter Eight: Lessons in Governing 87

Chapter Nine: A Change is Gonna Come 93

Chapter Ten: Much More than Teachers 107

Chapter Eleven: Building Strong Men 129

Dudley's 2022 Men's Out-door Track & Field Team Makes History ... 152

Chapter Twelve: Strong Leadership Makes a Difference 155

Chapter Thirteen: Memories and Traditions 175

Chapter Fourteen: All That and Then Some 208

All that Drama (The Dudley Thespians) 208

Lift Every Voice and Sing. Till Earth and Heaven Rings (The Choral Music Tradition) 214

That Band! (The Marching Band Tradition) 219

Dudley's Longest Tenured Band Directors 225

Chapter Fifteen: Dudley-Success Personified 232

And Still We Sing: Dudley Divas 237

Sing A Song (Men of Music) 252

Dudley's Civic Leaders 268

Chapter Sixteen: For Your Willingness to Serve, We Salute You 296
    J.B.D. Muster List All U.S. Military Branches 304
    Dudley's Connection to the B-1 Navy Band 326
    Dudley's Junior AFROTC Continues 330
    Family, God, and Country 343

Chapter Seventeen: Dudley's "New Kind" of Pioneers 347
    Dudley Women's In-door and Out-door Track & Field 364

Chapter Eighteen: Dudley Graduates Come Home 390
    Some Dudley Alumni Home to Stay 407
    A New Standard- Alumni Loyalty, Commitment & Service 412
    James B. Dudley Educational & Sports HOF/HOD 413

Chapter Nineteen: Panthers in Nontraditional Roles 415

Chapter Twenty: We Mean Business 430

Chapter Twenty-One: The Fight to Save Dudley 455

First Person Resources 463

Bibliography 468

Illustrations & Picture Sources 478

Index 485

Author's Notes 536

v

Dr. Jo Evans Lynn, Ed.D.

A PLACE WHERE SUCCESS WAS EXPECTED: FINAL EDITION

Preface

Whether we were called Negroes, Colored people, Blacks, or African Americans three things sustained us through it all: pride in ourselves as a people, faith in God, and a burning desire to learn. For we knew intrinsically that the minds of people who hunger and thirst for knowledge can never be enslaved. The desire to learn through the most trying, and in the South prohibited, circumstances meant that once an opportunity to learn presented itself- we grasped it with both hands. For most Black children, going to school every day unless we were "bout dead or had a fever of 104°" was a marching order. Perhaps Booker T. Washington said it best when he stated,

> "Few people who were not right in the midst of the scenes can form any exact idea of the intense desire which the people of my race showed for education; it was a whole race trying to go to school. Few were too young, and none too old, to make the attempt to learn. As fast as any kind of teachers could be secured, not only were day-schools filled but night-schools as well. The great ambition of the older people was to try to learn to read the Bible before they died. With this end in view, men and women who were fifty and seventy-five years old would be found in the night-schools. Sunday schools were formed soon after freedom, but the principal book studied in the Sunday school was the spelling book. Day—school, night—school, and Sunday—school were always crowded, and often many had to be turned away for want of room."

Nowhere in the southern part of the United States was this hunger and thirst for knowledge better exemplified than in Greensboro, North Carolina by the people and events that led to the first fully accredited high school for African Americans in the state. This book discusses how James Benson Dudley High School could easily have met all of the criteria on the National Register of Historic Sites. For a property to be eligible for the National Register, it must meet at least one of the four National Register primary criteria. Although James Benson Dudley High School apparently met all four criteria, only one was acknowledged in its formal placement on the National Register of Historic Places: Criterion C,

Dr. Jo Evans Lynn, Ed.D.

"Design/Construction". Information about architectural styles, association with various aspects of social history and commerce, and ownership are all integral parts of the nomination. Each submission contains a narrative section that provides a detailed physical description of the property and justifies why it is significant historically with regard either to local, state, or national history. The four National Register of Historic Places criteria include the following:

- Criterion A, "Event," the property must contribute to the major pattern of American history.
- Criterion B, "Person," is associated with significant people of the American past.
- Criterion C, "Design/Construction," concerns the distinctive characteristics of the building by its architecture and construction, including having high artistic value or being the work of a master.
- Criterion D, "Information potential," is satisfied if the property has yielded or may be likely to yield information important in prehistory or history.

It may have seemed to some people from up North and from other parts of the state that the Black folks in Greensboro, North Carolina were a bit uppity about the schools in their communities. The racism, segregation, and abject poverty of the Deep South failed to "keep them in their place." They owned homes, businesses, and massive brick churches. They were masters of taking a little bit of nothing and making something special out of it. Their parents took cast-off furniture from the homes of the wealthy families for whom they worked and re-upholstered or made fancy doilies to cover worn places until they had front rooms fit for Sunday Company. Their mothers could cut one chicken into enough pieces to feed families of nine or more. In spite of the circumstances around them, their parents instilled in them a sense of pride in themselves as Black people. They fortified the determination to make better lives for themselves and their children with old sayings like,

"You're God's children, and God doesn't make any junk."
"They can put us down, but nothing can keep us down, but ourselves"
"Overcoming is about keeping on coming long after everyone would've thought you'd have given up."
"The blacker the berry, the sweeter the juice."
"It's not where you start out, but where you end up that matters."

A PLACE WHERE SUCCESS WAS EXPECTED: FINAL EDITION

Yes, their parents, encouraged them to be proud of themselves as people of color, but more importantly, their parents' cajoling, strategizing, and demanding got "real" schools for their children. Sure, at first, the schools were one room, non-graded schools and the textbooks in those schools were as rare as hen's teeth but learning still took place. The children learned how to learn.

The elders believed in that old saying, "Give a man a fish and he'll have food for a day. Teach a man how to fish and he'll have food for life."

One of the teachers at Washington Street School told all of her students on the first day of school, "Reading is the key. Once you know how to read no one can keep you from learning all that you have enough sense to want to know."

Since most of us had "good sense" we wanted to learn. And because we were a people who hungered for knowledge, even when the schools were segregated, we still had good reason to be a bit uppity about the quality of learning that took place in the schools for Colored Children in Greensboro, North Carolina.

Dr. Jo Evans Lynn, Ed.D.

Chapter One

We Have Come: The Anti-Bellum Period.

The historical significance of what more than five generations of African Americans accomplished educationally in Greensboro, North Carolina predates the establishment of the school that was eventually named James Benson Dudley High School. During the majority of the slavery period in the South, there were no public-school systems. Woodson (1919) wrote the most definitive book on the education of Negroes before the Civil War. Woodson summarized,

> The questions, however, as to exactly what kind of training these Negroes should have, and how far it should go, were to the white race then as much a matter of perplexity as they are now. Believing that slaves could not be enlightened without developing in them a longing for liberty, not a few masters maintained that the more brutish the bondmen the more pliant they become for purposes of exploitation. It was this class of slaveholders that finally won the majority of southerners to their way of thinking and determined that Negroes should not be educated. The history of the education of the ante–bellum Negroes, therefore, falls into two periods. The first extends from the time of the introduction of slavery to the climax of the insurrectionary movement about 1835 when the majority of the people in this country answered in the affirmative the question whether or not it was prudent to educate their slaves. Then followed the second period, when the industrial revolution changed slavery from a patriarchal to an economic institution, and when intelligent Negroes, encouraged by abolitionists, made so many attempts to organize servile insurrections that the pendulum began to swing the other way. By this time, most southern white people reached the conclusion that it was impossible to cultivate the minds of Negroes without arousing overmuch self–assertion. P.3

Dr. Jo Evans Lynn, Ed.D.

The state of education for most whites in the South was not much better until 1839. A 1940 edition of the *North Carolina Standard* heralded the opening of North Carolina's first public schools:

For decades, reformers had been calling for free public education in North Carolina. In 1839, the General Assembly, now under Whig control, passed the North Carolina Public School Act. The act established primary schools, today called elementary schools. Students attended these schools for only a few years to learn reading, writing and arithmetic. The law followed many of the recommendations put forward by Archibald Murphey in 1817. Each county was to provide half of the funds to run a public school, and the state would contribute the rest of the money.

Since counties were responsible for raising part of the money, the proposed legislation had to be ratified or accepted by a majority of people in the county. The bill was put to the people in the election of 1839 and was approved by all but seven counties — Columbus, Davidson, Edgecombe, Lincoln, Warren, Wayne, and Yancey. In many counties it was ratified by an overwhelming vote, demonstrating that by the 1840s there was finally widespread public support to provide free education in North Carolina.

By 1850, there would be more than 2,500 public schools in North Carolina. The schools served both boys and girls though only white students — black children would not be served by public education until after the Civil War.

It must be noted that no other source claimed the establishment of 2,500 schools during this period. C.H. Wiley, the first General Superintendent of North Carolina's Common Schools, certified far fewer common schools. In his first report on the status of the Public Schools of North Carolina in 1854, he reported,

"No. of Colleges and Universities, 2
 No. of Academies and Grammar Schools, 141
 No. of Primary and Common (County) Schools, 632
 Whole No. of Schools, Academies & Colleges, 775"

Wiley's numbers are consistent with other accounts that stated that schools for poorer whites were in short supply before the Civil War. Wealthy whites saw no reason to educate poor white children who would eventually end up as paid laborers on farms or in mills beyond the primary school level (Woods, 1942). The Southern aristocracy who owned slaves hired governesses and tutors for their young children and sent their older children abroad, to private schools or to boarding schools that were located in the larger cities and towns throughout the south.

It was against the law to teach any slave child how to read or to write. According to Woods (1942), "The laws were emphatic in forbidding any kind of education to slaves, and in the main, these laws were tenaciously adhered to especially after the Nat Turner insurrection in Virginia." It appears that these prohibitive measures were mostly successful because although there is no actual record of the education of Negroes at this time, W.E.B. DuBois (1935) estimated that short of 150,000 of about one million slaves emancipated could read and write. Although Woodson (1919) who included all people of color in numbering nearly four million (both former slaves and freedmen) in the total number of blacks living in the United States immediately after the war, his estimate of close to one million literates, is still relatively small.

Until after the Civil War, education in the South beyond the primary level was mostly limited to those who could afford to pay tuition. Stockard (1902) stated that, "David Caldwell opened for wealthy white males the most eminent of these Classical Education schools in 1766." The poorer whites who needed public education seemed unwilling to promote the issue. A Quaker, Richard Mendenhall opened the only free public school for whites in Guilford County during the last two decades of the 18th century in his store in Jamestown (Stockard, 1902). Mendenhall taught all ages of white men and boys the rudiments of an education in a night school where he provided free books and tuition (Stockard, 1902). Woods (1942) documented the poor state of public education during this period. He stated,

> "North Carolina was the only state that provided for public instruction prior to the abolition of schools during the Civil War, but there was no appropriation, and the only direct result was the establishment of the state university. It was not until 1825 that a meager beginning was made toward defraying the cost of public schools by the establishment of a literary fund."

In the long run, the burden of public instruction came to rest 66upon the local authorities. Thus, the poor whites had almost as little opportunity to learn as the colored. The significant difference was that the poor whites were complacently content to remain in their ignorant state of being, while the colored, old and young, were straining every nerve, facing every danger for the sake of a little book learning."

The general complacency about educating poor whites and blacks remained until 1875. North Carolina opened a few Common Schools or public schools in the state for whites during the 1840s. The first Common School in the Piedmont area was inaugurated in 1840 in Rockingham County. Guilford County opened its first Common School in 1841, but during the Civil War, these schools were closed (Arnett, 1955). During the Civil War and the period of Reconstruction, the children of the poorer white population went altogether without schooling. There was no facility to take care of their education, and the white parents refused to send their children to the denominational schools that were established for freed slaves, Native Americans (Catholic Schools) and their children (Woods, 1942). Most white parents did not have the funds to hire tutors for their children or to send them to private schools (Woods, 1942).

In the Stockard book, *History of Guilford County, North Carolina*, which contains 36 pages on the history of education in Guilford County, there are only two notations about the education of Negroes prior to the Civil War. In the first statement, Stockard notes that in the Minute Book of Court Pleas and Quarter Sessions 1804, on page 300: *"Ordered that a child of color, aged six, born free, named Hannah to be bound to James Dicks until she reaches the full age of eighteen years. He is to teach her to read and to give her freedom dues." P. 78* It was a common practice during this period in history that poor orphans, both black and white, be placed in homes as bondsmen. In the other notation about the education of slaves during the pre-Civil War period, Stockard states,

> From 1820 until 1830 George C. Mendenhall was the most prominent man in this section of the state lawyer, farmer, wealthy slave owner, and teacher. On his farm, Negroes were trained as special workmen: carpentry, harness making, shoemaking, and tailoring, cooking, agriculture reached a high state of perfection. The problem of the education of Negroes was solved. Pp. 81-82

The final statement in the above quote reflects what was to remain the accepted practice for the education of blacks in the South until after the Civil War.

A PLACE WHERE SUCCESS WAS EXPECTED: FINAL EDITION

However, in spite of the prohibitions against teaching slave children how to read and to write, a few slaves managed to learn these basic skills. Hester James (1860-1969), who was born into slavery, often related stories about how one of her brothers had learned more from the tutors than his young master learned. All that he learned; he secretly taught the other slave children. Another unintended source of knowledge came from the slave owners. The White Mistresses on the large plantations considered it their Christian duty to teach the slaves Bible scriptures, and many of the slaves used this knowledge to learn to read books other than the Bible (Woods, 1942). This talent for taking a fist full of flour and making biscuits "from little much"- is a unique attribute of Black folks. A few slave owners like Edward Dudley in Handover County in North Carolina started schools for the children of their house slaves (Woodson, 1890).

Many of the citizens of Greensboro were Quakers and did not own slaves. One of the most active links of the Underground Railroad in Guilford County was housed at Mendenhall Plantation in Jamestown, North Carolina.

Picture Courtesy of Mendenhall Plantation, Jamestown, N.C.

Mendenhall Plantation was once home to Quaker pacifist Richard Mendenhall. The main house is a two-story, Quaker-style home that was built in 1811. During a tour of the plantation, modern day visitors can see numerous outbuildings, as well as an example of a false-bottom wagon used to transport runaway slaves to freedom via the Underground Railroad.

Chapter Two

Our New Day Begun: Post Civil War Education

After the Civil War, according to the laws passed by the U. S. Congress in 1865 and 1866, no seceding southern state was allowed to be restored to the Union unless it formed and established a new constitution. According to the laws enacted by the Congress for the requirement of restoration to the Union, seceding states were required to meet certain standards (Woods, 1942). During the framing of the new constitutions of the seceding southern states, public school systems were included in the different state constitutions for the first time in their history (Woods, 1942). It took seceding states as long as ten years to frame their new state constitutions and to have them approved by the Congress of the United States. Although North Carolina rejoined the Union in 1868, it was not until 1875 that public schools for whites and blacks officially opened in the state (Stockard, 1902).

In the meantime, from 1866-1874, Northern men and women were sent as teachers into the South, by the different church denominations and benevolent societies to open schools for the children of the recently emancipated slaves (Johnson, 1890). Although the denominations supplied the teachers and sites for the schools, attendance was not free. Johnson (1890) documented how most of the students supplemented the cost of their education with their labor. Johnson wrote, "In most of the schools for colored people in the South assign certain hours each day in which the students are to labor. Some institutions do not spend one cent for domestic labor during the whole of the school terms." In addition to the domestic work, students worked on the school farm to supply garden products for their tables and sometimes made brick enough to put up new buildings (Johnson, 1890).

When students progressed beyond the community schools that usually ended at the equivalent of 6th-8th grade, parents paid tuition for their children to attend normal school/high school at Hampton Institute in

A PLACE WHERE SUCCESS WAS EXPECTED: FINAL EDITION

Hampton, Virginia (1868), Bennett Seminary (Founded in 1873, High School Started in 1879), and Livingstone College in Salisbury, (1879 -then called Zion Wesley Institute) (Craig, 1941). Many local blacks attended day school at Bennett Seminary. Johnson (1890) stated that for the colored schools the expense of tuition, board, lodging, laundry-work, and incidentals was over $12 per month (and in some cases it is as low as $6). These fees were paid by fathers who worked in local foundries and mills (Craig, 1941) and by mothers who performed various forms of domestic labor (Johnson, 1890). Johnson claimed, "Thousands of faithful mothers spent many weary nights at the ironing-board and washtub, to get money to help their children obtain an education." According to Craig (1941), this focus on educating their children beyond the elementary level led to 60 per cent of Colored children in communities like Warnersville and Jonesboro attending college.

After 1874, many of the schools for black children were the direct result of the parents and community leaders saving money to build their schools and hiring teachers. Craig (1941) noted that the parents in Warnersville provided housing for the teacher and her two assistants. Another example of the parents continuing to provide educational facilities beyond those supplied by the denominations is that of the Fairview Community. In 1891, the Quakers established the High Point Normal & Industrial Institute for African Americans (Eventually became William Penn High School). By 1902, the school no longer had room for all the children in the area. Black families in the southern area of the city opened Fairview School and paid for its teachers.

The determination of the former slaves to educate themselves and their children is well documented (Craig, 1941; Johnson, 1890; Woodson, 1919; Woods, 1942). Johnson (1890) noted that although less than one million of the former slaves were literate in 1866, by 1890 nearly half of the eight million Negroes in the United States, both former slaves and freedmen could read and write. Craig (1941) documented that in some black communities that number had reached over 60% by the early 1900s. In areas of Guilford County where relatively large numbers of blacks lived, churches and black leaders started schools for their children. Predominately black communities like Goshen, Poplar Grove, Terra Cotta, and Mt. Zion had one to three room schools' decades before the county started public schools. All of the schools in the county outside of the city limits of High Point and Thomasville later served as feeder schools to James B. Dudley High School. The Goshen School, which had grades 1-9, later became Rena Bullock School named for a longtime first-grade teacher at the Goshen School. Like Lincoln Junior High School and J.C. Price School, Rena Bullock School had a band and was a rival for the other two junior high schools in athletics. Rena Bullock was the only one located outside the city limits. It was located in southeast Guilford County and served grades 1-9 until 1967. After that, it was a Junior High School (Grades 7-9) until it closed in 1987 (Buchanan, 2001).

Picture Courtesy of Joseph Rodriguez

Rena Bullock School on Davis Mill Road in Guilford County.

The following picture of the Rena Bullock School's First Grade Class of 1953-54 with teacher Mrs. Dot Harris Furcron eventually became a part of Dudley's Graduating Class of 1965.

A PLACE WHERE SUCCESS WAS EXPECTED: FINAL EDITION

Picture Courtesy of the Rena Bullock Reunion 2015

Mrs. Dot Harris Furcron's First Grade Class 1953-54: Charles Gladney, Christine Haith, Jackie Shoffner, Mildred Warren, Harold Evans (standing), Carol Enzlow, Reginald Cathey, Charlie Moore, Michael Lilly, Elliot Johnson, Larry Pankey, Jimmy Headen, Howard "Pop" Hall, Ernest Isley (standing), Virginia Mark, Sylvania Rogers, Bobby Moore, Harold Enzlow, Mary Lou Goins, Nancy Owens, Tony Hall.

Yardley Warner

A Quaker Friend whose name was Yardley Warner of Philadelphia, Pennsylvania purchased about one hundred acres of land in the immediate suburbs of the southern section of the town of Greensboro in 1866. This was where most of the recently freed slaves from Guilford County and the surrounding area had come to live. He had the tract divided into lots of the dimension of 50x125 feet, which he sold for a moderate amount allowing the freed slaves to pay small portions of the fee over a period. He felt that this taught the former slaves valuable lessons about saving money and about buying homes.

Harmon Unthank
by H. Griffin

There is no doubt that Warner helped the new freedmen to make a life for themselves. However, the leadership of one of their own race, Harmon Unthank, was equally as beneficial. Harmon Unthank, a former slave, became the leader of the Warnersville Community after Warner left to establish similar communities in Tennessee (Craig, 1941). According to Craig (1941), "Older residents of the neighborhood, who were toddlers when their fathers bought lots from the Philadelphia Friends, referred to him as the boss." Unthank was one of the early purchasers of a lot in the subdivision and he helped other former slaves buy property in the settlement.

A PLACE WHERE SUCCESS WAS EXPECTED: FINAL EDITION

Picture Courtesy of the Warnersville Community Coalition

Harmon Unthank House, c.1960 at 163 West McCulloch Street

Unthank not only promoted landownership and entrepreneurship, but he also encouraged education for all ages. Craig stated,

> "These new landholders, so recently slaves who in most cases could not read or write must have been inspired to give their children the advantages of education. For the records show that the majority of them not only sent their children to the private schools which the northerners established, and the local government later took over, but to the various colleges and institutes which sprang up for higher education of the Negroes. Hampton Institute in Virginia [and] Livingston College at Salisbury were attended by many and later when Bennett College was established in Greensboro, still greater numbers studied there as day students. Many of them became teachers in their community. An instance of the type of service which was apparent in the community from the beginning extending to the second generation and is found currently in Hannah Payne's daughter, Sylvia P. Ruff. Ruff was a teacher in the Moore school of the Greensboro system, and lives with her mother on McCulloch Street in the very heart of Warnersville."

It was in fact, Unthank who gave the community its name (Craig, 1941). When he was asked one day what the name of the Colored settlement was, he could not give an answer, but after he went home and thought about it, he decided to call it Warnersville. The next day, he asked one of the teachers to paint Warnersville on a board and attached it to the schoolhouse. Once the name was published in the newspaper, it has been used for generations to honor its founder, Yardley Warner.

In Warnersville and other black communities, education stood as the key to economic elevation. Margo (1990) concluded, "Schooling expanded a black man's economic options by increasing his probability of holding a nonfarm job in the South or moving from the South. Illiterates had fewer options, and most were condemned to a life of very low incomes."

Douglas and Amanda Johnson were typical residents of Warnersville during the late 19th and early 20th century.

Douglas Johnson

Amanda Johnson

Amanda Carruthers Johnson was born about 1860 in Mecklenburg County, grew up as the oldest daughter in a family of seven children. She became a teacher and eventually moved to Guilford County. Where she taught at Percy Street School. The first graded school in the state.

Amanda's husband Douglas Johnson worked as a mail carrier and railway postal clerk and is listed as a Warnersville resident in the 1884 city directory. By the mid-1890s. the couple lived in this large two-story house at 803 South Ashe Street.

Pictures Courtesy of Greensboro History Museum

A PLACE WHERE SUCCESS WAS EXPECTED: FINAL EDITION

The Quakers or the Society of Friends, with headquarters in Philadelphia, Pa., were the first Northern denomination to send teachers for ex-slaves to Greensboro, North Carolina sometime between 1866 and 1868. Next followed the Freedmen's Aid and the Southern Educational Society of the Methodist Episcopal Church, headquarters in Cincinnati, Ohio; and the Freedmen's Aid under the Presbyterian Church, headquarters in Pittsburgh, Pa. Parochial schools were opened in the churches for Negroes of these two denominations, around 1870—1872, which had previously been established in Greensboro, a year or two after the close of the Civil War.

The Northern Lutherans in 1884 built a church in Warnersville, and also opened a parochial school in the community. Two private schools during this period were started and taught for a limited time in Providence Baptist Church and in what was named at the time Boone's Chapel of the A. M. E. Church on Regan's Street. Another group of forty charter members led by Dr. Goler organized Trinity AME Zion Church in Greensboro in 1891. The first Trinity AME Zion church was an impressive brick edifice that was known around town as "Big Zion". It was the largest brick structure owned by a black congregation in North Carolina. Many years before, around 1865, a smaller AME Zion church was built at 306 North Church Street, in Salisbury, North Carolina using the same architectural design. The church in Greensboro was demolished during redevelopment in 1966, but the church in Salisbury has been beautifully maintained in its original glory. One needs only to go to Salisbury, North Carolina to get a sense of how "Big Zion" looked.

During the years before public schools were established, missionary schools and Sunday schools served as the primary learning facilities for blacks. There were no grade levels in these early schools and school age children learned alongside adults who were learning the basics of reading, writing, and arithmetic for the first time. "Big Zion," the former site of Trinity AME Zion Church later relocated to Florida Street in Greensboro, held evening and Sunday school classes in which adults and children learned to read.

Left: Trinity AME Zion 1891-1966 "Big Zion." Redevelopment in 1966 led to the demise of "Big Zion" and other massive brick churches that existed in communities like Warnersville during this era of Black History in Greensboro.

The Palace Theater and almost every other historic landmark in the predominately Black neighborhoods that dated back to the mid- 1800s were demolished during this time. Trinity was relocated to Florida and Larkin Streets.

In 1870, when Greensboro was estimated to have a population of about 2,000 residents, one-third of whom were Colored, the town was chartered by the state legislature to become a city (Arnett, 1955). And by the new constitution, the Greensboro Public School System was originated (Woods, 1942). The City Board of Education decided that they were not financially able at the time to erect buildings for the school children of both race groups. Therefore, they were forced by the new constitution to make an arrangement with the Northern Presbyterian Board and the Society of Friends to cooperate with them in continuing the instruction of the Colored pupils in the respective places where they were taught before the State of North Carolina had inaugurated the public school system (Woods, 1942). Although the public schools of Greensboro, North Carolina continued to be segregated until the late 1960s like other public schools in the South, because of the leadership of educated freedmen, African American businessmen and White missionaries, the Negro Public Schools of Greensboro were always a cut above other schools for blacks in the South.

> The Greensboro City School System was a pioneer in public education. The charter which established a school district was ratified March 28, 1870, Section 74. The city document reads as follows:
>
> "That the corporate limits of the City shall constitute a school district, and that all taxes levied upon citizens by the State for school purposes, shall be expended in conformity with the regulations of the State, in establishing graded schools within the city, and should

this amount thus realized not be sufficient to keep the schools open eight months in the year, in that event the commissioners shall appropriate a sufficient amount of money from the funds on hand belonging to the city to mediate the deficiency."

Charles Henry Moore
Educator & Civic Leader

According to Smith (2011), "One cannot talk about public education for African Americans in the City of Greensboro without beginning with one man- Charles Moore (1855-1952)." Moore came back to his home state of North Carolina after graduating from Amherst in 1873. Moore spent the rest of his life working against educational and financial inequality. In addition to his work at North Carolina Agricultural and Technical State University, he was the first principal of the first "Negro graded school" in the state and was instrumental in helping to open the first hospital in the Negro Community of the city, L. Richardson Memorial Hospital in 1926 (Smith, 2011).

Percy Street School opened in 1875 in a one-room church. It was the first graded school in the state opening one month before the Lindsay Street School for whites. A permanent building for Percy Street School for Negro children was erected in Greensboro in 1880 five years after the first permanent graded public school, the Lindsay Street School for Whites, opened. Nevertheless, before this building was erected, Percy Street School was a functioning graded school. There were only three teachers, including Charles Moore trying to teach 150 pupils in the same room under the same roof in the St. James Presbyterian Church, where the parochial school originated years previously. From 1875 until 1880, Moore and the other teachers worked hard to teach under the most unfavorable conditions imaginable. Moore decided that the children deserved better, and he was finally successful in his many appeals to the City Board of Education in getting them to build a separate building for the Colored grade school children. The new school was a brick building of one story and three rooms situated on Percy Street. It was the first graded school building for colored children in the State of North Carolina.

Dr. Jo Evans Lynn, Ed.D.

Picture Courtesy of Price School Scrapbook, 1922-1984

The first Negro graded school which was known as Percy Street School, originally started in 1875 in a one-room church and later moved in 1880 to three one-story rooms to which a two-story front was later added. The lower back end of the above building was the original separate brick building. It was not only the first Negro graded school in the state it was also the first graded school in the state of North Carolina.

In 1891 the corporate limits of Greensboro were extended. The population had increased and, as a result, the Asheboro Street School (later known as David Caldwell School was opened. At about this same time another school for Negro children was built. This structure, commonly referred to as Old Ash Street School, was located in the southwest section of the city known as Warnersville. The Ashe Street School in Southwest Greensboro became J. C. Price School in later years.

A PLACE WHERE SUCCESS WAS EXPECTED: FINAL EDITION

Pictures Courtesy of Price School Scrapbook, 1922-1984

Above: Around 1893 the entire student body and staff of Ashe Street School pose for their yearly photograph. The school was located in the southwest section of Greensboro which is known as the Warnersville Community. **Left:** A "senior" or eighth grade class poses with teachers Reverend Lawrence (left end of first row) and Mrs. Williams (right end of back row).

Bennett Seminary also was a site where the children of former slaves were educated before the establishment of a public-school system. Bennett Seminary was founded in 1873 as a coeducational institution. Its first sessions were held in the basement of Warnersville Methodist Episcopal Church North, now known as St. Matthews United Methodist Church, in Greensboro. The school was founded through the inspiration of newly emancipated slaves. Mr. W. J. Parker served as principal. The Freedmen's Aid and Southern Education Society of the Methodist Episcopal Church assumed responsibility for support of the school in 1874. African American members of the Methodist Church at Greensboro helped raise funds for land and a school building. Contributions fell short of the goal. Lyman Bennett, a businessman from Troy, New York, donated $10,000 for the purchase of land and the erection of a building large enough to house classrooms and also serve as a dormitory. Shortly after that, Bennett died of pneumonia while seeking funds for the purchase of a school bell. The institution was named Bennett Seminary in memory of Bennett, and the first building was named Bennett Hall.

Picture Courtesy of Archives Department of Bennett College

Bennett Hall was the first Building on the campus of Bennett Seminary which later became Bennett College for Women.

Professor Edward O. Thayer, of Boston, Massachusetts, became its principal in 1877, and associated with him were two or three other teachers. During the Thayer Administration, the school grew though only local pupils were enrolled. In 1889, The Reverend Charles N. Grandison was elected president of Bennett Seminary, the first African American president. Grandison was also the first African American president of any of the institutions founded by the Freedmen's Aid Society (The Carolina Peacemaker, 1995).

During the period from 1879-1926, Bennett Seminary/College had the only normal school (program for training elementary level teachers) and high school programs for African American students within the city limits of Greensboro. The Normal School Department at Bennett Seminary began in 1879 and qualified teachers for Colored elementary schools (The Carolina Peacemaker, 1995). Most of the teachers who graduated from the normal school program were from 16-18 years of age. Although the school was coeducational at the time, most of the graduates were females. By 1901, the college department had grown from 11 in 1888 to 222 college students (The Carolina Peacemaker, 1995).

In 1926, The Women's Home Missionary Society joined with the Board of Education of the Church to make Bennett College in Greensboro, N.C., a college for women. At that time, both the coeducational normal school and the public high school for Negroes were moved to other sites. The females in the normal school department continued in the Elementary Education Department at Bennett College, and the males went to the State Normal Schools for Coloreds in other parts of the state. Most of the students in the Public High School for Negroes in Greensboro moved to Washington Street School. A few of the male students who had been attending the high school on Bennett College's Campus elected to attend North Carolina Agricultural and Technical College, which had been converted to an all-male institution during this time, 1915-1926 (Nxumalo,1995).

Although it was still co-educational, by 1922 more than two thirds of the graduates of Bennett were females.

Picture Courtesy of Archives Department of Bennett College

North Carolina opened a Normal School for White Women in Greensboro in 1891. The Colored State Normal Schools at Winston-Salem, Fayetteville and Elizabeth City were maintained by the State for the purpose of training teachers for the Colored elementary public schools of North Carolina. The school at Winston-Salem was established in 1895; the school at Elizabeth City in 1891, and the school at Fayetteville in 1877. Many of the teachers in the early schools for Colored children in Greensboro, North Carolina, were graduates of these programs.

For many years, Bennett also included a coeducational college program which limited the number of normal and high school students that were accepted by early 1920.

Carolina Hall was built as a male dormitory while Dr. Jordan Chavis was president (1892-1905)

Picture Courtesy of Archives Department of Bennett College

As the population of Greensboro increased, the numbers of school age children increased. Consequently, four more rooms were added to the three-room building on Percy Street. And several other primary public schools were built, but education beyond the eighth-grade or ninth-grade level was limited to those who could "get in" the limited spaces at the private Bennett Seminary.

In 1883 Guilford County adopted graded school legislation modeled on those approved by Goldsboro and Durham to ensure that special taxes for schools, including "taxes paid on white property and polls should be applied exclusively to the support of White schools only, and that the taxes paid on Colored property and polls should be applied to the maintenance of Colored schools only" (Noble, 1930). Around 1890, a complaint was made to the City Council that public-school monies were being used to support the high school/normal school department at Bennett Seminary although there were not sufficient Colored property and polls to support payments for Colored students beyond the 8th grade.

The city of Greensboro had supported the elementary program established by the Methodist Church at Bennett Seminary (College) since 1875 and extended this support to a few students who lived inside the city limits in the high school program which started there in 1879. Jenkins, (1979) documented in an article, *Dudley...50 years later*, the city's early support of high school for Negroes. He wrote, "The city didn't start such a school (a high school), at least not then, but Greensboro did pay Bennett a supplement based on the number of city residents in their program." Bennett's records document that there were never more than 12 Negro secondary students whose tuition was paid by the city. Although the high school/normal school program at Bennett continued after public payments ended, the growth and development of the Industrial Education Department (1906-1916) of Palmer Memorial Institute in Sedalia (about eight miles southeast of Greensboro) cost Bennett many of its non- seminary prep male students. Payments by the City of

A PLACE WHERE SUCCESS WAS EXPECTED: FINAL EDITION

Greensboro did not resume until after 1899, when George Adonijah Grimsley arranged to purchase the St. Agnes Catholic Church building on North Forbis Street in order to establish Greensboro High School for the White students (Byrd, 2017).

Although Palmer Memorial Institute opened in 1902, it was not until the period between 1906-1910 when the Domestic Science and Industrial Arts Departments expanded that more parents in Greensboro began to see the school as a viable option to Bennett College, Hampton Institute, and Livingston. The opening of the $150,000 Alice Freeman Palmer Building made Palmer Memorial Institute the school of choice for Greensboro's rising upper class of Blacks who could afford to pay to educate their children beyond 9th grade level. Daniel (1931) described the Palmer Building,

> The building when completed cost about $150,000. This three-story fireproof structure contains offices and classrooms with modern equipment for the various departments of the school. On the lower floor are the science and home economics laboratories, the practice dining room and domestic art room–all bright and well lit. The art collection, the first of any Negro school in the South, is located here as well as the school library and auditorium. The auditorium contains two hundred and thirty seats, which cost three dollars apiece. Individuals paid for these seats and named them, thereby giving inspiration to each student who occupies one. As a result of these struggles, the Alice Freeman Palmer Building, the most modern Negro school building in North Carolina at that time, was dedicated on April 9, 1922.

Picture From Women Builders 1931

Alice Freeman Palmer Building 1922

Dr. Charlotte Hawkins Brown was ahead of her time. Long before Rosa Parks sat down on the bus, Dr. Charlotte Hawkins Brown, the founder of Palmer Memorial Institute, (A private boarding school for Blacks) would drive up to the Paragon Restaurant on Bessemer Avenue and demand to be served. It was the forties and segregation was the Law of the Land.

John Harris, a deacon recalled for a Black History article in the *At the Wells* monthly newsletter at Wells Memorial COGIC (February 2006),

Dr. Charlotte Hawkins Brown, 1918

"She drove up in a big car and suddenly all the other car hops had to go to the bathroom. I wondered why they were letting the "new kid" get one of the cars that was sure to leave a big tip. I soon found out—Dr. Brown was big trouble. She would drive up to the front of the restaurant and she would not leave until she was served. We had a back door where black people could be served, but she wouldn't go there. She almost got me fired. My boss called me in after I took her special order—a chicken salad sandwich on toast with brown bread. Mr. Claude Bailey, the owner, told me to tell her to go around to the back. But I told him that since she and I were the same color. It didn't feel right for me to tell her that. Since he never saw fit to tell her himself, I continued to serve her.

The school that she founded is now a museum, a National Historic Site, and a state park, but perhaps her greatest legacy is her spirit of equality. All of her students learned, "there is nobody better than you unless you allow them to be" (Harris, 2006).

In the twenty-first century, it is easy to see why a strong Black woman with such an attitude was so unpopular with the predominately male Black educational establishment in Guildford County. For many years, they summerly dismissed Brown and her school, although the reputation of Palmer Memorial Institute continued to grow among Blacks throughout the nation.

A movement began that would change Greensboro's limited support of Negroes at the secondary level started with a report on the status of education for Blacks in North Carolina in 1916. Charles Moore's 1916 inspection and report on rural schools in North Carolina was groundbreaking and showed that thousands of public dollars earmarked for the education of black students had gone instead to build schools, hire teachers and increase resources for white students (Moore, 1916). Wherever Moore traveled, he encouraged people in African American communities to "take charge" of educating their children by demanding that tax money is spent on their children and by becoming better educated themselves. This kind of self-determination and willingness to "stand-up" for a proper education for

A PLACE WHERE SUCCESS WAS EXPECTED: FINAL EDITION

children of color has continued in predominately Negro communities for over five generations.

The earliest planned neighborhood for blacks in the state, the Warnersville Community, was bustling with businesses and churches with workers and members who were driven to have their children better educated. The main streets in the Warnersville community boosted all of the businesses that this self-contained community needed, and the churches were some of the largest brick edifices for worship owned by blacks in the state.

Picture Courtesy of the Warnersville Community Coalition

800 Block of Ash Street in Warnersville

By the 1960's many of the businesses along the 800 Block of Ashe Street had been serving the community for several generations.

(Left) **St. Matthews United Methodist Church** which was located at 601 Ashe Street was organized in 1866. It has the distinction of being the oldest and largest African American Church in the Western North Carolina Conference of its denomination. Members have always been dedicated to the educational, civic, and social life of the community. In 1873, Bennett College was organized in the basement of St. Matthews. The church organized the first Boy Scout troop (#441) for African Americans in Greensboro.

(Left) **New Zion Missionary Baptist Church** which was founded in 1897. It was located at 1127 S. Cedar St. and has remained a major contributor to the community even when it was relocated to Asheboro Street (Now Martin Luther King Blvd.). The church built another beautiful edifice at 908 Martin Luther King Blvd in 2016. The church's many community outreach ministries include: A Food Bank, a Prison Ministry, and a Health and Wellness Ministry.

(Left) **Shiloh Baptist Church** founded in 1892 at 730 Ashe Street was one of the largest African American congregations in North Carolina. Its pastors have always served as both religious and civic leaders. The church was relocated to South Elm-Eugene Street but has continued to serve the community with scholarships and many other humanitarian programs.

Pictures Courtesy of the Warnersville Community Coalition

There was also a thriving Negro community in southeast Greensboro that included several churches and businesses that were owned and operated by Blacks. Many of the neighborhoods of the 1880s, near downtown, were not as segregated as they came to be later, and black and white families lived in the same areas. One such area was the one that developed on East Market Street around Bennett Seminary (Bennett College). Such prominent white citizens as Mayor A.P. Eckel lived on the southeast corner of Washington and Davie Streets and Ralph Gorrell, a grandson of the man who provided the site for Greensboro, also chose the southeast for his home. The first paved street in the Negro community was named Gorrell Street. It was around 1926 when the last of the prominent white families moved out of the neighborhood to the Irving Park Community that was under development along North Elm Street (Fripp, 1998).

Less affluent neighborhoods also cropped up. The Cones created villages around Proximity and White Oak Mills and built a separate village for black employees that was called East White Oak (Fripp, 1997). A one room grade school was established there in 1887 for grades 1-6. In 1916, East White Oak School was built at 1801 10th Street. Few students could afford schooling beyond this point, and they were not encouraged to do so since boys and girls usually started working in the mills or in the homes of wealthy families when they were about the age of fourteen.

A PLACE WHERE SUCCESS WAS EXPECTED: FINAL EDITION

Picture: Benjamin Filene

East White Oak School, built in 1916

Pictured above is East White Oak School. Built in 1916, it was later used as East White Oak Community Center. It is a historic school building for African American students. One-story additions were constructed in the 1920s or 1930s to form a square-shaped building. The school closed in 1946 and subsequently housed a YMCA before becoming a community center. It was listed on the National Register of Historic Places in 1992.

Picture Courtesy of The Carolina Peacemaker 1995

This is a class of 3rd-4th graders. The students are: (Left to Right) **Back Row**- Geraldine Darden, Gladys Hampton, Billie Jean Mason, Beth Helen Grier, Grances Raines, Maxine Caddell, Helen McCain, teacher Sallie L. Jones. **Front Row** (Left to Right): Janie Mae Harrison, Luvenia Turner, Peggy McTier, Willie Lee Harrison, Sarah Graves, Geraldine Caddell, Clementine Caddell, Charlotte Alston, Doris Guy, Billie McGibbony.

Another thriving Black community was Terra Cotta, known to its residents as "The Pines," which was created as segregated company housing for black families that moved to Greensboro for work in the Boren Brick Plant. Owned by the Boren family, the factory encompassed the social and economic lives of the Terra Cotta residents through a company store, sponsored community baseball team, and two churches. Many former residents remember their days there fondly, something UNCG Professor Benjamin Filene said could be hard to reconcile side-by-side with the real poverty people experienced. In describing the community, Dennis L. Waddell noted,

Terra Cotta was established in the mid1880s when W. C. Boren, along with others, founded the Pomona Terra Cotta Company. Terra Cotta was similar to other mill towns that were common during the country's early industrial period. The owners laid out a community and constructed homes for the workers who labored at the plant. The community was located about five miles outside and southwest of the city of Greensboro in the unincorporated community of Pomona in Guilford County, North Carolina. The men who lived in the community were the primary labor force for the plant. They and their families lived in a company built, and company-owned wood frame or red clay blockhouses. The wood was cut from local pine trees, and the blocks of the houses were made at the Pomona Terra Cotta Company. The housing conditions were impoverished, and the homes had no toilets, running water, or electricity.

Education for Black children in this area was limited to a school in which three teachers taught all primary grade levels through 8th grade. In Pomona, John Van Lindley–who owned the Pomona Nursery and the Terra Cotta Company, and who was director of the Cotton Mill–erected a schoolhouse for the children of white mill employees at his expense (Balliett 1925; Arnett 1973:97; Greensboro Daily News, February 18, 1960). In other rural communities such as Summerfield, Mount Zion, and Pleasant Garden, small community schools such as Goshen School were operated by church denominations and community leaders until Guilford County began to open public schools for blacks in 1887. By 1904, there were 24 schools for Blacks in the county with most serving students in grades 1-9.

In 1893, the Agricultural and Mechanical College (now North Carolina Agricultural and Technical State University) opened in Greensboro on a site northeast of Bennett College. Chartered by the state in 1891, the school was temporarily located in Raleigh on the campus of Shaw University. The school's first president J.O. Crosby designed its first significant building, which was named after the school's second President, James Benson Dudley (Fripp, 1997). A new generation of better educated, professional Blacks in the community increased the need for better housing and educational facilities for Negro children in Greensboro. A group of leaders in the Black community began to appear regularly at meetings of the City Council requesting funds for a separate public high school division at Bennett Seminary. The Greensboro City Council had agreed to pay the tuition for a few (Bennett's records show that there were never more than twelve) Negro children to attend school at Bennett beyond 8th grade back in 1879. Most of the council members felt that this accommodation was more than sufficient.

A PLACE WHERE SUCCESS WAS EXPECTED: FINAL EDITION

To fully understand the changes that took place in Greensboro, North Carolina, in educating people of color during the next fifty years, one must "see" what race relations were really like. By the 1900s, a subtle shift began in how Blacks related to the inequities of racism, especially in urban areas like Greensboro. Black North Carolinians, who lived during World War I, had witnessed the beginning at the turn of the century of a "Jim Crow" society, with its pillars of legal segregation, political disfranchisement, and racial discrimination. Most were old enough to remember the feelings of euphoria and hope of the strides promised by emancipation and then Reconstruction in the 1870s. By 1900, much of those feelings had faded due to violent white racism, Democratic political subversion, and economic hardship. Nevertheless, Blacks in Greensboro and other urban areas of North Carolina forged ahead in the 1900s, building their communities within the restrictions imposed by white racism. Even during those times, they continued to push for more inclusion in the larger society.

In Greensboro, as in other parts of the Deep South, Blacks saw education as the key to progress. They worked together to pool their resources to support black schools and colleges, filling the gaps left by white philanthropy and public subsidies. While most Blacks struggled to make a living as farmers, usually as tenants and sharecroppers, urban Blacks did substantially better. Blacks working in the mills were reported to earn as much as $4.00 a week! As workers spread the word to family members and friends about this bounty, it caused a wave of African American migration to towns and cities to take industrial jobs, especially in furniture and tobacco manufacturing. Although the company housing was impoverished and the Company Stores took most of the money earned, city living was still better because it gave their children a better chance to be educated. The urban Black population also fostered the growth of the black professional class. These professionals, along with ministers and educators, became leaders in the Black communities and served as emissaries to the white power structure.

Greensboro's early-twentieth-century race relations and racial policy were relatively moderate compared to the rest of the Deep South. The white elite tolerated a degree of Black economic power, educational achievement, and even political participation, as long as white supremacy remained unchallenged, and the Black community appeared sufficiently subservient and grateful for the benevolence. By the time of World War I, urban Black civic leaders had learned the rules of the game. What historian William Chafe has termed a "progressive" system that emphasized "civilities" over "civil rights" –or proper racial etiquette over real equality–and played it as best they could. At the same time, African Americans in North Carolina and across the South recognized the oppression they lived with daily. One poem by Paul Laurence Dunbar, *We Wear the Mask*, speaks eloquently of this period of race relations and how African Americans managed to live and thrive through it all.

We wear the mask that grins and lies,

Dr. Jo Evans Lynn, Ed.D.

It hides our cheeks and shades our eyes, --
This debt we pay to human guile.
With torn and bleeding hearts we smile,
And mouth with myriad subtleties.
Why should the world be overwise?
In counting all our tears and sighs?
Nay, let them only see us, while
We wear the mask.

We smile, but, O great Christ, our cries,
To thee from tortured souls arise.
We sing, but oh the clay is vile,
Beneath our feet, and long the mile.
We wear the mask!
But let the world dream otherwise.

Chapter Three

From Behind the Masks…

So, through much of the early twentieth century, Black people continued to "wear the mask." To this generation of African Americans, World War I provided a valuable opportunity to prove to white America their worth as citizens and thus their moral claim to more rights and opportunities. African Americans served their state and nation both at home and abroad during the war. A few prominent Black North Carolinians felt it was hypocritical, however, for African Americans to sacrifice to make the world safe for democracy while forced to endure Jim Crow conditions at home. At the beginning of the war, some white editorialists worried that German spies might use similar arguments to stir up disloyalty amongst the African American population. The state's Black leaders like James Benson Dudley quickly dispelled such fears. Instead, they rallied their communities to conserve already scarce resources and to dip into already meager savings to help the war effort. In fact, Kate M. Herring (1918), the Director of Publicity for the North Carolina War Savings Committee, noted that, "Black North Carolinians have bought and have pledged to buy War Savings Stamps far more extensively in comparison with their ability than the white people."

African American labor also contributed to the war effort and tried, with limited success, to use the war to better their economic lot. Black men and women helped to keep North Carolina's tobacco factories running during the war. They also tried to obtain better, higher paying jobs in textile mills, shipyards, and other war industries that had been vacated for the duration of the war by white men. Long-standing practices of occupational segregation and discrimination, however, hampered Black advancement.

Shenk (2008) noted that Black workers were not treated fairly by the new Federal agencies that were supposed to ensure fair treatment of all wartime workers. In eastern North Carolina, the state and federal governments instituted a kind of forced labor system on African American farm workers. A new "Work or Fight" program required black women and any black men unfit for military service to work for whichever white farmer or planter local officials assigned them to for whatever wage the employer deemed fit.

In addition to their economic contribution to the war effort, African American men accounted for nearly one-quarter of North Carolina's military role (142,505 of the 480,491 men registered for the draft in the state, and 20,350 of the 86,457 Tar Heels mustered into service). The fact that these numbers roughly parallel the African American percentage of the population suggests that local Selective Service boards were not discriminatory in their application of the draft as they were in the Deep South. There, local draft boards sometimes protected White men by registering black draftees in their place. Both the U.S. Army and Navy relegated black servicemen to segregated companies commanded by white officers. African American troops also endured the added burdens of the Army's discriminatory supply and pay policies.

The experience of World War I changed the African American community and race relations across the country, and to a greater degree in Greensboro and other urban areas than in other parts of North Carolina and in the Deep South, over the next decade. After the Armistice in November 1918, many African Americans heeded W. E. B. DuBois' charge not just to return from fighting, but to "return fighting" against Southern racism. At an Emancipation Day ceremony in Raleigh in January 1919, a crowd of 3,000 passed resolutions condemning lynching and attacking segregation. Through the 1920s, the annual commemorations of emancipation as well as the Armistice ending World War I remained occasions for rallies. Editorials in the Black press in Greensboro, Durham and Raleigh frequently called for improvements in, if not an end to, the Jim Crow system.

White North Carolinians listened with concern to the outbursts of Black protests after the war, but they managed to preserve both white supremacy and the myth that Black North Carolinians were contented with legal segregation and Jim Crow. North Carolina's postwar reconsideration of racial relations and racial policy took place in the context of the nationwide "Red Scare" between 1918 and 1921, touched off by fears of communist and foreign subversion.

North Carolina did not experience the waves of abuse of Black veterans and lynching of Black men that swept across the South and, with one notable exception, was spared the race riots that erupted elsewhere in the country at the end of the war. The exception occurred in Winston-Salem on November 17, 1918. A white female textile worker claimed she had been raped and beaten by a Black man. Police apprehended a suspect who was an out-of-town vagrant. The man protested his innocence. As was the pattern in such cases across the South, a white lynch mob converged on the jail intent on meting out their rough justice. The beleaguered constables found an unusual and unwanted ally in a contingent of armed Black men who rushed in to fend off the white mob. In the ensuing riot, five men were killed, and several Black businesses and homes were destroyed. The Forsyth County Home Guard, bolstered by Home Guards from around the state, intervened after a few days to restore order. The black vagrant survived and was proven innocent.

For the most part, after World War I, local race relations and racial policy in North Carolina were determined, as they had been before the war, by the "better classes" of both races. Black and white businessmen, educators, and civic leaders met to ensure that the channels of civil communication and white philanthropy remained open while the underlying structure of segregation and discrimination remained intact.

In 1922 the school that was to become what one resident of that area called "the beating heart of Warnersville" replaced the Old Ashe Street School. The Joseph Charles Price School was named after a Black religious leader and educator from North Carolina. Lorcey Henderson was the first principal of the school which served students in grades 1-9 from 1922-1931. From the time it was built until David Dallas Jones Elementary School was built, J.C. Price was the primary school for Blacks in Warnersville.

Courtesy of the Greensboro Historical Museum
Mr. A. H. Peeler

In 1932 Abraham H. Peeler became principal, and only grades 3-9 were offered. Abraham H. Peeler was born in Warnersville on May 23, 1904. His father was the pastor of St. Matthews United Methodist Church in Warnersville, and his mother was a schoolteacher in the community.

Mr. Peeler received his master's degree from Columbia University and furthered his education at Ohio State University and the University of Wisconsin. He remained the principal of the school for the next 37 years, until his retirement in 1969.

Courtesy of the Greensboro Historical Museum
Joseph Charles Price School inaugural First Grade Class in 1922

Courtesy of the Greensboro Historical Museum

Joseph Charles Price School during the 1930s

In 1940, the auditorium was added to J.C. Price School. In 1942, a broadcast radio station was established under the leadership of principal Peeler. This addition made J.C. Price one of only two schools in Greensboro to have a radio station at the time. In 1946 the Education Policies Commission of the National Education Association from Washington D.C. was touring elementary schools across the nation, looking for innovative teaching methods. J. C. Price was the only school in North Carolina that they visited.

A PLACE WHERE SUCCESS WAS EXPECTED: FINAL EDITION

Mr. Peeler was very involved in other aspects of the Black community. He was one of the leaders in helping to create the first city park in Greensboro for African Americans, Nocho Park. He was also instrumental in the development of Camp Carlson in the Lake Brandt area of Guilford County, which was at the time the only camp for Blacks in North Carolina.

Picture Courtesy Warnersville Community Coalition

Melvin C. Swann

When Peeler retired in 1969, Melvin C. Swann became the principal. Before becoming principal, Swann began his career at Price as a health and science teacher in 1960. He also coached basketball, baseball, and football. Seven years later, he became assistant principal.

From 1959 until Jones School opened, Price offered grades 3-9 at the school. After Jones School opened, J. C. Price became a junior high school offering grades 7-9 until it was closed in the 1983-1984 school year.

In 1923, the Greensboro City Council finally relented to pressure applied by a group of Black business leaders. It commissioned a full public high school division for Negro Children established on the Bennett College Campus. The much larger high school program was a dramatic addition to the limited number of Black students for whom the city had paid tuition to attend high school at Bennett Seminary from 1879-1890 and again from 1899-1923. John Allen Tarpley, who had come to Greensboro in 1922 to teach biology and Latin at Bennett College, was named principal of the Negro High School Division at Bennett College in 1923.

A graduate of Wiley College in Marshall, Texas, Tarpley received a master's degree from Ohio State University and the University of Michigan and an honorary doctorate from Wiley. Since he graduated from Wiley College at 17, Tarpley was younger than some of his students at Bennett. He became principal of the Negro High School in Greensboro at the age of 22. The High School division remained on Bennett College's campus until 1926, when Bennett College began the transition from a co-educational institution that offered preparatory courses, a high school department, and a college-level curriculum to a college for women.

Dr. Jo Evans Lynn, Ed.D.

Picture Courtesy of Archives Department of Bennett College

During the years that Bennett Seminary/College was co-educational, its baseball team played games against schools such as Hampton Institute (now Hampton University) in Hampton, Virginia that had similar educational programs for Negroes. There were also similar programs in Winston Salem, Elizabeth City, and Fayetteville, North Carolina. Hampton Institute records show that team members ranged in age from 14-17 (Harper's New Monthly Magazine, 1873). Bennett Seminary/College was also renowned for the contributions made by its graduates.

From its inception, Bennett College produced outstanding graduates. Stowell (1922) wrote,
> Throughout its history, it has been characterized by the devotion of its Colored constituency to it and by the usefulness of the lives of its graduates. It records among its alumni more than twenty doctors and a goodly number of merchants, teachers, dentists, college professors, farmers, postal clerks, and others. In the turning of men to the ministry, Bennett College has an enviable record, having sent more graduates to Gammon Theological Seminary than any other school. Both of the Negro Bishops elected at the 1920 General Conference of the Methodist Episcopal Church, Bishop Matthew W. Clair, Sr., and Bishop Robert E. Jones, are listed as alumni of Bennett.

A PLACE WHERE SUCCESS WAS EXPECTED: FINAL EDITION

Picture Courtesy of Bennett College Archives

The above picture of the Student Body is shown in a narrative of Bennett College's early history as a Seminary and High/Normal school.

Another development that acerbated the need for additional educational opportunities for Blacks was the opening of a hospital near Bennett College. Charles H. Moore, a veteran Greensboro city schoolteacher for whom a city school was named, is credited with having begun the movement for a Negro hospital to serve the needs of the African American citizens of the city. Dr. S. P. Sebastian, a practicing physician who with physicians J.W.V. Cordice and C. C. Stewart had operated the private Trinity Hospital for Negroes in Detroit, Michigan, and layman Watson Law were two other Negro leaders of the pioneer group. In January of 1923, these men were included in a panel of individuals that organized the Greensboro Negro Hospital Association.

ATTRACTIVE HOSPITAL AND HOMES IN NOCHO

By Daily News Staff Photographer.

Shown above at the left is a recently finished home on Benbow Road. In the center is the L. Richardson Memorial Hospital, completed and furnished at the cost of about $150,000. The hospital is said to be the most modernly equipped of any Negro hospital in America. On the right is the home of S.P. Sebastian. Below, on the left, is a group of houses on East Gorrell Street, the one in the foreground being the home of Jesse Wright. On the right are two stucco homes recently completed on Benbow Road. (Daily News Staff, 1929)

Dr. Simon Powell Sebastian
Martha J. O. Sebastian Collection, Bluford Library and Archives and Special Collections, NC A&T State University. Used with permission.

After obtaining his medical doctoral degree from Leonard Medical School at Shaw University in 1912, Simon Powell Sebastian returned to Greensboro to practice medicine. Dr. Sebastian was employed again by A&T in 1919 to serve as college physician, filling the role left by Dr. Samuel Benjamin Jones after the First World War. With two other doctors, Sebastian opened the private Trinity Hospital for Negroes in 1918. Over a course of 4 years, Sebastian co-founded the historic L. Richardson Memorial Hospital in Greensboro

On May 28, 1927, L. Richardson Memorial Hospital opened. The hospital received donations from families in Greensboro. Mrs. Lunsford

A PLACE WHERE SUCCESS WAS EXPECTED: FINAL EDITION

Richardson's family donated $50,000.00 to assist with building the hospital. Mrs. Emanuel Sternberger contributed $10,000.00 to purchase equipment for the operating room and X-Ray Department. Additionally, donations received from the Rosenwald and Duke Funds were used to finance a nurses' residence built in 1929. The hospital which always accepted charity cases did not have an endowment and finances were always a problem. Although the old hospital was vacated in 1966 when the hospital was moved to a new facility, it served as a nursing facility until 1996. The restored building is used as a low-income apartment complex.

Shortly after the hospital opened, the Nocho Park neighborhood opened in the same area. At the time, it was considered an exclusive Black residential development. It included a 12-acre park. Nocho Park was the first recreational area set aside for the Negro community. This 12-acre area extended from Gorrell Street almost three-eighths of a mile on the east side of Benbow Road and East Side Drive. By 1951, the area was best known for the Windsor Community Center. Although the Nocho Community was planned by a White real estate firm, it was named for Jacob R. Nocho. Nocho served as the principal of the free African American school held at St. James's Presbyterian Church on Church Street between 1868 and 1872. He died in 1912. Architect F. A. Mayfield designed many of the neighborhood's homes, including the home shown on page 41.

This Nocho Park home that was built on Benbow Road in 1927 with high ceilings, front porch, dining area, and two bedrooms. It was considered a "dream" home for a new generation of better educated more affluent Blacks who bought homes in this exclusive neighborhood.

A colloquial term for this era for the Black Upper Class or anything that was first class in quality was "Benbow Road good." King V. Cheek a 1954 graduate of Dudley, described his family which was typical of this community during the early 1900s-1960s in a 2011 article in History Makers,

> "Our parents instilled respect for education in each of their five children. Great things were expected of us. But no one could foresee

that my brother James and I would grow up to lead some of the major educational institutions in the land.

I was named after my father, King Virgil Cheek, Sr. He was a Baptist minister. My father was a very proud person who wanted to care for his family in ways that being the minister of a small Baptist church would not allow. So, he worked with the Railway Express Agency most of his working years. My mother is Lee Ella Williams Cheek. She was a schoolteacher and later became an insurance broker. She was the first licensed black female insurance broker in North Carolina." (p.1)

With public schools like Washington Street School (1914), and denominational schools Bennett Seminary/College High School/Normal School (1879) and St. Mary's Catholic School (1928), the children in the Nocho Community received a very good educational foundation. King V. Cheek spoke fondly of his education at Washington Street School. Cheek (2011) wrote,

"School was very important in our family. All of my teachers influenced me because, you see, at that time, teachers were icons, and black teachers were almost spiritual figures and not just confined to the classroom. They were part of your life. They visited your home, met with your parents. They were concerned about all dimensions of your development.

In the second grade, I had a teacher, Mrs. Baker, who was very suspicious of me and my talents. She convinced the system to give me tests, which I didn't want to take. And I only took them because her pretty eyes convinced me to. That's when I discovered I was a sexist at age seven because she looked at me with her pretty eyes, and I couldn't resist. So, I took the test, and I scored off the charts, which really surprised them." (p.2)

Most of the students at Washington Street School and the other schools during this time could relate stories about teachers who went beyond the usual expectations of the job. It should be noted that "success" for the five Cheek children, while all were based on their education in the segregated schools of that period, advanced along different lines. Their only sister Helen Cheek Dean used her skills as a seamstress to work in one of the most exclusive department stores Downtown. She also made prom dresses, cotillion gowns, and wedding dresses for three generations of women in the community.

Within the same general area of the Nocho Community lay the business heart of the east Greensboro section of the Black community. The

A PLACE WHERE SUCCESS WAS EXPECTED: FINAL EDITION

railroad underpass at East Market Street was the dividing line between Downtown and a thriving Black community, complete with stores, churches, a theater, restaurants, and homes. One of the most popular restaurants in the area was the Half Moon Cafeteria at 1109 East Market Street. At the address, 1909, East Market was the Jones Grocery that was managed by Osbey Smith and his wife, Elizabeth. J. W. Barksdale and W.V. Hinnant owned the store. Perhaps the most popular spot in the area was the Palace Theatre at 907 East Market Street. It was a major gathering spot in the community until it was razed for redevelopment in 1962.

I attended the Palace Theater regularly as a child with my parents. My father loved Westerns and although Friday night was his night on the town, Saturday night was usually reserved for a family outing to the latest feature at the Palace Theater. I do not think my father attended a movie theater after The Palace Theater was razed in 1962. He refused to pay his "good money" as he called it to attend the theaters for Whites Downtown even though there were separate entrances and balcony seating for blacks at the Carolina and National Theaters.

G.H. Fripp, "The Palace Theater", **Greensboro**, p. 92

The Palace Theater was an important gathering spot for Black couples and families until 1962.

I wrote a fictional account of my only visit to the Carolina Theater while it was segregated in my book, *The Promise of Friendship*. Although the characters were fictional and it was my brother Phillip who got us thrown out rather than the fictional character, the feelings that that particular incident carved into my spirit were real.

During the time that the High School for Negroes in Greensboro was housed at Washington Street School, in the original building that was two stories, a movement began to build an actual high school building for Negro children. Washington Street School had been built for 400-450 students and with 75-100 students added from the High School, the school was overcrowded. The Black community became, even more, dissatisfied with the lack of a "real" high school building for their children.

"There became an agitation on the part of the Negroes for a high school," Dr. John Tarpley told a reporter for the Greensboro Daily News in 1979. Tarpley joined with students and other leaders in the Black community in a movement to gain a high school building with a separate campus. Their first step was to use the expertise of Tarpley and other Negro educators to develop a proposal for the school. Once the group was satisfied with the program, they presented it to the superintendent of the Greensboro City Schools, Fred Archer. As Dr. John Tarpley recalled in an article written by Jim Jenkins for the Greensboro Daily News,

> "We got with them and began to show them why they should get a high school for black folks, but they didn't have enough energetic support for it. But Fred Archer said he thought it would be a good time to get a double-headed sort of thing. So, he used it (the proposal presented for the high school for Negroes) to get a white high school."

As Tarpley remembered it, the proposal for a separate high school for Blacks in effect resulted in the building of Dudley and also what became Greensboro Senior High School and is now Grimsley Senior High School. Perhaps a timeline comparing the establishment of these two schools, which are the oldest public high schools in Greensboro, will crystalize how extraordinary this development was for people less than a full generation out of slavery.

A PLACE WHERE SUCCESS WAS EXPECTED: FINAL EDITION

Comparative Analysis of the Post-Civil War Establishment Factors for the Two Earliest Greensboro Public High Schools

YEAR	EVENTS LEADING TO THE HIGH SCHOOL for NEGROES in GREENSBORO Now: James Benson Dudley High School	EVENTS LEADING TO GREENSBORO SENIOR HIGH SCHOOL Now: Grimsley Senior High School
1866	Post-Civil War, public school systems are included in Southern states' constitutions for the first time. A few public schools for whites had opened in North Carolina in 1840, but those closed during the Civil War.	
1867	The Quakers are first Northern denomination to send teachers for former slaves to Greensboro	
1868	North Carolina officially reenters the Union. However, like other Southern States, North Carolina drags out the process of establishing a state-run public-school system for the next eight years.	
1870	The Freedmen's Aid and the Southern Educational Society of the Methodist Episcopal Church, headquarters in Cincinnati, Ohio establish Parochial schools in the churches for Negroes.	Post-Civil War Federally mandated public schools in North Carolina remain in the developmental stage. The children of wealthy white families attend private boarding schools.
1872	The Freedmen's Aid under the Presbyterian Church, headquartered in Pittsburgh, PA. establishes Parochial schools in the churches for Negroes	
1873	**Bennett Seminary was founded as a coeducational institution. Its first sessions were held in the basement of Warnersville Methodist Episcopal Church North in the Warnersville Community. The school was founded through the inspiration of newly emancipated slaves. Mr. W.J. Parker served as principal**	
1874	The Freedmen's Aid and Southern Education Society of the Methodist Episcopal Church assumed responsibility for support of Bennett Seminary in 1874.	

1875	**The Percy Street School, a graded school for Negroes, began a month before the Lindsay Street School in a one-room church becoming the first graded school in North Carolina.**	Greensboro establishes Lindsay Street School, the state's first permanent public graded school for whites. In graded schools, unlike those that came before, education and skill sets are broken into several levels or grades.
1877		St. Agnes Catholic Church School opens to serve the Native American population of Guilford County.
1879	Normal School and High School Departments open at Bennett Seminary to train teachers for black children. **Due to a lack of funds, Greensboro City Council agrees to pay expenses for Negro Students who lived inside the city limits to attend Normal (High) School at Bennett.**	
1880	**A local tax supplement funds 120 days of public-school instruction.**	
1881	Jesse R. Wharton becomes the first Guilford County Superintendent of Schools. The position is primarily responsible for guiding and managing the school tax fund. The hiring and firing of teachers and principals of schools and most other school-based decisions remain in the hands of the local community. This management system will continue mostly unchanged but not without strife well into the 20th Century.	
1883	Guilford County adopted graded school legislation modeled on those approved by Goldsboro and Durham to ensure that special taxes for schools, including "taxes paid on white property and polls should be applied exclusively to the support of White schools only, and that the taxes paid on Colored property and polls should be applied to the maintenance of Colored schools only" (Noble, 1930)	
1885	State legislature establishes boards of education to supervise the state's public-school system. Guilford County's first board of education consisted of Professor J.A. Holt, Dr. J.A. McLean, and Dr. Nereus Mendenhall.	
1890	**Greensboro City Council discontinues paying (Bennett's records show that there were never more than twelve) for Negro children to attend public high school at Bennett Seminary.**	

A PLACE WHERE SUCCESS WAS EXPECTED: FINAL EDITION

1891	The Agricultural and Mechanical College (now North Carolina A&T State University) chartered by the state in 1891, the school was temporarily located in Raleigh on the campus of Shaw University. In 1891 the Asheboro Street School (later known as David Caldwell School was opened.	
1892	Another school for Negro children was built. This structure, commonly referred to as Old Ash Street School, was located in the southwest section of the city known as Warnersville.	
1893	The Agricultural and Mechanical College opened in Greensboro on a site northeast of Bennett College.	
1897	Public graded school for African American students opens at the High Point Normal and Industrial Institute (later becomes William Penn High School) with about 169 students attending.	
1899	**Greensboro resumes payments to Bennett's High School Department for Negro children. Had originally made payments from 1879-1890.**	Superintendent George A. Grimsley buys the high school department at St. Agnes Catholic Church School to add high school courses for White students at Lindsay Street School. Since 1877, the school served the native American population of Guilford County. Native American students could no longer attend high school there after the purchase by Grimsley.
1902	Having outgrown the capacity of the High Point Normal & Industrial Institute, an African American school established by the Quakers, families in the southern area of the city open Fairview School. Charlotte Hawkins Brown founded Palmer Memorial Institute in Sedalia, near Greensboro, which became one of the finest private college preparatory schools for black students in the United States. It closed in 1971	

1904	24 Public Schools for Negroes open in the Guilford County School System.	87 Public Schools open for whites in the Guilford County School System.
1907	Guilford County provides some high school courses for black students. High school for Negro children already existed in Sedalia, High Point, and on the campus of Bennett College.	Guilford County Board of Education announces the locations of the first high schools. Jamestown, which would serve the western area, and Pleasant Garden, which would serve the east. These would-be additions to schools that already existed in these communities. The Pleasant Garden School had already established some high school courses for students.
1914	Washington Street School opens for grades 1-9.	
1915	North Carolina Agricultural and Technical College starts a Normal School Program for Colored men to learn to teach elementary school children.	
1919	**Greensboro passes a Jim Crow ordinance that prohibits black people from purchasing homes and establishing businesses in white-dominated blocks.**	
1922	The J.C. Price School "the beating heart of Warnersville" was established. Lorcey Henderson was the first principal of the school which served students in grades 1-9 from 1922-1931 and 7-9 as a junior high school from 1932-1987.	
1923	The Greensboro City School Board establishes a full high school for blacks at Bennett College naming John A. Tarpley as the principal.	
1926	Bennett Seminary becomes Bennett College for Women, and the high school moves to Washington Street School and A&T (Males Only).	
1927	Tarpley and a group of concerned citizens present Superintendent Fred Archer a plan and curriculum for a high school for Negroes. Archer uses the plan as leverage to get the city to build a high school for whites and one for blacks. David Hartmann commissioned to design both schools.	

A PLACE WHERE SUCCESS WAS EXPECTED: FINAL EDITION

1928	The Daughters of Charity sent three sisters who began the teaching apostolate in September 1928 at St. Mary's Parish School.	
1928	**Building begins on both schools designed by David Hartmann**	
1929	**The much smaller new edifice opens in January of 1929 and the school is named James Benson Dudley High School in December.**	The much larger new edifice for Greensboro Senior High School is ready to open in the fall of 1929.

Figure 1. The events leading to the establishment of the two oldest public high schools in Guilford County.

The information in **Figure 1** comes directly from several primary sources: The Financial Records of Bennett Seminary/Bennett College during the presidencies of Edward O. Thayer (1877-1881), the Reverend Wilbur F. Steele (1881-1889), the Reverend Charles N. Grandison (1889-1892), Dr. Jordan Chavis (1892-1905), the Reverend Silas A. Peeler (1905-1913), Professor James E. Wallace (1913-1915), and the Reverend Frank Tigg (1915-1926). A master's thesis that was written by Maurice F. Woods in 1942 titled *A History of Education in Greensboro, North Carolina: As It Pertains to the American Negro in Greensboro, North Carolina* at Atlanta University in Atlanta, Georgia was also helpful. A 1979, article by Jim Jenkins, Dudley…50 Years Later, also supplied valuable documentation. A History of Greensboro/Grimsley Senior High School by Peter Byrd of the class of 1974; and an Updated History of Dudley High School by Claudette Burroughs-White were both useful resources.

Dr. Jo Evans Lynn, Ed.D.

Chapter Four

Striving on…A High School Is Built

The high school first known as the High School for Negroes in Greensboro was designed and planned for an eighty-acre tract of land on the edge of the Nocho Community. Although most of the acreage was within a reasonable walking distance of the black communities, there was some grumbling. One of the first members of Dudley's staff, Vance Chavis (Jenkins, 1979) explained,

> "Many of the residents thought the school had been built too far out in the country. And there were no paved streets then. I remember we had to brush branches back from the trees to go down the road. Of course, there weren't but four automobiles going there at the time, anyway." (p. D20)

The school, like Greensboro Senior High School, now Grimsley Senior High School, was designed by noted Greensboro architect, Charles C. Hartmann. Construction started in 1928 and the school opened in 1929. The original plan consisted of one part, the three-tiered Main Building, which was built in 1928, and the future Auditorium, which was added sometime between 1929 and 1930. In spite of conflicting reports, at least, the exterior walls had been added at this point because, in a picture of the first graduating class, the Class of 1930, the graduates are standing on the outside corner of the north end of the Main Building. The original auditorium seated 1,000 on two levels and also contained a small classroom.

David Hartmann commissioned by Greensboro City Schools 1927
The Original Architectural Drawing of the High School for Negroes in Greensboro

James Benson Dudley High School was officially named on December 9, 1929, after the second president of North Carolina Agricultural and Technical College (now North Carolina Agricultural and Technical State

University). According to Dr. Tarpley, the school opened in its new building a full semester ahead of the new White school, Greensboro Senior High School (Jenkins, 1979).

The Man For Whom the School was Named: James Benson Dudley

James Benson Dudley was born into slavery on November 2, 1859, in Wilmington, New Hanover County, North Carolina. His parents John Bishop and Annie Hatch Dudley were owned by Edward B. Dudley the Governor of North Carolina from 1836 to 1841. As the child of "house" slaves of the former governor, Dudley enjoyed a less difficult childhood than other slaves (Nxumalo, 1995). The governor greatly influenced Dudley. One of the governor's ideas was that everyone should be educated Dudley took these ideas to heart, and they affected his approach to education for the rest of his life (Arnett, 1973).

James Benson Dudley

Because most of the schools in the area were shut down after the American Civil War due to insufficient funding, Dudley was not able to attend school until 1867 when the Freedmen's Bureau funded a missionary school in his area. Dudley was one of the first students to enroll. Under the tutelage and encouragement of Ella Roper from New England, he excelled in his early education. He later attended public schools when they opened in his area and learned Latin. After going through the public-school system, Dudley attended the Institute for Colored Youth in Philadelphia, Pennsylvania. For college, Dudley attended Shaw University in Raleigh, North Carolina. Throughout his education, he focused on learning to become an educator. In 1880, at age 21, Dudley passed the North Carolina state exam required to obtain a teacher's certificate. Later he attended Harvard's summer school and gained an M.A. from Livingstone College and an LL.D. from Wilberforce University (Arnett, 1973).

Dudley went straight out of college to work as a teacher in 1880. His first teaching position was in the first-grade classroom in Sampson County. The following year, while he was still only 21 years old, due to his success, he was elected principal of Peabody Graded School in Wilmington, North Carolina. The school at this time was described as being one of two "very good public schools for African Americans" in the area. He spent the next fifteen years teaching in Wilmington. He was also President of the State Teachers' Association for Negroes for six years. For twenty years, he was the foreign correspondent for the Grand Lodge of Masons. Like many former slaves and freedmen, Dudley identified with the party of Abraham Lincoln and during his lifetime, the Republican Party remained the party of liberal carpetbaggers (Northerners who moved to the South after the Civil War). He also represented the Republican Party at several conventions. In 1896, he was selected to attend the Republican National Convention in St. Louis, Missouri. As an influential person in the Republican Party, as well as having connections with the Farmer's Alliance, he helped to pass a bill in 1891 that led to the establishment of The Agricultural and Mechanical College for the Colored Race, which was later renamed North Carolina Agricultural and Technical State University.

In 1895, the North Carolina legislature appointed Dudley to the Board of Trustees for the college. Later that year he was made the secretary of the board, a position he served in until 1896 when the President, John O. Crosby, resigned. In his letter of resignation Crosby said, "I have taken the school as far as I can. I am a builder, not an educator. It is time for a visionary to take us into the next century" (Nxumalo, 1995). At the next meeting of the board, Dudley was voted unanimously to become the second President of the college and to be the educational visionary to take the college into the twentieth century. Dudley inherited a school with only two buildings and 58 students. While President, Dudley focused on modifying the curriculum. He believed that it was best to aim the curriculum towards jobs that were currently available. He wanted the men and women who attended his college to be able to get jobs and "raise the standard of living among their people." His additions to the curriculum included the teaching of carpentry, wood turning, bricklaying, blacksmithing, animal husbandry, horticulture and floriculture, mattress and broom making, shoe making, poultry raising, tailoring, electrical engineering, and domestic science. Dudley also added an entire teaching department to the school that taught pupils to be teachers while placing special emphasis on "courtesy, manners, and an appreciation of culture in general" (Nxumalo, 1995).

In 1912 Dudley, with the help of the director of the Agricultural Division of the College, Professor J.H. Bluford, organized the Farmers' Union and Co-operative Society. This institution sponsored local unions in each county of the state. The aim of the society, which was described as having raised the living standards of African American farms in the area, was "to discourage the credit and tenant farming system among Negro farmers in North Carolina. Their aim was also to assist them in the buying and selling of products; to control methods of production and distribution of farm products; and to secure uniform prices." According to my great grandmother, Hester James, "The credit and tenant farming systems were nothing, but another form of slavery." The owners of the large farms that had once been plantations rented plots of land to former slaves and built company stores that supplied seeds, farm equipment, clothing and staples like flour, salt, sugar, etc. Since the owners of the stores kept the books that showed what the tenant farmers owed, and most of the farmers could not read, the debt was always more than their crops earned, thus "tying" them to the land year after year.

In 1915-1916 academic term the college changed its name to "Agricultural and Technical College." The change was provoked by the college being in debt due to not having sufficient students enrolled to support it. Many people in the area wanted "professional or classical education, many parents wished their sons to become preachers, lawyers, teachers, or physicians." The overhaul was Dudley's approach to addressing all of the problems (Nxumalo, 1995). He also began offering a course of study suited to the ability and needs of students. Another issue had been that many people opposed the co-educational student body. As a result, when the college reopened, it was as an all-male college (Nxumalo, 1995).

As the college prospered under Dudley's visionary leadership, legislative appropriations were greatly increased, and building after building was added to the campus plant (Nxumalo, 1995). Philander Priestley Claxton, one-time United States commissioner of education, noted that the "Agricultural and Technical College in Greensboro was one of the best schools for Negroes to be found anywhere." During Dudley's 29 years in the presidency, the college campus grew in area from twenty-six acres to one hundred and twenty-five acres, including farmland and the number of buildings expanded from two to thirteen. Dudley was also a leader in the Bethel A.M.E. Church in Greensboro, serving as a trustee. His wife led the Missionary Department and established its first missionary divisions. At the time of his death in 1925, there were over 500 students enrolled at A&T (Nxumalo, 1995).

In naming the High School for Negroes in Greensboro for James Benson Dudley, the Greensboro School Board acknowledged his educational, social, and political leadership in the city, state, and nation. England (1995) noted, "Dr. Dudley is remembered in many memorials in Greensboro including the street where he lived, and his birthday is celebrated at A&T as Dudley Day."

An Educational Institution Evolves

The exterior front of James B. Dudley High School (1957) had no central front entrance until 1978. Until then, the North Stairwell led up to the upper floors and the South Stairwell led down. There were Senior Safety Patrols on duty between classes, before and after school to ensure that this rule was followed except during fire drills.

John A. Tarpley, who had served as the principal of the High School for Negroes in Greensboro while it was located on the campus of the Bennett College, retained his position as principal when the new high school building was completed. James Benson Dudley High School Principal was a post that he held until he retired in 1965. When the high school building opened in 1929, there were 88 sophomores (Students who had completed the equivalent of 8th or 9th grade), 64 juniors, and 39 seniors (Jenkins, 1979). Seniors were eleventh graders until 1947 when the 12th grade was added to prevent new graduates from competing for jobs with soldiers returning from World War II. Until the school system changed to the middle school format, the 9th grade in junior high school was the freshman year of high school with 9th graders receiving their first high school credits in English, history, physical science, Algebra I, and Home Economics (girls) or Industrial Arts (boys).

During the next ten years, more and more of the wealthier Negro parents were willing to transfer their children from Palmer Memorial Institute, a private residential secondary school for Negroes in nearby Sedalia, North Carolina to Dudley High School. The fact that Benbow Road in the Nocho Park Community became the housing equivalent of owning a Cadillac also helped the growth of the school. Dudley was built in what was to become the geographic center of the "Colored Community" and this contributed to its growing status as the educational, social, and political center of the community.

The reputations of Bennett College, the Agricultural & Technical College (North Carolina A&T State University), James Benson Dudley High School and the availability of jobs in the mills encouraged Black families to relocate to Greensboro. The fact that Dudley existed as a byproduct of segregation did not seem to matter to its academic status because Dudley was not only an excellent school for Blacks; it was an excellent school -period.

A PLACE WHERE SUCCESS WAS EXPECTED: FINAL EDITION

This excellence in academics was real even though the school's books were always hand-me-downs from the all-white Greensboro Senior High School and the rest of Dudley's campus was built piecemeal over a period of 32 years. During the forty-one years before integration in 1970-71, less than 2% of any class dropped out. Students did not stay because they were getting a simplified or watered-down education (Tarpley, 1979). In 1926 while still on the Washington Street site, the high school became the first fully accredited high school for Negroes in the state of North Carolina (Coley, 1966). It was reaccredited in 1934 by the Southern Association of Accreditation which had by that time become the most prestigious association of its kind (Coley, 1966).

(Left-Right) Dudley's first principal, Dr. John A. Tarpley 1923-1965 (including the years that he was principal while the school was located on the campus of Bennett College and Washington Street School) and assistant principal Mr. Franklin Brown. Brown became Dudley's second principal (1965-1976).

While the Senior High School for whites built at the same time as the High School for Negroes was hailed as a "Million Dollar" school, only about $200,000.00 was allotted for Dudley. Of that amount, $172,000.00 was spent on construction. However, the differences in cost were mostly in size rather than in the quality of the exterior features. The same, mostly Black, brick masons and carpenters crafted both buildings, and the bricks came from the same company in Burlington, North Carolina. James Robert Cathcart, who worked as a plasterer for the construction company that built both schools, recalled elderly Black workers bragging about how they ensured that the school for their children was just as good as the one built for Whites. He said, "They said some of them did extra pointing up (a masonry term for correcting mistakes or adding finishing touches) and labor on their own time."

The strong academic programs at Dudley also encouraged graduates of Bennett College and North Carolina A&T College to remain as residents of Greensboro to work and to provide better educational opportunities for their children. After the school opened on its current site, Tarpley designed a curriculum that was the same during his tenure as principal at the school. The curriculum included standard courses, industrial/mechanical arts, and agriculture and liberal arts courses. Tarpley said in an article titled, *Dudley, Fifty Years Later*,

> "We went pretty heavily on some of the practical courses and industrial arts, carpentry, and auto mechanics. I worked on the concept that education ought to have a relation to life situations. We operated on the belief that we ought to educate a person to help him in what he was doing in life, not to live in the skies." (Jenkins, 1979)

So many students wanted to go to school at Dudley High School that Tarpley often had to hire additional teachers during the school year. Tarpley explained, "Public education hadn't caught fire in those days. So, we never had any problem getting teachers. In fact, at one time I had more teachers with college degrees than they had at the white school." (Jenkins, 1979)

In 1932, the school board added to Tarpley's duties as Dudley's principal the job of supervising all the black schools in the system. He set about improving faculties by hiring only college graduates and insisting on further education for teachers who were already working in the schools. Within a year, all the black elementary schools were accredited by the state education officials and in 1936, James Benson Dudley High School became North Carolina's first fully accredited high school for Blacks (Adding state accreditation to its 1934 Southern Association Accreditation).

During the 1950s, the school continued to grow in membership when the Morningside Homes Projects was built. After World War II, many of the returning soldiers moved with their families to urban areas to attend College on the G.I. Bill or to find work. In order to fulfill President Truman's promise of decent housing for soldiers who had served their country, government subsidized housing, or public housing was built in cities throughout the country. The first two public housing developments in Greensboro, North Carolina were completed in 1951 as segregated communities. Smith Homes served the White community while Morningside Homes served African Americans.

Morningside Homes was built in the eastern section of Greensboro (About two city blocks from Dudley), and it included 400 units. The units contained 1-4 bedrooms. For many of its occupants, these townhouses or single level units represented a step up in housing because each room was heated with a radiator and the kitchens were large enough for a dining table and were equipped with modern electric appliances. With the government subsidy, the rent which included all utilities was about $33.00 a month for a 4-bedroom unit. Until the Greensboro City Schools were fully integrated in the 1970-1971 school year, all of the high school students in Morningside Homes attended Dudley High School.

Over the next four decades, Tarpley built Dudley from a fledgling high school with 16 teachers into a striving high school with 96 teachers that was the pride of Greensboro's Black Community and whose reputation as a first-class educational institution spread beyond North Carolina. Many black families from other areas of the state moved to Greensboro, solely because they wanted their children to attend Dudley High School. Such was the case with the parents of Elreta Melton (aka. Judge Alexander) who moved from Reidsville where her father was pastoring a church in Rockingham County, North Carolina so that, "Elreta and her siblings could get the best education available."

One of the richest assets of James B. Dudley High School and the other schools in black communities during this time was community support. It was a well-known fact that the segregated schools were resource-poor when compared to the schools for whites. However, the research of Cecelski (1994), Craig, 1941, Emerson (2003), Hessling (1993), Walker (1996), Walker (2000), Wilson (1997), and Wilson and Segall (2001) documented that from the late 1800s until desegregation, these schools were rich in community support. Cecelski (1994) documented one of the most intensive examples of black community support of the schools in their community. He wrote,

> "The 1968-69 school boycott in Hyde County (North Carolina) was one of the most sustained and successful protests of the civil rights movement. For a year, the county's black citizens refused to send their children to school in protest of a desegregation plan that required closing two historically black schools in their remote coastal community. These closures were seen as undermining the traditional heritage of the black community. Parents and students held daily nonviolent protests for five months, led marches on the state capitol in Raleigh, and drove the Ku Klux Klan out of the county in a gunfight that marked the end of public toleration of open Klan meetings in Hyde County. The eventual preservation of the two schools gave black citizens a power base in the new configuration of schools in the county and a voice in educational policy." (p.1)

Dudley and the other schools were especially rich in educational support from the African American teachers, administrators, and local businesses. The teachers and administrators lived and attended church in the communities where they worked, and their children attended the schools. The churches and businesses advertised in the school's newspaper and yearbooks; sponsored athletic teams and clubs and were actively involved in major school activities.

Dudley's reputation as a first-rate academic institution was so well established by the late 1930s that Paul Laurence Dunbar High School in Washington, D.C. was the only public high school that ranked highly enough academically to be mentioned in the same breath with Dudley (Coley, 1966). During the decades from the 1930s through the 1950s both schools were fully accredited and unlike most high schools during that time were initially established as high schools rather than initially being established as multi-grade schools.

The curriculum that Tarpley designed for the students at the school prepared students to proceed directly from high school to professional careers as master carpenters, brick masons, auto mechanics, seamstresses, tailors, practical nurses, etc. or to continue to undergraduate programs. One student, David Moore (1962) noted, "Students graduated from Dudley with the equivalent of an associate degree from a community or technical/industrial arts college today."

Early Faculty of James B. Dudley High School

This photograph, with the title "Dudley Teachers Plan Experiment," appeared in the June 29, 1940 edition of the *Norfolk New Journal and Guide*: Top row: W. F. Taylor, William A. Goldsborough, Fannie K. Gordon, W. W. Johnson, Vance H. Chavis (GEB Fellow 1946-1947); Third row: N. E. McLean, Pearl Garrett, L. L. Humphrey, N. D. Arnette, D. L. Boger; Second row: Mildred A. Colson, Alma P. White, R. M. Glover, Ester D. Hollomon, L. F. Wood, Ernest L. Raiford; Front row: J. R. Davis, Juanita Jones, Nelle Artis (Coley), John A. Tarpley, Blanche Taylor Grant, A. M. Farrison, Gladys F. Rogers.

The school was established in 1879 when the Greensboro City Council agreed to pay for a few Negro students to attend high school on the campus of Bennett Seminary. This handful of Negro students (male and female) were the first students in Guilford County to receive a free public education beyond the eight-grade level.

In 1923, it became a high school for all Negro students within the city limits with an enrollment of between 100-150 students. It was the first full public High School for Negroes operated by the Greensboro City School System; the school was located on the campus of co-educational Bennett College until it became Bennett College for Women. The high school had a fine faculty even before it was officially named. The faculty started the year

A PLACE WHERE SUCCESS WAS EXPECTED: FINAL EDITION

with 16 teachers, but by year's end there were 22 teachers. The first faculty was made up of many outstanding individuals. The average tenure of this staff was 34.5 years with Vance Chavis (Top right of picture on page 51) leaving to become the assistant principal of Lincoln Junior High School after only 26 years. Chavis became principal of Lincoln one year later. Another teacher from this early group was Nelle Artis (Coley) remaining at Dudley for 38 years of her teaching career.

Teachers in the Greensboro City Schools did not always get equal salaries. Until 1931, North Carolina paid teachers based on experience, whether or not they had a "full" class, and their education level. Davis (2010) stated, "The salary range for White North Carolina teachers in 1933 was $45 to $90 per month. African American teachers had a different scale: $35 to $70." Woods (1942) stated, "The latest data (1941) on salaries paid Negro teachers from State funds show a total of $69,469——-an average of $817.28 per year." The separate pay scale remained in effect until the schools in the state were fully integrated in 1970."

By 1939 there were about seven hundred students enrolled at Dudley High School. By 1959, there were 1,000 students at Dudley and in 1962, the first group of "War Babies" or future "Baby Boomers" entered Dudley. That class, 1965, at 406 graduates remained the largest class to ever graduate from Dudley until 1977. In the forty years between1923-1966 the graduation rate remained steady at 98% (Coley, 1966). In 1947, the 12th grade was added to all the high schools in the state to prevent soldiers returning from World War II from having to compete with recent high school graduates for jobs. Christine Thompson, who would have graduated from Dillard High School in Goldsboro, North Carolina that year said, "We were mad as all get out. How would you have felt if you'd been looking forward to graduating and suddenly there was a 13th grade? You have to remember that a lot of girls got married right out of high school back then. They messed up a lot of people's plans."

Although the 12th grade was added to all graded schools in the United States in 1947, there were still only three grade levels at Dudley High School (10th, 11th, and 12th) because junior high school was still at either J.C. Price, Washington Street School (until 1955), Rena Bullock School, Palmer Memorial Institute, or Lincoln Junior High School. During this period, 9th graders began earning high school credit while in junior high school.

Dr. Jo Evans Lynn, Ed.D.

Chapter Five

A Place Where Success Was Expected...

The Main Building on the school's campus is a significant three-story brick building with well-developed brick detail, including quoins, corbels, blind arcades, and segmental arches. Some characteristics of the façade of Dudley's original Main Building, the heavy brackets, moldings, and arches reflect Gothic Revival Style and Modern Style that are typical of designs by Charles C. Hartmann. Dudley is one of only three schools designed by Hartmann. Multiple pilasters rising above its flat roof adds variety to its symmetrical design. The exterior of Dudley's Auditorium pictured on the next page is exactly as it was designed by Charles Hartmann and added to the Main Building between 1929 and 1930.

Since the Gothic Revival Style thrived at the end of the 19th century, James Benson High School looked a bit "old" even when it was brand new. The double doors at the north and south ends of the front of the Main Building were the original entrances to the school. These entrances are adorned with two-inch-thick marble tiles. Dudley also has segmental arched windows and molded sashes. The bricks are laid in a common bond. However, there are intricate designs set into the brickwork above the original entrances.

Exterior view of the James B. Dudley High School Auditorium (2005)

Although it was part of Charles Hartmann's original design, the First Gym was not added to the Main Building until 1936. Since the bricks came from the same company that had supplied the bricks for the original structure, it is

A PLACE WHERE SUCCESS WAS EXPECTED: FINAL EDITION

impossible to detect where these additions were joined to the Main Building. The former gym wing has undergone dramatic alterations since its construction in 1936. The gymnasium was very small with a basketball court that was 40ft. X 80ft. or two small cross courts. The dressing rooms, lockers, and showers were along the east wall of the gym, and two small offices were on opposite sides of the three 12 ft. windows at the front of the Gym. Those windows were bricked in during the 1991 renovation that converted the first Gym into the Dudley Open Magnet School. The bricks were removed in the newest Whole School Modernization (2001).

Since the First Gym never had any permanent seating, all "big" games were played in Moore's Gym on the campus of the then Agricultural and Technical College that was located on 102 acres between Dudley Street and Benbow Road off East Market Street. The First Gym became the Women's Gym when the Main Gymnasium was completed in March of 1959. Until the larger cafeteria was built around 1956, Senior Proms were held in the First Gym.

The school is visible from Highway 29 North and its dark red bricks and imposing architecture have been a landmark for generations of travelers through the city and state. On the right side of the Main Building, there are two structures. One is the Main Dudley Gymnasium, 1959 (named the Chester Bradley Gymnasium in 2003, after a former Dudley football coach, biology teacher, and administrator). The other building is the Auxiliary Gym (named the G. E. Dye Multiplex Athletic Building in 2003 after Georgene E. Dye the woman who founded and coached numerous athletic programs for women at Dudley). The nominations for the naming of these buildings were made by the

Dr. Jo Evans Lynn, Ed.D.

Dudley Project Team that provided school-based oversight during the Whole School Modernization of Dudley 2002-2004. Connected to the back of the Main Building by way of a breezeway were the North and South Annexes with the Cafeteria standing between the far ends of both buildings. The North Annex originally contained home economics classes, custom sewing classes, nursing classes, the Dean of Women's Office, a family life class that was required for all male and female seniors, the band room, and the chorus room.

The South Annex originally contained vocational classes that included auto mechanics, carpentry, masonry, and agriculture classes. To the right of the Main Building were the Science and English Buildings. The Science Building was erected in 1964, renovated in 1991 and again in 2004. Until the 2004 Whole School Modernization, the Science Building contained ten classrooms with labs, two smaller specialized classrooms with labs, and a two-story Library/Media Center. The 2004 renovation converted the Library/Media Center to an Auto Mechanics Classroom and Shop.

The Main Building of Dudley was renovated in 1991; the heating system was updated, the first-floor classrooms were converted to offices. The First Gym or Girl's Gym was remodeled to accommodate classrooms for the Dudley Open Magnet School (1992-1995) which was later called the Engineering, Education, and Health Science Academy at Dudley. The original open plan of the gym was changed, and a second story was added. Where there was a single open space, seven classrooms were added on the first level, and four classrooms were created on the second level. A staircase was installed in the southwest corner. A few changes were made in the rooms along the east wall where classrooms and offices already existed.

Although a central entrance was added to the front of the Main Building in 1978, the façade retains all of its architectural integrity because no major structural changes have ever been made to the exterior of the building. Although additions were made to the school in 1956, 1958, 1959, 1960, 1962, and in 1978, the Main Building remained the primary structure that people identified as "Dudley." The front of the Main Building has remained essentially the same for over 85 years. It seems odd then that after the additions to the campus during the Whole School Modernization that some people are saying that James B. Dudley High School closed at the end of the 2001-2002 school year, and a New Dudley took its place. This belief simply is not true.

A PLACE WHERE SUCCESS WAS EXPECTED: FINAL EDITION

During the entire Whole School Modernization process, the school remained open, and, in fact, there were classes in both the English Building and Science Building. It was only after the rest of the school moved back across the street from Lincoln that renovation began to the Science Building. The English Building was not converted to a Ninth Grade Academy until 2013.

Eastern Guilford High School burnt to the ground, and its student body was spread out from one end of the county to the other while it was being rebuilt, yet everyone still refers to it as Eastern Guilford High School, not New Eastern Guilford. While Grimsley Senior High School has undergone an, even more, elaborate renovation than Dudley, there appears to be no evidence of anyone referring to the school as the "New Grimsley." Perhaps this is true because the additions to Grimsley Senior High School were handled by a local architect, Clinton Gravely, who very carefully followed the original Charles Hartmann design in designing additions to the campus.

The term "New Dudley" is offensive because the term "new" implies that what is here is something Gantt Huberman Architects and Interior Designers and the Guilford County School Board produced. Too many generations of Black folks in Greensboro have toiled too hard for every brick; for every advancement for Black folks to abandon what they

fought to give their children and future generations. The James Benson Dudley High School that resulted from the efforts of five generations of African American citizens of Greensboro, North Carolina is still here!

Harvey Gantt, the architect who designed the facilities that replaced the North Annex, South Annex and cafeteria included in the Whole School Modernization of Dudley told the Construction Committee that it would be too expensive to reproduce exact replicas of the original façade. He did, however, promise that the new part would be closely reminiscent of the original design. It seems that some things have not changed since 1929. No expense was spared in continuing the authenticity and faithfulness to Charles Hartmann's original design when renovations were done at Grimsley Senior High School while "Doing the best we can with the money we received" was the key phrase repeated time and again to the Construction Committee at Dudley.

The front of the Main Building still has its intricate, handcrafted, well-developed brick detail, including quoins, corbels, blind arcades, and segmental arches. Some characteristics of the façade of Dudley's Main Building such as the heavy brackets, moldings, and arches reflect Gothic Revival Style and Modern Style that are typical of the designs of Charles Hartmann. On the other hand, the façade of the addition that replaced the North Annex, South Annex, and Cafeteria has a prefabricated arch and cement slabs on top that makes it resemble many of the buildings on the campus of Moses Cone Hospital.

Front of James B. Dudley H. S. facing Lincoln Street.

Gantt Huberman Architects and Interior Designers

Back of James B. Dudley H. S. facing Willow Road.

Chapter Six

Academically Speaking...

Given the circumstances under which Dudley became a high school- segregated school, substandard books, used equipment, and facilities that became "cramped" after the first two years, the level of the academic programs was extraordinary. As Dr. Tarpley stated, "The law said the schools shall be racially segregated, but they shall be equal. They saw to it that they were separate, but they didn't give a darn about whether they were equal." Nothing remotely resembling equality in facilities, equipment, books, and other educational supplies were freely given to the African American population of Greensboro without protracted battles.

Here's how Vance Chavis (Jenkins, 1979), who joined the school's staff in its first year as a science teacher, described those early years:

> "I was hired to teach general science, but I taught biology, physics, chemistry, and civics along the way. There had to be more diversity on the faculty because most of the people on the faculty had gone to liberal arts colleges. But we had people on the faculty from Fisk University in Nashville, Tennessee, Smith College in New England, Hampton Institute, all over. Many of them had come south to get jobs.
>
> But that faculty often had to make do with less than adequate equipment. Both schools were new, but the white school was sort of a Cadillac, and the Black school was a Buick. I know from experience that a lot of the science equipment was old equipment moved from the other schools. A lot of it was still there when I left in 1955.
>
> And a wooden structure served as a cafeteria, industrial arts building and classroom. We had to make do. The basketball players would have to practice at another school at night, and the teachers would have to take them down there. But in many ways, they were easier times for teachers---Vietnam, racial troubles and an increasingly complex society were yet to develop to their fullest. It seems to me that teachers were given more respect back then than

now. The worst word I ever heard was 'darn.' There seemed to be a greater thirst for knowledge. The students had to take more required courses, and we tested them often—they had to learn a lot of poems.

Faced with fewer conflicts, most teachers were at Dudley to stay. We saw it as a "calling." It was about all we could do at the time (College educated Blacks), and we devoted all our energy to it. There was the real love of teaching. And the students seemed to pick their favorite teachers to emulate."

Chavis' account of the early period of the school, at its present, is related here only to demonstrate the hard work, intelligence, dedication, and creativity that went into making James B. Dudley High School a world-class educational institution. It was the intent of some of the Southern whites that even after slavery ended, former slaves and freedmen would feel inferior because they were given less with which to learn. Because of the efforts of John A. Tarpley and the early group of teachers those intended feelings of inferiority evolved into the building blocks of determination and pride in what Blacks could achieve both as individuals and as people of color. Tarpley (Jenkins, 1979) described his staff's efforts to build self-esteem in their students,

"We had to give a lot of thought to inspiring them on the basis of 'you can do it. Because you're black doesn't mean you don't have the ability.' Even then, we had courses in Negro history, and it was an eye-opener to some of those students to see and read about those who had made it."

Throughout their years at Dudley, one of the most important lessons that the students learned was that success was an expected outcome of their education. Success was not measured by whether or not students attended college after graduating, but by their body of work as self-actualizing citizens whether they were brick masons, carpenters, teachers, principals, preachers, practical nurses, doctors, lawyers, or business owners.

One student, Gloria Evans, recalled that one of the last announcements Tarpley made as principal over the school's intercom was that the auto mechanics team had won the state championship in Raleigh. He sounded particularly excited that this was the third year in a row that Dudley's students had won. She also noted, "He didn't seem half as excited when he announced that two more students had earned full college scholarships." Auto mechanics and practical nursing were two of the many programs offered at Dudley that enabled students to begin their careers right out of high school.

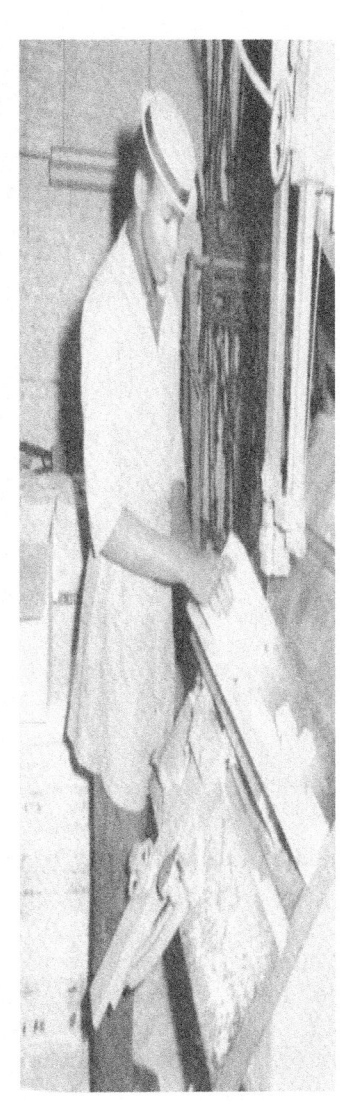

A PLACE WHERE SUCCESS WAS EXPECTED: FINAL EDITION

1967 ICT Classes in Action

Left: Zimmerman Price is practicing his craft as a Baker's Apprentice.

Right: Ronald Vample is shown working as a Woodworking Machine Operator.

Dr. Jo Evans Lynn, Ed.D.

Junior Class Practical Nurses of Dudley High School at L. Richardson Hospital

Shown above is the Junior Class of Student Practical Nurses of Dudley High School, while doing their clinical practice at L. Richardson Memorial Hospital. Standing left to right are Misses Marlene Wadlington, Barbara Jeffries, Bobbie McClure, Harriett Hatchett, Inola Leach, Mrs. Burge, Assistant Director of Nursing Service, L. Richardson Hospital; Misses Sandra Correia, Agnes Davis, Catherine Johnson, Marsha Blakney and Josephine Hayes. Standing in the center is their coordinator-instructor, Miss Janice Feemster. Not pictured: Brenda Jones (Graduating Class of 1962)

A PLACE WHERE SUCCESS WAS EXPECTED: FINAL EDITION

Distributive Education

In this program students learned all sorts of jobs.

Top Left: Lorenzo Caldwell at Saslow's Jewelry

Right: Patricia Gilmer at Gillespie School.

Center Left: Elsie Wharton works behind the counter at Meyer's Department Store.

Center Right: Ronald Miller at Lane Drug Store and **Bottom:** Billy Griffin and Joe Coley at Wesley Long Hospital.

Many of the students like Zenobia Haygood Barnes went on to work at jobs that they started in Distributive Education for 25-30 years.

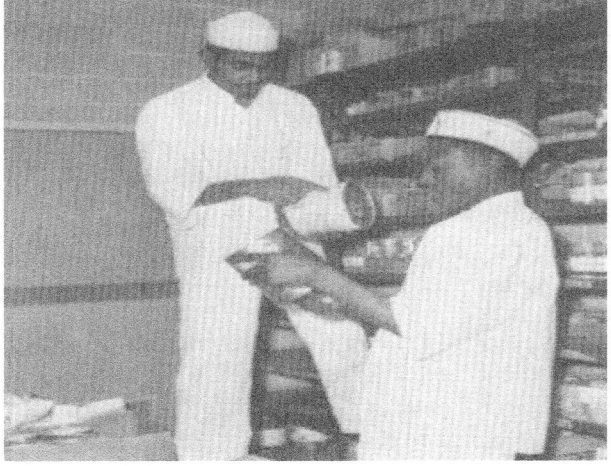

When former teachers and students are asked to describe Dudley's first principal, Dr. John A. Tarpley some of the same terms appear over and over again:

"John A. Tarpley was one of the most *influential* persons at Dudley." Kathryn Paylor (Miss Dudley 1932)

"Tarpley was a *great strategist* in his relations with school superintendents and boards." Vance Chavis (Former Dudley teacher (26 years), Lincoln Junior High School's second principal, and Greensboro City Councilman)

"He was a *strict disciplinarian*… To me he was a tremendous *teacher*---even when he wasn't formally in that role. He just imparted so much coping information." Robert Meadows (Dudley student, Class of 1954, President- Black Child Development, School Board Member)

Dr. John A. Tarpley, Principal

"He was *supportive* of his teachers. I'll never forget that about him." Bill Whites (Dudley teacher, Assistant Principal at Grimsley Senior High School)

No matter the odds, Tarpley fought for Dudley. Tarpley was quite a strategist when it came to fighting to get resources for the school. Each year when it was time to submit a budget for the next school year to the school board, Tarpley would go to the meeting with two budgets. The first one he presented contained what teachers referred to as their "wish list"- the latest science equipment, new textbooks, a fully equipped cafeteria, enough library books to meet or maintain accreditation standards, and for the gym that had been a part of the original plan to finally be completed (The First Gym in the Main Building was not completed until 1936). He knew that the board would reject the first budget. His second budget contained the essentials that the school needed. Since the board had made such a production of refusing his first list, they usually ended up giving him everything in his second budget (Tarpley, 1979).

Tarpley's strategizing was not limited to the budget. Once, when the new Dudley cafeteria was stocked with only half the necessary chairs and tables, Vance Chavis recalled, Tarpley posted a boldly lettered sign on the wall noting that "the cafeteria has not been fully equipped because the superintendent says the funds are not available at this time." By the time the students went home and reported this to their parents, the message finally got through to the School Board that Dudley would not be short changed.

A PLACE WHERE SUCCESS WAS EXPECTED: FINAL EDITION

Dr. Tarpley treated his teachers with a calculated mixture of public support and private discipline. Bill Whites used to tell the teachers under his supervision at Grimsley Senior High School this story to explain how Dr. Tarpley helped to shape his administrative style:

"I was a first-year teacher fresh out of the military. One day this student got really angry about something that happened in class. When I intervened, the student stepped over to me. When he raised his right fist, I knocked him out. I could have stopped him without doing that, but I didn't think. I just reacted like a soldier instead of a teacher. We revived him, and he went on to his next class.

But I knew that once that boy got home and told his father what had happened my career as a teacher was over. When a good part of the next morning passed without anything happening, I began to think that maybe the boy who was over 6 feet tall was too ashamed to tell his parents. My hopes died when I looked up and saw Mr. Brown, the assistant principal, coming into my classroom.

"Whites," he said, "Mr. Tarpley wants to see you in his office. I'll stay with your class."

All the way to his office, I kept thinking about how I was going to take care of a wife and children with no job. When I got to his office, the boy and his father were there. Tarpley barely looked at me before he started talking.

"Mr. (------), I suppose you're here for your boy to apologize and for you to explain how you raised a child disrespectful enough to try to hit one of my teachers."

The man stammered too shocked to say anything.

"I tell you what," Tarpley said, "take that disrespectful young man home and we'll let you know when or if ever we'll allow him to come back to this school."

Then he turned to me and said, "Whites, see them out of the building and then come back here."

I was grinning like a Cheshire cat when I got back to his office thinking I was off the hook.

Then Tarpley said, "What the hell is wrong with you? If you ever put me in a position like that again, they'll be looking for pieces of you all over the state."

Mr. Whites finished the story with,

"I tell you that story to let you know that I will support you as much as I can for as long as I can. Just don't put me in a position like that too many times. Don't think I got away "Scot free" after that tongue lashing. I think I was on probation with Tarpley until he retired."

Mrs. Coley, who taught English at Dudley, told a similar story about how Dr. Tarpley handled one young teacher's lapse:

"In a conference with the teacher and the parents of a student who was having problems, Tarpley asked the teacher to retrieve the "handy register" in which every teacher was required to keep attendance and academic records. The register was blank. The teacher had kept records on various scraps of paper.

He turned those blank pages and ad-libbed just as if the records were all there so as to keep from embarrassing the teacher. But when the parents left, he severely reprimanded the teacher and made her transcribe all the records immediately.

He had this way of clearing his throat— 'Ahem, ahem—that let you know something terrible was coming."

The term innovative is not often applied to black principals and teachers from that era. Following the No Child Left Behind Act of 2001 (NCLB) schools across the nation began to implement an innovative strategy for improving the overall performance of public schools. New! Innovative! This new innovative method of improving the educational outcomes of an entire school had been in place at Dudley for decades. In 1942, Dr. Tarpley submitted the following description of his staff's efforts to improve educational outcomes at Dudley that later appeared in the Secondary School Study News Bulletin, *To and From Our Schools* (Vol. 1, No. 2)

A PLACE WHERE SUCCESS WAS EXPECTED: FINAL EDITION

Dudley High Examines Curriculum

The entire staff of Dudley High is concerned with two professional problems.
1) Attempting to make a more careful evaluation of our curriculum with specific reference to our school philosophy.
2) Attempting to develop plans and procedure for making wider and more effective use of our audio-visual aid facilities.
The following is the plan under which we are working with the evaluation phase of our program:
A) We are reviewing our general philosophy for the purpose of added interpretation and classification.
B) We are holding two types of weekly staff meetings—general staff meetings and departmental staff meetings.
In the general staff meetings we are engaging in a series of discussions, having exhibits and demonstrations, etc. on approved procedures and techniques for measuring pupil growth. Special attention will be given to the study of measuring growth in "attitude," "appreciations," "habits" and "skills."

More than fifty years ahead of the *innovative school improvement plans* that were implemented around the nation after the No Child Left Behind Law was enacted in 2001, Tarpley implemented his plan for Dudley.

Some of the teachers were equally innovative. For example, Mrs. Nelle Artis Coley had a procedure for individualizing instruction that she used at the beginning of each school year, in which she interviewed each student. During this interview, she asked a few questions about grammar, literature, and one's goals in life. Then she explained what each student had to do to make an "A" "B" or "C" in her class. At the end of the session, each student had to sign a contract. These three contracts that were available would determine the maximum grade a student could expect to receive in the class.

On the "A" Contract the student agreed to write at least four major essays each grading period, make a 95 or higher on every test, design and put up a bulletin board that was based on the unit that the class was studying at the time, spend two hours a week tutoring an assigned student, and to select an author who was not included in the literature book to develop and make a ten-minute presentation that would make our classmates want to read the author's works. The three other students in my class who signed the "A" Contract agreed with me that the most unfair part of the contract was that the test grades of the person you tutored were factored into your test grade. Mrs. Coley followed her explanation of the contract with a brief speech about why she expected any student who was truly serious about attending college to sign the "A" Contract.

The "B" Contract was scaled down a bit to three essays a grading period, 87-94 on every test and no tutoring. It was rumored that the "C" contract said that a student would come to class every day and make at least an 80 on every test. No one in their "right" mind will admit to actually signing a "C" contract because of the speech Mrs. Coley made before handing a student a "C" contract. She would start out by saying something like, "I cannot imagine what path in life is open to a person so lazy and with such a low opinion of their ability to accept that the best they can do in life is to be "average." She would continue to expound on how little respect and appreciation for the hard work of one's parents the selection of an expected grade of "C" demonstrated. She seemed to be almost omnipotent because she could tell a student how hard their parents worked using concrete examples. After she finished, no one would admit to being unthankful or stupid enough to look Mrs. Coley in the eye and sign a "C" contract.

Mrs. Coley was doing this way back in the 1950s, but individualizing instruction did not become a popular strategy for instruction until the 1970s. It should also be noted here that the primary authors that were not included in our textbooks were people of color. Her strategy introduced students to Paul Laurence Dunbar, Countee Cullen, and other Harlem Renaissance writers besides Langston Hughes.

Mrs. Rosa T. Yourse  **Mrs. Annie M. Gillespie**

Not only were the teachers at Dudley innovative and competent, but they were also demanding. My sister, Gloria, and I have had a running argument for years about whether Mrs. Gillespie, Mrs. Yourse or Mrs. Coley was the most demanding English teacher at Dudley. In an Alumni Association Meeting, February 20, 2016, it was announced that Mrs. Rosa T. Yourse had died. Someone commented that right after integration he was working with a young white man who was attending Grimsley Senior High School. The man asked him whether or not he was taught by Mrs. Yourse while she was at Dudley. When he answered, "No, but she was my homeroom teacher. I liked her." The young man said, "Well, she is about to work us to death." Some of us around the table exclaimed, "She wasn't nearly as hard as Mrs. Coley." Someone else mentioned that Mrs. Gillespie was more demanding than either of the other two teachers. The truth is: All of Dudley's teachers were demanding. They demanded our best from us. No matter where we lived, Dudley Heights, Lincoln Heights, Morningside Homes, Ray Warren Homes, Hampton Homes, or along Benbow Road. We were expected to work hard and study. Most of us endeavored to live up to their expectations.

For 97 years (1923-76), the curriculum for black high school students in Greensboro was designed to prepare students for work or further academic study and a well-rounded life with required core subjects all students took and both liberal arts and industrial/mechanical arts electives. Dr. Tarpley made no exceptions for anyone in the required core courses. When one of Dudley's top academic students, senior James E. Cheek, who later became president of both Shaw University and Howard University, refused to meet the school's physical education requirement, Tarpley would not compromise. Cheek left Dudley and finished his senior year at Immanuel Lutheran School with a secondary diploma in 1950.

All of the electives, both industrial and liberal arts, were available to all Dudley High School students and an "F" in any core subject meant that a student was required to repeat the entire grade unless the student attended school during the summer. Since it cost the phenomenal amount of $75 to attend summer school (The fee in 1968 when the minimum wage was $1.25 an hour for factory workers and even less for domestic workers), students worked hard during the regular school year.

Overview of Course Offerings at Dudley through 1978

Core Subjects	Industrial Arts Electives	Liberal Arts/Electives
4 English Courses 3 Math Courses 2 History Courses 2 Science Courses 3 Physical Education Courses 1 Family Life Course 1 Home Economics (Females) 1 Industrial Arts (Males) 2 Foreign Language Courses	Carpentry/Wood Working (1929-1976) Masonry (1941-1978) Practical Nursing (1950-1963) Agriculture (1929-1969) Horticulture (1929-1978) Electronics (1950-1970) Auto Mechanics (1942-1978) Custom Sewing/Tailoring (1929-1971) Home Economics Business (Typing, Shorthand, etc.) Distributive Education, Driver's Education	Chemistry, Physics French III, Spanish III Latin I & II Drama I, II, III (1971-1978) Journalism (Newspaper & Yearbook) Trigonometry, Calculus Marching Band I, II, III; Orchestra I, II, III Chorus I, II, III Modern Dance (1971-1978) Art I, II, III

Grading Scale: 95-100 A   94-90 B   89-80 C   79-70 D   69-under F

One of the most successful practical education programs for females at Dudley during the early- 1950s through 1963 was the practical nursing program. It was a two-year program for juniors and seniors in which skills and hands-on learning experiences were taught at L. Richardson Memorial Hospital.

Picture Courtesy of Linda Glasgow

Combined 1962 and 1963 James B. Dudley High School Practical Nursing Classes

From Left To Right: Senior Practical Nursing Class (1962)-Barbara Jeffries, Harriett Hatchett, Marlene Wadlington, Sandra Correia, Brenda Jones, Bobbie McClure, Inola Leech, Agnes Davis, Mrs. McGibonney, Instructor, Junior Practical Nursing Class-Mary Anne Coleman, Junior Practical Nursing Class Instructor, Lenora Summers, Sandra Smith, Ms. Rambus, Lenora Donnell, Bernice Vincent, Margaret James, Linda Glasgow, Addy Lindsay, Shirley King, Gloria Pickens, and Gayle Richard. Due to contention about the restructuring of the curriculum, the Class of 1963 was the final graduating class in the program.

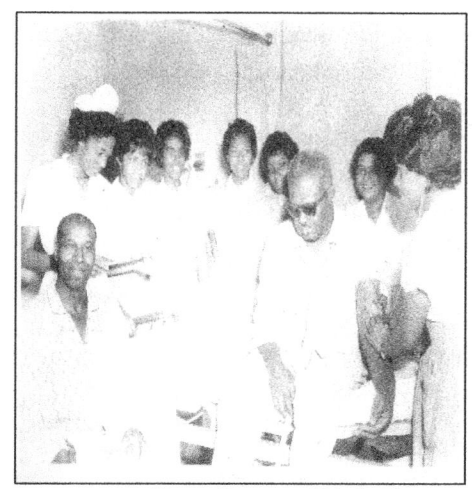

A PLACE WHERE SUCCESS WAS EXPECTED: FINAL EDITION

Picture Courtesy of Linda Glasgow

According to 1963 graduate Linda Glasgow, "The instructors were excellent and the practical learning experiences that we had at L. Richardson Hospital prepared us to pass the state test. Many of the students in those classes like Lenora Donnell, and Gloria Pickens, went on to become Registered Nurses. I had a very rewarding career as a Licensed Practical Nurse working at L. Richardson Hospital and Moses Cone Hospital." **At left:** Dudley 1963 Practical Nursing students "practice" taking a patient's blood pressure.

Although the course descriptions and curriculums of some of the courses have changed tremendously, most of the basic concepts are much the same as in the 1950s and 1960s. For example, although Distributive Education is now called marketing, its student goals are very similar. The marketing curriculum features a state approved vocational education program of instruction which enables students to study various functions of marketing about their particular career interests. Participation in marketing courses also provides students with the opportunities to write a resume, utilize computer skills, refine communication and public speaking skills, simulate career or college interviews and exercise knowledge and skills gained through on-the-job work experiences. These were the same curriculum features listed in the 1966 Distributive Education curriculum.

Another factor that contributed to the strength of the curriculum at Dudley was the academic strength of the programs at Lincoln Junior High School, J.C. Price School, and Rena Bullock School. All three schools had outstanding mathematics, music, English, industrial arts, and home economics departments. All three schools even had marching bands, and J.C. Price had a jazz band. Each spring, the major field trips of the Junior High School seniors (9th graders) were matinee performances of the Dudley Thespians, the Modern Dance Company, and the Dudley Choir's and Orchestra's Christmas Recital.

Although the girls wore white dresses, and the boys wore suits, the celebration marking the students leaving junior high school and going to

Dr. Jo Evans Lynn, Ed.D.

Dudley was called a Continuation Exercise rather than a graduation. Students went to Dudley as sophomores with 5-6 high school credits.

Tarpley and the teachers at Dudley were practical, but they never stopped working and dreaming that Dudley would someday have the kind of facilities that the students deserved. They worked hard to improve their skills with over 60% of the teachers earning master's degrees in the subjects that they taught and 100% of the teachers teaching only in the areas in which they were certified by 1948 (Tarpley, 1979). The speech that Dr. Tarpley gave on the evening that the football stadium at Dudley was dedicated and officially named in his honor eloquently sums up what he dreamed of accomplishing during his time at the helm of the school:

Ladies and Gentlemen:

The dedication of a school facility is a rare occasion for all of us. This dedication tonight is certainly a rare and happy event for me.

When I became the first principal of Dudley, I was filled with youth, ambition, and dreams. I dreamed of making James B. Dudley High School a tribute to this community, and I dreamed of students being challenged and set on the right course for the greatest possible development. I was fortunate. I wasn't just dreaming. I was blessed with the tools for making Dudley great. One of Dudley's assets was its dynamic, capable, dedicated faculty. Another great asset was the group of parents who supported the school. The majority of Dudley's parents believed that students should learn to turn stumbling blocks into stepping-stones. The parents, also, believed that a sound education was the best possible shield for blunting the attacks from prejudice and injustices.

I have enjoyed seeing many of my dreams fulfilled. Dudley High School won top awards, year after year, in dramatics, in music, in scholarship, and in athletics. Some of our athletes went on to gain national recognition such as Lou Hudson, Curley Neal, and Charlie Sanders. I feel certain that those fellows and others are rejoicing tonight over the tremendous improvements which have been made in the facilities for the athletic program.

Yes, I dreamed of greatness for Dudley, and I saw that dream come true. Those were happy years. Tonight, you are dedicating Tarpley

A PLACE WHERE SUCCESS WAS EXPECTED: FINAL EDITION

Stadium. This is a cherished honor which was never included in my dreams. I am grateful, and I am touched by your actions. I accept this honor with sincere thanks to the members of the Board of Education, to the wonderful people of the community, and to all of my great friends who have contributed to the success of my professional career. May God bless you and love you all. (Transcript of speech is the property of David Moore)

Chapter Seven

Petition Again and Again, Until…

For many years, the Dudley Parent Teacher Association had unsuccessfully petitioned the Superintendent of Schools, Mr. Ben L. Smith, and the Greensboro Board of Education to build a gymnasium at the high school that would accommodate the crowds that wanted to see the men's basketball team play. During this period, Dudley had several outstanding multi-sports players who excelled in basketball. Players like Freddie (Curley) Neal drew huge crowds that even Moore's Gymnasium on A&T State University's Campus was too small to accommodate. A gym had been promised since the late 1930s, and there was much bitterness in the black community over the delay.

In 1957-58 the PTA under the leadership of Ezell Blair, Sr. (the father of Ezell Blair, Jr. of the Greensboro Four) who taught drafting at the school, forced the Board of Education to agree to allow the Dudley High School basketball team to play its home games at the all-white, then Greensboro Senior High School's Gymnasium until Dudley High School had an appropriate facility. At the time, Dudley outstanding player Fred Neal (a.k.a. Curly Neal) was receiving tremendous statewide and national press. Much of the publicity about the facility in which a player of his caliber was forced to play was negative since Dr. Tarpley made sure that the games that would receive the most coverage were played in the school's gym which had no seating. The Board's change of heart may have had as much to do with the negative statewide and national press coverage as with anything the PTA threatened.

A PLACE WHERE SUCCESS WAS EXPECTED: FINAL EDITION

Picture Courtesy Harlem Globetrotters

Freddie "Curley Neal's signature shaved head, magical shooting, and dribbling captured the imagination of fans around the world. During his career with the Globetrotters (1963-1985) he played in more than 6,000 games in 97 countries.

During the 1957-58 school year, the Dudley basketball team played three home games at the Greensboro Senior High School Gymnasium. Dudley's team playing in Greensboro Senior High's Gymnasium produced a harsh reaction in the white community. Racial tension remained high even after construction began on Dudley's Main Gymnasium. The players did not seem to be to upset about the ruckus because that year Dudley won the state AAA Championship in basketball.

The James B. Dudley Senior High School Gymnasium, built in 1959, meets National Register Criterion C in the area of architecture. The steel-framed groin vaulted building with four brick elevations displaying corrugated glass fiber-reinforced polyester panels stands as an exceptional example of the Modernist movement in school planning and design in Greensboro. Project architect W. Edward Jenkins (1923-1987), a 1949 graduate of North Carolina Agricultural and Technical College's architectural engineering program, worked for the firm of Loewenstein-Atkinson Architects, ALA from 1949 to 1961. The firm was the only one in Greensboro in the 1950s that hired African American architects. Jenkins designed the gym during a period when architecture schools and architectural journals espoused the use of innovative laminated wood and thin-shell concrete vaulted forms, but local school systems typically chose more utilitarian designs namely flat-roofed, brick buildings for classrooms and physical education facilities. African American architects of the period, including Jenkins, saw modernism as a new beginning and as a symbol of the promise the future held for African Americans in the segregated South. Jenkins perhaps felt the need to make the gymnasium's design something extra special due to all the racial turmoil that surrounded the decision to build the gym.

The Main Gymnasium rose like a phoenix out of what was once the city dump. Its three-tier Foundation demonstrates the African American precept of "making something out of nothing." When the building's architect discovered that the ground on which it was to be built was unstable, he designed and made a stable foundation by removing almost two stories of soil and pouring three separate levels of cement and reinforcing each level with steel. Jenkins's use of arch columns set on concrete bearing plates to support two massive intersecting steel arches that form the principal roofline remains a unique design in institutional architecture in Greensboro.

So innovative was the design that the National Association of School Architects chose a scale model of the gym to display at their annual conference in Atlantic City in 1959. The following year, the American Institute of Steel Construction awarded the Dudley High School Gymnasium one of Twelve Architectural Awards of Excellence for the outstanding aesthetic in design in structural steel. The local chapter of the American Institute of Architects bestowed the award on Lowenstein-Atkinson Architects at its meeting in the fall of 1960. Jenkins operated his practice in Greensboro from 1962 until his death in 1987. Among his Greensboro commissions were a prominent Modernist residence for civil rights lawyer Kenneth Lee at 1021 Broad Avenue in Greensboro, St. Mathews Methodist Church on Florida Street, and the football stadium and Business and Math Building at North Carolina A&T State University. He also designed several post offices and numerous churches including the White Rock Baptist Church in Durham. The Dudley High School gymnasium met Criteria Consideration C because of its exceptional importance as a steel-vaulted free-span Modernist design in Greensboro and was placed on the National Register of Historic Places in 2003.

A PLACE WHERE SUCCESS WAS EXPECTED: FINAL EDITION

Back View of Main Gymnasium 1959   **Front View of Main Gymnasium 1959**

Gantt Huberman Architects and Interior Designers

Lincoln Street View of the Main Gymnasium. The Main Gym was named the *Chester Bradley Gymnasium* in 2003

The latest Modernization of James B. Dudley High School left the Main Gym's historic exterior virtually unchanged on three sides. An extension was added to the front that includes a breezeway connecting the Gym to the Main Building. The design of the breezeway mimics the historic design of the roof of the Gymnasium. The interior was altered to enlarge dressing rooms, weight rooms and training areas, create offices, equipment storage, and a laundry room. Over 600 permanent seats were removed when the stairs that allowed people to move from the upper to lower level were taken out on the 'Home side" and Visitor's side of the gymnasium.

Dr. Jo Evans Lynn, Ed.D.

The "Get and Take" of Every Renovation or Addition to the Campus:

Top left: In the 1972 picture taken during a Pep Rally (Motivational Seminar), Dudley students are sitting ten rows deep on the lower level of the Main Gymnasium. Openings in the railings led to stairs that allowed spectators to move from level to level to go to concession stands and bathrooms. Openings also allowed Senior Band Members to majestically move from the lower level to join the Band seated on the upper level during graduation.

Bottom left: In the renovation, there is no access to the lower level by way of similar interior stairs in the seating area and the lower seating is only five rows deep. When one takes into consideration that both teams, their families and special guests sit on the same lower side, seating is even further reduced. New lights, a score board, paint, and refinishing the floor were the only other changes to this part of the gymnasium.

Gantt Huberman Architects and Interior Designers

With every addition or renovation of James B. Dudley High School, something was lost. The Chester Bradley Gymnasium gained better training and weight rooms, better locker-rooms for both the home and visiting teams,

A PLACE WHERE SUCCESS WAS EXPECTED: FINAL EDITION

additional classrooms, bathrooms, equipment rooms, a laundry facility, and offices for the coaches and physical education instructors. The significant loss was in seating. The Main Gymnasium had seating in 1959 for 2,500 spectators. This size made it large enough for graduation ceremonies, concerts, and pep rallies that the entire student body could attend.

In the renovation, the stairs that allowed spectators to move from the upper levels to lower levels were removed along with about 600 seats.

Dudley's football stadium remained unfinished for 38 years. Construction began in 1941 but every year the administration was forced to choose between spending to complete the stadium and other academic priorities.

In 1967, the Greensboro Yankees moved their team from Greensboro, and the city went over ten years without a team. In 1978, a group of Greensboro businessmen and city leaders began negotiations with the Cincinnati Reds to have their Class A Baseball Team use the stadium.

The condition of the field was a major problem. With a high school team and a college team using the field for football and baseball, and the hot North Carolina summers, the field needed to be re-sodded frequently. A partial solution to the problem was to finally complete Dudley High School's Football Stadium. So, in 1979 Dudley's football team finally had a "home field" on campus- The John A. Tarpley Stadium.

During the many years that Dudley played in War Memorial Stadium, every home game was played in front of overflow crowds. Big rival games against teams like William Penn High School in High Point, North Carolina and Atkins High School in Winston Salem, North Carolina were always packed and the stadium which had a capacity of only 7,500 could not begin to hold the crowds that always included the bands from both schools.

Chapter Eight

Lessons in Governing...

The Student Government at Dudley helped to develop the social consciousness of students who would later become civic leaders in the local community and state. In the fall of 1959, the Dudley High School Student Association consisted of approximately 1,000 students in grades ten through twelve. Students became members of the Association by enrolling in the school. Before the 1959-60 school year, the Student Association had never met en masse or all together on a regular basis. The Association was governed by a student council, consisting of two chambers: a house of representatives comprised of the chief executive officers of each curricular organization chartered by the Association; and a Senate comprised of six senators, two elected from each class by direct popular vote of the entire Association. The executive officers of the Association were elected by the council during the first meeting following the elections in September of 1959. Tommy Johnson (1961), the first elected Student Body President of the Dudley Student Government Association wrote an account of the first full meeting. He wrote,

> The first meeting of the council was presided over by Mr. Franklin Brown, Dean of Boys, and teacher of radio. When he opened the house for nominations of presidential candidates, a vigorous discussion arose, and it was the consensus of the House that the president should be elected by the direct popular vote of the Association. Mr. Brown explained to the House that the change that the council contemplated required an amendment by the Association to alter the Constitution and that such a complicated process that had never been used before would take no less than six months to complete. The house proceeded to elect a president who then appointed a Constitution Committee Chairman, who, by resolution of the House was authorized to appoint a committee that would draft the necessary amendment and implement the required constitutional procedures. One of the amendment provisions was that the proposed amendment should be submitted by the drafters to the assembled student body for discussion on at least three occasions. Those meetings took place in January, February, and March of 1960.

> The drafting of the proposed amendment took place in a series of meetings of the Constitution Committee from October of 1959

through January of 1960 in the radio shop room with Mr. Franklin Brown serving as the advisor. The students on the committee understood the social and political ramifications of the task they were undertaking. They felt that they were about to forge a new kind of relationship between the Student Association and the School's administration. There was a strong sense of a need to do everything with great care.

This account makes it clear that political activism is a vital part of James B. Dudley High School. The only Civil Rights fatality in Greensboro, Willie Grimes (May 22, 1969) was directly connected to the refusal by Dudley's administration to allow a student, Claude Barnes, to run as a candidate for student body president. It was Barnes' position that the Administration, by setting the criteria for candidacy, were in effect deciding who would be elected. He felt that any student who wanted to run for office should be allowed to do so. This way, it would be up to the students to elect the person who would do the best job.

Barnes ran as a write-in candidate and won by over five hundred votes (747 votes).

There was only one official candidate for student body president on the ballot, Connie Herbin. The Administration gave the election to Connie Herbin, the official candidate with the most "official" votes (236 votes), and the campus erupted in protest. When A&T student leader Nelson Johnson and other A&T students got involved, the protest spread to A&T's campus. The governor called in the National Guard. Willie Grimes, a junior at A&T, was shot in the head during the turmoil. Barnes and several other students, including Ervin Brisbon, were expelled, but a new era of student activism began at Dudley. Now, any rising senior who wants to run for President of the Student Government at Dudley is allowed to run.

A PLACE WHERE SUCCESS WAS EXPECTED: FINAL EDITION

Connie Herbin was declared the 1969 Student Government President by the Administration although he lost the election by over five hundred votes.

Claude Barnes ran for office as a write in candidate and won in spite of the fact that the Administration refused to put his name of the ballot. He later taught history at A &T.

Dudley's teachers were political and social leaders in the community. Vance Chavis, Nelle Coley, Rev. Otis Hairston, Sr., Ida Jenkins, and George Simkins, Sr. have buildings named in their honor (The Vance Chavis Library, Hairston Middle School, the Coley-Jenkins Extended Living Facility, and the George Simkins, Sr. Elementary School). Several Dudley students and teachers have held local and state public offices: Vance Chavis- Greensboro City Council, Warren Dorsett-Guilford County Commissioner, Yvonne Johnson- Greensboro City Councilwoman and Mayor, and Amos Quick-Guilford County School Board and State Legislator. Dudley's first Band Director, James Benton Parsons was appointed by John F. Kennedy as the first Black federal district judge appointed with life tenure in 1961. Another Dudley graduate, Lou Hudson was the first African American to be elected to the State Legislature in Utah. An article by Lewis Brandon for the February 2002 issue of the Panther's Claw Newspaper stated:

> One book about the Sit-in Movement, Lunch at the 5 & 10, "The Four" mentions Dudley High School over thirty times. Why? Simply put, James B. Dudley High School produced two of the four members of the A&T Four: Ezell Blair, Jr., and David Richmond. One of the other two, Franklin McCain attended Dudley during his junior year in high school, when his family moved to Greensboro. However, the following summer his family moved back to Washington, D.C. and he graduated from Eastern High School in Washington, D.C. The other two young men graduated in 1959 from Dudley High School. They left Dudley with a strong sense of civic pride and the knowledge that a few individuals could make a difference.
>
> Two years earlier, 1957-58, the Dudley PTA under the leadership of Ezell Blair, Sr. (the father of Jirbrell Khazan, formerly Ezell Blair, Jr.) who taught drafting at the school forced the Board of Education to agree to allow the Dudley High School basketball team to play its home games at the all-white, then Greensboro Senior High

School's Gymnasium until Dudley had an appropriate facility. During the 1957-58 school year, Dudley played three home games at Greensboro Senior High (Grimsley). This produced a harsh reaction in the white community. Racial tension remained high even after construction began on Dudley's Main Gymnasium.

At one point, construction was halted when the PTA protested the decision of the board to set a tile rather than a hardwood floor. The PTA won. No doubt, these victories helped produce the kind of mindset that all four young men needed on February 1, 1960.

Picture from Greensboro Visitor's Center

Left to Right: David Richmond, Dudley graduate 1959, Franklin McCain, attended Dudley during his sophomore and junior years, Ezell Blair, Jr. (Jibrell Khazan), Dudley graduate 1959 and Joseph McNeil. It seems fitting that their courageous act is immortalized in front of the building on North Carolina A&T State University's campus honoring the man for whom James Benson Dudley High School was named.

Other students from A&T State University and Bennett College joined them. Bennett College students played a vital role in the organization and planning of future demonstrations. Bennett's

Student Government President, Gloria Brown, along with Edward Pitt of A&T, co-chaired the Student Executive Committee for Justice (SECJ), which served as the planning committee for the demonstrations. Of the 45 students arrested on April 21, 1960, 13 were Bennett College students. Dudley High School students, under the leadership of William "Bill" Thomas, continued the demonstrations after many A&T and Bennett students returned home for the summer.

The successful desegregation of Woolworth, S.H. Kress, Meyer's Department Store Tea Room (Dudley students added this facility to the demonstration), and Walgreen Drug Store in July of 1960 can be attributed to the persistence of Dudley students. Many of the Dudley students subsequently enrolled at A&T and Bennett and became the nucleus for the formation of the CORE chapter and the demonstrations of 1962 and 1963. William "Bill" Thomas became the Chairman of CORE and the leader of the 1962-63 Greensboro Demonstrations (Brandon, 2002).

One of the most important duties of each newly elected Student Government Association has long been to either reaffirm or make amendments to the Dudley Student Manifesto which documents the ideals and values that members of the student body are expected to adhere to not only while in school, but also in life long after they graduate.

Dudley Student Manifesto

We the Panthers of James Benson Dudley High School, consent to establish an ongoing foundation for students to continue tradition with a new attitude—an attitude of superiority and not inferiority, we as fellow Panther's pledge to:
1. Model Academic Excellence
2. Always Have Self-Motivation
3. Show Respect for All
4. Promote School Peace
5. Display Complete Honesty
6. Exhibit dedication to school cleanliness
7. Demonstrate Humbleness of Character
8. Strive for social effectiveness
9. Reflect a willingness to help others
10. Maintain true Panther Pride

Dr. Jo Evans Lynn, Ed.D.

In the words of James Benson Dudley, "The true status of a school is measured by the success of its students." To all who experience the rich tradition of Dudley High, the Student Government Association challenges you to uphold these standards.

Student Government Association, Cedric Owens, President (The Panther Yearbook: 2000 Millennium Edition, p.127)

Chapter Nine

A Change Is Gonna Come...

One of the most important outcomes of the "Battle for the Gym" was the reassurance that the strategy of a unified, nonviolent movement for equal rights for Black people could work. The "pitched battle" over race relations- the battle beyond the individual and small community struggle- that began during slavery had continued through the years. There were leaders in the Black community like James B. Dudley, who worked for acceptance, education, and financial independence through hard work rather than for equality. Most Blacks during this time were Republicans because it had been the party of Abraham Lincoln. The Southern Democrats were the opposite of the 1860s Republican party of Lincoln and African Americans found it hard to identify with the party that placed Confederate flags over State Houses, erected statues to Confederate generals, and put laws legalizing segregation on the books. The political dynamics changed with the election of John F. Kennedy in 1962 when the Dixiecrats (staunch segregationists) of George Wallace joined the Southern Republican Party rather than remain Democrats.

Dudley, president of the A&M College (later to become North Carolina A&T State University), spoke out against segregation as early as 1914, however, in most matters of race relations he counseled patience and nonresistance. Many requests by Blacks for better living conditions, like those expressed by Dudley, were left unanswered by the white community until decades later. The segregationist philosophy of "separate but equal" had been upheld in the famous 1896 Supreme Court decision "Plessy vs. Ferguson," in which the Court ruled that the state of Louisiana had the right to require different railroad cars for blacks and whites. The "Plessy" decision eventually led to widespread adoption of segregated restaurants, public bathrooms, water fountains and other facilities. "Separate but equal" was eventually overturned in the 1954 Supreme Court Case "Brown vs. Board of Education," but Jim Crow's legacy would continue to endure in Greensboro until the 1970s.

Many influential black citizens of Greensboro denounced the city's system of racial segregation during the turn of the century. White Quakers also continued to work for racial equality during this time. Many of the requests for better living conditions, better-equipped schools, were left unanswered by the white community. This dissatisfaction certainly played a part in fueling local blacks to start a city branch of the NAACP in 1917, one of the first three branches to be chartered in North Carolina (Greensboro NAACP, 2015).

Regardless of the mounting presence of racial segregation in the early 1900s, a substantial number of economically independent black citizens in Greensboro were able to discover ways to influence political affairs in a mostly white-run city. The neighborhoods around Dudley High School were steadily becoming a strong economic and political force in the city. In fact, during the 1930s the Black middle class in Greensboro (together with those in Raleigh, Durham, Charlotte, and Winston-Salem) comprised most of the Black voters in the state. In some eastern North Carolina towns, black voting was practically nonexistent until the post-World War II period.

The strengthening of the Black middle class in the area around Dudley also helped to encourage a more militant atmosphere. During the mid-to-late 1950s, the Dudley Heights and Lincoln Heights areas began to develop with housing for Greensboro's strong middle class of Blacks. Dudley Heights is located between Lee Street (now Gate City Boulevard) and East Florida Street. Many of the new homes were purchased by Blacks who were the first in their family to own a home. They took great pride in their lawns and maintaining their homes. By this time, Washington Street School was bursting at the seams and had to have split sessions with half the student body attending school in the morning and the other half in the afternoon. As a remedy for this, Lincoln Junior High School opened in 1955, and F. D. Bluford Elementary School (Named after the third president of North Carolina A&T State University) followed in 1956.

Underpinning this political shift in Greensboro, the more organized battle to end segregation and discrimination in the South began in 1930. In 1930, the National Association for the Advancement of Colored People had concluded that Black Americans and their White allies would support a direct attack on racial inequalities in American education. A grant of $100,000 from the American Fund for Public Service aided the NAACP. They used the money from this grant to establish a "war chest" specifically for this purpose. The group hired Nathan Ross Margold, a former assistant United States attorney in New York, to complete a full study of the Negro's legal status. The 1931 Margold Report proposed to attack the doctrine of separate but equal by challenging the inherent inequality of segregation in publicly funded primary and secondary schools.

Charles Hamilton Houston, however, recognized the pervasiveness of racism and believed that they needed first to establish a series of legal precedents. He modified the Margold Report by beginning the NAACP's legal campaign with lawsuits for equal facilities in graduate and professional schools. The following excerpt from the information packet published by the

A PLACE WHERE SUCCESS WAS EXPECTED: FINAL EDITION

U.S. Department of State, International Information Program (2015) Free at Last: The U.S. Civil Rights Movement, details this period of the movement:

Charles Hamilton Houston was born in 1895 in Washington, D.C. A brilliant student, he graduated as a valedictorian from Amherst College at the age of 19, then served in a segregated U.S. Army unit during the First World War. After his brush with racism in the Army, Houston determined to make the fight for civil rights his life's calling. Returning home, he studied law at Harvard University, becoming the first African American editor of its prestigious law review. He would go on to earn a Ph.D. in juridical science at Harvard and a Doctor of Civil Law degree from the University of Madrid in Spain.

Thurgood Marshall (left) and Houstor (center), with Donald Gaines Murray plaintiff in a key civil rights case.

Houston believed that an attorney's proper vocation was to wield the law as an instrument for securing justice. "A lawyer's either a social engineer or he's a parasite on society," he argued. In 1924, Houston began teaching part time at Howard University Law School, the Washington, D.C. institution responsible, by some accounts, for training fully three-fourths of the African American attorneys then practicing. By 1929, Houston headed the law school.

In just six years, Houston radically improved the education of African American law students, earned full accreditation for the school, and produced a group of lawyers trained in civil rights law. In the book Black Profiles, George R. Metcalf writes that Houston took the job to turn Howard into "a West Point [a popular name for the United States Military Academy] of Negro leadership so that Negroes could gain equality by fighting segregation in the courts."

Meanwhile, the National Association for the Advancement of Colored People was laying the groundwork for a legal challenge to the separate-but-equal doctrine approved in the Supreme Court's 1896 Plessy decision. On Houston's recommendation, the organization engaged former U.S. Attorney Nathan Ross Margold to study the practical workings of separate but equal in the South. Margold's report — 218 legal-sized-pages long — was completed in 1931. It documented woeful inequality in state expenditures between white and black segregated schools.

In 1934, Houston accepted the position of NAACP special counsel. He surrounded himself with a select group of young, mostly Howard-trained lawyers, among them James Nabrit, Spottswood Robinson III, A. Leon Higginbotham, Robert Carter, William Hastie, George E.C. Hayes, Jack Greenberg, and Oliver Hill. With his young protégé Thurgood Marshall often in tow, Houston began to tour the South, armed with a camera and a portable typewriter. Marshall later recalled that he and Houston traveled in Houston's car: "There was no place to eat, no place to sleep. We slept in the car, and we ate fruit." This could be dangerous work, but the visual record Houston compiled, and the data amassed by Margold would anchor a new legal strategy: If the facilities allocated to blacks were not equal to those afforded whites, Houston reasoned, segregationist states were not meeting even the Plessy standard. Separate but equal logically required those states either to improve drastically the black facilities, a hugely expensive undertaking or else integrate.

This equalization strategy bore fruit in 1935, when Houston and Marshall prevailed in a Maryland case, Murray v. Pearson. The African American plaintiff challenged his rejection by the segregated University of Maryland law school. The university's lawyers argued that the school met the separate but equal requirement by granting qualified black applicant's scholarships to enroll at out-of-state law schools. The state courts rejected this argument. While they were not yet prepared to rule against segregated public schools, they did hold that Maryland's out-of-state option was not an equal opportunity. Maryland's law school was ordered to admit qualified African American students. The triumph was especially sweet for Marshall, who numbered himself among the qualified blacks rejected by the school.

Houston retired from the NAACP in 1940 because of ill-health, and he died in 1950. "We owe it all to Charlie," Marshall later remarked. While Houston's prize student would lead the final legal assault on segregation, it was Houston, the teacher, who devised the strategy and illuminated the path. His students continued the fight.

Following the success of the suit against the University of Maryland law school, Marshall turned to North Carolina and a case in which J. Kenneth Lee was a plaintiff. In this case Thurgood Marshall, still the chief legal counselor with the NAACP's Legal Defense Fund, argued to desegregate UNC's law school, opening the university's doors for entry to other black students.

A PLACE WHERE SUCCESS WAS EXPECTED: FINAL EDITION

Kenneth Lee Papers, #482, Southern Historical Collection, The Wilson Library UNC at Chapel Hill

(Left to Right) Harvey Beech and J. Kenneth Lee during registration for UNC's law school in 1951.

Upon graduation from UNC's law school, J. Kenneth Lee argued civil rights cases across North Carolina. As a civil rights attorney, Lee represented more than 1,700 defendants in civil disobedience cases during the civil rights movement. One of his earliest civil rights cases was one in which he represented five black girls in the fight to attend the all-white Gillespie Park Elementary in 1957, making Greensboro one of the first cities in the Southeast to desegregate its all-white public schools under a freedom of choice plan. Lee represented the majority of the civil disobedience cases in North Carolina that started with the Woolworth sit-ins of 1960 and included the arrest of his own son, Michael (McLaughlin, 2018).

African American veterans across the nation came back from World War II with a greater desire to end racial injustice. Blacks optimistically expected that if the United States were willing to fight against Nazism and the persecution of Jewish people in Europe, then it would likewise be influenced to improve race relations in America as well. In Greensboro, black veterans came back home with similar attitudes, and as a result, both NAACP membership and voter registration exploded in the years after 1945. The Greensboro Citizens Association (GCA) was formed among black citizens in 1949 and propelled one of Greensboro's most successful voter registration campaigns. In the 1949 city election, two black candidates survived the primary for the first time. Blacks had discovered the power of voting as a block. In 1951, Dr. William Hampton was elected as the first black member of Greensboro City Council, receiving more than half of the votes cast; he was reelected in 1953.

Black political activism continued to manifest itself in rising civil rights protests during the late 1950s and 1960s. Following the Brown v. Board of Education decision of 1954, that outlawed public school segregation, race relations in Greensboro began to change. The post-1954 era would primarily be marked by a series of direct-action demonstrations in which blacks demanded jobs, better educational facilities, and basic civil rights. During this period, a few whites in Greensboro volunteered to improve race relations by desegregating their restaurants, providing support for school integration, and campaigning for the election of blacks to the school board. But generally, these volunteer efforts were limited, and the pace of improved racial relations was unsatisfactory to most in the black community. The majority of whites in Greensboro seemed to prefer gradual integration as reflected in North Carolina's Pearsall Plan for school desegregation. The Pearsall Plan was the General Assembly of North Carolina's alternative to whites attending integrated public schools. It called for small numbers of black students to volunteer to attend all-white schools.

In 1954, Greensboro became the first city in the South to announce its planned compliance with the Supreme Court's ruling. In actuality, desegregation was not enacted in Greensboro until 1970 (sixteen years later), making it one of the last cities in the South to end segregation of public schools. From 1955 until 1969, many of North Carolina's school districts, including Greensboro's avoided real desegregation by consenting to token desegregation and enacting illusive "freedom of choice" and pupil assignment plans.

Although it is seldom acknowledged or talked about, many students gave up their dreams of becoming Dudley students to do what they believed was paving the way for "real" desegregation during the "freedom of choice" era. In 1963, Mr. Chavis visited the top two classes of ninth graders at Lincoln Junior High School. He gave an impassioned speech about how it was the responsibility of the best and the brightest Colored students to go to Grimsley and Smith to integrate those schools. He talked about all those who had struggled and died for the kind of freedom that we only had to go to school and do our best to achieve maybe not for ourselves, but for future generations.

JBD

I could just see myself sacrificing my place in the trombone section in Dudley's band to make a difference for future generations. But when I asked my dad about going to Ben L. Smith High School he said, "You know your Mama is crazy when it comes to someone messing with her children. If one of those (he used the "c" word) spits on you, she'll go over there and tear that school down. I don't know how much it would take to get her out of jail."

A PLACE WHERE SUCCESS WAS EXPECTED: FINAL EDITION

I remembered what had happened in second grade when a teacher wouldn't assign me a reader, and I never mentioned going to B.L. Smith High School again. However, two of my friends, Toni Jordan, and Victor Tynes, Jr. did voluntarily transfer to Smith High School. I did not realize until years later what a great sacrifice they had made. Victor Tynes was one of the most gifted musicians I have ever known. He could play the saxophone, the French horn, the trumpet, the trombone, and the bass horn. He was our drum major at Lincoln Junior High School and during band class, he was our band director's, Mr. Harris, assistant. He was also a straight-A student and president of the student council.

All he talked about our ninth-grade year was finally getting a chance to be in the band at Dudley and someday being the drum major. He sacrificed that dream. Here is his story:

It was mid-summer, and I was home from college and standing at the bus stop on the corner of Bragg Street and Asheboro Street (now Martin Luther King Blvd.) waiting for the bus when this man started talking to me. I ignored him. He had all this facial hair and a big unkempt natural. Then he said, "Oh, now you want to act like you don't know me, Jo Ann."

"I don't know you. Leave me alone," I didn't bother to look up from the book I was pretending to read.

"I'm Victor. Victor Tynes," he said.

I started to tell him that he was lying. The Victor Tynes that I knew was voted Best Dressed and Best-Looking Boy in our ninth-grade class, but when I looked up, there was something about his eyes that told me that he wasn't lying.
Since I've never been known for being tactful, I asked, "What happened to you?"
He didn't say anything until we'd gotten on the bus and taken our seats.
"Those three years at Smith were the worst days of my life. I would raise my hand to answer a question, and if none of the white students raised their hands, the teacher would answer the question rather than calling on me. You know both of my parents are college-educated, and I would have both of them read over my work before I turned it in, but every time I got back a paper, it would have a C or a D. No marks or lines drawn through anything, just a letter grade. Finally, my mother took me to Mrs. Coley's house one evening and asked her to look at my paper. She told me to make a couple of changes, but otherwise, she said it was perfect. I finally thought I would get the kind of grade that I was used to getting back at Lincoln, but when the paper was returned a couple of days later, it had a C- on it. When I asked the teacher very politely to show me what I had done wrong so that I wouldn't keep making the same mistakes, she threatened to write me up

for insubordination. It never got any better the whole time I was there. I had never felt the things that they made me feel- like I wasn't smart- Like I was somehow less than others."

I did not know what to say to him. His eyes looked so sad and pitiful. We sat without talking until I got off at my stop.

Dudley Class of 1967 Souvenir Book, Thornhill Holmes et.al
(Left) Toni Jordan and classmates at Ben L. Smith Senior High School celebrate their 50th Year after graduation.

I know now what I should have said, "Thank you."
"Thank you, Victor, Toni, and all the other black students who gave up the years that for the rest of us were some of the most enjoyable learning experiences of our lives."

In 1968, the U.S. Supreme Court outlawed "freedom of choice" plans across the South, and in 1970, a federal court ordered Greensboro's schools to desegregate. By that time, a new progressive leadership on the school board and the Chamber of Commerce, led by former Greensboro College trustee Al Lineberry, Sr., pledged to not only abide by the court ruling but to use school desegregation as a means for a more genuine racial reconciliation in Greensboro.

When integration came to James B. Dudley High School, many expected a situation much like what had happened to William Penn High School to become the fate of Dudley. William Penn High School was the cornerstone of High Point's African American community for more than 70 years and was the city's black high school. When the white students who had been redistricted to the school in 1968 refused to attend the school, it was closed as though it had never existed. In spite of the turbulent racial backdrop

A PLACE WHERE SUCCESS WAS EXPECTED: FINAL EDITION

of the 1970s, Dudley integrated almost seamlessly. The people closest to the school during this time attributed this to three factors.

First, the staff and administration of the school were a unique blend of seasoned personnel and young educators. As part of the process of integration, the three white high schools in Greensboro were allowed to protect two-thirds of their staff from being moved. Dudley was not allowed to protect any staff members. Grimsley, Page and Smith administrators were allowed to move the teachers that they felt were the cream of Dudley's staff to their schools. The older staff members like Mrs. Coley and Mrs. Wells at Dudley and the other three high schools felt that they had been judged too old to be effective. When integration stated, they had something to prove. The younger teachers at Dudley and from the other three high schools felt that they had been judged too inexperienced to be selected or placed on the "Protected List." They had something to prove too. All the teachers were determined to prove that the white students who were redistricted to Dudley were going to get the best education available anywhere- the same quality education that Dudley's students had been getting for years. The administrative staff was equally determined to make integration work. Principal Franklin Brown, assistants, Mr. Chester Bradley, and Mr. James Howell demonstrated a level of fairness in their discipline and treatment of students of both races that encouraged an atmosphere of cooperation.

The staff of Dudley were fair and inclusive of all the students. For example, when one of the counselors found out that several of the white female students had been looking forward to playing on their old high school's field hockey team, she asked around and found out that one of the new teachers had played the sport in college. And miraculously, there was a Lady Panthers Field Hockey Team. Without quotas, the clubs and organizations at the school represented the school's new racial makeup- 60% Black and 40% White. Barbara Swann, president of the Dudley Girl's Athletic Association, recalled this period at Dudley this way,

> "I played basketball, volleyball, softball, field hockey, and ran track. When you are part of a team, you don't see yourself as a member of a certain race. Teammates are teammates. I enjoyed being at Dudley."

Dudley Girls' Field Hockey Team

1st Row L-R: Barbara Swann, Miranda Wilson, Sharon Bailey, Pam Phoenix.
2nd Row L-R: Susan Wilson, Gwen Platt, Lynn Myers, Sandra Simpson.
3rd Row L-R: Patty Sims, Gayla Kelly, Robin Neal. Absent are Laurie Fogleman and Eloise Davis

Without a doubt, some of the best examples of inclusiveness of all students without regard to race or social status could be found in all of the groups selected and coached by Miss Dye. Without using a quota system, the Cheerleaders, Modern Dance Group, and Pantherettes reflected the 60% Black and 40% White racial makeup of Dudley.

A PLACE WHERE SUCCESS WAS EXPECTED: FINAL EDITION

The 1972-73 Dudley Pantherettes

    The second factor that probably ensured the almost seamless integration of Dudley was the mixture of whites and blacks that were redistricted to Dudley. The whites who had been redistricted to Dudley lived mostly in the mill communities near Cone Mills and in other mill communities. The redistricting plan for Dudley sent most of Nocho Park including Benbow Road and Warnersville to Grimsley Senior High School and left most of the African American students at Dudley those from Dudley Heights, Lincoln Heights, Kings Forest, and the few remaining private homes in predominately black neighborhoods. For some reason, none of the Projects were placed in Dudley's School District. This mixture of black and white students meant that both the white and black students at Dudley came from mostly middle class, working families that had similar educational goals and career goals- that their children be self-actualizing citizens capable of either going to work right out of high school or going to college.

Many of the white students viewed the industrial and mechanical arts and academic programs at Dudley as an opportunity for economic and social advancement. For members of both races, this was a totally new experience. Benjamin A. Evans, a sophomore at Dudley the first year of integration, said,

> "The first couple of months were hard. We had to get used to white students at our school. I guess they had to get used to us too, and there were a few fights- mostly the same kids who just didn't want whites going to our school and there were some tough white boys too who stood up for themselves. But what really made a difference was being around each other and figuring out that we really weren't all that different. By the end of the first year, it wasn't anything special to see black and white kids hanging out together between classes or after school. When we got to be seniors, the white kids who stayed were just Dudley students like the rest of us."

The third factor was that the high skills vocational and industrial arts classes at Dudley prepared students to move directly from high school to the workforce. Classes like auto mechanics, woodworking, electronics, custom sewing, and horticulture were overloaded with students from both races. The Vocational Industrial Clubs of America (VICA) that served the trade, industrial, technical, and health students and Distributive Education Clubs of America (DECA) actually had larger numbers of whites than blacks in membership (1972-73). The cultural arts programs also offered additional opportunities for students, especially female students, to participate were also attractive to many students.

During the early seventies, the post-integration James Benson Dudley High School was a unique group of middle-class blacks and whites that made integration "work."

A PLACE WHERE SUCCESS WAS EXPECTED: FINAL EDITION

Top left: Tom Matkins and Edith Gonsavles participate in Home Economics Wedding. **Top right:** Jim "Cosell" announces Student-Faculty game. **Bottom left:** Students work on a group project. **Bottom right:** 1972-73 Dudley Stage Band conducted by Mr. Wise. Its musicians were as follows: David Fox –piano; Evert Bruner-guitar; Wayne Sain-bass; Joe Lambeth-drums; Tracy Spoon, Chuck Simpson, Bobby Laughlin, Ron Johnson, Fred Trulove-trumpets; Brad Simpson, Mike Braswell-alto sax; Lin Buie-tenor sax; Joel Woody- baritone sax; and Mike Oakley trombone.

The 2015-2016 Automotive Vehicle Technology Team (AVT) at Dudley seems to confirm that the current racial make-up of Dudley (95% African American) is not an indictment of the failure of integration, but a consequence of removing from the traditional curriculum practical industrial courses. Such courses encourage students of all races to want to attend a high school. Until the Auto Mechanics Class was revived, there was a less than 1% non-African American population at the school.

Dr. Jo Evans Lynn, Ed.D.

Photos Courtesy of Ivan Cutler

Dudley High School students Justin Williams, Jorge Prieto, Joshua Hill, Jetson Randall-Peangmeth, Camin Randall-Peangmeth, and Jeremy Peangmeth

Photos Courtesy of Ivan Cutler

Rick Lewis, CTE Educator/Automotive Instructor with students David Alaya, Thui Romah, Deborah Vincent (club advisor), Daniel Romero, Joanna Ziegler, Y'China (DHS Engineering Instructor) at Shell Competition

Chapter Ten

Much More than Teachers...

Dudley has always been fortunate to have dedicated teachers who were willing to give their personal time and resources. For most of the first 91 years of the school's existence, there were no stipends or extra pay for advisors or faculty coaches for clubs and non-revenue athletic programs. Before integration, coaches for revenue sports made as little as $100 for an entire season. So, teachers who were willing to give countless hours so that Dudley's students could participate in extracurricular activities were a very special breed.

NELLE ARTIS COLEY began her teaching career in eastern North Carolina after completing training to be a teacher at the Normal School at Bennett Seminary. After she returned home to Greensboro to teach at Washington Street School, she graduated from Bennett College in 1931 as a member of one of its first graduating classes after it became a college for women. She taught at Dudley from 1935-1973. She was the first president of the local and state Negro Teacher's Association. While a teacher at Dudley, she served as Department Chairperson of the English Department for over 25 years, Advisor for the National Honor Society, the Junior Marshals, and the Dudley Ladies. She was "Ma Coley" to thousands of men and women around the world.

She was active in numerous professional and civic organizations which included the American Association of University Women, the National Council of Negro Women, the NAACP, Bennett College Alumnae Association, the Classroom Teachers Association of Greensboro, and the North Carolina Teachers Association. In 1992, Mrs. Coley was honored by the Delta Sigma Theta Sorority, Inc. in its "Salute to Great Teachers" and in 1998, she was honored by having Project Homestead build a residential complex named the Coley-Jenkins Independent Living Center. Mrs. Coley was a devoted member of Providence Baptist Church where she served as a Sunday

School Teacher, Trustee, library volunteer and member of the Philathea Missionary Circle, and the Providence Service Guild.

Mrs. Coley is shown at the center of the first row with the 1965-66 Junior Marshals.

While the group was advised by Mrs. Coley, the Dudley Junior Marshals served as hosts for many school activities including assemblies, evening programs, and graduation exercises. The members were chosen in the spring of their sophomore year to participate during their junior and senior years at Dudley. It was always a prestigious group. Early candidates were required to have the following qualities: willingness to accept responsibility, dependability, courtesy, alertness, neatness, and good posture. The requirements for candidates changed during the 1980s limiting membership to the top 15 academic scholars of the rising Junior Class, and their active role became limited to Honor Society Inductions and graduation exercises.

When she came to Dudley in the fall of 1973 to replace Mrs. Nelle Coley, who had retired in the spring of that year, Janis Baines was surprised to find Mrs. Coley sitting in her classroom. Baines recalled,

> "She looked at me up and down very sternly. I answered her questions about my education very respectfully. Then she said,

A PLACE WHERE SUCCESS WAS EXPECTED: FINAL EDITION

"You'll do. You have tall shoes to fill and very high expectations to meet. The students deserve your best, and I expect nothing less."

Mrs. Coley's innovative teaching style- peer tutoring, learning contracts, group projects- have finally been acknowledged as the "right" way to teach.

Picture Courtesy of Chavis Library

VANCE H. CHAVIS was born January 14, 1906, in Wadesboro, North Carolina. He was educated in the Anson County School System and attended the High School Department of Biddle University (now Johnson C. Smith University). He continued his education at Johnson C. Smith University, earning a Bachelor of Science degree. At North Carolina Central University he received a master's degree in public health. He also studied at the University of North Carolina at Chapel Hill, the University of North Carolina at Greensboro, North Carolina A&T State University, and the University of Wisconsin.

Chavis was one of the first members of Dudley's staff when it opened on Lincoln Street. Chavis taught physics, general science, and biology at James B. Dudley High School from 1929 to 1955. He was appointed assistant principal at Lincoln Junior High School in 1955 and in 1957 was promoted to principal. Chavis remained in that position until his retirement in 1969. Chavis was known first as an educator but was also a leader in the local civil rights movement. He was an early member of the NAACP in the 1930s, and he in 1949, was integral in organizing the Greensboro Citizens Association. He was also an active member of the Democratic Party at both state and local levels, serving on the state Democratic Executive Committee and as a precinct chairman. From 1969 to 1973, he was a member of the Greensboro City Council. Chavis received numerous awards and honors, including Johnson C. Smith University's Alumni Centennial Award for outstanding achievement in community relations and a certificate of meritorious service from the City of Greensboro for his efforts on the Redevelopment Commission; Chavis was the first African American male in the United States to be appointed to a redevelopment commission. The Southeast Branch of the Greensboro Public Library was renamed in his honor.

GEORGENE E. DYE joined the Dudley staff straight out of Hampton Institute (Hampton University, Hampton, Virginia) in the fall of 1951. From that day until the day she died, on campus on September 10, 1977, she was married to Dudley. Although Dudley had majorettes and cheerleaders when she arrived, most people agree that she redefined both groups.

She felt that beauty and grace were important, but she also believed that majorettes and cheerleaders were athletes. With an instructor who believed that a female could be both physically fit and feminine, it was not surprising that many of her girls were also members of the first Lady Panthers Varsity Basketball Team and the *Lady Panthers Track Team.*

Miss Dye devoted countless after-school hours to extra-curricular activities. She strove for perfection and was responsible for innumerable contributions to the Dudley community and Greensboro. She was both loved and respected for all that she did for the young ladies at Dudley and in the community. She was so much more than a teacher.

A PLACE WHERE SUCCESS WAS EXPECTED: FINAL EDITION

The 1972-73 Squad was typical of Dye's Cheerleading squads. This squad co-headed by Anne Barbour and Roselyn Roberson spent many long hard hours of practice during the summer and after school to perfect their cheering performances. The athletic skill and grace demanded by Dye of all her squads did not come easily and she spent as many hours as needed working with them.

All of the squads after integration reflected Dye's determination not to use quotas. She said, "I will select members as I always have-solely on their merit, talent, and willingness to learn.

Miss Dye helped to expand the role of young women at Dudley when she founded a new auxiliary for the band, the Pantherettes. My sister, Mary Louise Anderson, recalls the tryouts,

> "I think there were about 100 girls there the first day. We were all excited because other than the girls who got to be majorettes or cheerleaders there just wasn't that much for girls to do. That first day of tryouts was so hard, half that number showed up the second day. When Miss Dye posted the list of the girls

who had made it, I was so excited that I had made it that I couldn't wait until I got home. But when I told Mama, she talked to Bishop Wells about it, and they decided that it wasn't appropriate for me to be in a group wearing that skimpy costume and dancing in public. I was so hurt."

The Pantherettes of James Benson Dudley have received numerous awards for their versatility and style. Now, every high-stepping marching band in the area has a similar group. Dudley was the training ground for many of the Golden Delights of North Carolina A&T State University and similar squads at other colleges and universities for many years.

The First Pantherettes 1966-67

In 1966, this new Auxiliary to Dudley's band gave 20 additional young ladies an opportunity to participate in an extracurricular activity. The high-spirited, high-kicking Pantherettes performed precision marching and dance routines at football games and in parades.

A PLACE WHERE SUCCESS WAS EXPECTED: FINAL EDITION

THE DUDLEY MODERN DANCE GROUP (1957)

OFFICERS

President………….. Juanita Tatum
Vice President…......Maurice Drake
Secretary................ Roberta Clarke
Treasurer.....................Rosa Jeffries
Manager............Jacqueline Florence
Directress.................. Miss G. E. Dye

Joan Bass	Hattie Logan
Barbara Byrd	Iris Lyons
Sirley Craven	Mary F. Reese
Barbara Guy	Mary Moragne
Ann Florence	Blondean Orbert
Elizabeth Harris	Ruby Russell
Shirley Hinnant	Verdie Wilkes
Bettye Jones	Barbara Robinson
Jean Ledwell	

Although she coached the Pantherettes and the cheerleaders, the Dudley Modern Dance Group was her "baby." It was the James B. Dudley Modern Dance Group that was the first group of women that she founded in 1957. Under the direction of Miss Dye, its twenty-seven to thirty members learned to express themselves with grace and charm through dancing. The dance group enabled the young ladies to discipline not only their bodies but their ethics and personalities. The girls put into action unselfishness, loyalty, and school pride to have a Company of dancers that moved together as one.

Every performance by her Modern Dance Group was a culturally enriching experience for the audience. M.L. Heard, the principal of Monroe High School, in Albany Georgia, said of her dancers, "The Performance by these talented young people will do much to enhance the cultural life of our community." In fact, any community group in Greensboro, and towns far and near, that wanted to ensure that a fundraiser was a success requested a performance by the Dudley Dance Group.

In April of 1964, the Entrée Nous Social Club in her hometown of Albany, Georgia, invited the Dudley Modern Dance Company to help with their Shoe Project. The idea of the Shoe Project came about because many of the high school dropouts in the area stated that a lack of shoes to attend school during the winter months had caused them to get so far behind that they finally gave up on getting an education. The club's goal was to raise enough money to buy shoes to keep a few students in school. However, a single performance by the Dudley Modern Dance Company raised enough money to start an endowed fund that provides not only shoes but also other necessities for needy students to this very day.

The programs for the performances by the Dudley Modern Dance Group were international journeys that enriched the lives of people whose itinerary seldom included any places beyond the Deep South. For example, for their 1964 Dance Recital Miss Dye choreographed a ballet from Ferrante and Techier; Coming Home Baby, a Jazz piece by Herbie Mann, My Lord What a Morning, a spiritual by Harry Belafonte; The Four Struthers Tap, a Broadway-style selection by Hugo Winterhalter; and A Tribute to America Through Dance- "No Man Is an Island", "Give Me Your Tired, Your Poor," and "Battle Hymn of the Republic."

A Night of Dance, a benefit performance for the Shoe Project, was only one of many benefit performances by the Dudley Modern Dance Group under Miss Dye's direction. Becoming a member of the Dudley Dance Group enhanced the lives of hundreds of young ladies. Miss Dye stressed that the body was a beautiful instrument that each had a responsibility to care for and to develop whatever talents their body had been given. One personal story personifies, for me, her willingness to help every student achieve his or her goals:

> *"I remember when I heard that Dudley was going to start a Girls' Basketball Team. I told Miss Dye that I was going to try-out. She did not discourage me although I had been in her physical education class for both my 10th and 11th-grade years, and she was well aware of my limitations as an athlete. She said, "Come early. I'll work with you."*

A PLACE WHERE SUCCESS WAS EXPECTED: FINAL EDITION

> *Even though I did not make the team, having her use over an hour of her time giving me lessons in the basics of women's basketball, gave me the confidence I needed to try some things that I would never have attempted."*

She made her students feel comfortable and capable.

Not only did she make outstanding contributions to Dudley High School as the advisor to the Cheerleaders, Pantherettes, Majorettes, Modern Dance Group, Pep Club, and the School Spirit Committee, but she also made outstanding contributions to the community:

- She was a physical education teacher at James Benson Dudley High School for all twenty-six years of her teaching career, 1951-1977.
- She founded the Dudley Modern Dance Group, Junior Varsity Cheerleaders, Dudley Pantherettes, Dudley Pep Club, and Dudley Flag Girls.
- She helped select and coach Dudley's first Girls Varsity Basketball Team.
- She was the first African American member of the board of directors of the Greensboro Civic Ballet.
- As a member of the Alpha Kappa Alpha Sorority, she choreographed the Annual Alpha Kappa Alpha Cotillion in Greensboro and High Point for over twenty years. This program not only provides social and cultural enrichment for young ladies, but it also helps provide scholarship money for the participants.
- She taught dance as a volunteer to children at Windsor Community Center for more than twenty years. Many of these young dancers later became members of the Dudley Modern Dance Group. One, Cheryl Gould, who took lessons from Miss Dye as a child and later became a member of the Dance Group, was a physical education/health and modern dance teacher at Dudley.
- In 1970, shortly after the Greensboro City Schools were fully integrated, Miss Dye received a letter of commendation for her wise and fair selection of the members of the Cheerleading, Pantherettes, Majorettes and Dudley Modern Dance Group. During a time of confusion and turmoil, Georgene Dye refused to set quotas for whites or blacks in the groups she directed. She said, "I will select members as I always have solely on their merit, talent, and willingness to learn."

No teacher could have survived in the same community, at the same school for twenty-six years, especially an attractive, single woman, unless her character was beyond reproach. Miss Dye not only survived, but she was also well respected by all who knew her. For the hundreds of young ladies, she taught and directed during her years at Dudley, she was a role model. Comfortable in a body that at the time was considered skinny, she helped us see that to be beautiful one had first to see the beauty in herself. The fifties were a time when many of the old intra-racial prejudices between fair and dark skin blacks still existed. Miss Dye changed this at Dudley. Pictures of her dancers, cheerleaders, and majorettes show many faces that could never have passed the "brown paper bag test".

As a teacher, she made physical education more than something one had to take. She called us to line up with, "Ladies, Ladies. It is time." Every young lady arrived for inspection in a freshly pressed jumpsuit, clean Bobbie socks and white polished tennis shoes with clean shoelaces. She expected us to look and act like ladies at all times. She did not allow us to say that we had been "sweating" after our activities. Although we practically ran to the showers after class, we only admitted to having "perspired profusely." She was a lady and every girl who came in contact with her wanted to follow her example.

Several of the young ladies that she taught and directed loved her so much and were so impressed by her that they decided to become physical education teachers or dance instructors. One such student is Mrs. Cheryl Robinson Gould, a 1978 graduate of Dudley. Mrs. Gould followed in the steps of her role model as Dudley's modern dance teacher and as minister of Sacred Dance at Mount Zion Baptist Church in Greensboro.

Miss Dye was a fitness freak before it was cool. She had the strict self-discipline to still fit into her college clothes when she was well into her forties. One could not doubt her ability to mold a group of young women from diverse backgrounds into a single unit through dance after attending a performance of her dancers. It takes honesty and integrity to win the hearts and full cooperation of so many young people.

She made every department in the school a part of every dance performance. The seamstresses in the custom sewing classes made the costumes; the carpentry classes built the set or made some props; the business classes designed and typed the programs; art classes designed and painted backdrops. Musicians from the band supplied some of the music. There was always, at least, one dance to a vocal selection sung by one or more members of the chorus; and if she did not manage to find something for her coworkers to do directly, she asked him or her to come and help her out with the audience on the night of the show. Teachers and administrators gladly cooperated because no one wanted to be left out. No matter how small, it was an honor to play a part in one of her productions.

One Dudley alumnus and former Dudley math teacher, Calvin Strachan, remembers the air of cooperation that surrounded Georgene Dye this way,

> "I remember how excited our electronics class was to do the lights and sound effects for her programs. It was more than getting close to those fine dancers; it was being a part of an event that special. If she asked for you, by name, the next season, you could brag about it to all your friends."

Her stand, after integration, on the selection of the members of the groups she directed was so fair and racially unbiased that she helped to foster a sense of belonging and equality among the 40% of Dudley's student body that just happened to be white. If a student made one of her groups, no one doubted that she was supposed to be there.

Miss Dye's dedication to her work at Dudley was extraordinary. According to those who talked to her that day, she was not feeling very well on her last day of work, but she came because new members had just been selected for one of her groups and she wanted to talk personally to any of the girls or their parents who had questions. When she died of a cerebral hemorrhage on September 10, 1977, it took seven people (Two cheerleading coaches, two coaches for the Pantherettes, one dance director, one majorette instructor/advisor, and one physical education teacher) to do all that she had once done for Dudley (Lynn, 2004). Miss Dye was inducted posthumously into the James B. Dudley Sports and Educational Hall of Fame/Hall of Distinction in 2019.

Dr. Jo Evans Lynn, Ed.D.

In 1970, during a time of confusion and turmoil in some schools, Georgene Dye refused to set quotas for whites or blacks in the groups she directed. She said, "I will select members as I always have- solely on their merit, talent, and willingness to learn."

Senior Modern Dancers 1972-73

A PLACE WHERE SUCCESS WAS EXPECTED: FINAL EDITION

JANIS BAINES came to Dudley in 1973 as a new teacher replacing Dudley teaching legend Mrs. Nelle Coley. During her 31 years at Dudley, she created a legacy of her own. In honoring her 31 years teaching at Dudley by dedicating the 2004 Yearbook to her, the Yearbook Staff wrote,

"Once in a while, an extraordinary teacher comes along, who seems to be able to do everything well. Usually, it is not until the end of his or her tenure that we realize the full measure of his or her worth.

Although we appreciated Mrs. Baines before she retired in the spring of 2003, we could never thank her enough for the many wonderful and admired things that she did. As English Department Chairperson, as Yearbook Advisor, as the mentor to future and present teachers, and as a classroom teacher, she definitely made her mark on the grounds of Dudley High School. So, thank you, Mrs. Baines, just for being you!!!"

She served as the advisor for the Panther Yearbook for ten years and co-advisor with her successor Lori Bolds for the 2003 Yearbook. Her senior Academy students presented outstanding presentations during Black History Month that for many years were the major theatric performances at Dudley. She also led the way for all seniors to make presentations of Senior Projects long before it became a requirement for graduation statewide. Baines was one of the first teachers at Dudley to receive her National Board Certification and was the Guilford County Teacher of the Year in 1997. She also served as coordinating teacher to dozens of new English teachers. Jennifer Broome complimented her mentorship,

"Janis Baines was more than my co-operating teacher. She was a mentor, a mom away from home, and a true friend. When I was student teaching, she made sure I had the resources, administrative support, and knowledge to instruct students successfully."

Dr. Jo Evans Lynn, Ed.D.

Juniors in Mrs. Baines 11 Honors American Literature Classes present original productions highlighting the progress of African Americans throughout history.

A PLACE WHERE SUCCESS WAS EXPECTED: FINAL EDITION

GWENDOLYN SPINKS BENTON, a 1967 graduate of James B. Dudley High School, returned to Dudley to teach English in 1980 and spent the next 24 years making a difference in the lives of the students at Dudley. She understood how important extracurricular activities are to creating an enriched academic experience in high school. While a student at Dudley, she was a member of the Junior Marshals, the Dudley Modern Dance Company, the Spanish Club, the Safety Patrol Force, and a majorette with the Dudley Marching Band. Before she graduated from high school, she had already decided to become a teacher. She was a member of the Future Teachers of America. One fellow teacher, Stanley Johnson (Dudley, 1967) says that she started her teaching career with him, "I probably wouldn't have graduated from Dudley if it hadn't been for Gwen. I didn't care much about going to school, but Gwen would make sure that I got there every day, and she kept me encouraged. It is hard to fail when someone believes in you that way."

Her husband Charles Benton was a member of the same graduating class and these high school sweethearts attended North Carolina A&T State University together. All three of their children, Charles E. (1990), Shatarra (1994), and Byron (2000) graduated from Dudley.

Gwendolyn Spinks' husband, Charles Benton at Dudley. They were classmates and members of the Class of 1967.

Charles Benton, 1967

Gwendolyn Spinks, 1967

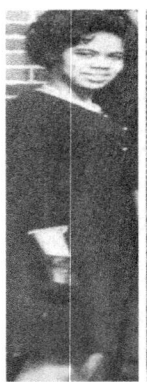

Dr. Jo Evans Lynn, Ed.D.

Gwen is pictured, **above from left to right**: as a member of the Junior Marshals, a Dudley Majorette (Front Row), as a member of the Future Teachers of America (Left, end of the top row).

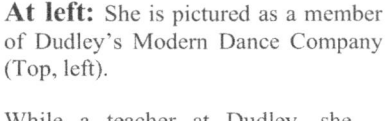

At left: She is pictured as a member of Dudley's Modern Dance Company (Top, left).

While a teacher at Dudley, she served as faculty advisor for many clubs, organizations, and student activities. Since her son, Byron L. Benton was a member of the band, she was also an active "Band Parent."

Pictured Top left: Mrs. Benton served with Mrs. Kerr as the advisors for the Dudley Ladies. It is a service organization whose mission is: "To foster the development of young women who will become ideal ladies exemplifying self-confidence, demanding excellence, role modeling for other female students and ultimately becoming leaders who will affect positive influences through exposure to a world of new ideas, a positive environment, and multi-cultural appreciation."

At Bottom: Benton is pictured at the 1988, Dudley Prom. She served as Junior Class Advisor in planning the prom.

A PLACE WHERE SUCCESS WAS EXPECTED: FINAL EDITION

Recent- More Than Teachers at Dudley

To those who think the teachers featured earlier in this chapter were the last of their breed of caring, effective teachers, there are many such teachers, staff members and administrators at Dudley.

BONITA GREENE HARGETT graduated from Dudley in 1983. While a student at Dudley, she was a Varsity cheerleader, a Dudley Student Government Association member, and performed with the Dudley Dance Company. As a student-athlete, she was on the Dudley Swim Team. She also served on the Greensboro Youth Council, the Steering Committee, and as a student representative on the PTSA Executive Board. She was selected to be on the Homecoming Court and listed in Who's Who Among Greensboro Youth.

She graduated from North Carolina State University with a BS in Business Management in 1987. She was certified in Business Education in 2006 at North Carolina A&T State University and earned an MS in School Administration from High Point University in 2010. She taught Business Education at Dudley for 18 years and at Andrews High School for two years. In 2014, Hargett began serving at Dudley as the Career Development Coordinator. Hargett has been very active in the Dudley High School community serving as Department Chairperson (Career & Technical Education), Superintendent Advisory Representative, NTHS Advisor (National Technical Honor Society), SGA Advisor (Student Government Association), and as Class Advisor (Freshman, Sophomore, Junior & Senior). Hargett has also served as HSTW Representative (High Schools That Work) and Site-Based Leadership Committee, Facilitator of the Career Expo at Dudley, and assisting in creating Business Partnerships with Dudley High School. Her community outreach also includes serving as the representative for High Schools that Work and Jack and Jill Co-advisor. Hargett has also been very active in the local community as a Delta Sigma Theta Sorority member, Jabberwock Bonding Co-Chair, the National Association of Negro Business and Professional Women, and Bethel A. M. E. Church. She is also a member of The Links, Incorporated an American invitation-only social and service organization of upper-class Black women. It is the largest and most influential organization of Black women in the US. Members include multiple prominent women, including Kamala Harris, Marian Wright Edelman, and Betty Shabazz,

In their desire to give the Seniors at Dudley as close as possible to a "real senior experience, during the 2020-2022 COVID Pandemic, Hargett worked with other administrators and staff members to plan and facilitate a zoom graduation ceremony, Spirit Week, and other Senior Class activities. She also serves as Homecoming Parade Coordinator, JV Cheerleading Coach, and Assistant Golf Coach.

Hargett was elected to the James B. Dudley Hall of Fame/ Hall of Distinction in 2019.

Pictures Courtesy B. Hargett

ABOVE LEFT: Ms. Hargett and students receiving gift cards for their hard work in the Learning Hub where Hargett serves as the Learning Hub Champion.

ABOVE RIGHT: As the Career Development Coordinator, Hargett assists in creating Business Partnerships with Dudley. One such partnership is with the Samet Corporation which is one of the leading Commercial & Industrial General Contractors, Design & Builders and Construction Managers in the Southeast. Pictured above: Ms. Hargett (First Row, Far Right) with Dudley's Apprentice students at Samet with Johnny Siger, Samet President (Second Row Far Right).

Equestrianship/ horseback riding is not a common sport for African American children.

Here, Ms. Hargett (Far Left) is seen giving back to community by teaching children the basics of grooming and learning about horses. The first step to becoming an equestrian.

Picture Courtesy of B. Hargett

A PLACE WHERE SUCCESS WAS EXPECTED: FINAL EDITION

MAURICE D. HAMILTON was born September 7, 1976. He graduated from Dudley on June 5, 1994, as a 2nd generation Dudley Graduate (Mother, Esther Hamilton, Class of 1965). While a student at Dudley, Hamilton was active in the Marching Band (Trumpet Co-Section Leader), the Concert Band (1st Chair on both Trumpet and French Horn), the Jazz Band, the Dudley Student Council (Class Representative), and Jr. Civitan's (Served as President Senior Year - 1993 -1994).

After graduation, Mr. Hamilton served his country in the United States Army. During his eight-year tour in the military (Five Years Active Duty & Three Years U.S. Army Reserves) Mr. Hamilton served as a Mechanized Infantryman.

After being Honorably Discharged, Hamilton attended North Carolina Agricultural & Technical State University. In 2008, Mr. Hamilton graduated with honors (Cum Laude) with a Bachelor of Arts in History with a concentration in African American Studies.

Proud of his roles as husband, father, teacher, mentor, community leader & Dudley Alumni.

Mr. Hamilton's passion for helping and working with young people directs the trajectory of his community service and profession as a teacher. Mr. Hamilton has been a member of the Prince Hall Masonic Family since 1998. He has served in various leadership positions on the local, state, and national levels. Hamilton's involvement, especially with the Knights of Pythagoras (Masonic Mentoring Group), has afforded him opportunities to give back to his community, especially with the youth, through service, leadership, and mentorship.

As a Life Member of Bethel AME Church, he served on the Board of Trustees, the Audio/Visual & Tech Ministry, Security Team, the Sons of Allen Men's Ministry, and Boy Scouts Troop 723 at Bethel AME Church. He also served the Old North State Council Boy Scouts of America as a former Executive Board Member.

Left: Rev. Dr. Martin Luther King, Jr. Drum Major for Justice Band Competition, Tampa Florida, January 1994 - 1st Place Best Band in the Nation. **Center:** B PHI B Trumpet Section- Dudley High School Marching Band 1993-1994 Edition. **Right**: Maurice. Hamilton before Band Practice -Senior Year- Fall 1993.

Dr. Jo Evans Lynn, Ed.D.

Top: National Honor Society Induction Fall 2021 (Committee Member); **Center Left:** Hamilton leading Marching band of Thunder as Assistant Band Director; **Center Left:** Assistant Director Maurice Hamilton before 2019 Homecoming Parade; **Bottom:** 2019 - 2020 Edition of the Dudley High School Marching Band of Thunder under the direction of Mr. Roger D. Jackson, Jr., Director of Bands.

A PLACE WHERE SUCCESS WAS EXPECTED: FINAL EDITION

JESSICA MARTIN-OATES was born in Peru, Indiana, to her mother, Jacquelyne (Smith alum), and her military father, Walter Martin (Dudley Alum)—who at the time was stationed in Germany.

When her father retired, they settled in Greensboro, where she followed the legacy of attending Lincoln, then Dudley. Martin-Oates comes from a line of Dudley graduates. On her mother's side: grandmother Veoila Archie-Bennett and her uncle Prentiss Bennett. On her dad's side: Grandfather Walter Martin Sr; father and his brother Jeffery Martin. All three of her brothers also graduated from Dudley. Her oldest daughter, Kayla, graduated in 2021 from Dudley, and her son, Terrence Jr., will graduate in 2023.

Martin-Oates graduated from Dudley in 2002. While a student at Dudley, she was in the National Honor Society, Dudley Ladies, Computer Club, Junior Marshals, Key Club. She also served as Squadron Commander of the Junior ROTC and was Captain of the Girls Soccer Team. After graduation, she attended Guilford College, where she had a double major in English and Secondary Education. Martin-Oates will complete a master's degree from Garner Webb University in Teacher Leadership, Curriculum, and Instruction-Urban Education in May of 2023.

Left: During the JROTC Banquet in 2002, as a senior squadron commander of JROTC, she is pictured passing on the job of squadron commander for next year to her brother Warren Martin.

Right: Double picture- Martin Oates- Is shown Coming back from the Academy Beach Trip & Graduation Picture with honor cords and NHS stole

For eight years, she has taught English I, Honors English I, and Honors Teacher Cadet I & II at Dudley. When asked what encouraged her to teach at Dudley, she responded, "When I came back to Greensboro, I decided to substitute teach.

When I came to Dudley, I could see there was a need for teachers who knew these kids, the history, and who cared. Our pride is infectious! If students don't see our love for our school, then they will not have a love for their school, and we already have enough against us." At Dudley, she serves as co-advisor to the National Honor Society.

If her students forget everything else, she has taught them, she says, "I want them never to forget Dudley is a family and never go without anything. Someone here has what you need, whether knowledge, food, clothing, or job experience—help is only an ask away.

Celestine G. Bennett
Dudley High School
EC Teacher

CELESTINE G. BENNETT, an Exceptional Children's teacher at Dudley, is one of many such teachers and administrators still at Dudley. She received her undergraduate degree from New Jersey City University, Jersey City, NJ, and her graduate degree in Educational Leadership from St. Elizabeth College in Morristown, NJ. The 2020-2021 school year marks her 22nd year as a Special Education Teacher. Bennett began her teaching career in Newark, New Jersey, teaching every grade level, from grammar to high school.

She described her passion for teaching this way, "If I allowed my mom to tell the story, she would say I was born to teach. She often shares with people how as a child, I would line up my dolls and teddy bears on my bed to teach them their ABC(s)and 123(s). My memory of why I wanted to enter the educational profession had everything to do with my desire to teach students who were negatively impacted by their disability, either by the school system or society. I wanted to create a nurturing learning environment for them and foster the belief that they could and would learn with my help and support."

Bennett explains moving from New Jersey to North Carolina by saying, "In 2011, I moved from New Jersey to North Carolina to be closer to family and raise my two daughters. I was offered a job as an EC Teacher at Andrews High School, where I taught for five years before transferring to Dudley High School."

When asked, How is teaching at Dudley different? Bennett stated, "Working at Dudley High School has been very rewarding. I enjoy and embrace the rich legacy that many alumni members have fostered, passed down to our current students. I admire the *Panther Pride* many of our young adult students exhibit in our school and community.

Chapter Eleven

Building Strong Men ...

'It is easier to build strong children, than to repair broken men." Fredrick Douglass

During the more than 143 years since its founding on the campus of Bennett Seminary in 1879, the administrators, teachers, and coaches have done an outstanding job of producing men of great character, skill, and determination to excel. The Men of Dudley have excelled in every walk of life-doctors, master carpenters, lawyers, accountants, architects, entrepreneurs, professional athletes, teachers, ministers, master mechanics, politicians, college professors, master musicians, brick masons… The list goes on and on. During the last twenty years with more than 70% of African American males being reared in homes with young single mothers there is an even greater need for men who are willing and able to mentor and to serve as role models. Fortunately, James B. Dudley High School has always had men who fulfill this need.

CHESTER BRADLEY coached Dudley High School to a state football championship in November 1951. The Panthers beat Durham Hillside 13-6 in front of an overflow crowd at War Memorial Stadium. Although this was a great game, most of the men who played for him agree that not even that great game had as much of an impact on their lives as Chester Bradley.

"He was the type of coach that wanted fellas to learn what life was all about," said Lonnie Winston, a senior on that championship team. "Winning was not his top priority. Character building was his thing."

Bradley started his teaching career at Dudley as a biology teacher in 1945. He was an assistant principal from 1967-1982. He served as Dudley's second associate principal during the turbulent years of integration. Bradley was the first African American member of the North Carolina Coaches Association.

He introduced several generations of students to golf and helped Coach Dudley's first golf team. Bradley developed Dudley's first fitness program for its football players using his resourcefulness to make a tackling dummy with a heavy cement bucket hanging from it.

Bradley was a pastor by trade and never said a profane word. He did not drink or smoke either. Guilford Westmoreland, one of Bradley's players, said that was reason enough for him not to take up those vices. Westmoreland continued, "Bradley met with his players and talked about their lives every morning- lessons in respecting yourself and those around you would never be forgotten."

"He was a person you didn't want to disappoint," said Eddie Favors, a straight-A student who was one of the several brains-over-brawn players on Bradley's 1951 team. The 1951 team stands out as one of Dudley's best teams ever for other reasons. In 1950, the Eastern Region of the NCHSAC had two undefeated teams- Dudley and Durham Hillside. The Conference Administrators selected Hillside to represent the Conference in the State Playoff. The following year, the Conference changed the age requirements so that several of Dudley's top players aged out. The changes also placed Dudley and Hillside in different Regions. Bradley coached his team to an undefeated season and a State Championship anyway.

Oakley, another one of Bradley's players that later got into coaching, said of him, "Bradley and his assistant, William Furcron, knew plenty of football and passed that knowledge on to their players. He believed that you didn't have to degrade or demoralize a person to get him to do right. You can influence by showing them, drilling them. He was good at that. I try to reflect these things in my coaching style."

Dudley's coaches were not paid much, and they didn't have very much of a football budget. Although Dudley's stadium was started in 1941, it was not completed until 1979, when Bradley was no longer coaching. Getting a football team over to War Memorial Stadium was no easy task. Bradley was resourceful.

The first five years he served as assistant principal proved that he was a man of fairness. After integration, his stand on the treatment of all students at the school was so fair and racially unbiased that he helped foster a sense of belonging and equality among the 40% of Dudley's student body that just happened to be white.

A PLACE WHERE SUCCESS WAS EXPECTED: FINAL EDITION

Picture & Text Courtesy of Mr. Eddie Favors

The James B. Dudley Undefeated 1951 State Championship Team

(Back row-left to right) 1. Johnny Blackwell (DB); 2. Peter Morehead (DB); 3. Eddie Favors (RB); 4. Lloyd Oakley (FB); 5. James Thomas (FB), 6. Robert Bingham (RB); 7. ?? Jones (QB); 8. Bobby Little (RB):
(Front row-left to right) 1. Herman Williams (OE); 2. Johnny Evans I; 3. Leo Cardwell (T); 4. ?? (T); 5. Nosco Wright (G); 6. George Grier I; 7. Bobby Echols (G); 8. ?? Whiteside (G); 9. Eugene Coleman (T); 10. Lonnie Winston (T); 11. Robert Hughes (DE). **Not Pictured:** Jimmy Neal (DB), Charles Hutton (QB), Guilford Westmoreland (QB)

WILLIAM J. FURCRON taught, coached, and served as Athletic Director at Dudley. When a professional player, Charlie Sanders, gives a high school coach credit for his success, it speaks to what an extraordinary man and coach the individual was. In his 2007 NFL Enshrinement Speech, Charlie Sanders said,

Coach William Furcron, my senior high school coach, was very instrumental in my athletic career. I thank him for all that I learned from him. He was a true mentor, a man that only wanted the best for a young black athlete growing up at such a difficult time. To coach boys, a gentle giant, who with a paddle in his hand could improve your twitch and your quick get off. I still feel some of the things he was trying to tell me (smiling)."

Teacher, Coach & Athletic Director

William (Bill) Furcron coached in both football and basketball programs at Dudley for a generation, with his teams playing for four state titles and winning twice in a seven-year span from 1956-1961. One of the teams that he coached during that span is considered one of the greatest in high school basketball history. However, when asked to name a team that had given him some of his proudest moments as a coach Furcron said,

"The 1968-69 Football Team. Thirty players from our State Championship Team were redistricted away from us. No one gave us a chance to do much of anything that year, but the young men on that team were determined to have a good season. They were what team play was all about."

Three of the athletes on the very talented 1961-62 basketball team were Curly Neal, Lou Hudson, and Charlie Sanders, all of whom have been inducted into the Guilford County Sports Hall of Fame. He also coached the basketball team to a State Runner-Up in 1956. As Athletic Director and Head Football Coach, he coached the 1966-67 Football Team to a State Co-Championship title in the North Carolina High School Athletic Conference. This title was particularly "sweet" because not even the local Greensboro Daily News or Greensboro Record had given Dudley a fighting chance against an undefeated Fike High School team that had 305lb. twins who played both sides of the ball.

A PLACE WHERE SUCCESS WAS EXPECTED: FINAL EDITION

In 1967, his team moved from the North Carolina High School Athletic Conference to the North Carolina High School Athletic Association (When the schools were segregated, the NCHSAC was the conference that schools like Dudley played in. It dissolved in the summer of 1968). In 1968, Furcron coached his football team to a City Co-Championship and Conference Co-Championship. No one except the coaches and the team had given them a chance to succeed that season. Furcron said, "Redistricting had started and 30 of our players from the previous year's championship team were playing for other teams. They didn't know how determined that made the players who were left to prove everyone wrong."

His team made it to the first round of the State playoffs where they lost to Fike High School 21-14. As Athletic Director, he expressed a keen interest in the education of his athletes. To allow his athletes ample time to study, he had all athletes take gym during the last class period of the day. During this period, athletes were required to do their homework and study. Also, those athletes who were struggling with their studies were tutored by other athletes. This practice resulted in record numbers of athletes making the A and B honor rolls (Robinson, 2013). To prepare his athletes for college, he encouraged them to take the PSAT in their junior year to prepare for the SAT. Under his watch, all Dudley athletes were required to dress and conduct themselves like ladies and gentlemen at all times. Dudley athletes today are still required to meet that standard.

Honors: Guilford County Sports Hall of Fame Class of 2007, the Dudley High School Field House was named in his honor in 2013. Professional Experience: James B. Dudley High School Athletic Director, Head Football and Basketball Coach, Chemistry Teacher, and Advisor to Honor Society (Robinson, 2013).

WILLIAM "BILL" BOYERS taught physical education and coached at Dudley from 1956 until 1995. Although he officially retired in 1995, it was as though he never left Dudley. He was a regular substitute, and he proctored for exams until he became ill. He stood near the sidelines-never in the stands during football games long after he was no longer actively coaching. To say that he had an impact on the lives of the athletes and students that he coached would be an understatement. During his tenure as a coach and a teacher, he felt that preparing the young men he worked with for the realities of life was as important as the skills they learned during practice or on the playing field. Life, according to Boyers, was tough and not always fair. Stahle Vincent, the first African American to play quarterback at Rice University, described his experience under Boyers in an article by Jeff Mills. He said,

"He was a tough man who competed until the whistle blew, and he expected his players to be the same way. Our practices were very hard. In fact, the toughest practices I had during my entire football career were the ones during my first year at Dudley. Mr. Boyers would tell us afterward that he was getting us ready to face a world that was hard and not always fair."

TRACK AND FIELD 1967

First Row: W. Bratcher, K. Shipp, N. Tate, L. Shaw, F. Noble, J. Russell, M. Young, S. Brower. **Second Row:** M. Tate, P. Nichols, W. Wesley, J. Smith, J. Shoffner, A. Crawford, Coach Boyers.

Boyers believed that mental and physical toughness were primary keys to success. NFL Hall of Famer, Charlie Sanders mentioned Boyers by name as one of the coaches who had a significant impact on his life and playing career. Boyers coached football for 35 years, was the school's track coach for 34 years, the wrestling coach for 20 years, a basketball coach for five years and a baseball coach for a year. The track at Dudley was named in his honor in 2013, and he was elected to the James B. Dudley Sports Hall of Fame/ Hall of Distinction.

MARVIN H. WATKINS graduated from Dudley in 1952. He earned a bachelor's degree in history and English from A&T in 1958 and a master's degree in education in 1962. Watkins was among the first Dudley graduates hired by Dr. Tarpley. He taught history at Dudley where he was named Dean of Boys. He led the change of the title of the position from Dean of Boys to Dean of Men: acknowledging the role of high school teachers and administrators in grooming the male students at Dudley to grow academically and socially into men who contributed leadership in their homes and communities.

In In 1962, Superintendent Phillip Weaver convinced the School Board to allow former students who had dropped out of high school and students who had been incarcerated to reenroll in high school. Dr. Tarpley would not allow such students to come to Dudley. So, he set Watkins the task of developing a night school program for young adult students. Watkins developed the program and served as coordinator of The Evening School for Young Adults at Dudley High School. The program which started in 1963 was so successful with students who had dropped out of the other Greensboro High Schools because Dudley offered courses like auto mechanics, electronics, carpentry, brick masonry and custom sewing which allowed graduates to prepare for higher paying jobs. The program was closed in 1965 because the interracial mix of students did not sit well with the administrators of the then segregated school system.

Watkins served as assistant to the president for development at Bennett College for six years. He also served an administrative internship with Piedmont University in Winston-Salem. He joined the A&T administrative staff in 1976 as assistant director of the Office of Research Administration.

Watkins served as director of research administration at N.C. A&T for 12 years, before being promoted to associate vice chancellor for research. The announcement was made by Dr. Edward B. Fort, chancellor of A&T. In the announcement Fort said, "Mr. Watkins has rendered outstanding service in the area of research administration. We are confident that he will continue to assist our new vice chancellor for research in achieving our announced goal of $40 million in extramural funding by the year 2000. Watkins a native of Greensboro, has played a leadership role in the generation of more than $148 million in research and development projects at A&T during the past decade."

JONATHAN MCKEE, SR. When former coach and athletic director Jonathan McKee, Sr., died one of the most notable comments made about his legacy was, "Hundreds of men who played for him lost one of the guiding influences in their lives." He was many things during his adult life, but perhaps the most impactful of those titles was the term Coach. "We always called him Coach, but he was much more than that,' former Dudley student Ray Crosby said. "He became a friend of mine. But I still called him Coach." (Harden, E., 2006)

Coach McKee was a Retired U.S. Army Reserves Major, serving in that capacity from 1954-1980. He worked in Virginia as a teacher and coach for several years before joining the staff at Greensboro's Dudley High School, where he was a Head Football, Basketball and Golf Coach, also serving as the school's athletic director for a time (Strunk, R. 2021).

McKee was an outstanding and well-respected coach, earning the Coach of the Year award in 1976 in the Central 4A Conference and Division 8. His Basketball team brought home the 1960-1961 Basketball District and State Championships, compiling a 22-2 record. In 1963, he led Dudley to a state runner-up finish and conference championship on the hardwood.

Then on the diamond, Dudley's 1964 baseball team won the conference and State championships in the NCHSAC. One year later, in 1965, his baseball team again took the 4A State Championship in the NCHSAC (W. A. Vincent, 2022). McKee's football teams posted a 90-46-3 record, winning the conference championship in 1966 and 1967, and advancing to the state finals in 1966 where they tied for the State Championship (J.T. Barber High School tied 6-6 for Co- State Championship).

A PLACE WHERE SUCCESS WAS EXPECTED: FINAL EDITION

Outside of his accolades for coaching, McKee was a well-respected community leader, earning the Emporia Extravaganza Award in 1984 and a Carolina Peace Maker Award. He served on the Board of Directors for the NC Coaches Association from 1978-1980 and was once selected as the NCCA Man of the Year. In 1975, he was recognized by the NCCA for 20 years of outstanding service. In addition to his role at the school and in the coaching community, McKee was a pillar of his church community, serving as a deacon at United Institutional Baptist Church.

McKee saw Dudley through a period when the school merged, along with other black high schools in the NCHSAC, into the NCHSAA and desegregation. Jonah McKee, his twin brother, told the *Greensboro News & Record* in an interview after his brother's death, that it wasn't uncommon for him to get a phone call in the middle of the night from the police needing help during the downtown civil unrest in the late 1960's and early 1970's. "They'd call him and ask him to come down and mediate," Jonah told the **News & Record's Ed Hardin** back in 2006. "They needed a man who could come and calm things down. Jonathan would do that. He was more than a football coach. He was … a great man."

1964 State Baseball Champions

Picture Courtesy of W. Anthony Vincent

NELSON MACOMSOM AKA Mr. Make. He was born in Gaffney, South Carolina. He graduated from A&T College, now known as N.C. A&T State university, in Greensboro, North Carolina in the class of 1939.

Macomson began teaching at James B. Dudley High School in 1941. He started the Brick Masonry Program at Dudley in 1941 and was the instructor through 1956. In 1956, he started the Auto Mechanics Program and was an instructor until his retirement. His students won numerous trophies including the North Carolina Auto Mechanics State Competition for consecutive years (1963, 1964, 1965). He also served as the Chairperson of the Vocational Education Department for many years.

During his 35 years of tenure at Dudley High, he also drove the school activity bus from 1950-1966. This was a second-hand bus that was painted blue (school colors) and was given the nickname "The Blue Goose". The bus was well known for its mechanical problems; thus "Mr. Make" would carry spare parts used to repair "The Blue Goose" as he transported the sports teams, choir, drama, and other such groups to in-town and out-of-town activities. There were many occasions on which those spare parts had to be utilized.

As a teacher "Mr. Make" was of the firm belief that youth would greatly benefit from acquiring a trade or skill to carry over into adulthood. Toward the end of his teaching career, in the 1970s, he had some female students in his auto mechanics classes.

After his retirement in 1976, Mr. Macomson spent the remaining 20 years of his life dedicating his finances and time to Hayes Taylor YMCA on East Market Street and to various other organizations that are geared toward programs that provide encouragement to the youth of the community. In 1993, he was awarded "Man of the Year Trophy" by Hayes Taylor YMCA. The Auto Mechanics Facility at Dudley was named in his honor.

Mr. Macomsom's classes were crowded with students desiring skilled instruction that would enable them to get practical experience for a future job.

One of Mr. Macomsom's former students, Bernard Fowler said of his expertise, "That man was so good; he could just listen to a car running and tell you exactly what was wrong and how to fix it."

A PLACE WHERE SUCCESS WAS EXPECTED: FINAL EDITION

Andrew Scales

**Nelson Macomson
Chairperson**

VOCATIONAL EDUCATION classes produced blooming master craftsmen in Auto Mechanics, Carpentry, and Brick Masonry.

Lonnie Reynolds

Picture Courtesy Panther Yearbook 1967

Dr. Jo Evans Lynn, Ed.D.

Edward H. Greene

John O. Bigelow

The VOCATIONAL EDUCATION classes at Dudley prepared students to go directly from graduation to jobs in Electronics, Masonry, Carpentry, Auto Mechanics, and Agriculture.

Warren Dorsett

Picture Courtesy Panther Yearbook 1967

A PLACE WHERE SUCCESS WAS EXPECTED: FINAL EDITION

WILLIAM "BILL" WHITES was an assistant coach to Dudley's Varsity Baseball Teams State Championships in 1964 and 1965 and later served as head coach during the late 1960's. Whites served as both a football and basketball official for the Central Intercollegiate Athletic Association (CIAA) for thirty-four years and was inducted into the CIAA Official Hall of Fame in 1998. In addition to the CIAA, Whites served as an official with the Atlantic Coast Conference, Conference of Carolina, Old Dixie Conference, Southern Conference as well as the MEAC. He was appointed the coordinator for women's officials of the MEAC in 1995 and served in that capacity until his death. "Mr. Whites was a consummate professional and an even better person." stated MEAC Commissioner Dennis Thomas. "Bill made a difference. He influenced the lives of so many people in a positive way."

In addition to his passion for officiating, Whites loved influencing the youth. He retired from Grimsley High School (NC) where he served as the assistant principal. He also dedicated his time as a swim instructor and lifeguard at the Windsor Community Center and Hayes Taylor YMCA and worked with social organizations including the Flexible Social Club and Meals on Wheels. Whites, a 1963 graduate of North Carolina A&T State University, was also a proud veteran of the United State Marine Corp. He was a member of Kappa Alpha Psi Fraternity and became a life member.

Baseball

Baseball Players from left to right, FRONT ROW: John Guy, Larry Boone, Raymond Pettiford, Garry Russell, SECOND ROW: Anthony Waldrum, Garcia Howard, Earl Caldwell, Reginald Booker, Claude Patterson, Ronnie Willie THIRD ROW: Joseph Herring, Micheal Hall, Joseph Davis, Roger Brice, Abner Donnell, Gerald Johnson, Manager

Coach Bill Whites is pictured on the right side of the back row.

Dr. Jo Evans Lynn, Ed.D.

MARVIN LAMBERT or "Coach Lamb" as he was affectionately called graduated from Dudley in the class of 1970. He received his B.S. Degree in Health and Physical Education and an M.S. Degree in Guidance and Administration from North Carolina A&T State University.

His work experience included service with the National Summer Youth Sports Program, the JTPA, a tour of duty as an officer in the United States Air Force, and as an assistant supervisor and counselor for the federal government's ACTION Program. He was a guidance counselor in the Winston-Salem Forsyth County School System, and he retired as a guidance counselor after 29 years of service (20 at Dudley).

For 21 years he worked with the Men's Track Team at Dudley, taking the helm as head coach in 1992. He built a solid program leading his teams from Little Four City Champions to numerous other high school and college invitational victories. During his tenure, his teams compiled a regular season record of 131 wins against 16 losses; his teams won six Conference Championships; and secured a State Runner-up Title. He was selected "Coach of the Year" on six different occasions (Bolds & Lynn, 2004)

Coach Lambert pictured with the last Dudley Track Team he coached in 2004. Most of his track teams seemed to be loaded with natural talent. However, it took a coach like him to help convert natural talent into the high level of performance that produces champions. Some of his former track athletics say that he taught them how to work hard enough and feel confident enough to make it to the next level (Bolds &Lynn, 2004).

A PLACE WHERE SUCCESS WAS EXPECTED: FINAL EDITION

DAVID PRICE head coach for men's basketball for 21 years retiring in 2012. Price is a native of Leaksville, North Carlina where he attended Stoneville High School where he played basketball and was named Best Defensive Player, All-Conference, All-County and played in the State championship game. He was also recognized by Street and Smith Magazine. Davis graduated from Stoneville High School in 1969 and from Winston-Salem State University in 1974. He later received his Master of Science degree from North Carolina A&T State University.

Teams coached by Price have amassed a 78.12 winning percentage and played in five state championship games and won the state championship three times. Dudley won back-to-back state championships in 2005 and '06 at the 3-A level and took the 4-A championship in 1996. In the 1996 State Championship game the final score was Dudley 76, Richmond Senior 68 (OT): Vincent Whitt and MVP Braxton Williams scored 24 points each for the Panthers (29-2) in the 4-A title game. Brendan Haywood blocked nine shots.

The Panthers were 3-A runners-up in 2000 and in 2004. Price's teams complied a career record 668-217 in 29 seasons as assistant and head coach. This record includes the years he served as an assistant and head coach at Stoneville High School and as an assistant basketball coach and football coach at Morehead High School. Price has received numerous caching awards: NCHSAA Regional Award, Conference Coach of the Year and Guilford County Coach of the Year. Price has coached in numerous other All-Star events: Coca Cola All Star Game in Muncie, Indiana (1996), Kentucky Derby All -Star Basketball Game (2002), Commonwealth Classic in Richmond, VA (2005), and the Jordan Classic in Madison Square Garden, NY (2006).

The Historically Black High Schools Classic held Saturday, January 15, 2021, at Dudley High School featured four games and a cheerleading competition. Dudley honored former coach David Price, who guided the Panthers to three NCHSAA boys state titles and two other championship game appearances.

QUENTIN CROSBY graduated from Dudley in 1997 as one of the top wrestlers in the program. Wrestling has never been as popular as football or basketball at Dudley, however, the love, and passion for the sport that Quentin Crosby brought to the program as its head coach raised wrestling to new heights.

During his freshman year at A&T, Crosby learned that Dudley no longer had a wrestling team. He came back the next year and helped restart the program and served as an assistant to Kevin Green throughout his years in college. Crosby became the Head Wrestling Coach at Dudley in 2001 after he graduated from A&T. His enthusiasm for the sport was contagious, so getting young people to come out for wrestling was not the hard part. Keeping them involved was.

Greensboro Daily News 2008

Crosby considered the powerhouse wrestling programs at Morehead High School in Eden and Ragsdale High School in Jamestown and concluded that the keys to success were coaches who put in endless hours of work; wrestlers who compete year-round; and former wrestlers who return to help sustain the tradition. All of the keys to success were present under Quentin Crosby. He worked endless hours, and he created a feeder program, Panther Kids Wrestling, as an offseason club team. It was not only a feeder program; it generated among current and future Dudley wrestlers the kind of passion

A PLACE WHERE SUCCESS WAS EXPECTED: FINAL EDITION

Crosby had for the sport. He kept his wrestlers involved in every aspect of the Super 32 Challenge. Like every nonrevenue sport, there was always a shortage of funds. His wrestlers worked tirelessly to raise money for travel and to pay entry fees to out-of-season tournaments. Crosby even paid out of his pocket when necessary.

When he was only 28 years old, he began a wrestling match with a deadly opponent: cancer. In September of 2007, persistent stomach cramps led to an unexpected diagnosis: Carcinoid tumors were growing on the lining of his small intestine and his liver (Greensboro News & Record, 2008). The disease was a particularly challenging circumstance for a man who had been a high-energy person all his life. He lost his final match in August of 2013. However, he went out as a winner because those who knew him remember him as someone who spent his life helping others and as someone who, against all odds, built a winning wrestling program at James Benson Dudley High School.

Quentin Crosby was inducted into the James B. Dudley High School Hall of Fame/Distinction in 2013. Interested alumni and friends may contribute to the nonprofit that he started to benefit the Wrestling Program at Dudley at www.pantherkids.moonfruit.com or contact Dudley's wrestling coach.

STEVEN T. DAVIS. Dudley has won seven state championship titles in football. Teams coached by Steven T. Davis have won five of them. Davis started his coaching career at Page High School under Marion Kirby and assistant coach Frank Starling. After joining Dudley as an assistant in 2001, Davis was promoted to the head coaching spot in 2004. He quickly found success with a state championship berth in 2004. Davis went on to lead the Panthers to state titles in 2007, 2008, 2013, 2016 and 2021. Davis was named the head coach of the North Carolina team for the 2018 Shrine Bowl, which took place in Spartanburg, S.C.

When asked which of his coaches had the greatest impact on his coaching style Davis said, "My former college coach Bill Hayes when I played football for him at N.C. A&T… He taught me how to get the most of my X's and O's in the game of football… What I learned from him really helped me as a coach. I liked how he managed his coaches and players."

The 2023-2024 school year marked 28 years coaching and 19 years as head coach at James B. Dudley High School. When asked what he found most rewarding about coaching Davis did not mention all the championships. He said,

> "When the guys go off into the real world and graduate and come back and say, thank you Coach Davis. We did it. I did not see back then the lesson that you were trying to teach me, but I see it now…"

It is clear that the small-town work ethic that Davis brought with him from Calhoun Falls, South Carolina has been tremendously effective in coaching the young men at Dudley. Steven Davis understands how being an athlete can change the trajectory of a man's life. Davis played for Calhoun Falls during the program's glory years under coach Dennis Botts. Davis played quarterback and defensive back and went on to a Division III opportunity at Chowan University in Murfreesboro, North Carolina (Rolstad, 2018).

Davis later transferred to play defensive back at North Carolina A&T, a historically black university that competed in the Division I Mid-East Athletic Conference (MEAC). Playing at that level made Davis even more proud of his small-town beginnings.

A PLACE WHERE SUCCESS WAS EXPECTED: FINAL EDITION

The longtime football coach has come a long way since he lined up for the Blue Flashes on Friday nights, and he continues to afford young athletes the same opportunities he capitalized on when he spent Fridays and Saturdays under the lights (Rolstad, 2018).

Davis's players value the hard work that it takes to succeed. Dudley has produced more players that have played and are still playing in the NFL than any other high school in North Carolina, (Charlie Sanders, Stahle Vincent, John Guy, Jeff Davis, Marques Douglas, Demario Pressley, David Amerson, Kenny Okoro, Emanuel Moseley, Matt McCain & Hendon Hooker). However, it is the opportunity to use the skills that they develop at Dudley to move on to greater opportunities in life that Davis truly values.

Davis says, "Football and athletics itself was just a way out for me. And I can honestly say, if I didn't play athletics, I don't know if I would have gone to school. It was one of those things where the opportunity presented itself and once, I got in there I think I was fortunate enough to take advantage of it and here I am today." (Rolstad, 2018)

Davis makes sure that his players know that the games they compete in at Dudley help prepare them for a better life off the field. Davis's players know that playing for Dudley is an honor for which they have to work hard to prove themselves worthy.

The Coach and his assistants understand that they are more than coaches. They are mentors and role models. Calhoun Falls football assistant coach Earl Wright helped raise Davis, along with his wife and Davis's grandparents. When Wright and his wife worked night shifts, Davis babysat his cousins at their house.

Wright said Davis was always a good student and athlete. Davis was an all-state basketball player and also played baseball. Wright said, "What it will do is let somebody else know that, hey, just because you come from a small town doesn't mean that you have to have small-town dreams. With you having the mindset to go ahead and do the best you can, and continue to strive to move forward, you can do anything. The world can be your home" (Rolstad, 2018).

Coach Davis and his assistant coaches have built a program that has been one of the state's best during his 19-year tenure. His teams have an .849 percent winning rate.

Steven Davis and Steven Davis II (Deuce)

All championship games are special. However, 2021 was even more special, Coach Davis won a title with his son on the roster, Steven Davis II, better known as Deuce.

"Deuce has been on the sidelines for the other championship games as a ball boy, as a little boy," said Coach Davis. "For him to be playing this year, is very special for me."

Coach said he doesn't treat him any differently than the rest of the guys.

"At home. I'm dad," said Coach Davis. "On the field, I'm coach. I tell him you have to work for everything you get."

"It's the perfect scenario for me," said Deuce. "That's the best way I could go out my senior year."

"I'll be proud both ways being his coach, but so proud of him as a father, just to watch him grow and he's doing good in school," said Coach Davis.

Win or lose, Coach Davis is proud of his son.

"Just proud of him and he knows that" said Coach Davis.

KENNETH FERRIERA, NEWS & RECORD

A PLACE WHERE SUCCESS WAS EXPECTED: FINAL EDITION

"He's one of the best dad's I think I could have," said Deuce.

The father and son left Chapel Hill with a championship, beating J.H. Rose 69-40

"It's an honor to do it with my son," said Coach Davis.

"It's the perfect scenario for me," said Deuce. "That's the best way I could go out my senior year."

"I'll be proud both ways being his coach, but so proud of him as a father, just to watch him grow and he's doing good in school," said Coach Davis (Sirera, J., 2021).

Win or lose, Coach Davis is proud of his son.

"Just proud of him and he knows that" said Coach Davis.

As a senior, Davis II was a defensive leader on the team. Brandon Anderson, Dudley's longtime defensive coordinator, says, "Deuce is our leader right now. He's the one getting everybody lined up, checking coverages, because he's been around the program so long and he knows the defense."

Kenneth Ferriera. Greensboro News & Record

Above: Dudley's Steven Davis II runs back an interception during the first half of the Panthers' 20-6 win at Statesville in the NCHSSA Class 3-A playoffs. Davis led Dudley with four interceptions during the 2021 Season and broke-up 16 passes.

In the highest scoring neutral site State Championship Game in history, the Dudley Panthers blasted J.H. Rose 69-40 to win the school's seventh Football State Championship and fifth title in NCHSAA play. The Panthers were led by quarterback Jahmier Slade who rushed for 98 yards and three touchdowns and throwing for two more with 115 yards passing on his way to winning MVP for the game.

Picture Courtesy NCHSSA

Dr. Jo Evans Lynn, Ed.D.

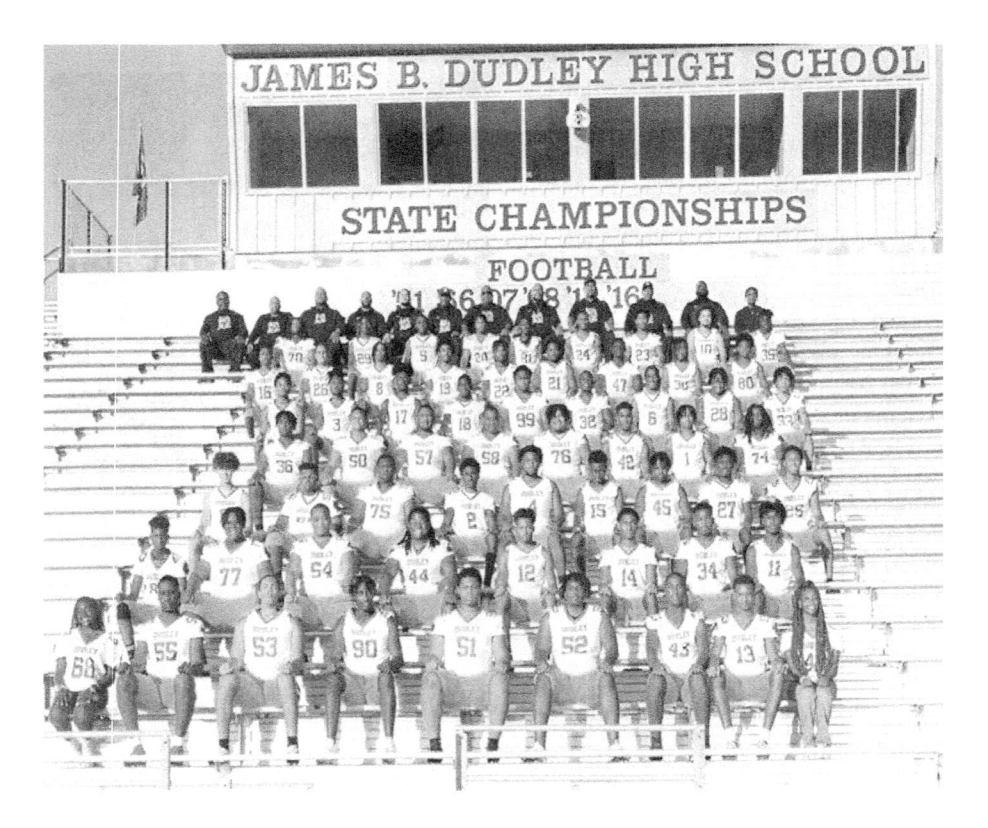

ROW 1 (Left to Right): Milan Foxx, Student Manager, 55- Trevon Humphrey, 53-Soti Woodson, 90-Dominque Wilson, 51-Malcolm Kennion (OL, DL), 52- Darius McLendon, 43-Yero Woodson, 13-Savoi Edwards, Deja Robinson, Student Manager; **ROW 2 (Left-Right):**83-Abdul Baylor (K), 77-Jaden Buie (OL), 54- Jaden Lane (OL), 44- Jhyheem Pittman (DL), 12- Shawn Seagraves (DB), 14-Shannon Edwards, Jr. (WR), 34-Braden McCall (LB,DE), 11-Nasir Newkirk (YR,DB); **ROW 3(Left-Right):** 9-Domaine Vann (QB), 60-Joshua Palmer (OL), 75-Todd Hargrove (OL); 2-Steven Davis, II (DB), 4-Jaylan Richmond (LB, FB), 15- Sofiyan Oumarou (DB), 45-Darryl Dawkins (LB, DE), 27-Le'Ezra Brown (WR, DB), 25- Cameron Baldwin (LB,RB); **ROW 4 (Left-Right):** 36-Austin Lloyd (DL, FB), 50- Johnathan Neal (OL,DL), 57-Braxton Smith (OL,DL), 58-Jordan Miller (OL, DL), 76-A'Mon McManus (OL, DL), 42-Brian Siner (LB), 1-Jahmier Slade (QB), 74-Seth Lawrence **ROW 5 (LEFT to Right):** 7-Elvis berry (DB), 3-Mehki Wall (WR,DB), 17-DJ Parker (WR,DB), 18- Koredell Bartley (WR,DB), 99-Logan Wright (DL,FB), 32-Kafi Abass (LB), 6-K.J. Morehead (ATH), 28-Cihiem Graham (LB), 23-Tyler Moore (RB), **ROW 6 (Left to Right):** 16-Antonio Lee, Jr. (QB), 26-Corey Jones (DB), 8-R.J. Baker (ATH), 19-Trey Green (DB), , 26-Corey Jones (DB), 21-Jeremiah Barnes (RB), 47-Tayshawn Glover (DL), 30-Jaylin Williams (RB), 80-Tommy Westbrook (WR);
Row 7(Left to Right): 70-Cedrick Commander (OL), 29-Lorenzo Southern, Jr., 5-Michael Shaw (RB), 24- Asha Bonds (RB), 23-Tyler Moore (RB), 10-Jorga Lara (WR), 35-Dwayne Reese.
Top Row (Left to Right): (Assistant Coaches, Head Coach & Student Manager) Brandon Anderson (AC), Pat Neal, Marcus Alford, Antonio Hall, Denorris Best (AC), Calvin Davis, Lewis Walker, Steve McCormick, Steven Davis (HC), Richard Powell, Artouris Bryant, and Mia Shaw.

A PLACE WHERE SUCCESS WAS EXPECTED: FINAL EDITION

Picture Courtesy of Greensboro Times 2021 December Edition

Dudley set a record for most points scored in an NCHSAA championship, breaking an 18-year-old record, and the Panthers topped the 60-point mark five times during the 2021 season. Dudley High School, which won its first state title in five years, had 62 points with two minutes and nine seconds left in the third quarter. Panthers senior QB Jahmier Slade was championship MVP, after he ran 11 times for 98 yards and three touchdowns. He threw for 115 yards and two touchdowns. The Panthers tied an NCHSAA state championship game record for most points in a half (Greensboro Times, 2021).

Dr. Jo Evans Lynn, Ed.D.

Dudley's 2022 Men's Track and Field Team Makes History

Some of Dudley's most outstanding male athletes have been members of the Dudley Men's Track and Field Team. Several had actually won 1st place in their event- Jerome Gantt (Shot Put, 1966) and Harvey Clanton (Discus, 1967), and Clarence Grier (High Jump,1963), but Dudley's men had never won a State Championship in Track and Field until the 2022 Men's Track and Field Team did it. Dudley senior Isaiah Monroe turned in an MVP performance to lead the Panthers to the 2022 NCSHAA Men's Out-door Track and Field Championship in the Class 3-A division.

Running on the track at N.C. A&T, Monroe won the 100-, 200-and 400-meter races and anchored the Panthers' winning 4X400 relay team in a dominating performance. Steven Davis II won the high jump for Dudley as the Panthers finished with 80 team points to easily outdistance runner-up Croatan (51.5).

Picture Courtesy of WOODY MARSHALL, NEWS & RECORD

Dudley's Isaiah Monroe (left) wins the NCHSAA Class 3-A men's championship in the 100-meter dash with a time of 10.91 seconds. Monroe also won the 200 and 400 and ran the anchor leg on the winning 4X400 relay to help the Panthers claim the team title.

The 2022 Dudley Panthers were a force to be reckoned with at the 3A Men's Championships as the Panthers won five of the meet's events including the final event of the day, the 4X400 Relay. The Panthers put an exclamation point on their dominant performance, winning the relay in 3:22.40 as Steven Davis II, Asa Bonds, Michael Shaw, and Larry Monroe combined to blow away the field. Isaiah Monroe set a new 3A State Meet Record in the 200 Meter Dash when he crossed in 21.12 seconds. His time eclipsed the time of 21.20 seconds posted by Warren County's Randy Jordan which had stood for over 36 years.

A PLACE WHERE SUCCESS WAS EXPECTED: FINAL EDITION

Picture Courtesy of NCHSAA Pictures

Front Row, Left-Right: Gregsha' Lee, Tequille Jackson, BJ Felix, James Pinnix

Top Row, Left-Right: Steven Davis II, Jonathan Smith, Larry Monroe, Elvis Berry, Asa Bonds, Le'Ezra Brown, Micheal Shaw

Coaches- Gregsha' Lee (Track Director & Vertical Jumps Coach), Tequille Jackson (Boy's Head Coach), BJ Felix (Boys Asst. Head Coach), James Pinnix (Horizontal Jumps Coach)

Dr. Jo Evans Lynn, Ed.D.

2022 N. C. STATE CHAMPIONS 3A MEN'S OUTDOOR TRACK AND FIELD TEAM

Aaron Spears

Abishek Pradhan

Adeniyi Adegorioye

Alijah Tibbs

Asa Bond

Ayden Foxx

David Blackmon

Denzel Foster

Derrick Hicks

Devin Dow

Devin Mims

Donyel Parker

Elvis Berry

Isaiah Monroe

Jahariee Paschal

Jahmier Slade

Jalile Elliott

Jeremiah McLaurin

Jonathan Smith

Kameron Baldwin

Keyaun Dow

Koredell Bartley

Langston Wood

Larry Monroe

Le'ezra Brown

Michael Shaw

Nasir Newlink

Rory Baker

Shawn Seagraves

Steven Davis II

Tashawn Neal

Terrance Oates

Trey Green

Tylei Woolard

Chapter Twelve

Strong Leadership Makes a Difference

During its first fifty-three years as a public high school for students both inside and outside of the city limits of Greensboro, the Greensboro High School for Negroes a.k.a. James Benson Dudley High School had only two principals. Serving as the leader of a high school such as Dudley is an extremely difficult role because not only must the principal perform all the ordinary functions of a principal, but he or she must also embody the community's image of the school. All fourteen of Dudley's principals 1923-2023 brought something different to the table in this respect.

Dr. John Allen Tarpley
1st Principal
1923-1965

Dr. JOHN ALLEN TARPLEY was named the principal of the Greensboro High School for Negroes in 1923 while the high school was located on the campus of Bennett Seminary. Before this, beginning in 1879, the Negro public high school students whose tuition was paid by the city of Greensboro, fell under the leadership of the president of Bennett Seminary. Tarpley and other community leaders lobbied the Greensboro City Council to build an edifice for the high school for years. The agitation for a school building intensified after Bennett became a college for women in 1926, and the upper grades joined the ninth grade at Washington Street School. A few male students attended the Normal School on the campus of North Carolina A&T State University.

When the school building was completed in 1929 and occupied by students the Tuesday after New Year's Day, January 2, 1929, Tarpley continued in the role of principal until his retirement in 1965. Tarpley created the curriculum for the school, which remained the same throughout his tenure as principal. He also hired the school's first teaching staff, many of whom taught at Dudley for more than thirty years.

There was never any doubt during the Tarpley years as to who was the dominant leader at Dudley. He led by example. He was always positive and enthusiastic about the potential of the students, the capabilities of his staff, and the contributions of the school to the community. His hand was always in the day-to-day activities of the school. However, he did not micromanage; he hired competent teachers and allowed them to do their jobs.

He improved the quality of instruction not only at Dudley but also in all the Greensboro Negro Public Schools for which he served as superintendent (1932-1948). Insisting by 1936 that all teachers be college graduates and that they teach only in the area(s) for which they were certified. He also encouraged teachers to continue their education at the graduate level. By 1942, James B. Dudley High School had more teachers with master's degrees than any other high school in the state (Tarpley, 1979).

He was involved in the community and paid close attention to what his constituents were saying. For example, although he favored a curriculum that was heavy on vocational courses, he listened to his constituents, who insisted that all students needed cultural arts and foreign languages to be well-educated citizens. During the Tarpley years, the feeling of Dudley's students and the community that it served was that of pride and complete togetherness.

Mr. Franklin Brown
Dudley's 2nd Principal
1965-1976

When **MR. FRANKLIN BROWN** became James B. Dudley High School's second principal in 1965, he had the impossible task of following a legend. He had two primary advantages when he was named principal: he knew the school and community, and he had served for two generations under Tarpley's leadership.

Brown had been a member of Dudley's staff since 1937 teaching Radio and Electronics and had also served as Dean of Men and Assistant Principal. Although he served as principal during one of the most turbulent periods of the school's history, most of the staff, students, and parents considered him an effective leader. The 1973 Panther Yearbook noted,

A PLACE WHERE SUCCESS WAS EXPECTED: FINAL EDITION

> "In spite of its heavy work burden, a capable administrative staff always has time to communicate with students. Mr. Franklin J. Brown can be seen many times during the day talking with students around the campus. He has a genuine interest in all the students and will aid in any way possible."

An effective leader is available to teachers, staff members, parents, students, and community members. A good leader stays calm in difficult situations and puts the needs of the school first. His leadership abilities were certainly some of the most valuable aspects of Brown's character that helped Dudley survive the conflict over the 1969 Student Election and the transition to integration during the 1970-71 school year. Tia Hodge, a Dudley graduate, wrote about this period in a 1979 article, Dudley's History Reflects Change,

> "In 1971 one of the greatest changes in the history of education took place, 1971 was the year of desegregation. Many Dudley students did not like the idea of white students coming to their school; neither did the whites like being forced to come to Dudley. For a period of time, Dudley was a place of apprehension. None of the students knew what to expect from one another. It was a time when numerous hostile racial feelings surfaced, but because of Mr. Brown and his assistant principals, Mr. Chester Bradley and Mr. James Howell, desegregation took place with minimum racial disturbances."

Through one of the most turbulent periods in the school's history this kind, and gentle man proved to be an effective leader.

Mr. Earl H. Crotts
Dudley's 3rd Principal,
1976-1980

MR. EARL H. CROTTS succeeded Mr. Franklin Brown as principal of Dudley in the fall of 1976 becoming the first white man to serve as principal of Dudley. He had been an assistant principal at Page Senior High School, and he brought with him from Page Mr. Francis Nolan to serve as assistant principal in charge of curriculum. Mr. Chester Bradley, who had been on the Dudley faculty since 1945, continued as the assistant principal in charge of student affairs and school buses.

Mr. Crotts saw his mission at Dudley as one to change Dudley from what was still a "community" school to one that served a broader range of students. He did this by reducing

Dudley's course offerings to a very rudimentary level. He said in an article shortly after his arrival,

> "After years of new- this, and new that, and much experimentation in school curriculums through the country, there is a return to basics across the board. There's been a real demand from parents that the kids have more basic skills, and I think people at the colleges have demanded it as well. A couple of years ago, the people in Chapel Hill and other places were raising cane about not getting people who could write and express themselves." (Hodge, 1979)

Crotts sort to "return" Dudley to a place it had never been. While the segregated white schools had been experimenting with all sorts of "new" curriculum ideas, the curriculum at Dudley remained the same for over 50 years. Since Chapel Hill was 99.9% white at this time, one would have to assume that the students who were going to college there unable to write and express themselves were not African American students.

The academic "bar" at Dudley had never been set as low as it was during Crotts' tenure. Even when the school was located on Bennett Seminary's campus and the students were the sons and daughters of former slaves, students who advanced to the normal school (high school) level were expected to have mastered the basics of reading and writing. In keeping with his goal to return to the basics, Crotts allowed Dudley's auto mechanics, modern dance, carpentry, masonry, and drama departments to be moved to the newly opened Phillip Weaver Education Center and ended custom sewing and Family Life Classes. After these changes had been made, many of the white students who had at first been forced to come to Dudley, but had stayed because of the exceptional vocational, industrial arts classes, and expanded opportunities to participate in extracurricular activities like Drama and Modern Dance began to leave Dudley.

JBD

A PLACE WHERE SUCCESS WAS EXPECTED: FINAL EDITION

In 1980, **MS. LINDA MCDOUGLE** became the principal of Dudley High School. She was Dudley's first female principal. Linda Wilson McDougle was born in Burlington, North Carolina, where she grew up on a farm with her parents and three sisters. In 1962, she graduated from an all-black high school, Jordan Sellars High School, at the top of her class and graduated in 1966 from North Carolina Central University.

After graduating, she began work as an earth science teacher at a predominantly all-white school called Jackson Junior High School in Greensboro, North Carolina, which is now known as Jackson Middle School. In 1970, she earned a master's degree in education from the University of North Carolina at Greensboro and two years later was promoted to assistant principal at Jackson Junior High School.

Ms. Linda Wilson McDougle
Dudley's 4th Principal, 1980-1986

In a 1983 interview with Scott Stalmasek, student reporter for the school's newspaper, the Panther's Claw, McDougle listed her concerns for the 1983-84 school year: "Outstanding grades, a winning sports season, and making sure that students were aware that Dudley is the best school in the city and that their actions needed to show this, whether they were on campus or in the community." She also stated,

> "I hope the students continue to say all the good things that Dudley has to offer to the community and to keep up the school spirit. Also, I want the students to strive for their maximum potential in academics and athletics."

McDougle helped implement the Science and Math Open School and Dudley's membership stabilized during her tenure as principal. She retired as the Associate Superintendent of Guilford County Schools.

Principal McDougle **(fourth from left)** with **(L-R)** Mr. Johnson, Mr. Barbour, Mrs. Hudson, Mrs. Viele, Mrs. Gibbs, Mrs. Harris, Mr. Allen, and Mrs. Garcia.

JBD

Mr. Robert Saunders
Dudley's 5th Principal
1986-1989

MR. ROBERT (BOB) SAUNDERS became Dudley's fifth principal in 1986. Saunders was a native of Lynchburg, Va. He coached football and was the assistant principal at Johnson Junior High School in Washington D.C. He was also the principal of Jackson Junior High School in Greensboro before coming to Dudley.

Mr. Saunders was known as a caring, diligent, and dedicated person. Staff members described him as a strong leader who made himself available to the students and staff. His commitment to serving youth and his enrichment of their lives serve as his legacy.

There was a resurgence in sports during the late 1980s under Mr. Saunders. Dudley played for two State 4-A Championships in football and was runner-up in two 3-A Championship games in basketball.

A PLACE WHERE SUCCESS WAS EXPECTED: FINAL EDITION

Mr. Lenwood Edwards
Dudley's 6th Principal
1989-1993

MR. LENWOOD E. EDWARDS became Dudley's sixth principal in 1989. Several of the people interviewed for a biographical segment about him referred to Mr. Edwards as "Dudley's most beloved principal." He was a genuine "people person" who had a gift for helping young people find that special something in themselves. Wayne Robinson, a student he coached at Greensboro Day said of him, "He put me on the path for everything else I accomplished."

It did not seem to matter to Mr. Edwards whether a student was a top academic student or one who was barely getting by; he remembered every student's name and he had the same smile and words of encouragement for everyone. His positive attitude about Dudley and its students seemed to breathe new life into Dudley. He did not come with the attitude that Dudley needed "fixing" but rather with the belief that Dudley had great students who wanted to learn and competent teachers who were there to teach them. The students and staff responded to his attitude in the way that people live up to the expectations of those whom they respect.

After graduating from Greene County Training School in Snow Hill, he earned a Bachelor of Science degree in Physical Education from Johnson C. Smith University. He was on the football team and was a superb punter. At one point, he held the highest punting average in the conference. He later earned post-graduate degrees from Springfield College (Masters of Sports Medicine and Administration) and North Carolina A&T State University (Master of Education in School Administration). Also, he pursued various doctoral courses in the field of Educational Counseling at the University of North Carolina at Greensboro.

Edwards was a consummate educator, motivator, coach, and mentor in the Edgecombe County Schools and the Guilford County Schools for over 40 years. His assignments included: Pattillo High School of Tarboro, North Carolina, Lincoln Junior High School, Kiser Middle School, Page High School, Joyner Elementary School and Foust Elementary School in Greensboro. He was the first African American athletic director at Greensboro Day School. In all of these positions, he seemed to have found a way to "connect" with young people.

JBD

Mr. Larry F. Lewis
Dudley's 7th Principal
1993-1999

MR. LARRY F. LEWIS became Dudley's 7th principal in 1993. He led the school during the School Merger of the Greensboro City Schools and the Guilford County Schools. Mr. Lewis was known for a management style that consisted primarily of acknowledging that Dudley had an excellent faculty when he became principal and hiring the "right" people to fill the infrequent openings on the staff. (When I came to Dudley in 1997, I was one of only seven new teachers that year). Mr. Lewis allowed good teachers to do their jobs. His strategy seemed to work. During his tenure, Dudley High School had three consecutive winners of the title Guilford County Teacher of the Year.

DHS principal Larry Lewis poses with (left to right) Janis Baines, Teacher of the Year 1997, Dr. Patricia Legrand, Teacher of the Year 1999, and Mr. Tony Watlington the Teacher of the Year 1998.

A PLACE WHERE SUCCESS WAS EXPECTED: FINAL EDITION

MR. KEN THOMPSON was Dudley's 8th principal serving in that capacity from 1999-2001. He attended North Carolina Central University earning a Bachelor of Arts in History and Geography with focus on intermediate grades in 1971. He also attended the University of North Carolina at Charlotte completing his teacher certification in 1973. Mr. Thompson worked for several years in Charlotte-Mecklenburg before moving his family to Greensboro where he enrolled at the University of North Carolina at Greensboro. It was there that he completed a master's degree program leading to a Master of Education degree focusing on Educational Administration in 1989.

Mr. Kenneth Thompson
Dudley's 8th Principal
1999-2001

Thompson led what he felt was the School Board's plan to bring Dudley into the 21st Century. After the battle to save the school had been won, I had a long talk with him. I felt that most of the members of the Construction Committee, who voted to demolish the entire campus, sincerely believed that their decision would give the community a school with better facilities, more educational space, and much needed technological updates. After months of reviewing various reports, I felt that Mr. Thompson and a few others were aware, at the time that the Committee voted, that the school that the Construction Committee had been shown would not be the one that was built. The final "New Dudley Plan" would have been an Academy for 1,200 students, an auditorium with a capacity for 350, and a new gym with a capacity of 700.

I never had been able to reconcile the man who had fought so hard to demolish the entire campus transforming it into an academy with a limited number of African American students and in all likelihood an entirely new staff with the man who introduced himself at our first Faculty meeting. That man said, "We have the finest students, the finest teachers, and the finest parents to be found anywhere." So, the first time we talked one on one after the "dust" had settled over whether to destroy or renovate the campus, I asked him the question that disturbed me the most about what had nearly happened to Dudley. I asked him, "Did you know what would have happened if the entire campus had been demolished?"

He said, "It seemed like the best plan to me. For years Black folks went to Second Ward in Charlotte, and that's exactly what happened to our old school. The old school was demolished, and the students went to other schools. Mrs. Lynn, the world didn't come to an end."

The Plaque Ceremony for Second Ward School that served Black Charlotte teenagers in grades 7-12 from 1923-1969. This is part of the *Second Ward Consolidated High School* Reunion each year.

Dr. Tony Watlington
Dudley's 9th Principal
2001-2004

DR. TONY WATLINGTON became Dudley's 9th principal in 2001. He had taught Honors American History, World Geography, World History, Government and Economics (ELPSA) at Dudley for four years before leaving to become principal of Fairview Elementary School. While at Dudley, he served as Social Studies Department Co-Chairperson; on the Instructional Senate/Leadership Team; as Special Programs Coordinator; as Ninth-Grade Program Coordinator; he was on the Dudley Math Science, and Technology Academy curriculum committee; on the Southern Association of Colleges and Schools (SACS) as the Committee Chairperson, as the Scholarship Committee Chairperson and as the High I.Q. Team Coach. So, when he returned to Dudley as principal, he had a clear understanding of the dynamics of the school and the community that it served.

A PLACE WHERE SUCCESS WAS EXPECTED: FINAL EDITION

In some ways his administration was very reflective of the administrative style of Dr. Tarpley. As a former history teacher, he was very conscious of Dudley's historical and academic legacy in the community. He saw Dudley as one school and its students as one student body–as a complete entity rather than as the Academy and the rest of the school. During his first speech to the faculty he said,

"**Every** Dudley student deserves the same opportunity to learn and to develop to the fullest of their potential. I agree with the man for whom this school was named, 'The true measure of the status of a school is the success of its students.' It will be our goal to ensure the success of every student not only while they are in school, but also their future success as self-actualizing citizens."

Like Dr. Tarpley, he developed and implemented policies, programs, and curriculum activities, in a manner that promoted the educational development of each student and the professional development of each staff member. The teachers were required to turn in lesson plans for the coming week every Friday, and each department was responsible for presenting a strategy that had been effective in teaching, testing, or studying in their discipline, but that could also be used effectively in other disciplines. Teachers also attended workshops and a summer seminar to learn new strategies for teaching students with learning disabilities.

During his tenure as principal, the school system realized that several years of a policy that required students to repeat certain grade levels if they did not pass the end of grade tests had produced a toxic environment at the middle school level. Some students, mostly males, as old as 17 were in school with 10 and eleven-year-olds. The school system decided to establish a pre-high school level that sent these older students to high school at all of the high schools except Grimsley Senior High School. Grimsley's principal, Jane Teague, flatly refused to accept students who had not completed middle school. Her refusal meant that Kiser Middle School students were split among the other three high schools within the city limits.

Teague was right, the students were neither academically nor socially ready for high school. Instead of simply suspending the students until a case could be made for putting them out of school or keeping them in self-contained classes away from the rest of the student body, Watlington hired two former eighth grade teachers and two additional special education teachers and encouraged the students' inclusion in electives like drama and chorus. When this proved not to be enough to meet the needs of some of the students, Watlington worked with North Carolina A&T State University to develop an All-Male Academy and with Bennett College to establish an All-Female

Academy. All of the academy's first students were Dudley students and the first teachers in the programs were Dudley teachers who initially used their planning periods to teach the students on A&T's and Bennett's campuses.

Like Tarpley, Watlington was a results-oriented principal. When the Valedictorian and Salutatorian complained to him that although they both had received "A" grades in their AP Physics class both of them had scored a Level 1 instead of the Level 3 that they needed to get college credit for the course; Watlington replaced a very popular mathematics teacher. The next year, Dudley's AP Physics' class scored an 87% passing rate- the highest in the school system. That same year, under the new department chairperson, Mr. Stanley Johnson, Dudley's passing rate on the Biology I End of Course Test was 97%.

Another change in the academic set-up during Watlington's tenure was the transition of all of Guilford County's High Schools, except Grimsley Senior High School, to block scheduling. One of Grimsley's parents who was also on the Guilford County School Board had done her doctoral study on the effect of block scheduling on the academic performance of students in higher level courses (Advance Placement and International Baccalaureate) and found that examination scores dropped significantly when block scheduling was used. When the scores at several of the high schools dropped for the first time in years after the change to block scheduling, Dudley High School, Page High School, and Northwest High School all applied to the school board to return to six-periods-full- year course scheduling. Dudley's application was denied.

One of the most difficult tasks of Watlington's tenure as principal was moving most of the classes and the student body to Lincoln Middle School's campus during the Whole School Modernization of the Dudley High School campus. In a statement in the 2003 Dudley Yearbook, Watlington stated,

> "As principal of Dudley High School, my goal is to work in partnership with all Dudley stakeholders to create a school culture and climate wherein all students can do their very best. During the next two years, we will face new challenges and opportunities as the newly renovated Dudley High School is completed. Let us meet these challenges and opportunities with pride and commitment as we continue to build Dudley's historical legacy." As W.E.B. DuBois once commented, "With all, we accomplish all."

As he worked with the Construction Committee, he planned to develop courses and programs that would make Dudley High School relevant for all its students whether or not their plans included going to college or going straight into the workforce after high school. His plans for the curriculum included high-tech vocational education in auto mechanics, childcare and early childhood education, engineering, technology, and performance arts. The Ninth Grade Academy was to be on the second and third floors of the Main Building. The Drama Department included facilities and space to teach lighting, sound, costume design and set design. The theater was equipped with a state-of-the-art lighting and sound system, an extra-large backstage entrance that would allow prefabricated sets to be rolled on and off stage, dressing rooms, and even a catwalk above the stage that would allow elaborate presentations.

However, shortly before the students and staff were scheduled to move back to Dudley's campus after the renovation, Mr. Watlington was transferred to the Middle College at GTCC and those spaces in the drama department were used to store ROTC uniforms and textbooks.

JBD

Dr. Phyllis Martin
Dudley's 10th Principal
2004-2008

DR. PHYLLIS MARTIN became Dudley's 10th principal and the first Dudley graduate to serve as principal (Dudley Class of 1969). She said that she accepted the challenge of coming to Dudley because of her heritage and the ties she had to Dudley. Her father was just one of the many members of her family to graduate from Dudley. While a student at Dudley, she participated in several activities. She was a Junior Marshal, a library assistant, a safety patrol officer, and a Thespian. She said of her teachers at Dudley, "Teachers were different when I was at Dudley. Teachers had a sense of raising their students like second parents."

Before coming to Dudley, Martin served as principal of Cone Elementary school and Jackson Middle School. During her tenure as principal, she supervised the return of the student body to Dudley's campus after the 2-year renovation. For the first time, department chairpersons were named by the principal rather than elected by their co-workers in the department. Martin also led the movement to have Dudley students wear uniforms and relocated most of the ninth-grade core subjects to the English Building.

Mr. Jesse Pratt
Dudley's 11th Principal
2008-2015

MR. JESSE PRATT became Dudley's 11th principal in 2008. His tenure in the position of 6 years and eight months means that he served the second longest term as Dudley's principal since Mr. Brown retired in 1976.

Before coming to Dudley, he served as principal of the Middle College at A&T for two and a half years. He also served as the principal of Allen Middle School for two and a half years and as the principal of Southeast Middle School in the Winton-Salem Forsyth County School System, and for six years as the principal of Allen Jay Middle School in High Point, North Carolina.

During his tenure as principal, he rewarded improved test scores by ending the practice of students wearing uniforms, relaxed the standards for students to enter Dudley's Academy, and expanded the role of the Attendance Officer so that the numbers of students completing end-of-course tests increased significantly.

A PLACE WHERE SUCCESS WAS EXPECTED: FINAL EDITION

Mr. Rodney Wilds
Dudley's 12th Principal
2015-2020

MR. RODNEY WILDS transferred from Andrews High School in High Point, North Carolina in 2015, to become Dudley's 12th principal. While a student at Dudley, he was active in Future Business Leaders of America (FBLA) and the Spanish Club. He graduated from Dudley in 1984. After graduating from Dudley, he attended North Carolina A&T State University earning a bachelor's degree. He also holds a Master of School Administration degree from the University of North Carolina at Chapel Hill.

Test performance has been a primary focus of the Guilford County School System since 2001 when the No Child Left Behind Law was passed. After being nominated for Guilford County Schools (GCS) Principal of the Year in 2009, Wilds was appointed principal of T. Wingate Andrews High School in High Point, North Carolina. Test performance at Andrews improved under his leadership. Wilds also is credited with improving the learning environment and perceptions of Andrews. He also was recognized as Guilford's 2013 Secondary Principal of the Year.

Before this appointment, Mr. Wilds served three years as principal at Jackson Middle School in Greensboro, North Carolina where he was the instructional leader for one of the most poverty impacted middle schools in the third largest school district in the state. During his tenure at Jackson Middle School, Rodney led his faculty to meet 100% of Adequate Yearly Progress (AYP) targets in 2008 and 2009. Jackson Middle School increased their math proficiency by 18 percentage points and Algebra I proficiency by 44 percent in one academic year. Additionally, Wilds implemented an extremely successful assessment model that supported the availability of real-time information on student mastery.

Before this position, he served two years at Summerfield Elementary School in Summerfield, North Carolina. While under Mr. Wilds' leadership, Summerfield Elementary achieved state recognition for being a School of Excellence for seven consecutive years. Rodney aided his faculty in meeting 100% of AYP targets for two consecutive years, and the school was recognized for achieving High Growth Status in 2004-2006.

Mr. Wilds served on the GCS Superintendent's Principal Advisory Council as well as several project teams assembled to ensure successful implementation of the initiatives outlined in the district's first strategic plan. Wilds also served as a School Administration Internship Site Supervisor, and as Assistant Principal at Monticello-Brown Summit Elementary School. He taught at Page High School for ten years. Wilds presented at the Annual GCS Leadership Institute, the Annual Association for Supervision and Curriculum Development Conference in Orlando, Florida, and served on the GCS School Climate Task Force.

When asked whether or not he planned any changes for Dudley he responded, "Yes, after I have been here awhile to see what is needed." It was clear early in his first school year at Dudley that things were changing. According to long time Dudley teacher, Virginia Griffin,

> "It just "feels" different. The students are moving from class to class with a sense of purpose. Rules have been set. Students know what will happen if they misbehave. It makes a difference because students react to our expectations. It is clear that he expects only the best of Dudley's students. The English teachers are even teaching the Alma Marta again. I can see that old time Dudley Pride coming back."

Wilds left Dudley in 2020 to become a member of Guilford County Schools Administrative staff.

jBd

Lisé Timmons Mclaughlin
Dudley's 13th Principal
2020-2023

LISÉ TIMMONS MCLAUGHLIN, former principal at the Academy at Smith, became the 13th principal of James B. Dudley High School. Timmons McLaughlin holds an EDS in educational leadership from Wingate University, a master's degree in education, curriculum, and supervision from UNC-Charlotte, as well as a bachelor's degree in secondary education from UNC-Charlotte.

While at the Academy at Smith, Timmons McLaughlin led the successful implementation of the Academy of Biomedical Technology, one of five signature academies in the Guilford County Schools System. Under her leadership, parent and community

A PLACE WHERE SUCCESS WAS EXPECTED: FINAL EDITION

involvement increased, school culture noticeably improved, and the school consistently achieved a 100% graduation rate. Prior to joining the Academy at Smith, she served as assistant principal and interim principal at Page High School; where the school's student proficiency score increased, and discipline suspensions and referrals decreased during her tenure. Prior to school leadership Mrs. Timmons McLaughlin worked at the district office as a School Support Administrator and AIG Director for GCS Gifted and Talented Program.

With the Covid-19 pandemic, the 2020-21 school year was one of the more challenging school years. Timmons Mclaughlin felt well suited to meet every challenge; she found creative ways to improve virtual learning, engage community stakeholders, and encourage students while inspiring and reassuring staff. V. Raymond Smith, a teacher at Dudley said of Timmons Mclaughlin's leadership during the challenging 2020-21 school year,

> "I'm thankful for you and the Gold Team for your guidance, understanding, and love shown throughout this tough, but "will be done", school year. I'm glad to be a faculty member of such an educational institution, as well as, having you as our leader!"

Timmons Mclaughlin said of her leadership, "I am determined to preserve/ and perpetuate the legacy and long-standing tradition of James B. Dudley Senior High School definitely being "THE" place where success is expected."

Timmons McLaughlin left Dudley on Medical Leave in April of 2023.

Dr. Marcus Gause, Ph.D.

Dudley's 14th Principal

During the first 44 years of its existence (1879-1922) the high school founded on the campus of Bennett College was administered by seven presidents of Bennett Seminary/College. In 1923, the high school's first principal was named. John A. Tarpley served as principal for the next 42 years. The next principal, Franklin Brown, served for eleven years. Since then, the longest serving principal, Larry F. Lewis, served for seven years. Dudley's 14th principal, Dr. Marcus Gause, the 8th in the last 30 years, brings both the "Ole time Dudley Spirit" and a new spirit of "Hope for even greater success."

{Updated excerpt from: Sowing Seeds of Love: Dr. Marcus Gause by Hannah Ray, June 2, 2022}

During the last 18 years in education, Dr. Gause has learned what students carry with them long after they turn their tassels: *love*. He says, "If I can teach them the power of love then I feel like we are well on our way to creating a productive citizen," says Dr. Gause. "Loving and understanding provides you with a different relationship with your neighbors who live in your community."

For Dr. Gause, it's the love that was planted in his own life that led him down this path – the path of being an administrator, a student advocate, a community leader, and even a viral singing sensation.

When Dr. Gause was just a boy growing up in Supply, North Carolina, his grandmother would often have him work on their farm. In the afternoons after school, and even some early mornings before he left for school, Dr. Gause would be charged with herding the pigs back into their pen and rebuilding the parts that had been broken.

"I learned the value of hard work," Dr. Gause says of his childhood. "And I learned some critical thinking skills because trying to get a 400-to-500-pound pig back into a pen is not easy!"

It was on this farm, raised by his grandmother who never had higher than an eighth-grade education, and in his church that Dr. Gause also learned

A PLACE WHERE SUCCESS WAS EXPECTED: FINAL EDITION

an analogy that would stick with him throughout his life: you reap what you sow.

"If you plant love, you'll get love. If you plant hate, you'll get hate," Dr. Gause says. "Whatever it is that you plant, those things will come back to life."

Many years later, Dr. Gause found himself working as a substitute teacher and then eventually as an administrator in Orange County. While he didn't have a lifelong desire to work as an educator, over and over again, life confirmed to Dr. Gause that he had a way of getting through to even the toughest to reach students.

After leaving a career at the Bureau of Engraving and Printing under the U.S. Treasury Department, Dr. Gause went on to work in administration at Dudley High School and the Middle College at A&T State University, as well as working closely with Title I, a federal program that aids educationally and economically disadvantaged students. Eventually, he was offered the principalship at Andrews.

But as Dr. Gause began to learn about the challenges facing High Point, including growing food insecurity, he was uncertain about his ability to make the transition and lead at Andrews.

"I had a conversation with my dad... about this transition, and he said, "If not you, then who? And if not now, then when?"' Dr. Gause recalls. "Those words have stayed with me forever."

And it was within the first year of his principalship at Andrews that Dr. Gause had to watch his father battle and ultimately pass away from cancer. When his first graduation day at Andrews came around on Father's Day weekend – his first Father's Day without his dad – Dr. Gause found a way to gain strength and honor his father through their shared love of music.

That was the first graduation that I sang at. I think I sang to get me through that day, that moment," he remembers. "One of the songs that I remember my dad listening to was 'You've Got a Friend in Me.' It was kind of off the cuff. I didn't expect it, and I hadn't planned for it."

But in the years to come, Dr. Gause would honor the tradition every year, remembering his father, celebrating his students, and reminding his students to believe in themselves – just as his father had challenged him.

"I challenged youth to do just that – to believe," says Dr. Gause. "Believe in the impossible, believe you have the power to be able to change your circumstances. Believe you can be whatever you decided you want to be. You might not have to take the path that everybody else has taken, but if you simply believe in yourself, that's more than half the battle. The other half is for us to teach you how to get there."

For Dr. Gause, "us" includes a lot more than just the faculty and staff; it includes the entire Greensboro community. Because while the problems facing some Dudley's students are heavy, they are often outweighed by the readiness of Alumni, surrounding neighborhood, and friends of Dudley to help meet those needs.

In his last assignment at Andrews High School Dr. Gause worked to meet the challenge. "It was a challenge to get all of the needs met very quickly," he recalls. Along with some of his faculty and staff, Dr. Gause began making "house calls," going door-to-door to make parents and families aware of the resources Andrews offered, and to hear first-hand what needs they were facing. Armed with more information, Dr. Gause sought out partnerships in the city to make sure the barriers to education were reduced.

Dr. Gause hopes that with the support of the Dudley community, Alumni, and faculty his administration will be able to encourage our students to become contributing citizens, making an impact, and following their dreams.

"We wish him success in leading the young men and women at Dudley to be the best they can be. We wish him joy in knowing that he is making a difference in the lives of so many young people, but most of all we wish he will be here long enough to achieve the love and reverence that the hard work and long tenure gave Dr. John Allen Tarpley."

Chapter Thirteen

Memories and Traditions

Every high school has its traditions, and all its students have memories that make them smile, laugh, or cry years later. Before integration and busing, most of the members of any graduating class had been sharing memories long before we came to Dudley. We had attended elementary and junior high schools at Washington Street School, Lincoln Junior High School, Hampton Elementary, J.C. Price School, Jones Elementary, East White Oak School, Goshen School, Rena Bullock School, Poplar Grove School, Bluford Elementary, and Mt. Zion Elementary. We knew where we had been. We knew who we were. We knew where we were going. We knew that we were going to succeed in school and life. The following are just a few of the memories and traditions that we shared.

Singing the Black National Anthem and saying the Pledge of Allegiance

We sang the *Black National Anthem* and said the *Pledge of Allegiance to the Flag of the United States of America* at the start of every school day, before every major event and every not so major event. For us, both of these pieces had very special meanings. The words of the Black National Anthem, *Lift Every Voice and Sing* (written as a poem by James Weldon Johnson in 1899 and put to music by his brother John Rosamond Johnson in 1900) served as potent reminders of our joint history as a people- not only of what we had suffered, but also of what we had accomplished. To us, it was every bit as patriotic as the *Star-Spangled Banner*.

Lift Every Voice and Sing

Lift every voice and sing
Till earth and
Heaven ring
Ring with the harmonies of
Liberty;
Let our rejoicing rise,
High as

Dr. Jo Evans Lynn, Ed.D.

The listening skies, let it resound loud as the
Rolling sea
Sing a song full of faith that the
Dark past has taught us,
Sing a song full of
The hope that the present has brought
Us;
Facing the rising sun of our new day
Begun,
Let us march on till victory is
Won.

Stony the road we trod,
Bitter the
Chast'ning rod,
Felt in the day that hope
Unborn had died;
Yet with a steady
Beat,
Have not our weary feet,
Come to the
Place on which our fathers sighed?
We have
Come over a way that with tears has been
Watered,
We have come, treading our path
Through the blood of the slaughtered,
Out from
The gloomy past, till now we stand at
Last
Where the white gleam of our star is
Cast.

God of our weary years,
God of
Our silent tears,
Thou who has brought us thus
Far on the way;
Thou who has by thy
Might,
Led us into the light,
Keep

us
Forever in the path, we pray

Lest our feet
Stray from the places, our God, where we met
Thee,
Least our hearts, drunk with the wine of
The world, we forget thee,
Shadowed beneath thy
Hand,
May we forever stand,
True to our
God,
True to our native land.

The Pledge of Allegiance: *"I pledge allegiance to the Flag of the United States of America and to the Republic for which it stands, one nation, under God, indivisible, with liberty and justice for all."*

This Pledge represented our assurance that we were full citizens of the United States of America and that although parts of the country had not kept its promise to us; we still stood firm in the belief and hope that one day the promise of liberty and justice for all would be a reality.

Baccalaureate Sermons and Four-Hour Graduations

Each year, on the Sunday before their graduation, James B. Dudley High School seniors marched into the Auditorium or Main Gymnasium and listened to a sermon delivered by pastors like Reverend Howard A. Chubbs, Reverend Cecil Bishop, and Reverend Otis Hairston, Sr. Not all of the ministers came from local churches. From 1930-1941, Dudley held two Baccalaureate Sermons and graduations each year-one mid-year in December and another at the end of the year in May. Dr. Tarpley noted, "Demand was so high that we had to have two graduations a year to make room for all the students who wanted to attend Dudley."

Dr. Jo Evans Lynn, Ed.D.

Senior Edition
THE PANTHER'S CLAW
Sit Lux

THE JAMES B. DUDLEY HIGH SCHOOL, GREENSBORO, N. C., JANUARY, 1941

1941 MID-YEAR GRADUATING CLASS

Left to right, Front Row: James Avery, Mary Whitsett, Alice Holt, Margaret Young, Doris McCain, Lottie Gilmer, Sarah Moses, Helen Frazier, Cora Brooks, Essie Hardy, Lubertha McNair, Harold Cotton.
  Second Row: Elsworth Barnes, William Miller, Jessie Jeffers, Arthur Garrison, Alice Harris, Oscar Fisher, Dorothy Maxwell, Robert Morrow, Gladys Davis, Louise Glover, Ruby Rhinehart, Elizabeth Donnell, Dolores Riggsbee, Nettie Robinson.
  Third Row: Lewis Carson, Charles Stewart, William Hall, John Stewart, Augusta Benton, Watson Foster, Robert Jones, Edward Jeffries, John Williams, Janie Beatty, Mary Thompson, Gertrude Jones and Esther Jones.
  Members of the Senior Class who do not appear on the picture are Brazalia Small and Flora Thompson.

Herbin (1958) noted that baccalaureate sermons like the ones delivered at Dudley were common throughout high schools and colleges all over the world. The 1965 Baccalaureate speaker Reverend Morris H. Tynes was from Chicago, Illinois. Several of the Baccalaureate speakers like Reverend Morris H. Tynes and the Reverend Cecil Bishop later gained national and international fame. The Reverend Morris H. Tynes spoke during Martin Luther King, Jr.'s funeral at Ebenezer Baptist Church and the Reverend Cecil Bishop, the pastor of Trinity AME Zion Church in Greensboro, North Carolina when he delivered the 1962 Baccalaureate sermon was elevated to the episcopacy by the Forty-First Quadrennial Session of the General Conference of the African Methodist Episcopal Zion Church in 1980 and consecrated the 78th Bishop in the line of Succession.

A PLACE WHERE SUCCESS WAS EXPECTED: FINAL EDITION

Notable Baccalaureate Speakers

The Reverend Morris H. Tynes (Baccalaureate speaker 1965) stands next to Dr. Martin Luther King during the Montgomery March. Tynes' recorded sermon "Shake it off" was the first recorded sermon to become a national best seller.

Rev. Cecil Bishop

At Left: The 1962 Dudley Baccalaureate Speaker, The Reverend Cecil Bishop then pastor of Trinity AME Zion Church in Greensboro became a National Bishop of the AME Zion Church. **At Right:** The 1967 Baccalaureate Speaker was the new young pastor of Providence Baptist Church in Greensboro. He led the building of a new edifice and moved the church from Harrison Auditorium on A&T's campus and served as pastor for 49 years.

Rev. Howard Chubbs

Rev. Beatha
Dudley's *Last Baccalaureate Speaker*

According to Herbin (1958), all the sermons were based on universal messages: "Remember who you are and where you came from." "Be aware of your potential and of what was placed in you from the day you were born." "Keep the faith of your fathers." "Know thy self." The messages were meant to foster spiritual and emotional courage in facing what for every senior would be a new world of challenges as either independent young adults in the workforce or as undergraduates in college.

Dr. Jo Evans Lynn, Ed.D.

Graduations were *commencement exercises* that celebrated the students who were going directly into the workforce as well as those who were continuing to college. There was no rush to finish these ceremonies. Speeches were not limited to 3-5 minutes and the graduation speaker was someone who was highly respected in the community for their success. For many years, Dr. Tarpley delivered the graduation address. In 1962, three years before his retirement, he delivered his last such address:

> Graduation time usually ushers into one's Life many paradoxical experiences. The most exciting announcement comes to the senior when he has been made certain that all requirements for graduation have been satisfied and that the diploma has been signed and *is* waiting to be delivered. But what sad emotions begin to surge in when friends, pals, and teachers begin to say words of parting.
>
> Why this paradox? Why on yesterday did you thrill with joy over the thought of receiving a diploma, but on today accept the diploma in tears of sadness? One reason has its normal and natural justification. To depart from friends normally and naturally brings a sense of sadness. As principal of this fine Class of 1962, I too sense this same kind of paradoxical and mixed feelings. You are close to our hearts. We would like for you to stay but our purpose all the while has been to prepare you for going. Our sentiments bid you stay but our logic bids you to go to a higher and more mature calling. We breathe a sigh and brush the tears away. But "not so fast" comes the voice of another conflicting emotional surge. Cold logic rushes in again but this time it too reverses its direction of reasoning. Questions like these are posed: "Have you told each of these 1962 graduates exactly what this new and more adult world is like?" "Does each one know that he will no longer be accorded considerations as are accorded children?" "Do these who are going to college know that at college each will be left to his own and progress reports and achievement evaluations will not be colored with the abundances in charity such as has been the case in high school?" "Do these who are assuming (now or in a few years) the role of marriage and family responsibility really know how profound the obligations are that must be assumed?"

In the face of this new set of complex questions we find ourselves mixed up in emotions all over again. This time we begin to search to recall a little poem that we learned just well enough to memorize for a morning recitation in class. We have forgotten it now, but we go back and read it and it has so much more meaning now than it had when we first memorized it.

"One ship goes east, another west, by the selfsame wind that blows.
It is not the gale, but the set of the sail that tells the way my ship goes." (Wilcox, 1916)

As your principal it makes me sad to see you go but I know you must go. As you depart, I shall think of each of you as a ship putting out to sea. Dudley has served as a tugboat to push you on out toward the mighty deep. You have crossed the bay. The mighty ocean stretches out before you. Set sails in a manner that will ensure that your legacy will be as rich and fulfilling as you can make it. Thank you.

The 3-5-minute time limit set for graduation speakers under the Guilford County Schools format does not allow time to develop or deliver speeches with the depth of emotion or insight of Dr. Tarpley's last graduation address.

Student Bus Drivers

Until busing for integration started, in the black community, within the Dudley attendance zone, the school bus drivers were high school juniors and seniors. Although most of the students within the city limits walked to school there were a few exceptions. Two of my siblings and I were in high school at Dudley or in junior high school at Lincoln when we moved to 914 East Bragg Street. We were incensed because the house our parents bought was one house down from the cut-off for riding the school bus from the Warnersville Community. We had to walk nearly three miles to school.

The student drivers were especially trained by Mr. Holley or Mr. Whites, the Driver Education Teachers, and their bus routes started and ended in their communities with the buses being parked at their houses. During this period, there was not one single serious accident and only a few breakdowns. As late as the 1966-67 school year, female bus drivers were rare. Patricia Aldridge, Dudley's first female bus driver described her experience in a 1965 issue of the Panther's Claw:

Girl Bus Driver Describes Job

Being a girl bus driver is like being a novelty. It is a thrilling experience. Everyone has been wonderful to me. All have been understanding and unprejudiced. My fellow bus drivers have treated me **like** their queen. Not only have the bus drivers been nice but most of the other drivers that I met on the city streets, were also. They were very courteous and friendly.

Many consider that it is hard for *a* girl to drive a bus but it's just the opposite. The only difference between driving a bus and a car is that the vehicle is larger, the steering is a little harder and one has to judge the distance differently. The only other difficulty comes with the passengers. A girl has to be firm in order to maintain order on her bus, which is essential for safe driving.

I feel that more girls should have this experience. For I feel that this responsibility will help develop a girl for the responsibilities in the future.

I have to give the credit for my success to Mr. W. Whites, my driver education teacher, and Mr. John Henry, the director of Dudley's school bus drivers.

Patricia Aldridge 12-B

STUDENT BUS DRIVERS (1966-67)

A PLACE WHERE SUCCESS WAS EXPECTED: FINAL EDITION

The Dudley Cheer Book

Once upon a time, Cheerleaders led cheers that everyone knew. Every sophomore was given a copy of the Dudley Cheer Book during Orientation, and any upperclassman could stop a "Soph" before or after school or during lunchtime and demand to hear any cheer from the book. One of the cheers, the longest one, "called out" the names of all the players. A home game at James B. Dudley High School "rocked the house" and could be heard at least a half mile away.

Cheers from the Dudley Cheer Book

Cheer #1 WE ARE!

Cheerleaders: Everywhere we go
Dudley: Everywhere we go,
Cheerleaders: People want to know
Dudley: People want to know,
Cheerleaders: Who we are
Dudley: Who we are,
Cheerleaders: We are the Panthers

Dudley: We are the Panthers.
Cheerleaders: The mighty, mighty Panthers

All: We are the Panthers. The Mighty, mighty Panthers!

Kick That Ball

Did you see James Jones kick that ball? Yes. He kicked it and that ain't all Hey Gang! James is real gone; James is a real gone guy.

Say Stewart, Chavis, Wright too They are three that know what to do. It's a fact when James comes to kick, the other team is licked. *Say... verse again substituting names of other players*

Who you Rooting For?

2-4-6"-Who do we appreciate?

3-6-9-   Who are we behind?

Cl. Who you rooting for? Dudley High School

Sch. Dudley High

Cl. A Little louder (say it 4 times)

Sch. Dudley High

Cl. A Little   softer (say it 4 times)

Sch. Dudley

Dr. Jo Evans Lynn, Ed.D.

All together -oh-h-h Shuh-now

Team <u>Yea</u> Team	1-2-3-4
T-E-A-M Yea Team	1_2-–-4
T-E-A-M Yea Team	**2-3-1-4**
T-E-A-M Yea team	Who for?

What For?

Team, Team, Team, Fight (Repeat)   Who you going to root for?

J.B. Dudley High (Repeat)

Let's   Go Dudley
Let's   Go Dudley
Let's   Co Dudley
Let's   Go Dudley
Come   on Dudley Let's'
Go (Repeat)

<u>We'll   Win</u> By, Golly
We'll win. By Golly.
We'll win
We'll win. By Golly.
We'll win
We'll win. By Golly.
We'll win
We'll win. By Golly.
We'll win
(Repeat)

Hold that Line.

Hold that Line.

Hold that Line.

Hold that Line.

Hold that Line.

Fight. Fight. Fight. (Repeat)

A PLACE WHERE SUCCESS WAS EXPECTED: FINAL EDITION

"Blue Goose" (1948-1966)

Some of the favorite memories of the older generations are of the "Blue Goose."

"The Blue Goose" was finally retired in 1966, but it remained on campus until the summer of 1968. The bus was purchased in 1948 from the Rehoboth Methodist Church for $800. For over 18 years, it served as the only form of transportation for the sports teams, the Dudley Thespians, the Debate Team, and music departments. The Blue Goose traveled extensively throughout North Carolina. Its first trip was to Winston-Salem in 1948. Its last trip was to Burlington. Ashville was the "Gooses" longest trip, and the War Memorial Stadium her shortest (Panther, 1967).

Although the "Goose" was ages old when it was purchased, its breakdowns were relatively few. The auto mechanics department kept it on the road for over 18 long hard years. Mr. Macomson, the auto mechanics teacher said that his most memorable breakdown was when "the Blue Goose" conked out just outside of High Point on a return trip from Concord. The bus was not towed in until 7:00 A.M. the next morning and it took most of the night to get all the students' home (Panther, 1967). None of the repairs to the Blue Goose were necessitated due to accidents.

Dr. Jo Evans Lynn, Ed.D.

"In the Stone"

Douglas Powell
Lincoln Junior High Band Director/ Dudley Assistant Band Director

Assistant band directors seldom find their names mentioned in the traditions of a school. However, alumni cannot mention one of the most revered traditions of the James B. Dudley High School Marching Band without bringing up the name of Douglas Powell. Powell arranged Dudley's field performance of Earth Wind and Fire's "In the Stone." Powell was the Band Director at Lincoln Middle School and an Assistant Band Director at Dudley for thirty years. One of his former students at Lincoln, Pamela Truesdale, said of him, "He taught me so much. He made sure that we were ready to maintain the tradition of excellence when we got to Dudley. All that time we spent marching up and down Lincoln Street helped develop a work ethic that has stayed with me."

Nearly every marching band in America, whether corps style or high-stepping style, played their version of EWF's hit song through the 1980s and 1990s. What made Dudley's arrangement special was Powell's compilation of "In the Stone" and Michael Jackson's "Can't Stop 'til You Get Enough." No alumni band get-to-gather is complete until everyone rocks to "In the Stone" the way only Dudley can do it.

Sophomore/Freshman Orientation

For over 79 years the entering class, that until 1986 were sophomores, were required to spend one or two days prior to the beginning of the school year being introduced to the life and expectations of Dudley students. Students learned the rules that governed moving from class to class in the allotted 2 minutes- there was no time to talk, socialize, or go back to get books from a locker. Students learned the Alma Mata and every cheer in the Dudley Cheer Book. Every teacher who taught sophomore and later freshman classes met with the students to explain the curriculum, the teacher's expectations, and specifics about homework and grading. Students were issued their lockers and books so that on the first official day of classes they were held accountable for being prepared and on time for class.

A PLACE WHERE SUCCESS WAS EXPECTED: FINAL EDITION

The Members of the 1972 Sophomore Class attend a session of Sophomore Orientation in the Main Gymnasium

The most memorable sessions were the ones led by the cheerleaders and Pep Band and the Dudley Style Presentation by the Student Council. During the 1930s, 1940s, 1950s, and 1960s young ladies were not allowed to wear pants to school and young men were not allowed to wear jeans or T-shirts. During the orientation, all the clubs and organizations competed for new members by offering special incentives like engraved pens, pencils, note paper, and Dudley memorabilia like mini footballs and megaphones sponsored by local businesses.

Homecoming Parades and Spirit Week

Although most football games were packed, Homecoming brought even bigger crowds. Homecoming has always been a special event at Dudley and until the early 2000s, only the local Christmas Parade and A&T's Homecoming Parade came close to the grandeur of Dudley's Homecoming Parade which started on campus, proceeded to Elm Street, circled around Market Street, and ended up at War Memorial Stadium.

The following article from the November 1953, Issue of the Panther's Claw Newspaper gives a detailed description of that year's Homecoming Parade:

Dr. Jo Evans Lynn, Ed.D.

N. C., NOVEMBER, 1953   **NUMBER 1**

Many Applaud Homecoming Queen And Gay Floats In Colorful Parade

Choruses of praise and applause were received on every corner as the annual homecoming parade of the Dudley High school cruised through some of the main streets of Greensboro.

The spot light was focused on "Miss HomeComing", Inez Fox riding in a black and red convertible. "Miss Dudley High," Barbara Martin, a picture of elegance, rode in a blue convertible.

Contributing their part to the parade, high stepping majorettes supported by bands from the Wm. Penn, Price, Lincoln and Dudley schools performed for the cheering crowds.

Colorful floats decorated by various clubs and classes met the approval of all who saw them.

The music department entered a float of white with red and black streamers. The green and white float presented by the marshals supplied dignity. Lovely seniorites riding a float of yellow, red and purple added color to the parade. "Miss Conservative" in a red convertivle displayed her beauty. "Build with bricks" was the theme used by the auto mechanics department. The New Farmers of America's float of yellow and black, The National Honor Society and Y-Teen float of blue and white. The Debating and Electrical appliances floats of pink and blue, The Hi-Y and New Homemakers Of America's float of light blue, and the 10-H class float of yellow and green showed the fine art of hard working students and teachers. The industrial arts float of yellow and orange, the art club float of pink and black, the Commercial club's float of white, the Crown and Sceptre and Dramatic of blue and gold, The office Staff of pink and brown, the 9-D class with imitation flowers and the Diversified Occupations float of red and grey all added splendor to the parade. Two floats, Y Teens blue and the Safety Council of colorful streamers were entered by the Lincoln school. Students of the driver education class drove their car. The fire department lent a fire truck which was used by the fire patrol. The Charles Moore school Y Teens also marched. Catchy steps were performed by the cheerleaders and pep club dressed in the school colors of blue and gold. Boy scouts helped to direct traffic.

This description of the "gay" or "bright and happy" floats makes it clear that the Dudley Homecoming Parade was a very special Community Event. Every department, club and organization in the school was represented and many local businesses and civic groups also participated. All of the elementary schools and junior high schools like Charles Moore School, Lincoln, and J.C. Price also participated.

Some years, the parade included as many as five bands: The James B. Dudley High School Marching Band, the rival team's band, Lincoln Junior High School's Band, The North Carolina A &T State University Marching Band and, in later years, the Dudley Alumni Band. There were also numerous floats made by all the clubs and organizations, and dozens of decorated cars carrying the queens and local dignitaries. Although most of the floats were crafted by student groups, a few of the more professional looking ones were rented or purchased from float companies.

A PLACE WHERE SUCCESS WAS EXPECTED: FINAL EDITION

Winsor Community Center Cheerleaders strut and cheer in the 2004 Dudley Homecoming Parade

Community groups and organizations also looked forward to participating in the parade. Winsor Community Center and Warnersville Community Center always had multiple units in Dudley's homecoming parade. Most of the businesses and churches in the community surrounding Dudley also participated in the parade. There were flatbed trucks loaded with little league football teams and cheerleaders making frequent stops to perform. A crowd favorite was the Dudley Air Force ROTC Drill Team. Street vendors also sold hotdogs, cotton candy, popcorn, and other treats along the parade route.

Dr. Jo Evans Lynn, Ed.D.

Dudley AFROTC Cadets proudly march in the 2001 Homecoming Parade.

Mr. Nobles, Dudley's Head Custodian, rides in the 1988 Homecoming Parade

During the late 1940s through 1950s female auxiliaries, majorettes & flag girls, were added to the band. Beginning in the 1966-67 school year, the Pantherettes were an exciting new Auxiliary to the Marching Band.

At Left: Christine Winchester, Gee Gee Moore, Kim Morton, Erica Gregg, and Pam Jones lead the Flag Girls stepping high in the 1988 Homecoming Parade.

A PLACE WHERE SUCCESS WAS EXPECTED: FINAL EDITION

Chris Goins leads the Alumni Band in the 2004 parade

The Dudley Science Club was one of many clubs in the 1988 parade.

Center: From its inception in 1956, the James B. Dudley Pep Club was not only a feature in every Homecoming Parade but also regularly attended home basketball and football games.
Bottom Left: The Future Nurses "represent" in the 1992 parade.

Every Homecoming Parade was not only a school event, but also a community event that brought all of the local churches, community centers, and businesses together.

Dr. Jo Evans Lynn, Ed.D.

Above: Before the Pantherettes and Flag Girls were combined into a single unit, being a Flag Girl gave 15 additional students an opportunity to participate in an extracurricular activity and to strut in the Homecoming Parade.

Nearly every class or student group found some way to participate in the Homecoming Parade. It did not matter if that participation came in the form of sitting on the back of a hastily decorated pick-up truck. **Center Left:** Dudley Open School) or marching as a unit **Center Right:** Blaque Queens Step Team. **Bottom:** FCCLA (Family, Career, and Community Leaders of America) Participants in the 2002 Homecoming Parade.

And of course, the finest Dudley Homecoming Parades always end with the James B. Dudley High School Alumni Marching Band!

The Homecoming Parade was one of the many events of "Spirit Week." McPherson (1983), described the 1983 Spirit Week,

> "This year's theme "The Panthers together always 'Puttin' on the Ritz" was evidenced throughout the week by each day's activity. The week started off with "Dress-Up Day" on Monday, "Punk Rock Day," Tuesday; "Kiddy/PJ Day," Wednesday; "Grimsley Grit Day," Thursday, and "Blue & Gold Day" on Friday, the final day of Homecoming week.
>
> The evening festivities began with the annual Homecoming Parade and culminated with the Homecoming Dance.
>
> The annual Homecoming Game kicked-off at 7:30 p.m., and the halftime activities consisted of spectacular performances by the band, majorettes, and Pantherettes. The halftime activities culminated with the presentation of 'Miss Dudley,' Wendy Jacobs and her escort, 'Mr. Dudley,' Von Evans, along with this year's Homecoming Court."

Although the theme changed each year, the level of school spirit and participation always remained high.

Dr. Jo Evans Lynn, Ed.D.

Class Songs

Beginning in 1940, every senior class had an original Class Song written by a member of the graduating class. Although this yearly tradition ended with the Class of 1967, there were brief attempts to revive the tradition in 1970 and 1971 with Class Songs written by Robert Dilworth with music written by seniors in Mrs. Richmond's music class (Pamela Fruster Stewart, 1971). However, this author could find no evidence of either the 1970 or 1971 Class actually adopting a Class Song written by Dilworth or any other senior as their Class Song. Nevertheless, every time we sing Dudley's Alma Mater a legacy from this tradition lives on. The Alma Mater was written by Doris M. Townes as the Class Song for the Class of 1944 and was later adopted as the school's song.

James Benson Dudley High School Alma Mater
by Doris M. Townes (1944)

Dear Dudley High, our Alma Mater true,
Deep thoughts of love, we'll always have for you.
We shall strive on, as others too, have done.
And in thy strength life's victories will be won.
Our Dudley High, we'll ever praise and love thee.

Success ahead through open doors we see.
Foundations built; our lives will forge ahead.
On love and kindness have our young souls fed.
Strength of our life, Dear Mother, and our home,
Be thou our light, in all our years to come.
Our Dudley High, we'll ever praise and love thee.
Success ahead, through open doors we see.

The process of selecting a class song was such a monumental task for a senior class that it is immortalized in a fictional account in the book, *The Promise of Friendship*. Here is an excerpt:

The James B. Dudley High School Class of '67' was good to go. All they had to do during this meeting was to select a class gift and a class song. It should have been simple, but the class officers couldn't agree on anything.

"Let's vote one more time on the gift, all in favor of donating funds for a football stadium, raise your hands."

Six hands went up.

"All those in favor of donating benches for the quadrangle, raise your hands."

Six hands went up.

"Who didn't vote this time?"

"Josephine," they chorused as everyone looked at her.

"I don't particularly like either choice. Only guys can go out in the quadrangle to smoke. I'm not voting our money for something; I'd have to come over here at night to sit on."

"Then why won't you vote for the stadium?"

"Who's going to know we paid all that money ten years from now?

"What if we donate a plaque that says: Major Contribution by the Class of Sixty-seven," Elmer Haygood suggested.

"That sounds fair," she admitted.

"Okay all in favor of the stadium raise your hands," Richard rushed to get it done before she changed her mind.

Seven hands went up.

"Now, we will listen to the submissions for class song and then we'll vote. I won't tell you who wrote each song until after we vote," Richard was glad to have things finally moving again. Maybe they would get home before midnight.

"This is song Number One," he passed out copies of the lyrics as he walked over and opened the door to admit the junior class members who had been selected and trained by the composer or composers of the song to present their masterpiece. Richard put the first group's record on and started the music. They began...

Boogie, Boogie,
We're gonna get up out of here.
Boogie, Boogie,
We're gonna get away from here.
Boogie, Boogie,
We're gonna give a great big cheer.
Boogie, Boogie,
Yell, loud so everyone hears.
Boogie, Boogie,
We're getting away from here.
Boogie, Boogie.

During the entire song they moved to the tune of the "Horse" dancing the latest dance, the "Pony." The thirteen class officers sat in stunned silence long moments after they left.

"That song made *The Vegetable Song* from my second-grade play sound like a masterpiece," Josephine broke the silence.

"Silly, is the word that comes to mind," Linda Alexander added.

"I thought it was kind of catchy," Olivia said, elbowing Gail into agreement.

"It was different, not syrupy and sentimental like most class songs," Rosaline threw in her two cents worth.

"Well, that's true," Ted Shoffner gave it tentative approval.

"The choreography was good. I could see us bringing the house down with that," Ella Knight joined the misguided souls.

"Now, wait a minute," Josephine spoke up, they were getting too close to a seven-member majority, "I don't know about the rest of you, but I will be needing my diploma to go to Shaw University this fall. If we sing that song, we will be the first class in the history of the world to have graduation and nobody gets a diploma."

"She's right. All we get is a rolled-up piece of paper until we turn in our robes," Blanche Tate cautioned.

"Maybe the next one will be better suited to our needs," Richard diplomatically moved on.

"You may begin," he said to Beverly Greenlee. She sang to the tune of "Oh, Danny Boy."

Our thanks to you dear Dudley
For you have taught was well.
We praise Thee dear Dudley.
Our love will never fail.
Good-bye, good-bye.
We salute you on high.
Our love for you dear Dudley
Will never, ever die.
We will keep you in our hearts.
Though today we part.
Good-bye, good-bye.
We salute you on high.

"That's more like it," Josephine was emphatic in her praise.

"I say vote for it now. I don't need to hear the other one," Ella immediately changed sides.

"I move..." Elmer began.

"It wouldn't be fair not to at least listen to the last one," Beverly Lanier used her own quiet form of diplomacy to reason with them. Since she only spoke when it was very important, they agreed to listen to the last song.

"Annette, Robert," Richard pointed them to the front of the library and started their music, after passing out the lyrics.

Josephine realized it was different from the start. The prelude was original rather than the tune of a well-known song. Annette announced that it was to be sung in alternating parts with the female voices beginning and the male and female voices coming together for the last stanza. As they sang, each word of the lyrics propelled Josephine closer to the edge of her seat.

Fragile children begin school.
Not knowing where the path
Of knowledge will lead,
Or what the years will reveal,
But soon hands and hearts.
Are joined in the growing,
And through the promise of friendship
Forever are bound.

There were times when we thought,
We'd outgrown all that you taught.
But the next minute, you placed
A new challenge before us,
And pushed us to finish the race,
Heads up, our faces
Warm in the glow of the sun,
And the knowing that the promise of friendship
Binds us forever to you.

Of all we know now
Only of one thing, we are sure.
Our lives are richer because of your presence.
Though we leave you with a token,
And heartfelt thanks earnestly spoken.
We take with us so much more,
    The truth of what can never be taken

For within us you are bound.

The lamp of learning burns ever brighter.
Chains of ignorance we have cast off.
The door to the future is opened wider.
We go through it gladly knowing,
'Ere we go we are bound.
Linked by the promise,
The promise of friendship
Links us forever to you.

"That was beautiful. Just beautiful," Beverly said.

"It was more than that. It is hauntingly exquisite. The melody flows through you. It's..."

"We all heard it," Richard cut Jackie Lane off. Let a musician get started talking about music and we'll be here all night, he thought.

Josephine said nothing. For the first time in her life, she was struck totally speechless.

"All in favor of *Song Number One*, raise your hand," Richard started the voting.

Two hands went up. The rest of the officers breathed a sigh of relief.

"All in favor of *Song Number Two*, raise your hand," Four hands went up.

"All in favor of Song Number Three, raise your hand."

Six hands went up. Heads turned to Josephine. She was the only one who hadn't voted for any of the songs.

"What is it now?" Richard asked her in disgust.

"You loved the second song a few minutes ago," someone reminded her.

"What are all of Y'all talking about?" She hadn't realized they were voting. Her mind was busy pulling out and unwrapping all the memories the song had invoked.

"I can't believe you. We're voting on the songs. Vote," Richard commanded losing patience.

"The last one. I vote for the last one. How could anyone be dumb enough to vote for one of the others after hearing that one," Josephine's tone made the ones who had voted for the first two songs mighty glad she hadn't been paying attention.

"That settles it. Our class song is, "The Promise of Friendship" written and composed by Kenneth J. Weeks.

The meeting was adjourned after that…

A PLACE WHERE SUCCESS WAS EXPECTED: SECOND EDITION

Of course, the lyrics of the fictional piece are different from the Graduation Song of 1967, which was truly beautiful, but the fictional excerpt helps outsiders understand how competitive the process of composing and selecting a class song was. Each class took this particular duty very seriously because it was *our song*. Each class song uniquely represented the things about Dudley and our overall education that were important to that particular class.

Kenneth J. Wyrtch

JBD

THOUGH WE MUST LEAVE
(Graduation Song 1967)
Lyrics and Music by Kenneth J. Wyrtch

Boys - Though we must leave, there is a love that lives within our hearts,
Girls - That makes our tears- our tears begin to flow for thee,
Boys - Forever we'll remember.
Girls - Forever we'll remember thee.

All -   O our Dudley, our Dudley High
          We'll sing thy praises upward high.
          May your light ever stay with us,
          Be it ever to stay with us.

Boys – Be ye ever shinning bright through the storms and blackened nights.
Girls – The things you've taught, the things you bore, you've been.
Boys- Be ye it evermore.
Girls- Be ye it evermore.

All-   O our Dudley, our Dudley High
          We'll sing thy praises upward high.
          May your light ever stay with us,
          Be it ever to stay with us.

          We love thee- We love thee,
          For having faith, strong holding patience.
          and love

Boys- Now we must leave –our joys are fill'd with sorrow.

Dr. Jo Evans Lynn, Ed.D.

Girls- Now we must leave – our joys are fill'd with sorrow.
Boys – Through our joy is having sorrow near
Girls – Dear God in heaven please hear.

All-   As we trudge the road before us,
             We will accept your blessing as you'll have it…
             Goodbye, goodbye our Dudley High.

No one seems to know why this particular tradition ended. However, my classmates and I speculate that after the amazing Graduation Song of 1967, other classes realized that they had no chance of creating a song that came close to ours and just gave up. How could they be expected to match perfection? The 1967 Graduation Song's author, Kenneth J. Wyrtch stated,

"The music and words of this song carry significant value. It is the only 'original song' written by a Dudley student and graduate at that time. This song is notably different from our Alma Mater in that its music is not based on another hymn's; that is, "Be Still My Soul. Mrs. Richmond sat next to me on the piano bench and helped me pick out the right cords as I hummed it to her."

Wyrtch's song was so good, in fact, that the Class of 1968 chose to sing *"To Dream the Impossible Dream"* from the musical *The Man of Lamancha* rather than write an original class song of their own. Even though they based their selection on the Temptations' rendition of the song, if you listen to Luther Vandross' rendition of the song you will understand why the Class of 1968 chose it as their Class Song. The lyrics truly speak to the lifelong quest to reach the highest level of success that is expected of every Dudley graduate.

Prom Night

The First Gymnasium in the Main Building has been transformed into "An Evening in Paris." Cut-outs in a dark purple, almost black fabric spread across the ceiling imitates stars shining through the night sky and elaborate center pieces on each table look like mini–Eifel Towers.

It is Prom Night at James B. Dudley High School. No need for the addition of the terms "junior" or "senior" because the underclassmen know that Prom is strictly a senior affair. There are no limousines and the couples either arrive in a "borrowed" family car or are dropped off by a parent. There are punch bowls, tiny sandwiches, and a live band playing the most popular songs of the day. A professional photographer is set up in front of a backdrop of a romantic Paris scene. This night will create memories that will last a lifetime. Most of the young ladies are wearing gowns that were made by a local seamstress or by a relative and the young men are wearing a rented tuxedo or their "Sunday best."

Vaughn Walls and Gloria D. Evans at 1965 Prom.

Although the Dudley High School Prom was held on campus until 1967, when the class opted to move off campus, it was certainly a lavish affair and for most of the seniors it was their first formal affair. The Prom in the black community was a direct outgrowth of the Debutante Cotillion which had been held in upper class black communities since the early 1900s. Lawrence Otis Graham, in his book <u>Our Kind of People: Inside America's Black Upper Classes</u>, said that "The nation has had black millionaires since the 1880s and that those families eventually sought out or created debutante cotillions and social clubs so their children could meet other affluent black children." In Greensboro, the black upper class evolved around the establishment of North Carolina Agricultural and Mechanical College (now North Carolina A&T State University), Bennett Seminary (now Bennett College), L. Richardson Memorial Hospital, Palmer Memorial Institute, the private school in Sedalia, the black business owners, and the administrators and teachers at James B. Dudley High School.

By the late 1970's juniors had become an intricate part of the Prom. In fact, the Junior Class at Dudley raised money for the prom, selected the theme, and the menu. Although it was still seen as the "big night" for the

Dr. Jo Evans Lynn, Ed.D.

seniors with the Prom Queen and King being popular members of the senior class, each junior class saw it as their mission to give the seniors the kind of prom **they** wanted to have the following year. The 1989 Dudley Yearbook commented on the hard work done by the junior class in preparing the 1988 Prom. It said:

> "Till the End of Time" proved to be a night to remember. The junior class worked diligently from sunrise to sunset to convert the Bryan Park Recreational Building into a creation nestled in glimmering shades of purple, lavender, and silver. On that magical May 20th night, the event was highlighted by the appearance of "Jazzy Jeff" and "The Fresh Prince." Those who wanted to satisfy hunger found quick relief by sampling the "Moonlight Delites" – Heartbeat drummettes, heavenly melon, Luv squares, starry mints, cupid chips, and passion punch. Those who attended the 1988 prom will savor memories "Till the End of Time."

During 1980s through mid-nineties, juniors planned and decorated for the prom.

Left: At the 1988 Prom Jennifer Russom and date Curtis Dickens dance the night away.

Right: Shena Sims, Prom Queen is escorted by Stephen Lee.

Picture Courtesy Dudley High School Homepage 2015

Dudley seniors and their guests wait to enter the Regency Room in Downtown Greensboro for the 2015 Prom.

Today's proms are expensive, all-night affairs, with after-prom activities often extending into dawn of the next day. Limousines, Stretch Hummers, fancy designer dresses, and glamorous ballrooms are now prom-night standards. The simple dinner for two before the prom has become an elaborate dinner party requiring reservations for several couples.

Dr. Jo Evans Lynn, Ed.D.

Strong Leadership from the Dudley PTA & PTSA

For many, many years the James B. Dudley High School PTAs or PTSAs were "forces with which to be reckoned." Since most of the teachers lived in the communities around the school, very often the president of the Dudley PTA/PTSA was a teacher at the school who also had a child attending Dudley. Although the associations worked with each administration, they also worked to be part of the educational leadership of the school. In an October 1983 article in the Panther's Claw, newly elected PTSA president, Mr. George Allen said,

> "Your Dudley PTSA Board has chosen the theme, 'Working Together in Our PTSA.' We feel positive that by working jointly we will be instrumental in providing the needed educational direction and combating many of the hidden and exposed pitfalls." (p.1)

His goal for membership that year was at least 650 members.

The Chester Bradley Gymnasium is only one example of the effectiveness of the PTAs and PTSAs at Dudley. Through the years, they have worked with the various Alumni Chapters, and booster clubs to help buy band uniforms, help with pre-game feeding of athletes, and to provide scholarships. For three straight years (1957-1959), the PTSA made its primary goal the building of a gymnasium. They petitioned the School Board, attended every School Board meeting submitting their request over and over again. And perhaps more importantly, they went to the national press.

Mr. Ezell A. Blair, Sr.
PTA President
1957-1958

Mr. Blair was a Vocational Education teacher, PTA leader and father of 1959 graduate and A&T Four, member Jerell Khazan a.k.a. Ezell Blair, Jr. He was one of a large number of Dudley teachers who not only taught but also demonstrated civic awareness and activism. The book <u>Lunch at the 5 & 10</u> mentions that several of the planning sessions for the Sit-in Movement were held at his home. The PTA Board that he led as president also played a major part in the building of Dudley's Main Gymnasium, The Chester A. Bradley Gymnasium.

Mr. George Allen
PTSA President 1983-84

Mr. Allen was a Social Studies teacher at Dudley. Under his leadership during the 1983-84 school year, Dudley's PTSA made history by teaming up with the alumni chapters located in many parts of the United States under the national leadership of Miss Lola McAdoo, the president of the National Alumni Association in helping the PTSA fulfill its goals. Those goals included at least 650 active members, a budget of no less than $5,000, and substantially increasing the amounts given in scholarships (Wright, 1983).

The Christmas Programs

In 2003, then Dudley music teacher Pamela Stewart revived one of the school's most cherished traditions, the Christmas Concert. During this time, Dudley was undergoing a Whole School Modernization and was without an auditorium large enough to host the program. The concert was held at New Zion Missionary Baptist Church. This move allowed a return to songs that express the meaning of Christmas with the spirit and joy of the traditional Christmas programs that were held in Dudley's Auditorium at 3:30p.m. on the second Sunday in December for over fifty years. The music recalled a time when the program was not called by generic terms like "Holiday Program" or "Winter Festival" and the songs were not odes to Santa Claus, Saint Nick, or Red Nosed Reindeers.

Every year, there was a modern "twist" to the story, but at some point, a strong voice would recite Luke 2:1-13 from the King James Version of the Bible,

And it came to pass in those days, that there went out a decree from Caesar Augustus, that all the world should be taxed...

Most of the people in the audience spoke the words silently along with the narrator because those words were as familiar to us as the songs- *Silent Night, Sweet Little Jesus Child, Away in the Manger, We Three Kings, and Joy to the World...* We did not know that the songs ranged from Old Negro Spirituals to complex classical musical arrangements. We only knew that the music was so beautiful and potent that it could reach places in one's spirit usually reserved for prayer.

Dr. Jo Evans Lynn, Ed.D.

FACULTY ASSISTANTS

Choreography - - - - - - - - Miss G. E. Dye

Costume Designer - - - Mrs. J. J. Goldsborough

Costuming - - - - - - - - - Mrs. M. S. Henry

                                  Mrs. W. M. McLaughlin

Make Up - - - - - - - - Miss L. Carpenter

                                  Mrs. A. W. Stoart

                                  Mrs. B. J. Wells

Programs - - - - - - - - Mrs. W. B. Mayo

Staging - - - - - - - - - Mr. P. J. Brown

Ushers - - - - - - - - - Mrs. M. A. Coley

Organ: Compliments of Harvey West Music Company

The Story of Christmas
By H. Alexander Matthews

PAGEANT CHARACTERS

Shepherds —————————— James Byrd
 George Harrison
 Hubert Graham
 Franklin Sherrill

Angel of the Lord —————— Randolyn Johnson

Other Angels —————————— Peggie McLaughlin
 Loretta Montgomery
 Brenda Shoffner

Mary —————————————— Yvonne Jeffries

Joseph ————————————— Ralph Moore

Kings ————————————— Charles Morton
 Alphonzo Scott
 Owen Williams

HUMANITY

Children —————————— David Florence
 Mary Susan Stuart

Boy Scout —————————— Horvey Alston

Newsboy —————————— Perry Holt

Student —————————— Beverly Smith

Physician —————————— Jesse Johnson

Nurse —————————— Betty Goins

Mechanic —————————— Howard Avant

A Business Man —————— Andrew Johnson

A Minister —————————— Tommy Johnson

THE CHOIR

Sophomores

Byrd, James
Fawcett, Amos
Fisher, Janice
Giles, Robert
Hall, Ted
Holloway, Hubert
Jackson, Alena
Jackson, John
Meadow, Eugene
McLaughlin, Ronnie
Owens, William
Walden, Carolyn
Warren, Judy
White, Iva
White, Reginald
Williamson, Norma
Wynn, James

Juniors

Artis, Alfreda
Borge, Paul
Covington, Shirley
Crawford, Charlayne
Ledbourutte, Henry
Greene, Hubert
Harrison, George
Jones, Linda
Martin, Teressa
McClenton, Paulette
McCallum, Earline
McKoy, Evangeline
McLaughlin, Peggy
Morton, Charles

Juniors (Cont.)

Pass, George
Pettiford, Harvey
Scott, Alphonzo
Shepherd, James
Sherrill, Franklin
Shoffner, Brenda
Simms, Lucein
Wade, Curtis
Ware, Thessolonia

Seniors

Alston, Mamie
Burnes, Bertha
Brown, Cleo
Ellis, Alfreda
Florence, Davetta
Fros, Dorothenia
Graham, Hubert
Hines, Olivia
Hood, Shirley
Johnson, Randolyn
Lowry, Elizabeth
Montgomery, Loretta
Oliver, James
Turner, Gwendolyn
Tyson, Lucein
Vincent, Clyde
Wiku, John
Wright, Nazar

Dr. Jo Evans Lynn, Ed.D.

Chapter Fourteen

All that and Then Some!

No book about James Benson Dudley High School would be complete without a chapter devoted to the arts. We simply acknowledge the "gifts" that are a unique part of who we are as a people.

All That Drama!

From 1942 until 1970, the Dudley Thespians was one of the many clubs at Dudley. The group usually presented two plays a year- a fall and a spring production. The Thespians under the direction of Mrs. Barbara Wells, an English teacher, won the North Carolina Drama Competition for so many consecutive years that the trophy was retired to Dudley in 1963. Drama did not become an elective until Dudley was integrated in 1970-71. Until then, as former Thespian Roberta Washington recalls, "We met after school or during the last period of the day which was usually when study halls and club meetings were held."

Mrs. Barbara Wells

Many of Lincoln's Junior High School students recall the excitement of attending a matinee of one the plays. The Thespians presented musicals like *Showboat*, comedies like *Arsenic and Old Lace*, and moving dramatic performances like *Spoon River Anthology*.

When the school integrated in the 1970-1971 school year, drama became an academic course, but in 1978, Dudley's drama program and many other programs (Modern Dance, Auto Mechanics, Brick Masonry, Carpentry, etc.) were moved to Weaver Center so that all the students in the Greensboro City Schools had access to the courses

Dr. Jo Evans Lynn, Ed.D.

THE DUDLEY THESPIANS
1957

Walter Johnson as Rets Harkins, Shirley Hinnant as Judith, Delores Gary as Sarah.

Harold Hairston as Clem, Shirley Hinnant as Judith. Winners of Best Actor and Best Actress Awards in District Festival.

Shirley Hinnant as Judith, Nancy Lewis as Cathy, Jerome Gaither as Norrie.

Staff and Cast of Drama Festival Play "Fog On The Valley"

KNEELING L-R: Jerome Gaither, Harold Hairston, Lazelle Free, Walter Johnson

STANDING L-R: Claudette Graves, Delores Gary, Catherine Hinson, Nancy Lewis, Mary Doggett, Catherine Bruner, Barbara Byrd, Flora Mebane, Margaret Wynn, Ann Florence, Shirley Hinnant, and Diane Bell

Dr. Jo Evans Lynn, Ed.D.

In 2000, the Dudley Thespians returned to Dudley with *To Become…*, a play about the present and historical struggles of African American men in America.

Dudley High School Thespians present "To Become…"
March 10, 2000

The Thespians bring an original production to the Dudley High School Stage to honor Black History Month

The play was the first full scale production by the Dudley Thespians since 1978. Starring Lt. Col. Lacy Free (seated right) who was a Dudley Thespian in 1954 as "Pops" and Dudley band director, Mr. Brian Millsapp (Seated second from left) in dual roles: Alvin Bethune & W.E.B. DuBois. Other cast members: Felix F. Colon, Tonya Williamson, Davis Milton, Mia Michelle Evans, April Franklin, Quentin Green, Ezikel A. Mitchell, Johnnie Jefferson, Chantel Percell, Christopher Watson, John Brian Heath, Nathaniel Pickard, Misty Bigelow, Sharonda Breeden, Dwinique Peters, Laquonda Oboe, Steven Stroud, Nyenwance Johnson, and Dorethea Taylor.

The first full drama production presented by the Dudley Thespians in over 20 years was almost like "old times" because the production combined the efforts of Dudley students, teachers, alumni, parents, and the community. The play was sponsored by the Dudley Key Club and its sponsor, the Greensboro Kiwanis Club. Ms. Dorethea Taylor, a 1999 graduate of Bennett College, served as director. As a Bennett Belle, she majored in music. She did her student teaching at Dudley. It was Ms. Taylor's "vision" and drive that brought the play, *To Become…* to Dudley's stage. A less determined or less committed person might have looked at all the things

Dudley did not have at the time: a sound system, set slats, costumes, etc. and said, "Forget it!" Taylor was as determined as the Thespians' advisor to give Dudley's actors and singers their chance to shine. Through all the last-minute defections, she continued to say, 'We can do this." She literally pulled people in and infected them with her *we-can-do-this-attitude*.

Although the play is a musical, only a few of the cast members actually sang senior Tanya Williamson, juniors Mia Michelle Evans, April Franklin, and freshman Chantel Percell. A Dudley teacher, Brian Millsapp, who was in his fifth year as band director at Dudley at the time, was especially helpful. He not only played dual roles, but he was also instrumental in encouraging several band and orchestra members to join the Thespians. One band member, drum major, Christopher Watson took a speaking role two days before opening night. Another cast member Felix F. Colon accepted the leading role of Joebee three days before the first performance after the abrupt defection of the original lead actor. He brought such a fresh and unique interpretation to the part, that he truly became "Joebee." A former co-worker of Mrs. Lynn, Mr. Richard Zaruba, the drama teacher at Grimsley, not only loaned Dudley salts to construct the set for the play, but he also came over and helped with the building of a professional-looking set.

The most experienced actor in the cast was Lt. Col. Lazelle Free. Free was a Dudley Thespian from 1954-1957. He said that his most exciting role while at Dudley was in "Showboat." After graduating from Dudley in 1957, Free attended West Virginia State College and was a member of the WVSC Players for two years. After retiring from the Army, he was an ROTC instructor at A&T State University and the senior Army ROTC Instructor at Grimsley Senior High School. The Thespians were lucky that this talented actor agreed to play the role of "Pops" which he played in the premier of "To Become a Man" at Grimsley in 1996. Parents like Mrs. Franklin collected props and costumes and 1971 Dudley alumni Phillip R. Evans helped build the set.

Drama became an elective at Dudley in 2002 when block scheduling began. There still was no sound system and no budget to build sets or to buy props or costumes.

Dr. Jo Evans Lynn, Ed.D.

Nevertheless, the first production, a play by August Wilson, was hailed as the finest at Dudley since Mrs. Wells retired. The 2002 Dudley Yearbook proclaimed,

> "The Dudley Thespians present a winner! Mrs. Jo Lynn's drama students presented a moving rendition of a story of a family adventure. Cast members gave 100% as they told the story with compassion and exuberance."

The Piano Lesson

The Boy Willie Cast: Christopher Holland, Venita Burwell, Christopher Richardson, Malcolm Taylor, Craig Boykin, Ebony Gilliard, Daniel Ferguson, and Jacquelin Hall.

The Bernice Cast: Toyin Afeila, Christopher Holland, Christopher Richardson, Malcolm Taylor, Marsallis Prescott, Ebony Gilliard, Daniel Ferguson, and Chantal Percell.

At Right: Christopher Holland stars as Boy Willie

A PLACE WHERE SUCCESS WAS EXPECTED: FINAL EDITION

August Wilson's, THE PIANO LESSON

The main symbol of the play, the piano, is coveted by Boy Willie who learns the value of family. Boy Willie, Chris Holland, and Lyman, Craig Boykin, try to sneak the piano out of the house.

Boy Willie talks to his niece, Ebony Gilliard, as he constructs a dolly for moving the piano.

Bernice, Venita Burwell, does not fall for Avery's, Daniel Butler Ferguson, lines as he tries to "woo" her.

The stage personnel, Shevon Sanders, Jerica Womack, and Sheree Boykin pose with the wardrobe people, Laurean Davis, Nicole Worthington, and Ashley Tonkins, and make-up and publicity, Crystal Garinger, Natalie Siler, Omeshia Bowens, Nicole McCullough, and Chris Mickens.

"Lift Every Voice and Sing. Till Earth and Heaven Rings..."
Dudley's Vocal Music Department (1930 and beyond)

Choral Music has been a part of the James B. Dudley High School tradition since Dr. Tarpley hired its first music teacher, **MRS. N.D. ARNETTE,** in 1930. Like most music teachers of that time, she was a proficient piano player and continued to teach music and direct various choirs at Dudley through the early 1950s. In 1931, Dr. Tarpley added another music teacher, Mrs. Eloise Logan Penn. Mrs. Penn was already a music teacher at Washington Street School in the Greensboro City School System at the time. Although she was officially the music teacher for grades 7-9 at Washington Street School, she worked with the high school students while the high school grade levels were temporarily located on the Washington Street School campus during the two and a half years after Bennett became a college for women (1926-1929).

Picture Courtesy of Samuel Penn Pass
Mrs. Eloise Logan Penn

MRS. ELOISE LOGAN PENN was a graduate of Fisk University, with a major in music, she later earned her master's degree in music education from the Columbia University School of Music. In 1922 she joined the Greensboro City School System as a music teacher for grades 7-9 at Washington Street School. In 1946 she was named Supervisor of Music for all the schools in the Negro City Schools.

Other school systems in the state also used her as a consultant to their music education programs. For many years she was in charge of the music program at Dudley High School, and when Dudley's band director was inducted into the military to serve as director of a Navy band during World War II, Mrs. Penn was the school's band director during the war years. When the war ended, Mrs. Penn was named full-time supervisor of music for the city schools, a position in which she continued until her retirement in 1966.

A PLACE WHERE SUCCESS WAS EXPECTED: FINAL EDITION

Many persons employed by the Board of Education of Greensboro remained in the service of the schools for a long period of years perhaps several remained with the schools as long as or longer than Mrs. Penn, but it is probably true that she is the only person who spent a complete adult life, a period spanning more than forty years, employed by the local schools. All of her adult life she knew and did no other work except with the children, the teachers, the supervisors, and the administrators of the Greensboro City Schools.

Picture Courtesy of Samuel Penn Pass

Officer Sam Penn, the husband of Mrs. Eloise Logan Penn and the first African American policeman on the Greensboro City Police Force poses with his wife and the 1938 James B. Dudley High School Girls' Choir

Mrs. Penn loved Greensboro and its people. She made herself a part of many civic, social, and cultural activities of the community. Music was her life; music was her work, and music was her hobby. She was co-founder and organizer of the widely acclaimed Greensboro Men's Glee Club, which she directed for a long span of years. She was prominently connected with the development of the choir and music program for her church, the Providence Baptist Church, in Greensboro. Her last assignment in this area was as director of its young people's choir. A member of the Delta Sigma Theta Sorority, she arranged the music for the Delta Sigma Theta "Sweetheart Song."

JULIA RUTH MORRISON RICHMOND became Dudley's Choir Director and music teacher in 1955 after Mrs. N. D. Arnette retired. Born June 21, 1926, in Iredell County, North Carolina, she was the youngest of ten children born to Pless Edward Morrison and Lula Belle Houpe. Having completed high school at Morningside in Statesville, NC, she continued her education and received the BA and MA degrees in music and English at North Carolina Central University in Durham, NC. Further study was done at the University of North Carolina in Greensboro, which qualified her for the supervision of music in North Carolina. She was an outstanding soprano and choral director. During her tenure at Dudley, she taught thousands of students the art of singing choral music.

After her retirement she continued to live in Greensboro, North Carolina where she was a long-time member of St. James Presbyterian Church (U.S.A.), 820 Ross Avenue. As a member of Saint James, she was the first elder to chair the Community Affairs Committee which gave the church greater presence in the Triad area. She established College Church Sundays which attracted hundreds of college students to the church. Other church work included: Sunday School teacher, Vacation Bible School teacher, Stephen ministry, Sisters for All Seasons ministry, member and moderator of the Essie B. Meares Bible Study Circle, and Presbyterian Women mission communicator. Mrs. Richmond taught and directed the Children Singers, the Teen Singers, and the Chancel Choir. She organized, taught, and directed the Women's' Choir and served as coordinator of the Music Liturgical Arts ministry for many years.

She also remained active in the community. Mrs. Richmond was affiliated with the NC Retired Governmental Employees Association, the American Association of Retired Persons, and she was an Alpha Kappa Alpha woman. She was a member of the Board of Directors of Greensboro Urban Ministry and served as chairperson for several years. She also chaired Greater Greensboro CROP Walk and, for many years, she helped raise thousands of dollars to build Greensboro Urban Ministries on Lee Street, Partnership Village on Greenbriar Road and Pathways Center on Church

Street. She also served as chairperson of the Board of Advisors for Friends Homes, Inc. She sang with the Greensboro Oratorio Society, the Glenn Burleigh Concert Choir, and the Black Caucus Choir of Salem Presbytery.

In recognition of her exemplary service to the State of North Carolina and to her community that was above and beyond the call of duty and made a significant impact and strengthened North Carolina, she was awarded the Order of the Long Leaf Pine by Governor Pat McCrory in June of 2016.

Carolyn Walden Munchus (Class of 1962) who was a piano accompanist for numerous concerts and programs while she attended Dudley noted, "Mrs. Richmond tutored me in theory to help me transition to college music theory classes by requiring that I learn all the major and minor scales, key signatures, chords, and intervals. I appreciated this additional work even more after I saw how much it helped me to be successful in the theory classes."

Mrs. Richmond directs the Freshman Choir (1966)

Shannon Stewart Minor of the Class of 1996 wrote a moving tribute to Mrs. Richmond's tenure and the Choral Music Tradition at Dudley under Mr. Cheek for the 2005 Panther's Claw Yearbook. She wrote,

"My experience at Dudley was a dream come true because I grew up knowing about Dudley and all of its traditions from my parents who graduated from Dudley.

I had been told about the strictness of the choir in the late 60s and 70s by my mother, who had been taught by Julia Ruth Richmond. When I went to the audition with Mrs. Brenda Hodge, I had big shoes to fill. I did just that. I was accepted to participate in the Honors Vocal Ensemble and Camerata Singers as a sophomore and I participated through my senior year.

The experience of participating in a choir at Dudley is one that I will never forget. It awarded me the opportunity to travel and represent my school and community in several venues. We participated in the Orlando Music Festival in the spring of 1995. Our group was the only group of color to participate. Because of the rich traditions that Dudley holds, our director, Mr. Cheek, chose the most difficult level of music for us to perform. We placed first in the Music Festival.

Because of my involvement in the choir, I learned the value of the high school experience. I learned to respect all kinds of music and cultures. I also learned to represent the best high school in the land with pride and dignity. It was a rewarding experience that will forever be imbedded in my memory." (Minor, 2005)

Shannon Stewart Minor with her parents, Pamela Stewart & Charles Stewart. Both graduated from Dudley in 1971.

That Band!
The Dudley's Marching Band of Thunder

Historically black college North Carolina A&T State University and the B1 Navy Band both played a major part in the evolution of what we now know as Dudley's Marching Band of Thunder. The director of the B-1 Navy Band was the first band director at Dudley, James Parsons.

The B1 Navy Band was formed from a nucleus of North Carolina A&T College students and graduates, the band was comprised of "the best, most talented musicians in North Carolina." Nine students from Dudley High School also joined, six with their parents' consent, and the Dudley band director, James Benton Parsons became B-1's bandmaster (though he was never afforded that rank) after A&T's director Bernard Mason failed to pass the Navy physical. Bernard Mason remained at North Carolina A & T as band director while many of his former students were off to Raleigh for enlistment.

Picture Courtesy of B-1 Navy Band Achieves

Dudley High School's first band director, James Parsons teaches young student while a member of the B-1 Navy Band.

Picture Courtesy of Photographic Archives, North Carolina Collection, UNC-CH

The B-1 Navy Band Marches in Chapel Hill led by Bandmaster/Drum Major James Parsons

Dr. Jo Evans Lynn, Ed.D.

Parsons had a talent for being able to stand in front of a whole band and pick out the one guy with a bad note. This is a particularly ironic skill given the story bandsmen tell of the two times the Navy tried to replace B-1's bandmaster, James Parsons, with a white bandmaster. In each instance, during rehearsal for the "National Anthem" prior to a big public event, one reed would squawk, the bandmaster would stop, fuss, and start again, only to have another one squawk, and the process would go on until the white bandmaster would give up in exasperation, never able to find the culprit(s). And each time, the baton came back to Parsons (Fountain, R.A. November 29, 2023).

That Parsons never was afforded the rank of Chief Musician rankled many of the men in B-1. He was put up for it by his commanding officers three times, each denied, once in 1942 at Chapel Hill and then in 1944 and 1945 at Manana, though on some Navy forms he is mistakenly accorded that rank he was the only African American leading one of the Navy's 100+ black bands. One of the requirements for future bandsmen to earn that rank was graduation from the Navy's School of Music, which was closed to blacks until after World War II. The rank of Musician, of course, was closed to blacks and would not be open to them until B-1's collective induction in 1942 (Albright, Alex. 2013)

Applications made for Chief on Parsons' behalf tried to satisfy the School of Music requirement by appealing that his conservatory training and experience more than qualified him for the position. The Navy first said he couldn't be Chief because he had not served at sea; then, when he had completed that requirement by serving at Pearl Harbor, the Navy said he couldn't be promoted to Chief because he had not served 6 years. He mustered out of the Navy in November 1945 at Great Lakes in Chicago.

Years later, Parsons was nominated by President John F. Kennedy on August 10, 1961, to a seat on the **United States District Court for the Northern District of Illinois**. He was confirmed by the **United States Senate** on August 30, 1961, and received his commission the same day, becoming the first African American to serve as a U.S. district judge in a U.S. district court.

JBD

After Parsons' Induction into the Navy, Mrs. Eloise Logan Penn served as band director. Parsons was followed by Warmouth Gibbs, Jr., and James D. Morgan who were both B-1 band mates.

A PLACE WHERE SUCCESS WAS EXPECTED: FINAL EDITION

During the early years, A&T's "old" uniforms often became Dudley's "new" uniforms. It was not a big stretch since the schools' colors are the same: gold and Navy blue. Many A&T Blue & Gold Marching Machine Members are former Dudley band members who come back as volunteers to work with current band members. The unique style of marching referred to as "show-style" has allowed Dudley's band to make their mark at many events throughout the years. Dudley's marching band has been known for generations for their skill in musicianship, choreography, and precision in formations and of course for their high stepping. Their high stepping consists of bringing their leg to a 90-degree angle and then pointing the toe at the ground, as they march forward. This is known in the band world as a "chair" (Malone, 1996).

A&T's Marching band, which started in 1918, was well established when Dudley's Band was established in 1930. Mrs. Eloise Logan Penn who arranged the music for the Delta Sigma Theta, "Sweetheart Song" served as band director during the World War II years while Parsons served in the military as the director of the B-1 Navy Band. Mrs. Penn led the band and the rest of the Music Department at Dudley until she left to become the director of music for the Greensboro Negro Public School System in 1946. At that time, Warmouth Gibbs, Jr. the son of A&T State University's 4th president, was hired as band director. In 1956 Mr. Morgan was hired as band director. Like all the other teaching positions at Dudley during the first six decades of the band's existence, the position of Band Director was one that was held with pride and tremendous staying power with early band directors remaining for an average of 16.5 years.

JBD

Warmouth T. Gibbs, Jr. was Dudley's third band director. Although Dudley followed A&T's lead in many aspects of music and style, Dudley added majorettes in 1948, while A&T did not add this auxiliary until the mid-1960s (History of the Machine, 2015). Adding majorettes as a female auxiliary to the band and moving the band from the military corps style to the high stepping marching/show band style were innovations of Warmouth T. Gibbs, Jr. According to Fine (2003), stepping is based on a long and rich tradition in African-based communities that use movement, words and sounds to communicate allegiance to a group. It draws movements from African foot dances, such as Gumboot, originally conceived by miners in South Africa as an alternative

Mr. Warmouth T. Gibbs, Jr.

to drumming, which was banned by authorities. The stepping tradition in the United States grew out of song and dance rituals practiced by historically African American fraternities and sororities, beginning in the early 1900s (Fine, 2003).

As a member of Omega Psi Phi Fraternity, Gibbs had participated in stepping while in college. Because he had also been a member of the B-1 Navy Band, he kept the precision of the military corps style of marching that Parsons had established and added some of the dance movements of stepping. By the early 1950s, the high-stepping show band style was firmly established at James B. Dudley High School.

High Steppers at Homecoming

Picture Courtesy of Juanita Brown

James B. Dudley High School, November 1950. Left to right: Len McLaughlin, drum major; Loretta Free, Thelma Simpson, Dorothy Brice, Juanita Brown, Doris Mae Capps, and Doris Brice. Not shown is Tiyette Neal.

A PLACE WHERE SUCCESS WAS EXPECTED: FINAL EDITION

The position of drum major has always been a highly sort after position. The drum major's duty is to conduct the band, sometimes using a large baton or mace. In most school bands, the drum major is the student leader of the band, followed by students within the band that lead a section. Dudley was also ahead of the times in its selection of a female drum major. Many Historically black colleges did not have a female drum major until the late 1990s or early 2000s, *Dudley's first female drum major, Kathleen Winchester was high stepping during the 1958-1959 school year.*

Once Dudley had only one auxiliary –the majorettes who were added to the band in 1948. The flag girls who were required to have been members of the band were added sometime during the 1950s and the Pantherettes were added in 1966. The Pantherettes are a dance line that consists of young ladies who present choreographic movements to the music as it is performed. They add flare and excitement to the performance. The flag lines add color and decoration to the formations on the field with their precision flag twirling and marching.

Dudley's 1966-67 Female Drum Major

Although Dudley, like most other High School bands, evolved from military bands, high step marching has been the band's marching style since the late 1940s. High step marching is a high-energy, high-effort, crowd-pleasing style of marching. When combined with the strong sound of a full marching band, it helps create field shows that bring audiences to their feet. Many bands have transitioned to corps style marching because high step marching is more challenging than other styles, requiring more effort by the marcher and because it is the preferred style of the once all-white schools that all except James B. Dudley and three of the other historically black high schools (Durham Hillside, Fayetteville E.E. Smith, and Winston-Salem Carver) in North Carolina have been assimilated into historically White high schools. In the high-stepping style of marching the musician needs to not only play their instrument well but also needs to be able to lift their feet high on every step and make sharp turns. It is a very powerful form of marching, and the musicians get in great shape. While high stepping requires more effort than other forms of marching, it is much more exciting for the audience. Band directors that choose high step teach showmanship and lead bands that entertain crowds of all kinds, especially football crowds. Corps style is generally appreciated by band people or military people to the exclusion of most other crowds.

Now that most of the historically black high schools no longer exist, there are not as many band competitions for high-stepping style bands as there are for corps style bands. This lack of competition has never been a problem for Dudley's Band since it allows the band to learn and perform more music and often put on a different show at each home football game, which is far more entertaining for the crowd. The crowds at many of Dudley's competitors often stay to watch Dudley's field show during halftime and leave for refreshments when their band performs because corps style bands learn one competitive performance a year and use it over and over again for the entire season.

Dudley's Longest Tenured Band Directors

James D. Morgan was born July 1, 1915, in Tuckahoe, North Carolina. He decided to attend North Carolina A&T after A&T's band performed at his high school. "I sat there and looked at that band and admired their sounds," he told the Greensboro Record's Bruce Washburn, "and fell in love with instrumental music. That did it."

He put himself through college at A&T by cooking, cleaning, and doing housework for the school's bursar. After graduating in 1941, he became the assistant director of the B-1 Navy Band and became famous for his strut as drum major. John Clark, who still leads the dance band started by his brother, Doug Clark, and the Hot Nuts, recalled that as kids they loved seeing the B-1 Navy Band parade from its barracks past their house in route to the UNC campus where they'd play colors for the Navy's preflight cadets. "Doug and I and all the kids in the neighborhood would run out to Robinson Street when we heard the band coming," Jon Clark recalled, "and we followed them as far as we could. Doug wanted to be just like Morgan."

Cadet James D. Morgan, B-1 Navy Band, 1941

A PLACE WHERE SUCCESS WAS EXPECTED: FINAL EDITION

Fellow B-1 veteran Huey Lawrence still gets excited when he describes Morgan's strut: "He's leaning back past being straight back, I mean he's' leaning back so that his hat's' almost hitting the ground, and straight, too! But past parallel to the ground."

After the war, Morgan taught at several schools in North Carolina--Rocky Point, Yanceyville, Asheboro, and Greensboro--and in Virginia at Albert Harris High School in Martinsville. He also directed choirs at Harris High and the Men's' Choir at Providence Baptist Church in Greensboro, where he was a beloved music teacher for 37 years.

Mr. James D. Morgan,
Portrait by Dudley student Ed Lineberry, 1978

Also, while in Greensboro, he taught music at several recreation centers and supervised a show wagon for the Parks & Rec Department, traveling around to city parks to produce programs that featured performances by community children.

Mr. Morgan was the band director at James B. Dudley High School for twenty-two years, from 1956-1978. Throughout his years of instruction, he taught band classes, managed homeroom classes, and provided supportive activities related to numerous events that occurred at the school and throughout the community. Instrumental music was an intricate part of most of the traditional programs at Dudley.

Under his leadership, the marching and concert bands performed in parades and rendered musical selections for special programs as well as the usual ones. Special programs included those honoring administrators, students, and teachers. The usual programs included various assemblies, awards day, senior class day, holiday programs, and commencement activities. For many years, Mr. Morgan conducted the capping ceremony for the senior class. Dressed in all-white attire, he would stand in a chair or on a platform. Facing the senior class, he would direct them to put on their caps and flip their tassels with precision and unity. Even after his retirement from Dudley, he returned year after year to lead this traditional activity. He did this until he could no longer climb up in a chair or up on a platform. Mr. Morgan worked tirelessly for many hours beyond the school day.

Hours were spent in afterschool band practice whether it was for parades or concerts. On any given school day, the band would march up and down Lincoln Street, down Willow Road and all around the open field that is now Tarpley Stadium. Between Mr. Morgan and Georgene Dye, who directed the majorettes, cheerleaders and Pantherettes, band members had very serious physical workouts on a daily basis. The concert season was even more demanding. It required being in the band room for what sometimes seemed like an eternity, practicing the same selections over and over until each piece was memorized and could almost be played without the music. After that, it was on to the auditorium or the gym to sit for long hours going over the same selections again, to make sure the band sounded its best. Mr. Morgan believed in practice, practice, practice.

His approach to teaching band was greatly influenced by his years of service in the B-1 U.S. Navy Band during World War II. He believed in the band as a military-like organization, required to perform music in an appropriate manner. He cringed at the sight of band members getting on the ground or putting their instruments on the ground. The band had to be neatly clad and marching with precision in straight lines at all times. He did not like seeing band uniforms all over the city before or after an event. He required that band uniforms never left the band room unless they were worn immediately for an event. Students had to dress in the band room area. After the event, the students had to return to the band room and leave the uniforms there. Uniforms were to be stored neatly and cleaned often. After all, they were expensive and not an easy purchase for Dudley. Although the uniforms during the 50s and 60s were made of wool and extremely hot during the early games of the football season, Dudley's Band never dressed down. Mr. Morgan made sure to get longevity from the uniforms.

The fruit of his labor manifested itself in awesome parades down the old "Dudley" Street, now Bennett Street, from the Hayes Taylor YMCA to War Memorial Stadium for football games. The band looked good and performed in the Christmas parades, Veteran's' Day Parades, A&T Homecoming parades (The band often led this parade. Mr. Walter Carlson, who was A&T's' band director for over 40 years, was a B-1 U.S. Navy Band mate during WWII. This was the first African American Navy Band. The director of the B-1 band had also been a band director at Dudley, James Parsons. Other B-1 band mates who directed the James B. Dudley High School band were Shelton Williams and Warmouth Gibbs, Jr. The band took many trips with the football teams to add support to their efforts. The band played at every home basketball game. Travel to many cities to compete in band contests was part of the band agenda.

Mr. Morgan was dedicated to the school, his co-workers, and especially his students. He thought of students as "his" children. He was firm, but fair, caring and nurturing. "My fondest high school memories are of being in the band with Daddy," his daughter Chapelle Morgan Davis commented, "I must admit that at times I was a little jealous of the time and attention he lavished on his students. Looking back, I appreciate his keen interest in his students and his high expectations of them. We all needed this at a time in our lives when we craved guidance beyond the classroom. We all needed our teachers to be our parents away from home. Teachers at Dudley High School always showed that they cared for their students and James D. Morgan, Jr. was no exception." (Chapelle Morgan Davis, Daughter, Dudley Class of 1965)

Dr. Jo Evans Lynn, Ed.D.

"Chief" Shelton Williams
(1966-1993)

Before becoming the assistant band director at Dudley in 1966, Mr. Shelton "Chief" Williams taught at J.C. Price 1959 through 1966. While there, he taught English, math, and band. Mr. Williams taught by the standard course of study that was in place at that time because he wanted to make sure he was teaching the right thing to the students (Williams, 2009).

Unlike many of his fellow teachers, Mr. Williams did not live in the Warnersville Community. He lived at 1923 Julian Street and described his community as a typical strong black community which saw the typical adverse effects of segregation.

Mr. Williams had a few memories of the after-school activities. He recalled a student vs. teacher basketball game and being able to put the middle school band in the Greensboro Christmas parade as well.

In an interview in 2009, he explained that when he was at Price, the quality of Price's educational program was at its highest peak. Despite that, Mr. Williams said, "There were things that Price school wanted to do but could not due to segregation." After leaving Price, Mr. Williams went on to teach at Lincoln Junior High School, then to Dudley High School, where he led the marching band.

Mr. Shelton "Chief" Williams
Assistant Band Director (1966-1978)
Head Band Director, 1978-1993

When Mr. Williams became band director, Mr. W. Arthur Wise took over his former roles with the orchestra and jazz band. For several years, the James B. Dudley High School Marching Band served as the official home band for Guilford College.

In 1972, the band finally received its long-awaited new uniforms. The uniforms were designed so that they could be used for marching and converted to formal concert uniforms. The band had suffered slightly in enrollment because of busing dropping to 114 members. Mr. Williams was determined to prove that this would in no way change the quality of the band's performances. The band worked and demonstrated that it was the most spectacular band in the Piedmont area by winning accolades for every performance.

During Mr. Williams' tenure as band director, the Marching Band won several awards and honors. In 1993 the Dudley High School Marching Band won top honors and the first-place trophy during the fifth annual Martin Luther King Jr. Drum Major for Justice Festival of Bands competition on Jan. 18, 1993, in St. Petersburg, Fla.

The contest sponsored by the Southern Christian Leadership Conference drew approximately 20 top high school bands from high schools across the nation, including the St. Augustine (Fla.) High School Band and the Lakewood High School Band. Dudley's was the only Marching Band from North Carolina that competed.

Approximately 86 of the band's 142 members participated in the competition, according to Dudley band director Shelton Williams. Their music for the contest included "Under Pressure," "Skin I'm In," and "Before I Let Go."

Williams said the win in 1993 topped a slate of memorable performances by the band over the last four years, including a Sea World performance in Orlando in 1990; the National Peach Bowl Parade in Atlanta in 1989; Gov. Jim Martin's

"Chief" and drum majors proudly display the first-place trophy.

Inaugural Parade in 1989; repeated appearances since 1985 in the Mardi Gras Parade in New Orleans, and the band's celebrated appearance in Paris in 1989 in France's Bicentennial Celebration Parade. The parade in Paris was televised internationally.

Williams was chief director of the band for 20 of the 32 years he was on the Dudley faculty. He spent the first twelve years as assistant band director and instructor for the percussion section of the band.

MR. BRIAN MILLSAPP
(1995-2001)

Brian Millsapp. When he was hired in 1995, Brian Millsapp became Dudley's youngest Band Director earning the assignment with an outstanding recommendation from A&T State University's long-time Band Director, Dr. Johnny Hodges. Millsapp had just received a Bachelor of Science Degree in Music Education from North Carolina A&T State University with high honors in 1995. In 2000, he received his master's in music education from the University of North Carolina at Greensboro.

At Dudley, Millsapp's bands received numerous superior ratings in chamber ensembles, concert, jazz, and marching bands. Dudley and A&T graduate Christopher Goins (1996) and Benjamin Mittman (1997) worked as Assistant Band Directors during Millsapp's tenure. Perhaps, the most outstanding features of the Marching Band during Millsapp's tenure was how hard they worked and the superb quality of their half-time performances. In 1997, my first year at Dudley, I came to campus often during the summer to work in my classroom. No matter how early I got there or how late I stayed there were several sections of the band on campus practicing. The band was nick named "The Marching Band of Thunder" during Millsapp's tenure.

During Millsapp's tenure, he started a festival known as the P.A.W.E. (Panthers Always Working toward Excellence) Classic. The festival was unique because it focused on both corps and traditional high-stepping style bands. Participating bands included E. E. Smith, 71st High School, Harding University High School, and Ben L. Smith High School. In 2001, he left Dudley to begin a collegiate career at Central State University in Wilberforce, Ohio. In 2004, his band at Central State was featured in the movie "Dave Chappelle's Block Party". In 2011, Brian Millsapp was named the Assistant Director of Bands at North Carolina A&T State University.

Millsapp was a member of Kappa Kappa Psi Honorary Band Fraternity, Inc., an Honorary Member of the Tau Beta Sigma National Band Sorority, Inc., Phi Mu Alpha Sinfonia Music Fraternity, and HBCU-NBDC (National Band Director's Consortium) and the N.C.M.E.N.C. Millsapp was born in Fort Lee, Virginia.

A PLACE WHERE SUCCESS WAS EXPECTED: FINAL EDITION

Above: An invitation to the P.A.W.E. Classic was a coveted honor. At left, **From Left to Right:** Willie Lewis, Demani Bell, and Elliot Yourse entertain the audience at the second annual P.A.W.E. Celebration.

Dedication, hard work, excellence in performance and showmanship are qualities that have made the James B. Dudley High School Marching Band one of the top high school bands in the nation for more than five generations.

Dr. Jo Evans Lynn, Ed.D.

Chapter Fifteen

Dudley: Success Personified...

For many years during the late 1800s black families moved to Greensboro so that their children could attend the schools that by this time were well established. Greensboro was known in the black community as a "college town" with two colleges for blacks: Bennett College and Agricultural & Mechanical College (later North Carolina A&T State University). Blacks also had four separate normal/high schools that they could attend: the Normal School Program at Bennett Seminary (1879-1926), Agricultural & Mechanical College Normal School for Males (1915-1928), Palmer Memorial Institute in Sedalia (1902-1970), and The Negro High School in Greensboro- later named James Benson Dudley High School (1879-Present). All of these schools, except Dudley, were private schools that charged tuition and had buildings for students to "board" or live on campus. Beginning in 1879, the Greensboro City School Board paid tuition for some of the city's Negro students to attend high school at Bennett Seminary and from 1923-1926 for a coeducational high school for 150 students on the Bennett College Campus. For a brief period, while Dudley's Main Building was being built, after Bennett became a college for women the school system paid for a few male upperclassmen to attend the Normal School at the Agricultural and Mechanical College (1926-1928).

It would be impossible to cite by name and accomplishments all of James B. Dudley High School's successful students. Instead, this book includes some of the most famous and a few not so famous alumni who served to pave the road to success for future generations. Some sacrificed more than others- the star Dudley quarterback who gave up a sure starting position at a historically black college to be switched to a half-back position or the tremendously talented basketball player who never felt "welcomed" back home because he gave up a scholarship to a historically black college to pave the way for other black athletes at larger white institutions. Dudley produced many Jackie Robinsons in a vast number of arenas. Here are just a few of them.

Picture Greensboro News & Record

Judge Elreta Alexander-Ralston (Class of 1934)

No one who met her personally would ever deny that **Judge A** was a "real character." Her personality filled a room. The first time I saw her was at my sister's graduation in 1965 when she was the guest speaker. She wore a fitted red jersey dress that was cut daringly low in the back. My mother and the other older women whispered in shocked outrage while the men smiled appreciatively. But when she stood to speak, that outfit did not prevent her from captivating over 2,000 people with what she had to say.

Elreta Melton was born in Smithfield, North Carolina on March 21, 1919. Her family moved to Greensboro, and she graduated from Dudley High School at the age of 15 in 1934 and from A&T State University at 18 with a degree in music.

At an A&T dance, she met a handsome young doctor-to-be named Girardeau "Tony" Alexander. They were married in Chester, South Carolina in a civil ceremony.

Unhappy in her marriage, she applied to Columbia University. She was the first black woman accepted to the Columbia University School of Law. She graduated with a law degree in 1945. She was the first black woman to argue a case before the state Supreme Court. She was also the nation's first black woman to be elected to the bench, serving as a District Court Judge from 1968-1981 (Duncan, 1988).

It seemed odd that my personal account of the first time I came in contact with Judge Elreta Alexander mirrors Nancy McLaughlin's account of being in the presence of this great lady. Both of us began with a description of the way she looked and ended with proof of what made her so uniquely authentic. In the article, **'Speak now, darlin' Bold and brazen, breaking barriers was Elreta Alexander's bread and butter. So was the law**, McLaughlin says, *from the back row of the colored section.*

"Ms. Alexander, you can sit up here with us," a white lawyer intoned as the others coming in with her began filling in a row at the front of the courtroom.

Attorney Elreta Alexander-Ralston kept walking.

In walked a Black lady wearing a full-length mink coat and matching hat. 1960s shut up, including the high school students with their civics teacher, who all got a show

"She said, 'Oh, no. I prefer to sit amongst my people' — and swung that coat across her seat like it was a trench coat," recalled Joe Williams, who was one of those admiring students. "The whole class went back to school wanting to be lawyers."

When **KING V. CHEEK** was a child, everyone called him "dummy." In a 2011 article he described this aspect of his childhood. Cheek wrote,

"For me personally, growing up was a little frustrating because I really was not considered normal. I was technically branded as retarded. The community and, to some extent, I think, even my parents questioned whether I had all my faculties because I had a tongue-tied physical deficiency, and I could not speak until I was 6 or 7 years old.

And when you can't talk, people simply assume there's something wrong with your head. I have congenital cataracts, which don't really bother me. That contributed to what was perceived as an abnormality because I didn't have glasses at the time. I didn't bother letting anybody know that I really had difficulty seeing. I just decided it wasn't their business. So, I just ignored it and dealt with it in my way.

I found that there were some advantages to having people perceive you as not being like other children. When you're called a dummy and people think you're a dummy, they ignore you. So, you can do pretty much what you want to do. I learned on my own, and I took charge of my own development. I knew I was not abnormal or retarded. At a very early age I started developing my own agenda, deciding what I wanted to do with my life." (p.3)

Well qualified and caring teachers at Washington Street School, Lincoln Junior High School, and James B. Dudley High School discovered that he was actually a gifted student. King Virgil Cheek became an author and lifelong educator. Cheek was born on May 26, 1937, in Weldon, North Carolina. His father was a Baptist minister, and his mother was the first black female insurance broker in North Carolina. He attended Washington Street Elementary School and became a child evangelist at twelve years old while attending Lincoln Junior High. Cheek received his high school diploma from Dudley High School in 1955, where he was a member of the debate team.

Recruited by his mentor, Dr. Benjamin Mayes, he attended Bates College in Lewiston, Maine, and earned his Bachelor of Arts degree in economics in 1959. He went on to earn his master's degree from the University of Chicago in 1967. Cheek earned his law degree from the University of Chicago in 1969. He was active in the Civil Rights movement, participating in the March on Washington and passed up a number of lucrative offers to practice law and chose instead to teach at a Black college in the South.

At the age of twenty-seven, Cheek became a dean and vice president at Shaw University under his brother, Dr. James Cheek, who was president of the university at that time. Of that experience he King V. Cheek wrote,

"Working with him was a phenomenal growth experience. I learned something and developed something that became a part of my life force. I was able to be a vice president and separate my relationship with him as a brother from my role as an employee and as a vice president ---subordinate to him. Learning how to do that, both philosophically and emotionally, was a very powerful experience, and one that has never deserted me."

He held the post until 1969, when he was appointed president. Cheek served as president at Shaw University until 1971. That year, Cheek was named president of Morgan State University in Baltimore, Maryland, where he remained until 1974. From 1974 through 1976, he was vice president of

Union for Experimenting Colleges and Universities; Cheek served as president of the organization from 1976-78. His focus then shifted to leadership development; along with a colleague they developed the Center for Leadership and Career Development in Washington, D.C., in 1978. From 1985 until 1996, Cheek served in a number of posts at New York Institute of Technology including social sciences professor, dean of graduate studies and vice president of academic affairs.

From 2001 until 2003, Cheek served as the chancellor of New York College of Health Professionals. He is the author of numerous books, chapters and articles including *Quadra soul,* four novels that explore four dimensions of the human spirit. He is also the recipient of innumerable awards and honors. In November of 2014, Cheek was a guest speaker at the 2014 Corporate Citizenship Conference.

And Still We Sing: Dudley Divas

Dudley's First Diva!
Margaret Tynes
(Dudley, 1936)

Margaret Tynes was the daughter of Dr. J. W. Tynes, a longtime pastor of Providence Baptist Church in Greensboro, North Carolina. She was Dudley's first Diva. She had an international career as a singer in opera, jazz, and theater for over fifty years. Tynes began her operatic career at the New York City Opera. Her early principal roles were in *Carmen*, *Aida* and in *Verdi's Macbeth*.

Tynes was a 1936 graduate of James B. Dudley High School. While at student at Dudley, she sang in the chorus under the direction of Mrs. Eloise Logan Penn. She graduated from North Carolina A&T State University with a BA in music in 1939 and from Columbia University in 1944 with a master's degree.

While living and performing in New York, Tynes starred as Harry Belafonte's leading lady in an off-Broadway show that he produced called *Sing Man, Sing!* She recorded a jazz suite called *A Drum is a Woman* with Duke Ellington and made several appearances on *The Ed Sullivan Show*. In 1961, she gained international fame as Salomé at the Spoleto Festival of the Two Worlds in Italy.

She made her home in Milan, Italy for more than forty years with her Czech-born architect husband.

During that time, she appeared repeatedly with the leading opera companies of Europe and the United States. Tynes returned home to Greensboro in 1981 to present a free concert in the Harrison Auditorium at A&T State University as the opening event of the inauguration of Dr. Edward Fort as the school's 9th president.

Picture Courtesy of Brown-Reid

EVA FOSTER was Dudley's first jazz and blues diva. She was the daughter of Reverend Joseph Oscar Foster and Eva Turner Foster. Because her father was an AME minister, the family moved frequently and did not move to Greensboro until she was ten years old. She attended Washington Street School from the 5th through 9th grade. As a young girl and throughout the rest of her life, she attended Bethel AME Church in Greensboro. Her talent as a singer became apparent during her 10th grade year when she performed in a vocal concert (Brown-Reid, 2014). Mrs. Pearl Garrett Bradley, the drama teacher, served as Eva's mentor recognizing her talent and encouraging her to perform soap-opera skits on WBIG Greensboro's only radio station during the 1940s (Brown-Reid, 2014).

While a student at Dudley, Eva Foster played the French horn in the marching band. She graduated from Dudley in 1941. Eva completed her Bachelor of Arts degree in education at North Carolina A&T State University in 1946.

Eva became a part of the strong jazz culture in North Carolina during the late 1940s and 1950s. John Coltrane, Ben Collier, Max Roach, Thelonious Monk, Billy Strayhorn, Nina Simone, Eve Cornelius, and Lois Deloatch were just a few of the more than one hundred noted jazz singers and musicians from North Carolina during this era. Foster's first appearance on a jazz stage was at *The Club Mombassa* a popular night spot for Colored people in Greensboro during the late 1940s and early 1950s.

When Foster decided to take her career as a jazz singer beyond the local scene, she performed in several East coast cities including Philadelphia, Atlantic City, Washington D.C., and New York City- Harlem. Her greatest early success was winning first-place at the Apollo's Harlem Amateur Hour in 1948 (Brown-Reid, 2014). Foster rose to national acclaim with her first hit single, "You'll Never Know," with the Van Perry Quintet on the Atlantic Records Label.

While she was a member of the Van Perry Quintet, she performed at the Blue Mirror Club in Washington, D.C. She also performed with dancer and actor, Vance Gregory Hines at the Carolina Theater, and comedienne Pigmeat Markham at the Apollo Theater (Brown-Reid, 2014).

A PLACE WHERE SUCCESS WAS EXPECTED: FINAL EDITION

INEZ FOXX. In 1953 Inez Fox (They added the other "x" when they became famous) shocked the school by upsetting a senior tradition. Fox was a sophomore when she was overwhelmingly chosen as Homecoming Queen of 1953-54. This was the first and only time in the school's history that this honor went to a non-senior. Her popularity was evidenced when she polled 307 votes, approximately half of the 629 votes cast.

While a student at Dudley, she was a member of the Dudley Thespians. After graduating from Dudley, in 1960 Inez traveled to New York City and recorded for Brunswick Records using the name Inez Johnston, but with little success.

In early 1963, she teamed up with her older brother Charlie Foxx and the pair introduced themselves to Henry "Juggy" Murray, the owner of Sue Records, and sang for him their arrangement of the traditional lullaby "Hush, Little Baby." The song, re-titled "Mockingbird" was released in 1963 and made the Top 10 on both the US rhythm and blues and pop charts. It was their most successful record, and was later covered by artists including Aretha Franklin, James Taylor and Carly Simon, Dusty Springfield, Etta James with Taj Mahal, and Toby Keith.

The record company, keen to promote Inez Foxx as a solo singer, issued later recordings under her name alone, despite the presence of two voices on the records. Perhaps because "Mockingbird" was seen as a novelty record, the pair had difficulty following it up, although "Ask Me" and "Hurt by Love" made the lower reaches of the US charts, and "Hurt by Love" also reached the United Kingdom's chart. In 1966 the pair joined *Musicor* Records and recorded for its subsidiary label, Dynamo. They returned to the pop charts in 1967 with "(1-2-3-4-5-6-7) Count the Days" and became known for their exciting live performances. A highlight was Inez's rendition of "I Stand Accused", which finished with a supposedly distraught Inez singing the last verse, while being carried offstage by Charlie. They toured extensively in Europe and their music played a key role in the development of the Northern Soul movement.

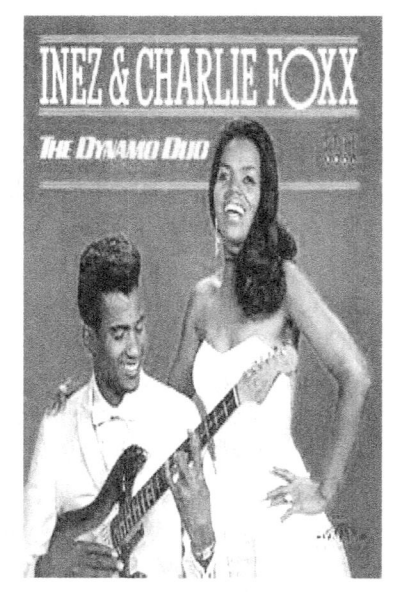

Inez Foxx married songwriter and producer Luther Dixon in the late 1960s. Together they wrote, and he produced, the Platters' mid-1960s return to hit making with the single "I Love You 1000 Times." Luther Dixon produced Inez and Charlie's 1967 Dynamo album *Come by Here*.

Inez also had some success recording on her own, beginning in 1969, but her popularity faded in the 1970s. Charlie was already working as a songwriter and record producer when they finally disbanded their act. Inez continued to record as a solo singer for Volt Records in the 1970s.

Inez & Charlie Foxx

Inez & Charlie Foxx

Although her top hit *Mockingbird* was sung as a duet with her brother, she had an outstanding solo career with two hits, *I had a talk with My Man* and *Circuits Overloaded*, which made it to the US R&B Top 100 List.

ELVIRA GREEN (Class of 1958) was born in Macon, North Carolina. Her parents later moved to Greensboro. Both of her parents were college graduates. Green's parents attended North Carolina Central University. Her father was a concert pianist, and her mother sang and played the violin while in college. Green said of her learning experiences growing up, "As a child, we were taught that English was only one of the languages that we would speak. We were encouraged to appreciate people of other cultures not only through their ethnicity but through their language as well."

She graduated from James B. Dudley High School in 1958. She then attended North Carolina Central University where she majored in music and minored in French. After graduating from NCCU, Green took the advice of Afrika Hayes, then NCCU music instructor and daughter of singer Roland Hayes, and went to Washington D.C. to study voice with baritone Todd Duncan. Green moved to New York to continue her studies with Afrika Hayes and Lola Wilson Hayes. Wilson Hayes was affiliated with the Metropolitan Opera's program. After a number of

Elvira Green in Broadway Costume

years, Green was invited to the Metropolitan Opera where she performed with the Met for a total of 19 years between 1966 and 1990. She also sang with the San Francisco Opera.

Since leaving the stage, Elvira Green has taken her mezzo-soprano voice, performance experience and love of music to NCCU as a scholar-in-residence in their Department of Music.

Picture Courtesy of Ursula Robinson

THELMA LIVONIA SPRUILL ROBINSON BURWELL graduated from Dudley in 1957. She grew up in the Warnersville Community and attended Jones Elementary School and J.C. Price Junior High School. While attending J.C. Price Junior High School, she became a member of the school Glee Club. It was there, that her enormous talent and beautiful operatic voice came into fruition. Her music teacher encouraged her to share her talent and helped her tremendously by giving her voice lessons.

Once Thelma started singing, she never stopped. She went on to join James B. Dudley High School's treasured chorus and to give her first recital while a student there. Even as a Bennett Belle she was a star commanding the attention of the music department and local audiences.

She was one of Bennett College's Songbirds as well as a soloist at Wells Memorial Church of God in Christ. She sang for Bishop Wyoming Wells in Memphis at the National Convocation, for the AIMS National Convention and for Bishop Woolard. She started playing piano for services at Brown's Funeral home at the age of 15.

NANCY BAKER CARREE WILSON graduated from Dudley in the class of 1966. While a student at Dudley, she was active in DECA. She was the first music director for Evangel Fellowship COGIC in Greensboro, North Carolina. Her musical credits include hosting "Gospel Expo," a television program which aired on ABC and Fox for over twenty years and recording with several Christian artists such as: Bishop Larry Trotter & Sweet Holy Spirit (Chicago, IL), Co-Pastor Debra Morton & the Women of Excellence Choir (New Orleans, LA) and Pastor Chris Brinson and the Ensemble (Kernersville, NC). In 2003, Wilson recorded live in Chicago at Sweet Holy Spirit Church where Bishop Larry Trotter served as pastor. Her project, released in March of 2004, was appropriately titled, *Nancy Wilson-Designed for Worship*. One song from that album, "If You Could See Me Now," has become an anthem of comfort for the final rites of Saints throughout the country. She served as pastor of New Beginnings Christian Fellowship from its inception in 1994. She is the mother of noted gospel singer Isaac Carree.

Most of the non-COGIC Christian music fans in the Triad remember Nancy Baker Carree Wilson as the charismatic hostess of Gospel Expo. However, she also served faithfully as a Pastor for more than twenty years.

YVONNE HAYGOOD SMITH

Yvonne participated in numerous musical endeavors in the Warnersville Community and Greensboro City Schools. Following graduation from James B. Dudley High School in 1964, she attended North Carolina Agricultural and Technical State University.

Yvonne and her immediate family joined Wells Temple Church of God in Christ under the pastorate of Bishop Wyoming Wells and continued to serve under Bishop Ithiel Clemmons, Bishop Leroy Jackson Woolard, and Dr. Herman G. Platt. She was Minister of Music, choir director, musician, soloist, and musical trainer for over 50 years. She also served as Minister of Music for the Greater North Carolina Jurisdiction of the Church of God in Christ. She worked with many local state and national church and community choirs from the age of 12. She traveled yearly on tours to Europe with The Ethel Caffie Singers.

She was a gifted and anointed writer, arranger, singer, musician, and choir director. She resisted many lucrative opportunities and encouragement to use her God-given talents otherwise. Instead, Yvonne used her musical gifts to help build self-esteem and pride among the youth of

Greensboro. She organized the *We Are One Choir* involving youth from public housing communities. She was led to do so out of a concern over what she observed as growing potential for gang development and rivalry between these communities. This project received recognition from the North Carolina Governor's Office and was adopted as a cultural program with the City of Greensboro.

As the first director/trainer of the award-winning North Carolina A&T State University Fellowship Gospel Choir from 1969 through 1982, Yvonne was directly responsible for musical performance, development of presentation and several recordings. N.C. A&T's Fellowship Gospel Choir, during her tenure, received national acclaim at the Annual Black College Workshop in Atlanta, Georgia, and the National Black Music Collegiate Gospel Choir Competition in New York City.

Although Yvonne could play piano "by ear" at a young age, she gave Mrs. Richmond credit for helping her to refine her skills while she was at Dudley High School

Dr. Jo Evans Lynn, Ed.D.

Toni Cameron Vincent: Dudley's Prima Ballerina

In 1966, when the curtain opened for a dance number near the end of Dudley's Modern Dance Company's Annual Spring Recital there was only one dancer on stage. This was not the norm for one of Miss Dye's elaborate Modern Dance productions. Nor was the tutu worn by the dancer the typical costume of the Dudley Modern Dance Company. Some members of the audience grumbled wondering what a single dancer (A sophomore as someone noted) could give an audience unaccustomed to ballet.

Picture Courtesy of Kenneth J. Wyrtch

Toni Cameron prima ballerina assoluta the most exceptional Dudley dancer of her generation

Toni Cameron gave most of the members of the audience their first taste of Classical Ballet. She took command of the stage. From the moment she started to dance, Toni Cameron became, for many years, my definition of "poetry in motion."

A PLACE WHERE SUCCESS WAS EXPECTED: FINAL EDITION

While a student at Dudley, Toni was an honor student, one of the original members of the Dudley Pantherettes, Miss Varsity, and a Dudley Thespian. She was also an accomplished visual artist and administrator. After graduating from Dudley in 1968, she became the first African American to be selected to the Governor's School of the Arts Performance Division for ballet. She did further professional study at the Boston Conservatory of Music where she performed with the Boston Dance Theater. She earned a Bachelor of Arts degree in Dance with a minor in drama. She performed with the Greensboro Civic Ballet. Toni Cameron was the first Dudley graduate to earn the title prima ballerina assoluta. Prima ballerina assoluta is a title awarded to the most notable of female ballet dancers. To be recognized as a prima ballerina assoluta is a rare honor.

An excerpt from "At the Wells" The Wells Memorial COGIC Newsletter, 2/9/2009

THE HAYGOOD SISTERS

"They're singing," that's all we needed to hear, and my sisters and I would rush to the window of the Little Girls' room (Mary, Sandra & Daisy) to hear an impromptu concert by the Haygood Sisters. Although, they sang some church songs, they also sang some of the popular songs of the day– nothing risqué— just soft soulful ballads that spoke to the hearts and dreams of young girls. Our window was right above their front room, so we had great seats on the side of the bed. We wanted to sing just like **them. They were the "big" girls and** our role models, but even though our mother bought us a piano, we failed in forming a singing group because only Sandra could really sing.

We were connected to the Haygoods by the fact that we lived in the same building in the Morningside Homes Projects during a time when each block of homes was truly a village. Their mother was the neighborhood, Mom. We went to Sister Haygood when we were hurt and sometimes when we weren't because her treatment for every ailment was a big hug and a piece of sweet potato pie.

We were also connected to the Haygoods by the fact that we attended Wells Temple. This was also during a time when a church family was truly "family". We took delegates for Convocation into our homes, and no one had anything on us when it came

Front: (Left to right): Margaret, Marie, and Malois. Back: (Left to right) Sara, Yvonne, and Zenobia

to packing one of the two or three cars owned by church members with as many people as each could hold.

I never stopped admiring the Haygood sisters and I always looked forward to hearing them sing in church on Sundays. The older Haygood girls were far enough ahead of me in school that I never considered them my contemporaries, but Yvonne was different. She was only three years older than me. She was close enough in age that her struggles mimicked mine and her "walk" seemed close to my own. Yvonne was family– Morningside Homes Family -- Wells Temple Family and Dudley High School Family- a body can't get any closer than that without being a blood relative.

BARBARA WEATHERS is an American Rhythm and Blues/soul singer. She was born December 7, 1963. Her first band was Covacus, a Greensboro, North Carolina band that is relatively well known in the southeast. Performing with Covacus was enough to gain her the attention of the management team of Atlantic Starr. The talented Barbara Weathers was hired by Atlantic Starr in 1985. The band's album As *the Band Turns* Atlantic Starr's first post Bryant album and sixth album overall -- found the outfit unveiling a smaller lineup that consisted of Weathers, lead singer/guitarist David Lewis, lead singer/keyboardist Wayne Lewis, trombonist/percussionist Jonathan Lewis, and percussionist/flutist Joseph Phillips. Weathers sang on two of Atlantic Starr's biggest hits, "Always" and "Secret Lovers". Her smooth vocals can also be heard on many of the group's soulful ballads. Weathers left Atlantic Starr in 1987 to pursue a solo career.

On leaving Atlantic Starr, Weathers released a self-titled solo album on Reprise Records with help from the singer-songwriter/record producer of Earth, Wind, and Fire, Maurice White, among other well-established musicians. The album consisted mainly of dance music numbers but was led off by the mid-tempo singles "The Master Key" and "Our Love Will Last Forever." Weathers utilized her ability to sing in the whistle register on

Photo credit: Jeff Katz

In 1985 Weathers joined **Atlantic Starr L-R**: David, Wayne, & Jonathan Lewis, and Joseph Phillips

Album Cover: Solo Album -Barbara WEATHERS

the album's operatic closing song "Our Love Runs Deep." The whistle register is the highest register of the human voice. With proper vocal training, it is possible for women within all voice types to develop this part of the voice, but few can sing it as naturally as Barbara Weathers.

Dr. Jo Evans Lynn, Ed.D.

Three Generations Spreading the Gospel

Picture Courtesy of Amber Headen

Generations Gospel Group: From left to right- **Mary Elizabeth Weathers Legette, Amber Lassiter Headen, Mia Lassiter Medlock, Tanya Legette Lassiter**

MARY ELIZABETH (LIZ) WEATHERS LEGETTE was a 1956 Dudley graduate. Her family called her Liz but to the rest of the world she was known as "Widdie". She never met a stranger and always had an open door. Whether a person was family (it didn't matter how far down the line a connection was), a neighbor, a friend, or a friend of a friend she would welcome them into her heart and home with open arms. She owned a store near downtown Greensboro for many years called Inspirational Creations where she enjoyed meeting new people and blessing people with hand-made crafts.

Widdie was also known as the restaurant evangelist because anywhere she went, she was excited to tell people about the goodness of Jesus and to give her testimony. One of her good friends, Mary Anderson, says of Widdie's ministry,

> "The first time we were out to dinner together she went over to talk to a man who was sitting by himself at Stephanie's, a soul food restaurant in Greensboro. I was amazed to see someone actively practicing their faith like that because usually when someone is sitting alone in a place that crowded, it means that they want to be left alone. But with a few words and that smile of hers, she had the man smiling and promising to go to church somewhere next Sunday. After years of watching her minister that way I understood the

courage that it took to practice one's faith even in places where it might not be accepted or welcomed." Widdie was like that because she was able to meet a person exactly where they were with no judgment - with welcoming arms.

Liz was very well known for her powerful singing voice that she used to spread the gospel in churches throughout North Carolina and Virginia. Every Sunday morning, she led the Praise and Worship section of the service at United Institutional Baptist Church. With her daughter and a couple of her granddaughters, she sang with a group named *Generations*. There were three generations represented in the group. Her granddaughter Amber Headen says of the group, "We loved being able to sing and minister together wherever we could."

Dr. Jo Evans Lynn, Ed.D.

Sing A Song, Full of the Faith that the Dark Past Has Taught Us...

'Historically, black music has influenced other cultures and other genres and created other genres." Miguel

There is something about "us" as a people that can only be expressed in our music. It does not matter whether its drums, vocals, or other musical instruments, our experiences as a people have placed in us and in our music something which while often imitated can never be totally replicated. Shortly after the second edition of A Place Where Success Was Expected was published Kenneth Wyrtch called me. He was always my greatest fan and my biggest critic. I appreciated both his compliments and his criticisms because both came with what he called recommendations.

Kenneth said, "You did an outstanding job with the Dudley Divas. I especially like the piece about Eva Foster, but (There was always a "but") you could have had the same kind of section about the male musicians and singers."

I pointed out the inclusion of J. Alphonse Nicholson. He insisted that there were dozens more before Nicholson, but Kenneth passed away before he could send me his list... With the help of Virginia Griffin, Chuck Cotton, and James Yourse I have completed this addition to the book.

Charlie Foxx,
Singer & Producer

CHARLIE FOXX. While brother pairings are commonplace enough in rock and pop groups, sister-brother teams occur less frequently. Inez and Charlie Foxx, whose single "Mockingbird" became a perennial Sixties favorite, were the sibling rhythm 'n' blues duo par excellence, regularly visiting Britain and earning more than a cult following amongst mods and northern soul fanatics (Perrone, 1998).

Born in 1939, Charlie Foxx came from a large family (he had four sisters and two brothers). He first sang at Dudley High School and with the Gospel Tide Choir in his native Greensboro, North Carolina. Tall and handsome, Charlie played football and basketball, and shared with his sister Inez an interest in music. By 1959, they had both graduated and started to compose together, while performing the odd date in local clubs. Inez recorded "A Feeling" for the Brunswick label in 1962 (as Inez Johnson) but joined forces with Charlie when they moved to New York the following year (Perrone, 1998).

Outside a restaurant, they bumped into Henry "Juggy Murray" Jones, who had set up the Sue R&B imprint, signing artists such as Don Covay, Jimmy McGriff and Ike and Tina Turner. Inez and Charlie Foxx were keen to join the label and told Murray they had a hit song. He invited them to his office near the legendary Brill Building (the New York hit factory where Carole King and Neil Sedaka honed their songwriting skills). Charlie's guitar had a broken string but their "let's-do-the-show-right-here" attitude impressed Murray (Perrone, 1998).

He liked their call-and-response number loosely based around a Bo Diddley shuffle and an old nursery rhyme even more. Charlie started with "Mock", answered by Inez singing "Yeah". Charlie came back with "King", Inez still jiving "Yeah", Charlie sang "Bird", Inez went "Yeah" again and so on and so forth. Within a few minutes, Juggy Murray called the arranger Bert Keyes to set up a session date and offered the brother and sister team a deal with one caveat: he wanted to bill Inez as a solo artist at first.

The pair agreed and "Mockingbird", released on Symbol, a Sue subsidiary, proved an instant smash, crossing over from the rhythm 'n' blues market into the US pop charts and eventually reaching No 7 by September 1963. Elated by his new charges' success, Juggy Murray allowed the Charlie and Inez Foxx moniker to appear on subsequent soundalike singles like "Hi Diddle Diddle", "Ask Me", "Jaybirds", "Hummingbird", "He's the One You Love", and "La De Dah, I Love You", none of which matched the success of their first hit (Perrone, 1998).

In Britain, Inez and Charlie Foxx made an immediate impact on the soul scene but took a while to penetrate the mainstream consciousness. After leasing a few recordings to Decca's London/American label, Juggy struck a licensing deal with Chris Blackwell at Island Records, who had heard "Mockingbird" on the radio in Jamaica. The hip disc jockey and producer Guy Stevens was appointed British label manager for Sue and turned the Foxx single into a club classic (Perrone, 1998).

July 1964 saw Inez and Charlie Foxx promoting their Top 40 single "Hurt by Love" and Mockingbird album on a British tour, backed by the Spencer Davis Group, and then recording "Here We Go Round the Mulberry Bush". They played the Cavern Club in Liverpool, and appeared on television on Ready, Steady Go! and generated a great deal of interest. So successful proved the first trip that they came back a few months later to support the Rolling Stones.

However, Guy Stevens had started to use the Sue UK logo for tracks from other sources by the likes of Elmore James, Larry Williams, and Billy Preston. Juggy Murray felt that was a clear breach of their agreement and returned to London/American in late 1965. This switch probably affected the international popularity of the Foxxes, who nevertheless came up with "My Momma Told Me", a fine single, and the album Inez and Charles Foxx (Perrone,1998).

In 1967, the duo switched to Musicor's soul subsidiary Dynamo for minor hits such as "I Ain't Going for That" and "(1-2-3-4-5-6-7) Count the Days", and Come By Here, a nice album containing stand-out tracks such as "No Stranger To Love", a dramatic cover of Jerry Butler's "I Stand Accused" and "I Love You 1,000 Times" (later adapted by the vocal group the Platters), all issued in Britain on Direction, a CBS budget label. Subsequently, "Baby Give It To Me" and the gritty, self-produced "You Fixed My Heartache" fared less well and the Foxxes disbanded in 1969. Charlie was already working as a song writer and producer before they disbanded. **Charlie Foxx died from leukemia in 1998, at the age of 58.**

JBD

A PLACE WHERE SUCCESS WAS EXPECTED: FINAL EDITION

HAROLD CHARLES COTTON, JR. AKA CHUCK COTTON. For over five decades, Chuck Cotton provided the backbeat for a slew of local bands, as well as being the pulse for long-haul road dawg Bob Margolin and C.J. Chenier (Britt, 2021).

Cotton's soulful vocals and in-the-pocket percussive skills have enhanced the sound of in-town aggregations including Buddha Hat, Sky Kings, Messengers of Deliverance, and recently with House of Dues as well as Matt Hill and his band. Cotton teamed up with pianist Clark Stern for a Durham-based residency for years and is a member of Tim and Denise Duffy's Music Maker foundation, backing artists including Guitar Gabriel, who introduced Duffy to the local musical community that initiated the foundation (Britt, 2021).

Picture Courtesy of Carey Sound

Before he started playing drums, Cotton expressed himself through horns starting in elementary school. "Everybody was trying out instruments, and first, I told my mom I wanted to play the trombone. They gave me a trombone to take home, and Mom was like, 'I like the saxophone better.' She said, 'Yeah, we'll buy you a saxophone.' So that's what I started out playing."

Cotton's alto skills and soulful curiosity led him downtown to the Record Center on the corner of Washington and Elm where he and a trumpet-playing friend would buy 45s of the soul men and women they overheard on local radio station WEAL.

"We would learn all the horn lines from James Brown, Otis Redding, whatever was popular. We would do that so when we did get out there with those older guys, they were impressed that we knew the lines because we'd been practicing all the time."

Cotton and friends formed The Band Justice in high school, getting small gigs around town, including the Lion's Den on West Market Street that was where Biscuitville is now.

Cotton's first foray into out-of-town show business brought him down-to-Earth, grounded by his parents for an unscheduled overnight stay. Hooking up with Chuck King and the Cadillacs was a crash course in musical cool (Britt, 2021).

"They were older, and they all had processes, and I don't think we had been two years away from playing little league baseball. I must have been about 14 years old."

King and the Cadillacs were regulars in local establishments such as the Carlotta and El Rocco and the Silver Slipper in Liberty as well as performing at small joints out in the country.

Chuck Cotton beats the "soul" out of those drums at El Rocco Club and Restaurant in Greensboro.

"Then we had a breakdown one night coming from one of those places," Cotton recalls. It was the first time he had spent all night away from his parents' house by himself. "It was back in the day when you just couldn't be walking up to no house if you didn't know who was living there, definitely if you were Black," Cotton says. "We weren't really taking that into account because we were younger and the man who was in charge of the band, he took off walking. He came back around close to daylight; somebody had called a tow truck. When I got home that Sunday morning, and I hadn't been seen since Saturday night, of course my parents were in a panic. My dad just told me, 'Park that horn under the bed until marching band season.'"

"Unfortunately, I got distracted by the pull of one or the other, be in school and play, do the right thing, or be in these little bands, and I chose to be in the bands." Chocolate Funk was one of those bands, a '70s era funk/soul band. "We used to wear outfits and play in the Cosmos (club) all Down East in Wilson and Rocky Mount. We had four horns, a singer out front and a rhythm section — a 10-piece band."

Local guitarist Carlos Morales got him to switch over to drums, and local recording engineer Phil Nelson heard the duo, telling them, "I like you guys, and I like these little ideas you're trying to put down."

"I got hold of a little raggedy drum set and Phil had drums, so we would go there every day and he would just record us putting out whatever, our little ideas," Cotton says. "When we got with Phil, we didn't even have a name. It was just me and Carlos."

Coming out of Chocolate Funk, Cotton hooked up with Funkhouse through Morales, who had gotten in with the Reidsville-based bandmembers, relatives of Miles Davis's second wife, Betty Davis. The band only played locally, with a regular Thursday gig at the Cosmos club. That gig got to be a drop-in spot for the Sentinel Boys, Bobby Kelly, Scott Manring, Dennis Worley, David Licht.

"We all used to get together, sometimes socially," Cotton says. "They had never been playing in front of an all-black crowd, and we used to have fun. At the end of the night, we'd get together and jam."

Sam Frazier dropped into Cotton's orbit through the Messengers of Deliverance, a motley amalgamation of local talent and scrambled genres fronted by harpist/singer David "Driveway" Moore and a rotating cast of guitarists including Arhoolie vet Max Drake, Scott Manring, Danny Morris, with bassist Chris Carroll and Cotton on drums. The band's Tuesday night residency at The Blind Tiger attracted Frazier, who lived nearby and began to drop in and jam.

"When it comes to musicians, one of the best things you can say about them is that they're easy to play with," says Sam Frazier. "Chuck is a really good example of that. He's so good at what he does, it makes your job so much easier. That's the highest praise you can give to anybody. And he's a shufflin' fool, too. He's got the best shuffle around. It jacks me up and makes me play a certain way, and I love it every time."

Cotton had joined Bob Margolin then and was touring the world. "It was the first time I'd actually been on the road and stayed away from home for days, and I was married and wanted to be home more. So, I got up with Chris Carroll and Sam, and we started doing Buddha Hat." The band didn't have a name for a while, but that didn't stop them from building a loyal local following. "Greensboro has been a place where people have always appreciated local music" Cotton says. "So, me and Sam, when we got together, we started playing off and on for quite few years, 20 years or better."

Another local, guitarist Tim Betts, had linked up Cotton with Clifton Chenier's son C.J. for about two years before Margolin took him on the road playing with legends such as Pinetop, Perkins Jimmy Rogers, Fingers Taylor, Dion, and The Fabulous Thunderbirds, as well as recording with Margolin on a slew of records.

He was still doing about 20 dates a year with Margolin before COVID hit. Now he's done some virtual things for a church in Reidsville and has done some projects with Tim and Denise Duffy's Music Maker foundation, which helps out local and regional musicians in need, providing financial as well as career support. Cotton was a beneficiary of their largesse in 2018 when an EF-2 tornado deposited several trees on his house, destroying it.

Cotton had been helping out the foundation since its beginning, playing with founding partner Guitar Gabriel, who once told "Rolling Stone" that, "I've played so much guitar it'd make your ass hurt."

"Mr. Gabe was an older feller, but I tell you what, when he got on stage, he was good for about three or four hours straight," Cotton says.

But for now, Cotton is trying to keep his own engine in gear. "Just trying to keep the wheels moving till we can get back into doing what we were doing, because music is really about all I've been doing for the past 20 years. Been kinda rough going, but we're gonna make it."

A PLACE WHERE SUCCESS WAS EXPECTED: FINAL EDITION

Picture Courtesy of James "Coffee" Yourse

Coffee grinds so fine, he's been the mainstay for many bands. Finding a song, he can't play on his magical keys would be a bet you don't want to take.

JAMES YOURSE AKA COFFEE YOURSE was born in 1951 at L. Richardson Hospital delivered by Dr. Evans. He attended David D. Caldwell Elementary School during a time when Washington Street School was so overcrowded that students took turns going to school the second or first half of the school day. To ease crowding, Black students were allowed to attend school at segregated David D. Caldwell school in a separate add-on that had no cafeteria or library.

He attended Lincoln Junior High School for 7th- 9th grades. Lincoln had a fantastic Band Program taught by Mr. Harris. Yourse says of Mr. Harris, "He was an excellent teacher. He wanted each of his students not to just play an instrument, he wanted us to master our instruments to the point that the music and the high stepping style of marching became part of us. Yourse graduated from James B. Dudley High School in 1968 and later graduated from Johnson C. Smith University. He attended graduate school at North Carolina A&T State University.

Yourse came from a strong musical family since his father and his Aunt (Name) were Master Musicians. Both his father and his aunt served as his role models. Yourse says, "They could play amazing piano. My Father's military involvement with the B-1 Preflight Navy Band introduced me to the trumpet and marching bands. He also played in the Rhythm Vets with Walter Carlson who was another Master Musician. Their dance and jazz band skills amazed me." I took piano lessons from Dr. Charlotte Alston, a Professor and Chairperson of the Music Department at Bennett College. Dr. Alston also directed the Bennett Belles and advanced the choir's national reputation. Yourse says of Dr. Alston, "I profited from Her love of Classical Music."

At Dudley High School, the Band Director, Mr. Morgan, allowed Yourse to explore musical leadership by participating in the Concert, Marching, and Jazz Bands. Yourse also gives some of the credit for his development as a Master Musician to his experiences while a student at Johnson C. Smith University in Charlotte, North Carolina. He says, "While in Charlotte at JCSU, I learned from Professor Davenport as well as Professor Jackie Hairston. The musicians in Charlotte embraced me and taught me how to gig at places like the Excelsior, Birdcage, Soul21 as well as Myers Park Country Club." For those who are not musicians, a "gig" means a live performance or engagement for a musician or group playing popular or jazz music- especially one that is temporary.

When Yourse graduated from JCSU he started playing with Chocolate Funk and working with Dudley's Band. His next opportunity in performing was given to him by Richard Bowling, a Greensboro entrepreneur and owner of Cosmos Supper Club. Bowling hired Yourse to provide music for the Sunday talent show. Working with the musicians at Cosmos led to the formation of Covacus. Covacus was made up of seven very talented, seasoned musicians. The group has more than twenty years of concerts and serving as the opening act for greats like the Ohio players, Cameo, Midnite Starr, Atlantic Starr, and Alanis Morrisette. Covacus has performed sorority and fraternity parties from Princeton to the University of Alabama. Covacus performs many variations of music from jazz, reggae, pop, Rock, and Beach music. However, their most popular music to perform is high energy Funk, and R&B. For a long time Covacus was the hottest show on the east coast.

Picture Courtesy of CareySound

Audiences were blown away by Covacus. Just about everybody in the band with the exception of Coffee (Far-Left seated at keyboard) was still in high school. They opened the show on the main stage at the Cosmos with George Bishop's PA and his band The Mighty Majors. Covacus had 11 members including Barbra Weathers (Center Vocalist) who would later sing for Atlantic Star before moving on to a solo career.

Picture Courtesy of James Coffee Yourse

Promo-Portrait of *Sweet Dreams*- James Coffee Yourse is third from right.

Years later Yourse continued to play with his group Sweet Dreams that he and Fred Mills formed. Yourse is on the touring roster for the NC Arts Council, the MUSEP program in Greensboro, as well as music director for events for the International Civil Rights Museum. In updating his music career Yourse says, "Perhaps my most satisfying event was supplying music for the NC Democratic Party pre-inaugural ball for President Obama's first election in Washington DC. Yourse says, "I still love Music."

ISAAC CARREE, III is a singer, producer, and song writer. He was born on April 28, 1973. Carree attended Dudley with the Class of 1993 through the 10th grade, and he is a product of the Greenfield Homes Community. Carree and his siblings attended Wells Temple/Memorial Church of God in Christ in Greensboro.

The Carree Children and other Sunday School mates on the steps of Wells Temple/Memorial COGIC. Left to Right: Kimberly Carree, Angela Williams, Angela L. Carree, Isaac Carree, and Janel L. Lynn.

Isaac Carree began his music career as a soloist with John P. Kee & New Life Community Choir, before co-founding the award-winning contemporary gospel group, Men of Standard. Over the next decade, the group went on to record five albums, releasing numerous hit singles including "Trust in God" and "In Your Will," before taking a hiatus to pursue individual endeavors.

Contemporary Gospel Group **MEN OF STANDARD** (Isaac Carree is second from left). The two founding members, Isaac Carree and Lowell Curtis Pye Sr. met while members of John P. Kee's New Life Community Choir. Next, Michael Bacon, a Dallas-based music producer, joined the group. Bryan Pierce, the fourth member to climb aboard, was a youth pastor at Pastor Paul Morton's Greater St. Stephens Church in New Orleans.

A PLACE WHERE SUCCESS WAS EXPECTED: FINAL EDITION

In 2011, Isaac Carree released his debut solo album, *Uncommon Me*. This much anticipated album received groundbreaking acclaim. It debuted at #1 on Billboard's Gospel Albums chart, #48 on the Billboard 200 and #5 on the Independent Albums chart. The project's hit single, "In the Middle," peaked at #1 on Gospel radio, where it remained for 8 consecutive weeks, becoming a beloved praise party anthem across the nation. The album Uncommon Me earned Carree the prestigious Stellar Award for Producer of the Year, along with four more nominations, including Contemporary Male Vocalist of the Year and New Artist of the Year.

During the next two years, Carree toured extensively in the U.S., opening for Steve Harvey and Kirk Franklin in a 7-city comedy/music arena tour, and as a featured guest on the Go Get It Tour with gospel duo Mary-Mary. He also participated in the historic King's Men Tour, sponsored by Live Nation, featuring Kirk Franklin, Donnie McClurkin, Marvin Sapp, and Israel Houghton.

"I've grown a lot since I released my first solo album," says Carree. "I got to a place where I needed to reset some things in my life, personally and professionally, in order to be who God made me to be, and to do everything God has for me to do."

With new management, a new distribution deal and the restructuring of his own label, Door 6 Entertainment, Isaac Carree boldly released RESET in 2013, solidifying his position as one of gospel music's leading male vocalists.

J. ALPONSE NICHOLSON

Percussionist & Actor

Dudley, 2008

J. ALPHONSE NICHOLSON graduated from James B. Dudley High School in 2008. Nicholson considers himself both a percussionist and an actor. When discussing his love of music, he says, "It started at home with my mother and my father investing in my music abilities by having drums in the house, guitar, piano. As I got older, my mother continued to push that.

"I played drums in the church. I was on the drumline in middle school and high school. The schools that I went to in Greensboro were predominantly Black and full of culture. I cultivated that pretty heavily at James B. Dudley High School where I had some amazing mentors. During my teen years, even though I didn't know that I wanted to be an actor at that time, a lot of those seeds were planted in me then."

He attended North Carolina Central University for three years where he majored in theater. Although he is very proud of his hometown, he realized that it was not the best place to be in order to pursue a career in entertainment. In 2013, he relocated to New York City in order to give himself easier access to opportunities within the industry.

For nearly a decade, J. Alphonse Nicholson has entertained viewers on both the screen and the stage. Over the years, he has appeared in shows like *Chicago P.D.* and movies like *Just Mercy*. While his resume is already very impressive, it got even better when he appeared as a serious regular in the Starz show, *P-Valley*. The show follows a group of strippers and other employees at a fictional strip club in the Mississippi Delta.

REGINALD N. JOHNSON graduated from Dudley in 2009. While a student at Dudley, he served as Drum Major, Captain of UMOJA Male Step Team, and as Mr. Dudley. He attended North Carolina A&T State University where he was Mister A&T and Mister HBCU. He graduated in 2013 from A&T with a Bachelor of Fine Arts, Professional Theater degree. Post graduation, Johnson relocated to Atlanta GA, where he is the CEO of his start-up company Inward Discovery, as a creative entrepreneur, actor, and dancer. In 2018, Johnson became the state representative for Georgia as Mr. Georgia in the Mr. United States pageant and competition. During this week-long leadership conference and competition Johnson received many awards for his community service incentives and platform. Johnson finished 1st runner up in the nation and now serves on the administrative team for the organization as a board member and partner.

Picture Courtesy of Reginal H. Johnson

Reginald N. Johnson on set of movie musical, The Color Purple which opened in December of 2023.

Collectively Johnson has held 6 major titles in leadership and appeared on numerous national television shows including Lee Daniels 'Star' on FOX, MTV's 'Wild N Out', 'Wendy Williams', BET's 'American Soul' as one of 'The Pips', 'Coming to America 2', and his most recent role in the featured film, 'The Color Purple'. Johnson has also danced and worked with a variety of musical artists such as Musiq Soul Child, India Arie, P-Diddy, Missy Elliott, T.I, Jacquees, and many others.

Blessed to have worked with so many artists, Johnson's gifts have afforded him the opportunity to travel the world from Africa to Japan over to Europe and all throughout the Caribbean teaching and performing.

Johnson continues to expand his artistic empire through his company Inward Discovery, a young thriving company comprising the many innovative and creative talents that Johnson has to provide. As a businessman, leader, and artist, Johnson commits his life to serving the public with a resilient force that changes lives through the universal the universal healing power of the arts.

During the years after his graduation, he worked at his craft in acting and dancing. Finally, in 2023 his determination and perseverance in the face of what might have been overwhelming odds Johnson got his big break. Johnson says his road to the big screen began in high school. "I would be remised not to mention that it started at Dudley," Johnson said. "It's been a full circle moment of just so many dots that have been connected from like teachers and administrators and past coaches and professors who all poured into me and now again they're just seeing the fruits of their labor in this moment," Johnson said. "Not that they haven't seen the other highlights, but this one is on a world stage.

A world stage that has now afforded Johnson the opportunity to work with names including Oprah Winfrey, Taraji P. Hensen and High Point native Fantasia.

"When I found out that she was Celie and I was doing The Color Purple, my heart went 'Wow'!" Johnson said.

"And so, you have this excellence all around and I feel as though everyone was hand-picked to be a part of this project and all of us have equally contributed to the masterpiece that I know will be timeless for years. Like, it's bigger than us."

Johnson's role is in the last scene of the movie, an ensemble dancer set in the 1940s.

He has a message for young actors and actresses, or anyone chasing a dream. It's simple: to never give up.

VONII BRISTOW, a native of Greensboro and 2010 graduate of Dudley High School, appeared in the movie "Surviving Compton: Dre, Suge and Michel'le on the television network Lifetime.

The film is a biopic of singer Michel'le Toussaint. Bristow portrays the hip hop artist Ice Cube.

Bristow began acting at Dudley under the drama instruction of Drennan R. Paylor. After graduation, he attended Winston-Salem State University where he performed in stage plays. He joined the Actors Group led by actor Burgess Jenkins.

Bristow's film career started with a lead role in the feature film "Find A Way," in 2013 which was directed by Jenkins, and he played opposite Omari Hardwick in "A Christmas Blessing," a made-for-television movie.

Since graduating WSSU, Bristow has had roles in the television series *Survivor's Remorse*, *Halt and Catch Fire*, *Saints and Sinners*, and several other made for television movies.

Bristow also appeared in the FX series "Atlanta" and as Young Jabari in three episodes (2016-2017) of "Saints and Sinners." Bristow is also a writer and producer of the "short" movies *Sometimes* (2019) and *The Deal* (2019).

Dr. Jo Evans Lynn, Ed.D.

Dudley's Community and Civic Leaders

EMMA LOU MORGAN MCADOO was born May 18, 1914, and was a member of the first graduating class of James B. Dudley High School in 1930. She married Hilton McAdoo during the Great Depression, and it was not until the age of 30 that she was able to continue her education at North Carolina A&T State University. She was an outstanding community leader until her death in 2012 at the age of 97.

Mrs. McAdoo was a retired educator with the Greensboro City Schools/Head Start Program and a graduate of North Carolina A&T State University.

As a lifetime member of Union Memorial United Methodist Church, Ms. McAdoo served as chairperson of the Finance Committee, past president of the United Methodist Women, and was former district president of the Women's Society of Christian Services.

Mrs. McAdoo served on additional committees and community organizations including being a charter member of Greensboro's Black Child Development Institute. As a charter member, Mrs. McAdoo joined its founder Sarah Herbin in pursuing the group's mission to serve as advocates for disadvantaged black children by recruiting, screening, training, and mobilizing a cadre of volunteers who serve children in the community, providing them with free one-on-one academic assistance, offering them opportunities for family enrichment, opening doors for access to community resources, and reigniting the spirit of volunteerism. Former Vice President of Eastside Community Club, member of the Everachievers' Retired Teachers, member of North Carolina A&T State University Gate City Alumni Chapter, member of James B. Dudley Senior High School National Alumni Association, past presidents/secretary for the PTA's at Washington Elementary, Lincoln Middle, James B. Dudley High School and Bennett College, and as a storyteller at Uhuru Bookstore.

Her many awards included the Urban Ministry Five Year Service Award, named Honorary Board Member of United Daycare Services Project Independence, recipient of four Mission pins for Service from the United

Methodist Women, National Council of Negro Women certificate, Union Memorial United Methodist Church Kindergarten Service Award (1980-1986), Las Amigas, Inc. Service Rendered to the Community Award, Head start Outstanding Teacher Award, 1993 Mother of the Year Award - Union Memorial United Methodist Church, inducted into the African American Women of Distinction Hall of Fame, inducted into the Grassroots Hall of Fame 'Women of the Village' and was honored by Greensboro Unit of Church Women United on May Friendship Day for her contributions to the Piedmont Community. To honor her many years of service, on Mrs. McAdoo's 90th birthday, her family established the Emma Morgan McAdoo Scholarship Fund for graduating seniors at James B. Dudley Senior High School.

2015 Emma Morgan McAdoo Scholarship

(L-R) Lola Anne McAdoo (Class of 1954, past Dudley Alumni Association President, and daughter of Emma McAdoo), Destiny Baldwin, 2015 Award Recipient, and Yasten Burton (Miss Dudley 2006 and grand-daughter of Emma McAdoo).

Dr. Jo Evans Lynn, Ed.D.

NANNIE MCADOO-DICK worked at the Main Library in downtown Greensboro where she served as the young adult reference librarian, becoming the first African American professional on the staff and the first Young Adult Librarian. She retired from the City of Greensboro after 24 ½ years of service. She graduated from James B. Dudley High School in 1936 and from Bennett College in 1942. She received her degree in Library Science from North Carolina Central University.

Dick has received numerous awards from Bennett College, Church Women United of Greensboro, and Hayes-Taylor YMCA. Dick is a role model for youth through her work with Bennett College, United Methodist Women, and Holmes Grove United Methodist Church. After her retirement, she continued to work with young people through her church, her alma mater, and in the community. Dick was active in such organizations as the Bennett College Alumnae Association, Azalea Garden Club, Church Women United of Greensboro, and Hayes-Taylor YMCA. She was a volunteer with Mobile Meals and was Chaplain for eight years for the James B. Dudley National Alumni Association. She also received several awards including Lady of the Year in 1992 from the Hayes-Taylor YMCA and the Bennett Ideal Award from the Bennett College National Alumnae Association. Based on a nomination by the Project Team of Dudley High School, the media center was named The Nannie McAdoo-Dick Media Center in her honor in 2006.

JBD

A PLACE WHERE SUCCESS WAS EXPECTED: FINAL EDITION

DAVID W. MOREHEAD was born September 9, 1918, in Greensboro, North Carolina. He graduated from Dudley High School in 1936 and went to work at Pomona Terra Cotta Company. He then worked at Vick Chemical and later earned a bachelor's degree in sociology from North Carolina A&T State University.

David Morehead spent much of his career with the Hayes-Taylor YMCA in Greensboro, a facility built to serve the black population. Morehead was initially hired as an assistant, but within a few years was appointed youth director. In 1949, he became the executive director, a position he held until 1971. Under his leadership, the YMCA became a meeting place for civil rights activists and leaders of both races. From 1971 to 1986, Morehead served as director of consumer affairs and Community Services in Greensboro at the state office of the U.S. Department of Housing and Urban Affairs. He later became a partner in Carolina Woods, a housing development for low- and moderate-income people, and worked on a project to find better health care for the elderly. Morehead also served on the North Carolina A&T State University Board of Trustees for a record twenty-one years. In 1968, the Greensboro Chamber of Commerce presented Morehead with the Nat Greene Award for community contributions. The Hayes-Taylor YMCA swimming pool was dedicated in honor of Morehead. In February 1999, the Morehead-Simkins Independent Living Center, apartments for low-income and elderly people, was dedicated in his honor. Morehead died on December 24, 2003, at the age of 85 (Civil Rights Digital Library, 2013).

Dr. Jo Evans Lynn, Ed.D.

The "Good Shepherd" Dr. Otis L. Hairston, Sr. (1936)

The Reverend Otis L. Hairston Sr. was born on April 28, 1918, in Greensboro, North Carolina. He graduated from Dudley High School and then attended Shaw University in Raleigh, N.C., where he earned a bachelor's degree in journalism in 1941.

In 1958, he returned to Greensboro, where he succeeded his father, the Reverend J. T. Hairston, as pastor of historic African American Shiloh Baptist Church. He led the church, one of Greensboro's oldest African American congregations, for thirty-four years. Under his leadership, the church developed programs and ministries that served the congregation and the community as well.

Reverend Hairston allowed civil rights meetings and activities to be held at the church when other pastors were hesitant to do so. In alliance with the federal government, Hairston and his congregation helped to construct the first non-profit housing complex, the J. T. Hairston Apartments, in Greensboro. Through his efforts, Hairston helped to start an active day care program and to establish the J.T. Hairston Memorial Scholarship Fund. Hairston was also instrumental in rallying members of the Greensboro community to take part in the burgeoning civil rights movement. He led several marches and peaceful demonstrations in 1963 against segregated businesses in downtown Greensboro in which hundreds of arrests were made, including Hairston's own son, Otis Hairston Jr. Hairston's devotion to the community-at-large was seen in the various organizations and institutions with which he was involved: Industries of the Blind,

A PLACE WHERE SUCCESS WAS EXPECTED: FINAL EDITION

Greensboro Chamber of Commerce, Greensboro School Board, Greensboro Urban Ministry, and the United Way. Hairston was a charter member of the Greensboro Human Relations Commission and also served on the General Baptist State Convention, the Progressive National Baptist Convention, and the State Democratic Party. Hairston was also on the Board of Trustees of Bennett College and Shaw University, which awarded him the Honorary Doctor of Divinity degree in 1968, in addition to the Distinguished Alumni Award. Hairston's other honors include the Peacemaker Award, the Distinguished Service Award from the North Carolina Council of Churches, and the NAACP "Man of the Year Award." In 2001, a new middle school in southeast Greensboro was posthumously named in his honor.

Greensboro Daily Photo, Feb. 05, 2012

This is the edifice of Shiloh Baptist Church located at 1210 South Eugene Street. The original church (See page 20) was located at 730 Ashe Street. Shiloh Baptist, located in the Warnersville community, has a rich history and held a legendary place in the Civil Rights struggles of the 1960's.

GEORGE C. SIMKINS, JR. was born in Greensboro, North Carolina, on August 23, 1924, the first child of George C. Simkins Sr., a dentist and community leader, and Guyrene Tyson Simkins, an educator. He grew up in sports and was a natural athlete and was even a nationally ranked badminton player. Simkins graduated from Dudley High School in Greensboro in 1940, before matriculating into Herzl Junior College in Chicago, and then Talladega College, from which he graduated. He earned his dentistry degree from Meharry School of Dentistry in 1948 and completed his rotating internship at Jersey City Medical Center. Simkins opened a private dentistry practice upon returning to Greensboro and joined the Guilford County Health Department, becoming the first African American employed there.

George C. Simkins, Jr., was community leader and civil rights activist. During the 1950s, he won several significant desegregation lawsuits and was, for a quarter of a century, the president of the Greensboro branch of the National Association for the Advancement of Colored People (NAACP). Beginning in 1955, Simkins used the courts and local referenda to compel the desegregation of recreational facilities, schools, and hospitals and end discrimination in the delivery of public housing, banking services, and city services. One of the first cases he was involved in was about the rights of blacks to use the public Gillespie Golf Course.

On February 24, 1970, Dr. George C. Simkins and close to a dozen black parents filed a legal suit demanding immediate desegregation of Greensboro's schools. The next April Judge Edward Stanley ruled in favor of Simkins and the black parents and ordered the Greensboro School Board to offer a plan for complete desegregation by June 18, 1971, to be implemented in the subsequent school year. The school board, under the leadership of new chairman Al Lineberry, submitted a plan which left five schools all white and three mostly black. The NAACP offered its own proposal to Judge Stanley in which all schools would have the same racial proportions. After gaining the school board's consent, Stanley chose the NAACP's plan as the preferred model to carry out the mandated integration of Greensboro's schools. This meant that Dudley had a ratio of 60% Black and 40% White. The redistricting plan left wealthy white neighborhoods in formerly all-white schools. From 1971-1978, when Weaver Education Center opened, this ratio held.

In 2015 a new school near the community where he lived was named in his honor. On the school's website, a brief history of the reason for naming the school to honor George C. Simkins, Jr. captures the greatness of a local Civil Rights Legend. It says,

He fought to make sure that all people were treated fairly at our local hospitals, libraries, tennis courts, and golf courses. He even helped to make sure that all students—no matter the color of their skin---re able to ride the buses safely to schools here in Guilford County. Dr. Simkins was a local hero and he once lived near the community where the school named in his honor now stands.

Picture Courtesy of Chaves Interiors, LLC

George C. Simkins, Jr. Elementary School

ALFRED KNIGHTON (TONY) STANLEY was born July 15, 1937, in Dudley, N.C. He was the youngest of five children of the Rev. Joseph Taylor Stanley, a congregationalist minister, and Kathryn Turrentine Stanley. He graduated from James B. Dudley High School in 1955. Rev. Stanley graduated from Yale Divinity School in 1962 and then returned home to Greensboro, N.C. He believed that it was important that he return amid growing tensions over civil rights protests. He said, "Here I am in the nice, beautiful North, and my people are fighting this revolution."

Greensboro had drawn national acclaim in 1960 when students at the city's historically black colleges led sit-ins at Woolworth's because they had been denied service on the basis of their race. According to Bernstein (2013), "When the community did nothing more to integrate many of its theaters, emporiums and other public accommodations, the pickets and protests continued afresh." Chafe (1980) declared in the book *Civilities and Civil Rights*, "Demonstrations in Greensboro were larger than anywhere else in country except Birmingham, Alabama. There were 1,400 people in jail in the spring of 1963."

Rev. Stanley charged into this environment, serving as a respected adviser to the students who really drove the civil rights movement in the city and proving instrumental in bringing the black establishment behind the demonstrations (Bernstein, 2013). Chafe said, "There was a generation gap, and if you could show that people like Rev. Stanley were behind the effort, reinforcing it, it meant you had a lot of other people, members of the establishment, willing to be supportive."

Rev. Stanley worked at North Carolina A&T State University and Bennett College. He also became a local official with the Congress of Racial Equality (CORE), a civil rights group, and sat on Greensboro's human rights commission. According to Bernstein (2013), "Unlike Rev Martin Luther King, Rev. Stanley was not a spell-binding orator, and it was not in his nature to argue with anyone." His role in the Civil Rights Protests in Greensboro was more intellectual: calculating when activists would proceed with utmost caution and when they would risk mass arrests with the intent of flooding the city's jails. Such a dramatic gesture, he said, would "break the back of the whole damn thing."

Rev. Stanley knew that the civil rights efforts in Greensboro lacked someone to galvanize the struggle in a consistent way, and he helped identify

A PLACE WHERE SUCCESS WAS EXPECTED: FINAL EDITION

the charismatic potential of Jesse Jackson, then a popular campus athlete and student body president at North Carolina A&T State University. Jesse Jackson later became a minister, civil rights leader, and presidential candidate. *"We needed Jesse as a football player the girls loved," Rev. Stanley told Chafe. "We woke him up one day and he has been protesting ever since."*

In an interview, Jackson called Rev. Stanley his "closest teacher" before he became involved in civil rights marches led by the Rev. Martin Luther King Jr. "He was young enough for us to relate to but old enough to set parameters for us," Jackson said. "He had the capacity to interpret our struggle bigger than just the daily march."

Jackson said that white government officials threatened the school with budget cuts and loss of accreditation if the university president did not more forcefully prohibit student protests. When state legislators targeted the school, Jackson said, Rev. Stanley helped persuade the students not to back down. *"At the crossroads, you must take the right choice and must be willing to make sacrifice," Jackson recalled Rev. Stanley advising. "He was saying, 'What good is a degree without dignity?'"*

Jesse Jackson says that Rev. Stanley changed the way he viewed the ministry. He said, "I was inclined to pursue a career in law before Rev. Stanley steered me toward a religious vocation. I had a limited definition of the ministry," said Jackson. "He saw it as a call to do service, to do justice to exalt people. He said the ministry is much broader than the law, said its Genesis and Revelation and beyond — the sum total of life."

Rev. Stanley left Greensboro in 1966 to become an associate pastor of Plymouth Congregational United Church of Christ in Detroit. Two years later, he was called to lead Peoples Congregational United Church of Christ in Washington, D.C., in the shadow of its longest serving pastor, the Rev. Arthur Fletcher Elmes, and at a time when the city was on the brink of race riots. During his 38 years as senior minister at People, Rev. Stanley displayed an intellect and a compassion that could open doors and bridge differenced. His was a progressive ministry for the masses rather than for the few, the friends, the more faithful, the more fortunate. He had an undying love for and an interest in children, including his own three. People's Church became home to a day care center, a community credit union and D.C.'s largest Boy Scout and Girl Scout programs. It expanded a scholarship program that still recognizes church and community graduates from pre-school to Ph.D. Classic Negro spirituals, urban gospel and jazz became common musical fare, along with sermons of national leaders and his own, in which he characteristically blended biblical teachings with folk wisdom and current events in a manner that nurtured Christian souls. The church membership grew threefold, and Peoples built a new sanctuary that he described as "an

African hut of cathedral proportions." The Rev. Dr. Stanley, who received a doctorate degree from Howard University in 1974, extended his service and leadership beyond the church's Petworth neighborhood. He accepted the many calls to public service in the district and to continuing community concerns and was a regional and national leader in the United Church of Christ.

Attorney David M. Dansby, Jr.

He served as the attorney for the Civil Rights Cases that overturned the Freedom of Choice Legislation that circumvented integration for more than 15 years.

DAVID M. DANSBY, JR. was a member of Dudley's graduating class of 1957 and was the Class Valedictorian. This Dudley graduating class was well ahead of the formal Civil Rights movement, he was one of its many members who ventured out to attend predominately white institutions of higher learning. After graduation, he attended the University of North Carolina-Chapel Hill where he became the first African American to receive an undergraduate degree, a Bachelor of Arts, in 1961, He continued in the University of North-Chapel Hill (UNC-CH) School of Law and achieved his Juris Doctor Degree in 1964. With this degree, he became the first African American to receive two (2) degrees from UNC-CH.

Dansby was a life member of the NAACP and served two terms as President of the Greensboro Branch of the NAACP. He was also a Charter Member of the UNC-CH Branch of the NAACP and served a term as its President. As a member of this group, he was the first UNC-CH student to join picket lines to desegregate restaurants in Orange County. Dansby led efforts to get African Americans hired in the Guilford County Courts. As a public Defender, Dansby's office, was featured in the Civil Rights Documentary "Majority of One". In 1989 he received the Dudley the High School's "Humanitarian Award (Dudley National Alumni Association, 2015).

Dansby also served as Past Master of the C.W. Lawrence Lodge No. 837. He served 15 years as Grand Attorney for Prince Hall Grand Lodge of North Carolina. In 2012, he received International Civil Rights Museum's "Unsung Hero Award." In 2015, he was elected to the James B. Dudley Sports and Educational Hall of Fame/Distinction.

CLAUDETTE BURROUGHS-WHITE was born in Greensboro, North Carolina, on May 1, 1940. She graduated from Dudley High School in 1957 and then matriculated at Woman's College (now The University of North Carolina at Greensboro), where she joined two other women as the first African American students to attend the school. While a student at Woman's College, Burroughs-White joined the February 1960 sit-in at Woolworth's the day after four NC A&T State University college students began the movement.

After a brief time in Philadelphia following her graduation in 1961, Burroughs-White returned to Greensboro to work as a probation officer with the Domestic Relations Court of Guilford County. She continued working with children and families in the court system as supervisor of the 18th Judicial District Juvenile Services Division until her retirement in 1994. Burroughs-White also served the community as a city councilwoman from 1994 until 2005, where her most lauded achievement was closing the White Street Landfill. She served on the Governor's Crime Commission from 1997 until 2005 and was on the board of the Greensboro Commission on the Status of Women. Her civic involvements included the United Way of Greensboro, the Tar Heel Triad Girl Scout Council, the YWCA Advisory Board, and the National Conference of Community and Justice Board. She was the recipient of the Sertoma Club Service to Mankind Award in 1990, the North Carolina Outstanding Juvenile Service Award in 1988, the African American Woman of Distinction Award in 1993, and the state Democratic Women's STAR award. She posthumously received the National Conference for Community Justice Brotherhood/Sisterhood Citation Award in 2007. She was the first president of the Dudley Alumni Association.

RICHARD BOWLING graduated from Dudley in 1957. He was one of the first African Americans to attend and graduate from North Carolina State University. Bowling majored in Electrical Engineering. He created *Other Voices*. *Other Voices* is a leadership program designed to create an awareness of multicultural issues in Greensboro. He was the owner of the Cosmos Clubs and Restaurants and a shopping center. Bowling was the innovator behind the idea of an alumni association and consolidated reunion and presented his idea to a meeting of other Dudley Alumni at the Cosmos Club and Restaurant in 1975. Bowling and a pioneering group representing several Classes of Alumni worked on the original Dudley Reunion Steering Committee.

Business Owner and Served Six Terms as James B. Dudley High School's National Alumni Association President

This group planned and helped implement the first Dudley Consolidated Class Reunion. The reunion took place the weekend of July 23-25, 1976, at the Cosmos Club in Greensboro, North Carolina. Dudley's first two principals, Dr. John A. Tarpley and Mr. Franklin Brown were honored on that occasion. During the first reunion meeting on July 24, 1976, those present confirmed the desire to create an alumni association. Officers were elected, and they served as the steering committee until the writing of the proposed constitution and by-laws. Claudette Burroughs White of the Class of 1957 was elected president.

Back Row, left to right: Richard Bowling-1957, Cleveland Wright-1950, Claudette Burroughs White-1957, Andrew Johnson-1940, Ben Poole-1939, **Front Row, left to right:** Reginald Whitsett-1962, Harvey Pettiford-1961, Doris Vincent-1968, Zenobia Goldston-1949, John Harris-1948, Maurice Woods-1930, Daryl Smith-1966, Daisy Hood-1953, unnamed, Ernestine Donnell-1952, and not pictured Howard Stewart-

In 2014, Bowing was elected to serve his sixth term as the president of the Dudley Alumni Association. He has also served as the national president of the American Bridge Association, Inc.

KENNETH FREE, SR. graduated from Dudley in 1954, earning a baseball scholarship to A&T College. After two years in the Army, he played in the Negro League for The Raleigh Tigers during the 1959 season and played in the East/West All-Star game in Chicago's famous Comiskey Park. That game highlighted the Negro League season and drew 45-50 thousand people and all the Major League scouts. He started the 1960 season traveling with Negro League icon Satchell Paige, who is a member of the Major League Baseball Hall of Fame. Free finished the 1960 season by signing a pro contract with Hickory of the Western Carolina League. In 1961, the NY Mets were approved as an MLB expansion team, bought the contract, and assigned Free to their farm team, The Raleigh Caps of the Carolina League.

MEAC's First Fulltime Commissioner

He began his venture into athletics management as a community center director at Windsor Community Center for the Greensboro Parks and Recreation Department. He then moved up to become a regional Parks/Recreation consultant for the state of North Carolina Department of Natural and Economic Resources. Through his professional administrative prowess and grave concern for youth and intercollegiate athletics, Free became the first full-time commissioner of the MEAC in 1978 and reigned until June 1996. He made Greensboro the conference headquarters early in his tenure. Free was instrumental in the drive for MEAC institutions to attain NCAA Division I status, which became a reality in 1980. In 1987, he was named to the powerful NCAA Division I Men's Basketball Selection Committee, becoming the first African American appointed to that group. After his MEAC run, Free served as Commissioner of the Eastern Intercollegiate Athletic Association (EIAC) from 1996-2006.

In 1986, Free received the North Carolina Recreation and Parks Society prestigious FELLOW AWARD, the highest honor in that association. Also, during his eight years with the state of North Carolina, he received the ORDER OF THE LONG LEAF PINE from the late Governor James Holshouser. Most recently, he served on the Greensboro Parks and Recreation

Pictures Courtesy of J. C. Cotton

Harold Cotton, Sr. standing at podium during Dudley's 60th Jubilee in 1988.

HAROLD CHARLES COTTON, SR. graduated from Dudley in 1941. He attended Immanuel Lutheran College in Greensboro, N. C., and North Carolina A&T State University. Cotton also attended the Chicago School of Shoe Rebuilding where he earned a diploma in hat blocking and cleaning. His expertise in hat blocking led Cotton to launch his business, Bob's Hatters in 1953. Bob's Hatters became a mainstay in downtown Greensboro for more than 50 years.

Cotton was a civil and human rights advocate and served as president of the Greensboro Chapter of the NAACP. He was an active member of St. Stephen United Church of Christ. His dedication to the church and the United Church of Christ led to his appointment as the first president of the United Black Christians, which provides a voice for African American members and churches within the UCC. As president of the Dudley Alumni Association for 10 years, he provided leadership for the inaugural Consolidated Reunion and Dudley's 60th Jubilee Anniversary in 1988. His distinctive contributions in support of Dudley and political and social justice for Greensboro residents are featured in a multi-media presentation, *American Enterprise*, in the National Museum of American History at the Smithsonian in Washington, D.C.

Cotton was a member of Invincible Lodge No. 251 PHA, Greensboro Consistory No. 106, Khalif Temple No. 144. For more than a decade, he coached and mentored youth who participated in the organization's Little League baseball program. He was a scoutmaster for the Boy Scouts troop at St. Stephen and he served on the board of the Old North State Council, which oversees troops in Guilford and several other counties. Cotton contributed to scholarship programs at Dudley, NCA&T, St. Stephen, and other institutions that aligned with his steadfast commitment to expanding educational opportunities for area residents. He had a stellar career as an athlete and played football and basketball at Dudley. He played on several semi-pro baseball teams and was a champion boxer in high school, college, and during his military service. He was also known for his dancing talents and he surprised and delighted audiences with his tap dance routines in a

A PLACE WHERE SUCCESS WAS EXPECTED: FINAL EDITION

local production of "Tap Dance Kid." His performance led to "tap" demonstrations at local schools, churches, senior centers, and other venues.

Cotton and his wife of 54 years, Mary (Dudley Class of '44), had three sons, Harold Jr. (Chuck), a gifted musician and recording artist; Craig, a public relations specialist; and Michael, a veterinarian and college professor. Harold Jr. graduated from Dudley in 1971 (Cotton, 2021).

WARREN DORSETT served on the Guilford County Board of Commissioners from 1993-2002. Dorsett, a former Industrial Arts teacher at James B. Dudley High School, took the seat of his wife, former state Sen. Katie Dorsett, on the Board of Commissioners in early 1993. She resigned from that board after former North Carolina Governor Jim Hunt appointed her secretary of the North Carolina Department of Administration.

The county commissioners' districts have shifted since he served on the board, but Warren Dorsett, like his wife, represented District 9, which included much of the eastern section of Greensboro. Dorsett was 66 when he joined the board. While Dorsett was running for his third term on the Board, in a prepared statement, Dorsett said that if elected he would work to consolidate more city and county services, such as planning and law enforcement. He also said he would work to attract more economic development and assure that women and minorities get a fair share of jobs. Throughout his terms on the Board, Dorsett fought to fulfil those promises. In 2002, he didn't seek reelection after serving as a commissioner for nearly a decade.

In 1997 while serving as a county commissioner Dorsett found himself in the unusual position of suing the Guilford County Board of Commissioners. Dorsett and Isaac Barnett filed a lawsuit against the Board of Commissioners after they were both removed from the Guilford County Board of Social Services. Dorsett and Barnett were returned to the board as part of a complicated political deal, and they dropped the lawsuit.

Before becoming a county commissioner, Dorsett served on the Greensboro Zoning Commission and also served as a precinct chairman for the Democratic Party.

Guilford County Register of Deeds Jeff Thigpen, a former Democratic commissioner who served with Dorsett on the Board of Commissioners from 1998 to 2002, said he remembers well the lively discussions he had in those years with Dorsett, Commissioner Skip Alston, and former Commissioner Bob Landreth, who died in 2018. Thigpen said Dorsett was dedicated to the Democratic Party and what it stood for.

"He was really committed to education in Guilford County and really committed to the issues of the Department of Social Services," Thigpen said. "He was an advocate for Democratic ideals."

WALTER THANIEL JOHNSON, JR., was born and raised in Greensboro, NC, where he graduated from James B. Dudley High School in 1957. In 1961, he graduated from North Carolina Agricultural & Technical College with a degree in Engineering Physics where he was student body president and member of the ROTC. He made history by becoming the first African American student to enroll in Duke University through the School of Law in the Fall of 1961.

After law school, Walter began his service as a Captain in the USJAG Corp at Stewart Air Force base in Newburgh, NY. After completion of his military service, Walter moved back to his hometown of Greensboro where he began his law career as a Solicitor (now known as an Assistant District Attorney) for the State of North Carolina. Later, he went into private practice until 1980 when he was called into government service by then Governor Jim Hunt as the first African American to serve as Chairman of the NC Parole Commission. During the course of his legal career, Walter taught at both Duke Law School and NC Central School of Law as an adjunct professor. After Walter's service with the State, he opened his own law practice where he protected the rights of many until his retirement in 2004.

Walter was a member of several boards and organizations. He was a proud member of Omega Psi Phi for over 60 years. He was a member of the Greensboro Sports Council, Greensboro Men's Club, Black Lawyers Association, Sigma Pi Phi Fraternity (The Boule), Greensboro Bar Association, UNCG Board of Trustees, Academy of Trial Lawyers, Gold Helmet Club, Dudley Alumni Association, NCA&T Alumni Association,

Inmate Grievance Committee, Greensboro Planning Commission, a proud Driftwood, and a plethora of other boards and organizations.

Walter was a pioneer and a trailblazer. He served as the first African American Chairman of the Greensboro Public School's School Board in the late 1960s. He also developed businesses in chemical production and contracting. He was a founding member of BARJO Chemicals, Inc., and his contracting company was responsible for building affordable housing in Northeast Greensboro. Walter was a lifelong member of Providence Baptist Church where he served multiple terms on the Board of Trustees as well as attorney for the church.

Greensboro, North Carolina's 1st African American Mayor

YVONNE JOHNSON, a Dudley graduate in 1960, was the mayor of Greensboro, North Carolina from 2007 until 2009. She was previously a member of the Greensboro City Council for 14 years, beginning in 1993, and Mayor Pro-Tem for six years. Johnson was the first African American to serve as Greensboro's mayor.

Johnson lost her reelection bid in 2009 to Republican political newcomer Bill Knight. In 2011, she ran for an at-large city council seat, having garnered the most votes of any candidate in the October 2011 city primary. In the November 2011 election, Johnson won the majority of the at-large vote, reclaiming her city council position of Mayor Pro-Tem. she won a new term in the general election in November 2017.

In February 2010, the Greensboro Economic Development Alliance (GEDA) awarded her with the Stanley Frank Lifetime Achievement Award. She is the Executive Director of One Step Further, a non-profit United Way Agency in Greensboro that provides mediation and court alternative programs to Greensboro's Youth. Yvonne served on the board of directors for Malachi House and was the Women's Resource Center's first president. She has also served on boards for Foster Friends, Sports Dreams, and the Greensboro Art's Council.

GLADYS FAULKS SHIPMAN was a native of Guilford County and was born on September 9, 1945, to AJ Faulks and Eugenia Grier Faulks. She was educated in the local public schools and graduated from James B. Dudley High School, class of 1963.

Gladys was the President, CEO and Executive Director of Shipman Family Home Care, Inc. She founded this company in 1987 which has become the largest minority home care provider in North Carolina.

Shipman was the first woman to serve as vice president for the North Carolina Chapter of the NAACP and was also the first woman to serve as president of the organization's Greensboro chapter. As one of the founding members of the International Civil Rights Center and Museum, she worked tirelessly to make sure the lunch counter, where she protested segregation during the 1960 Sit-in Movement, would serve as a place for education and truth for generations to come (Mclaughin, 2021).

Credit: WFMY

Gladys Shipman was the first woman to serve as Vice President of the NC NAACP. Shipman is pictured with Rev. William J. Barber who also served on the NC NAACP and now co-chairs the Poor People's Campaign: A National Call for Moral Revival

A PLACE WHERE SUCCESS WAS EXPECTED: FINAL EDITION

Her fight for equality and social justice continued throughout her life serving on a number of executive boards and councils, while also receiving several note-worthy civil rights awards, including the prestigious Medgar W. Evers Award from the Civil Rights Advocacy Training Institute. Shipman also received the Alston-Jones International Civil and Human Rights Award as well as the NCAT Hall of Fame Honorary Award of Excellence (Mclaughlin, 2021).

She was a life member of the Lady Sertoma Club and the NAACP, the philanthropist helped organize the first annual Martin Luther King Jr. breakfast and parade. During election years she helped promote the Underground Railroad, a transportation service to the polls. She fought for and financially supported causes that helped people who were struggling and empowered women.

Candidates for various political offices over the years often stopped by Shipman's office to get her endorsement or to hear what she had to say about issues in the community. As president of the NAACP, she also led the investigation into allegations by black Greensboro police officers years ago that they had been targeted by a covert police intelligence squad.

Shipman is a past recipient of the NC A&T SU Hall of Fame Honorary Award of Excellence, Greensboro Chamber of Commerce Women in Business Award, Civil Rights Advocacy Training Institute Medgar W. Evers Award and the McDonalds African American Achievement Entrepreneur Award. She was also inducted into the Hall of Distinction at James Benson Dudley High School (Class of 1963).

Guilford County Councilman Skip Alston mentioned Shipman giving a second chance to people coming out of prison, by helping them find jobs — or giving them one. She often took homeless people off the street and helped them find housing. Shipman also served as his campaign manager over the years.

LISA JOHNSON-TOMKINS
Clerk of Superior Court

LISA JOHNSON-TONKINS graduated from Dudley in 1991. She received her Bachelor of Arts (B.A.), in Public Relations Advertising and Applied Communication from North Carolina A&T State University in 1994 and her Doctor of Law (J.D.) from North Carolina Central University in 2003. She worked briefly at her father's law firm, Walter Johnson, Jr. and then became an associate attorney with Higgins, Benjamin, Eagles & Adams, P.L.L.C. The areas of law in which she practiced were bankruptcy, business, and real estate, criminal, civil and child support. These areas of specialty gave her a unique body of experience for a successful bid for the office of Clerk of Superior Court in 2014 and reelection in 2016.

The job title may be "clerk," but Johnson-Tonkins has judicial duties as well. Clerks of Superior Court in North Carolina issue arrest and search warrants and, like magistrates, can take guilty pleas for a variety of minor offenses. Clerks conduct proceedings including adoptions, incompetency determinations and partitions of land. And they serve as probate judges. These tasks are in addition to the office's actual clerical functions: administering oaths, keeping court records, providing court dates, accepting court fees, and providing court-related information to people working in the judicial system and the public.

DAVID MOORE graduated from Dudley High School in 1962. While a student at Dudley, he was Captain of the Drum Line under the direction of Mr. James Morgan who served as the band director in charge of the percussion and jazz bands during that time. He attended NC A&T State University and Guilford Technical Community College.

In 1990, David began his quest to help young children succeed in life by volunteering to mentor them. Since the early 1990s, David has mentored over 3,000 youth in Guilford County Schools (including Dudley High, Washington Street Elementary, Peck Elementary, Foust Elementary, Kiser Middle, Hairston Middle, Bessemer Elementary and Wiley Elementary). He has also mentored at Hayes-Taylor YMCA and in the community. Moore received Certificates of Appreciation from most of the schools for the countless hours of volunteer work at their schools.

To further his goal to help young children, David Co-Founded: Men-Tors Association, Inc.; BOTSO (Brothers Organized to Serve Others), Hayes-Taylor Y-Men's Club and Men of Dudley Mentoring Group. David assisted the In-School Suspension Personnel at Dudley for two years. Also, he has found time to serve in the following positions: Executive Director and Past Chairman of the Board of Mentors Association, Inc., Head of Security Team and Member of Trustee Board for Bethel AME Church, President of Hayes Taylor Y-Men's Club (Hayes-Taylor YMCA), Member of James B. Dudley Hall of Fame/Hall of Distinction Board, Member Alumni Band at North Carolina A & T State University and Dudley High School, Past President of the Postal Retirement Club, Past President and Shop Steward for National Postal Mail Handlers Union, Local 305, Past Shop Steward for National Postal Mail Handlers Union, Local 98 and he was one of the original members of the Committee to Save Dudley.

Moore received the National Alumni Service Award for 2015, and he was inducted into the Dudley Hall of Fame/Hall of Distinction in 2015.

BEVERLY MILLER EARLE of the Class of 1961 became the first African American woman to represent Mecklenburg County in the North Carolina State House of Representatives. She was first elected in 1994. Earle was also the first black woman to serve as House Majority Whip. By 2016 she was serving her 7th term representing District 101 which has one of the largest urban populations in the state. In the State Legislature, she serves as Health Chair of the National Caucus of Black State Legislators and as 1st Vice Chair of the North Carolina Democratic Party. She also represents her District on several committees: Aging, Agriculture, Alcoholic Beverage Control, Appropriations, Banking, Insurance and Public Utilities and the Subcommittee on Appropriations, Health, and Human Services.

She attended North Carolina A&T State University where she earned a degree in Social Science. Earle retired after 30 years at Bell South Services and in addition to her legislative duties is the owner of Earle and Associates. Earle was elected to the James B. Dudley Sports Hall of Fame/ Hall of Distinction.

REGINALD R. REEVES graduated from Dudley in 1943. In 1947, Reeves was a member of the first group of eight officers in the North Carolina A & T State University Army ROTC division commissioned into the Infantry branch. According to Hamilton (2016), Lt. Col. Reginald Reeves, said that the ROTC program was quite different back in his day than what it is today. Reeves said,

"The students get a lot more training today than what we did back then," he said. "They also have choices. There was only Infantry in my time. After we commissioned, we went to Fort Benning and that was it."

Reeves, spent 20 years with the Army Reserve as a Civil Affairs Officer in Idaho.

A PLACE WHERE SUCCESS WAS EXPECTED: FINAL EDITION

He was inducted into the A&T Military Hall of Fame in 2003.

His humanitarian activities include working with local business leaders to facilitate the donation of more than $300,000 in 2011 to be distributed to soup kitchens and various homeless shelters and charities (Ramseth, 2014). The food drives led to collecting used computers for migrant workers' schools, and ultimately hundreds of computers to be sent to poor school districts in Mississippi. These drives also facilitated the opening of offices in Idaho Falls and Boise to assist low-income persons obtain free medication from pharmaceutical manufacturers worth $10 million in 2009 and 2010. Ramseth (2014) noted that,

> "His international work included encouraging a sugar company in Guatemala to build a computer laboratory at three schools, and to hire teachers for them. He also helped facilitate about $1,850,000 worth of hospital and medical supplies being delivered to Vietnam. Drawing on high-level contacts and friends in the military, and in the medical community, similar projects provided development and medical supplies for the Virgin Islands, Nepal, and Ghana."

Reeves received one of the nation's highest awards for volunteerism — the Outstanding Public Service Award. It was awarded by Gen. Martin Dempsey, chairman of the Joint Chiefs of Staff. The medal was presented to Reeves in November of 2014 at a ceremony in Ketchum by Lt. Col. Richard Goodman, commander of the 389th Fighter Squadron at Mountain Home Air Force Base. The award cited the Military Medicine Program, which helped thousands of military retirees, spouses and widows get their prescriptions filled. It talks about the $1.5 million worth of hospital equipment Reeves gathered and shipped to Cao Bang, Vietnam. And it also mentions the 200 lbs. of blood Reeves donated through the years to the Red Cross (Ramseth, 2014).

"He likely saved almost 800 lives by donating 33 gallons of blood through the Red Cross," the citation said.

The citation also discusses the pro bono legal work Reeves provides for eastern Idaho veterans.

"My name got passed around the veteran's community," he said. "I get calls from up and down the Snake River Valley, and from the central part of the state."

Even as Reeves gets older, West said the scope of his charity work always is expanding. The Sun Valley Charitable Foundation has grown from a one-man show (Reeves) to a team of 24 volunteers picking up groceries and fanning out across eastern Idaho.

"I see a need, and I try to fulfill it," Reeves said. "My mantra is, 'Service to others is the rent we pay for the space we occupy.' And this is my way of paying the rent."

His other awards include Commander's Award for Public Service, The Outstanding Civilian Service medal, Alumni Hall of Fame, University of Idaho, Military Hall of Fame, North Carolina, A. &T. State University. South Central Idaho District Health Department, 2004 Health Hero, Governor's Brightest Stat Award for Public Service, 2002, City of Sun Valley Humanitarian Award, 2009 Red Cross, Donor of 30 gallons of whole blood.

Asked about public service, Reeves quoted Winston Churchill: "From what you earn, you can make a living. From what you give, you can make a life."

JOSEPH A. WILLIAMS was born October 16, 1944, the son of Andrew Williams II, and Jacqueline McDonald Williams. His father, a professor at North Carolina A&T State University, was the inventor of the Ames-Williams cranial drill, a device used for emergency relief of intracranial pressure in patients who have had a stroke or other severe brain injuries.

His mother was an instructor at Grimsley Senior High School. Joseph Williams graduated from James B. Dudley High School in 1963. He attended North Carolina A&T State University where he earned a B.S. in Industrial Technology in 1967. From 1970-1972, he attended North Carolina Central School of Law where he received his Juris Doctor degree. After completing law school, he became a Law Clerk with Frye, Johnson & Barbee, Attorneys from 1973-1975. In 1975, he became Assistant District Attorney for Guilford County, North Carolina with his primary areas of responsibility being the trial of criminal cases at the District and Superior Court levels. In 1977, he became a District Court Judge serving the 18th Judicial District in Greensboro, North Carolina.

One of his most notable cases settled a project liability case for eight (8) million dollars. At the time, the award was made it was the largest case involving a product in North Carolina history. Locally, his most notable civil case was representing approximately 13,500 citizens of Northeast Guilford

County and successfully defeating a landfill zoning request before the Guilford County Board of Commissioners in 2003. He also represented the town of Oak Ridge and successfully defeated a landfill zoning request before the Guilford County Board of Commissioners in 2004.

AMOS LEWIS QUICK, III, served as an Associate Pastor of the New Light Missionary Baptist Church and as the Senior Pastor of Calvary Baptist Church in High Point, NC. He is a native of Greensboro, and 1986 graduate of Dudley. Since graduating from the University of North Carolina at Wilmington with a degree in Psychology, Quick has made a distinguished career for himself in the community, public, and religious service (Temple Emanuel, 2014).

After successful early careers in comedy and radio, Quick later dedicated his life to be a positive influence on the lives of children and their families. After spending time on the staff at the Black Child Development Institute, he continued with his desire and passion for helping young people at the Greensboro Salvation Army Boys and Girls Club. There, he has worked to meet the growing needs of children and their parents in the community. Through a variety of athletic and personal development activities, his programs helped students gain self-confidence, improve public speaking skills, build character, and be recognized for excellence in academics. His work helped create a safe environment for children to develop into responsible, productive, and caring young people. Quick also created a Parent Advisory Council to get ideas and feedback from parents about problems affecting them and also helped educate parents on the importance of staying involved in their children's lives and how to effectively deal with difficult family situations (Temple Emanuel, 2014).

Quick became a Board Member of the Guildford County Board of Education in 2004. Described as outspoken and having strong opinions, he believed that the board's primary challenge was to focus on the needs, interests, and challenges of each child. He also personally worked hard on breaking down stereotypes. His hard work and dedication resulted in him being elected to the School Board for an eighth consecutive term and appointed as Vice-Chairman in December 2012.

In addition to all his community work, Rev. Quick is also a dedicated member the local religious community. With a strong religious background and education, after spending more than three years studying as a "Minister in Training," Reverend Quick was appointed as the Associate Pastor of New Light Missionary Baptist Church, in Greensboro, North Carolina in September of 2011. He was inducted into the Dudley Hall of Fame /Hall of Distinction in 2015. In 2016, he was elected to serve in the North Carolina House representing District 58.

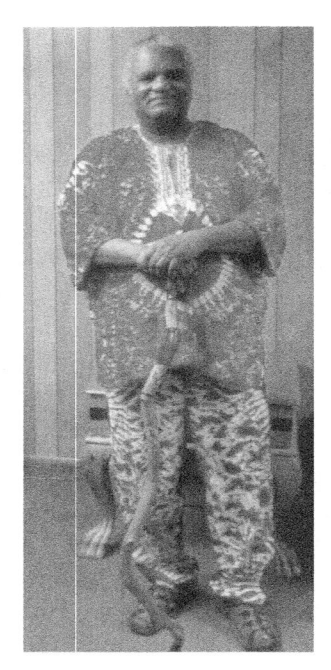

EZEKIEL BEN-ISRAEL-A.K.A. ROBERT BENSON DUREN, II attended the Greensboro City Schools graduating from James B. Dudley High School in 1972. He served in the United States Air Force as a Conscientious Objector. Although he refused to carry a gun, he served honorably as an orderly at military hospitals in Texas and in Turkey. He has a B.A. in Industrial Technology, Manufacturing from North Carolina A&T State University and an M.S. in Counseling Psychology, Oral Roberts University. He is a Certified Counselor. He is a member and Associate Pastor at Trinity AME Zion Church. Ben-Israel is a community activist working with local groups including the Operation Transparency's Protection Brigade asked for and forced the City Council to release the police video on the **Jose Charles case.** He recounted his experiences in the military in the book *The Art of the Hustle: Lessons in Becoming a Man.*

Jose Rodriguez, Greensboro News & Record

Operation Transparency's Protection Brigade asking the City Council to release the police video on the Jose Charles case

A PLACE WHERE SUCCESS WAS EXPECTED: FINAL EDITION

Jose Rodriguez, Greensboro News & Record

The Rev. Ezekiel Ben-Israel speaks during the Operation Transparency's Protection Brigade asking the City Council to release the police video on the Jose Charles case, at the Melvin Municipal Office Building on Wednesday, April 12, 2017, in Greensboro, N.C. After a brief press conference, the crowd of about 40 people went to the council's executive office to deliver packets of information. At first denied entry, the Rev. Nelson Johnson spoke to Greensboro Police Deputy Chief James Hinson Jr. who came out of the locked door to speak to the crowd and afterward let them in to make their delivery (Rodriguez, 2017).

Dr. Jo Evans Lynn, Ed.D.

Chapter Sixteen

For Your Willingness to Serve, We Salute You

Although there is evidence that Blacks fought in every war involving the Colonies of North America and the United States of America, information about Blacks from Greensboro, North Carolina, or Guilford County, who served in the military before the end of slavery is not as well documented by historians. Perhaps, this was because many of the blacks from Southern states who fought on both sides of the wars from 1775-1866 were slaves who had escaped to the North during the time that "slave takers" or bounty hunters were common. For them, anonymity was a matter of life or death. So, we begin with a general discussion of Blacks in the military and continue with the military contributions of Black graduates of the Bennett Seminary where the school that became Dudley High School was established in 1879 and end with more recent Dudley graduates' service in the military.

African Americans as slaves and freemen served on both sides during the Revolutionary War. Nash (2012) stated that recent research concludes there were about 9,000 black Patriot soldiers, counting the Continental Army and Navy, and state militia units, as well as privateers, waggoneers in the Army, servants to officers, and spies. Raphael (2001) noted that while thousands of Blacks did join the Loyalist cause, "A far larger number, free as well as slave, tried to further their interests by siding with the patriots."

Black soldiers served in northern militias from the outset of the war, but the South forbade participation by blacks, where slave-owners feared arming slaves. Lord Dunmore, the Royal Governor of Virginia, issued an emancipation proclamation in November 1775, promising freedom to runaway slaves who fought for the British; Sir Henry Clinton issued a similar edict in New York in 1779 (Selig, 1997). Over 100,000 slaves escaped to the British lines, although possibly as few as 1,000 served under arms. Many of the rest served as orderlies, mechanics, laborers, servants, scouts, and guides, although more than half died in smallpox epidemics that swept the British forces, and many were driven out of the British lines when food ran low. Many descendants of Black Loyalists now live in Canada and Sierra Leone. Many of the Black Loyalists performed military service in the British Army, particularly as part of the only Black regiment of the war the Black Pioneers, and others served non-military roles (Selig, 1997).

In response, and because of manpower shortages, General George Washington lifted the ban on black enlistment in the Continental Army in January of 1776. All-black units formed in Rhode Island and Massachusetts; many were slaves promised freedom for serving instead of their masters; another all-African American unit came from Haiti with French forces. At least 5,000 African American soldiers fought as Revolutionaries, and at least, 20,000 served with the British. Peter Salem and Salem Poor are the most noted of the African American Patriots during this era, and Colonel Tye was perhaps the most prominent Black Loyalist.

According to Gray (2011), black volunteers also served with various groups of the South Carolina guerrilla units, including that of the "Swamp Fox", Francis Marion, half of whose force sometimes consisted of free Blacks. Gray also noted that these Black troops made a critical difference in the fighting in the swamps and kept Marion's guerrillas useful even when many of his White soldiers were down with malaria or yellow fever. Shaw and Donnelly (2002) described the exploits of the first black American to fight in the Marines, John Martin, also known as Keto, the slave of a Delaware man, recruited in April 1776 without his owner's permission by Captain of the Marines Miles Pennington of the Continental brig USS Reprisal. Shaw and Donnelly also stated that Martin served with the Marine platoon on the Reprisal for a year and a half and took part in many ship-to-ship battles including boardings with hand-to-hand combat, but he was lost with the rest of his unit when the brig sank in October 1777 (Shaw & Donnelly, 2002). At least 12 other black men served with various American Marine units in 1776–1777; more may have been in service but not identified as blacks in the records. However, in 1798 when the United States Marine Corps (USMC) was officially re-instituted, Secretary of War James McHenry specified in its rules: Negro, Mulatto or Indian to be enlisted" (Shaw & Donnelly, 2002). Marine Commandant William Ward Burrows instructed his recruiters regarding USMC racial policy, "You can make use of Blacks and Mulattoes while you recruit, but you cannot enlist them" (Shaw & Donnelley, 2002). This policy was in line with long-standing British naval practice which set a higher standard of unit cohesion for Marines, the unit to be made up of only one race so that the members would remain loyal, maintain shipboard discipline, and help put down mutinies (Shaw & Donnelly, 2002). The USMC maintained this policy until 1942 when all military units were officially integrated (MacGregor, 1981; Morris, 1969).

A painting owned by the United States History and Art Museum titled *Battle of Lake Erie* depicts One of Perry's African American oarsmen in the boat and another African American sailor in the water.

Gordon of the Corps d'Afrique in uniform

The Timeline of Events for African Americans in the U.S. Army (2015) states that during the War of 1812 about one-quarter of the personnel in the American naval squadrons of the *Battle of Lake Erie* were black, and a portrait rendering of the battle on the wall of the Nation's Capital and the rotunda of Ohio's Capitol show that blacks played a significant role in it. Hannibal Collins a freed slave and Oliver Hazard Perry's personal servant, is thought to be the oarsman in William Henry Powell's *Battle of Lake Erie*. Collins earned his freedom as a veteran of the Revolutionary War, having fought in the Battle of Road Island. He accompanied Perry for the rest of Perry's naval career and was with him at Perry's death in Trinidad in 1819.

The law of 1792, which generally prohibited enlistment of blacks in the Army became the United States Army's official policy until 1862. The only exception to this Army policy was Louisiana, which gained an exemption at the time of its purchase through a treaty provision, which allowed it to opt out of the operation of any law, which ran counter to its traditions and customs. Louisiana permitted the existence of separate black militia units which drew its enlistees from freed blacks. Although Louisiana was a slave state, there were 4,600 free Blacks by 1809, many of whom had emigrated from Santo Domingo as veterans of the Haitian Revolution. All free Blacks who owned any property worth at least $300 or paid taxes for the past two years were recruited. Although the law in Louisiana only permitted Whites to be officers in this battalion, three Black second lieutenants still existed.

Governor William C.C. Claiborne of Louisiana needed to defend his territory against a rumored British attack, and he firmly believed in the ability of the Black soldier. He even made sure that General Andrew Jackson understood this, noting that under the Spanish the free Blacks had been very reliable. Of Jackson's 6,000 troops defending Louisiana, 500 were free Blacks. The battle would end up a stalemate, and soon the British would give up on their plan to capture the U.S., given the stiff determination encountered in all areas of the North American battlefield (Battle, 1932).

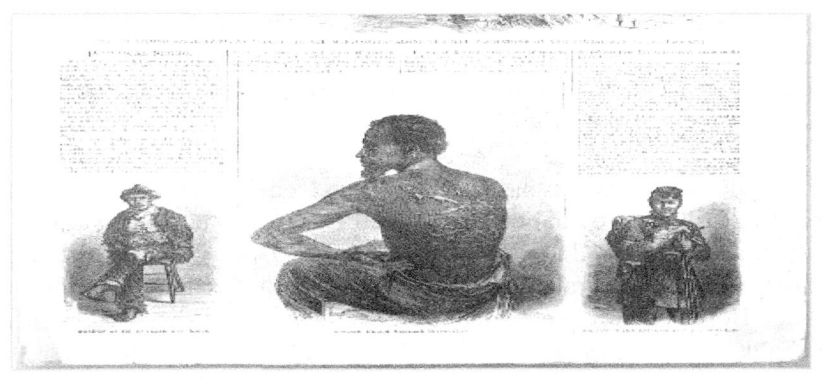

"Gordon, scourged back, Harper's weekly, 1863 July 4, p 429.

    Gordon, or Whipped Peter, was a slave on a Louisiana plantation who made his escape from bondage in March 1863, he became a contraband and went on to serve as a soldier in the United States Colored Troops. *Contraband* was a term commonly used in the United States military during the American Civil War to describe a new status for certain escaped slaves or those who affiliated with Union forces.
    The Army (and the United States Congress) determined that the US would not return escaped slaves who went to Union lines and classified them as contraband. The carte-de-visite (A type of small photograph which was patented in Paris, France by photographer André Adolphe Eugéne Disdéri in 1854). Photographs showing Gordon's flagellation scars were frequently used by abolitionists throughout the United States and internationally (Selig, 1997). In July 1863, these images appeared in an article about Gordon published in *Harper's Weekly*, the most widely read journal during the Civil War (Chambers & Anderson, 1999). The pictures of Gordon's back provided Northerners with visual evidence of brutal treatment of slaves and inspired many free blacks to enlist in the Union Army.

The courage displayed by colored troops during the Civil War played an important role in African Americans gaining new rights. As the abolitionist Frederick Douglass wrote:

"Once let the black man get upon his person the brass letter, U.S., let him get an eagle on his button, and a musket on his shoulder and bullets in his pocket, there is no power on earth that can deny that he has earned the right to citizenship." (Frederick Douglass)

Corning (1987) noted that, "Approximately 180,000 African Americans comprising 163 units served in the Union Army during the Civil War, and many more African Americans served in the Union Navy." Both free African Americans and runaway slaves joined the fight. On July 17, 1862, Congress passed two acts allowing the enlistment of African Americans, but official enrollment occurred only after the September 1862 issuance of the Emancipation Proclamation.

The U.S. Congress passed the Second Confiscation Act in July 1862. It freed slaves whose owners were in rebellion against the United States, and a militia act empowered the President to use freed slaves in any capacity in the army. President Abraham Lincoln was concerned with public opinion in the four Border States that remained in the Union, as they had numerous slaveholders, as well as with northern Democrats who supported the war but were less supportive of abolition than many northern Republicans. Lincoln opposed early efforts to recruit black soldiers, although he accepted the Army's using them as paid workers.

The Union Army's setbacks in battles over the summer of 1862 led Lincoln to emancipate all slaves in states at war with the Union. In September 1862, Lincoln issued his preliminary Emancipation Proclamation, announcing that all slaves in rebellious states would be free as of January 1. Recruitment of colored regiments began in full force following the Proclamation of January 1863.

According to Cornish (1987) the United States War Department issued General Order Number 143 on May 22, 1863, establishing the Bureau of Colored Troops to facilitate the recruitment of African American soldiers to fight for the Union Army. Regiments, including infantry, cavalry, engineers, light artillery, and heavy artillery units, were recruited from all states of the Union and became known as the United States Colored Troops (USCT).

Gray commented that, "Approximately 175 regiments comprising more than 178,000 free blacks and freedmen served during the last two years of the war." Their service bolstered the Union war effort at a critical time. By war's end, the men of the USCT composed nearly one tenth of all Union troops. The USCT suffered 2,751 combat casualties during the war, and 68,178 losses from all causes. Disease caused the most fatalities for all troops, black and white.

USCT regiments were led by white officers, and rank advancement was limited for black soldiers. The Supervisory Committee for Recruiting Colored Regiments in Philadelphia opened the Free Military Academy for Applicants for the Command of Colored Troops at the end of 1863. For a time, black soldiers received less pay than their white counterparts, but they (and their supporters) lobbied and gained equal pay. Notable members of USCT regiments included Martin Robinson Delany, and the sons of Frederick Douglass.

In general, white soldiers and officers believed that black men lacked the courage to fight and fight well. In October 1862, African American soldiers of the 1st Kansas Colored Volunteers silenced their critics by repulsing attacking Confederates at the battle of Island Mound, Missouri. By August 1863, 14 Negro Regiments were in the field and ready for service. At the battle of Port Hudson, Louisiana, May 27, 1863, the African American soldiers bravely advanced over open ground in the face of deadly artillery fire. Although the attack failed, the black solders proved their capability to withstand the heat of battle (American Civil War.com, 2012).

On July 17, 1863, at Honey Springs, Indian Territory, now Oklahoma, the 1st Kansas Colored fought with courage again. Union troops under General James Blunt ran into a strong Confederate force under General Douglas Cooper. After a two-hour bloody engagement, Cooper's soldiers retreated. The 1st Kansas, which had held the center of the Union line, advanced to within fifty paces of the Confederate line and exchanged fire for some twenty minutes until the Confederates broke and ran. General Blunt wrote after the battle,

> "I never saw such fighting as was done by the Negro regiment.... The question that Negroes will fight is settled; besides, they make better solders in every respect than any troops I have ever had under my command."

The most widely known battle fought by African Americans was the assault on Fort Wagner South Carolina, by the 54th Massachusetts on July 18, 1863. The 54th Massachusetts was made up of 1000 black men from 24 states including North Carolina. The 54th volunteered to lead the assault on the strongly fortified Confederate positions. The soldiers of the 54th scaled the fort's parapet and were only driven back after brutal hand-to-hand combat. During the battle, Sgt. William H. Carney, a former slave, became the first of many black men to later earn the Medal of Honor. After the regimental commander, Col. Shaw, was killed, Carney climbed the fort's parapet and retrieved the Union Flag from the slain flag bearer. In spite of being wounded in the arm, chest, and legs, he planted the flag atop the fort, which encouraged his fellow Soldiers

Although black soldiers proved themselves as reputable soldiers, discrimination in pay and other areas remained widespread. According to the Militia Act of 1862, soldiers of African descent were to receive $10.00 a month, plus a clothing allowance of $3.50. Many regiments struggled for equal pay, some refusing any money until June 15, 1864, when Congress granted equal pay for all black soldiers (American Civil War.com, 2012).

Dyer (1908) stated that, "African American soldiers participated in every major campaign of 1864-1865 except Sherman's invasion of Georgia." The year 1864 was especially eventful for African American troops. On April 12, 1864, at Fort Pillow, Tennessee,

Confederate General Nathan Bedford Forrest led his 2,500 men against the Union-held fortification, occupied by 292 black and 285 white soldiers. After driving in the Union pickets and giving the garrison an opportunity to surrender, Forrest's men swarmed into the fort with little difficulty and drove the Federals down the river's bluff into a deadly crossfire. Casualties were high and only sixty-two of the U.S. Colored Troops survived the fight. Many accused the Confederates of perpetuating a massacre of black troops, and the controversy continues today. The battle cry for the Negro soldier east of the Mississippi River became "Remember Fort Pillow!" (American Civil War.com, 2012)

The Battle of New Market Heights, Virginia (Chaffin's Farm) became one of the most heroic engagements involving African Americans. On September 29, 1864, the African American division of the Eighteenth Corps, after being pinned down by Confederate artillery fire for about 30 minutes, charged the earthworks and rushed up the slopes of the heights. During the hour-long engagement, the division suffered tremendous casualties. Of the sixteen African Americans who were awarded the Medal of Honor during the Civil War, fourteen received the honor as a result of their actions at New Market Heights (American Civil War.com, 2012).

In January 1864, General Patrick Cleburne and several other Confederate officers in the Army of the Tennessee proposed using slaves as soldiers since the Union was using black troops. Cleburne recommended offering slaves their freedom if they fought and survived. Confederate President Jefferson Davis refused to consider Cleburne's proposal and forbade further discussion of the idea. The concept, however, did not die. By the fall of 1864, the South was losing more and more ground, and some believed that only by arming the slaves could defeat be averted. On March 13, the Confederate Congress passed General Order 14, and President Davis signed the order into law. The order was issued March 23, 1865, but only a few African American companies were raised, and the war ended before they could be used in battle (American Civil War.com, 2012)

A number of African Americans in the Army during the Mexican American War were servants of the officers who received government compensation for the services of their servants or slaves. Also, soldiers from the Louisiana Battalion of Free Men of Color participated in this war. African Americans also served on a number of naval vessels during the Mexican American War, including the U.S.S. Treasure, and the U.S.S. Columbus.

The men and women of Bennett Seminary (1873), Bennett College Normal School (1879), Greensboro High School for Negroes at Bennett College (1823-1826), and later James B. Dudley High School have participated in the armed services of the United States during the last 146 years. However, the battle for integration and for recognition of the accomplishments of black soldiers has been a slow process. The U.S. armed forces remained segregated through World War I. Still, many African Americans eagerly volunteered to join the Allied cause following America's entry into the war. By the time of the armistice with Germany on November 11, 1918, over 350,000 African Americans had served with the American Expeditionary Force on the Western Front.

Many Dudley teachers, students, and graduates served in the military during World War II and in the wars since then. Three of Dudley's first four band directors, Parsons, Gibbs, and Morgan were all members of the B-1 Navy Band. The following is as complete a list of James Benson Dudley High School students and graduates that have served in the military as I was able to document during more than ten years of research. All of the individuals listed on the following chart either attended Dudley on its current site or while the upper grades were located on the campus of Washington Street School or Bennett Seminary/College. Some may have ended their formal education after 9th grade which was not unusual during 1920s, 1930s, 1940s, and early 1950s. The older children in large families often went to work in the local mills at the age of fourteen to help support their families. High school attendance beyond the 9th grade was considered a privilege often reserved for the younger siblings.

Dr. Jo Evans Lynn, Ed.D.

James B. Dudley High School Muster List of Service in All Branches of the U.S. Military

Name	Branch	Military Action/WAR
Adams, John M.	U.S. Navy	WWII
Adams, Jr. Willie	U.S. Air Force	Vietnam
Adger, Willie Howard, LCpl	U.S. Marine Corps	Vietnam (KIA)
Aikens, Jessie James	U.S. Navy	WWII
Akridge, Lindwood J., Pfc.	U.S. Army	WWII
Aldrich, Isaiah, Cpl.	U.S. Army	WWII
Alexander, James Robert	U.S. Navy	WWII
Alexander, Nathaniel	U.S. Army	WWII
Allen, Joseph Daniel	U.S. Navy	WWII
Allison, James Odair	U.S. Army	WWII
Alston, James	U.S. Army	Vietnam- Bronze Star
Alston, Pearlie Caldwell	U.S. Army	WWII
Alston, Thomas	U.S. Navy	WWII
Ancrum, Lonnie	U.S. Army	WWII
Anderson, Harry	U.S. Army	Vietnam
Anderson, Ceab Eleisus	U.S. Army	WWII
Anderson, George Lesley	U.S. Army	WWII
Anderson, Jerry Lee	U.S. Navy	WWII
Anderson, Julius, Sgt.	U.S. Army	WWII
Anderson, Melvin	U.S. Navy	WWII
Anderson, Vaughn Allen	U.S. Army	WWII
Anderson, William James	U.S. Navy	WWII
Attaway, Eugean	U.S. Navy	WWII
Austin, Michael, Sgt.	U.S. Army	Radio Operator
Avery, Fred Douglas Jr.	U.S. Army	WWII
Banks, Herman	U.S. Army	WWII
Barksdale, Anthony L.	U.S. Army	Vietnam
Barksdale, James Odell	U.S. Navy	WWII
Bason, Henry Bernard	U.S. Navy	WWII
Bass, George, Jr.	U.S. Navy	WWII
Beam, Robert Lee	U.S. Army	
Bennett, Bennett, Jr.	U.S. Navy	WWII
Bennett, Wilson	U.S. Army	Vietnam

Blackwell, James E.	U.S. Army Airforce	WWII
Blair, Ezell Alexander	U.S. Army	WWII
Boger, Dellie Lee, Sgt.	U.S. Army	WWII
Bost, Alfred	U.S. Air Force	
Bowden, Zack Alven	U.S. Navy	WWII
Bowen, Larry	U.S. Marine Corps	Vietnam
Boyd, Samuel Wilson	U.S. Navy	WWII
Bratcher, David	U.S. Army	
Brame, Theolis Edward	U.S. Navy	WWII
Brice, Phillip	U.S. Navy	1970-1978
Brice, Willie Henry	U.S. Army	WWII
Briggs, Jean	U.S. Army	20+ years of Service
Brittain, William C.	U.S. Army Airforce	WWII
Brooks, Alfred Russell	U.S. Army Airforce	WWII
Brooks, Hubert	U.S. Army	WWII
Brooks, James	U.S. Army	Vietnam
Brooks, John Henry	U.S. Navy	WWII
Brower, Robert Emmons	U.S. Navy	WWII
Brown, James L.	U.S. Navy	WWII
Brown, Jerry	U.S. Navy	Vietnam
Brown, Nathaniel	U.S. Army Airforce	WWII
Brown, Nathaniel	U.S. Navy	Vietnam
Bruce, Samuel Martin, 1stLt	U.S. Army Airforce	WWII
Bruner, Ron	U.S. Army	Military Police, Fort Ritchie, MD
Burge, Paul Charles	U.S. Army	WWII
Burkes, Andrew Jackson	U.S. Army	WWII
Burkes, Nathaniel	U.S. Army & Army Reserves	17 Years of Service
Burnett, Clayton	U.S. Army	Vietnam
Burton, Edgar Cornell	U.S. Army	WWII
Butler, Thomas, Jr.	U.S. Army	WWII
Byrd, George	U.S. Navy	WWII
Byers, John Edward	U.S. Navy	WWII
Bynum. William	U.S. Army	Vietnam
Bynum, Willie Clyde	U.S. Navy	WWII
Caldwell, Christopher	U.S. Army	4 years
Calvert, Benjamin	U.S. Navy	Vietnam
Campbell, Edward	U.S. Navy	WWII
Cannon, John Bradford	U.S. Navy	WWII

Carmack, Reuben, Pfc.	U.S. Army	WWII
Carr, Victor	U.S. Army	Vietnam
Carter, Herman	U.S. Army	WWII
Carter, Raymiene Hobbs	U.S. Air Force	8 Years of Service
Carter, James Redson	U.S. Navy	WWII
Carter, Maurice	U.S. Army	
Carter, Thomas Nathaniel, Sgt.	U.S. Army	WWII
Chappelle, James B.	U.S. Navy	WWII
Chavis, Limuel Andrew	U.S. Navy	WWII
Cathey, Lonnie	U.S. Army	WWII
Cathey, Jr. Lonnie	U.S. Navy/ Navy Reserves	21 Years of Service
Chavis, Douglas	U.S. Air Force	Vietnam
Cheek, Charlie, Pvt.	U.S. Army	WWII
Cherry, Jasper	U.S. Army	WWII
Chisolm, James	U.S. Marine Corps	1969-1971
Clapp, Rufus C.	U.S. Navy	WWII
Clark, Walter	U.S. Army	WWII
Clark, William D.	U.S. Army	WWII
Clinard, Aldine, Sr.	U.S. Army	3 Years of Service
Cochran, Johnnie Albert	U.S. Army	WWII
Cole, Lee Woodruff	U.S. Army	WWII
Cole, Robert, Sgt.	U.S. Army	WWII
Coleman, Charles Ellis	U.S. Navy	WWII
Compton, Lewis Alfonzo	U.S. Army	WWII
Compton, Lovette Frank	U.S. Army	WWII
Cook, Theodore	U.S. Navy	WWII
Cooper, Ellis	U.S. Marine Corps	Stationed in Santiago California
Cooper, Kathleen Young	U.S. Army/Army Reserves/ U.S.P.H.S.	28 Years of Service
Cornelius, Frederick	U.S. Army	
Cotton, Harold Charles	U.S. Army	WWII
Couch, Herman	U.S. Army	Tour of Duty/Fort Bragg
Courts, Willie Benjamin	U.S. Navy	WWII
Covington, James	U.S. Navy	WWII
Covington, Wilbert	U.S. Army	WWII
Crawford, Ramious	U.S. Army	WWII
Crawford, Waldo, Jr.	U.S. Navy	WWII

A PLACE WHERE SUCCESS WAS EXPECTED: FINAL EDITION

Crosby, Jr. Raymond Brian, Captain	U.S. Navy	USS TYPHOON, Patrol Coastal Squadron One
Crockett, Ozzie		
Cunningham, Jack	U.S. Navy	WWII
Cummings, Calvin Henry, Jr.	U.S. Army	WWII
Cummings, Clarence	U.S. Army	WWII
Cummings, Herbert James, Cpl.	U.S. Army	WWII
Currie, David	U.S. Army	WWII
Davis Algood, Willeena Joyce, LTC	U.S. Army, Nurse Corps	Vietnam
Davis, James	U.S. Army	Vietnam
Davis, Roscoe	U.S. Army	Vietnam
Day, James Arthur	U.S. Navy	WWII
Davis, James A.	U.S. Army	Combat service Dominican Republic 1965
Dejurnette, Willie	U.S. Navy	WWII
Dillard, James Rawley	U.S. Navy	WWII
Dilworth, Wesley	U.S. Navy	WWII
Dixon, Richard	U.S. Navy	WWII
Donnell, Earlton Charles	U.S. Army	WWII
Donnell, Earlton Charles, Jr.	U.S. Air Force	Guam/Vietnam
Donnell, Larry	U.S. Marine Corps	Germany & Vietnam
Donnell, William R.	U.S. Navy	WWII
Dorsett, James	U.S. Army	WWII
Dorsett, James Earl, Pvt.	U.S. Army	WWII
Douglas, James Alton	U.S. Army	2 years
Douglas-Shaw, Patty	U.S. Army	20+ Years of Service
Douglas, Theodore, Seaman, 1st class	U.S. Navy	WWII
Dukes, Randolph	U.S. Army	
Dumas, Willie, Jr.	U.S. Navy	WWII
Duren, Robert Benson, III	U.S. Army	Medic
Echols, Everett Rufel, Sgt.	U.S. Army	WWII
Echols, Theodore, Cpl.	U.S. Army	WWII
Eichelberger, William Leon	U.S. Army	WWII
Ellis, Charles Robert	U.S. Army	WWII

Ellis, David Edward	U.S. Army	WWII
Ellis, Samuel Junius	U.S. Army	WWII
Enslow, Benjamin Harold	U.S. Army	Vietnam
Epps, Bonnie Well	U.S. Army	WWII
Ervin, Clarence	U.S. Army	WWII
Evans, Benjamin A.	U.S. Army	Tour of Duty
Evans, Carl Sebastain	U.S. Navy	WWII
Evans, David	U.S. Army	WWII
Evans, Fernard	U.S. Marine Corps	
Evans, Joseph Spencer	U.S. Army	WWII
Evans, Leon	U.S. Army	WWII
Evans, Robert	U.S. Army	Vietnam
Everett, Donzell	U.S. Marine Corps	
Fairley, Thomas A.	U.S. Army	WWII
Farrington, Artis	U.S. U.S. Coast Guard	1969-1995
Farrington, John William	U.S. Army	WWII
Farrington, Johnnie William	U.S. Army	WWII
Ferguson, Arthur W.	U.S. Army	WWII
Ferrell, Willie Lee	U.S. Navy	WWII
Fewell, Chester D., PFC	7th Marine Corps	Vietnam (KIA)
Fields, James, MSgt.	U.S. Army Airforce	Vietnam
Fisher, John Louis	U.S. Navy	WWII
Florence, John Howard	U.S. Army	WWII
Florence, David Lewis	U.S. Navy	WWII
Florence, Robert	U.S. Army	WWII
Foster, Paul	U.S. Navy	WWII
Foster, Watson Eugene	U.S. Navy	WWII
Foster, William Eddie	U.S. Navy	WWII
Foushee, Clifford	U.S. Army	WWII
Foust, Corbet, Jr., Pfc	U.S. Army	WWII
Foust, Felton	U.S. Army	WWII
Foust, Oliver Durham	U.S. Navy	WWII
Foust, Theodore Christopher	U.S. Navy	WWII
Free, Douglas Walter, Jr.	U.S. Army	WWII
Free, Kenneth, Sr.	U.S. Army	Tour of Duty
Free, Lazelle "Lacy", Lt. Colonel	U.S. Army	20 years Active Duty, ROTC Instructor N.C. A&T State University

A PLACE WHERE SUCCESS WAS EXPECTED: FINAL EDITION

		& Grimsley Senior High School
Freeman, Julius Lawrence, Jr.	*U. S. Navy*	*WWII*
Freeman, Rogers	*U.S. Army*	*WWII*
Freeman, Wilton Edward	*U.S. Navy*	*WWII*
Fryar, Gregory	*U.S. Army*	*Tour of Duty*
Fryer, Willie Odell	*U.S. Navy*	*WWII*
Fuller, Fred William	*U.S. Army*	*WWII*
Fuller, Harold Clarence	*U.S. Army*	*WWII*
Fuller, Matthew Elijah	*U.S. Army*	*WWII*
Fuller, Monroe	*U.S. Army*	*WWII*
Funderburk, Jr., Henry Clay	*U.S. Army*	*E5 Machines*
Furcron, William James	*U.S. Army*	*WWII*
Gaffin, Fletcher James	*U.S. Navy*	*WWII*
Galloway, LeRoy	*U.S. Army*	*WWII*
Galloway, Wallace Lee	*U.S. Army*	*WWII*
Garrett, William Roosevelt	*U.S. Army*	*WWII*
Garrison, Arthur	*U.S. Navy*	*WWII*
Garrison, James	*U.S. Navy*	*WWII*
Garrison, Vernon, Pfc.	*U.S. Army*	*WWII*
Gee, Arthur	*U.S. Airforce*	*Vietnam*
Gibbs, Chandler Dorsey	*U.S. Navy*	*WWII*
Gibbs, Warmoth Thomas, Jr.	*U.S. Navy*	*B1-Navy Band*
Gibbs, Moses James	*U.S. Army*	*WWII*
Gibson, Lloyd Norris	*U.S. Army*	*WWII*
Giles, Samuel, Sgt.	*U.S. Army*	*WWII*
Gilmer, John Samuel	*U.S. Navy*	*B1-Navy Band*
Gilmer, Melvin Josephis	*U.S. Army*	*WWII*
Gilmer, Paul	*U.S. Army*	*Vietnam*
Gilmore, Walter Mac, Jr.	*U.S. Navy*	*WWII*
Gilreath, Herman Kessler	*U.S. Navy*	*WWII*
Gilreath, Thomas Howard	*U.S. Army*	*WWII*
Gilyard, Ronald	*U.S. Air Force*	
Gladney, Larry	*U.S. Army*	
Glasgow, Jesse Louis	*U.S. Navy*	*WWII*
Glenn, John W.	*U.S. Navy*	*WWII*

Glover, Carl Well	U.S. Navy	WWII
Glover, Edwin	U.S. Marine Corp/Marine Corp Reserves	10 years of Service
Goins, Frank	U.S. Navy	WWII
Goins, John Vernon, Pfc.	U.S. Army	WWII
Goldston, James	U.S. Army	WWII
Gorrell, Richard	U.S. Army	WWII
Graham, Elmer	U.S. Army	WWII
Graham, Ernest Eugene	U.S. Navy	WWII
Graham, Gentry, SP4	U.S. Army	Vietnam (KIA)
Graham, Scott	U.S. Navy	WWII
Graham, Walter	U.S. Army	1968-1970
Graves, Arthur Alexander	U.S. Navy	WWII
Graves, Eddie	U.S. Army	Vietnam
Graves, Marvin	U.S. Navy	5 Years of Service
Green, Richard B., P.O. Second Class	U.S. Navy	WWII
Greenlee, David, Jr.	U.S. Army	WWII
Greer, Charles E.	U.S. Army	Vietnam
Griffin, Eddie	U.S. Navy	WWII
Groves, Willie Lee, Jr.	U.S. Navy	WWII
Gunn, William Hamilton	U.S. Navy	WWII
Hagey, James Theodore	U.S. Army	WWII
Hairston, Gattis Valentine	U.S. Army	WWII
Haith, Carlacy	U.S. Navy	WWII
Haith, George Henry	U.S. Navy	WWII
Haith, Henry Clayton, Jr.	U.S. Navy	WWII
Haith, Lacy, Lt. Col	U.S. Army	Tour of Duty
Haith, Sammy	U.S. Army	WWII
Haith, Walter Filmore	U.S. Navy	WWII
Hall, Alan Dale	U.S. Marine Corps	Honorable Discharge Disabled
Hall, Howard Russell (Pop), Sgt.	Marines	Vietnam
Hamilton, Maurice D.	U.S. Army	Desert Storm 5years Active Duty, 3 years Reserves
Hargraves, Rodney L.	U.S. Marine Corps	4 years of Service
Hargraves, William	Army Airforce	WWII
Hargett, Frederick Alexander, Jr.	U.S. Navy	WWII

A PLACE WHERE SUCCESS WAS EXPECTED: FINAL EDITION

Harris, Clayton	U.S. Army	1972-1987
Harris, Claude Swanson	U.S. Army	WWII
Harris, Daniel, Pvt.	U.S. Army	WWII
Harris, James Edward	U.S. Navy	WWII
Harrison, James Thomas	U.S. Army	WWII
Harrison, John Allen, Sgt.	U.S. Army	WWII
Harris, Clarence Elmer	U.S. Navy	WWII
Harris, John W.	U.S. Navy	WWII
Harris, Otto Delano	U.S. Navy	WWII- B1 Navy Band
Harshaw, Eugene Horatius	U.S. Navy	WWII
Hart, James	U.S. Army	Vietnam
Harvey, Frederick	U.S. Navy	WWII
Haulsey, Robert Lynn	U.S. Army	WWII
Hawkins, James Robert, Jr.	U.S. Army	WWII
Haygood, Hillis" Buddy"	U.S. Air Force	Vietnam (Distinguished Flying Cross)
Haynes, John Washington	U.S. Navy	WWII
Haywood, Herbert	U.S.Army	Vietnam
Headen, Albert Elmer	U.S. Army	WWII
Headen, Arthur	U.S. Army	WWII
Headen, David	U.S. Army	WWII
Headen, Jarvis Searcy	U.S. Army	WWII
Headen, Sandy	U.S. Army	WWII
Heggie, Bromot D. Clent "Brammie," pl	U.S. Army	WWII
Henderson, Eugene R.	U.S. Army	WWII
Henry, Roosevelt	U.S. Navy	WWII
Herbin, John William	U.S. Army	WWII
Herbin, Ralph H., Sgt.	U.S. Marine Corps	Vietnam
Herring, Wray Rapheal	U.S. Navy	B-1 Navy Band
Hester, Elvester, Pfc.	U.S. Army 503rd Infantry	Vietnam (KIA)
Hester, Perry	U.S. Army	Tour of Duty/ Vietnam
Hester, Preston	U.S. Army	Tour of Duty/Vietnam
Hightower, John P., Tech 5th ^{G}rade	U.S. Army	WWII
Hicks, Robert Lee, T/Sgt.	U.S. Army	WWII

Hicks, Donald	U.S. Marine Corps	
Hicks, Ronald	U.S. Marine Corps	
Hodge, John Wesley	U.S. Army	WWII
Holley, Jacqueline	U.S. Army	5 years of Service
Holloway, Joseph	U.S. Army	Tour of Duty/ Vietnam
Holt, John Lewis "Buddy"	U.S. Army	WWII
Holt, Richard	U.S. Amy	10 years of Service
Holt, Roger F.	U.S. Navy	B-1 Navy Band
Hood, Arthur L., MSgt.	U.S. Air Force/National Guard	26 years of Service
Hood, Floyd Harry, Seaman 2nd Class	U.S. Navy	WWII
Hood, Leonard	U.S. Army	Tour of Duty/ Vietnam
Hood, Reginald	U.S. Navy	Tour of Duty/Vietnam
Hooker, Percy William	U.S. Army	WWII
Hooper, Clarence	U.S. Army	WWII
Howard, James	U.S. Marine Corps	Tour of Duty/ Vietnam
Hundley, Harry C., Cpl.	U.S. Army	WWII
Huntley, James	U.S. Navy	
Hyman, Ishmael Hubbard	U.S. Navy	WWII
Ingram, James Zachariah	U.S. Army	WWII
Ingram, Samuel, Jr.	U.S. Navy	WWII
Ireland, Walter Henry	U.S. Navy	WWII
Isley, Ernest L. Sr., SMSgt.	U.S. Air Force	
Jackson, Herbert	U.S. Army	
Jackson, Manning Limuel	U.S. Army	WWII
Jackson, Willie James	U.S. Army	
James, Maco	U.S. Navy	WWII
Jarrell, Nevada, MSG	U.S. Marine Corps	Marine Security Guard
Jefferies, Joe	U.S. Army	WWII
Jenkins, Abraham	U.S. Army Airforce	WWII
Jenkins, Lewis	U.S. Navy	WWII
Jenkins, Lewis Wilson	U.S. Navy	WWII

A PLACE WHERE SUCCESS WAS EXPECTED: FINAL EDITION

Jenkins, Roger Waddell, PFC	U.S. Army	Vietnam (KIA)
Jennings, Elbert	U.S. Air Force	1974-1994
Johnson, Andrew, Lt. Col.	U.S. Army Air Force, Tuskegee Airman	WWII Korean War Vietnam (Fighter Pilot)
Johnson, Carl Lee	U.S. Army	WWII
Johnson, Charles, Jr.	U.S. Army	WWII
Johnson, Clifton G., Lt. Col.	U.S. Air Force	25 years of Service
Johnson, Jesse, Jr. Senior Master Sergeant	U.S. Air Force	Vietnam Logistic Program/System Analyst
Johnson, Lowaren	U.S. Army	6 years of Service
Johnson, Mark E.	U.S. Marine Corps	15 years Military Police & Correctional Specialist
Johnson, Roger Charles	U.S. Army Airforce	WWII
Johnson, Sarah E.	U.S. Army Nurse Corps	
Johnson, Walter Lee	U.S. Army	WWII
Johnson, Walter Thaniel Jr, Captain	USJAG Corp	Tour of Duty
Johnson, Wayman (aka Slack)	U.S. Army	First Air Calvary Division, Vietnam War
Johnson, Wendell, Lt. Col.	U.S. Air Force	19 Years of Service 8/10/1992 Died in Crash of Practice Flight
Johnson, Weldon, Jr.	U.S. Army	WWII
Jones, David Dallas, Jr.	U.S. Army	WWII
Jones, Irvin, Pvt.	U.S. Army	WWII
Jones, John Henry, Cpl.	U.S. Army	WWII
Jones, Luther H.	U.S. Army	WWII
Jones, Paul Maurice	U.S. Navy	WWII
Jones, Richard Henry Lee	U.S. Navy	WWII
Jones, Theodore C.	U.S. Army	WWII
Jones, Thomas Franklin	U.S. Army	WWII
Jones, Warren	U.S. Army	Vietnam
Joyner, Ray Leo	U.S. Navy	WWII
Keith, Eddie J.	U.S. Army	WWII
Kelly, Evelyn	U.S. Army	1979-1997
Kendall, Gene, Rear Admiral	U.S. Navy	Commanded the USS SPHINX (ARL 24), the USS FLETCHER (DD 992), and the USS

Dr. Jo Evans Lynn, Ed.D.

		MOUNT WHITNEY (LCC 20), Flagship for Commander, Second Fleet.
Kitchen, James Ben	U.S. Navy	WWII
Lambert, Marvin	U.S. Airforce	Officer
Lawson, George Augustus, Cpl.	U.S. Army	WWII
Leadwell, Edison	U.S. Army	WWII
Lewis, George	U.S. Navy	
Lindsay, James Arthur, Cpl.	U.S. Army	WWII
Lindsay, Leroy, Jr., Cpl.	U.S. Army	WWII
Little, James Kelly, Jr.	U.S. Army Airforce	WWII
Lofton, Jr. Johnnie	U.S. Army	
Long, Charles Brimmer	U.S. Army	WWII
Long, Eugene Evans	U.S. Army	WWII
Long, Victor	U.S. Army	WWII
Lott, Arthur	U.S. Army	WWII
Lyles, Thomas Jefferson	U.S. Navy	WWII
Lyndsay, Ada E.	WAAC/WAC	WWII
Manning, James Douglas	U.S. Army	WWII
Manuel, Tommie Abner	U.S. Navy	WWII
Marsh, George, Jr.	U.S. Army	WWII
Martin, Holly	U.S. Army	WWII
Martin, Kenyatta, Lt. Col.	U.S. Navy	Graduate of U.S. Naval Academy, Commissioned Officer
Martin, Luther Matthew, Jr.	U.S. Army	WWII
Martin, Romie Russell	U.S. Army	WWII
Martin, Royster	U.S. Army	WWII
Matherson, Herman Angus	U.S. Army	WWII
Matier, Curtis Owens, Sp4	U.S. Army	Vietnam (KIA)
Maybrey, Walter P.	U.S. Army	WWII
Maynard, Hoyte Andrew	U.S. Army	WWII
Maynard, James Collins	U.S. Army	WWII
Maynard, Pete W.	U.S. Army	WWII
McAdoo, Charlie Homer	U.S. Army	WWII
McAdoo, Darryl	U.S. Army	20+ years of service

A PLACE WHERE SUCCESS WAS EXPECTED: FINAL EDITION

McAdoo, Harold Alexander, Dr.	U.S. Army Dental Corps U.S. Navy Dental Corps	30+ Years of service
McAdoo, Nathaniel Theodore	U.S. Army	WWII
McAdoo, Robert Allen	U.S. Army	WWII
McArthur, Theodore	U.S. Army	WWII
McBrayer, Charles Edward	U.S. Navy	WWII
McCain, Edward, Jr.	U.S. Army	WWII
Mclean, Samuel	U.S. Air Force	1974-1994
McClenton, Titus	U.S. Marine Corps	Vietnam
McClinton, Lee Ernest, Sgt.	U.S. Army	WWII
McCollum, Cicero Clarence J., Jr., Sgt.	U.S. Army	WWII
McCollum, Clarence	U.S. Army	WWII
McCoy, Henry Edward	U.S. Navy	WWII
McCrimmon, Henry T., Sgt.	U.S. Army 327th Infantry	Vietnam/KIA
McDaniel, Marion	U.S. Army	WWII
McEachern, James Willie	U.S. Navy	WWII
McKee, Sr. Jona, Lt. Col	U.S. Army	WWII, Korea, Vietnam
McMasters, John	U.S. Army	WWII
McNair, Gurnee Brooks	U.S. Army	WWII
McNair, James Elmer	U.S. Army	WWII
McNair, Melvin	U.S. Navy	WWII
McNair, Robert Walter	U.S. Navy	WWII
McNeil, Tommy Lee, Command Sergeant Major	U.S. Army	22 years of service
Means, Rudolph	U.S. Army Airforce	WWII
Mears, William G., Tech Sgt.	U.S. Army Airforce	WWII
Mebane, Charles	U.S. Army	Vietnam
Mebane, Henry	U.S. Army	

Melvin, Ennis Eugene	U.S. Navy	WWII
Miller, Ronald	U.S. Army/National Guard	33 Years of Service/ Vietnam Retired
Mills, Rivers	U.S. Navy	Tour of Duty/Vietnam
Mitchell, Bernard	U.S. Army	WWII
Mitchell, Filmore	U.S. Army	WWII
Mitchell, Irving Reed	U.S. Army	WWII
Mitchell, Talmadge Taliferro	U.S. Army	WWII
Mitchell, Rivera Grenville	U.S. Army	WWII
Moffett, Ernest William	U.S. Navy	WWII
Moore, Charlie	U.S. Army	Vietnam
Moore, Charlie Edward	U.S. Navy	WWII
Moore, Henry Clay	U.S. Army	WWII
Moore, James N.	U.S. Army	WWII
Moore, James Ware	U.S. Army	WWII
Moore, Perry	U.S. Army	Tour of Duty/Vietnam
Moore, Willie, Jr.	U.S. Army	WWII
Moravian, Willie Lee	U.S. Army	Vietnam
Morhead, Allen	U.S. Army	WWII
Morehead, Eugene, Pfc.	U.S. Army	WWII
Moorehead, Nathaniel Sylvester	U.S. Navy	WWII
Morrow, Calvin F.	U.S Navy	B1 Navy Band
Morton, Wilton Lee	U.S. Navy	WWII
Murdock, Curtis	U.S. Army	Tour of Duty
Murdock, Harold	U.S. Army	Tour of Duty
Murphy, Edgar B.	U.S. Army	WWII
Murphy, Hubert Webster	U.S. Navy	WWII
Murphy, Thomas Robert, Sgt.	U.S. Army	WWII
Nelson, Walter Emmett	U.S. Army	WWII
Nelson, William	U.S. Army	1973-1976
Nettles, Hurman Lee	U.S. Army	WWII
Newby, Jessie L.	U.S. Army	WWII
Newton, Gaither, Cpl.	U.S. Army	WWII
Nichols, Paul	U.S. Marine Corps	

A PLACE WHERE SUCCESS WAS EXPECTED: FINAL EDITION

Nobles, Charles Herman	U.S. Army	WWII
Norman, James	U.S. Navy	Tour of Duty/Vietnam
Oaks, Walter Edward	U.S. Army	WWII
Ogburn, Ralph Hardin	U.S. Navy	WWII
Orr, Richard	U.S. Navy	WWII
Orrell, Thomas Walter	U.S. Navy	WWII
Owens, Charles L., "Charlie"	".S. Army	WWII
Paden, Lula Mae	U.S. Army Nurse Corps	WWII
Palmer, Harrison	U.S. Army	WWII
Panky, Craig	U.S. Navy	WWII
Parker, Haywood William	U.S. Army	WWII
Pass, Peter Button	U.S. Army	WWII
Pass, Samuel Penn	U.S. Navy	Vietnam
Patterson, Richard Daniel	U.S. Navy	WWII
Patterson, James, Msgt.	U.S. Air Force	Vietnam
Payne, Clarence	U.S. Navy	WWII
Peay, Roscoe Henry, Sgt.	U.S. Army	WWII
Pennix, Horace D., Sr.	U.S. Army	E4
Pennix, Lewis	U.S. Air Force	1968-1972
Perkins, Larry	U.S. Army	Vietnam
Pettiford, Christmas	U.S. Army/ National Guard	SFC7 (TOC & Medical
Pettiford, Raymond	U.S. Navy	B-1 Navy Band
Pickett, Joseph W.	U.S. Army	1970-1973
Poole, Benjamin Franklin, Seaman 2nd Class	U.S. Navy	WWII
Platt, Herman George	U.S. Air Force/ U.S. Navy	U.S. Navy Chaplains' Corp, Japan -South Korea
Poole, William Perry	U.S. Army Airforce	WWII
Presley, Jerome	U.S. Navy	Tour of Duty/Vietnam
Preston, Elijah	U.S. Navy	WWII

Pressley, Donald	U.S. Marine Corps	Vietnam
Rambert, Robert	U.S. Air Force	Vietnam
Ramseur, William	U.S. Marine Corps	Congressional Medal of
Reeves, Reginald R. Lt. Col.	U.S. Army	Commissioned Officer, N.C. A ROTC, 20 years Army Reser Military Hall of Fame 2
Richmond, Dennis	Army	Vietnam
Richmond, Franklin	U.S. Marines	Vietnam
Richmond, Paul	U.S. Navy	Vietnam
Reynolds, Cleveland	U.S. Navy	WWII
Roberson, Ricardo	U.S. Navy	Tour of Duty/Vietnam
Robinson, Harold Sherman	U.S. Navy	WWII
Robinson, James Marcus, SGT.	U.S. Army	Vietnam (KIA)
Rogers, Aaron	U.S. Army	25 Years of Service/Reti
Rogers, Eugene James	U.S. Navy	WWII
Rucker, Alonzo	U.S. Marine Corps	Vietnam
Ruffin, Wilbur	U.S. Army	
Sanders, Joseph Arlanders	U.S. Navy	WWII
Sanders, Talmadge	U.S. Navy	WWII
Sandifer, Riley	U.S. Navy	WWII
Scott, James Backmos	U.S. Navy	B-1 Navy Band
Sellars, Dwight	U.S. Army E6	Vietnam
Shaw, Patty Douglas	U.S. Army	20 years of Service
Slade, Thomas Franklin	U.S. Navy	WWII
Slade, William, Cpl.	U.S. Army	WWII
Sides, Howard	U.S. Army	Tour of Duty/Vietnam
Siler, Harry	U.S. Army	5 Years of Service
Slade, William, Cpl.	9th Marine Corps	Vietnam (KIA)
Sligh, Alvin Carnell, PFC	U.S. Army	Vietnam
Smith, Herman, Maj.	U.S. Army	
Smith, Rayshawn	U.S. Air Force	22 years Air Traffic Contr
Smith, Marion	U.S. Marine Corps	20 years

A PLACE WHERE SUCCESS WAS EXPECTED: FINAL EDITION

Smith, Melvin Eugene	U.S. Navy	WWII
Smith, Nishel Alphonso	U.S. Navy	WWII
Smith, Percy	U.S. Air Force	25 Years of Service/Reti
Smith, Rayshawn	U.S. Air Force	20+ Years of Service
Smith, Ricky	U.S. Coast Guard/ Army Reserve/ Air Force Reserve	22 Years of Service
Smith, Tom	U.S. Navy	WWII
Smith, Walter (Red)	U.S. Army	Vietnam
Smith, William	U.S. Army	
Spaulding, Vernon	U.S. Army	Tour of Duty/Vietnam
Spencer, Joe Lee	U.S. Navy	WWII
Spencer, Oscar Alexander	U.S. Navy	WWII
Spinks, Burley Junior	U.S. Navy	WWII
Sprinkle, Grover	U.S. Army	WWII
Spruill, John Emanuel	*U.S. Army*	*WWII*
Staley, Douglas	*U.S. Army*	*1969-1979*
Staley, Rick Redwine	*U.S. Coast Guard*	*4 Years of Service*
Stanford, Lemuel Alson	*U.S. Army*	*WWII*
Staton, Norris	*U.S. Army*	*Germany & Vietnam*
Steele, Johnnie Willard	*U.S. Army*	*WWII*
Stephens, Hodgist Walter	*U.S. Army*	*WWII*
Stephens, Hodgist	*U.S. Air Force*	*24 Years of Service/Retired*
Stephens, Thurston	*U.S. Army*	*WWII*
Stevenson, Charles Ronald	*U.S. Marines E6*	*Vietnam (MP)*
Stewart, John	*U.S. Navy*	*Vietnam*
Stimpson, Michael	*U.S. Marine Corps*	*1968-1974*
Stratford, Allen Lee	*U.S. Navy*	*WWII*
Stratford, Willie, Cpl.	*U.S. Army*	*WWII*
Street, Marquis	*U.S. Army*	*Vietnam*
Strickland, Frank Burnie	*U.S. Navy*	*WWII*
Stroud, Anderson, Jr.	*U.S. Army*	*WWII*
Stroud, Virgil Calvin, Staff Sgt.	*U.S. Army*	*WWII*

Stubblefield, Charles, Sgt.	*U.S. Army*	*WWII*
Summers, Cleophus	*U.S. Army*	*WWII*
Summers, Norman Evan Gelist, Cpl.	*U.S. Army*	*WWII*
Swann, Robert	*U.S. Army*	
Sweeney, James Edwin	*U.S. Army*	*WWII*
Swift, James Thelbert	*U.S. Navy*	*WWII*
Swinson, C. L.	*U.S. Army*	*WWII*
Tarpley, Tillery Deroy	*U.S. Navy*	*WWII*
Tate, Kaye Frances	*U.S. Army*	*SP5*
Tatum, Gregory R.	*U.S. Navy*	*9 years of Service & Persian Gulf*
Taylor, Aaron	*U.S. Navy*	*WWII*
Taylor, Abram Dearborn	*U.S. Army*	*WWII*
Taylor, Darrell	*U.S. Marine Corps*	*20+ years of service*
Taylor, David Eugene	*U.S. Army*	*WWII*
Taylor, Halley B., Capt.	*U.S. Army*	*WWII*
Taylor, Frank	*U.S. Army*	*WWII*
Taylor, George Preston	*U.S. Army*	*WWII*
Thompson, Andrew, Jr.	*U.S. Army*	*WWII*
Thompson, James	*U.S. Marine Corps*	*Tour of Duty*
Thompson, Julius, Cpl.	*U.S. Army*	*WWII*
Thompson, Linwood	*U.S. Marine Corps*	*Tour of Duty/Vietnam*
Thompson, Melvin	*U.S. Marine Corps*	*1968-1970*
Thompson, Otis	*U.S. Army*	*Vietnam*
Todd, Bobby	*U.S. Army*	*WWII*
Torain, David	*U.S. Army*	*WWII*
Toshumba, Roberta Wright, Warrant Officer	*U.S. National Guard*	*20+ years*
Totton, Claude Lemuel	*U.S. Army*	*WWII*
Totton, Eric Eugene	*U.S. Navy*	*WWII*
Totton, Raymond Daniel	*U.S. Army*	*WWII*
Townsend, Freddie B.	*U.S. Army*	
Troxler, John Wesley	*U.S. Army*	*WWII*
Troxler, Nehemiah	*U.S. Army*	*WWII*
Troxler, Samuel	*U.S. Army*	*WWII*
Turner, Calvin Coolidge	*U.S. Army*	*WWII*
Turner, Johnnie, Jr.	*U.S. Army*	*WWII*
Turner, Ralph Henry	*U.S. Army*	*WWII*

A PLACE WHERE SUCCESS WAS EXPECTED: FINAL EDITION

Tynes, Victor Horace, 1st Sgt.	U.S. Army	WWII
Tyson, John Charlie Franklin, Jr.	U.S. Navy	WWII
Tyson, Lucien Manuel, Cpl.	U.S. Army	WWII
Vample, Huey	U.S. Army	Tour of Duty/Vietnam
Van Deberry, Michael	U.S. Air Force	
Vanlue, Mitchell Jennings, Lillie, LTC	U.S. Army	
Vincent, Aubrey William	U.S. Army	WWII
Vincent, William Anthony	U.S. Marine Corps	Six Years of Service
Vincent, Thomas Coleman	U.S. Navy	WWII
Waddell, Alphonso	U.S. Army	WWII
Waddell, Hazel	U.S. Army	WWII
Waddell, London	U.S. Army	WWII
Wade, Edward W.	U.S. Navy	WWII
Waldrum, Walter, Jr.	U.S. Marine Corps	Tour of Duty/Vietnam
Walker, Bernard Wesley	U.S. Army	WWII
Walker, Larry	U.S. Army	
Walker, William Kenney	U.S. Army Airforce	WWII
Wallace, Irving Van	Army	WWII
Wallington, George Heyward, PFC	U.S. Marine Corps	Vietnam
Walls, Harold	U.S. Army	Two years
Warren, Cecil	U.S. Marine Corps	Tour of Duty
Warren, Roscoe	U.S. Army	WWII
Washington, Robert Lee, Lt.	U.S. Army Airforce	WWII
Watkins, Bernard, Cpl.	U.S. Army	WWII
Watkins, John	U.S. Army	WWII
Watkins, Junius June	U.S. Army	WWII
Watkins, Perry Windell	U.S. Navy	WWII
Watkins, Samuel Stuart, Jr., Cpl.	U.S. Army	WWII
Watkins, Ulysses	U.S. Army	WWII
Watts, Joseph	U.S. Army	Korean War
Weaver, Charles	U.S. Coast Guard	26 years of Service
Webster, Elmer Leon	U.S. Army	WWII
Weidman, Horace	U.S. Navy	WWII

Wells, Wendell DeAlton, Lt.	U.S. Army Airforce	WWII
Westbrook, Lowell Tennyson	U.S. Army	WWII
Westbrook, Purcell	U.S. Navy	WWII
Westmoreland, Bernard	U.S. Airforce	20 years of Service
Whitaker, Mose	U.S. Army	WWII
White, Albert	U.S. Navy	WWII
White, Albert J.	U.S. Army	WWII
White, Erwin	U.S. Air Force	1 Year of Service
White, Gurney	U.S. Army	Vietnam
White, Hammie	U.S. Army	WWII
White, James	U.S. Navy	WWII
White, Lenwood Clark, Tech Sgt.	U.S. Army	WWII
White, Louis	U.S. Air Force	1969-1990
White, Michael	U.S. Army	Vietnam
Whitfield, David Jarvis	U.S. Army	WWII
Whiteside, Dwayne A. Lt. Col	U.S. Marine Corps	Operation Enduring Freedom
Whitfield, Toussaint Philip	U.S. Navy	WWII
Whitt, Robert	U.S. Air Force	Vietnam
Whitt, Thadford	U.S. Army	
Whitworth, Samuel, Jr.	U.S. Navy	WWII
Wiggins, Lester	U.S. Marine Corps	4 Years of Service
Wiggins, Robert	U.S. Army	Tour of Duty
Wike, Sylvester	U.S. Air Force	Vietnam
Wiley, Albert, Jr.	U.S. Army	WWII
Wiley, Andrew Preston	U.S. Navy	WWII
Wilkins, John Thomas	U.S. Army	WWII
Williams, Adell	U.S. Army	WWII
Williams, Emanuel	U.S. Navy	WWII
Williams, Homer L.	U.S. Army	WWII
Williams, James Cecil	U.S. Air Force	Vietnam
Williams, John Champlain Brown	U.S. Navy	WWII
Williams, Quinnie R.	U.S. Navy	Vietnam
Williams, Robert	U.S. Army	WWII
Williams, Ronald, Sr.	U.S. Navy	
Williams, Rufus, Sp4	U.S. Army	Vietnam
Williams, Samuel James	U.S. Navy	WWII
Williams, Warren	U.S. Army	Korean War
Williams, Yardhick, Jr.	U.S. Army	WWII
Williamson, George H.	U.S. Army	WWII
Williamson, John	U.S. Navy	WWII

A PLACE WHERE SUCCESS WAS EXPECTED: FINAL EDITION

Williamson, John Wesley	U.S. Army	WWII
Williamson, Paul Douglas, Sp4	U.S. Army	Vietnam
Williamson, Roscoe	U.S. Army	WWII
Williamson, Sherman Ulysses	U.S. Navy	WWII
Williamson, Wesley	U.S. Navy	4 Years of Service
Wilson, Stephanie Querida-Quinn/Hoyes, Col	U.S. Air Force	20+ Years of Service
Winchester, Joel	U.S. Army	
Witherspoon, Robert	U.S. Marine Corps	3 years
Womble, John Woodrow	U.S. Army Airforce	WWII
Wooden, Ralph Lee	U.S. Army Airforce	WWII
Woods, Jessie James	U.S. Navy	WWII
Wooley, James Lee	U.S. Army	WWII
Wooley, William Thomas, Sgt.	U.S. Army	WWII
Worthy, Philip	U.S. Navy	WWII
Wright, Donald	U.S. Marines	Vietnam
Wright, George Lesley	U.S. Navy	WWII
Wright, John Wesley, Cpl.	U.S. Army Airforce	WWII
Wright Toshumba, Roberta	U.S. National Guard	20+ Years of Service
Wyche, Julius Dorman	U.S. Army	WWII
Wynn, John	U.S. Army	20 years of Service
Young, Fred, Staff Sergeant	U.S. Army	Vietnam
Young, Richard Harold	U.S. Navy	WWII
Yourse, Albert	U.S. Army	WWII
Yourse, Julius, Cpl.	U.S. Army	WWII

Dr. Jo Evans Lynn, Ed.D.

They Gave All...

We will never forget what they "gave" for God and Country.

LCPL. WILLIE HOWARD ADGER, MARINE CORPS

PFC. CHESTER DECATUR FEWELL, MARINE CORPS SP4.

GENTRY GRAHAM, ARMY

PFC. ELVESTER HESTER, JR. ARMY

PFC. ROGER WADDELL JENKINS, PFC ARMY

SP4. CURTIS OWENS MATIER, ARMY SP4

SGT. HENRY THURMAN MCCRIMMON, ARMY

SGT. JAMES MARCUS ROBINSON, ARMY

CPL. WILLIAM SLADE, MARINE CORPS

ST. SGT. FRED YOUNG, ARMY

We Can Fly!
Lt. Colonel Andrew Johnson (1940)

Andrew Johnson, Jr. a Dudley graduate in 1940 was one of the famed Tuskegee airmen during World War II. The Tuskegee airmen were the first black pilots in the U.S. military. They trained at the famous Tuskegee Institute in Alabama, where the Army Air Corps established the first training base for black pilots in 1941. It was called the Tuskegee Experiment because the prevailing thinking among white Americans at the time was that Blacks did not have the aptitude to fly airplanes.

After high school, where he had been a member of a state champion debate team, Johnson attended Fayetteville State Teachers College. With World War II raging, Johnson decided he wanted to enter the military, specifically, to become a pilot. "He took the test and was told he didn't score high enough," his daughter said. Still eager to serve his country, he moved to Philadelphia and joined some uncles who were already working in the Navy shipyard. While he was in Pennsylvania, someone reviewed his scores.

"Who told you that you didn't score high enough?" Lili Johnson said her father was told. "These are some of the highest scores we've ever seen. Come on in."

So south he went to Alabama. The attrition rate was not high for black trainees: Of 75 that started in Johnson's class, only 14 earned their pilot's wings.

He joined the 99th Fighter Squadron, comprised of Tuskegee Airmen, as a replacement fighter pilot in Italy in February 1945, near the end of World War II; he served as a fighter pilot in Korea for 18 months; and he saw seven months of duty — and flew 135 combat missions — in Vietnam, where he was a squadron commander flying assault transport planes.

He retired from the U.S. Air Force more than 20 years later, in 1965, holding the rank of lieutenant colonel. He returned home to Greensboro, went back to school, and earned a master's degree, then was an ROTC instructor at James B. Dudley High School until his retirement in 1975; one year his unit was honored as one of the top 11 in the nation.

Dr. Jo Evans Lynn, Ed.D.

B-1 Navy Band, Distinguished Service in the Military: The "Real" Fighting Began at Home

Picture Courtesy of B-1 Navy Band R.A. Fountain

Formed from a nucleus of North Carolina A&T College students and graduates, the band was comprised of "the best, most talented musicians in North Carolina."

There were nine students from Dudley High School who were recruited to join, six of them with their parents' consent, and three others were recent graduates. The Dudley band director, James B. Parsons became B-1's bandmaster (though he was never afforded that rank) after A&T's director failed to pass the Navy's physical exam. Bandsmen trained at Norfolk and served at Chapel Hill with the Navy's pre-flight school from August 1942 to May 1944, when they were transferred to Manana Barracks at Pearl Harbor, the largest posting of African American servicemen in the world.

DUDLEY'S CONNECTION TO THE FIRST B1-NAVY BAND

Pictures Courtesy of B-1 Muster List Band Achieves

Top Left-Right: Otto Harris, Roy H. Lake, John S. Gilmer, Calvin F. Morrow, James B. Scott, and Raymond Pettiford needed their parents' permission to join. **Bottom Left-Right:** Wray Rapheal Herring, Roger F. Holt, and Warmouth T. Gibbs, Jr. had graduated from Dudley, James Parsons, and James Morgan (Gibbs, Parsons, and Morgan were James B. Dudley H.S. Band Directors.

A PLACE WHERE SUCCESS WAS EXPECTED: FINAL EDITION

In addition to being the first African Americans to serve in the modern Navy at a general rating, B-1 also was the first Navy band whose members were not graduates of the Navy's School of Music, which did not admit blacks until after the war. In spite of the fact that segregationist laws prevented the bandsmen from being housed on the UNC campus or eating their meals there, they also became the first African Americans to work on the campus in a professional capacity–that is, as in the Navy, in non-servant occupations.

Picture Courtesy of B-1 Band Photographs Achieves

B-1 Navy Band practices on campus of in Chapel Hill

Picture Courtesy of B-1 Band Photographs Achieves

Work detail in Chapel Hill, L to R: John Carlson, Warmouth T. Gibbs, Jr., & Thomas Gavin. Wray Herring Collection, Special Collections, East Carolina University

Dr. Jo Evans Lynn, Ed.D.

Roy H. Lake: Setting a New Standard of Service to God & Country

Roger H. Lake
*Mus2c, clarinet,
Greensboro, Dudley
High School*

Roy H. Lake (1923-2018) was a civil servant, musician, and veteran of the United States Navy. Lake was born May 6, 1923, in Jefferson, South Carolina, the only child of William and Sadie Lake. Like the parents of Judge Elreta Alexander-Ralston (Class of 1934), Lake's parents moved to Greensboro, N.C. where the public schools for Negroes offered education beyond the elementary school level and he attended James B. Dudley High School. Lake played clarinet in Dudley's band under its first band director, James Parsons. He graduated in 1942 before the twelfth grade was added in 1947.

On May 27, 1942, Lake was recruited to join the United States Navy B-1 Band as a clarinetist. The U.S. Navy B-1 Band was the first all-African American Navy Band during World War II. He was known to his fellow service members by the nickname "Bably Lake."

Pictures Courtesy of B-1 Navy Band Achieves UNC Chapel Hill
Roger H. Lake (Top Left End Row) playing clarinet with the B-1 Navy Band in Chapel Hill, North Carolina.

A PLACE WHERE SUCCESS WAS EXPECTED: FINAL EDITION

    Following his service in the Navy, Lake attended North Carolina A&T State University and graduated with a degree in electrical engineering. After graduating, Lake went on to work at the U.S. Patent and Trademark Office. He eventually became the Chief of the Semi-conductor and Space Discharge Systems and Devices Division - the first time in the Patent Office's 125-year history a person of color served in that capacity. Lake retired in 1980.

Dudley's Junior AFROTC: A Proud Tradition Continues...

Dudley's Junior AFJROTC is the oldest JROTC unit in Guilford County and the second oldest AFJROTC unit in North Carolina. Our unit was established in August 1967.

Lt. Col. Andrew Johnson, the first Senior Aerospace Science Instructor, retired in June 1975.

Lt Col William M. Davis III replaced Lt. Col. Johnson and served until 1996. Lt Col Ronald Murphy served for one year until 1997 and was replaced by Lt Col Thomas Clarke who served until 1998. The next SASI, Lt Col Wayne Davidson served from 1998 until he retired in 2015. CMSgt Bell, the first Aerospace Science Instructor, served approximately three years. His replacement was MSgt James Savage, who served until 1991. Assistant Aerospace Science Instructor, MSgt Nevada Jarrell replaced MSgt Savage.

The Unit has won numerous awards over the years. Maxwell AFB selects the top units yearly, presenting Honor or Meritorious citations. Dudley has received the Highest Award Unit fifteen times and the Second Highest Award twelve times.

The Dudley AFJROTC Cadet Corps participates in a wide variety of school and community activities. These activities include raising the flag at the Annual Sit-In Movement Breakfast, participating in the Campus Clean-up Program; acting as teacher aides for the Guilford County Saturday Enrichment Program; an annual visit to an area nursing home; serving as pages for several regional and state educational/teacher conferences and workshops and presenting Colors at many school, community, and civic functions. They also participate in several parades each year.

The AFJROTC program reaches students on all levels academically with programs for the college-bound,

Left to Right: Lins Brewington and Cadet Richard Williams stand next to Mrs. Henry Frye and former State Supreme Court Justice Henry Frye

to programs for students who want to go directly into the workforce to those who want a military career. Many past students have completed college, and several have been commissioned in various branches of the military. The prime objective of the program has always been the brightest future possible for all its participants.

Dudley's AF ROTC Participates in Dudley's Homecoming Parade

NEVADA JARRELL graduated from Dudley in 1971. His Secondary Awards/ Honors & Leadership include being elected Vice-president of AVA. Vice-President of the Auto Mechanics Club, and Drill Team Commander of Dudley Junior ROTC (3 years). He also was a member of the Esquires Social Club; a member of the Red Cross Club and he was a Spirit Committee-Member. Jarrell was honored to serve as Homeroom Officer and Library President.

Jarrell served in the US Air Force. The highest rank he achieved was Master Sergeant. His numerous military honors and awards include the Air Force Commendation Medal w/two bronze oak leaf clusters; Air Force Outstanding Unit Award w/two bronze oak leaf clusters, Air Force Organization Excellence Award, Air Force Good Conduct Medal w/four oak leaf clusters; National Defense Service medal, Overseas Short Tour Ribbon, Air Force Longevity Service Award Ribbon w/three oak leaf clusters, Non-Commissioned Officer (NCO); Professional Military Education Graduation Ribbon w/one oak leaf cluster, Air Force Training Ribbon, served a term of one year in support of Operation Desert Shield and Desert Storm, and Inducted into the Senior Non-commissioned Officer's Fraternity.

Jarrell's Community Involvement includes serving as a volunteer at Hayes Taylor YMCA Vo; Dudley High School Student Mentor (Under Leadership of Mister David Moore); Jarrell has maintained his connection to

Dudley as an Air Force Junior ROTC Instructor at James B. Dudley High School (1991-2011). He is an active member of the Dudley Alumni Class of 1971. He was especially active in the Class of 1971-50th Anniversary Activities.

Jarrell's Academic Accomplishments include attending the Non-Commissioned Officer Leadership Academy (Lackland Air Force Base), Non-commissioned Officers Leadership School. Tactical Air Command NCO Leadership School (Shaw Air Force Base), Air Training Command Non-Commissioned Officer Academy, Community College of the Air Force, Air Force Junior Instructor School, Attended A&T State University, Sacramento City College, Consumes River College, Phillips University,

During his career he received many career-related awards, honors, or certifications: Outstanding Instructor of the Year Award of the Air Force Jr. ROTC Program at Dudley High School 1998-1999, 2008-2009. Certificate of Recognition for 20 Years of Dedicated Service to the ROTC Program, Nominated for Teacher of the year, nominated 2002 Alumni King, Dudley Alumni Consolidated Reunion. Further Information to Strengthen Application: While employed at Dudley High School, he served on committees that included the Scholarship Board, Awards Committee, and was involved in the establishment of the North Carolina Officer's Leadership School at Fort Bragg, NC. I also worked with my alumni Classmates of 1971 to raise funds for scholarships which were presented to qualified seniors upon graduation. "Working at Dudley as the Air Force Jr ROTC instructor, my mission was to make this unit one of the best units in the state. I helped accomplish that mission. From October 1991 to October 2011, James B. Dudley High School NC 201 continued to be one of the best ROTC units in the state. In 2008, the unit was awarded the highest award possible, The Distinguished Unit Award. Many of his cadets have gone on to careers as lawyers, administrators, doctors, and successful business personnel. Jarrell said, "This makes me proud as I know that I and the other wonderful faculty and staff at Dudley had a part in that. To this day, I still hear from many of my former students."

A PLACE WHERE SUCCESS WAS EXPECTED: FINAL EDITION

LT. COLONEL LAZELLE E. FREE was born in Harrisburg, Pennsylvania on January 27, 1940, to Lee W. and Margaret M. Free, and later the family moved to Greensboro, NC, where he was raised as a lifelong member of Celia Phelps Memorial United Methodist Church. He graduated from James B. Dudley High School in 1957 and received his BA degree from West Virginia State University (then College) in 1961, where he served his community as a member of Omega Psi Phi Fraternity and later served his country in the United States Army. He was commissioned as a 2nd Lieutenant.

Picture Courtesy of 1994 Whirligig

Lt. Col. Free served twenty years in the United States Army, completing two tours of duty in the Republic of Vietnam in 1964 and 1969. When he was wounded in Vietnam in 1966, he said that he could feel the prayers of his family, and that his faith in that moment - "like a breath of fresh air," as he once said - carried him back home. During his time stateside, he taught ROTC at Hampton University and met and married his first wife, the late Doris Morse Free in 1965. In 1969, he returned to Vietnam. His active-duty assignments included Tank Platoon Leader, Company Commander, and Chief Minority Recruiting Officer. "The Colonel," as his family called him, earned wide-ranging military honors that include two awards of the Bronze Medal for Meritorious Service; two Army Commendation Medals; Purple Heart; National Defense Service Medal; Armed Forces Reserve Medal; Combat Infantryman's Badge and Vietnamese Honor Medal.

He was assigned to North Carolina A & T State University ROTC from 1975-1979. In 1980, he expanded his family by marrying Hannah R. Free. In 1981, he obtained a Master of Arts degree in Public Affairs from Webster College (St. Louis, Missouri); and in 1985, he received a Master of Science degree from North Carolina A & T State University. After retiring from active duty in 1982, he was employed by Guilford County Schools as the Senior Army Instructor at Grimsley High School. He retired from Guilford County Schools after 19 years, having revived a thriving program for integrated students at the once-segregated school, changing the lives of hundreds of students, many of whom are still active in the military. In the fall of 1987, Lazelle fulfilled a dream by founding and operating Lacy and Sons, Inc. Transportation Services, a successful company that was "on the move" for over two decades.

Always active in his community, he supported the local Hayes Taylor YMCA, and he was honored by the Boy Scouts of America with the Whitney M. Young, Jr. Award for service. An avid sportsman, he also served on the Greensboro Sports Commission for many years. He was inducted into the James B. Dudley Hall of Distinction on October 21, 2017.

GENE KENDALL, REAR ADMIRAL, USN (Ret.) President and CEO of Admiral K Consulting was a 1963 graduate of Dudley High School. He then attended Duke University from 1963-1965. Kendall enlisted in the Navy and later earned a master's in engineering physics from the University of Kansas (1968-1971). He began his naval career as an enlisted man in 1966. He completed Nuclear Power Training in 1968 and was commissioned from the Naval Enlisted Scientific Education Program at the University of Kansas where he earned his B.S. in Engineering Physics. He went on to earn his Master of Engineering Physics Degree before he received his first officer assignment in 1972. An accomplished leader, Rear Admiral Kendall commanded the USS SPHINX (ARL 24), the USS FLETCHER (DD 992), and the USS MOUNT WHITNEY (LCC 20), also Flagship for Commander, Second Fleet. Ashore, Rear Admiral Kendall led in the academic arena as well. During his tour at the Surface Warfare Officer School in Newport, RI, he was Founding Director, Engineering Officer of the Watch course and Director, Engineering Specialty Training. He went on to become the Special Assistant to the Chief of Naval Operations in Washington, DC, where he helped to guide the navy's policies in the area of equal opportunity and minority affairs. Rear Admiral Kendall's next tour of duty was as Director, Division of Mathematics and Science, U.S. Naval Academy in Annapolis, MD, where he has the distinction of being the first African American, and the first non-Naval Academy graduate ever to lead a major academic division.

He next helped the navy determine its best course and strategy over the next 20 to 30 years as a Fellow with the Chief of Naval Operation's Strategic Studies Group XV at the Naval War College in Newport RI. Rear Admiral Kendall's last tour before his retirement in 2001 was as Deputy Director for Operations, Joint Staff, and National Military Command Center at The Pentagon in Washington DC. In 1996 when he was promoted, Rear Admiral Kendall became the 12th African American in the history of the United States Navy to achieve the rank of Rear Admiral (Admiral K Consulting, 2011).

DR. HAROLD ALEXANDER MCADOO graduated from Dudley High School in 1966. He earned a Bachelor of Science degree from North Carolina Central University and went on to earn a Doctor of Dental Surgery (DDS) degree from Howard University in 1978. Immediately upon graduation from dental school, he joined the U.S. Navy and completed a one (1) year General Dental Practice Rotation. He also completed a two (2) year residency program in Advanced Comprehensive General Dentistry while serving in the U.S. Army. Throughout his dental career, he participated in continuing education courses, conferences, and seminars. These enabled him to remain well-informed of emerging dental issues, treatments, and related practices.

After providing dental services for more than thirty-one (31) years to the military community, Dr. McAdoo retired at the rank of Colonel-06 from the U.S. Army Dental Corps in 2002. He would continue to provide dental services for an additional (14) fourteen plus years as a private dental practitioner to the civilian community. He retired from private practice in 2013. Since his retirement, he has continued to provide dental services to the North Carolina Department of Corrections population on a part-time basis.

Dr. McAdoo has received numerous awards. His military awards include a Bronze Star Medal, Meritorious Service Awards, a Kuwait

Liberation Medal, National Defense Service Medals, an Army Commendation Medal, an Army Good Conduct Medal, an Armed Forces Expeditionary Medal, a Southwest Asia Service Medal with 3 Bronze Service Stars, a Humanitarian Service Medal, an Armed Forces Reserve Medal, an Expert Field Medical Badge, an Airborne Parachutist Badge, and an Army Service Ribbon.

Dr. McAdoo has also made significant contributions as a dentist, both here at home and abroad. He developed and facilitated dental service, albeit part-time, by opening the first "Emergency only Dental Clinic" in the United States, Pinehurst, North Carolina in 1998.

COMMANDER KENYATTA O. MARTIN graduated from Dudley in 1997. Martin says that two of the most important positive aspects of his development into the man he became where BOTSO (Brothers Organized to Serve Others) and the outstanding math and science teachers at Dudley High School.

While he was a student at Dudley, he was a defensive end and linebacker on the football team. During his senior year, he accepted an appointment to the United States Naval Academy in Annapolis, Maryland. Martin graduated from the Naval Academy in 2001 with a degree in industrial engineering and served as a commissioned officer in the Navy for more than 15 years both on active duty and in the Reserves.

Martin continued to mentor African American boys and young men the way that the older men in BOTSO mentored him. In a meeting of the Council of Elders, Martin said, "The men in BOTSO were like a team of fathers to me and the other boys in the program. They took us on field trips and made sure that we understood the logistics of growing up as a Black man in America and that we knew how important it was to go to school and get a good education. I want to do that for my generation and the next generation of Black men."

A PLACE WHERE SUCCESS WAS EXPECTED: FINAL EDITION

LT. COL. DWAYNE A. WHITESIDE was born in Greensboro, North Carolina and graduated from James B. Dudley High School in 1979. Having attended grade school in the community and even college, Whiteside graduated from North Carolina Agricultural and Technical State University in 1983. He met his wife Verona while attending James B. Dudley High School in 1977 and married her in 1985.

"I was born and resided in Greensboro all the way through college," said Whiteside with a smile. "I am a no kidding a product of the community."

Courtesy Defense Video & Imagery D.S.

Whiteside decided to enlist in the Marine Corps reserve early in his college years based on rhetoric from Eddie McLenn, his brother-in-law, already a Marine, whose stories convinced him to sign up for recruit training in 1980. After leaving the Marines McLenn worked as a supervisor for the U.S. Postal Service in Greensboro. "He would come home fired up with boot camp stories," Whiteside remarked. "And he seemed so different and dedicated to the Marine Corps ethos. I always felt something was different."

According to Whiteside, his entire neighborhood, it seemed, had joined the Marine Corps, both men and women. His own government service extended beyond thirty years, which included duty as an infantryman, engineer, security guard, aide de camp and several tours to Iraq and Afghanistan, both in support and command roles.

"Some of the reservists come from the unit I started with," said Whiteside of his current Marines who deployed with him. "It's come full circle and now some of those Marines are out here with me."

He surpassed his mid-deployment milestone in the Helmand province while stationed at Camp Leatherneck in Afghanistan with Combat Logistics Regiment 2, Regional Command (Southwest), based out of Camp Lejeune, N.C., in support of Operation Enduring Freedom in 2013. His personal decorations include the Meritorious Service Medal with Gold Star in lieu of fifth award, the Navy and Marine Corps Commendation Medal with Gold Star, Joint Service Achievement Medal, and the Navy and Marine Corps Achievement Medal (Defense Video & Imagery Distribution System, 2013).

Courtesy Defense Video & Imagery D.S.

Col. Wolford **(left)**, the new commanding officer, accepts the regimental colors for Combat Logistics Regiment 2, 2nd Marine Logistics Group from Col. Whiteside during a change of command ceremony aboard Camp Lejeune, N.C., June 18, 2014. Whiteside commanded CLR-2 for nearly two years.

LCdr. HERMAN G. PLATT graduated from Dudley in 1972. In 1974, he accepted the call to ministry while serving with the Air Force in Okinawa, Japan. After returning to the United States for a short time, in 1978, he was ordained by Bishop Ithiel Clemmons at Wells Memorial COGIC. He returned to Okinawa, Japan, on a second tour and was made pastor of Calvary COGIC by Bishop Archie Buchanan. Operating as District Superintendent, Elders Council president, and fulfilling other duties, he established the church as the headquarters church for the Japan Jurisdiction. While in the Air Force, he achieved the rank of Master Sergeant, and later while in the Navy, he attained the rank of Lieutenant Commander.

In 1984, Elder Platt founded and established the work of the COGIC at the Upper Room Church in Son Tong City, Ozan Korea. Platt returned to the United States and completed seminary training at the Southern Baptist Theological Seminary

LCdr. HERMAN G. PLATT

graduating with a master's degree in divinity. Following graduation, Elder Platt transferred to the United States Navy Chaplains' Corp and served until his retirement from the military with 28 years of service.

Platt holds a Doctor of Philosophy degree from Brentwick University of the United Kingdom where he graduated Magna Cum Laude and is a candidate for the Doctor of Ministry degree from Regent University in Virginia Beach, VA. He holds a Master of Divinity degree from Southwestern Theological Seminary, Fort Worth, TX, a Bachelor of Science degree from the University of Maryland, College Park, MD, and he holds a certificate of completion as a Clinical Pastoral Education Clinician for the United States Navy. He has undertaken additional studies toward a master's degree in human resources at the University of Oklahoma, Norman, OK.

In April of 2000, Elder Platt was appointed pastor of Wells Memorial COGIC in Greensboro, NC. during the annual State Convocation and formerly came to Wells as pastor during May of that year. Under his leadership, the church's community outreach expanded through the Street and Prison Ministries, Children's Ministry (The Wealthy Place), Couple's Ministry, Single's Ministry, College Ministry, and Food Bank. Platt became a Superintendent over the Winton-Salem District in 2014.

Supt. Herman G. Platt,
Pastor Wells Memorial
COGIC

CAPTAIN RAYMOND BRIAN CROSBY graduated from Dudley in 1997. His activities and Honors while a student at Dudley include Dudley Fellows, the Beta Club, National Honor Society, Varsity Football, Wrestling, Baseball. Crosby was All-Conference in Wrestling, and All-Conference and All-County Football. He was the 1996 and 1997 Male Athlete of the Year. He also served as Captain of the Football, Wrestling and Baseball teams during Senior seasons.

During his senior year, he accepted an appointment to the United States Naval Academy in Annapolis, Maryland. His post Naval Postgraduate School achievements include USNA -2001/ NPS-2007; BS, English, MS-Systems Engineering Analysis; and Joint Professional Military Education.

Since graduating Crosby has served in the United States Navy. His highest Rank: Captain (O-6). His military honors include the Navy Achievement Medal, the Navy Commendation Medal (x2), three Meritorious Service Medals, a National Defense Medal, a Global War on Terrorism Service Medal, and a Global War on Terror Expeditionary Medal. In 2014, while in command of USS TYHOON received Battle Effectiveness Award, recognizing USS TYPHOON as the top performing ship in Patrol Coastal Squadron One; Twice recognized as the #1 Commanding Officer in the squadron. Crosby's community involvement include Membership on the Surface Navy Association, National Naval Officers Association, Kappa Alpha Psi Fraternity, Inc., Naval Academy Minority Association; Assistant Cub Scout Den Leader Pack 289, Dumfries, VA; and Cub Scout Den Leader Pack 535, Jacksonville, FL.; He served as a weekly speaker during a virtual summer program during the summer of 2020 in the midst of COVID to help students across North Carolina, South Carolina, and Georgia (Dr. T. D. Pressley). He volunteers as a motivational speaker to classes and has continued to donate his time and money to various programs and activities at Dudley.

A PLACE WHERE SUCCESS WAS EXPECTED: FINAL EDITION

COL. STEPHANIE QUERIDA QUINN HOYES WILSON graduated from Dudley in 1997. Her activities and honors while a student at Dudley include serving as Senior Class Parliamentarian and membership in several organizations: Dudley Ladies; Beta Club; National Honor Society; Dudley High School Marching Band; Dudley JR. ROTC (Cadet Commander), and the Drama Club.

Wilson attended Clemson University and earned a Bachelor of Science degree in Biology (2001); Embry University- Riddle Astronautical University (2004); University of the Rockies (2017: and the Air War College (2022). Post-secondary honors and awards include achieving Academic Distinction as a Master of Aerospace, Academic Distinction/Honors for PayD, Writing Award for Best Contribution to Leadership Research for Paper Titled: After the Flag, Post-Squadron Command Resiliency- Later published in the online journal; and Air University Military Instructor of the Year.

While serving in the United States Air Force Wilson achieved the rank of Colonel.

Courtesy Defense Video & Imagery D.S.

Col. Stephanie Q. Wilson (center), incoming 309th Missile Maintenance Group commander, accepts the guidon from Brig. Gen. Richard W. Gibbs, Ogden Air Logistics Complex commander, during a change of command ceremony June 22, 2023, at Hill Air Force Base, Utah. As part of the OO-ALC, the mission of 309th MMXG spans seven states and five Air Force bases around the country with over 750 personnel. (U.S. Air Force photo by Cynthia Griggs)

Wherever she is stationed in the Military, Wilson finds ways to serve the community. Examples of her service include developing and running the Black History Month contest for high School Students; being an Habitat for

Humanity Volunteer; annually collecting rolling suitcases for foster children-and individuals around the country, plus sending rolling suit cases to the local Child Services/CASA wherever she was stationed; using her promotion ceremony to collect school supplies for local children-over $500 worth of goods and supplies donated; participating in hurricane clean-up. She distributed food with the Salvation Army to those in need on her personal time; she participated in March of Dimes/Walk to End Alzheimer's/MS? Breast Cancer; volunteered to develop a 5k Walk/Run for local school in New Mexico; donated through Class Gifts to Dudley High School; and is a much-requested Speaker/Volunteer through-out the country. Wilson was the First female Air Force Air War College Class President AY22; Cheyenne Trophy – best military in region for mission and volunteer (Team won when I was squadron commander).

Her military awards include the Melbourne-Palm Bay New Female Engineer Award; Secretary of Air Force Leadership Award, Meritorious Service Award (Six times); Air Force Commendation (Two Times); Joint Service Achievement Medal; Military Outstanding Unit Award (Six times); AF Organizational Excellence Award (2 times); Military Outstanding Volunteer Service; Nuclear Deterrence Service Medal. She is also active in the Delta Sigma Theta Sorority serving as the Physical and mental Wellness Lead at Colorado Springs Alumnae Chapter and as Delta Sigma Theta- Decorations Chair for Community Scholarship Event (JBD Educational & Sports HOF.HOD).

Lt. Col. Clifton Girard Johnson

Clifton Girard Johnson (Center) in uniform, chatting with 1969 classmates.

Johnson graduated from James Benson Dudley High School in 1969. He was one of Dudley's first Air Force ROTC Cadets. He graduated from North Carolina A&T State University in 1974 with a B.S in Engineering. He also has a master's degree from Troy State University. He served 25 years in the United States Air Force as a systems inspector.

Lt. Col. Wendell Johnson

Johnson graduated from James Benson Dudley High School in 1970. He shared a love of model planes and ROTC with his brother, Clifton. He joined the Air Force and stayed in as a Career Man for 19 years. The brothers made the rank of lieutenant colonel on the same day. Wendell was a commander of academics at the fighter weapons school- the operations officer of the 57th Wing's F-15E Division at Nellis Air Force Base in Nevada.

*Lt. Col. Clifton Girard Johnson contributed the following selection to the book, **The Art of the Hustle. Lessons in Becoming a Man***

The Panther 1969 Yearbook

Clifton and Wendell Johnson started their military careers in Dudley's Airforce ROTC Unit.

Family, God, and Country
A Brother and a Friend

If you live long enough, there will be dark days. Some of those dark days will be of your own making and others will come down on you so hard and so fast that you feel as though heaven and hell are caving in on you at the same time. Some of the darkest days of my young adult life were of my own making.

I had graduated from James B. Dudley High School in 1969 and was a freshman at North Carolina A&T State University. Since my family lived in Greensboro, my parents saw no reason for me to live on campus.

My father had always had a very strict set of what he called his "House

Rules." I was a grown man-18 years old. None of my new friends had curfews. Anyway, parties didn't really get started until after 10:00p.m. It didn't make sense to me that a grown man- a college man- should have the same curfew that he'd had in high school.

The first night I stayed out late, my Dad was waiting up for me.

He said, "Did you forget that this is my house and my rules?"

"I said, "No, sir." And when he didn't say anything else, I went on to bed.

The next time, all he said was, "My house. My rules."

The third time I came home late, my clothes were packed up on the front porch. The house was dark and for the first time the doors were locked. None of us kids had ever needed keys because my mother did not work outside the home and at night we were required to be in before my Dad locked the doors before going to bed. I gathered my clothes and went to spend the rest of that night on the floor in a friend's room in Scott Hall.

I waited until I knew that my dad would be home from work the next day before going to talk to my parents. I knew that even if my mother wanted me to come back, she would not go against Dad's wishes. When Dad got home, I asked him why he'd put me out without warning.

He said, "I told you twice. My house. My Rules. Any child of mine who's too grown to follow my rules can't live here."

I think he wanted me to promise that I would never stay out late again and beg him to take me back. I didn't say a word.

I went and found a friend who didn't like staying on campus and we rented an apartment together. I had to get two more jobs to cover my share of the bills and buy food. I say two more jobs because I already had a work-study job on campus working in the cafeteria. Having to work two additional jobs while going to college sucked almost all the fun out of college. I wasn't all that big on having fun anyway. Two of the nights that I'd stayed out late I was in Scott Hall swapping tales with a couple of guys. I wasn't really a party person.

Anyway, I had a very solid reason for wanting to do well in college. One of my teachers at Dudley had said, "Clifton, you are never going to amount to anything because you have a bad attitude. You'll probably end up on the street." I made up my mind that day that I would graduate from college and go back and wave my diploma in her face. So, I worked three jobs so that I could stay on my own and make my own "house rules." I graduated in 1974 with a degree in engineering and entered the United States Air Force as a commissioned officer.

A PLACE WHERE SUCCESS WAS EXPECTED: FINAL EDITION

****

August 10, 1992, was one of those dark days that hit my body and spirit so hard that I couldn't see an end to the hurt. That was the day that my brother and best friend Lt. Col. Wendell "Sheik" Johnson died. Even after I left home, we were as close as we'd ever been. Every kid who grows up in a home as strict and structured as ours needs a friend. You know what I mean, someone you can complain and let off steam to without worrying that what you say will go any further. Someone who will take your side right or wrong, but let you know, without dressing it up, when you are wrong. Wendell was that someone for me - a friend and brother.

Growing up with Wendell was a grounding force in my life. We grew up in the Dudley Heights section of Greensboro, North Carolina on Ross Court. It was a very close-knit community of strong, middle class, working families. Our parents were very much involved in our education at Bluford Elementary, Lincoln Junior High School and James B. Dudley High School. We attended Grace Lutheran Church and the community, schools and church added even more structure to what our parents gave us at home.

My parents lived in the same house that we grew up in the rest of their lives and my brother Wendell planned every family Reunion to coincide with his three weeks of leave. I cannot put into words how much that "home place" means to me now. I understand now that it was more than just a place of "house rules"- it was, and still is, about family. It is about making the kinds of shared memories that help you get through those dark, dark days when the ones you shared them with are gone.

At family get-togethers we talk about how Wendell would always be the one to step in and stop any disagreements before fists started to fly. We laugh about how we would tease him about the time when he was five and climbed behind the wheel of Dad's car, released the brake, and rolled the car down a hill and into a tree. We smile knowing that if that had been any of us kids other than Wendell, we probably would not have made it to our next birthday. We speak quietly when we remember how he was so much into every activity at Grace Lutheran Church that our parents were convinced that he was going into the ministry.

No family gathering is complete until each of us reminisces about the many small acts of kindness Wendell was known for doing without being asked. We talk about how he was always willing to help out-doing more than his share of any task. Then we get quiet remembering that it was his willingness to work, although he was technically still on leave that led to his death. You see, he went to work on August 10,

1992, on a practice flight in place of the scheduled systems officer who called out because of a family emergency. Yes, there are some memories that all of us- his family, his friends, his co-workers share, but there are some that only Wendell and I shared.

I suppose that among siblings there are always differences in the way "blood" connects. There were six of us, but Wendell was special in different ways to each of us. Wendell and I were each other's best friend. Neither of us ever made a major decision without running it by the other one. We shared a love of model planes and ROTC. We joined the Air Force together and stayed in as Career Men (Wendell 19 years and me 25 years). We made the rank of lieutenant colonel on the same day. We both loved our job assignments in the military. Wendell was a commander of academics at the fighter weapons school- the operations officer of the 57th Wing's F-15E Division at Nellis Air Force Base in Nevada. I was a systems inspector whose job required me to travel to military bases all over the world. Although I was only home thirty days a year, Wendell and I remained close.

There is a certain camaraderie among men in the military. It comes with the structure and tight discipline. It's there in the preparation for duty. It is bread in the loyalty to our country and the trust that in times of danger we have each other's back.

Wendell and I had all that long before we joined the military.

Lt. Col. Clifton Girard Johnson

The "Colonel" was the first African American, as well as the first member of the U.S. Air Force to head a Defense Logistics Agency security / support force.

Chapter Seventeen

Dudley's "New Kind of Pioneers"

The late 1950s and 1960s ushered in the era of a new kind of pioneer: the brave souls who volunteered to cross racial and social lines to integrate the educational institutions of the South. Hardy young pioneers like Claudette B. White, Gene Kendall, Walter Johnson, David Dansby, and many others deliberately placed themselves in social and educational situations that set legal and social precedents that paved the way for future generations. All of them were young by any standards, and all of them were what Mr. Chavis, the principal of Lincoln Junior High School, referred to as the "best and the brightest" of their generation. It was not surprising that many of these pioneers were student athletes because the title "student" always came first at Dudley.

I learned that lesson about high academic standards before I became a student at Dudley. When I was in the ninth grade at Lincoln Junior High School, all everyone was talking about one day was the fact that Dudley's star basketball player would not be able to play in the championship game Friday night because he'd received a "D" in a core subject.

"I bet everyone is mad at that teacher," I said to my sister Gloria who was a junior at Dudley.

"Mad at the teacher for what? Teachers don't give grades; students make grades. She gave him what he made. We're angry at him. He knows the rules. He let his team down and the whole school down," Gloria sounded condescending as though she would have expected even a mere 9th grader to understand such a simple concept.

Generations of Dudley Student-Athletes understood that they had to have a minimum "C" average in all core subjects (English, Mathematics, Science, etc.) to participate in team sports long before High School Athletics Associations set uniform academic standards in the early 1980s. Eddie Favors, a star player on Dudley's first undefeated team to win a State Championship says, "The 1951 Football team was special in a lot of ways. One of them being that several members of this team were honor students and three or four were members of the National Honor Society."

However, it was more than the high academic standards that enabled Dudley's athletes to excel in what were at the time extremely hostile environments. Joyce Spruill summed it up during a December 9, 2015, meeting at Jones Elementary School. She said,

> "Sports is the great equalizer. Physical education and sports, if taught correctly, cuts across social, cultural, economic, and racial lines. When someone is a member of a team- they have a sense of belonging, and it does not matter who their parents are as long as they perform. Team spirit can transform a school and unite a student body like nothing else."

For all of the Dudley Pioneers who ventured forth to colleges and universities like UNC-Chapel Hill, Duke University, UNC-Greensboro, North Carolina State University, Wake Forest University, Rice University and the University of Minnesota, their paths in life were "marked" by the paths that they chose and for all of us their paths marked the way for better resources and extended career choices. To the Dudley Pioneers who were the first to integrate numerous fields, we are forever proud to walk the path your courage marked for us.

THOMAS EDISON ALSTON (January 31, 1926 – December 30, 1993) was a Major League Baseball first baseman who played for the St. Louis Cardinals from 1954 to 1957, the first African American to do so. A native of Greensboro, North Carolina, he stood 6'5' "200 cm) and weighed 210 pounds (95 kg).

Alston was acquired by St. Louis via a trade with the San Diego Padres of the Pacific Coast League, where he played in 180 games in 1953, on January 26, 1954, after team president Gussie Busch told manager Eddie Stankey to find a black player. Not only did Busch think excluding blacks from baseball was morally wrong, his company Anheuser-Busch, which had bought the team a year earlier to keep them from moving to Milwaukee, sold more beer to African American patrons than any other brewery, leading him to fear the effect of a boycott.

Busch was somewhat disappointed by Alston because he did not live up to the on-field exploits of Jackie Robinson and because when he reported to the Cardinals, the team learned he was two years older than the Padres had claimed. Busch demanded they return $20,000 the Cardinals had included with the trade to account for two seasons that Busch believed the team could not get from Alston.

A PLACE WHERE SUCCESS WAS EXPECTED: FINAL EDITION

When he made his Major League debut (April 13, 1954, at Sportsman Park), he became the first black player in St. Louis Cardinals history. He played in 66 games during his rookie season, batting .246 with 4 home runs and 34 runs batted in. After that, he got into 25 more games over the course of the next three seasons. He spent most of his major league career splitting time between the majors and the Class AAA Omaha Cardinals, where he had a .306 batting average and 21 home runs in 1956.

Career totals for 91 games include a .244 batting average (66-for-271), 4 home runs, 36 RBIs, 30 runs scored, and an on-base percentage of .311. In his 81 appearances at first, he handled 680 out of 689 total chances_ successfully for a fielding percentage of .987, just slightly under the league average during his era.

In 1990, Southern singer/songwriter and poet Bruce Piephoff recorded a song which told the story of Tom Alston's' journey to the big leagues and the years that followed. The song was titled "B's Foot in the Door."

LOU HUDSON. "The best basketball player Dudley has ever produced," was how his coach, Mr. Furcron, described his star player in 1962.

Louis Clyde Hudson was born on July 11, 1944, in Greensboro, N.C. He was a multisport star at Dudley High School playing football and basketball. He was one of the top basketball prospects in the state as a senior in 1962. When he graduated from Dudley, Hudson planned to play for North Carolina A&T State University, but when the University of Minnesota offered him a scholarship, an A&T coach told him to accept it. "He told me I should take this opportunity to play in the big time, that I was good enough for that," Hudson told *The Charlotte Observer* in 2009. "And he was right."

As a junior at Minnesota, Hudson averaged 24.8 points and 10.7 rebounds and was named an all-American while leading the Golden Gophers to a second-place finish in the Big Ten. He played much of his senior season with a cast on his shooting hand after breaking a bone in his right wrist, but he still averaged 19 points per game, often shooting left-handed. He had played hurt before. In a 1964 defeat of Purdue, he scored 36 points, 24 of them after hitting his head on the backboard, an injury that required stitches during the game. His jersey number 14 was later retired in Minnesota and in Atlanta, where the Hawks first played in the 1968-69 season.

Drafted fourth overall by the Hawks in 1966, when they were based in St. Louis, he was the first Dudley basketball player to be drafted in the first round. He was also drafted by the Dallas Cowboys in 1966. Hudson was a 6-foot-5 swingman who could play guard or small forward. According to Yardley (2014), "He was known as Sweet Lou, not least because his "sweet" jump shot that left his hands quickly, high over his head and went down oh so smoothly."

Odum (2014) stated, "Hudson went on to average at least 24 points per game for five consecutive seasons beginning in 1969-70. His NBA career average was 20.2. Hudson spent his last two seasons playing for the Los Angeles Lakers." In his final season, 1978-79, he shot 51.7 percent. His number 23 jersey is one of only three numbers retired by the Atlanta Hawks.

After his playing career, Hudson moved to Park City, Utah, where he pursued business interests and started a recreational program, the Growth League. "It teaches life skills through basketball," he told *The Times*. "They spend an hour in the classroom and an hour in the gym." In 2003, an association of retired NBA players named him the humanitarian of the year. In Park City, Hudson was elected to the City Council in 1993. He is believed to have been the first African American elected official in Utah. His campaign signs read, "Sweet Lou for You."

He was inducted in the North Carolina Sports Hall of Fame in 1988. Hudson was a college and pro basketball star. He broke his wrist as a senior but still made third-team AP all-American. Hudson scored 1,329 points in his college career, averaging 20.4 points per game. He was the leading scorer for U.S. gold-medal team, 1965 World University Games. Fourth pick, 1966 NBA draft, by St. Louis Hawks. Member of all-rookie team, 1967. Stayed with franchise when it moved to Atlanta after 1968 season, playing through 1977. With Los Angeles Lakers, 1978–1979. Second-team all-NBA, 1970. Played in six all-star games, scoring 66 points. Finished in top five scorers three times. Peak of 27.1 points per game, 1973. NBA career total 17,940 points, average of 20.2 points per game. Nicknamed Sweet Lou. He was inducted into the NBA Hall of Fame in September of 2022.

A PLACE WHERE SUCCESS WAS EXPECTED: FINAL EDITION

CHARLES ALVIN SANDERS. (August 25, 1946-July 2, 2015) Charlie Sanders embodied the term "Dudley Student Athlete." No matter how far he went in life or how many accolades he earned, he remembered his Dudley roots and gave credit to the coaches and teachers at Dudley. Mills (2011) described one of the many times Charlie Sanders came home to Dudley. Sanders returned to the Hometown Hall of Famer Ceremony in November of 2011. Dudley got a plaque honoring one of its own, a star at the University of Minnesota and All-Pro tight end for the Detroit Lions from 1968-1977. Sanders got a chance to tell stories of sacrifice. Mills wrote:

Sanders, who lives in the Detroit suburbs, saw a changed Dudley. He saw other plaques honoring his coaches and mentors; men named Boyers and McKee and Furcron.

And he was moved.
"I was astounded. My first thought was," Sanders began, his voice cracking. He cleared his throat. "Your life was touched by greatness. Those three men were instrumental in my life."
The coaches, Sanders said, didn't want their athletes to waste opportunities they themselves never had as young men.
"They taught values," Sanders said. "Even today, I look back and say, 'I learned that in high school from this teacher or that coach.' It was a tough time back then for young black athletes. The coaches were fundamentally sound and stern. Rarely did you see a soft side of them. They had to project that tough image."
Sanders can be tough, too.
He challenged the students in the room to work to overcome problems created by his generation.
He told them the story of his father, Nathan, a farmer-turned-engineer who valued education above all. A man who raised three sons on his own after Sanders' mother died when he was 2. A tough professor at N.C. A&T "who even gave Jesse (Jackson) an F once."

Sanders shares his father's value on education.

"Your mind can be your greatest asset or your biggest liability," he said. "It's the only tool out there that the more you use it, the sharper it gets. And the less you use it, the duller it gets."

"Fifty years ago, I sat in those same wooden seats, wondering where my life was going," Sanders told the students. "Fifty years later, I look around this room and realize: Who I am, where I've been, what I've learned — all of it started right here."

These words give us an indication of some of the reasons why many people refer to Charles Sanders as not only one of the best student-athletes Dudley has yet to produce but also as one of Dudley's finest men.

Sanders was a member of Dudley High School Class of 1964. While a student at Dudley, Sanders was one of the few athletes that lettered in three major sports for three years. As a member of the football team, he played tight-end and was also a punter. In 1964, he was selected to the State Shrine All-Star Game. Charles was a starter in that game as a tight-end and also won the position as starting punter. As a member of the varsity basketball team, he worked his way into the starting lineup as a sophomore. Charles led Dudley to two District Championships and two appearances in the State 4A playoffs. Charles was also a star baseball player at the first base position. He led his team to two straight State 4A Baseball Championships.

Drafted by the Lions in the third round from the University of Minnesota in 1968, Charles Alvin Sanders was the only rookie that season selected to play in the Pro Bowl, and he finished second to then-teammate Earl McCullough for NFL Rookie of the Year honors. In his first season, he hauled in 40 passes for 533 yards and scored one touchdown, and perhaps the single-greatest game of his career occurred in the season finale when he grabbed 10 receptions for 133 yards against Washington. He would prove during his career his extraordinary ability by combining great leaping ability, big hands, strength, speed, and elusiveness—traits not common for tight ends of his era. Sanders was one of the first tight ends who brought experience in both high school and college of having played at the varsity level both football and basketball.

Picture Courtesy of NFL Pictures

As great of a player as Sanders was on the field, he had an even greater presence off the field helping countless charitable organizations. Sanders, who was the Lions' Assistant Director of Pro Personnel and affiliated with the Lions in various capacities for 40 years, was always committed to assisting community efforts. While a player, Sanders annually supported the

A PLACE WHERE SUCCESS WAS EXPECTED: FINAL EDITION

March of Dimes and was a United Way spokesman for the team. Throughout his life, he continued to assist many charities but focused his efforts on two that were particularly close to his heart - –the Family2Family Foundation of Michigan and the Charlie Sanders Scholarship Foundation. The Charlie Sanders Scholarship Foundation began in 2007 after a successful fundraiser with the Rochester (Mich.) Community House. The Foundation annually funds at least, two college scholarships for high school students in Oakland County. In time, Sanders hoped to expand the scholarships to all of Michigan as well as North Carolina, his home state.

Charlie Sanders was the first athlete from Dudley to be inducted into the NFL Pro Football Hall of Fame in 2007. He was also inducted as a member of the North Carolina Sports Hall of Fame. In 2003, Charles was inducted into the Dudley High School Educational and Sports Hall of Fame.

Picture Courtesy of the NFL Hall of Fame

Dr. Jo Evans Lynn, Ed.D.

JOHN GUY is a former football player, coach, recruiter, and front office executive with a career that spans more than 36 years. His career featured tenures with 6 NCAA Division I college football programs as well as 4 NFL teams. He worked alongside Hall of Fame owners, head coaches, and assistant coaches as well as guided many former players along their paths to the sport's highest honors, including NCAA Division I All-American Awards, NFL Pro Bowls, and both the NFL and College Football Hall of Fame.

As a partner with Vanguard Sports Group, Guy oversaw the Professional Development of players. He helped to empower them to navigate their career challenges and assisted them as they transitioned from the professional arena to life off the field.

During John's nine years in the front office of the Buffalo Bills, he served as the Vice President of Pro Personnel and Pro Personnel Director. Guy worked alongside the Director of Player Engagement, overseeing player development towards building empowerment and self-awareness, along with teaching and strengthening vital media skills and promoting professionalism both on and off the field.

His 26-year coaching career culminated with the Oakland Raiders in 1998, where he served for three seasons as Assistant Defensive Line Coach. From 1992-1994, John was Special Teams Coordinator for the Pittsburgh Steelers. The team compiled a winning season record over two seasons, reaching the playoffs each year. John was a finalist for the NFL's Special Teams Coach of the Year Award in 1993, voted on by his peers.

Before making the transition to the NFL, John was the Assistant Head Coach at the University of Kentucky for three years. He was one of the first African American in Southeastern Conference (SEC) history to earn that position. While at Alabama he coached the outside linebackers producing at the time one of the best outside linebacking corps, led by the late Derrick Thomas, Hall of Fame Inductee. Equally important, John led defensive units at Duke University and Georgia Tech and was one of the youngest coaches in the NCAA ranks. He served as a Graduate Assistant Coach and later became Assistant Defensive Line Coach at the University of North Carolina at Chapel Hill from 1973-1978. Guy was one of the top college recruiters in both the ACC and SEC.

John earned a Bachelor of Science Degree from North Carolina A&T State University and started at free safety and placekicker from 1969-1973. He attended graduate school at the University of North Carolina at Chapel Hill in Physical Education from 1973-1974. In 2003, John was among the first NFL front-office executives to complete the league's Program for Managers at Stanford University.

John is a speaker at the collegiate and professional coaching events. He has been a guest lecturer at both national and international symposiums. He is a mentor to rising front-office executives and football stars of tomorrow while living in Sarasota, Florida

KENNETH "BUTCH" HENRY was a standout quarterback at Dudley in 1964. Both his parents were on Dudley's staff. His mother, Mae Sue Henry, was the Chairperson of the Home Economics Department and Dean of Women and his father John D. Henry was a guidance counselor.

Mae Sue Henry   **Mr. John D. Henry**

Butch Henry was smart and had, according to his coaches at Dudley, all the qualifications for the highly skilled position of quarterback.

Butch Henry became one of the first African American students to attend Wake Forest University on an athletic scholarship in 1964. When he went to Wake Forest University he was switched to halfback, perhaps because it was simply too soon to place a black man in the leadership position of quarterback on a predominately white football team. Even though he was playing a new position, Henry was a standout football player for the Deacons (Puckett, 2009). Kenneth Butch Henry ushered in the era of integrated sports teams at

Wake Forest and on other teams in the Atlantic Coast Conference.

Dr. Jo Evans Lynn, Ed.D.

STAHLE VINCENT took the term "student athlete" to new heights. He was a 1969 graduate of James B. Dudley High School. At Dudley, he was president of the National Honor Society, Senior Class President, Semi-finalist: National Scholar-Athlete of the Year, American Academy of Achievement, Dallas, Texas, Grant Award (leadership, academics and athletics), 3- Year letterman in football, basketball and baseball, MVP: baseball – three years, football – two years, All City in football and baseball, All Conference in football, Conference Player of the Year in football, All State in football, All Southeast in football and Honorable Mention All-American in football.

JBD

In addition to becoming the first African American to play quarterback at Rice University, he received many other honors. Among his honors and accomplishments at Rice are these: the George Martin Award as 1971 Most Valuable Player for Rice football, Rice nominee for Kern Tips Award presented by the Humble Football Network, several times member of President's Honor roll, served as a Fellow of Will Rice College (a key student advisor to the Master of College), SWC Academic All-Conference selection when only a sophomore, captain of his intramural basketball championship team, majored in commerce with consistent strong grades, aspired to an executive position in business after football (Drafted by Pittsburgh Steelers). In 1971 he set the SWC all-time record for most carries in a season (243), in 1971 set Rice all-time record most yards net rushing in a season (945), had an amazing 4-for-4 with 2 TDs for passing mark via halfback pass in 1971. Vincent also set additional Rice records such as: Most rushing plays for a season, most total plays (rush and pass), and the most rushing plays in a game.

Following his Graduation from Rice, Vincent was drafted by the Pittsburgh Steelers (he suffered a career-ending knee injury). He then got his master's degree in management at the University of Massachusetts after which he operated a men's clothing store (owner/operator) in Greensboro. He started his human resources career in 1984 with Cone Mills, a diversified textile manufacturer, located in Greensboro, NC, and as of 2007, is currently Director of Human Resources and Labor Relations for Cone Denim, a division of the International Textile Group, headquartered in Greensboro, NC. He received the Senior Professional in Human Resources (SPHR) certification in 2003.

He was a Charter Member of the James B. Dudley High School Educational Sports Hall of Fame.

Very active in the Dudley community, Vincent has served on numerous civic boards and committees for many years. He was also a volunteer youth sports coach for 20 years. He enjoys outside activities, especially bicycling.

He said, "I went to Rice looking for the same experiences as other college-bound teenagers. What I encountered was a unique set of challenges that prepared me for life after college." Stahle Vincent lived up to the qualities and expectations of those who recognized that he was an exceptional scholar athlete long before he reached the college level.

JOYCE SPRUILL is a pioneer in women's athletics and sports administration. During her time at Dudley, the basketball team on which she was the leading scorer was undefeated in 1970 and won the Citywide Championship. She was also a member of the Citywide Track Championship Team in 1970. In 1968, she set a softball throwing record at 235ft.

For her outstanding performances in three sports, she was named Dudley's Female Athlete of the Year in 1970. In the 1970-71 season, she became the first Black Female to be named Women's Softball MVP for the Greensboro Parks and Recreation Department. As a senior at Dudley, she was the only high school student invited to participate in the Annual Women's Athletic Association Sports Weekend hosted by A&T State University.

Although Title IX passed in 1970, it was not until 1975 when the Department of Health Education and Welfare (HEW) published the final regulations detailing the Title IX enforcement procedures for colleges and universities that received Federal assistance that most colleges got serious about providing equal opportunities in sports for women. During those years, Spruill was a standout in basketball at North Carolina A&T State University. When Spruill attended A&T, she captained the basketball team for four years and was the leading scorer during her last three years (Hayden, 1977). She continued to show her leadership skills by serving as Coordinator of Female Sports for the Intramural Department and coaching Lindley Junior High School to 2nd place while still a student at A&T.

Joyce Spruill scores during game at NC A&T State University

A PLACE WHERE SUCCESS WAS EXPECTED: FINAL EDITION

Pictures Courtesy Joyce Spruill

Far Left: Joyce Spruill as a star athlete at North Carolina A&T State University. **Center:** The year after graduation she became the AD of the Women's Sports Department. **Left:** Joyce is pictured with the Assistant Women's Basketball Coach.

Pictures Courtesy Joyce Spruill

Spruill graduated from A&T in 1975, the last year that women's basketball had intramural status. She was named A&T's first Women's Athletics Director and the Women's Basketball coach right out of college. That first year she says that the hardest part of her new position was the transition from student to a member of the athletic department. In an interview with Hayden (1977), Spruill said,

"The players I coached were the same ones I played with. I got more respect from the freshmen because they didn't know me. That year there were a lot of personality conflicts. The next year was fantastic. There was more spirit, more togetherness, and it was family-like. It was a group of girls who loved to play basketball. We are family, and we talk about whatever's wrong." p.14

Nicknamed the Aggiettes, the new Women's Athletics Program started out as a Division III NCAIA team. Coach Spruill is affectionately recognized as the mother of NCA&T Women's Basketball Program. According to Spruill, "Support for women's teams at A&T was tremendous. An average of over 1,000 spectators came out for each game. And when the women went against South Carolina State or a rival like Bennett College, Moore Gym was packed."

Dr. Jo Evans Lynn, Ed.D.

In addition to being Director of the Women's Athletic Program, she served in many other positions: volleyball coach, basketball coach, and softball coach. As the softball coach in 1979, she was the first African American coach of an HBCU to win an NCSIAW Division I State Softball Team Tournament. From 1988 until 2019, Joyce Spruill was a member of the Bennett College family. For 13 years, she served as basketball coach and volleyball coach and for a number of years as the Co-Chairperson of the Athletic Banquet, a Faculty Senate Member and Recruitment Committee Chairperson. She also held a faculty position in the Education Department, Advisor of Bennett College Student Association of Educators (SNCAE), Teacher Education Committee, and Faculty Development Committee.

In 1997, she became the first female inducted into North Carolina A&T State University's Sports Hall of Fame and in 2005, she was inducted into the James B. Dudley Sports and Educational Hall of Fame/Distinction

JBD

A PLACE WHERE SUCCESS WAS EXPECTED: FINAL EDITION

Pam Doggett: Simply The Best

Pam Doggett
James B. Dudley Track & Field Star Fall 1983- Spring 1986

Entering her first year at Dudley, 15-year-old sophomore Pam Doggett was already a national junior champion in the 100-meter hurdles and heptathlon. In her first Regionals at Dudley, she won two individual events and was a member of two winning relays. Her efforts helped the Panthers, who had not even fielded a team two years before, earn a third-place finish (Bulla, 1984).

"It's a real pleasure to coach a group of girls like this," said Dudley coach Lonnie Phifer. "It helps immeasurably to have somebody like Pam Doggett. Pam's one of a kind. She can do it all."

Doggett captured the 100- and 200-meter hurdles, establishing meet records in both events with times of 14.01 and 28.85, respectively She ran the second leg on Dudley's winning 400- and 800-relay teams, with a meet record coming in the former.

When she joined the Greensboro Pacesetters, she first concentrated on the 200 Yard-Dash in an All-Comers Meet. Because she was late to a meet not too long after that, Pacesetter's coach Charlie Brown entered her in a hurdles event to send a message. As it turned out, the "good sprinter was a great hurdler," according to Charlie Brown (Bulla, 1984).

The secret to Doggett's success was her year-round training, which came under Brown's guidance since she was in the sixth grade. Brown enters his athletes in The Athletics Congress (governing body of amateur track in the United States) and College meets. Doggett, for instance, finished second in the 100 hurdles in the prestigious Atlantic Coast Relays at N.C. State in March of 2024.

Brown says that such quality competition is not the only thing that molded the 5-2, 127-pound bundle of brawn into one of the nation's top young athletes.

"Parental support is the difference with Pam," Brown is quoted as saying of Doggett. "There are several factors that make a quality athlete, but this separates Pam from the others I've coached."

Pam Doggett established herself as one of the nation's top teenage sprinters of the 1980s. An eight-time high school state champion who set six meet records, she was named the NCHSAA Female Athlete of the Year in 1986 (for all sports), as well as the North Carolina Gatorade Track and Field Girls Athlete of the Year, and the MVP of the 1986 state 3A/4A Championships. Doggett made her mark at the international level in 1984 when she finished second at the USATF Juniors in the heptathlon and qualified for Team USA in the Pan American Junior Championships by placing third. Doggett was honored as one of "100 to Remember" at the NCHSAA Centennial Celebration in 2013 and inducted into the Dudley High School Hall of Fame in 2015 and the North Carolina High School Track and Field Hall of Fame in 2023.

NORTH CAROLINA HIGH SCHOOL TRACK & FIELD AND CROSS COUNTRY HALL OF FAME CLASS OF 2023

PAM DOGGETT, DUDLEY HIGH SCHOOL (GREENSBORO)
* NCHSAA Female Athlete of the Year, 1986 (for all sports)
*North Carolina Gatorade Track & Field Girls' Athlete of the Year (1986)
*3A/4A state meet MVP, 1986
*8-time state outdoor track champion (5 individual, 3 relay), setting 6 state meet records (there was no indoor meet when Doggett competed)
—won the 100-meter hurdles twice (1985 and 1986, setting an all-class record in 1986); 200-meter hurdles (1984, setting a state meet record); 300-meter hurdles (1985 and 1986, setting an all-class record of 42.00 in 1986 that stood for 25 years); 4×100-meter relay (1984); 4×200-meter relay (1984, setting a state meet record) and 4×400-meter relay (1986, setting a state meet record).
*1986 USATF National Junior Olympic Champion 100 m Hurdles
*1986 USATF National Junior Olympic Champion 4×100 Relay,
*1984, 2nd at USATF Juniors (under 20) in the heptathlon
*1984, 3rd at Pan Am Junior Championships in the heptathlon
*1984 USATF National Junior Olympic Champion 100 m Hurdles and national record in the heptathlon
*1983 USATF National Junior Olympic Champion 100 m Hurdles
*1983 USATF National Junior Olympic Champion Heptathlon

A PLACE WHERE SUCCESS WAS EXPECTED: FINAL EDITION

She was beyond a doubt one of the best track and field performers in North Carolina history who excelled at hurdles… The Dudley legend holds the second-best all-time mark in state in the 100-meter hurdles (when hurdles measured 30") and the eighth best all-time record in the 100-meter hurdles once the hurdles were increased to 33" in 1984. She additionally holds the third best mark in NC for the 300-meter intermediate hurdles and has posted a top 15 all-time long jump distance. She was also conference player of year in basketball as senior and won the inaugural Pat Best Memorial Trophy when she was named the NCHSAA Female Athlete of the Year in 1985-'86.

Pam Doggett of Greensboro Dudley set a national record in the 100-meter hurdles in 1986 when she won the NCHSAA championship in 13.88 seconds.

Although Our Domination of Women's Track and Field Began In the 1980s with Pam Doggett and Her Teammates, it continues...

Dr. Jo Evans Lynn, Ed.D.

Strong, Skilled, Relentless:

Dudley's Women Dominate in Sweep of State Indoor & Outdoor Track & Field

The women of James B. Dudley High School dominated Track and Field events in the State Championships during the period from 1984-1993 winning eight State Championships in 1984 (Out-door), 1985 (Out-door), 1986 (In-door), 1989 (In-door & Out-door Titles), 1990 (In-door & Out-door Titles), and 1993 Outdoor). Twenty years passed with the Women's track and field teams coming close like they did in 2022 coming only 5 points behind the eventual champions.

In 2023, domination returned with the Dudley women adding a tenth State Championship when Dudley's Women's Track and Field Team won the NCHSAA 3A State Championship at NC A&T State University to complete an indoor-outdoor sweep. It was the third sweep of both the In-door and Out-door State Track and Field Championship in the school's history with the previous times being in 1989 and 1990.

The Dudley Panthers used several second-place finishes to climb to the top of the team standings at the NCHSAA 3A Women's Track and Field Championships. Dudley scored a Team Total of 70 points. This placed them 21 points ahead of Statesville in second. Dudley junior Senadzi Rankin claimed second in the 100 Meter Hurdles and was a part of the relay team that included Dorothy Braswell, Tanzania Washington, and Nilijah Darden that took second in the 4×100. The Panthers also placed second in the 4×200 (Nathalya Daniels, Dorothy Braswell, Gabrielle Cheek, & Nilijah Darden) and took third in the 4×400 (Aa'Niyah Massey, Keianna Mims, Dorothy Braswell, Nathalya Daniels). Noelle Millner added second place in the discus.

Domination continued in 2024 when Dudley's Women's Track Team won their fourth sweep! The James B. Dudley High School women's track teams secured the 3A Woman's Indoor Track State Championship in 2024. They finished the day with **62 points**, beating out second-place Atkins' 44-point performance. The James B. Dudley High School female track teams also secured the 3A State Championship in Outdoor Track in 2024. They performed exceptionally well, with junior Jaylee Brown setting a state meet record in the 100-meter dash and claiming victory in the 200-meter dash. Additionally, Dudley's 4x100 and 4x200 relay teams took first place.

It is the Dudley women's seventh outdoor state title (1984, 1985, 1989, 1990, 1993, 2023 & 2024) and fifth In-door State Championship

(1986,1989,1990,2023 & 2024). It is the **fourth sweep** in the school's history with the previous times being in 1989, 1990, and 2023. These wins make the Dudley Women's Track & Field Team the ALL-TIME winningest sports team in the schools 145-year history (1879-2024).

2023 In-door Women's Track & Field State Champions

Row 1, Left-Right: Dynasty Franklin, Dorothy Braswell, Madison Crowder, Tequille Jackson, Tyla Gamble, Andre Rivers, James Pinnix

Row 2, Left to Right: BJ Felix, Nilijah Darden, Gabrielle Cheek, Derrick Wheeler, Robert Butler

Top Row, Left-Right: Kari Parker, Serenitie Johnson, Lyric Watkins, Nathalya Daniels, Tanzania Washington, Senadzi Rankin, Shamalia Carpenter, Jordan Johnson, Aa'Niyah Massey

Dr. Jo Evans Lynn, Ed.D.

2023 Out-door Women's Track & Field State Champions

Row 1, Left-Right: Dynasty Franklin, Dorothy Franklin, Serenitie Johnson, Senadzi Rankin, Gabrielle Cheek, Aa'Niyah Massey, Madison Crowder, BJ Felix

Row 2, Left to Right: Andre Rivers, James Pinnix, Robert Butler, Logan Speight, Noelle Millner, Briana Haith

Top Row, Left-Right: Nilijah Darden, Tanzania Washington, Tequille Jackson, Derrick Wheeler, Nathalya Daniels, Kieanna Mims, Lyric Watkins

A PLACE WHERE SUCCESS WAS EXPECTED: FINAL EDITION

2023 State Champions Women's Indoor & Outdoor State Track and Field

Aa'Niyah Massey
Alicia-Leilani Rodriguez
Amaya Wright
Ayomide Onadeji
Christina McKinney
Dorothy Braswell
Gabrielle Cheek
Jade Meekins
Jordan Johnson
Kaelin Brown
Kari Parker
Keianna Mims
Kendall Penniegraft
Logan Speight
Lyric Watkins

Misa Brumbly
Nathalya Daniels
Nilijah Darden
Noelle Millner
Paige McKinney
Rylee Jackson
Sanai Wells-Scott
Senadzi Rankin
Serenitie Johnson
Shamilia Carpenter
Tanzania Washington
Tyla Gamble
Zariah Jones

Coaches: Tequilla Jackson (Boys & Girls Head Coach), Robert Butler, James Pinnix, Bj Felix, Dynasty Franklin, Briana Haith, Andre Rivers, Derrick Wheeler

Throughout the school's history participation in sports has continued to serve as a gateway to outstanding careers. This gateway status has been true for several scholar-athletes who played sports professionally and for hundreds more scholar athletes who never played professionally, but have made tremendous social, civic, and cultural contributions at the local, state, and national levels.

JEFFREY "JEFF" E. DAVIS Day was acknowledged by Greensboro Mayor John Forbis on Tuesday, May 18, 1982. The James B. Dudley High School Athletic Department, Booster Club, and the school's National Alumni Association also took part in celebrating the occasion. The 1978 graduate of Dudley where he stood out in three sports. He played college football at Clemson University (1978-1982) and was drafted in the 5th round to play professionally for the Tampa Bay Buccaneers. While a student at Dudley, Davis lettered in basketball, track, and football. He was "All State" and "All Metro" in football his senior year. Dudley retired his number "70" and placed it in the school's trophy case.

Picture Courtesy of NFL Sports

During the Jeff Davis Day celebration, Davis said, "It was first of all because of someone I believe in... that's the Lord. He's really been good to me. He gave me a lot of good friends. This is what made me successful. Behind every good man there's a woman, I had two--—have had my mother and my grandmother.

Davis went on to praise J. A. McKee, Dudley's Athletic Director as his favorite coach and father image. "Kids today have to have heroes or role models to inspire them. Coach McKee looked at players not only for athletic ability, but as a person."

While he played and attended Clemson where he earned a degree in Industrial Technology, he received numerous honors and awards. He was Atlantic Coast Player of the Year his senior year, All Conference, Defensive Player of the Game- Orange Bowl; "All Star" East-West Shrine Game; and he was a member of the Gold Bowl Team. As a defensive lineman at Clemson, he helped them beat Nebraska in the Orange Bowl Game to win a

A PLACE WHERE SUCCESS WAS EXPECTED: FINAL EDITION

National Championship. After his NFL career, Davis worked for Clemson Head Football Coach Debo Swinney as a mentor and advisor (Hood. D., 2016)

The Tampa Bay Buccaneers chose Davis in the fifth round (128th Pick overall) of the 1982 NFL Draft, and he played for the Buccaneers from 1982-1987. He became a starter during his second season and led the team in tackles three times. He finished his career starting 72 of 83 games, and compiled 662 tackles, four sacks and three interceptions in his six-season pro career.

Greensboro Daily News, SPECIAL TO NITE REPORT, May 1982

Jeff Davis receives award from Lola McAdoo, president of Dudley Alumni Association

CLARENCE GRIER was a 1983 Dudley graduate. While a student at Dudley, he was a member of the National Honor Society and played in the Marching Band. As a scholar athlete, he played Varsity Basketball for three years and was All-Conference Basketball in 1982 and 1983 and an All – Metro Boys Basketball Selection – 1983. He was also a High Jumper on the track team. Grier is known for his collegiate career at Campbell University between 1985 and 1987. Grier was the holder of 30 school records at the time of his graduation and was named the Big South Conference Player of the Year as a senior in 1986-87. He scored the Highest Points ever in a Campbell Basketball Game – 39.

Picture Courtesy J.B.D. Hall of Fame

At 6'7" tall Grier played the forward position. The year he was named the Big South's top player, Grier scored a school single-season-record 739 points behind 24.6 points per game average, which ranked 12th nationally. He finished his two-year career with 1,087 points.

He was selected by the Houston Rockets in the 1987 NBA Draft, although he never ended up playing in the National Basketball Association. After a stint playing for the Continental Basketball Association's Quad City Thunder, Grier retired from basketball and became a Certified Public Accountant (CPA) licensed in the Commonwealth of Virginia and the State of North Carolina. He is a Chartered Global Management Accountant (CGMA), and a Certified Information Technology Professional (CITP). During his professional life, Grier has been an upper management professional and fiscal officer for several governmental organizations. Clarence has balanced budgets and completes financial statements for these organizations that received the highest award that be bestowed on a governmental organization by the Government Finance Officers Association (Distinguished Budget Award and Distinguished Award in Financial Reporting). While at Orange County, North Carolina, Clarence improved the County's Bond ratings from AA to AAA for all bond-rating agencies (Moody's, S&P, and Fitch) which made Orange County, North Carolina of only 24 Counties in the United States with an AAA bond rating from all three rating agencies. Most recently, at Guilford County, Clarence oversees the day to operations of 8 departments, two external agencies, is a member of the Say

Yes Education Planning Committee and is instrumental in the development of the County's budget.

In 2001, he was inducted into the Campbell University Hall of Fame and the James B. Dudley Sports and Educational Hall of Fame/Distinction in 2015.

JBD

WILLIAM JOSEPH N. "JOEY" CHEEK, a 1997 graduate, extended Dudley's long history of athletic prowess by becoming an Olympian. Cheek started skating at Skateland USA, in Greensboro, as an inline skater. As an inliner, he was a junior national champion. Cheek set national junior records in the 1,500 and 3,000 meters and was a member of two junior world inline teams. Joey Cheek began speed skating in 1995. When he decided to pursue speed skating at the next level, he had to move to Livonia, Michigan where he could practice speed skating year-round.

Even though he moved away, he continued his education at Dudley through correspondence. In 2002, he credited his teachers at Dudley, especially Mrs. Gwendolyn Benton, for going beyond the call of duty to help him earn his diploma.

Picture Courtesy of USA Olympics 2006

Cheek competed at the 1997 and 1998 World Junior Championships in speed skating, and his first senior international appearance was at the 2000 World Sprint Championships. Until then he had been an all-rounder but soon began focusing on the sprints. In 2002, Cheek was seventh at the World Sprint Championships, but three weeks later surprised the world by winning the bronze medal in the 1,000 at Salt Lake City. Though Cheek was frequently on the podium, he had no World Cup wins in races until 2006, when he finally broke through and won the World Sprint Championships. He followed that win a few weeks later by winning his gold medal in the Olympic 500 and silver in the Olympic 1,000.

Cheek's accomplishments off the ice may be more impressive. After the Torino gold medal, Cheek donated his $25,000 award to the humanitarian group "Right to Play", which had been founded by former Norwegian speed skating legend [Johann Olav Koss]. He also donated $15,000 from his silver medal to the same group. Cheek has founded Team Darfur, an international group of athletes committed to raising awareness about the crisis in Darfur in Sudan. He retired from skating after the Torino Winter Olympics and attended Princeton, where he studied economics and Chinese. Cheek's teammates chose him to carry the US flag at the 2006 Closing Ceremony. Cheek has stated that his goal is to be President of the United States.

MARQUES LAMONT DOUGLAS, a 1995 graduate of Dudley High School was born March 5, 1977, in Greensboro, North Carolina. He played college football at Howard University. Douglas played in the National Football League for 12 years as a defensive end. He was signed by the Baltimore Ravens as an undrafted free agent in 1999. Douglas played for the Ravens in 1999 and was traded to the New Orleans Saints for the 2000 season and then back to the Ravens for the next four years.

Douglas also played for the San Francisco 49ers (3 years), New York Jets (1 year), and the Tennessee Titans for his final year in the NFL in the United States. He later played for Rhein Fire, an NFL Europe team and was on the roster for the Miami Dolphins and Tampa Bay Buccaneers.

Picture Courtesy of NFL Pictures

He lives and works in Charlotte, North Carolina. Douglas said of his business pursuits, "I love to work in Real Estate. I also enjoy hosting my own radio show, every week. I have been a real estate professional for over 12 years." He owns Team Douglas Properties and is the founder and CEO of Game Plan Strategies. In 2015, Douglas returned to Dudley as the Keynote speaker for the Decision Day and Communities in Schools Awards Ceremony. He encouraged students to develop a "Game plan" for their lives that focuses on their careers beyond high school. He was inducted into the James B. Dudley Sports and Educational Hall of Fame/Distinction in 2013.

BRENDAN TODD HAYWOOD was born on November 27, 1979, in New York, NY, to Barbara Haywood. He lived in Manhattan, Brooklyn, Queens, and Kew Gardens and then to Greensboro, NC. He attended high school at James B. Dudley High School. In speaking of his transition on his official web site his mother, Barbara says, "Brendan had a Southern accent in two days after moving from NY to NC!" I'm sure he didn't want the other kids to tease him because he sounded different. In two or three days, he fit right in. The adjustment was no problem." Brendan was always taller than other kids - –hen he was just six months old, he was getting mistaken for a 1-year-old!"

His mother also noted, "Brendan also played baseball and football growing up. He started with T-ball and was gifted at hitting homeruns and then got into football in high school. He was a natural at tight end! Basketball proved to really be his sport though. Magic Johnson was his man! When he heard that Magic had HIV, he came home and I thought someone close had passed away, because he was so upset."

Picture Courtesy of NBA Pictures

Brendan is an only child and got involved with basketball when he was in junior high. He wasn't graceful or fast and was cut from the team.

A PLACE WHERE SUCCESS WAS EXPECTED: FINAL EDITION

Annoyed with Brendan being cut, Ms. Haywood took Brendan to the YMCA in Greensboro, in a predominantly black neighborhood. They taught him the game and he played with them for about two years.

Brendan went on to play basketball in high school and helped lead Dudley to a state 4A championship during his junior year by averaging 10 points and 10 rebounds (and was able to play at the Smith Center for the first time!) He set a single-season state record that year with 182 blocked shots. Brendan went to Nike camp and had the chance to meet and play with other future NBA players like Ron Artest, Larry Hughes, and Elton Brand.

As a senior, Brendan averaged 14.8 points, 11.7 rebounds and 6.7 blocks and shot 78% from the floor. He was a two-time all-county selection, News & Record Guilford Player of the Year, and the MVP of the 1996 Little Four Christmas Tournament. When Brendan was named as a McDonald's All-American, Dudley High surprised him with a special assembly to honor him. As a senior at Dudley, Brendan won the Gatorade North Carolina Basketball Player of the Year Award, and he even received a key to the city!

Picture Courtesy UNC Pictures

After graduation, Haywood enrolled at the University of North Carolina at Chapel Hill for the 1997–98 season. Haywood was recruited by legendary Tar Heel basketball coach Dean Smith, but the coach retired shortly after Haywood's arrival on campus and turned the job over to his assistant, Bill Guthridge. Haywood backed up Makkhar Ndiaye at the center position his freshman season and was the most-used bench player after the six rotating starters. That season, the Tar Heels advanced to the National Semifinals of the 1998 NCAA Men's Division I Basketball Tournament.

Haywood moved into the starting lineup during his sophomore season. At UNC, Haywood recorded the first triple-double in school history against the University of Miami on December 4, 2000, with 18 points, 14 rebounds and ten blocks (which was also a UNC record). He also finished his college basketball career as the Atlantic Coast Conference's all-time leader in field goal percentage (63.7%) and is the Tar Heels' 'll-time leader in blocked shots (304). During his senior year, Haywood was named to the All-Atlantic Coast Conference 2nd Team, and also was named 2nd Team All-America by the Sporting News.

Haywood was selected by the Cleveland Cavaliers with the 20th overall pick in the 2001 NBA draft. He was later traded to the Orlando Magic, who in turn traded him to the Washington Wizards. While playing as the Wizards' starting center for the next six years, Haywood began putting up career numbers in the 2007–08 season.

On February 13, 2010, Haywood was traded to the Dallas Mavericks. On July 9, 2010, Haywood re-signed with the Mavericks to a reported six-year, $55 million deal. The Mavericks went on to win the 2011 NBA championship.

Brendan has been active in the community ever since he was in high school as he participated in numerous church and youth group programs. While at UNC, he visited the Ronald McDonald House of Chapel Hill on a regular basis. Once he was scheduled to visit the House but planned to cancel because he was sick with a bad cold. Other Tar Heels who scheduled for same visit also had to cancel. When he learned that no one else was going to visit the sick children and families, he got out of his sick bed and visited the families and kids anyways!

Brendan has established a fund to assist single parent families. The fund, which is officially called the "Brendan Haywood Single Parents Fund," is set up with the Community Foundation of Greater Greensboro in North Carolina. Brendan opened the fund by contributing a donation of $25,000.00. He plans on soliciting additional donations to help him provide grants to fund programs that assist underprivileged single parent families in North Carolina and Texas.

Brendan has a firsthand understanding of the trials and hardships that sometimes accompany children from single parent families. "My mother raised me as a single parent and she worked twice as hard to make sure I always had the things I needed," says Brendan. "I've seen other children from single parent families who haven't been as fortunate as me and needed a little extra help. I'm hoping this fund will provide support for numerous single parent families on various levels and help them during those times when they need a helping hand."

In the fall of 2011, Brendan's Fund provided a Back-to-School Cookout for mothers and children from the Greensboro YWCA. He provided

Nike backpacks filled with school supplies and fed over 140 people at the cookout (The Official Website of Brendan Haywood, 2015).

JBD

DEMARIO LAMONTE PRESSLEY was born on November 3, 1985. He graduated from Dudley in 2004. While a student at Dudley, he was considered one of the top defensive backs in the nation. Preseason (2003) he was voted All-State, All-American, and All-Conference. He attended North Carolina State University on a Football Scholarship. Pressley earned a Bachelor of Science Degree in Sports Management. He was drafted by the New Orleans Saints in the fifth round of the 2008 NFL Draft. In 2010, he became. On February 22, 2011, Pressley was acquired by the Indianapolis Colts but was waived on August 16, 2011. He was claimed by Denver the next day. He finished the 2011 season with the Carolina Panthers and was promoted to the active roster on December 30, 2011. He played in the final game of the season. On April 11, 2012, Pressley signed with the Chicago Bears. On August 21, 2012, Pressley was waived/injured by the Bears, and subsequently reverted to injured reserve on August 22, 2012.

On Signing Day 2004, Pressley signed to play at N.C. State. DeMario is pictured with his grandmother, Rosalyn Baker (Dudley, 1965).

Courtesy of NFL Pictures

DEMARIO LAMONTE PRESSLEY

He became Dudley's first Super Bowl Champion when the New Orleans Saints won Super Bowl XLIV.

He is the creator and CEO of Press IT Forward, Inc., a nonprofit. He is also the Sports Development Director for the Greensboro Eagles (2010-present). The Greensboro Eagles is an athletic program that provides training for elite athletes.

The Greensboro Eagles offer a wholesome, enjoyable experience in sports while teaching the core values of athletic competition. These values include teamwork, good sportsmanship, discipline, and respect for others. They leverage their experience to help athletes achieve peak performance, enhancing their skill set so they may compete at the highest level. Since 2015, he has been the Director of Marketing and Promotions for StudentConnect, LLC. StudentConnect is a dedicated career community that connects students and graduates with companies looking to hire young talent for internships, part-time jobs, and graduate careers in Singapore & Hong Kong.

A PLACE WHERE SUCCESS WAS EXPECTED: FINAL EDITION

DAVID AMERSON was born in Honolulu, Hawaii. He graduated from Dudley High School in 2010 where he played on the Panthers football team. Amerson spent most of his high school career at safety for Coach Stephen Davis. He participated in the Shrine Bowl following his senior season. He finished the year with 55 tackles and six interceptions and also averaged 14 yards per punt return. He finished his junior season with 60 tackles and nine interceptions.

Amerson attended North Carolina State University, where he played from 2010 to 2012. As a true freshman in 2010, he started nine of 13 games and recorded 50 tackles. Through 11 games of his sophomore season in 2011, Amerson had 51 tackles and led the nation in interceptions with 13. Following the 2011 season, he received the Jack Tatum Trophy for the best college defensive back, first-team All-American honors from the Walter Camp Football Foundation and ESPN, and first-team All-ACC honors. At the inaugural Belk Bowl for the ACC Football Championship held in Charlotte on December 27, 2011, Amerson finished the game with five tackles, two interceptions, and one touchdown.

The Washington Redskins selected Amerson in the second round, with the 51st overall pick, of the 2013 NFL Draft. He was the highest selected North Carolina State defensive back since Dewayne Washington in 1994. He played three years for the Redskins. Amerson was claimed off waivers by the Oakland Raiders on September 22, 2015. He picked up the team's defensive scheme well and eventually became a starter for the Raiders. In Week 9, he recorded his first interception with for Raiders against the Pittsburg Steelers quarterback, Ben Roethlisberger. Amerson had a noticeably outstanding performance in the Week 12 win against the Tennessee Titans, where he recorded an interception and six pass deflections. His six deflections set a new single-game, franchise record. He was second in the NFL with 25 passes defended during the 2015 season and was named most improved player by Pro Football Focus.

According to Long (2016), "While David Amerson has only spent one season with the Silver and Black, he found a way to make the most out of the opportunity in front of him. The former North Carolina State standout managed to record four interceptions for the Raiders in 2015, finishing behind only the great Charles Woodson in the category.

Amerson gives back to the Dudley Community through The David Amerson Defending Hands Foundation, which hosts an annual youth football camp at Dudley High School. David Amerson leads the camp featuring current and former NFL athletes, who direct campers through various training methods and drills to help improve football skills and conditioning. Other former college athletes, high school, and Pop Warner coaches help as well.

EMMANUEL MOSELY: UNDEFEATED

49ers News 2018

Emmanuel Moseley was the first player during the Steven Davis era to play quarterback and defensive back.

Greensboro Daily News 2019

All faithful Dudley Alumni watched Super Bowl LIV to see every defensive play in which the Dudley's own Emmanuel Mosely (#41) was involved.

Mosely led the Dudley Panthers Football Team to their third undefeated season (15-0). As a senior, Moseley passed for 1,370 yards, rushed for 1,443 yards, and accounted for 47 total touchdowns at quarterback and recorded 28 tackles and four interceptions on defense.

Becoming the best player on a team at Dudley is never easy. According, to his coach Steven Davis, the head football coach at Dudley High School, Mosely was willing to do what needed to be done to get him there.

Coach Davis said, "He came in as a slim 9th grader, played on JV for a couple of years, but he wasn't afraid. He had a whole lot of heart

A PLACE WHERE SUCCESS WAS EXPECTED: FINAL EDITION

on the field, in the weight room, or wherever."

"He's a great football player, but the reason I knew he was going to be successful was because he's a great kid," said Davis.

Moseley led the Panthers to the 2013 4AAA State Championship.

"He might have been the first I had to play quarterback and defensive back, but I knew defensive back was his way to school, but on the other hand, he was our best athlete, so I played him at quarterback," said Davis.

Moseley got an opportunity to play for Tennessee as a cornerback and he made the most of it. He waited to hear his name called in the 2018 NFL Draft, but that moment never came.

Not long after, that chance finally came, in the form of a contract with the San Francisco 49ers.

"It's exciting," said Davis. "It gives the guys behind him hope to just continue to work hard, do the right thing, and the sky is the limit. Be ready when your number is called. Emmanuel didn't start the first two playoff games and now we're going to the Super Bowl with a starting defensive back from Dudley."

In Super Bowl LIV, Moseley recorded 5 tackles and 1 pass deflection in a 31-20 loss to the Kansas City Chiefs.

In Week 5, against the Carolina Panthers, Moseley suffered a season-ending torn left ACL. He was placed on injured reserve on October 15, 2022

On March 16, 2023, Moseley signed a one-year contract with the Detroit Lions. Still recovering from his injury sustained the prior season, he was placed on the physically unable to perform list on August 2.[30] In Week 5 of the 2023 season, against the Carolina Panthers, Moseley returned to play, but suffered a season-ending ACL tear in his right knee.

Corey Kimber and Eric Kimber Make It to the Professional Level

When **COREY KIMBER** was drafted by the San Diego Padres in the 25th round of the 2012 Major League Baseball Amateur Draft, it had been a long time since Reggie Ramert was drafted in the 33rd Round by the Blue Jays and even longer since Bill Bethea played on the minor league teams of Pittsburg and Atlanta (1953-1961). Not only was Cory drafted but he signed with a $120,000 bonus. Although Corey Kimber spent much of his first two seasons on the injured reserve list, he continued to work his way up to A level in the Minor League and moved up to the San Diego Padres single A affiliate Tri-City Devils in Seattle Washington.

His brother **ERIC KIMBER** signed a free-agent contract to pitch for the Kansas City Royals farm system. Eric, a pitcher, is also a former North Carolina Central Eagle. Although Kimber spent much of his three-year NCCU career in the outfield or infield, his opportunity at the professional level was as a pitcher. As a senior in 2015, the dynamic Eagle started 20 games at third base, 18 in left field, five at second base, two in right field, two at designated hitter and two as a pitcher. In three total pitching appearances that season, Kimber tossed just 5.0 innings.

A PLACE WHERE SUCCESS WAS EXPECTED: FINAL EDITION

Still, during his tryout just minutes away from his hometown, Kimber took full advantage of his 20 bullpen pitches by lighting the radar gun to between 92-94 miles per hour.

"The transition will be a challenge at first," Kimber said about making a full-time move to the mound. "(At NCCU) I was being used where I was needed, but now I can concentrate on pitching."

In three seasons at NCCU, Kimber accumulated 46.1 innings pitched in 19 appearances with 10 starts. Most of that work came in 2014 with 38.0 innings pitched in 14 appearances with seven starts.

"I feel like I have worked hard enough, and someone saw the effort," said Kimber, who graduated from NCCU in May of 2014 with a degree in psychology.

"The road was tough," he said about making the jump from Dudley High School to playing college baseball. "It humbled me – coming to college and having to work hard to earn a spot and keep a spot." Kimber was on the Kansas City Roster as a reserve pitcher when the team won the World Series in 2015.

Dr. Jo Evans Lynn, Ed.D.

Eric Hicks "The Helicopter" Gives Back

For the first time since its inception, James B. Dudley High School, and its feeder schools participated in the School Supply Give-a-Way at Peter's Auto Mall on South Main Street in High Point. Eric Hicks was responsible for making sure that Dudley was included in this massive School Supply Give-a-Way on Saturday, July 29, 2023, beginning at 8:00a.m.

When asked why it was so important to him that Dudley be included in the School Supply Give-a-Way, Hicks said, "When I saw how much was being sorted to give-out to churches and other local organizations, I asked if my school could be included too. The answer was a resounding, 'YES.' I know it's short notice, but it will be worth it if the school and students get what they need! It is important to me to give back in any way I can." Since items are packaged in bulk, everyone is encouraged to come in trucks or vans."

Eric attended James B. Dudley High School from 1998-2002. As a student at Dudley, Eric was a starting forward for three years. Eric was given the nickname "the Helicopter" by the legendary game announcer- Skip McCall, because of his phenomenal hang-time ability when going up for a dunk or a block. Eric received numerous honors and awards while playing at Dudley High School including: the single season shot-blocking record and the "most dunks in a single game". Both records still stand.

In 2000, he led the Men's Varsity Basketball team to state runner-up. "I loved that team", Eric says. He held the All-time leading scorer average. He was also a part of the 1000 points career club with an average of 31 points, 12 rebounds, and 7 blocks per game during his Senior year.

After graduating from James B. Dudley Sr. High School in 2002, Eric enrolled at the University of Cincinnati. He played basketball for the Bearcats for four (4) years under the leadership of coaches Bob Huggins, Andy Kennedy, and Frank Martin. His collegiate honors included the Oscar Robertson Awards for Cincinnati Bearcats, Honor Roll Award, Single Season Shot Block Record, and Humanitarian Award. When Eric played at Cincinnati, **Louisville head coach Rick Pitino was quoted as saying, "Eric Hicks is inch for inch, pound for pound the toughest ball player in America."**

After graduating from the University of Cincinnati, he played professionally for Telindus BC Oostende (Belgium), Polpak Swiecie (Poland), and CSK VVS Samara (Russia). He also had two stints in the NBA Summer League with the Miami Heat and Boston Celtics. **Honors:** Among the highlights of Hick's European career are a 2007 Belgian league championship and an appearance in the 2008 Polish league All-Star Game. He later played for Leite Río *Breogán*. In 2012, Hicks played football for the first time since he was in high school when he suited up for the Cincinnati Commandos of the United Indoor Football League as a wide receiver. **Hicks was inducted into the James B. Dudley High School Educational and Sports Hall of Fame on October 14, 2023.**

HENDON HOOKER. The expectations for Hooker have always been exceedingly high and he has proven again and again that he is more than up to the task. During the four years he played football at James B. Dudley High School, Hooker personified three aspects of the Dudley scholar athlete: work hard to enhance your God given talents; never give up; and believe that only your best is good enough. At 6ft. 5ins. tall and 210lbs he is what is considered to be the ideal height for a quarterback. During his high school career, he passed for 6,027 yards with 55 touchdowns and rushed for 2,975 yards and 48 touchdowns (Frey, 2022).

Pictures Courtesy of Greensboro News & Record

Hooker passed for 55 touchdowns and rushed for 2,975 yards and 48 touchdowns (Frey, 2022).

He finished his career as starting quarterback at Dudley's all-time passing leader and received NC Preps' All-State Player of the Year and was named to the Associated Press All-State team twice. During his years as starting quarterback, Dudley won two state championships. Hooker was awarded the 2016 championship MVP with 6 touchdowns. While playing football, he also played basketball for the high school, scoring over 1,000 points, and was named a three-time All-Metro conference selection. Finishing his career at Dudley, Hooker was a four-star recruit according to 247Sports and a three-star quarterback according to Rivals.com.

At the end of his high school career, Hooker received numerous offers to play in Power Five conferences. Power Five Colleges and universities are the highest ranked in college football in the United States. They are part of the Football Bowl Subdivision (FBS) of NCAA Division I, the highest level of collegiate football in the nation, and are considered the most "elite" conferences within that tier. After visiting Virginia Tech's campus, Hooker committed to them in 2016, stating, "When we set foot on the big stage, on that game field, it just felt right".

Academically, Hooker qualified for early graduation from high school in December of his Senior Year and was able to enroll in college early in the Spring of 2017 as a freshman. He completed four years of varsity football at Dudley earning State Championships in Football his freshman and senior years

At Virginia Tech Hooker competed with a redshirt freshman for the starting position at quarterback but would eventually end up getting redshirted before the beginning of the season in 2018. Hooker was named the starter in 2019 after their current quarterback threw seven interceptions in four games. Before Hendon started as quarterback at Virginia Tech, the Hokies started off with two wins and two losses, Hendon won five games when he played, allowing the Hokies to be eligible for a bowl game. Hooker helped Virginia Tech qualify for the Belk Bowl against Kentucky in the 2019 season. In Virginia Tech's 8–5 season in 2019, Hooker had 1,555 passing yards, 13 passing touchdowns, and two interceptions to go along with 123 carries for 356 rushing yards and five rushing touchdowns.

Picture Courtesy of Virginia Tech Sports

Dr. Jo Evans Lynn, Ed.D.

Picture Courtesy University of Tennessee Sports

In 2021, Hooker entered the Transfer Portal and transferred to the University of Tennessee under head coach Josh Heupel. He entered the 2021 season as the backup to Joe Milton. Milton suffered an injury against Pitt in the season's second game. Hooker came into the game in relief and helped lead Tennessee to a close loss to the Panthers took over the starting job and produced numerous productive outings for Tennessee. Hooker returned to the Volunteers in 2022 for his final collegiate season. He started the season with two passing touchdowns and two rushing touchdowns in a 59–10 victory over Ball State. In the following game against #17 Pitt, he passed for 325 yards and two touchdowns in the 34–27 overtime victory. Tennessee's successful start to the season gave them a #6 ranking to set up an undefeated showdown with longtime rival #3 Alabama. In that game Hendon passed for 385 yards, five passing touchdowns, and one interception in the 52–49 victory over the Crimson Tide. This was Tennessee's first victory over Alabama since 2006. With the score tied at 49 late in the fourth quarter, Hooker led a drive down the field with two clutch throws to Ramel Keyton and Bru McCoy to set up Chase McGrath's game-winning 40-yard field goal. For the first time in program history, Tennessee was named #1 in the first College Football Playoff rankings before a showdown with undefeated Georgia, which was ranked #1 in the AP Poll. Tennessee reached #2 in the AP Poll, their highest ranking since 2001.

Hooker's collegiate career ended abruptly against South Carolina when he suffered a torn ACL in a non-contact injury in the fourth quarter of the 63–38 loss. Hooker was instrumental for a resurgent season for the Tennessee Volunteers football program. Tennessee's 11 wins, of which Hooker was the starting quarterback for nine of them, were the most for the program since 2001 and tied for the second-most in school history

A PLACE WHERE SUCCESS WAS EXPECTED: FINAL EDITION

Picture Courtesy NFL Sports

Hooker was drafted by the Detroit Lions in the third round (68th overall) of the 2023 NFL Draft. The fact that he was drafted in spite of his ACL injury proves that Detroit has faith that he will do the work that it takes to make a full recovery. He was placed on the reserve/non-football injury list on July 20, 2023, and is expected to spend his Rookie Year working to rehab from the ACL injury. However, no one who knows Hendon Hooker doubts that he will be a starting quarterback in the NFL.

Dr. Jo Evans Lynn, Ed.D.

Chapter Eighteen

Dudley Graduates Come "Home..."

In years past, there have been as many as twelve former Dudley Panthers on the staff at James B. Dudley High School. There were five Dudley graduates on the staff including the principal Mr. Rodney Wilds during the 2015-2016 school year. Once the high school moved from Bennett's campus, Dr. Tarpley made it clear that Dudley was a high school that prepared students for professions beyond the traditional roles of teachers and preachers. Tarpley's graduation addresses encouraged Dudley graduates to broaden their horizons. Not very many Dudley graduates were hired to teach at Dudley during the early years of Dr. Tarpley's tenure as principal because there were always many more experienced applicants for the few openings on the staff. The few Dudley graduates who were hired during the last ten years of his administration, like Lonnie Reynolds, Ezell A. Blair, Sr., and Warren Dorsett each had specific skills in Vocal Education areas. Although Tarpley's focus on nontraditional roles did not change, during his last three years at Dudley, preparing for his retirement, Dr. Tarpley began to hire a new crop of teachers, many of whom were Dudley graduates.

These new teachers were different from the teachers who had been hired during the last thirty-nine years- they were younger and less experienced. Since teaching at Dudley had long been considered the "apex" of a teaching career, new hires were traditionally experienced teachers who had "paid their dues" often having taught for as many as twenty years before *finally* being hired to teach at Dudley. The teachers hired to teach during the 1964-1965 school year had not paid their dues; most were first year teachers' right out of out of college. Davetta Florance- Bristow, Virginia Griffin and Francine McAdoo Scott were included in this group of "new teachers".

Although they were fresh out of college, the Dudley graduates were well known to Dr. Tarpley. All of them had been outstanding students while at Dudley. Dr. Tarpley never lost the ability to identify every student by name or directly in relationship to one's siblings or parents who had attended Dudley. For example, I was always *Gloria Evans' Little Sister* in spite of the fact that I was more than a foot taller than Gloria.

A PLACE WHERE SUCCESS WAS EXPECTED: FINAL EDITION

DAVETTA FLORANCE-BRISTOW was hired to teach music at Dudley in 1964. She was a 1960 graduate of Dudley High School. While a student at Dudley, Florance-Bristow was a member of and soloist for the Dudley High School Choir all three years. It was extremely rare for a sophomore to "make" the main choir. Mrs. Julia Morrison Richmond was the director. The Dudley Mixed Chorus were state winners in the Annual Spring Music Festival from 1957-1960. When the Greensboro City School System integrated in 1970, she was transferred to Page Senior High School.

JBD

VIRGINIA GRIFFIN, who was also a 1960 graduate of Dudley, was hired to teach Spanish at Dudley in 1964. She described the experience, "We were thrilled to have been hired to teach at Dudley. The older teachers didn't like the idea of us coming in without having paid our dues as they had done. We had something to prove. We didn't hesitate to bring new ideas to the table. Oh, it wasn't that we didn't respect the teachers who were there before us- most of them had taught us. I think we were just beginning to prove ourselves when the schools integrated. All of the teachers who had come in with me got transferred to one of the other high schools. I was transferred to Smith High School- having to start all over again proving that I was capable of being an effective teacher. It wasn't easy. The teachers who had been there for a long time felt that they were better than us not simply because they were white but because they were the "select group" of teachers chosen by the principal to be protected from a transfer. I came to enjoy my teaching experience there, especially working with the students and touring Europe during the summer." Mrs. Griffin came back to teach Spanish at Dudley.

Dr. Jo Evans Lynn, Ed.D.

Pictures Courtesy of Virginia Griffin

The first Dudley student group to travel abroad went to Saltillo, Mexico in 1971. These students lived with the local families and studied at the Universidad International for two weeks. They immersed themselves in the culture and embraced the new experience The participants were Mrs. Virginia Griffin, Sharon Houston, Wanda Johnson, Michael Springs, Terrie Cochran, Regina Hairston, Theria Glover, Marsha Malone, Ingrid Hooper, Patricia McClenton, and Mrs. Bertha Jones.

Above: The Dudley student group that traveled to London, Paris, and Madrid in 2004. Pictured from **Left to Righ**t: Casey Barber, Ms. Virginia Weathers - Griffin, Demikia Surgeon, Brittany Lawson, and Whitney Neal. The back row: Michael Thomas and Melanese. Blanchard. Not seen is Mrs. Brenda Lawson.

A PLACE WHERE SUCCESS WAS EXPECTED: FINAL EDITION

FRANCINE MCADOO SCOTT was also a 1960 graduate of Dudley. While a student at Dudley, she was a member of the National Honor Society, Junior Marshals, Senior Safety Patrols, and a Library Assistant. She attended UNC Greensboro during the early years of integration. She said of her experience, "It wasn't easy. We had no social life. They made it clear that we did not belong in their social clubs or sororities. We attended parties and dances at A&T."

She was hired to teach English at Dudley. When asked why she left Dudley after only a couple of years she responded, "The hardest thing about teaching back then was finding work when school was out. There just weren't enough jobs – not for young black professionals back then. My brother had moved to Chicago after he graduated college to find work. So, the summer of 1967 I went up there to work for the summer. I met my husband and did not get back to Greensboro until 1996 and back to Dudley in 2001.

Because of her experience as a teacher, the Illinois State Employment Service offered Scott a job as a youth employment counselor. She provided resources and support for children in the Englewood community. During this time, the community had been identified as gang territory but through her work she was able to assist children with obtaining employment and improving their quality of life. Her Dudley High School southern charm enabled her to quickly establish relationships with the students, community leaders, and residents; and she was able to get students into jobs. This was the beginning of Francine's career in government.

Scott returned to Greensboro and to Dudley High School where she became the Site Coordinator for Communities in Schools. In this position, she was able to leverage all that she had learned in Chicago as she set about developing partnerships and strategies to assess and address the situations and issues that students were having who were failing or at risk of dropping out of school. When speaking of her role as coordinator, she says,

"I did everything possible to keep them in school. If a teen mother needed childcare while she attended school, I helped her find it. I developed Student Support Plans to fit each student's needs and goals." Francine further developed a partnership with North Carolina A&T State University School of Education, Student Services Office, and other departments to recruit NCA&T students to serve as classroom tutors and mentors for the students at Dudley High School. Also, through CIS' partnership with the UNCG and NCA&T Joint School of Social Work, social work interns worked with CIS students to address their personal needs, thus reducing failures and dropouts. During her tenure, at least 95% of the students in Communities In Schools (CIS) graduated from high school. Francine retired in 2018 and currently serves on the Board of Directors of Communities in Schools of Greater Greensboro.

I love it! My job as the Coordinator for the Communities in Schools Program for Dudley gives me the opportunity to help students not only stay in school but to graduate with a new sense of what they can accomplish in life."

JO ANN EVANS LYNN. After nearly 24 years as a teacher, I finally was presented with an opportunity to teach at Dudley. When Mr. Lewis called me about an opening in the English Department at Dudley, I did not have to think twice about transferring. When I graduated from Shaw University in December of 1970, there was a waiting list of teachers who were already in the Greensboro City Schools System who wanted to teach English at Dudley. Although I loved teaching at Clover Garden Elementary School, Eastern Alamance High School, and Grimsley Senior High School, finally having an opportunity to teach at my Alma Mata was a rewarding opportunity. It was worth the wait.

Throughout my teaching career, I always put into action the belief instilled in me while I attended Dudley: a broad education takes place during activities beyond the classroom. While a student at Dudley, I was a member of the French National Honor Society, the Student Government as Junior and Senior Class Representative, the Senior Safety Patrols, and a Library Assistant. I also finally learned how to play the trombone that I owned since being in the band at Lincoln Junior High School. I could play well enough to perform with the band during my graduation (Okay, I admit that the only song I learned to play well was *Pomp and Circumstance*. I thought it was so cool the way the senior band members looked marching up those steps to the upper level of the gymnasium).

As a teacher, I served as PTA president at Clover Garden Elementary School, Alamance County Teacher's Association School Representative and Treasurer, helped organize a college tour and developed an academic awards program for minority students at Grimsley Senior High School, where I also served as advisor to the Southeastern Consortium for Minorities in Engineering Organization and the Grimsley Step Team. I also and taught seventh grade English for several years in the Greensboro Area Math and Science Center Saturday Academy and Summer Programs at North Carolina A&T State University. At Dudley, I helped revive the Dudley Thespians and Panther's Claw Newspaper and coached the Debate Team and High I.Q. Team.

A PLACE WHERE SUCCESS WAS EXPECTED: FINAL EDITION

STANLEY JOHNSON graduated from Dudley in 1967. He states that he did not have a favorite subject while in school, and if it had not been for Gwen's intervention (Gwendolyn Spinks Benton), he probably would not have made it to school most days. During his years at Dudley, he was a standout on the swim team that practiced and swam its home meets in the "old" Winsor Center Pool that had a much larger Olympic size pool at the time. He was also an athletic trainer and like many students at Dudley held down a part-time job.

During a 2002 interview with *The Panther's Claw* Johnson said, "When I went to Dudley, the teachers were from the neighborhood. You knew them, and the staff was close-knit."

He also said that his favorite memory of Dudley is of the Blue Goose. This was the school's activity bus that many student groups including the band rode to games and competitions. He said, "The Blue Goose had a history of breaking down in route to at least one big game every year."

After he graduated from Dudley in 1967, he went on to attend North Carolina A&T State University. It was there that he obtained two degrees: one in Biology and one in Pre-Veterinarian Medicine. He also has a master's degree in biology.

Before his career at Dudley High, he taught for twelve years at the North Carolina School for the Deaf. At the beginning of the 1988-89 school year, Mr. Johnson decided to change his teaching style, so he came to Dudley. He taught biology, chemistry, physical science, and environmental science. That is every science course at Dudley except physics. Mr. Johnson says that his most memorable group of students was the graduating class of 1994. This group was special because of several outstanding science students, but especially because of one of its most dedicated students, Melba Paula (Howell, 2002).

During his years of being a student and teaching at Dudley, Mr. Johnson was under the administration of several principals. "The best was Dr. John Tarpley himself," said Johnson with a confident nod. He continued, "Dr. Tarpley was one of the most influential black men in Greensboro's black community, and he did so much for Dudley. As far as the concept of a "New Dudley" is concerned Johnson's comment was, "It's not the school that makes the students, but the students that make the school." (Howell, 2002)

In 2002, Johnson was Dudley's Teacher of the Year and in 2013 he was elected to the Dudley High School Hall of Distinction.

Dr. Jo Evans Lynn, Ed.D.

MARTHA CROCKETT DICK a 1966 graduate of Dudley attended North Carolina A&T State University. While a student at Dudley, her favorite subjects were Business and History. She was the Media Specialist at Dudley and the advisor to the Astra Club. She joined fourteen other teachers in chartering the Epsilon Upsilon Chapter, of Alpha Psi Omega National Sorority (Educators). As the Lead Media Specialist, she helped facilitate and organize visits of several major authors such as Marc Mathabane, the famed author of *Kaffir Boy* and Ernest Gaines the author of *A Lesson before Dying*. She also expanded the role of the media specialist by administering computer technology tests and Accelerated Reading Tests. She took great pride in adding to the African Heritage Art Collection of the Dudley Media Center with paintings of the Great Kings of Africa. During her tenure, Dick also ensured that the Media Center kept copies of all editions of the *Panther Yearbook* and archived copies of the *Panther's Claw Newspaper*. She was a long-time member of the Dudley Alumni Association where she served as secretary.

CHRISTOPHER "CHRIS" GOINS, a 1996 graduate of Dudley, was a member of the Marching Band, the Jazz Band, Dudley Fellows, Future Teachers of America, and the Symphonic Orchestra. He was also a Drum Major at both Dudley and North Carolina A&T State University. While a student at Dudley, he was also involved in the Student Government Organization, and Future Nurses (He says he joined the group solely because they went on "good" field trips). He was Mr. Dudley 1996. He remained active at Dudley as more than a history teacher. He served as North Carolina Association of Educators Representative for Dudley, UMOJA Male Step Team Advisor, and as assistant director with the Marching Band of Thunder. Goins was instrumental in the resurgence of the Dudley Alumni Band. For several years, he served as one of five past drum majors leading the Dudley Alumni Band during the Homecoming Parade. It became a tradition for the Alumni Band to end the Homecoming Parade and to perform after the game.

A PLACE WHERE SUCCESS WAS EXPECTED: FINAL EDITION

BENJAMIN MITTMAN, a 1997 graduate, was an earth science teacher at Dudley. According to his teachers, he was an outstanding student who participated in the Marching Band, the Jazz Band, and the Symphonic Band. He was also a member of the National Honor Society and the Beta Club. His favorite subjects while at Dudley were Biology and Chemistry. As a teacher at Dudley, he instructed students and enhanced knowledge of the Life Sciences. He served as a practical resource for students as well as parents for career development, as Assistant Band Director, Dudley High School Marching Band, as Assistant Track Coach, Co-Advisor of the UMOJA Male Step Team, and facilitated Freshmen Orientation for incoming freshmen. Mittman left Dudley to pursue his master's degree and later became a chemist at PETNET Solutions located in the Research Triangle located in the Raleigh-Durham, North Carolina area.

GLEN ANDERSON graduated from Dudley in 1996. Most of his classmates remember him as THE PANTHER mascot. His lively antics during games and Pep Rallies helped stir up the school spirit. He was also involved in the Diversity Club, Junior Civitan's, Dudley Fellows, Dudley Student Council, the National Honor Society, and the Wrestling Team. He taught biology and physical science at Dudley. He left Dudley to become an International Teaching Fellow in Japan.

Dr. Jo Evans Lynn, Ed.D.

GUILFORD WESTMORELAND played on Dudley's first undefeated football team (1950) and 1951 undefeated and State Championship Team. He not only returned to Dudley as an Administrative Assistant but remained in the community as one of the school's strongest supporters. He worked at James B. Dudley High School for 28 years. He began under Mr. Franklin Brown and served under six administrators as an administrative assistant under four principals. He served as a Bus Supervisor for 15 years. He was a coach of the junior varsity football team. He has received several awards and certificates from various organizations of Dudley. He was inducted in the Dudley Hall of Fame in 2005.

DAVID SURGEON graduated in the Dudley Class of 1960 and taught chemistry and biology at Dudley for more than twenty years. He served as Science Department Chairperson and Master Teacher- Mentor for new science teachers. He served as Academic Dean at Palmer Memorial Institute in Sedalia, NC. He taught Biology at Bennett College from 1971-1974. Surgeon began teaching at James B. Dudley High School in 1974. He served several years as Science Department chair and was an adviser to the James B. Dudley Student Government Association.

CHERYL ROBINSON GOUL, a physical education, health, and dance teacher, graduated from Dudley in 1972. While a student at Dudley, she was a cheerleader and was a member of the Dudley Modern Dance Company. Her favorite teacher was Ms. Georgene Dye. Goul graduated from North Carolina A&T State University where she majored in Health and Physical Education and Dance. She revived the Modern Dance Program at Dudley, served as Chairperson of the Athletic Department, and designed the curriculum for many of the health classes. In the community, she served as the Minister of Evangelical Dance at Mount Zion Baptist Church in Greensboro from its inception.

SGT. NEVADA JARRELL, who helped direct the AFROTC Program, was a 1971 graduate of Dudley. His favorite subject was history. While a student at Dudley, he was active in the AFROTC Program and has always credited it with the structure and direction that it gave him in life. He says, "The most important thing I learned from the program was how to be an effective leader." He served twenty years in the Air Force and came to Dudley in 1991. He was an Instructor of the Year for the Air Force twice, 1999 and 2001.

DESIREE FODRELL BEST graduated from Dudley in 1979. While a student at Dudley, she ran track and was a Pantherette.

She graduated from Winston Salem State University. In the spring of 2004, Dudley's certified teachers chose Desiree Best to represent them in the Teacher of the Year Competition. Even though it was her first-year teaching at Dudley, she came to Dudley with 17 years of experience teaching and coaching at Allen Middle School. She was also a National Board-Certified Teacher. This means that she was qualified to teach anywhere in the nation. Best was named the Best High School Teacher in Guilford County. Her principal Tony Watlington said,

> "I could tell that she was a special teacher by the very inviting and well-organized classroom she set up before her students arrived, However, I was even more impressed by her excellent classroom

management skills and the excellent EOC scores of her students." (Watlington, 2004)

In 2023, Desirée was elected president of the Greensboro Alumnae Chapter of Delta Sigma Theta Sorority, Incorporated. The chapter is more than 400 members strong. With their leadership, programs, and activities that fall under Delta Sigma Theta's Five Point Programmatic Thrust: Social Action, Delta GEMS, and Delta Academy, they are committed to public service in the community providing service that engages and inspires.

PAMELA STEWART, a 1971 graduate of Dudley served as both music teacher and assistant principal at Dudley. While a student at Dudley, she was active in the band, the orchestra, and was a soloist in the chorus.

After graduation, she attended Winston-Salem State University where she earned a Bachelor of Science Degree in Music Education (Vocal Concentration). She later earned a Master of School Administration degree from North Carolina A&T State University.

As an elementary music teacher, Pam served students in over twenty-five schools, exposing them to different genres of vocal and instrumental music. While teaching at Dudley, Stewart served as Chairperson of the Cultural Arts Department and was active in the Alumni Band. She became the principal at Falkner Elementary School in Greensboro, North Carolina in 2010.

ANGELA L. WILLIAMS, a 1993 graduate of Dudley became a teacher at Dudley in 2011 as a lateral entry teacher after having spent several years working in the Graphics Department at a major company in the Research Triangle. While a student at Dudley, she was active as a photographer on the Yearbook Staff and was a Pantherette her junior and senior year. She attended North Carolina A&T State University and graduated Summa Cum Laude with a 3.8-grade point average. She continued her graduate studies at North Carolina A&T State University in the Graphic Communication Systems Department on a research project designed to examine what changes needed to be made to science, engineering, technology, and mathematics curriculums on the secondary level to increase the numbers of women and African American professionals in those fields. She rose in record time to be elected by her peers as the Chairperson of the Technology Department and served as the advisor for the Women's Step Team.

1992-93 Pantherettes Squad, Angela L. Williams center of front row.

BRIAN SEAGRAVES is a 1991 graduate of Dudley. While a student at Dudley, Seagraves played on the football team and starred for the Panthers Basketball Team. In 1991, he was named conference player of the year and played in the East-West All-Star game. He played point guard at N.C. A&T State University for three seasons then served as an assistant basketball coach at Dudley for 15years. Dudley had three title runs during this period, from 1996 until 2011. Seagraves left for his first head coaching position at High Point Andrews. The Red Raiders went 20-7 under Seagraves (Formica, 2012).

Courtesy J.B.D. Hall of Fame

He became Dudley's Head Basketball Coach in 2012. During a news conference, shortly after Seagraves was named head coach he said, "It feels great to be home. This is my dream job. Coach Price has done such a great job here at Dudley; I have some big shoes to fill (Formica, 2012)." During his first three years, the team amassed a 41 and 22 record. After four seasons as head boys' basketball coach at Dudley, Brian Seagraves decided it was time for a change. The former Panthers and N.C. A&T player resigned to pursue opportunities as a college assistant coach. Seagraves moved on with a 59-40 record overall, 29-11 in conference play. His final Dudley team went 18-8, won the Metro 4-A regular-season title and reached the third round of the NCHSAA Class 4-A tournament.

RODNEY DOWE WESTMORELAND, Sr. was post humorously inducted into the James B. Dudley Hall of Fame on October 23, 2021. Induction into the Hall of Fame places Rodney Westmoreland in an exclusive group of superior scholar-athletes who embody the ultimate scholar athlete at James B. Dudley High School.

Westmoreland, a 1973 Dudley graduate was a three-sport athlete playing baseball, basketball, and football from his sophomore to his senior year. He served as Captain of the Men's Football Team, where he was recognized as Most Outstanding Player. Westmoreland also served as Co-Captain of the Basketball Team and was a pitcher on the Baseball Team. His talents were not limited to sports. Rodney was

Courtesy J.B.D. Hall of Fame

a member of the Dudley Choral Society where he served as an officer. He earned a Bachelor of Science degree from North Carolina A&T State University where he played Football.

In the Dudley Community, he was an Assistant Coach to Dudley's Men and Women's Basketball Teams. Westmoreland also served as Director of the AAU training program- Greensboro Galaxy/ Nothing But Basic Fundamentals Program where he coached and trained countless players of all ages and levels in both girls' and boys' programs. He was the Director of Facilities at North Carolina A&T State University in the Ronald E. McNair School of Engineering.

DENORRIS Q. L. BEST graduated from the James B. Dudley Early College Academies of Education, Engineering, and Health Sciences in 2007. He was always a well-rounded student involved in sports and other extracurricular activities. During his tenure, he served on the Freshmen Steering Committee and played a key role on the junior varsity and varsity football teams, junior varsity basketball team, and track team.

Upon graduation, Denorris entered North Carolina Agricultural and Technical State University (A&T) as a North Carolina Teaching Fellow and graduated from A&T with a Bachelor of Arts in Interdisciplinary Studies.

His love for mathematics allowed him to gain employment with Guilford County Schools as a math educator at Ferndale Middle where he was named Rookie Teacher of the Year. In 2019, he was afforded the opportunity to teach math at his alma mater, "Dear Dudley High," where he made a profound impact on the students and staff.

For more than 10 seasons Denorris served as wide receivers' coach, equipment manager, and statistician for Dudley's varsity football team. As a coach, he is most proud of the 2013, 2016, and 2021 seasons that concluded with Dudley being crowned NCHSAA 4-A champions.

ANNE CAROLYN BASKERVILLE REEDER graduated from James B. Dudley High School in 1976. Reeder earned a Bachelor of Science Degree in Social Work from the University of North Carolina at Greensboro. While pursuing her degree, Reeder was consistently on the Dean's List and received University Scholar recognition. She graduated Summa Cum Laude with Highest Honors. Reeder continued her education at North Carolina State University earning Licensure in the area of School Social Work. Anne holds lifetime memberships in the Phi Kappa Mu, National Social Work Honor Society and Omicron Nu, National Human Services Honor Society. Since 2012, Reeder serves Dudley High School as a Licensed School Social Worker, Dropout Prevention Counselor, and Homeless Student in Transition Liaison. Before moving to her current position, Reeder was the Lead Office Support and Administrative Assistant at Dudley High School. She also served Dudley High School as the School Treasurer, Accounts Payable, and Payroll Technician.

Reeder was awarded the Guilford County Employee of the Month Recognition in August 2014. She was also awarded the Guilford County Schools School Social Worker Community Service Award in December 2015. Reeder has served the Guilford County Schools District as a Member of the Guilford County Schools Crisis Team (2015-Present), and also served The Guilford County School District as a COVID-19 Youth Crisis Hotline Counselor from March 2020 to June 2020.

Reeder continues to participate in Community Outreach events assisting families, individuals, and older adults experiencing food insecurity and homelessness. She continues to make food deliveries while linking many to needed resources and services. Prior to the COVID-19 Pandemic, Reeder helped to sponsor a Community Holiday Gathering of older adults promoting connectivity, relationship building, togetherness, fellowship, and friendship. When Covid 19 limited face to face gatherings, Reeder continued to reach out and stay connected to older adults through phone calls and sending greeting cards on special days and special occasions.

She is a lifelong learner who continues her education in the areas of student and older adult mental health and family and student engagement from the University of North Carolina at Greensboro, Curtin University, and Harvard University, respectively.

Reeder's Family is Dudley Family Strong, since Anne's Mother, Seven Siblings, Husband, and Children are all Dudley Alumni.

A PLACE WHERE SUCCESS WAS EXPECTED: FINAL EDITION

ROBERT CARL JARRELL graduated from Dudley in 2003. His activities and honors while a student at Dudley: Trumpet Section Leader in the Marching Band of Thunder; Also served as the student conductor; Participated in the Jazz Band, Concert Band and Wind Ensemble. Represented the Marching Band during Homecoming activities as Mr. Band. He was a dedicated member of the Dudley Fellows (Junior & Senior years)- During this time, I was able to serve as a mentor for numerous students at Rankin Elementary School and participated in volunteer opportunities in the community through the Dudley Fellows. Robert served as a representative of James B. Dudley high School in Youth in Government at a convention in Raleigh, NC.; He maintained A/B Honor Roll throughout his four years at Dudley; He served as musician for the Panthers for Christ Organization, a group which performed at various churches in the community. He was a MACK Scholar, serving as a male peer mentor at Dudley; He served on the Yearbook Committee assisting with organizing pictures and selling ads for the 2002-2003 yearbook.; He produced and directed the musical stylings for each annual Mr. & Miss Dudley Pageant.

He graduated from North Carolina A&T State University with a BS in Music. He was a Member of the Greensboro Spiritual Renaissance Singers and served as Vice President. His community involvement: A part of the Greensboro Chapter of Gospel Music Workshop of America (GMWA). During his time with GMWA he served as the creative music director, which entails playing for the yearly NAACP Martin Luther King Jr. Day Gospel Fest. He served as one of the musical directors for the annual Christmas program at St. James Baptist Church. He has served as a Talent Judge for Jabberwock talent show for 4 years for the Greensboro Alumni Chapter of Delta Sigma Theta Jabberwock competition. I served as the coordinator of the 10-year class reunion for the Class of 2003; Currently serving on the 20-year Class 2003 Reunion Committee. In 2012, I launched an after-school music academy for the community called "Teach Me How Studio, LLC". In 2022, Teach Me How Studio, LLC (TMSH) celebrated 10 years of business providing affordable music lessons for ages 5 and up. TMHS offers piano, violin, drums, guitar, saxophone, and voice lessons.

As Chorus Teacher at James B. Dudley High School 2016-2021, he served on the Leadership team; Served as Co-chair of the Arts Department; Volunteering to provide music for various activities and programs at Dudley.

A PLACE WHERE SUCCESS WAS EXPECTED: FINAL EDITION

Some Dudley Alumni Are "Home to Stay"

There are more ways to "come home" to Dudley than as teachers, staff, or as administrators. Dozens of Dudley alumni have returned in many different capacities. Dale Tonkins (1971), Ray Crosby (1970), Mr. Isiah, and Juanita Brown (1951) are prime examples of the numerous Dudley alumni who remained vital parts of the school for many years after graduating. The Dudley Yearbook Staff in 2005 showed their appreciation by dedicating the yearbook to them. It read,

> We dedicate the 2005 Yearbook to all of the loyal supporters who volunteer hours of their time to benefit the students of Dudley; to all the people frying and serving fish and working concession stands at games; to all the parents and friends walking parade routes and carrying equipment with the band; to all those patient souls proctoring tests; and to the dozens of others doing hundreds of other helpful acts around the school, we say thank-you. Although some of these volunteers no longer have children or grandchildren at Dudley and some have never had children at Dudley, they all have made the students at Dudley their children. (p. 140)

Left: Ray Crosby (1970) was a member and leader in the Athletic Boosters of which he served as president for more than twenty years. He was also active in the Alumni Association and was inducted into the James B. Dudley Hall of Distinction in 2005. **Middle: Dale Tonkins** (1972) served multiple terms as president of the Dudley PTSA, on the Construction Committee, on the Committee to Save Dudley, and as a Charter member of the James B. Dudley Hall of Fame/ Hall of Distinction **Right:** Loyal Fans are there to "represent" no matter where our teams play.

Dr. Jo Evans Lynn, Ed.D.

Top right: Many students, parents, and community members volunteer to tutor and mentor Dudley students. **Top left**: Parental support is always strong. Parents, like the ones pictured here, make Senior Night special. **Bottom left:** Alumni Supportors march in the Homecoming Parade. Every graduating class has an active Alumni Chapter as long as a single member of the class remains. **Bottom right:** Band Boosters start with Summer Band Camp and work diligently to keep the band marching. They help by providng all kinds of physical, economic, and emotional support.

A PLACE WHERE SUCCESS WAS EXPECTED: FINAL EDITION

DR. MARK LEWIS FIELDS, M.D. After several years directing a trauma center in Rocky Mount, North Carolina, Dr. Mark Lewis Fields came home to Greensboro to serve as a Family Practitioner. Although he could have set up his practice anywhere in the city, he chose Southeast Greensboro. Once the thriving center of the Nocho Park Community, located near L. Richardson Memorial Hospital and Winsor Community Center, the area surrounding 1203 Gorrell Street has fallen on less prosperous times through the years. Dr. Fields' goal was to supply affordable health care long before the Affordable Care Act. He does this by setting his fees according to what his clients can afford to pay.

While a student at Dudley, Mark Fields was a member of the Marching Band and Dudley's AFJROTC Unit. Fields graduated from Dudley in 1971 and attended the UNC-Chapel Hill School of Medicine where he received his medical degree in 1981. He completed his internship and additional family practice training in Atlanta, Georgia at Morehouse. His practice is called Moja Health. According to the Merriam-Wester English Learner's Dictionary, in Swahili the term *moja* means "one". One of Dr. Fields patients, Donna Baker, described his "moja" or first-class medical service this way,

> "I was very pleased that he was willing to take me on short notice. He gave me options on how to proceed with care concerning finances. He spent time asking me questions and trying to find out all the information he could dealing with a new patient (me). I appreciate and look up to him for opening an office to help middle-income people. I have no insurance at this time (2010) and only paid half in cash compared to what I would have had to pay at Urgent Care or my regular doctor."

This kind of quality patient care has earned Dr. Mark Fields, who was ranked one of the Top 10 Doctors in the city (2014), other awards: Patients Choice Award (2014) and Compassionate Doctor Recognition (2014). He was also one of the founding members of the Committee to Save Dudley.

SONJA GAIL WESTMORELAND COBB

All That and More...

Few Dudley students or graduates have demonstrated more "staying power" than Sonja Gail Westmoreland Cobb (Dudley 1970). Her extra-curricular activities while a student at Dudley included participating in the Dudley Chorus, playing on the Dudley Powder-Puff Football Team, Serving as Point Guard on Dudley's Girls Basketball Team- Coaches Mrs. Harris & Ms. Dye, and being a member of the Dudley Modern Dance Company- Coach Ms. Dye.

Since she chose to continue her post-graduate studies at GTCC (1972) in Early Childcare Administration where she earned an associate degree, Gail remained on Dudley's Campus in a variety of positions for over 35 years. She served as an Administrative Support Specialist- (35 years). During that period of time, she also served as a Behavioral Exceptionality Teaching Assistant (19 years); a Front Office Assistant (5 years), and as an Attendance Office Assistant (12 years).

Her Involvement in the Dudley Community has always been extensive. James B. Dudley Alumni Association- Fiftieth Anniversary Honor Class 1970. She contributed to the 1970 Class's contribution to the Alumni Association's Scholarship Fund. She has coached James B. Dudley JV Basketball and has coached in many other capacities: Cheerleading Coach; Majorette Coach, Pantherette Coach, and Flag-girls Coach (5 years); Her other Community Involvement: Coached NC A&T State University Cheerleaders (10 years).

Gail has been a member of New Zion Missionary Baptist Church as an active member for over 60. At an early age she was a member of the Junior Choir and Usher Board. In later years she sang on the W. D. Johnson Choir; During Past years, she drove the Church van, worked with the Night Out Committee, visited the Sick and Shut-in and carried Seniors on errands.

A PLACE WHERE SUCCESS WAS EXPECTED: FINAL EDITION

Present ministries in which she serves: The Missionary Ministry, the Pastor's Aide Ministry. Community Leadership: Presently, she serves as Chairperson of the Trustee Ministry; and she is also presently Chairperson of the Deaconess Ministry.

The Deaconess Ministry of New Zion Missionary Baptist Church.

Deaconess Sonja Gail Cobb on right end of 5th row up (pillbox hat & double strain of pearls).

Dr. Jo Evans Lynn, Ed.D.

Setting a New Standard for Alumni Loyalty, Commitment & Service

The James B. Dudley High School National Alumni Association and local Dudley Alumni Chapters are essential to continuing to preserve and cherish the Dudley legacy. Their efforts in sponsoring the Consolidated Reunion represents a significant part of the legacy- keeping the connection between the thousands of Dudley alumni alive and vibrant. Through the years, they have worked with the various booster clubs to help buy band uniforms, supply pre-game meals for athletes, and in other areas to provide vital support for students and teachers. This group also offers college scholarships to deserving seniors.

In addition to presenting scholarships and organizing the Consolidated Class Reunion each year, the National Alumni Association serves the school and community in other areas. **Pictured above:** Standing-Reginald Whitsitt, Andrew Thompson, Mary Cotton & Kathryn Paylor. Seated: Lola McAdoo & Ernestine Donnell prepare gift packages for their February Project at Union Memorial Church to be delivered to Senior Citizens living in nursing homes. **Pictured at left:** The Dudley Alumni Association delivering gifts to Carter's Rest Home on Bessemer Avenue. From Left to Right: Julia Westmoreland, Loretta F. McKee, Lola McAdoo, Ernestine Donnell, and Mary Cotton.

James B. Dudley High School Educational and Sports Hall of Fame/Hall of Distinction

In the fall of 2000, a group of Dudley administrators, former coaches, students, and athletes met for the purpose of establishing a formal way of recognizing the outstanding accomplishments of Dudley Alumni and Friends of Dudley. Historically, Dudley High School Alumni and students have been trailblazers and risk-takers. Dudley has not only produced great athletes (Hall of Fame) but a long list of academic achievers, community, spiritual and civic leaders, performing artists and educators (Hall of Distinction). As a result of these meetings, the 20 Charter Members formed the James B. Dudley High School Educational and Sports Hall of Fame/Hall of Distinction, Inc., the first of its kind in North Carolina. The 20 Charter members included Glenn Booker, William Boyers, Roland Cardwell, Marché Clark, Ray Crosby, Eva Foster, Joe Godette, John Harris, Thomas Hasty, Melvin Henderson, Herbert Jackson, Everitt James, Melvin "Mud Tap" Johnson, Jonathan McKee, Helburn Meadows, Ken Thompson, Wilson Dale Tonkins, Stahle Vincent, Tony Watlington, and Willie Young

The first Induction Program and Banquet was held in 2001. Its 10th biennial Induction Program and Banquet was held in 2019. Thus far, there are 76 members in the Hall of Distinction and 54 members in the Hall of Fame. Since 2001, the "Hall" has awarded over $35,000 in scholar dollars to 58 students. (Stahle Vincent, 2021)

Photo courtesy

James B. Dudley High School Educational & Sports Hall of Fame/Hall of Distinction Members (2001-2021)

2023 Inductees James B. Dudley Educational and Sports Hall of Fame/Hall of Distinction

Top Row L-R: Steven T. Davis HOF-Coach, Jeffry B. Davis HOF, Kenyatta Owusu Martin HOD, Frank R. McNeill HOF-Coach

Front Row L-R: Raymond Brian Crosby HOD, Donald Wright HOF, Nevada Jarrell HOD & Robert C. Jarrell (HOD), not pictured Eric C. Hicks HOF, Johnathan Anthony McKee, Jr. HOF

Front Row L-R: Sonja Gail Westmoreland Cobb HOD, Stephanie Q. Wilson HOD, Dr. Janice Brewington HOD, Pamela Fruster Stewart HOD, **Second Row:** Mrs. Jonathan Anthony McKee (for Johnathan Anthony McKee, Jr.); **Third Row L-R:** Kathy Rouson Hairston HOD, Tiffany V. Tonkins HOF, Lisa Renee Richardson HOD, Ursula Robinson (For Thelma S. Robinson Burwell)

Chapter Nineteen

Panthers in Nontraditional Roles

Dudley graduates have continued to break down barriers and open doors by assuming nontraditional roles. L. Richardson Hospital brought an influx of highly trained medical staff. The growth of both North Carolina A&T State University and Bennett College, and the expanded more affluent and middle class African American communities in urban areas provided access to more nontraditional careers.

Courtesy UNCG Digital Library

MATTIE DONNELL HICKS was born in Greensboro, North Carolina on September 2, 1914, to John and Josephine Donnell. She was one of ten children. After graduating from Dudley High School in 1933, she enrolled at the Grady Hospital School of Nursing in Atlanta, Georgia (Trojanowski, 1999). Three years later she earned her diploma and began her career at a segregated, rural hospital in Gainesville, Georgia (Trojanowski,1999).

Trojanowski quoted Hicks saying that she, "Wanted to do something different in going into the military to try to help the soldiers with their wounds and all that". She joined the Army Nurse Corps on July 2, 1945, but served only a few weeks before World War II ended in August 1945. Hicks realized she enjoyed Army nursing, so she re-enlisted in March 1946 and stayed for twenty-one years.

Courtesy UNCG Digital Library

When the Korean War broke out, Hicks was assigned to the 11th Evacuation Hospital in Wonju, Korea on the eastern battlefront. During the war, approximately 540 Army Nurses served on the ground in Korea. Seriously wounded and ailing troops were air lifted to awaiting Navy hospital ships or evacuated to Army Hospitals in Japan and the United States for more intense treatment than was available in Korean MASH units or evacuation hospitals. Many Army nurses served in the newly created Mobile Army Surgical Hospitals (MASH) units close to the front. Hicks and other nurses in Evacuation Hospitals took wounded soldiers from the MASH units and provided longer term care. She recalled in an oral history interview with Trojanowski in 1999:

> "We enjoyed our work very much. One thing, we were kept busy because patients would be coming right off the battlefield because they had the helicopters to pick them up, bring them right to the hospital which saved a lot of their lives ... whenever a shipment would come in, you'd work ... if they were in real bad shape, they would ship them on right away. But if they were not in too bad shape, they would stay right there, and we'd take care of them."

Each Evacuation Hospital had a specialty area. The 11th Evacuation Hospital had a renal insufficiency unit and pioneered the use of renal dialysis. Hicks and her colleagues at the 11th Evacuation Hospital were among the first nurses to support patients with hemorrhagic fever on the first generation of artificial kidney machines. In addition to patients with renal disease and battlefield wounds, Hicks and her colleagues provided general car for soldiers and their family members with a variety of ailments. She recalled civilians coming to the hospitals with tuberculosis and gastro-intestinal distress.

> "We had to run a tube down their throat and clean – and get all the fluid and stuff out of their stomach. And you know, through that tube live worms would come through, Live!"

A PLACE WHERE SUCCESS WAS EXPECTED: FINAL EDITION

When asked about her social situation in Korea, including homesickness, cold temperatures, Spartan accommodations and serving in one of the first integrated units in US armed forces history, Hicks remembered, "When you're afraid, as most of us were, being in a theater where they were fighting and all that, you kind of act like a family".

After her tour in Korea, Hicks served wherever the Army Nurse Corps needed her. Her postings included hospitals in Japan, Ohio, Pennsylvania, Virginia, Germany, and North Carolina. She worked in medical surgical nursing and obstetrical nursing. She earned many medals for her courage and service including the World War II Victory Medal, the Korean Service Medal, the National Defense Service Medal, and Army Commendation Medal, the Armed Service Reserve Medal, a Meritorious Unit Citation, and a United Nations Service Medal.

In March 1966, Hicks retired from the Army having earned the rank of major. She returned to Greensboro and built a home. After her years of travel, she was ready to spend time with her extended family and childhood friends. She was dedicated to her church, spending many hours serving on committees, in the choir and helping fellow congregants in need. Hicks passed away on March 14, 2004.

JBD

RICHARD ALAN FIELDS, M.D. graduated from Dudley High School in 1967. While a student at Dudley, he served as Senior Class President, played on the Varsity Basketball Team, was President of the French National Honor Society and was a Junior Marshal and member of the National Honor Society. He graduated from Hampton Institute and the Duke University School of Medicine.

After receiving his credentials in Administrative Psychiatry after successfully completing the American Psychiatric Association examination in Toronto Canada, he served as director of the Neuse Mental Health Clinic in New Bern.

Richard Alan Fields, 1967

Fields founded Fields & Associates, Inc. (F&A) in 1996. He serves as its president, chief executive officer and senior consultant. Dr. Fields is a former hospital CEO and nationally recognized multi-board-certified psychiatrist with almost 40 years of leadership, treatment, and consultation experience across the public, private, and military sectors of the mental health field. Dr. Fields is the only psychiatrist ever to have actively surveyed for the Centers for Medicare and Medicaid Services (CMS) and The Joint Commission (TJC) concurrently for seven years. His experience includes 14 years as superintendent at one of the busiest state psychiatric hospitals in the country (more than 6,000 admissions per year at a 365-bed facility). He also has experience as a medical director in a variety of settings including a state psychiatric hospital, an inpatient treatment facility for mentally ill felons, a comprehensive community mental health center and a major metropolitan jail.

Dr. Fields has long recognized that it is difficult to find quality improvement and compliance information that is specifically relevant to behavioral healthcare organizations. For this reason, he has been developing a unique online resource to house and share such information among organization leaders and those responsible for quality/performance improvement, standards compliance, and survey readiness. The forum is called the State & Psychiatric Hospital Compliance Collaborative (SPHCC) and Dr. Fields serves as its executive director.

Dr. Richard A. Fields, M.D.

FAYE ADAMS-TAYLOR is perhaps the most acclaimed actress, poet, and storyteller to come out of Dudley. While a student at Dudley, she performed in starring roles with the Dudley Thespians, served as a student announcer, and worked in summer camps teaching theater to youth for Greensboro Parks and Recreation. Faye continued to perform through her college years at North Carolina A & T State University. She was the only freshman to perform in the first two productions with the Harrison Players in *Inherit the Wind* and *God's Trombones*. After she moved to Atlanta, she joined a community theatre company, The Proposition. She performed in *Olio, Willie Lobo*, Anton Chekov's *The Seagull*, and James Baldwin's *Amen Corner*. She won Best Supporting Actress by Atlanta Circle of Drama Critics. Faye toured the southeastern United States directing and co-starring in *Amen Corner*. Mr. Baldwin who attended a performance in 1981 at the M. L. King, Jr.'s *Kingfest*, said in an interview with the *Atlanta Daily World,* "Of all of the versions of my play that I have attended, Ms. Adams' interpretation is one of the best" (Adams-Taylor, 2011).

DEBRA L. LEE, media company chief executive, was born on August 8, 1955, in Fort Jackson, South Carolina to Richard and Delma Lee. In 1972, Lee graduated from James B. Dudley High School and later moved to the East Coast where she attended Brown University. During her junior year, Lee spent a year studying abroad in Southeast Asia in Thailand, Malaysia, and Indonesia. In 1976, after receiving her B.A. degree in political science with an emphasis on Asian politics, Lee attended Harvard University. She simultaneously earned her M.A. degree in public policy from the John F. Kennedy School of Government and her J.D. degree from Harvard Law School in 1980.

Then, Lee went to live in Washington, D.C. to complete a clerkship with the late Honorable Barrington Parker of the U.S. District Court for the District of Columbia. In 1981, she worked at the law firm, Steptoe & Johnson, as a regulatory lawyer. Five years later, Lee joined Black Entertainment Television (BET Networks) and created its legal department. During her tenure, Lee has played pivotal roles in the company's history, including executive vice president and general counsel of the legal affairs department; corporate secretary; and president and publisher of the publishing division. In 1996, Lee became president and chief operating officer; and, in 2005, she was named the chairman and chief executive officer. During her tenure, BET enjoyed some of its most explosive growth in ratings, revenue, and popularity. She led the network's evolution beyond its successful music programming into original movies, documentaries, concert specials, news, late-night talk shows and public policy coverage. Lee has also substantially expanded investment in marketing, advertising, digital, research and development.

Lee is one of the country's top female executives and served on the corporate board of directors of global businesses including Marriott International, Revlon, and Eastman Kodak Company. Lee is affiliated with several professional and civic organizations including the National Board of Directors for National Symphony Orchestra, the National Women's Law Center, and the Alvin Ailey Dance Theater. Lee was named Trustee Emeritus at Brown University, her alma mater.

Lee's honors include the 2001 Woman of the Year Award from Women in Cable and Telecommunications and the 2003 Distinguished Vanguard Award for Leadership from the NCTA, a first for an African-American female executive. Outside of the cable industry, Lee has also received special recognition, including the 2005 Madame C. J. Walker Award from Ebony magazine for best exemplifying the entrepreneurial spirit of the pioneering Black businesswoman (History Makers, 2012).

JBD

BRETT CLAYWELL is a professional actor, who graduated from Dudley in 1996. While a student at Dudley, he played basketball and was a point guard on Dudley's 1996 State Championship Basketball Team that starred Vincent Whitt, Brendan Haywood, and Braxton Williams. Brett Claywell is most well-known for his portrayal of young medical student Kyle Lewis on ABC's long-running daytime series, *One Life to Live*. He earned critical acclaim and national recognition, as well as a GLAAD award, for his turn as one of daytime's most talked about actors of 2010.

Claywell began acting at a young age, starting his acting career in the Children's Theater in Greensboro, North Carolina. He continued performing on the stage all the way up through college, where he studied theater at North Carolina State University while also earning a degree in Architecture. While at NC

State, he was a member of the Phi Delta Theta fraternity. Following his graduation, he moved to Wilmington, North Carolina to pursue a life as an actor. After few brief appearances on the WB's *Dawson Creek,* he won a role in the pilot of the CW's *One Tree Hill.* His portrayal of the character Tim Smith instantly made him a fan favorite and he remained so for all three seasons that he was on the show. He has also appeared in numerous episodes of the recent Joss Whedon show *Dollhouse* on FOX, where he appeared along with lead actress Eliza Dushku, Claywell has made multiple appearances in films, most notably *The Final Season,* where he co-starred with Sean Astin, Powers Boothe, Rachael Leigh Coo and Michael Angarano.

A PLACE WHERE SUCCESS WAS EXPECTED: FINAL EDITION

A NASA SPACE AND GLOBAL ENVIRONMENTAL SCIENTIST

DAVID C. WOODS graduated from Dudley in 1957. He earned a Bachelor of Science degree in Engineering Physics from North Carolina A&T State University in 1962 and a Master of Science in Physics from Old Dominion University in 1972. In 1962, he was employed as a Research Scientist at the NASA Langley Research Center in Hampton Virginia where he worked until his retirement in 2005. While working for NASA, he is credited with developing techniques, employing holographic interferometry, for locating disbands in NASA's solid propellant rocket motors. Holographic interferometry are measurements that can be applied to stress, strain, and vibration analysis, as well as to non-destructive testing. Such measurements are key to ensuring the structural integrity of materials and propellants used in space travel.

Woods also conducted extensive field studies using a specially equipped aircraft to assess the environmental impact of Space Shuttle effluents (liquid waste or sewage discharged into a river or the sea) during the first five Shuttle launches at the Kennedy Space Center. He organized and coordinated an international validation program for NASA's Lidar In-Space Technology Experiment LITE. Lidar is similar to the radar commonly used to track everything from airplanes in flight to thunderstorms. But instead of bouncing radio waves off its target, Lidar uses short pulses of laser light. Some of that light reflects off of tiny particles in the atmosphere and back to a telescope aligned with the laser. By precisely timing the Lidar "echo," and by measuring how much laser light is received by the telescope, scientists can accurately determine the location, distribution, and nature of the particles. The result of Wood's research is a revolutionary new tool for studying constituents in the atmosphere, from cloud droplets to industrial pollutants that are difficult to detect by other means. The LITE laser-based sensor in space helps scientists better understand global climate and how it might be changing. This involved scientists at numerous locations around the world making correlative measurements as Space Shuttle, with LITE on board, flew over their sites.

Woods developed and managed an Educational Outreach Program which conducted summer workshops for science teachers nationwide and visits to local schools. He published more than 50 technical papers in various scientific journals, contributed chapters to several books, and made numerous oral presentations at national and international conferences.

jBd

CLARENCE AVANT was born on February 25, 1931. Although his family lived in Climax, North Carolina, he was born in L. Richardson Hospital in Greensboro. He went to school through 9th grade at Goshen School before attending James B. Dudley High School for two years. At that time, in 1947, North Carolina, like other states, added a 12th grade to prevent high school graduates from competing with soldiers for jobs at the end of World War II. The additional year and family problems caused Avant to decide against spending an additional year in high school and at the age of sixteen, he moved to New Jersey to live with his aunt and cousin.

He began working as a manager at Teddy P's Lounge, owned by Teddy Powell, where he met the blues artist Little Willie John. Little Willie asked Avant to be his road manager, and because of Avant's skill in handling details more clients were added. In 1967, Avant helped sign William Stevenson with MGM, engineering the first joint venture between an African American artist and a major record company with the incorporation of Venture Records, Inc. into MGM Records in California.

Avant was famous for making advantageous deals for his clients. In 1968, Al Bell asked Avant to help in the sale of Stax Records to Gulf & Western. The deal was finalized for $4.3 million. The next year, Avant founded Sussex Records and bought the KAGB-FM radio station in 1973, both ventures closed in 1975. However, Avant maintained his passion for the music business and founded Tabu Productions in 1976. In 1987, Avant helped to promote Michael Jackson's first solo tour which grossed $125 million. He was named Chairman of the Board of Motown Records in 1993. One year later, Avant worked with a group of other notable African American investors to create a $20 million investment partnership in South Africa called New Age Beverages. New Age partnered with PepsiCo to build a bottling plant in South Africa, which would be completely run by South Africans.

A PLACE WHERE SUCCESS WAS EXPECTED: FINAL EDITION

Avant, along with Quincy Jones, received the Thurgood Marshall Lifetime Achievement Award in 1997. He was awarded an honorary doctorate from Morehouse College in 2003 and received the Living Legends Foundation Award in 2007. In 2010, he was inducted into the NAACP Hall of Fame. He has become known as the "Godfather" in the music business because of his willingness to aid newcomers in the industry. Through his mentoring, many of these people have become very successful and prestigious leaders in the music business.

JBD

ALLEN H. JOHNSON, III was born in April 1955 and graduated from Dudley in 1973. He spent most of his childhood in the Lincoln Heights community at 1602 Eastwood Avenue. Lincoln Heights was one of the neighborhoods of working middle class African American families that developed around James B. Dudley High School. The neighborhood, like most segregated black communities during that era, became a haven for African American families. Many of the families were first-time homeowners and there was tremendous pride in their properties, neighborhood, and schools.

While a student at Dudley, Johnson was a member of the Student Council, a Class Officer, a Junior Marshal, a member of the National Honor Society, the Panther's Claw Newspaper, and the Junior Airforce ROTC (The Panther, 1973).

After graduating from UNC Chapel Hill, Johnson joined the staff of the Greensboro News and Record eventually becoming Editorial Page Editor. His determination to remain starkly impartial on racial issues often placed him on the outs with groups like the Greensboro Truth and Reconciliation Commission and the Committee to Save Dudley. However, editorials written since mid-2015 reflect a blooming awareness and a connection to his roots as a son of the Lincoln Heights community. In a May 2018 editorial reflecting on the damage left by a tornado on the Eastern section of Greensboro, he wrote:

> *The community has continued to rally in ways that are downright inspiring. I wish we could come together like this to solve our*

longer-term problems that are not as swift and dramatic in their destruction: poverty, segregation, struggling schools. But no less harmful.
Whatever it is that makes us like this in a time of crisis I'd love to bottle.
Why must it take a tornado to bring out the best in us.

"To Be of Service Is to Lead."

PAMELA M. TRUESDALE
Class of 2003

Former First Lady Michelle Obama once said, "You may not always have a comfortable life, and you will not always be able to solve all the world's problems at once but don't ever underestimate the importance you can have because history has shown us that courage can be contagious, and hope can take on a life of its own."

The former First Lady's words resonate with me because I've always had a heart for service since I was a child who served on the guest ministries in the church and visited the sick and shut in. While at Dudley, I participated in the Female mentoring Program and both the Marching Band and Pep Band. In college, I returned to Dudley as a math tutor and judged senior projects. I believe "to be of service is to lead." In my brief lifetime, the United States has seen drastic change across all facets of life.

As I matriculate through my professional journey transferring skills learned both technical and social. On the job, I am working to break the 'glass ceiling' that hinders the presence and inclusion of minorities, especially women of color, in the corporate world. Unfortunately, change has been incremental as it relates to diversity and inclusion. As the country becomes increasingly diverse racially and economically, greater emphasis needs to be placed on identifying new markets and opportunities. I am working to bring awareness to corporate leaders because I feel business leaders must embrace and promote diversity. Still, a significant barrier exists in terms of a marketplace of ideas and communication. In today's politically correct environment, frank and honest conversation has been stifled and replaced with assumptions. As a Culture Ambassador for United Health Group, I am offering a voice for underrepresented and marginalized communities of color in the corporate world, offering insights that will drive collaboration, generate innovative ideas, and effect positive change to promote corporate sustainability.

To further my service, I serve on a nonprofit board called On Track Education. This group is dedicated to supporting the Guilford County School System and paying particular attention to marginalized children. They are equipping their parents with the resources they need to create a thriving environment for all stakeholders. Furthermore, I am an active member of the Pi Omicron Omega Chapter of Alpha Kappa Alpha Sorority, which initiated and formed a partnership with Alamance County Transportation Authority to provide scholarships for underprivileged women rides to and from their doctor appoints (supporting AKA program target of women's health). Additionally, I serve in Leadership Management as a Provisional Chair for the Junior League of Greensboro, mentoring new members through their first year in the League while promoting our vision of trained volunteers. Broadly, my commitments are rooted in my passion for equality, diversity, inclusivity, and volunteerism, which reflects in my civic engagement. (Essay by Pamela Truesdale, 2021)

Dr. Jo Evans Lynn, Ed.D.

WAYMAN BERNARD JOHNSON (AKA SLICK SLACK) a Dudley High School student through 1967 when he was drafted, Slack started his radio career with a 25-minute slot on WEAL, "the Big WEAL." He quickly became a conduit for Greensboro musicians, playing local records alongside artists such as James Brown, Solomon Burke, and Wilson Pickett. Although the charismatic Johnson would climb many industry ladders, arriving at the top of several, an interview in the News & Record from 1987 revealed that even the flashiest locals tended to keep Greensboro close to their hearts.

"It's funny coming home and realizing that it's the best place in the world," Slack said from Los Angeles. "I like Hollywood, but I'd rather be in Greensboro."

Johnson left Greensboro a three-minute memento of his stay — a 45 called "The Real Thing" by the Electric Express. Guitarist and songwriter Vic Hudson found that younger audiences from the Carlotta Supper Club and older audiences from the Elks Club responded favorably to the song's infectious riff. After Slack assured them that the song was indeed a hit, they approached Walter Copeland of Crescent City Studios at 1060 Gatewood Ave. with $60 in hand. Copeland was a reasonable man, but studio time was precious; his offer was firm: "I'll record one take." Luckily, the band's constant gigging and the informal nature of the composition yielded a hit for the mighty quartet. Released on Grady's Linco imprint, "The Real Thing" was picked up by Atlantic Records for distribution and sold more than 800,000 copies. This was an early triumph for Johnson, who cites "The Real Thing" as an important facet of his career's progression.

Slack left for Charlotte in 1972 for the evening drive time slot at WGIV-FM. While working at WGIV-FM in Charlotte, he was also on tour as the official MC for national recording artists such as Parliament-Funkadelic's, Gladys Knight & the Pips, Earth Wind and Fire, The Commodores, Chaka Khan, Brothers Johnson, The Isley Brothers, Stevie Wonder, Ike & Tina Turner, and other major recording artists.

"People would say, 'Slack, we were on this show with the Ohio Players the other day, and we smoked them!' and I used to always say, 'Well, what did they get paid and what did you get paid?' And don't get me wrong, I was so

A PLACE WHERE SUCCESS WAS EXPECTED: FINAL EDITION

proud for them. But even back then, my motto was, 'Let's not be No. 1 in Greensboro; let's be No. 1 in the world."

On the Slackson label, which he formed in 1997, he discovered Christopher Brinson and the Ensemble. He co-wrote and produced the hit single *"What if God Is Unhappy with Our Praise"* which earned a Grammy nomination.

Dr. Jo Evans Lynn, Ed.D.

Chapter Twenty

We Mean Business!

Since the early 1800's there were businesses owned by Colored people in Greensboro. From 1866- through the late 1960's communities like Warnersville and Jonesboro served the predominantly Colored residents in what was called the "Colored" parts of the city. In the 1920s, segregation laws and customs restricted public activities based on race. Signs marked such spaces as public bathrooms, train station waiting rooms, or sections in movie theaters for "white only" or "colored only." According to Tolbert (2007), "Despite the restrictions, African Americans started successful business communities and created vibrant neighborhoods in the segregated South."

Picture Courtesy UNCG Digital Library

The street scene of Elm Street in 1891 shows Black men going to or from their daily businesses as butchers, grocers, carpenters, blacksmiths, shoe/bootmakers, tailors, locksmiths, barbers, etc.

A PLACE WHERE SUCCESS WAS EXPECTED: FINAL EDITION

Corner stores in black neighborhoods had a little bit of this and a little bit of that from prescriptions, ready-made clothes, food staples (flour, sugar, rice, coffee, soft drinks, etc.) and every kid's favorite-a selection of hard candy, ice cream, and Baby Ruth candy bars.

Local grocery stores became the most common small businesses run by Black merchants. The independently owned grocers and other small businesses in the segregated neighborhoods were mainstays in their neighborhoods until chains began to open numerous stores. Chain stores—such as Sears, Roebuck and Company, F. W. Woolworth, and the Great Atlantic and Pacific Tea Company (A&P)—began to expand in the early 1900s. A chain is a company that runs many stores in different places, operating under the same name and selling the same merchandise. Chain stores created new ways to sell groceries—which meant stiff competition for smaller stores (Tolbert 2007).

In an attempt to save their businesses, in 1929 a group of African American grocers in Winston Salem joined a new cooperative business group called the Colored Merchants Association (CMA), which had begun in Alabama (Tolbert, 2007). On April 17 they announced in a local newspaper an ambitious plan to create "a movement looking towards the salvation of the Negro independent grocery stores, through cooperative buying and teaching the lesson and value of advertising." (Tolbert, 2007) The National Negro Business League, which Booker T. Washington had started in 1900 at Tuskegee Institute, promoted the grocers' efforts as a national model for

African American businessmen working in an increasingly competitive marketplace.

OFFICERS OF THE NATIONAL NEGRO BUSINESS LEAGUE, AT INDIANAPOLIS IN 1904.

In spite of segregation or maybe because segregation forced these neighborhoods to become totally self-reliant, through the late 1960's communities like Warnersville. Gilmore, Mont Zion, and Jonesboro served the predominantly Colored residents in these parts of the city. With the paving of Market Street and Gorrell Street, the areas around Bennett College and A&T College along Gorrell Street, Elm Street, and East Market Street teemed with businesses- Magnolia House Motel. Samson's Drug Store. Marie's Grill. The Busy Bee Cafe. Silver Streak Taxi Stand. The Palace Theater. Skylight Restaurant. L. Richardson Memorial Hospital. Ethel's Bake Shop. Pone Jones Billiards. The Half Moon. El Rocco Club & Restaurant. There was even a school of cosmetology- the Maco Beauty College.

One of Gorrell Street's most notable businesses of this era was the **Magnolia House Motel**, a Green Book-era accommodation with deep roots in Greensboro's Black community. Beyond its legendary hospitality, the Magnolia House has survived to witness Civil Rights history, political history, and a growing celebration of Black history (Biggs, 2021).

Magnolia House:

"The" Place to Be...

Picture Courtesy of Preservation Greensboro

The house itself was built in 1889 pre-dates the renowned motel. Although it was a private home from 1889-1949, one of its early occupants rented as many as six rooms. When Greensboro was home to the largest urban military base in the country during World War II, black soldiers and other black travelers had a limited number of places to stay. Greensboro's Green Book listings indicated limited accommodations for Black travelers. The Legion Club at 829 East Market Street was likely the largest hotel serving Black travelers. Smaller homes that took-in short-term boarders or travelers included those operated by T. Daniels at 912 East Market Street, Mrs. E. Evans at 906 East Market Street, Mrs. Lewis at 829 East Market Street, and I. W. Wooten at 423 Lindsay Street (Briggs, 2021).

Louie and Arthur Gist were the mid-twentieth century owners of Magnolia House. Arthur Taswell Gist was born in 1888 in Union, South Carolina to Lucy and Aaron Gist. He was a veteran of World War I and was trained as a brick mason. Louie was also a South Carolina native, born in 1908. She had two years of college education and earned income as a seamstress. The African American couple raised their family in Spartanburg, SC, but their eldest son attended NC A&T in the 1940s. By 1950, the family lived in the Gorrell Street house, also listed as the Magnolia House tourist home in the Greensboro city directory (Briggs, 2021).

In 1951, a new accommodation opened near the Magnolia House. Named the Plaza Manor Hotel, the facility located at 511 Martin Street was advertised as having hot and cold water, steam heat, and meals served. With nightly rates ranging from $2.00 for singles and $4.00 for double occupancy, this hotel targeted a middle-income market (Briggs, 2021).

In contrast, the Magnolia House catered to upper-income Black travelers. It was an immediate sensation. The Pittsburgh Courier reported in September 1951, "Mrs. Arthur Gist's [image, right] bridal luncheon at Magnolia House was superb…succulent was the word for the barbeque dinner…" The Magnolia House first appeared in the Green Book guide in 1955 and took its place at the top of the city's list for Black clientele.

Picture Courtesy of Sam Pass

Buddy Gist & Miles Davis

Throughout the 1950s and 1960s, Magnolia House was a distinguished and upscale accommodation for members of the entertainment industry and other celebrities. Historians have documented memories of James Brown playing with neighborhood children, Joe Tex signing autographs for fans on the front porch, and sightings of entertainers such as James Baldwin, Ray Charles, Sam Cooke, Jackie Robinson, and Ike and Tina Turner. Greensboro minister Donald Trapp remembered "It had Oriental carpets on the floor and a chandelier. It stayed full all the time, especially on weekends." (Briggs, 2021)

The house hosted numerous special events. In 1957, the house was the site of Black employees of Piedmont Natural Gas for their annual Christmas party and presentation of service awards. In 1960 it accommodated a reunion of veterans of World War I, where all such veterans were welcome. In 1968, the house served as the meeting location for the executive committee of the Democrat Club of Guilford County. The elder Gists took a role as political reformers in the city.

The tourist home also served as a touchstone to Civil Rights efforts, exemplified in May 1958 when the house was the site of the organizational meeting of the Guilford County Negro Democratic Club. Arthur Gist was elected treasurer. The club sought to coordinate with the Democratic Party and to meet Democratic candidates for public office during a time of Black empowerment in Greensboro. In July 1962, the house was a stop on the Freedom Drive in the south by the Congress of Racial Equality (CORE) to "end segregation at roadside restaurants". Principal targets of desegregation

A PLACE WHERE SUCCESS WAS EXPECTED: FINAL EDITION

were the Howard Johnson and Holiday Inn chains. The Magnolia House served as a training site for nonviolent protests, building on the civic engagement accomplished during the Woolworth Sit In demonstrations at area lunch counters of 1960.

The house was acquired by Sam Pass in 1996 from Grace Gist, Herman's widow. Sam Pass learned of the history of the house and developed a plan for a living history museum. Guests would not just examine the house as a museum, but could experience the landmark through learning, staying overnight, and dining…just as visitors had during the 1950s and 1960s. Today, the house is operated in tandem with his daughter, Natalie Pass-Miller, who continues to restore the site for continued use as an historic center for Greensboro.

Picture Courtesy of Samuel Penn Pass

The 21st Century Magnolia House is more than a "living" museum. It is the place to not only appreciate its past splendor, but to make new memories during wedding receptions, Sunday Brunches, book-club gatherings, and of course Weekend birthday celebrations with 10-20 of your closest friends.

Dr. Jo Evans Lynn, Ed.D.

Lillie Morehead Moore: She Meant Business!

Lillie Morehead Moore

Perhaps, one of the best-known female business owners during this era in the Gilmore section of the city was Lillie Moore who owned a building on McConnell Road that housed a Grocery Store, a beauty parlor, offered three rooms for rent on the second floor, and used the backyard to sell firewood and coal. My sister Gloria Evans remembers her this way,

"We were scared of her. Kids claimed she had eyes in the back of her head. I didn't believe it until one day when I was paying for my candy in the front of the store and without looking up, she yelled, "Put that back and stand there till I get to you."

She was yelling at a boy in the back of the store that I hadn't even noticed. The boy stood where he was. When she finished with me and my younger sisters. She let us out, pulled down the shade over the door's window, and we heard the door lock. I didn't know what to do- run get Officer Penn or go down to the bus stop to see if Mama's bus had left yet. While I was still trying to figure out what to do. The boy came out with two bags of groceries.

"I said, "Boy I'm gonna have my Aunt Daisy call the police on you. You had to kill her to get all that."

He said, "She's alright. She knows my dad got hurt on the job and ain't been able to work for a while. Please, he begged, don't tell anyone. She says if it gets out that she's given even a crumb of bread away, it'll be bad for her business.

Gloria finished, "It's a secret that I kept until Jo Ann was writing this book.

Lillie Moore's son, David Moore, Sr. had one of the most successful gardening businesses in Greensboro.

A PLACE WHERE SUCCESS WAS EXPECTED: FINAL EDITION

David Moore: An Extraordinary Gardener & Businessman!

David Moore
Tends Flowers In Prickett Yard

His son, David Moore contributed an excerpt about his father in the book, The Art of the Hustle: Lessons in Becoming a Man:

My father was the best gardener and landscaper in Greensboro, North Carolina. I am not just saying that. He won all kinds of awards and his gardens, especially his roses, were featured in the newspaper and even in a big-time magazine. All the rich White folks in those mansions out in Irving Park wanted him to work for them. He took great pride in his work.

Often, after another article came out about his beautiful roses, people would offer him as much as $500.00 a week to come and work for them, but he was loyal to his longtime customers. He could afford to be selective with his clients. I remember an important lesson that I learned about how he selected and kept his clients.

One time, shortly after I started working with my father, we were working in this rich lady's garden. She brought some members of her garden club out to see the garden. She pointed my dad out sayings, "David is the best yard boy in Greensboro."

First, I thought that maybe she had mistaken me for my dad, but then I realized that she couldn't see me because I was behind a fountain. It made me mad her calling my dad a "Yard Boy." I was the only "boy" out there, and I didn't much care for that term for myself because I was already doing a man's work.

Dad didn't say anything. He just kept digging around some plants. I wanted him to say something. I wanted him to bless her out and walk off the job.

He just nodded his head when one of the women that were with her complimented his roses.

The next week, when it was the day to go to that lady's garden, I expected my dad to drive right on by.

He didn't.

He went in and worked just like he always did. When he noticed that I was acting kind of slack-half cutting the grass- he said, "Don't make me take a switch to you boy. Do like I taught you to do."

When it was time for me to go up to the house and collect the check, Dad said, "I'll go."

I watched, expecting him to tell the lady that we wouldn't be back. When she tried to give him a check, he looked at it, shook his head, and handed it back to her. I couldn't hear what he said, but the lady fussed a while, but then went back into the house and came out with another check. Dad looked at it, nodded, turned around and walked back to the truck.

He didn't say a word. He just handed me the check. My eyes about popped out of my head. The check was for two times as much as he usually charged and instead of being made out to David Moore it was made out to Mr. David Moore. It made sense. A yard "boy" cost that lady twice as much as a gardener, and there was no mistaking Mr. David Moore for a "boy."

The lesson that I learned was that when you're really good at what you do, you can demand respect.

Lillie Moore & David Moore, Sr. and the other business owners along McConnell Road, and East Market Street reflected the history of the Black community.

Ash Street and the surrounding areas in Warnersville also had many successful businesses owned by Colored people. T.O. Stokes Senior owned a gas station. Mr. Vines owned a Dry Cleaner. Smith Funeral Home served families in Warnersville. Leroy Morgan had a Barber Shop - his son has a Barber Shop on MLK now. Scales' Pool Room. Tom's Take Home Carry Out Food. Fox Shoe Repair. Anderson's Grill and Sweet Shoppe. Hicks Snowball Stand. (Wynn, 2023)

There were several black owned businesses like tailor shops, barbershops, and hatters in Downtown Greensboro. Schlosser (2006) described black businesses in Downtown Greensboro.

Bob's Hatters and several barbershops and tailor shops were downtown's only black-owned businesses. Even so, they had to conform to segregationist customs or risk the wrath of city leaders. Black-owned barber shops could shave and cut the hair of white people only. At Bob's Hatters, black people were barred from sitting atop the shoeshine stand. They could drop off shoes or sit for a shine behind a curtain in the rear of the shop.

Harold Cotton, Sr. demonstrates his hat blocking skills.

In February 1960, while N.C. A&T and Bennett College students tried to integrate the Woolworth lunch counter downtown, Cotton without publicity integrated Bob's Hatters. A black Marine walked in and asked for a spit shine. Cotton told him to climb onto the stand.

When segregation was outlawed, those wanting proof it was ended only had to peek through the window of Bob's Hatters. Black and white people sat side by side on the stand talking sports, politics or whatever. Cotton and Gilyard joined in while polishing and buffing.

Yes, black owned businesses flourished in Greensboro for more than four generations. And then came Urban Renewal.

In Wilmington, North Carolina in 1898 and Tulsa, Oklahoma in 1921 it took thousands of armed White Supremacists to destroy wealthy Black and mixed-race businesses and communities. In Greensboro, they were more civilized about the mass destruction of majestic black churches, businesses, and homes that had been the "beating hearts" of the community. Benjamin Biggs in a blog for Preservation Greensboro eloquently described the effect of the so-called urban renewal on the Black community,

> From the perspective of those living in the twenty-first century, a community reinvestment plan that entails the destruction of the focus neighborhood seems to be a contradiction in terms. How can new life be brought into a community through revitalization if its housing, enterprises, sacred spaces, and cultural touchstones are destroyed?
>
> If urban renewal holds the reputation of demolition of neighborhoods such as East Greensboro…what exactly were planners and politicians of the era thinking?

At this point in our history, it really does not matter what they were thinking, the results were devastating. The original **Trinity AME Zion 1891-1966 "Big Zion"** was destroyed. Redevelopment in 1966 led to the demise of the Original Shiloh Baptist Church and other massive brick churches that existed in communities like Warnersville during this era of Black History in Greensboro. The Grand two-story homes like the one owned by Douglas & Amanda Johnson (pictured on page 16) which were some of the first homes owned by Freemen and former slaves in Greensboro were destroyed. The Palace Theater and other black owned businesses up and down Gorrell Steet, Market Street and almost every other historic landmark in the predominately Black neighborhoods that dated back to the mid- 1800s were demolished during this time. Trinity was relocated to Florida and Larkin Streets.

Nevertheless, through it all the spirit entrepreneurship still exists in us. Black owned businesses have continued to rise through hard work, determination, and the enduring expectation of success.

Art Ink Designs

Promotional Products

"Have You Got that Sprit? Yeah Man!

Arthur "Colley" Hood graduated from Dudley High School in 1965. There was never any doubt that Arthur had that "Ole Dudley High Spirit" because when he was a student at Dudley, Arthur became a vital part of numerous Dudley teams by participating in the best way that he could-as team manager. During his sophomore year, he was the manager for football, basketball, and track teams. He received a letter in all three sports. His junior and senior years he was the manager for football, basketball, and baseball. He was awarded a letter for each sport for each of those years. In the history of James B, Dudley High School, no other student has ever received nine letters while at Dudley High School as a student manager. Arthur says that his most exciting memory of that time was the 1964 and 1965 baseball teams winning the State Championship.

He later earned a Bachelor of Arts degree in Art Design from North Carolina A&T State University. Before becoming a full-time entrepreneur, Arthur spent 26 years in the United States Air Force. In 1979 Arthur relocated to Dallas Texas.

In 1980, Arthur started Art Ink Designs, a promotional products company. He first started the business by designing logos for small businesses. By demand, his clients began to ask for tee shirts for special events such as company picnics and retreats. And soon after that he began doing more promotional items such as coffee mugs, caps, uniforms, and business printing. Art Ink Designs are produced using several different mediums: embroidery, screen printing, and business printing. Overtime his business base has extended to producing items for HBCUs, HBHS', local, city, state contracts, and government agencies, schools, and North Carolina A&T State University Dallas/Ft. Worth Chapter Alumni.

Classic T-shirts   iPhone Soft Case   Dad Hats   Mouse Pads   Bucket Hats   Baseball Caps

Dr. Jo Evans Lynn, Ed.D.

It does not matter whether its clothing, gifts, stickers, mugs, phone cases, Hoodies, posters socks, stationery, office décor or wall art, Art Ink Designs custom designed products are artistically designed to meet the promotional needs of every client.

Phone 214-603-5117

Contact Information:

https://art-ink-promo-printyfy.me

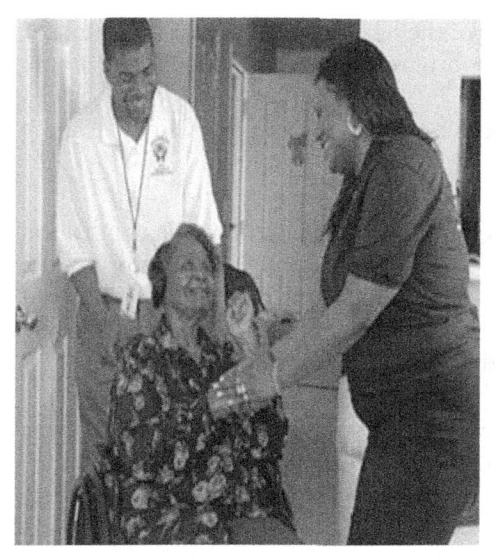

Shipman Family Home Care, Inc.

Their Clients Come First...

As a young mother, Gladys L. Shipman worked as an assistant manager at an apartment complex and part-time at a small agency that provided in-home healthcare aids. When the owner of the business got sick in the mid-80s, he asked Shipman to take over the business. She got a loan from Skip Alston and in three months doubled the clients. She hired people from her community. Through her hard work and determination to succeed for over 35 years Shipman Family Home Care provided personal healthcare. Shipman has been recognized as the largest minority-owned home care provider in the state of North Carolina. Shipman Family Home Care, Inc. has offices in about a dozen counties across the state. It has been Better Business Bureau Accredited since 1994.

Picture Courtesy of WCP Consulting & Communications

Picture Courtesy of WCP Consulting & Communications

Offices of Shipman Family Home Care, Inc. are located in Greensboro, Winston Salem/Forsyth County, Standford, Durham, Kinston County, High Point, Burlington, Durham, Richmond County and Reidsville.

Specializing in One-On-One Personal Care, their emphasis is on caring for their clients so that:

- Families can develop and make the best possible use of their time.
- Clients can make significant progress through a systematic home health program.
- As much emphasis as possible is placed on helping Clients to help themselves.

Since its inception in 1987, Shipman Family Home Care, Inc., has withstood the storms in the health care industry by sticking to the following principle: OUR CLIENTS COME FIRST! Building around this principle is a team of dedicated health care providers who make "Your Family... Our Family" they are never satisfied are never satisfied until their clients are satisfied.

Shipman Family Home Care consistently strives to identify in-home services that support people who may need to remain in their homes when disruptions are caused due to illness, disability, social disadvantage, and other problems affecting the quality of daily living.

Their **Personal Care** includes: a funded program of in-home care services for people with medical conditions that need help with daily living activities such as: bathing, dressing, grooming, toileting; errands / shopping; meal preparation; monitor medication; laundry / light housekeeping; home management; assist with scheduling doctor appointments; assist with walking and transfers

Under certain circumstances clients receive 60 hours per month in-home care by a certified nursing assistant (CNA) at no cost to the client or their family. To be eligible for a certified nursing assistant a client must:

- have a blue Medicaid card and
- have a medical need or
- you can pay privately

    Shipman also supplies respite care when family members need a break in caring for loved ones. They provide the care needed on the days or hours of your choosing.

Contact Information:

Phone +1 (336)272-7545

Email: sfcofnc@yahoo.com

ERNESTINE BENNETT, a graduate of Dudley's Class of 1964 received a Bachelor of Science Degree in Business Education from North Carolina A&T State University and attended graduate school at George Washington University in Public Administration.

She was the first African American Female Wendy's Old-Fashioned Hamburgers Franchisee selected in July 1993. Bennett purchased the first of her restaurants in March 1994. She expanded the business with a second acquisition in 1998 and built four new locations over the next six years. Bennett developed a system for delivering exceptional speed of service, resulting in double digit sales increases that became the standard and was adopted nationwide in the Wendy's system.

Prior to Wendy's, she had a 20+ year career in the federal government, Department of Health and Human Services, Social Security Administration. She took an early retirement to pursue her dream of becoming an entrepreneur.

Bennett has received many honors: Top 100 Women of Influence, Atlanta Business League, 2006; Infinity Broadcasting's 4th Annual "For Sisters Only" Community Service Award , 2004; Profiled by WSB TV for Black History Month, 2005; honored in "Salute to Living Legends", 2005; selected "Woman of the Year", Atlanta Business League, 2005; honored by the Southeastern Region AME Church for "Deliverance in Economic Development", 2008; "Above and Beyond Award" for outstanding Employer Support of the National Guard and Reserve, 2008; Who's Who in Black Atlanta, Master Achiever, 2004; Who's Who in Black Atlanta, Most Influential, 2005, 2006, 2007, 2009; Commissioner's Citation, DHHS, Social Security Administration, for Sustained Outstanding Contributions to the Modernized Disability System, 1993; Regional Commissioner's Citation, for

Highly Effective Contributions to SSA's Modernized Disability System, 1994 (James B. Dudley Hall of Fame, 2015).

She is president and CEO of E B Enterprise Unlimited, Inc. She sold the restaurants and retired from the QSR industry in 2009. Bennett continues to operate both holding Companies with other commercial ventures. She provides consulting to aspiring entrepreneurs, conducts workshops on "How to Become an entrepreneur", Bennett is also a Counselor with SCORE – Service Corps of Retired Executives/Entrepreneurs. (James B. Dudley Hall of Fame, 2015)

ROBERTA WASHINGTON at 1965 Dudley graduate is an American architect. While at Dudley, she was active in the Dudley Thespians and the Art Club. She is the founding principal of Roberta Washington Architects, PC, one of the only architecture firms in the United States led by an African American woman. She is a Commissioner on the New York City Landmarks Preservation Commission. Washington became interested in studying architecture after a chance encounter with a neighbor who was an architect. She described this life directing experience in a 2012 article for *Making a Place*. She Wrote,

"As a child I was attracted to drawing and art. In school, art was my favorite subject. When I was in the eighth grade, we had an English class assignment to interview three people who had occupations that we might want to pursue. I had thought I would become an artist, but I had a fast reality check with one of my teachers who convinced me that becoming an artist was difficult – but if you were black and female, it was all the more improbable. To be practical, I probably wanted to think about becoming an art teacher, I was told. I interviewed my art teacher. But I needed two more occupations to complete the assignment. I interviewed my Mom who worked at a hospital (in which I had no interest) and my mom suggested that I interview a new neighbor who was renting a house next door to us for a year. He was an architect who was teaching at North Carolina's historically black A & T College (which has since become a university).

Mr. Gray talked about how architecture expanded on art to create spaces and structures that could comfort the body, soothe the soul, and stir the spirit. Architecture, he said, was problem-solving. Good architecture could improve people's lives and their neighborhoods. He made it all sound incredibly cooler than becoming an artist. I was hooked. From then on, I had a name to describe what I really wanted to be in life. Architect.

When I told my high school guidance counselor that I wanted to become an architect she tried to convince me that architecture was a highly improbable field for a black person to choose. But because I had met a black architect, I was sure that it was possible. Although I didn't know it at the time, my chance meeting with Mr. Gray at the age of thirteen steered my life in a direction that I could not have imagined before. In the library I found a little AIA pamphlet "So You Want to Be an Architect" which I read and followed religiously. Until I entered college, I never encountered another architect."

Washington received her bachelor's degree in architecture from Howard University. She received a full scholarship along with 25 other African American students to Columbia University as a response to its campus race riots in 1968. There, she earned her master's degree in architecture. After earning her master's degree, she spent four years working on hospital and housing projects in Mozambique. During her education, she was active in organizations including the Women's Caucus at the AIA and Alliance of Women in Architecture. Forming bonds with fellow architects helped inspire Washington to work to ensure legacies of blacks and women aren't lost. To note, she has been researching and writing about Beverly Loraine Green and Georgia Louise Harris Brown since 1997.

Dr. Jo Evans Lynn, Ed.D.

Picture Courtesy of Roberta Washington Architects, PC
Roberta Washington Architects, PC established 1983 in Harlem, N.Y.

Roberta Washington Architects, PC was established in 1983 in the heart of Harlem as one of the few African American, woman-owned architectural firms in the country. The firm's primary work includes health and educational facilities and affordable housing projects. Projects include the renovation of dozens of abandoned apartment buildings in Harlem for low and middle-income tenants in addition to new moderate-income housing for home ownership, a specialty medical center, an MTA subway station, public school projects (including New Haven's first LEED Gold Certified School), museums and historic preservation projects.

Philanthropy and Loyalty

To Whom Much IS Given...

KATHY ROUSON HAIRSTON graduated from Dudley in 1971. While at Dudley, during her senior year she served as Vice-President of the Girls Chorus, Homeroom Secretary, Mixed Chorus Secretary, and Science Club Secretary. She completed her post-secondary studies at North Carolina A&T State University earning a Bachelor of Science degree in Social Services in 1975 and a Master of Science degree in Health and Physical Education from North Carolina A&T State University.

Kathy and her husband, John Hairston Sr., purchased their first McDonald's restaurant in Atlanta, Georgia, in 1986. They sold the Atlanta restaurant in 1989 and returned to Charlotte to build the first McDonald's restaurant in Mint Hill, N.C. They were the first black McDonald's owners/operators to be awarded a restaurant in the Charlottee area. The Hairstons would grow their business by purchasing ten more restaurants in and around Charlotte. They were McDonald's owners/operators for over 35 years. All through the years, the Hairstons gave back to their community in numerous ways- mentoring new owners/operators, sponsoring Little League Teams, sponsoring rooms at Ronald McDonald House for families with children in Levine Children's Hospital, volunteering at Ronald McDonald House of Charlotte the list goes on and on...

Kathy is a member of Rockwell A.M.E. Zion Church's trustee Board, finance Committee, and Deaconess Board member. Kathy is on the Board of Directors of the Foundation of N.C. A&T State

University. She has established two scholarship endowments to support students majoring in sociology and social work at N.C. A&T State University. In 2013, she was awarded The Alumni Achievement Award for career achievement and support of North Carolina A&T State University. The Hairstons made a multi-million, multi-year cash donation to N.C. A&T State University resulted in the naming of A&T's College of Health and Sciences to **The John R. and Kathy R. Hairston College of Health and Human Science**.

The Union Square-Cone Health, GTCC, NC A&T SU, and UNCG site offers state of the art *John R. and Kathy R. Hairston College of Health and Human Sciences*.

A PLACE WHERE SUCCESS WAS EXPECTED: FINAL EDITION

Scooping-Up Joy, Fun & Flavor...

Pictures Courtesy of Robert Jarrell

Co-Owners of Scoop Zone, Robert Jarrell, and Janneĕ Jarrell

ROBERT JARRELL graduated from Dudley High School with honors in 2003. He then earned a Bachelor of Arts degree in music from North Carolina A&T State University. Before becoming a full-time entrepreneur, Robert served as choral music director at Dudley High School from 2016-2021.

In 2008 Jarrell and his wife, Janneĕ started selling ice cream like the traditional ice cream trucks seen riding through your neighborhood. In 2018 they decided to revisit the ice cream business idea and rebrand themselves as Scoop Zone. They wanted to create a place that was fun and exciting that specialized in frozen treats and they did just that.

SCOOP ZONE is not a popsicle truck, and they do not sell cups of ice! The quality and variety of their frozen treats has made Scoop Zone the Triads favorite mobile ice cream parlor. Scoop Zone offers a variety of Blue Bell's scooped authentic ice cream flavors in cups and cones. They also offer cookie sandwiches, waffles cones, Cookie Monster sundae and their signature Rocket ball. Their Rocket ball is freshly made cotton candy wrapped in your favorite flavor of ice cream. Their Cookie Monster sundae is every cookie lover's dream come true! It is vanilla cookies and ice cream layered with cookie crumbles topped with whipped cream, chocolate drizzle and a chocolate chip cookie. For their non-dairy customers they also offer a variety of Italian ices.

The Jarrell's have been in business for five years. Over those five years, they have had two brick and mortar locations- one in downtown High Point and the other in the Four Seasons Mall in Greensboro. During the course of this journey, Scoop Zone has evolved from brick-and-mortar locations to mobile ice cream parlors. Janee and Robert both play a major role in the operations of Scoop Zone. Robert handles the day-to-day operations, booking, and maintenance. Janee handles the marketing, Human Resources, training staff and administrative duties. In 2023 their business employs 10 employees who are trained for working events. They have four ice cream units that are capable of handling small and large events.

When asked why they settled on the idea of an ice cream business the Jarrell's say, "We love ice cream! And we are passionate about bringing joy and happiness to others." These two factors have been the driving force behind Scoop Zone's success. **Their commitment to using high-quality ingredients and customer satisfaction has helped them build a loyal customer base and gain recognition throughout the local community.**

Their mobile business is more than the Ice Cream trucks that were the high point of summer days in Morningside Homes and other communities. Scoop Zone's four mobile units bring the party to all kinds of events. Iceberg, Snowball, Scoop Mobile. and their mobile Ice Cream Parlor fleet, are the perfect addition to any event to spice up the excitement! Their mobile Bounce House is perfect for any child's party and their Mobile giant screen takes Movie night to a new level of fun.

Scoop Zone's "Snowball" is one of three mobile units that delivers a vast number treats to all types of events.

The Scoop Zone ice cream trailer is called Scoop Mobile, and is a pushcart, allows the company to cater to a larger group of people.

A PLACE WHERE SUCCESS WAS EXPECTED: FINAL EDITION

Over the past five years, Scoop Zone has experienced significant growth and success. The company now has three ice cream vans, an ice cream trailer called **Scoop Mobile**, and a pushcart, allowing them to cater to more people. The fleet of mobile units allows Scoop Zone to serve delicious treats to various events and locations, including company events, festivals, birthday parties, and more.

Scoop Zone continues to grow and expand, with plans to launch new and exciting flavors in the coming months. The company strives to provide a memorable experience for their customers, whether it's through the delicious taste of their ice cream or the unique entertainment they offer.

Contact Information

Phone: (336) 338-5601

Website: https://scoopzone336.com/

Address: 1130 W Vandalia Rd Greensboro, NC, 27406-5740
United States

Dr. Jo Evans Lynn, Ed.D.

Pictures Courtesy of Robert Jarrell Jr.

Robert Jarrell, Jr. is the owner of Teach Me How Studios where teachers aim to inspire students of all ages through exceptional music education. Teach Me How Studio has a talented faculty that has created an innovative music program that offers flexible hours and a convenient location for families in the Greensboro Triad area. Teach Me How Studio encourages parents to allow their children to come to a place where the love of music is demonstrated in the caring skill and talent of our teachers. Our mission is for each of our students to discover their innate passion for music! For example, the Music Production Program highlights and exposes students to music production and song writing, audio engineering practices, the music industry, and technology. It is a comprehensive program that brings music performance and compositions with practical training in audio engineering.

They offer group and private lessons in a variety of instruments. Instruction includes but is not limited to piano, trumpet, drums, and wood wind instruments. We are dedicated to teaching and preparing students for careers in Performing Arts, and Electronic Music. We encourage students to explore instruments and discover their unique connection to them. We are a hands-on training facility.

Contact Information:
Address: 1130 W Vandalia Rd. Greensboro N.C. 27406
Phone: (336) 456-1099
Email: TeachMeHowToPlayPiano@gmail.com

Chapter Twenty-One

The Fight to Save Dudley...

It started with a twenty-two to one vote. The vote to demolish the entire campus-Main Building, Main Gymnasium, the North Annex, the South Annex, the Science Building, and the English Building. All of it. The one "NO" vote was that of Dudley High School alumnae, Jo Evans Lynn a 1967 Dudley graduate. Shortly after that vote Lynn and her sister, Gloria Evans, a 1965 graduate of Dudley, contacted the press to question why the public had not been notified of the imminent vote. After the emotional television appeal, the Evans sisters were joined by several activists who shared their common vision: to save James Benson Dudley High School for future generations (Baines, 2002).

Committee to Save Dudley Members

Front left to right: Mrs. Jo Evans Lynn, '67, Ms. Gloria Evans, '65, Ms. Heather Seifert. **Second row left to right**: Dr. Mark Fields, '71 & Mr. David Moore, '62; **Back Row, left to right:** Mr. Edwin White,'67, Mr. Erwin White, '67, Mrs. Jackie Kpeglo, Mr. Lewis Brandon, and Mr. John Hamilton, '54. **Not pictured**: Dr. Goldie Frinks Wells, Agnes Greene,'51, Glenn Booker, '78, and Phyllis Booker

There were numerous sentimental and practical reasons why the historic Main Building and award-winning Main Gymnasium should be saved. However, the three obvious reasons for keeping those buildings should have been enough to turn the tide to whole school modernization before the matter reached the second vote by the Guilford County School Board. First, three engineering studies by independent companies concluded that the buildings' exteriors were structurally sound. The Science Building,

English Building and Auxiliary Gym were relatively "new" having been completed in the early 1960s and mid-70s.

Secondly, there was simply not enough money approved for the project by the school board, 31.4 million, to build a new school of the size and quality of the one that it would replace. The project received 31.4 million dollars to complete a whole school modernization of Dudley. Only 24.6 million of that money could be used for actual construction (this is called the C-cap) and the rest must be set aside to furnish technology, furniture, and specialized equipment for the high-tech programs that were expected to be placed in the modernized Dudley facility. Since the community voted in 1998 during a meeting of over 300 concerned Dudley alumni and friends to keep the school on its current site at 1200 Lincoln Street rather than move it to Franklin Boulevard, the school board only allotted enough money to modernize the school.

Thirdly, the design that was sent to parents and alumni and placed on the Internet was a long way from what would have replaced Dudley if the community had allowed an entirely new school to be built. After the school board approved a new 278,000 square feet facility to replace Dudley, several issues came to light that made it fair to assume that the only way to get "new" was to accept a much smaller building constructed of materials that merely "met" state standards. For example, because of the amount of money that was allotted the new auditorium would only seat 350 (the same size of the auditorium at Weaver Center), the new main gymnasium would have only seated 700 (the same size as Smith High School's gymnasium), and the total student population would have been 1,200. The general use of high schools of this size is for an academy or charter school. This smaller size would have meant that most of the students in the communities around Dudley would have been redistricted to other high schools in the system.

Most of the construction committee that recommended destroying all the buildings on the campus and building a new school later reversed their decision based on this new information. Dale Tonkins, one committee member, said, "The school that Gantt is planning is nothing like the one we approved. If we had known he was going to do this, we would have stayed with restoring what we have."

A PLACE WHERE SUCCESS WAS EXPECTED: FINAL EDITION

Why was the whole school modernization the right option for Dudley? Simply speaking, it gave us the best of both worlds. The whole school modernization protects the historic structural and cultural integrity of the exterior of a building while providing all the modern amenities and technological advantages in the interior of a contemporary structure.

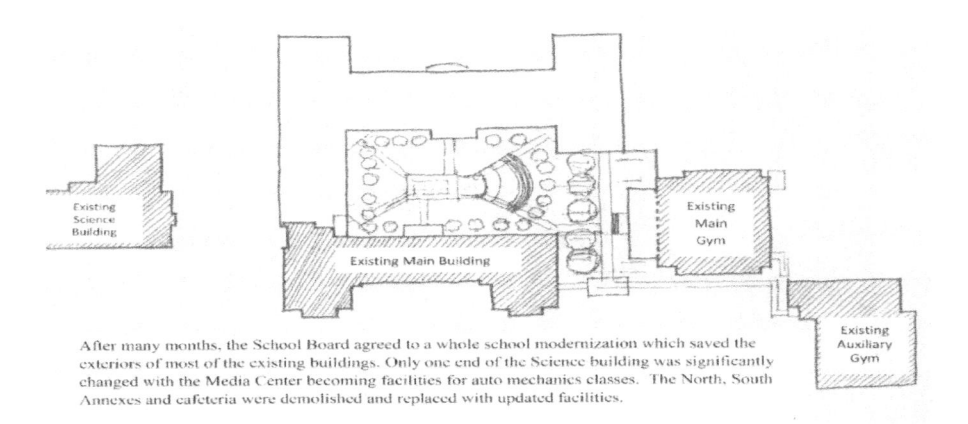

After many months, the School Board agreed to a whole school modernization which saved the exteriors of most of the existing buildings. Only one end of the Science building was significantly changed with the Media Center becoming facilities for auto mechanics classes. The North, South Annexes and cafeteria were demolished and replaced with updated facilities.

For facilities like Dudley's Main Building and Main Gymnasium this means removing some non-load bearing interior walls to restructure classrooms and labs for modern uses; adding keyed elevators for use by handicapped students and visitors; adding classrooms and other facilities for exciting new programs; and adding larger and better equipped cafeteria and media center spaces. This would also mean that all or most of the interior walls and flooring would be replaced and that all of the tiles and fixtures in the bathrooms and dressing rooms would be replaced with modern, state-of-the-art materials. However, in some cases where the old materials are not only in excellent shape, but also are far more valuable as antiques than any modern material would be, the architect could try to incorporate the old fixtures in the new design. For example, the seats in the auditorium are very expensive antiques, saving them and incorporating them into the modernized auditorium actually increased the value of the facility.

Dr. Jo Evans Lynn, Ed.D.

Although a few of seats needed repair, all except a few of the original seats with the blue JBD were reused in the modernized auditorium. They were reused because the seats are valuable antiques and even with the cost of refurbishing them were valued at more than five times the cost of any seats that are "standard" for new school auditoriums. The wrought iron frames of the seats are much sturdier than any that would have replaced them.

I must stop here to disburse a rumor that I heard about the renovation of the auditorium. No, the Construction Committee Members did not demand that we keep the old floor of the stage. We were told that there was not enough money in the budget for new flooring for a full-sized stage. The pictures at the left are before and after photos. The only seats with significant damage were on the front row were not reused but were removed to allow wheelchair access. Damage to the auditorium is not due to age but more likely due to workmanship of the construction company in charge of the Modernization. The roof was leaking when we moved back into the building. A couple of days before Open House there were puddles and water spots on the ceiling in the hallway leading from the auditorium to the main hall and outside my classroom. I went and got the On-site Construction Manager. The crew was still there working on converting the Old Media Center into the auto mechanics' class. He assured me that the problem would be repaired. But Mrs. Stephens, the custodian at the time, told me that all they did was replace the ceiling tiles.

Gantt Huberman Architects and Interior Designers

A PLACE WHERE SUCCESS WAS EXPECTED: FINAL EDITION

One would think that after the Whole School Modernization had been completed that the Battle to Save Dudley had been won. However, it seems that skirmishes must still be fought. On a return to campus after nearly a year's absence, I noticed that several trees had been planted in front of the Main Building. I asked a gentleman who was passing nearby, "What's that about?" I pointed to the trees.

"Beautification." He stated as he hurried by.

"Beautification? Beautification!" I fussed to my sister, Gloria. "How does one beautify a historic site by covering it up? I guess their next project will be collecting money to use modern technology to restore the nose on the Great Sphinx of Egypt or maybe they will gather funds to give the Taj Mahal a paint job since white marble is no longer in style." I ranted and raved all the way home and for about an hour after we got there.

I was angry and I was hurt because after all that we had gone through to save the school, there were still people who did not understand that the beauty of the building is in more than its architecture. The beauty is in the fact that it is still here and still a high school attended by young people who live in the communities around it. So much of our past has been loss. Buildings, like the old Lincoln Junior High School that still exist have been turned into Academies that limit access to children who live in the surrounding neighborhoods (Only 20% of the children living in the attendance zone around Dudley are allowed to enroll in Lincoln Academy). Jones Elementary School in the Warnersville Community has a very successful Spanish Immersion Magnet Program with over 400 students, but during the 2015-2016 school year there were only eight children from the neighborhoods around the school in that program.

Other schools like J.C. Price are closed and loss forever along with most of the communities around them. Most of Warnersville was razed during the late 1960s and 1970s. After J.C. Price was closed, the school system sold the property to Guilford Technical Community College which used the school as part of its campus until 2001. Greensboro College bought the property in 2003 as a site for a new football stadium. Warnersville Community leaders began to organize to plan to preserve the school. In the Introduction to the book, *Picturing Greensboro: Four Decades of the African American Community*, Otis L. Hairston, Jr. (2007) stated, "The threat to J.C. Price is significant, and images in this book reflect on much of the traditions and events in the African American community that have been lost due to a lack of effort by past and present generations to preserve our past." Johnny Hodge, then A&T State University Band Director and former Guilford County School Board member, and his wife Brenda Hodges (Retired Dudley High School teacher) joined many other citizens with ties to the Warnersville Community in an effort to save J.C. Price School. In the Hairston book, they wrote:

> In the very near future, a decision will be made whether to preserve or demolish J. C. Price School. The sad part about this issue is that few Guilford County citizens understand the historical significance of this location.

People in this area need to be informed about the contributions that J.C. Price School (and other segregated schools) made to the growth of public education in America. It is only by gaining sufficient knowledge and thorough insight that communities are able to make wise decisions about what can be destroyed and what should be preserved.

We've' heard on numerous occasions that "You can't appreciate your present unless you know something of your past."

His statement becomes particularly meaningful to those of us whose roots trace back to the old Warnersville community. In an age characterized by financial, social, and moral degradation, many of our black youth are finding it more and more difficult to find worthwhile connections to black history in Greensboro.

Never before in the history of this country have so many young black youths lost sight of what education and knowledge has meant for our race. Not only has there been a decline in their test scores, but their respect for education and leadership has come to an alarming halt. These problems are amplified by the fact that, over the past thirty years, black people in leadership roles have been carefully deleted from public school systems. Many blacks have been replaced by others who know little if anything about the motivations, the achievements, and the struggles of our ancestors.

J.C. Price School sits in the middle of the old Warnersville community where there are precious few reminders of this history of black people in Greensboro. Warnersville was the first black community in this county where people of color could own their own homes, build their own churches, own land, run their own businesses and educate their own children. J.C. Price served an important cultural function for children and adults who belonged to an authentic cultural minority.

Most often a teacher's appointment to a position at J.C. Price implied that the teacher was highly trained. They were considered by many to be the best in the field. Some of these teachers received their training in Guilford County, attended colleges and universities throughout the United States and often found their way back to J.C. Price to teach. Thus, the legacy was passed on; the people progressed.

Consider the contributions of the longtime Price principal, A. H. Peeler. Said one former Price student:

"During the 1950s few would dispute that Negroes were getting education inferior in quality to that provided for whites. Mr. Peeler never emphasized our lack. He always accentuated the positive and expected a lot from us. Our industrial arts department, our home economics department and our library were second to none in the state. We were pushed to excel, and we were motivated to always do our best that's the way Mr. Peeler was. And, most importantly, our parents trusted him."

Said Mr. Peeler:

> "I was born in Warnersville. My mother taught at the J. C. Price School. Our children attended J. C. Price School. It was my privilege to serve as principal of J.C. Price for thirty-nine years. I belong to this community and J.C. Price belongs to us."

A PLACE WHERE SUCCESS WAS EXPECTED: FINAL EDITION

A group of current and past residents of the Warnersville Community, former students, administrators, and teachers at J.C. Price School organized the *Warnersville Heritage & Music Festival* to raise awareness of the importance of Warnersville and J.C. Price to the community. The group began to make plans to add J.C. Price to the National Register of Historic Sites and contacted members of the Committee to Save Dudley about beginning the process and also organized a series of events designed to focus on the rich historic significance of the Warnersville Community. In response to the public support for preserving the school, Greensboro College announced that they had scaled back their plans to a smaller athletic facility that would preserve the Price building itself. In 2008, Greensboro College announced its intent to preserve the J.C. Price School. They said that once funding was secured for renovations, the proposed use of the former school (to be renamed the J.C. Price Lyceum) and property was to house educational and athletic activities, in addition to a community museum for Warnersville. The football stadium was removed from the plans. The people thought that the battle to save J.C. Price School had been won.

In spite of their promise, in 2010, Greensboro College abandoned those plans and sold the school to student housing developer Campus Crest for $3.75 million, according to county property records. The J.C. Price School was demolished in 2014. Efforts by the community to save the school by having it placed on the National Register of Historic Sites failed in part because during the time that Greensboro College promised to save the school, efforts ceased, and another school named for J.C. Price in Rowan County built in 1923 was given that honor in 2010. Because many of the historic structures in the community were destroyed during urban renewal, Warnersville could not apply for placement on the National Register of Historic Sites. However, in July of 2015, Warnersville received the first designation of *Heritage Community* in the state of North Carolina. Ladd (2015) stated, "That (the designation) was fitting, since it was residents of Warnersville who asked the city several years ago for a way to honor neighborhoods of historic significance that have lost many of their original structures."

We cannot assume that the battle to save Dudley has been won simply because the Main Building and Gymnasium are still there. One need only look at Lincoln Academy, once known as Lincoln Middle School to understand that there are ways to "take" a neighborhood school away from a community without tearing it down. Why is it important that the original Main Building be visible? The following story demonstrates what Dudley means to so many people:

During the battle to save Dudley, I spoke at a Preservation North Carolina Conference in Ashville, North Carolina. In my speech, I noted that we had lost the first round because the School Board had voted to follow the recommendation of the Building Committee to destroy the entire campus by relocating Dudley's students to other high schools and then build a new school. After my speech, a woman approached me and said,

"Don't stop fighting to save your school. We made the mistake of allowing W.E. B. Dubois High School to be taken from us because we were told that a new school would be built. However, when the new school was built, we were informed that white parents would not allow their children to attend a school named for a communist. There is no longer a W. E. B. Dubois High School in Wake County. Keep Dudley for all of us."

Of the more than 300 historically black high schools in North Carolina before integration only five remain: Hillside High School, Durham, E.E. Smith High School, Fayetteville, Carver High School, Winston-Salem, West Charlotte, Charlotte, and James B. Dudley High School in Greensboro. Although the permanent structures that housed the schools were all built in the early 1900s, only Carver, West Charlotte and Dudley are still located on those sites with the original main buildings intact. There is some debate as to which school was established first because Durham Hillside High School has always acknowledged its history from 1887 when it was called Whitted High School. On the other hand, Dudley historians have long ignored the fact that the High School for Negroes in Greensboro was established in 1879 when the Greensboro City Council agreed to pay for Negro students to attend high school at Bennett Seminary. This is why Hillside is generally noted as the oldest of the five historically black high schools still operating as high schools in North Carolina.

A PLACE WHERE SUCCESS WAS EXPECTED: FINAL EDITION

First Person Resources

Anderson, Mary Evans, Class of 1968, holds a Bachelor of Science in Business Management/E- from the University of Phoenix, a master's in business administration from the University of Phoenix and a Webmaster's Certification from Guilford College, Greensboro, North Carolina. She has helped individuals and small business owners develop websites for the past 11 years. She started a web design and web building online training site, Invest-N-Others. She was involved in DECA and Business courses at Dudley, 1965-1968.

Black, Crystal, Class of 1990, was a Pantherette at Dudley. She is the Greensboro Dudley Alumni Chapter President. She believed the vision for this book and supports the proposal to use most of the proceeds from the book to help establish an Endowment Fund for Dudley. She and Shannon Stewart Minor also helped with the final edits.

Bailey, Mark, Class of 1990, was a member of Dudley's Marching Band of Thunder under Mr. Shelton Williams. He graduated from North Carolina A&T State University. His assistance in proofing the book's cover, picture formatting, and contributions on how not to "date" the book with certain terminology and the inclusion of more recent Dudley graduates helped the book "cross" generations.

Coley, Nelle Artis, was a 1931 Bennett Belle. She was a Dudley High School English teacher for more than 40 years. She spoke to her classes frequently about the proud history of James Benson Dudley High School and why we should strive to live up to all that the term "Dudley Student" implied. Much of what I know about the early history of the school comes directly from this source.

Davis, Chapelle Morgan, Class of 1965, Librarian, Media Specialist, Page High School, and Greensboro Central Library. She provided most of the information about Mr. James D. Morgan in an article titled, "My Daddy: Mr. James D. Morgan, excerpts from which are included on pages 172-174.

Evans, Benjamin (Ben) Andrew, Class of 1973, entered the Army after graduation. While at Dudley, he was a member of the Student Council (10-11), Class Officer (10-11), Homeroom Officer (10-11), Office Assistant 10, Marching Band 10, Junior Achievement (10-11), Beautification Committee -10, and Art Club-10. He worked for 17 years at Guilford Mills as a Color Specialist.

Evans, Gloria Dean, Class of 1965. While a student at Dudley, she was a member of the Panther's Claw Staff. She graduated from the North Carolina A&T State University School of Nursing in 1970. She worked as a Registered Nurse for 37 years. She worked at L. Richardson Memorial Hospital (7 years) and Wesley Long Community Hospital (30 years). For serval years she co-edited and wrote the Health Section of the At The Wells the monthly newsletter of Wells Memorial Church of God in Christ. She was one of the founding members of the Committee to Save Dudley.

Favors, Eddie, Dudley graduate 1953. He served as Chief Dudley Safety Patrol (1952-1953). President of the Dudley Marshals. He was inducted in the National Honor Society (1951-52); Graduated with honors 1953; Starting Halfback and leading rusher (1951) undefeated State Football Champions (1951); College: Athletic Scholarship to North Carolina A&T State University; Lettered in Football (1954, 1955, 1956); Lettered in track (1956, 1957); Received Jack Gibson Trophy as Most Outstanding Senior Athlete 1957; President of the A&T Letterman's Club (1956-1957); Inducted into the NC A&T Sports Hall of Fame 2008; Graduated with honors with a B.S. in Mechanical Engineering (1957); Received National Science Foundation Fellowship Award for Graduate Studies. Professional Career and Honors: NC A&T Employer

(ME instructor) 1958-1962; US Patent Office 1962-1994 (Patent Examiner); Litman 1997-2014 (Patent Lawyer); Community: Banquet Speaker, 28th Dudley High Consolidated Reunion, 2003; Participated in tutoring program DC public schools 1979-83; EEO Counselor 1980-92He contributed information about the 1950, 1951, 1952 seasons of Dudley's Varsity football team.

Florance-Bristow, Davetta, was a 1960 graduate of Dudley High School. She was a member of and soloist for the Dudley High School Choir. Mrs. Julia Morrison Richmond was the director. While she was in the choir, they were state winners during that time; 1957-1960. She was a member of the Dance Group with Georgene Dye as teacher, coach, and choreographer. She was also a Majorette for the marching band under the direction of Mr. James Morgan, and a flutist for the concert band also under his direction.

She was a member of the Dudley Thespians, which was an outstanding state-winning Drama group, directed by Barbara J. Wells. She was a reporter for THE PANTHER'S'CLAW. The advisor was Luvenia Milling.

Gilmer, Paul, Class of 1965, A Vietnam Veteran, who researched and compiled the documentation for the 1965 Yearbook for the Class's 50th Anniversary Reunion on the Class Members who served in the Military. He is a realtor and is currently a member of the City of Greensboro Zoning Commission.

Glasgow, Linda, Class of 1963, was a student in Dudley's last class of Practical Nursing Students. Glasgow had a very successful career as a licensed practical nurse at L. Richardson Memorial Hospital and Moses Cone Memorial Hospital. She contributed a picture of the combined 1962 and 1963 Practical Nursing Students and their teachers in front of L. Richardson Memorial Hospital on its original site. She also supplied information about some of the graduates of the program and a picture of the 1963 Class in training at L. Richardson memorial Hospital.

Hamilton, Cassandra Feaster, Class of 1965, Dudley Cheer Book. Cassandra was a member of the National Honor Society, the Marching Band, the Dudley Modern Dance Group, Safety Patrols, a Junior Marshal, and she was elected Miss Homecoming her senior year. She graduated from Bennett College in 1969 and taught elementary school for 33 years as a 5th grade teacher and Title 1 Math instructor. She also hosted a live call-in television show for students to get help with their math homework.

Lee, Gregsha. A Durham native who graduated from Durham's City of Medicine Academy but competed in athletics for Southern Durham High School. In College, Lee competed in track and field at Oral Roberts University and earned her bachelor's degree from North Carolina A&T State University. She was a science teacher at Dudley High School for five years, as well as a track coach and an assistant to former athletics director Art Wade before becoming Athletic Director. She describes herself as a lifelong athlete. She says, "In college, my major was pre-physical therapy, so when I came in as a teacher through Teach for America it was, "Oh, you're qualified to teach science."

She spoke with the News & Record's Joe Sirera about her experiences as a teacher, coach and administrator and her goals for the Dudley athletics program include sending more of our student-athletes to the next level; getting some of our student-athletes to the student-athlete summit that the state offers, just so that they can get some of those experiences: and bridging the gap between school and athletics by creating a social media and marketing organization at Dudley.

A PLACE WHERE SUCCESS WAS EXPECTED: FINAL EDITION

Moore, David (Bunny), Class of 1962, Member of the Dudley High School Drum Line, and the A&T State University Drum Line. He supplied some Dudley memorabilia 1959-1988, Dudley Alumni Association pictures and newspaper clippings, Industrial Arts information and an excerpt about his father Dave Moore Sr. originally found in the book The Art of the Hustle: Lessons in Becoming a Man. Moore is a long-time community activist, 2015 Inductee Dudley Hall of Fame, Winner 2015 Alumni Service Award, volunteer, and mentor for students throughout the Guilford County School System.

Munchus, Carolyn Walden, Class of 1962, Mrs. Richmond, Dudley Christmas programs, and other Dudley Music Department Programs. After graduating from Dudley High School in 1962, Carolyn received a scholarship to Talladega College in Alabama and majored in music. Mrs. Richmond tutored her in theory to help her transition to college music theory classes by requiring that she learn all the major and minor scales, key signatures, chords, and intervals. Carolyn appreciated this additional work even more after she saw how much it helped her to be successful in the theory classes. Carolyn was selected to be an exchange student at the University of Iowa during her junior year. When she completed the exchange program, she transferred to Iowa and received her Bachelor of Music degree. She also completed the Master of Music degree at the University of Cincinnati. Carolyn taught music for several years before returning to Iowa to complete a master's degree in library science and after graduation, she began working as the Music/AV Cataloger in the Mervyn H. Sterne Library, University of Alabama at Birmingham. She retired in 2015 after working there for 37 years. Carolyn still shares her love of piano by playing for special services at First Congregational Church in Birmingham and for other special events. Every Christmas when she hears "Carol of the Bells," she remembers this as the final selection of the Dudley High Chorus at the special Christmas programs that filled the auditorium with beautiful music for the overflowing audiences of students, parents, and supporters of Dudley High.

Pass, Samuel Penn graduated from Dudley in 1970. He contributed the information about Mrs. Penn, Dudley's interim Band Director during World War II and its second music teacher. He served in the United States Navy on the USS Denebola from 1970 through 1972. He graduated from North Carolina A&T State University in 1998 with a Bachelor of Arts Degree in History. Pass earned an MSIT in Occupational Safety and Health in 2004 from the same university. Currently, he is employed at Duke University as a Fire Protection Specialist in the Fire Safety Division of the Occupational and Environmental Safety Office. Organizations with which he is currently affiliated: Omega Psi Phi Fraternity, Tau Omega Chapter, and the Dudley Alumni Association. Community service includes serving as president of the Concerned Citizens of Gorrell Street Neighborhood Association, the Greensboro Community Resource Board, and executive director of Magnolia House Motel.

Patterson, Veda Malia is a proud second-generation Dudley graduate from the Class of 1972. She received her undergraduate degree from Howard University and graduate degree from The American University. Veda retired from the Federal Government with over 32 years of service. She contributed a lead on Roy H. Lake that led to the expansion of several other articles: B1 Navy Band, James Parsons and Warmouth T. Gibbs, Jr. Veda is the. Co-founder Northern Virginia chapter National Political Congress of Black Women, vice president, 1993-1997, president, since 1997. Member Continental Socs., Inc. (Northern Virginia chapter vice president since 1993), Junior League Northern Virginia, Howard U. Alumni Association (Northern Virginia chapter charter member, past secretary, past vice president, president), and a member of Alpha Kappa Alpha Sorority.

Dr. Jo Evans Lynn, Ed.D.

A committed community and civic volunteer, Veda gives her time to several organizations. From her days at Dudley, Veda displayed a keen interest and love of history. This led to her declaration as a history minor in college. The preservation of history is one of her passions, as demonstrated by her donation of her majorette boots, baton, and class ring during her 50th year class reunion. The items are on display in the Dudley Media Center.

Truesdale, Pamela graduated from Dudley in 2003. Pamela helped me "see Mr. Powell and Dudley's Marching Band through the eyes of a 21st Century band member. She was an outstanding student who was elected to the National Honor Society during her sophomore year, a member of Dudley's marching band, and the Dudley Thespians. She has worked as a Project Analyst in Billing Operations at Laboratory Corporation of America. Pamela has 5+ years of professional experience in the financial and healthcare management sector, with extensive experience in analysis support for financial decisions efforts. She has a Bachelor of Science in Accounting from North Carolina Agricultural & Technical University and is enrolled in Elon University where she is pursuing her master's in business administration with a focus on Analytics.

Spruill, Joyce graduated from Dudley in 1971. is a pioneer in women's athletics and sports administration. During her time at Dudley, the basketball team on which she was the leading scorer was undefeated in 1970 and won the Citywide Championship. She was also a member of the Citywide Track Championship Team in 1970. In 1968, she set a softball throwing record at 235ft. For her outstanding performances in three sports, she was named Dudley's Female Athlete of the Year in 1970. In the 1970-71 season, she became the first Black Female to be named Women's Softball MVP for the Greensboro Parks and Recreation Department. As a senior at Dudley, she was the only high school student invited to participate in the Annual Women's Athletic Association Sports Weekend hosted by A&T State University.

Vincent, Stahle took the term "student athlete" to new heights. He was a 1969 graduate of James B. Dudley High School. At Dudley, he was president of the National Honor Society, Senior Class President, Semi-finalist: National Scholar-Athlete of the Year, American Academy of Achievement, Dallas, Texas, Grant Award (leadership, academics and athletics), 3- Year letterman in football, basketball and baseball, MVP: baseball – three years, football – two years, All City in football and baseball, All Conference in football, Conference Player of the Year in football, All State in football, All Southeast in football and Honorable Mention All-American in football. In addition to becoming the first African American to play quarterback at Rice University, he received many other honors. Vincent was a very conscientious facts checker especially in the areas of Dudley Athletics and coaches. He also contributed to the selection about the History of the James B. Dudley Educational and Sports Hall of Fame/Hall of Distinction.

Vincent, W. Anthony is a 1964 graduate of Dudley High School. He was a three-year letterman on the baseball team that won its first State Championship in 1964. He led the team in stolen bases, sacrifice bunts, total bases, and outfield putouts. Vincent got the only hit in a one-hitter semifinal game. He also had a .389 Batting average in 1964, his senior year. Vincent was selected to the Dudley All-Time Baseball Team as a Left Fielder. Vincent served six years in the U.S. Marine

A PLACE WHERE SUCCESS WAS EXPECTED: FINAL EDITION

Corps (Honorably discharged with the rank of Sergeant. He contributed valuable information about Dudley Athletics during the early 1960s.

Williams, Rufus E. graduated from Dudley in 1965. While a student at James B. Dudley High School, he was a three-sport athlete playing Varsity Basketball, Varsity Football and Varsity Baseball – 1963-1965; He was named the Dr. W. L. T. Miller Basketball Most Valuable Player 1964-65. Williams supplied information for the Dudley military participation for classmates other than members of the Class of 1965. He helped with the title options and rescued me when I misplaced Gloria's Class of 1965 50th Reunion Yearbook, by replacing it. He served in the United States Army in Vietnam and served as the president of the Class of 1965 and in that role served as chairperson for the Class of 1965 Reunion Committee.

Wynn, John F. is a native of Greensboro, NC and grew up in a house on the corner of Bilbro and Ashe Streets, which was in the Warnersville Community during the early 1950's. John was the fourth oldest child in the Wynn household of 11 children. He was educated and attended David D. Jones Elementary, J.C. Price Middle School and graduated from Dudley High School. Growing up in the Warnersville Community, one inspirational mentor to John that came to mind was Bill Bethea. This area was a thriving and tight knit community where many lives were shaped, and people were proud to be surrounded by African American business and homeowners that they could look up to.

Dr. Jo Evans Lynn, Ed.D.

Bibliography

Adams-Taylor, F. (2011). A. Faye Adams-Taylor Bio. Retrieved from: http://fayeadamstaylor.com/author.html

Admiral K Consulting (2011). Biographical Sketch: Rear Admiral Gene Kendall, Retrieved 12-05-2016, from: http://admkconsulting.com/13520.html.

Aldridge, P. (1965). A Girl Bus Driver Describes the Job (Article), The Panther's Claw: Dudley Student Newspaper.

Altoff, G. T. (1996). Amongst My Best Men: African Americans & the War of 1812, Put-In-Bay, Ohio: Perry Group Publishers.

Albright, Alex. (2013). The Forgotten First B-1 and the Integration of the Modern Navy, Fountain, NC: R.A. Fountain, 2013 Retrieved November 28,2023: https://rafountain.com/navy/bibliography/.

American Civil War.com (2012). History of the Colored Troops in the American Civil War, Sources: U.S. National Park Service & U.S. Library of Congress. Retrieved December 1, 2015, from: http://americancivilwar.com/colored/histofcoloredtroops.html

America's Reconstruction- People and Politics after the Civil War: The meaning of Freedom Black and White Responses after the War (2003). Retrieved August 8, 2015, from: http://www.digitalhistory.uh.edu/exhibits/reconstruction/section2/section2_school.html.

Annie E. Casey Foundation (2015). Kids Count Data Center (Project), Children Eligible for Free or Reduced Lunches by North Carolina School System. Retrieved December 23, 2015, from: http://datacenter.kidscount.org/data/tables/2239-percent-of-students-enrolled-in-free-and-reduced-lunch?loc=35#detailed/10/5010-5124/false/1021,909,857,105,118/any/4682

Arnett, E. S. (1955). Greensboro, North Carolina: The County Seat of Guilford. Chapel Hill: UNC Press.

Arnett, E. S. (1973). For Whom Our Public Schools Were Named, Greensboro, North Carolina, Greensboro, NC: Piedmont Press, pp. 181-191.

Ball, B. (2016). Controversial plan to allow for-profit charter school takeovers of low-performing NC schools re-emerges. N.C. Policy Watch, May 9, 2016. Retrieved from: http://www.ncpolicywatch.com/2016/01/27/controversial-plan-to-allow-for-profit-charter-school-takeovers-of-low-performing-nc-schools-re-emerges/

Balliett, Carl J. 1925. World Leadership in Denims. Through Thirty Years of Progress. Baltimore: Privately printed by the Thomsen-Ellis Co. for the Proximity Manufacturing Company. Company publication located at the Greensboro Public Library, Caldwell Jones Room.

Baines, J. (1993). Dudley High's Band takes first place in King Competition, The Panther 1993 (Yearbook): The Technique Is Sweet, pp.126-127.

Baines, J. (1993). Pantherettes, The Panther 1993 (Yearbook): The Technique Is Sweet, p.128.

Baines, J. (2002). The Panther 2002 (Yearbook): The Dawning of a New Era, pp.152-153.

Baines, J. (2002). The Panther 2002 (Yearbook), Yearbook Dedication, p. 78-79.

A PLACE WHERE SUCCESS WAS EXPECTED: FINAL EDITION

Barton, B.C. (1973). The Panther 1973 (Yearbook), Greensboro, North Carolina: James B. Dudley High School.

Battle, C. A. (1932). Rode Island African American Data: Hannibal Collins. Negroes of Rhode Island Genealogy Trails. Retrieved January 16, 2016, from: http://genealogytrails.com/ri/bio_collins.html.

Bernstein, A. (2013). A. Knighton Stanley, a civil rights leader and D.C. pastor, dies at 76 (Obituary). Washington D.C.: The Washington Post. Retrieved from: https://www.washingtonpost.com/local/obituaries/a-knighton-stanley-a-civil-rights-leader-and-dc-pastor-dies-at-76/2013/09/25/1ddabb36-25fc-11e3-ad0d-b7c8d2a594b9_story.html.

Biggs, B. (1921) The Magnolia House: A Pivotal Point of Greensboro History. Retrieved November 24, 2023 from: https://preservationgreensboro.org/the-manolia-house-a-pivotal-point-of-greensboro-history/

Bolds, L. & Lynn, J. (2004) Panther Yearbook: Do You Remember- 75th Anniversary, Sports Section, pp. 22-23.

Brandon, L. (2002). Dudley Has Historic Links to the Civil Rights Movement, The Panther's Claw: Special Dudley Black History Edition, Vol. 2002, February 2002, p. 1.

Briggs, B. (July 22, 2015). The Secrets of Nocho Park, Clinton Hills, and Benbow Park, Preservation Greensboro: Saving Treasured Places Bog, Retrieved 10-26-2023 from: https://preservationgreensboro.org/the- secrets-of-nocho- park- clinton-hills-and-benbow-park

Britt, B. (Dec.24,2020). Chuck Cotton's soulful backbeat (Article) Special to Go Triad. Retrieved February 4, 2021, from: https://greensboro.com/entertainment/chuck-cottons-soulful-backbeat/article_bdeaed3c-3e57-11eb-860b-93af8d2ba70a.html

Brock Historical Museum (2009). J.C. Price School: If these walls could talk; An oral history. Retrieved, March 15, 2015: https://museum.greensboro.edu:42001/jcpriceschool/history-of-the-school.php.

Browder, C. (2014). NC education spending on decades-long slide, Raleigh, North Carolina: WRAL.com, Retrieved from: http://www.wral.com/nc-education-spending-on-decades-long-slide/13795657/.

Brown-Reid, M. (2014). In Spite of It All: Eva The Diva Foster. North Charleston, South Carolina: CreateSpace Independent Publishing, 74 pp.

Buchanan, B. (2001). Students Recall Beloved School/Rena Bullock School Served Black Students in Southeast Guilford County In the 1950s and '60s. Greensboro, North Carolina: News & Record, December 28, 2001. Retrieved December 26, 2015, from: http://www.greensboro.com/students-recall-beloved-school-rena-bullock-school-served-black-students/article_1c64a614-690e-5b35-98e4-683431488188.html.

Bulla, David (Fri, May 11, 1984). Andrews team prevails; Doggett leads Panthers (Article), Greensboro News and Record

Bureau of Labor Statistics (2014). Table 6. Occupations with the most job growth, 2014-24. United States Department of Labor: Economic News Release. Retrieved from: http://www.bls.gov/news.release/ecopro.t06.htm.

Burroughs-White, C. (2007). History of James Benson Dudley High School. Dudley Alumni Association, Inc. 40th Consolidated Reunion Souvenir Journal, Alumni Weekend, July-17-19, 2015, p. 41.

Cecelski, D. (1994). Along the freedom road: Hyde County, North Carolina, and the fate of black schools in the South. Chapel Hill: The University of North Carolina Press.

Center for Research on Education Outcomes (2015). Urban Charter School Study Report on 41 Regions, Stanford, California: Stanford University, Retrieved from: http://urbancharters.stanford.edu/download/Urban%20Charter%20School%20Study%20Report%20on%2041%20Regions.pdf.

Chafe, W. H. (1980). Civilities and Civil Rights: Greensboro, North Carolina, and the Black Struggle for Freedom, USA: Oxford University Press, USA.

Chambers, J. W. & Anderson, F. (1999). The Oxford Companion to American Military History. Oxford, New York: Oxford University Press. ISN 978-0-19-507198-6.

Chapman, B. & Lestch (2013). Money for charter schools balloon during Mayor Bloomberg's tenure, New York, New York: New York Daily News, July 14, 2013. Retrieved from: http://www.nydailynews.com/authors?author=Corinne-Lestch

Cheek, K.V. (2011). How 2 Siblings Became College Presidents, From the History Makers Series, Posted September 20, 2011. Retrieved from: http://www.theroot.com/articles/culture/2011/09/black_college_presidents_the_cheek_brothers.html.

Civil Rights Digital Library (2013). Morehead, David W., 1918-2003: Biography. UGA Library Retrieved, February 29, 2016, from: http://crdl.usg.edu/people/m/morehead_david_w_1918_2003/

Coley, N. (1941). 1941 Mid-Year Graduating Class. The Panther's Claw. Volume 10, Number 2, p.1

Cornish, D. T. (1987). The Sable Arm: Black Troops in the Union Army, 1861-1865: Black Troops in the Union Army, 1861-65 (Modern War Studies), Lawrence, Kansas: University Press of Kansas.

Craig, N. (1941). Warnersville: Pioneer Venture in Homeownership by Means of Modest Charges and Long-Term Payments Started After the Civil War. Daily News (Greensboro), June 1, 8-9, sec. A.

Daniel, S. I. (1931). Women Builders. Washington, D.C.: Associated Publishers, Inc., Retrieved October 10, 2018 from: http://www.nchistoricsites.org/chb/pmi-growth.htm.

Davis, A. P. (2010). Public Schools in the Great Depression: Keeping the Doors Open, Reprinted with permission from The Tarheel Junior Historian, Spring 2010. Tar Heel Junior Historian Association, NC Museum of History. Retrieved September 2015, from: http://ncpedia.org/public-schools-great-depression.

Defense Video & Imagery Distribution System (2013). News: Greensboro, N.C., native leads Marines in Afghanistan, II Marine Expeditionary Force. Retrieved July 8, 2015, from: https://www.dvidshub.net/news/112548/greensboro-nc-native-leads-marines-afghanistan#.VowQdrUo6M8.

Dean, A.B. (2014). Immigrant children deserve excellent schooling too. Retrieved October 1, 2015, from: http://america.aljazeera.com/opinions/2014/1/charter-schools-shouldeducatenotdiscriminate.html.

Dempsey, A. (2002). Dudley's Joey Cheek Goes to the Olympics. The Panther's Claw (Newspaper), p.3.

Department of Student Affairs, North Carolina A&T State University (2015). History of the Machin: History of the North Carolina A&T State University Marching Band. Retrieved November 21, 2015: http://www.ncat.edu/student-affairs/student-services/marching-machine/about/history.html.

Drane, Gregory (2020). *An Oral History of the Navy Band B-1: The First All-Black Navy Band of World War II*. PhD dissertation. State College, PA: U of Pennsylvania, 2020.

DuBois, W.E.B. (1935). Black Reconstruction in America: An Essay Toward a History of the Part Which Black Folk Played in the Attempt to Reconstruct Democracy in America, 1860–1880, New York, New York: Harcourt Brace and Company Publishers, p.p. 59, 419, 465, 494, 503, 521, 675-709.

Dudley Alumni Association (2016). Dudley Honored Military. Retrieved from: https://www.alumniclass.com/dudleyhs/military-alumni-view.

Dunbar, P. L. (1896). Lyrics of Lowly Life, "We Wear the Mask." Touchstones: Literature and the Writing Process. Ed.

Dunbar, P.L. (1913). The Complete Poems of Paul Laurence Dunbar. New York: Dodd, Mead, and Company.

Duncan, A. (1988). Judge A (Article). Greensboro News & Record: Fashion, Weddings, Advice, Sunday, May 22, pp. G1-2.

Emerson, D. E. (2003). Education to subordinate-education to liberate: an historical study of the dual role of education for African Americans, 1865-1968.

England, Christina, Features Editor (1995). James B. Dudley Remembered, Panther's Claw: Vol. 5, No.3, p.1.

Fine, E. (2003). Soul Stepping: African American Step Shows. Chicago: University of Illinois Press.

Forgione, P.D. (1998). Center for Education Reform and Empower America Achievement in the United States: Progress Since A Nation at Risk? (Report), U.S. Commissioner of Education Statistics, National Center for Education Statistics, Office of Educational Research and Improvement, U.S. Department of Education.

Formica, B. (2012). Dudley High School Names Seagraves New Head Basketball Coach. Retrieved from: http://archive.digtriad.com/news/local/story.aspx?storyid=225443.

Fripp, G. H. (1982). Greensboro: A Chosen Center. Woodland Hills, California: Windsor Publications. Located at the Greensboro Public Library, Caldwell-Jones Room.

Fripp, G. H. (1997). Images of America: Greensboro. Charleston, South Carolina: Arcadia Publishing, p.45.

Ferguson, A. (December 10, 2021)."For him to be playing this year, it would be very special for me": Father and son compete for state title together (Feature **Story), WFMY** News 2, Retrieved January 29, 2022, from: https://www.wfmynews2.com/aricle/sports/father-and-son-in-dudley-championship-game/83-f9558f7a-8ddf-4d3c-93e6-360ee232ed35

Gant, G. W. (1967). The Panther 1967 (Yearbook), Greensboro, North Carolina.

George C. Simkins, Jr. Elementary School (2015). A History of George C. Simkins Elementary School. Retrieved February 5, 2016, from: http://www.edlinesites.net/pages/George_C_Simkins_Elementary

Gilmer, P. (2015). Class of 1965 Veterans, James B. Dudley High School Class of 1965 50th Reunion, Yearbook

Graham, L. G. (1999). Our Kind of People: Inside America's Black Upper Class. New York: HarperCollins Publishers.

Gray, J. M. (2011). "Francis Marion Foils the British," Military History Quarterly, pub. Aug. 3, 2011. Retrieved: November 11, 2015, from: http://www.historynet.com/up-from-the-swamp-francis-marion-foils-the-british.htm

Greensboro, NAACP (2015). History of the NAACP in North Carolina, Retrieved from: http://greensboro.naacp-nc.org/

Greensboro News & Record (2008). Dudley Wrestling Coach Meeting New Challenges (January). Retrieved from: http://super32.com/news/crosby.html.

News & Record E-Edition (July 10,1993). Watkins Named Associate Vice Chancellor for Research (Article). (Retrieved 12-28-2023 from: https://greensboro.com/watkins-named-associate-vice-chancellor-for-research/article_52ebbb32-eb10-5ac8-9a19-232034a02826.html

Guilford County Schools (2015). Thank you for Choosing Guilford County Schools- Congratulations to the Class of 2015 (Graduation Program Supplement), p.p.1-2.

Hamilton, B. (2016). NC A&T State University commemorates 100 years of ROTC with Hall of Fame Induction ceremony. Retrieved January 4, 2017, from: http://www.usar.army.mil/News/Article/722214/nc-at-state-university-commemorates-100-years- .

Harden, E. (8-15-2006). Ex-Dudley coach McKee dies at 78, Greensboro News and Record, Retrieved Jan,26, 2022 from: https://greensboro.com/sports_high_school/football/ex-dudley-coach-mckee-dies-at-78/article.26aa68e-5103-598e-9ad3-5b83d2303d2f.html

Harper's New Monthly Magazine (Oct. 1873). Hampton Normal and Agricultural Institute: Ball Team (Article). New York: New York, p.p. 3-17.

Harris, J. (2006). A Local BlackStory: Charlotte Hawkins Brown (Article), At The Wells, North Carolina: Greensboro, Volume No.2, Issue No. 10, p. 6.

Hartmann, C. (1927). Architectural Drawing: The Negro High School in Greensboro, North Carolina, Greensboro Public Schools.

Herbin, A. B. (1958). The Meaning of Commencement, The Future Outlook (Newspaper), Greensboro, North Carolina, Saturday, June 7, 1958, Vol. 17, No.24, p. 2.

Herring, K. M. (1918). How the Southern Negro is supporting the Government. New York: Outlook Company (North Carolina Collection, University at Chapel Hill), Detached from The Outlook, Vol.120 (Nov. 20, 1918), p. 452-453

A PLACE WHERE SUCCESS WAS EXPECTED: FINAL EDITION

Hessling, P. A. (1993). To be "The best school in town": An historical study of two Southern elementary schools. Unpublished doctoral dissertation, the University of North Carolina at Chapel Hill, Chapel Hill, North Carolina.

History Makers (2012). Debra Lee: Media Company Executive. Retrieved from: http://www.thehistorymakers.com/biography/debra-lee-1

History of the Machine (2015). The Blue and Gold Marching Machine of North Carolina A&T State University. Retrieved from: http://www.ncat.edu/student-affairs/student-services/marching-machine/about/history.html

Hodge, T. (1979). Dudley after 50 Years: Brief History of James B. Dudley High School.

Hood, A. (2015). In Memory of Charles A. Sanders, 40th Consolidated Reunion Souvenir Journal, Alumni Weekend, July 17-19, 2015, Theme: Going Back to the Future- "Where you were, where you are, and where you're going," p.60.

Hood, D. (2016). Davis Still Winning Championships (Webpage), Tigernet.com, Retrieved February 27, 2016, from: http://www.tigernet.com/story/football/Jeff-Davis-Still-Winning-Championships-14481.

Howell, P. (2002). Old Teacher, New School. The Panther's Claw News Paper, p.3.

IMDb (2015). Brett Claywell Biography (Mobile App). Retrieved December 16, 2015, from: http://www.imdb.com/name/nm1505775/bio.

James B. Dudley High School Educational and Sports Hall of Fame/Hall of Distinction (2015). Amos Quick, III Biography. Retrieved December 23, 2015, from: http://www.dudleyhofhod.org/#!2015-inductee-bios/gw4v1

James B. Dudley High School Educational and Sports Hall of Fame/Hall of Distinction (2015). David (Bunny) Moore Biography. Retrieved December 23, 2015, from: http://www.dudleyhofhod.org/#!2015-inductee-bios/gw4v1

James B. Dudley High School Educational and Sports Hall of Fame/Hall of Distinction (2015). David Dansby Biography, Retrieved December 23, 2015, from: http://www.dudleyhofhod.org/#!2015-inductee-bios/gw4v1.

James B. Dudley High School Educational and Sports Hall of Fame/Hall of Distinction (2015). Ernestine Bennett Biography. Retrieved December 23, 2015, from: http://www.dudleyhofhod.org/#!2015-inductee-bios/gw4v1.

James B. Dudley High School Educational and Sports Hall of Fame/Hall of Distinction (2015). Clarence Grier Biography. Retrieved December 23, 2015, from: http://www.dudleyhofhod.org/#!2015-inductee-bios/gw4v1

James B. Dudley High School Educational and Sports Hall of Fame/Hall of Distinction (2013). Brian Seagraves Biography. Retrieved December 23, 2015, from: http://www.dudleyhofhod.org/#!2015-inductee-bios/gw4v1

Jenkins, J. (1979). Dudley …50 Years Later, Greensboro News & Record, Section D: pp. 1 & 20, Col 1.

Johnson, III A. H. (May 2018) The Best of Us, Greensboro News & Record

Johnson, E. A. (1890). A School History of the Negro Race In America, From 1619 To 1890, With A Short Introduction As To The Origin Of The Race; Also, A Short Sketch Of Liberia: Electronic Edition, Academic Affairs Library, University of North Carolina at Chapel Hill, Raleigh, North Carolina: Edwards & Broughton, Printers and Binders, p.p. 153-159.

Johnson, J.W. & Johnson, J.R. (1900). Lift Every Voice and Sing: A Celebration of the Negro National Anthem at the Way back Machine (archived March 1, 2009), edited by Julian Bond and Sondra Kathryn Wilson. Retrieved May 1, 2015, from: https://web.archive.org/web/20090301050124/http://bookpage.com/0011bp/nonfiction/lift_every_voice_and_sing.html.

Johnson, R. H. (2019). Reginald N. Johnson: Creative Director/Dancer/Actor/CEO of Inward Discovery. Retrieved December 28, 2023, from: https://www.linkedin.com/in/reginald-n-johnson-46b86768/

Johnson, T. (1961). Account of the First General Meeting of the James B. Dudley High School Student Government Association (Fall 1959).

Johnson, W.B.(2020). Wayman Bernard (aka Slack) Johnson Music Industry Executive/Producer/Radio Personality.

Ladd, S. (July 22, 2015). Warnersville becomes the first city Heritage Community (Article). Greensboro News & Record Posted: Wednesday, July 22, 2015, http://www.greensboro.com/blogs/around_town/warnersville-becomes-first-city-heritage-community/article_ceda4b3b-0da2-558f-b428-a5e1b701e812.html.

Long, A. (2016). Oakland Raiders gave David Amerson new life (Article). Retrieved from: http://nflspinzone.com/2016/05/30/oakland-raiders-gave-david-amerson-new-life/.

Lynn, J. (1999). To Become… (Program to Benefit the Angel House Foundation). Greensboro, North Carolina: Dudley Key Club, Greensboro Kiwanis Club, & Dudley Thespians, p.p.1-6.

Lynn, J. (2004). Submission to the Guilford County School Board to Name the Auxiliary Gymnasium at James B. Dudley High School in Honor of Georgene Dye, March 5, 2004.

Lynn, J. (2009). The Haygood Sisters. At The Wells (Newsletter): Wells Memorial Church of God in Christ, Greensboro, N.C. Vol.3, February, page 8.

Lynn, J. (2011). The Promise of Friendship, Bloomington, Indiana: Westbow Press, p.p.180-184.

MacGregor, M. J. (1981). Integration of the Military, 1940-1965, Center of Military History, U.S. Army, ed. Government Printing Office, p.p. 100-102

Malone, J. (1996). Steppin' on the Blues. Chicago: University of Illinois Press.

Margo, R. A. (1990). Race and Schooling in the South, 1880-1950: Economic History (PDF), Chicago, Illinois: University of Chicago Press. Retrieved September 6, 2015, Out of Print Volume of the National Bureau of Economic Research: http://www.nber.org/chapters/c8792.pdf.

Margold, N. (1931). The Margold Report to the NAACP. New York, New York: American Fund for Public Service Records, Manuscripts and Archives, The New York Public Library, Astor, Lenox, and Tilden Foundations.

McLaughlin, Nancy (September 25, 2018). Fighter of racism. Mentor to many. J. Kenneth Lee 'stood at the front of the line all the time',' Retrieved October 3, 2018, from: https://www.greensboro.com/news/north_carolina/fighter-of-racism-mentor-to-many-j-kenneth-lee-stood/article_e60498a3-b693-5011-ab97-b888c08f8653.html from Greensboro News and Record.

McLaughlin, N. (January 30, 2021). Bold and brazen, breaking barriers was Elreta Alexander's bread and butter. So was the law. Lifestyles Section Greensboro Daily News. Retrieved from: https://greensboro.com/life/bold-and-brazen-breaking-barriers-was-elreta-alexanders-bread-and-butter-so-was-the-law/article_450b2e04-568a-11eb-bb09-4790c11ff24e.html.

McLaughlin, N. (Sept.14 2021). Gladys Shipman, first woman to serve as Greensboro's NAACP president, dies, Greensboro News & Record-E-edition, Retrieved, November 13, 2023 from: https://greensbor.com/news/local/gladys-shipman-first-woman-to-serve-as-greensboros-naacp-president-dies/article_12777f94-1591-11ec-9e-16-43d47957808e.html.

McPherson, K. (1983). Panthers "Puttin' on the Ritz" (Article), The Panther's Claw, Vol. 49: Number 1, October 1983, p.1.

Mencimer, S. (2013). North Carolina Home Schools to Get Public School Money, Political Mojo. Retrieved November 20, 2015, from: http://www.motherjones.com/mojo/2013/12/north-carolina-home-schools-public-vouchers

Mills, J. (2015). Charlie Sanders, proud of his Dudley roots, never forgot where he came from (VIDEO), Greensboro News & Record: Posted July 2, 2015. Retrieved November 17, 2015: http://www.greensboro.com/blogs/sports_extra/charlie-sanders-proud-of-his-dudley-roots-never-forgot-where/article_19af7b4a-2100-11e5-bb36-4b385ace0802.html

Mikkelson, Emily NC A&T alumnus featured in 'The Color Purple' musical movie. Retrieved December 18 from: https://www.msn.com/en-us/movies/other/nc-a-t-alumnus-featured-in-the-color-purple-musical-movie/ar-AA1UoQF

Mills, J. (2016). Bill Boyers, coaching legend at Dudley High, dies at 82. Greensboro, N.C.: Greensboro News and Record, March 2, 2016. Retrieved from: http://www.greensboro.com/sports/bill-boyers-coaching-legend-at-dudley-high-dies-at/article_60498d35-ca16-57f2-aaa7-0773f969e4df.html

Minor, S.S. (2005) My Dream Experience in Dudley's Chorus, The Panther 2005: Through the Fire, Clubs and Organization Section, p.103.

Moore, D. (2017). The Hustling Begins at an Early Age: The Spirit of a Menor (Excerpt about David Moore, Sr), Found in: The Art of the Hustle: Lessons in Becoming A Man by Council of Elders & Jo Evans Lynn, pp. 1-8.

Morris, S. (1969). How Blacks Upset the Marine Corps: "New Breed"-Leathernecks are tackling racist vestiges. Johnson Publishing Company: Ebony 25 (2), p.p.55-58.

Nash, G. B. (2012). The African Americans Revolution, in Oxford Handbook of the American Revolution, edited by Edward G Gray and Jane Kamensky, pp 250–70, at p 254.

National Geographic Learning (2001). Voice of Freedom: A Story about Frederick Douglass, National Geographic Learning; January 1, 2001. Retrieved January 16, 2016, from: http://www.americancivilwar.com/colored/frederick_douglass.html

NCAA Division I-A Player Defense Statistics-2011. Retrieved from: http://espn.go.com/collegefootball/statistics/player/_/stat/defense/sort/interceptions/year/2011/group/80

North Carolina Nursing History (2016). Mattie Donnell Hicks: Korean War Nurse, Bonne, North Carolina: Appalachian State University. Retrieved January 2016, from: http://nursinghistory.appstate.edu/mattie-donnell-hicks-korean-war-nurse.

North Carolina Standard (1840). North Carolina's first public school opens (February 12). Retrieved August 8, 2015, from: http://www.learnnc.org/lp/editions/nchist-newnation/4804.

Nxumalo, V. (1995). James B. Dudley High School: A Brief History. Carolina Peacemaker: African American History Section, p.p. 1&15.

Odum, C. (2014). Former Hawks All-Star Lou Hudson dies at 69. Retrieved from: http://sports.yahoo.com/news/former-hawks-star-lou-hudson-160516426--nba.html.

Panther (1967). Organizations: The Pantherettes-Article (Yearbook), pp. 178-179.

Panther (1967). The Blue Goose-Article (Yearbook), pp. 186-187.

Panther (1967). William J. Furcron, Director of Athletics- Article (Yearbook), p. 206

Panther 73 (1973). Capable Administration Aids Students-Article (Yearbook), p. 22.

Panther 73 (1973. Girls Field Hockey Has Winning Season- Article (Yearbook), pp. 58-59.

Panther 73 (1973). Activity Thaws Winter Chill-Article, Edith Gonsavles and Tom Matkins (Yearbook), p.p. 120-121.

Panther 73 (1973). Stage Band and Orchestra: Only the Beginning- Article (Yearbook), p. 147.

Panther 73 (1973). Pantherettes and Majorettes Display Skill and Grace- Article (Yearbook), p. 152.

Panther 73 (1973). Cheerleaders Help Build That Panther Spirit-Article (Yearbook), pp. 154-155.

Panther 73 (1973). Auto Mechanics: Trade or Hobby-Article (Yearbook), p. 166.

Panther 73 (1973). Senior Statistics: Evans Benjamin Andrew (Ben), p. 179.

Panther's Claw Newspaper (1953). Many Applaud Homecoming Queen and Gay Floats in Colorful Parade, November 1953, p.1.

Perrone, P. (November 1998). Obituary Charlie Foxx, The Independent, Retrieved February 2, 2022, from: Https://www.independent.co.uk/arts-entertainment/obituary-charlie-foxx-1182407.html

Puckett, J.R. (2009). From Greensboro VOICES Biography, "Hairston, Otis L., Sr. d." Retrieved from: October 9, 2008, http://library.uncg.edu/depts/archives/civrights/detail-bio.asp?bio=49.

Ramseth, L. (2014). Honor for I.F. Attorney and Army Veteran. Retrieved: January 4, 2017, from: http://www.postregister.com/articles/featured/2014/11/06/honor-if-attorney-and-army-veteran

Raphael, R. (2001). A People's' History of the American Revolution, New York, New York: Harper Collins, p 281.

Ray, Hannah (June 2, 2022). Sowing Seeds of Love: Dr. Marcus Gause Emagzine- High Point Discovered, from: https://www.highpointdiscovered.org/stories/sowing-seeds-of-love-dr-marcus-gause

Regester, Y. (2016). Dudley High's AVT Team rolls over competition at Shell's Eco-marathon. The Carolina Peacemaker: Thursday, April 28 to Wednesday. May 4, 2016, Vol. L, No.6, pp. 1A & 3A.

Reeves, Jesse S. "The Treaty of Guadalupe-Hidalgo," American Historical Review, Vol. 10, No. 2 (Jan. 1905), pp. 309–324.

A PLACE WHERE SUCCESS WAS EXPECTED: FINAL EDITION

Rich, M. (2012). Charter Schools Still Enroll Fewer Disabled Students. Retrieved from: http://www.nytimes.com/2012/06/20/education/in-charter-schools-fewer-with-disabilities.html?_r=0.

Robinson, K. (2013). Petition to name the new Field House, William J. Furcron Field House at Dudley High School.

Robinson, U. (2014). Thelma Livonia Spruill Robinson Burwell (Collage).

Rolstad, S. (August 5, 2018). A 4-time state champ, Steven Davis holds Calhoun Falls roots close (Article), Index Journal, Retrieved January 18, 2022, from: https://www.indexjournal.com/sports/a-4-time-champ-steven-davis-holds-calhoun-falls-roots-close/article_0c2d0c3a-4aee-5108-9e44-82d0177dbb09.htm

Salmasek, S. (1983). Interview with Mrs. McDougle (Article), The Panther's Claw, Vol. 49: Number 1, October 1983, p.1.

Sanders, C. A. (2007). NFL Enshrinement Speech to the Hall of Fame, Canton, Ohio.

Schott Foundation for Public Education (2014). Black Lives Matter: A Report of the Public Education of Black Boys. Retrieved December 12, 2015, from: http://blackboysreport.org/national-summary/.

Schlosser, J. (2006 updated 2015). Father and son keep Bob's Hatters shining, @ News & Record ,com. Retrieved from: Father and son keep Bob's Hatters shining (greensboro.com)

Second (2nd) Marine Logistics Group II Marine Expeditionary Force (2013). Lt. Col Dwayne A. Whiteside Commanding Officer, Combat Logistics Regiment 2 (News Release). Retrieved from: http://www.2ndmlg.marines.mil/News/PressReleaseView/tabid/6689/Article/517492/lt-col-dwayne-a-whiteside.aspx.

Selig, R. A. (1997). The Revolution's Black Soldiers (Article), American Revolution Organization. Retrieved December 31, 2015: http://www.americanrevolution.org/blk.php.

Shaw, H. I., Jr. & Donnelly, R. W. (2002). "Blacks in the Marine Corps" (PDF). Washington, DC: History and Museums Division, Headquarters USMC. Retrieved June 1, 2011.

Shenk, G. (2008). Work or Fight! Race, Gender, and the Draft in World War One Basingstoke, Palgrave Macmillan.

Sirera, J. (December2021) Journey's end: Dudley's Davises hope to share a state football championship, From the Joe Siera's five favorite stories of 2021, Retrieved January 31, 2022, from: https://greensboro.com/sports/high-school/journeys-end-dudleys-davises-hope-to-share-a-stste-football-championship/article_f67cb7b0-5923-11ec-b58e3411f7241.html

Sirera, J. (July 27, 2022). Gregsha Lee On Goals as Dudley Athletic Director: I Want It All... Retrieved December 7, 2023 from: https://greensboro.com/gregsha-lee-on-goals-as-dudleys-athletics-director-i-want-it-all/article_9bdd5aa0-01c-11ed-912-Sfd285560675.html

Sistrom, M., Payne, J., Brandon, L. & Lambert, L. A. (2007). If These Walls Could Talk: The History and Legacy of J.C. Price School, Brock Historical Museum, Greensboro College, J.C. Price Oral History Project.

Smith, A.B., Advisor (1941). 1941 Mid-Year Graduating Class (Picture), The Panther's Claw, Volume X, page 1.

Smith, A. B., Advisor (1953). Inez Fox, sophomore, Upsets Senior Tradition by Becoming 'Miss Homecoming,' The Panther's Claw, Volume XXII, page 1.

Smith, A. B., Advisor (1953). Many Applaud Homecoming Queen and Gay Floats in Colorful Parade, The Panther's Claw, Volume XXII, page 1.

Smith, J. P. (1984). Race and Human Capital, The American Economic Review: Vol. 74, No.4 (Sep. 1984), pp.685-698.

Smith, S. (2011). From the Biographical Files of Charles Henry Moore, December 14. Retrieved November 29, 2015: https://consecratedeminence.wordpress.com/2011/12/14/from-the-biographical-file-of-charles-henry-moore/

Stockard, S. W. (1902). The history of Guilford County, North Carolina, Knoxville, Tennessee: Gaut-Ogden Company, Printers. Retrieved April 1915 from: https://archive.org/details/historyofguilford00stoc (Digital publication, University of Chapel Hill.

Stowell, J. S. (1922). Methodist Adventures in Negro Education, Chapter 10: The Carolinas-Claflin College (South Carolina) and Bennett College (North Carolina), Chicago, Illinois: Illinois University Library, pp. 155- 162.

Strunk, R. (Feb19, 2021) Celebrating Black History/Jonathan McKee, Sr.- Dudley HS, NCSAA Black History, Retrieved January 26, from: https://www.nchsaa.org/news/2021-2-19/clebrating-black-history-jonathan-mckee-sr-dudley-hs

Student Government Association (2000). Student Manifesto, The Panther Yearbook: 2000 Millennium Edition, p.127.

Tarpley, J.A. (1942). Dudley High School Examines Curriculum (Article), Secondary School Study News Bulletin, To and From Our Schools (Vol. 1, No. 2).

Tarpley, J.A. (1962). Graduation Address to the 1962 Graduating Class of James B. Dudley High School, Original Script is part of the David Moore Collection of Dudley Memorabilia.

Tarpley, J.A. (1979). Dedication Ceremony for Tarpley Stadium (Speech). Unpublished Original Document Owned by David Moore.

Temple Emanuel (2014). Reverend Amos Quick, III Speaker, Martin Luther King, Jr. Shabbat Service January 17, 2014. Retrieved from: https://www.tegreensboro.org/mlk-shabbat-service-speaker-rev-amos-quick

The Carolina Peacemaker (1995). Education: From Humble Beginnings to National Prominence-Bennett College Founded 1873, Thursday, February 22, p. B11.

The National Center for Higher Education Management Systems (2016). College Participation Rates: College-Going Rates of High School Graduates Going Directly from High School. Retrieved from http://www.higheredinfo.org/dbrowser/index.php?submeasure=63&year=2010&level=nation&mode=data&state=0

The Official Website of Brendan Haywood (2015). Brendan Haywood Single Parents Fund. Retrieved December 12, 2015, from: http://www.bhaywood.com/ .

The Panther's Claw (2002). Dudley's Junior AFROTC a Proud Tradition Continues. Special Dudley Black History Edition: Vol.2002, Issue February 2002.

Timeline for the Events for African Americans in the U.S. Army (2015). 1812-1815: The War of 1812. Retrieved from: http://www.army.mil/africanamericans/timeline.html .

Tolbert, l. (2007). Colored Merchants Association "Challenging the Chain Stores." Tar Heel Junior Historian: Spring Issue. Retrieved from: https://www.ncpedia.org/industry/colored-merchant-assoc

Torpey, E. (2012). High Wages after High School without a College Degree. Office of Occupational Statistics and Employment Projections, BLS. Retrieved from: http://www.bls.gov/careeroutlook/2012/summer/art03.pdf

Trojanowski, H.J. (1999). Betty H. Carter Women Veterans Historical Project Oral History Collection: Mattie Donnell Hicks. Greensboro, N.C.: UNC-G Digital Collections: February 25, 1999. Retrieved from: http://libcdm.l.uncg.edu/cdm/singlem/collection/WVHP/id/4218/rec/1

Thornton, Jerry (21 June 1993). "James B. Parsons, 1st Black U.S. Judge". *Chicago Tribune*. Retrieved June 18, 2023.

Truesdale, P. (2021). To Serve Is to Lead (Introduction Essay), James B. Dudley Educational Sports Hall of Fame/ Hall of Distinction (2021 Cohort).

Unks, W. (December 2021). Deuce Is Our Leader, Lee Newspapers, Retrieved January 26, 2022, from: https://greensboro.com/sports/high-school/journeys-end-dudleys-davises-hope-to-share-a-stste-football-championship/article_f67cb7b0-5923-11ec-b58e3411f7241.html

United States Department of State, International Information Program (2015). Free at Last: U.S. Civil Rights Movement. Retrieved from: http://beijing.usembassy-china.org.cn/uploads/images/sSl_vt_egg5seuIxnH7z5A/free_at_last.pdf

United States War Department (1880-1901). The War of Rebellion: A Compilation of the Official Records of the Union and Confederate Armies. 128 Volumes. Washington: Government Printing Office.

Virginia Historical Society (2015). The Green Decision of 1968 (Webpage). Retrieved, February 2, 2016, from: http://www.vahistorical.org/collections-and-resources/virginia-history-explorer/civil-rights-movement-virginia/green-decision.

Waddell, D. L. (2016). Terra Cotta Heritage Foundation, Home Fires Still Burning at Terra Cotta (Article). Retrieved from: http://www.terracottaheritagefoundation.org/index.html.

Wagner, L. (2013). Vouchers gain ground; public loses in a final budget (Blog), North Carolina Policy Watch: News and Commentary on Public Policy in North Carolina. Retrieved July 7, 2015: http://www.ncpolicywatch.com/2013/07/25/vouchers-gain-ground-public-education-loses-in-final-budget/

Walker, V. S. (1996). Their highest potential: An African American school community in the segregated South. Chapel Hill, NC: The University of North Carolina Press.

Walker, V. S. (2000). Valued segregated schools for African American children in the South, 1935-1969: A review of common themes and characteristics. Review of Educational Research, 70(3), 253-285.

Washington, Roberta (2012). Feature: Roberta Washington, FAIA, Makes a Place. Retrieved October 12, 2015, from: http://www.bwaf.org/roberta-washington-faia-makes-a-place/

Watlington, T. (2004). Desiree Best, Guilford County High School Teacher of the Year, The Panther Yearbook 2004: Do You Remember- 75th Anniversary Edition, p.66.

WCP Consulting &Communications (2017). Shipman Family Home Care, Inc. (Website). Retrieved 11-14-2023, from: https//shipmanfhc.com/#team-section & https//shipmanfhc.com/#about-us section.

Wiley, C. H. (1854). First Annual Report of the General Superintendent of Common Schools (To Governor David S. Reid), Raleigh, North Carolina: W.W. Holden Printer of the State, p. 30.

Williams, Rudi (February 6, 2004). "Marine Corps' Magnetism Beckons Future General into World of Elite Warfighters". *Defense LINK News*. U.S. Department of Defense. Archived from the original on 2006-10-14. Retrieved 2020-10-15.

Williams, S. (2009). An Interview with a J.C. Price Teacher: Shelton Williams, Brock Historical Museum, J.C. Price School: If these walls could talk; An oral history. Retrieved, March 15, 2015: https://museum.greensboro.edu:42001/jcpriceschool/history-of-the-school.php.

Wilson, A. V. (1997). Forgotten Voices: Remembered experiences of cross-over teachers during desegregation in Austin, Texas, 1964-1971. Unpublished doctoral dissertation, the University of Texas at Austin, Austin, Texas.

Wilson, A. V., & Segall, W. E. (2001). Oh, do I remember: Experiences of teachers during the desegregation of Austin's schools, 1964-1971. New York: SUNY Press.

Wilson, C. (October 12, 2016). Dudley alum appears in Lifetime network movie, Greensboro News & Record, Retrieved 12-1-2020 from: Dudley alum appears in Lifetime network movie | Blog: Go Triad - –&E Extra | greensboroom.

Woods, Maurice F. (1942). A History of Education in Greensboro, North Carolina: As It Pertains to the American Negro in Greensboro, North Carolina (Thesis). Atlanta University: Atlanta, Georgia.

Woodson, C.G. (1919). The Education of the Negro Prior to 1861: A History of the Education of the Colored People of the United States from the Beginning of Slavery to the Civil War. E. Book Published 2004: http://andromeda.rutgers.edu/~natalieb/The_Education_Of_The_Negro_P.pdf

Wright, M., Advisor (1983). Your 1983-84 P.T.S.A. at Work for You! (Article), The Panther's Claw, Vol. 49: Number 1, October 1983, p.1.

Vaughan, Don (2015). "Changing Tunes." Periodical: *Military Officer*. Feb. 2015: 52-55, 70-71

Yardley, W. (2014). 'Sweet' Lou Hudson, Jump Shot Master with the Hawks, Dies at 69, April 12, 2014.

Yost, S.D. (January 16, 2019). Remembering Guilford County Commissioner Warren Dorsett, Retrieved February 12, 2022, from: https://www.rhinotimes.com/news/remembering-guilford-county-commissioner-warren-dorsett/

Illustrations:

"Gordon, scourged back, Harper's weekly, 1863 July 4, p429, bottom" "y Harper & Brothers, New York - Library of Congress, Native name Library of Congress Location Washington, D.C. Coordinates 38° 53′ 19″ N, 77° 00′ 17″ WEstablished1800Websitewww.loc.gov. Licensed under Public Domain via Commons - – ttps://commons.wikimedia.org/wiki/File:Gordon,_scourged_back,_Harper%27s_weekly,_1863_July_4,_p429,_bottom.jpg#/media/File:Gordon,_scourged_back,_Harper%27s_weekly,_1863_July_4,_p429,_bottom.jpg.

Hartmann, D. (1927). Original Architectural Drawing of the High School for Negroes in Greensboro, North Carolina. Commissioned by the Greensboro City Schools.

A PLACE WHERE SUCCESS WAS EXPECTED: FINAL EDITION

Achieved in the Guilford County Schools Construction Projects Facility, High Point, North Carolina.

Lineberry, Ed (1978). Portrait: Dudley Band Director James Morgan in Uniform

Pictures:

Archives Department of Bennett College, Carolina Hall. Retrieved from: http://contentdm.auctr.edu/cdm/ref/collection/BCHD/id/47.

Archives Department of Bennett College, Baseball Team. Retrieved from: http://contentdm.auctr.edu/cdm/singleitem/collection/BCHD/id/48/rec/1

Best of David Amerson 2015. Photo highlights of the blossoming cornerback, David Amerson, from the 2015-2016 season. Retrieved from: http://www.raiders.com/news/article-1/Cornerback-David-Amerson-Impresses-In-First-Season-As-A-Raider/99ad2055-dd4a-42e2-a70f-c69207fc9530#e2910450-727f-4b71-b64f-9f8befe8db00

Carey, K. (2010). Covacus Band at Cosmos (CareySound Website). Retrieved February 8, 2022 from: https://www.careysound.com/oldsite/company/history/index.html

Carolina Peacemaker (1995). Students at East White Oak School, Thursday, February 16-Wednesday, February 22, 1995, Taking A Step Back in Time, p. B13.

Chavis Library, Greensboro City Libraries, Vance Chavis (Formal Portrait).

Covacus (2022). Early Involvement of James Yourse (Picture). Retrieved Feb.9, 2022: https://www.facebook.com/photo.php?fbid=1011069342279068&set=a.362542047131804&type=3

Defense Video & Imagery Distribution System (2013). Lt. Col. Dwayne Whitehead. Retrieved from http://www.2ndmlg.marines.mil/News/PressReleaseView/tabid/6689/Article/517492/lt-col-dwayne-a-whiteside.aspx.

Ferriera, K.(December 2021) Steven Davis & Steven Davis II, Retrieved January 29, 2021, from: https://kennethferrieraphotography.comsingles/qay7sc2dvrz55avjybt5v6yuhipcn

George C. Simkins, Jr. Elementary School, http://chavezinteriors.com/portfolio-items/george-c-simkins-elementary-school/.

Greensboro Daily News, Jeff Davis & Lola McAdoo, Special TO NITE REPORT, May 1982

Greensboro News & Record, Judge Elreta Alexander in courtroom in 1969, May 22, 1988.

Greensboro, News & Record (October 12, 2016. Vonii Bristow (Carl Wilson Blog) 5da443620089b.image,

Greensboro News & Record (October 23, 2020). Richmond, Julia Ruth (Legacy Section), Retrieved November 5, 2020 from: https://www.legacy.com/us/obituaries/greensboro/name/julia-richmond-obituary?pid=196982347.

Holmes, B., Cathey, L., (2017). Rededicating, Reconnecting, Remembering (Class of 67 Souvenir Book), Toni Jordan & Smith High School Classmates.

J. Kenneth Lee Papers, #4782, Southern Historical Collection, The Wilson Library, University of North Carolina at Chapel Hill

James B. Dudley Home Page. Prom Night 2015.

James B. Dudley High School Educational and Sports Hall of Fame/Hall of Distinction (2015). Picture: Amos Quick, III. Retrieved December 23, 2015, from: http://www.dudleyhofhod.org/#!2015-inductee-bios/gw4v1.

James B. Dudley High School Educational and Sports Hall of Fame/Hall of Distinction (2015). Picture: David (Bunny) Moore. Retrieved December 23, 2015, from: http://www.dudleyhofhod.org/#!2015-inductee-bios/gw4v1.

Dr. Jo Evans Lynn, Ed.D.

James B. Dudley High School Educational and Sports Hall of Fame/Hall of Distinction (2015). Picture: David Dansby. Retrieved December 23, 2015, from: http://www.dudleyhofhod.org/#!2015-inductee-bios/gw4v1.

James B. Dudley High School Educational and Sports Hall of Fame/Hall of Distinction (2015). Picture: Ernestine Bennett. Retrieved December 23, 2015, from: http://www.dudleyhofhod.org/#!2015-inductee-bios/gw4v1.

James B. Dudley High School Educational and Sports Hall of Fame/Hall of Distinction (2015). Picture: Clarence Grier. Retrieved December 23, 2015, from: http://www.dudleyhofhod.org/#!2015-inductees/c1dni.

James B. Dudley High School Educational and Sports Hall of Fame/Hall of Distinction (2013). Picture: Quentin C. Crosby. Retrieved December 23, 2015, from: http://www.dudleyhofhod.org/#!2013-inductee-bios/gw4v1.

James B. Dudley High School Educational and Sports Hall of Fame/Hall of Distinction (2015). Picture: Clarence Grier. Retrieved December 23, 2015, from: http://www.dudleyhofhod.org/#!2015-inductee-bios/gw4v1.

James B. Dudley High School Educational and Sports Hall of Fame/Hall of Distinction (2013). Picture: Brian Seagraves. Retrieved December 23, 2015, from: http://www.dudleyhofhod.org/#!2013-inductee-bios/gw4v1.

James B. Dudley High School Educational and Sports Hall of Fame/Hall of Distinction (2013). Picture: Brian Seagraves. Retrieved December 23, 2015, from: http://www.dudleyhofhod.org/#!2013-inductee-bios/gw4v1.

James B. Dudley High School Educational and Sports Hall of Fame/Hall of Distinction (2023) Pictures: Brian Crosby, Nevada Jarrell, Robert Jarrell, Stephanie Wilson.

Johnson Reginald H. (2023). Picture on the Set of The Color Purple(Musical Movie)

Lemon. E. (January 9, 2009). Chuck Cotton of The Buzzkillz. Retrieved February 9, 2022, Dot-matrix Project from: https://live.staticflickr.com/3559/330141522_55ab6e39f_b.jpg

Mendenhall Plantation Home Place, Mendenhall Plantation (Front view). Retrieved from: http://mendenhallhomeplace.com/.

WCP Consulting & Communications (2020). Shipman Family Home Care, Inc

(Website) Front of Building, Patient Care, Retrieved 11-18-2023 from.

https://shipmanfhc.com

"Officers of the National Negro Business League in Indianapolis, 1904." Image ID: 1229313. Online in the New York Public Library Digital Gallery at http://digitalgallery.nypl.org/nypldigital/id?1229313 [2].

Pamela M. Truesdale (2021). Professional Linked-in Image, Retrieved March 28,2021 from: 10+ "Pamela Truesdale" profiles | LinkedIn

Panther (1967). English Department: Miss Francine McAdoo (Yearbook), p. 18.

Panther (1967). English Department: Mrs. Rosa T. Yourse (Yearbook), p.18.

Panther (1967). English Department: Mrs. Annie Gillespie (Yearbook), p.19.

Panther (1967). English Department: Mrs. Barbara Wells (Yearbook), p.18.

Panther (1967). Physical Education: Miss Georgene Dye (Yearbook), p. 27.

Panther (1967). Physical Education: Mr. William Boyers (Yearbook), p. 27.

Panther (1967). Home Economics: Mrs. Mae Sue Henry (Yearbook), p. 28.

Panther (1967). Vocational Education: Mr. Ezell A. Blair, Sr. (Yearbook), p. 26.

Panther (1967). Seniors: Charles Benton (Yearbook), p. 43.

A PLACE WHERE SUCCESS WAS EXPECTED: FINAL EDITION

Panther (1967). Seniors: Jo Ann Evans, (Yearbook), p. 49.

Panther (1967). Seniors: Richard Fields (Yearbook), p. 49.

Panther (1967). Seniors: Gwendolyn Spinks (Yearbook), p. 67.

Panther (1967). Organizations: Future Teachers-Gwendolyn Spinks Benton (Yearbook), p. 151.

Panther (1967). Organizations: Sophomore Choir, Mrs. Julia Richmond Directing (Yearbook), p.174.

Panther (1967). Organizations: Student Bus Drivers (Yearbook), p. 155.

Panther (1967. Organizations: Junior Marshals (Yearbook), p. 167

Panther (1967). Organizations: ICT In Action: Ronald Vample & Zimmerman Price (Yearbook), p.228.

Panther (1967). Organizations: Distributive Education: Elsie Wharton, Silvia Bethea, Lorenzo Caldwell, Patricia Gilmer, Billy Griffin, Joe Coley, and Ronald Miller (Yearbook), pp. 158-164.

Panther 1969 Yearbook, (1969), retrieved January 20, 2021 from: Yearbooks -High School, College and University Yearbooks Online (e-yearbook.com).

Panther 73 (1973). Modern Dancers Display Poise, Grace, Liquidity in Motion, at Rest or in Posed Forms- Pictorial (Yearbook), pp. 168-170.

Rena Bullock Reunion (2015), Dot Harris Furcron's First Grade Class 1953-54

Rodriguez, J. (August 1, 2007). Rena Bullock School (Goshen School), Greensboro News and Record.

Rodriguez, J. (April 12, 2017). Jose Charles Operation Transparency, Retrieved December 12, 2020 from: Jose Charles Operation Transparency | Gallery | greensboro.com.

Slick Slack Johnson (2020). Retrieved December 30, 2020, from: Home - –SlickSlackShowGram (theslickslackshowgram.com).

The Raliegh News & Observer (1986). Dudley High School's Pam Doggett.

UNCG Digital Collection: Mattie Donnell Hicks (Portrait 1950. Betty H. Carter Women Veterans Historical Project. Retrieved from: http://libcdm1.uncg.edu/cdm/singleitem/collection/WVHP/id/870/rec/.

UNCG Digital Collection: Mattie Donnell Hicks (Performing Nursing Duties, 1950). Betty H. Carter Women Veterans Historical Project. Retrieved from: http://libcdm1.uncg.edu/cdm/singleitem/collection/WVHP/id/873/rec/3.

Unks, W. (2021). Long Delayed high school Football season finally here, Four Teams to Watch, HSXtra High School Sports, Retrieved January 29, 2022, from: hpps://Greensboro.com/sports/high-school/long-delayed-high-school-football-season-is-finally-here/article_8b02d28-7627-11eb-b2cf-7bf73ea5f2d8.html

Unks, W. (2021). Dudley's Steven Davis II runs back an interception during the first half of the Panthers' 20-6 win at Statesville in the NCHSAA Class 3-A playoffs. Davis leads Dudley with four interceptions this season and has broken up 16 passes (Action Shot). Deuce Is Our Leader, Lee Newspapers, Retrieved January 26, 2022, from: https://greensboro.com/sports/high-school/journeys-end-dudleys-davises-hope-to-share-a-stste-football-championship/article_f67cb7b0-5923-11ec-b58e3411f7241.html

Warnersville Community Coalition, 800 Block Ashe Street. Yesterday, Today & Tomorrow, Warnersville Community 1st Heritage Community in North Carolina.

Warnersville Community Coalition, Warnersville Methodist Episcopal Church, Saint Matthews United Methodist Church, Inc. Yesterday, Today & Tomorrow, Warnersville Community 1st Heritage Community in North Carolina.

Dr. Jo Evans Lynn, Ed.D.

Warnersville Community Coalition, Shiloh Baptist Church at 730 Ashe Street, Yesterday, Today & Tomorrow, Warnersville Community 1st Heritage Community in North Carolina.

Warnersville Community Coalition, Harmon Unthank House, Yesterday, Today & Tomorrow, Warnersville Community 1st Heritage Community in North Carolina.

Whirligig (1994). A Whirl Through Time, "Rev It Up" Grimsley Staff, Lazelle Free Army ROTC, page 87.

A PLACE WHERE SUCCESS WAS EXPECTED: FINAL EDITION

INDEX

2-Steven Davis II, 150
3-Mehki Wall, 150
4AAAState Championship, 381
8-time state outdoor track champion, 362
9-Domaine Vann, 150
11-Nasir Newkirk, 150
16-Antonio Lee, 150
17-DJ Parker, 150
30-Jaylin Williams, 150
32-Kafi Abass, 150
34-Braden McCall, 150
35-Dwayne Reese, 150
36-Austin Lloyd, 150
40thConsolidated Reunion Souvenir Journal, 483
42-Brian Siner, 150
45-Darryl Dawkins, 150
51-Malcolm Kennion, 150
60-Joshua Palmer, 150
74-Seth Lawrence, 150
75-Todd Hargrove, 150
76-A'Mon McManus, 150
77-Jaden Buie, 150
83-Abdul Baylor, 150
90-degree angle, 221
90-Dominque Wilson, 150

A

Aa'Niyah Massey, 364–67
Aaron Gist, 433
abolitionist Frederick Douglass, 300
abolitionists, 5, 299
Academic Affairs Library, 484
Academic Dean, 398
academic programs, strong, 55
Academies and Grammar Schools, 6
Academy, Lincoln, 460, 463, 468
Academy Beach Trip & Graduation Picture, 127
Accelerated Reading Tests, 396
ACC Football Championship, 379
ACL injury, 389
actress Eliza Dushku, 422
Ada E. WAAC/WAC, 314
Adams-Taylor, 419, 478
Addy Lindsay, 76
Adegorioye Rory Baker, 154
Adell, 322
Adeniyi, 154
Adequate Yearly Progress (AYP), 169
Administrative Psychiatry, 418
Aerospace, 341
Affordable Care Act, 409
AFJROTC program, 330
AFJROTC unit, 330
African American business and homeowners, 477
African American Church, largest, 27
African American Community, 460
African American community and race relations, 34
African American History Section, 486
African American Mayor, 285
African American member, first, 115, 129
African American migration, 31
African American Patriots, 297

African American population, 33, 65
African American president, first, 22
African Americans, 1, 18–19, 21, 26–27, 31, 33–34, 37, 51–52, 81–82, 95–97, 296–98, 300–303, 424, 430–33, 489–90
 served, 56
African Americans Revolution, 485
African American Step, 481
African American students, 22, 29, 47, 103, 158, 163, 447
 qualified, 96
African American Woman of Distinction Award, 279
African American Women of Distinction Hall of Fame, 269
African foot dances, 221
African Heritage Art Collection, 396
African Methodist Episcopal Zion Church, 178
Afrika Hayes, 241
Afrique, 298
AFROTC Program, 399
Aggiettes, 359
Agricultural & Mechanical College, 232
Agricultural & Mechanical College Normal School, 232
Agricultural & Technical College, 54
AIA pamphlet, 447
Aida, 237
AIG Director, 171
Airborne Parachutist Badge, 336
Air Force, 304, 306–7, 311, 313, 315, 317–19, 322–23, 325, 338, 341, 343, 346, 399
Air Force Commendation, 342
Air Force Gladney, 309
Air Force Good Conduct Medal, 331
Air Force in Okinawa, 338
Air Force Jr ROTC instructor, 332
Air Force Junior Instructor School, 332
Air Force Junior ROTC Instructor, 332
Air Force Leadership Award, 342
Air Force Longevity Service Award Ribbon, 331
Air Force Organization Excellence Award, 331
Air Force Outstanding Unit Award, 331
Air Force ROTC Cadets, first, 343
Air Force Training Ribbon, 331
Air Force Vanlue, 321
Air Training Command Non-Commissioned Officer Academy, 332
Air University Military Instructor, 341
Air War College, 341
AJ Faulks, 286
Akridge, 304
Alamance County Teacher's Association School Representative and Treasurer, 394
Alamance County Transportation Authority, 427
Alan Dale, 310
Albany Georgia, 114
Albert Harris High School, 225
Albert J. U, 322
Albright, 220, 478
Aldridge, Patricia, 181–82
Alexander, Linda, 196
Alfonzo, 306
Alford, Marcus, 150
ALFRED KNIGHTON, 276

Alfred Russell, 305
Alice Freeman Palmer Building, 25
Alicia-Leilani Rodriguez, 367
Alijah Tibbs, 154
All City in football and baseball, 356, 476
all-class record, 362
All-Comers Meet, 361
All-Conference and All-County Football, 340
All-Conference Basketball, 370
All Conference in football, 356, 476
All-County Football, 340
Allegiance, pledge, 177
Allen, Robert, 315
All-Male Academy, 165
All Southeast in football and Honorable Mention All-American, 356
All Southeast in football and Honorable Mention All-American in football, 476
All Star East-West Shrine Game, 368
All-Star events, 143
All State, 368
All State in football, 356, 476
ALL-TIME winningest sports team, 365
Alma, 517
Alonzo, 318
Alpha Kappa Alpha, 216
Alpha Kappa Alpha Sorority, 115, 427, 475
Alpha Psi Omega National Sorority, 396
Alphonse Nicholson, 252, 264
ALPONSE NICHOLSON, 264
Alston, Charlotte, 29, 259
Alston-Jones International Civil, 287
Alston's, Tom, 349
Alum, Dudley, 127, 491
Alumni, Dudley, 280, 282, 380, 404, 407, 412–13, 457
Alumni Achievement Award, 450
Alumni Association, Howard U., 475
Alumni Band, 396, 400
Alumni Band clubs, 191
Alumni Hall of Fame, 292
Alumni Service Award, 475
Alumni Weekend, 480, 483
Alvin Ailey Dance Theater, 421
Alzheimer's/MS, 342
Amanda Carruthers Johnson, 16
Amanda Johnson, 16
Amanda's husband Douglas Johnson, 16
Amber Lassiter Headen, 250
AME minister, 238
Amen Corner, 419
American Academy, 356, 476
American Association of University Women, 107
American Bridge Association, 281
American Civil War, 51, 299, 478
American Economic Review, 488
American education, 94
American Enterprise, 282
American Expeditionary Force, 303
American Fund, 94
American Fund for Public Service Records, 485
American Historical Review, 487
American History, 2, 282
American Institute, 82
American Marine units, 297
American naval squadrons, 298
American Negro, 49, 491

American Psychiatric Association examination in Toronto Canada, 418
American Revolution, 485, 487
American Revolution Organization, 487
American Rhythm and Blues/soul singer, 249
American Soul, 265
America's Black Upper Classes, 201, 482
America's Reconstruction, 465
America's Reconstruction- People and Politics, 478
Amerson, 379–80
  selected, 379
Ames-Williams, 292
AME Zion Church, 17, 179
Amherst, 19
Amherst College, 95
AMOS LEWIS QUICK, III, 293
Amos Quick-Guilford County School Board, 89
ancestors, 461
Anderson, 149, 304, 319, 473, 480
  Brandon, 150
  Mary, 250
Anderson's Grill, 439
Andrew Preston, 322
Andrews, 169, 173, 305, 313–14, 320, 473
Andrew Scales, 139
Andrews High School, 123, 128, 169, 174
Andrews team, 479
Andrew Williams II, 292
Angarano, Michael, 422
Angela L. Williams, 401
Angel House Foundation, 484
Angus, 314
Annapolis, 334, 336, 340
Annette, 197
Annexes, first, 535
Annie Hatch Dudley, 51
Annie M. Gillespie, 74
Anniversary Activities, 332
Anniversary Edition, 490
Anniversary Reunion, 474
Annual Alpha Kappa Alpha Cotillion, 115
Annual Association, 170
Annual GCS Leadership Institute, 170
annual Homecoming Game, 193
annual Martin Luther King Jr, 229
Annual Sit-In Movement Breakfast, 330
Annual Spring Music Festival, 391
Annual Women's Athletic Association Sports Weekend, 358, 476
Anson County School System, 109
anthem, praise party, 263
Anthony, 476
Anti-Bellum Period, 5
antiques, expensive, 458
A&P, 431
Apollo's Harlem Amateur Hour, 238
Apollo Theater, 238
Appalachian State University, 486
AP Physics class, 166
AP Physics EOC passing rate, 471
Applaud Homecoming Queen, 486, 488
Appliance Repair, 471
Applied Communication, 288
Apprentice, 67
April Franklin, 210–11
A Proud Tradition, 330
Arcadia Publishing, 481

Archer, 48
Archibald Murphey, 6
Architectural Drawing, 482
Architectural Plans, 535
architecture, institutional, 82
Archives Department, 22–24, 38, 491
Aretha Franklin, 239
Arhoolie vet, 257
Arlanders, 318
Armed Forces Expeditionary Medal, 336
Armed Service Reserve Medal, 417
Army Air Corps, 325
Army Airforce, 310, 323
Army and Navy, 34
Army Bennett, 304
Army Commendation Medals, 333, 336, 417
Army Dental Corps, 335
Army Nurse Corps, 313, 415, 417
Army Nurses, 416
Army Reserves, 125, 290
Army Service Ribbon, 336
Arnett, 8, 18, 30, 51, 478
Arnette, 58, 214, 216
arranger Bert Keyes, 253
Art Club-10, 473
Art Design, 441
Artest, Ron, 375
Arthur Fletcher Elmes, 277
Arthur Gist, 433–34
Arthur L., 312
Arthur Taswell Gist, 433
Arthur W. U, 308
artificial kidney machines, 416
artillery, deadly, 301
Art Ink Designs, 441–42
  started, 441
art-ink-promo-printyfy.me, 442
artists, major recording, 428
Art Museum, 298
Arts degree in music, 451
Arts Department, 406
Asha Bonds, 150
Asheboro, 225
Asheboro Street, 28, 99
Asheboro Street School, 20, 47
Ashe Street, 27–28, 273, 477, 495
Ashe Street School, 21
Ashe Street School in Southwest Greensboro, 20
Ashore, 334
Ash Street, 439
Ash Street in Warnersville, 27
Ashville, 185, 463
Asian politics, 420
assemblies, 108, 225
assistant band directors, 126, 186, 228–30, 397
assistant coach Frank Starling, 146
Assistant Defensive Line Coach, 354
assistant director, 135, 396
Assistant Director Maurice Hamilton, 126
Assistant Director of Bands, 230
Assistant Director of Nursing Service, 68
Assistant District Attorney, 284, 292
Assistant Golf Coach, 124
Assistant Head Coach, 354
assistant manager, 443
Assistant Principal, 70, 156–57, 170
Assistant Track Coach, 397
Assistant Women's Basketball Coach, 359

Association, state Negro Teacher's, 107
Astin, Sean, 422
Astor, 485
Astra Club, 396
A&T Blue & Gold Marching Machine Members, 221
A&T coach, 349
A&T College, 138, 281, 432
A&T graduate Christopher Goins, 230
Athletic Banquet, 360
Athletic Director, 132–33
athletic director Jonathan McKee, 136
Athletics, Dudley, 476–77
Atkins High School, 86
Atlanta, 49, 229, 245, 267, 349–50, 382, 409, 415, 419, 449, 491
Atlanta Circle, 419
Atlanta Daily World, 419
Atlanta GA, 265
Atlanta Hawks, 350
Atlanta University, 491
Atlantic City, 82, 238
Atlantic Coast Conference, 141, 355, 376
Atlantic Coast Player, 368
Atlantic Coast Relays, prestigious, 361
Atlantic Records, 428
Atlantic Records Label, 238
Atlantic Star, 260
Atlantic Starr L-R, 249
A&T Letterman's Club, 473
A&T Military Hall of Fame, 291
A&T's' band director, 226
A&T's campus, 88, 179
A&T's College, 450
A&T's director, 219, 326
A&T's Homecoming Parade, 187
A&T State University, 90, 138, 211, 221, 230, 233, 237, 441, 450, 467, 476
A&T State University Band Director and former Guilford County School Board member, 461
A&T State University Drum Line, 475
A&T State University's Campus, 80
A&T student leader Nelson Johnson, 88
Attaway, 304
Attendance Office Assistant, 410
Attendance Officer, 168
attendance zone, 460
Attended A&T State University, 332
Attorney David, 278
Attorney Elreta Alexander-Ralston, 234
Attorney Nathan Ross Margold, 95
Aubrey, 321
Audio/Visual & Tech Ministry, 125
August Wilson, 212–13
Aunt Daisy, 436
Austin, 304, 490
Austin's schools, 490
Author's Notes, 535
auto mechanics, 56, 58, 62, 66, 75, 104, 135, 139–40, 167, 459, 469
Auto Mechanics Class, 105
Auto Mechanics Classroom and Shop, 62
Auto Mechanics Club, 331
Auto Mechanics Facility, 138
Auto Mechanics Program, 138
auto mechanics teacher, 185
Automotive/Aviation Services, 471

Automotive Vehicle Technology Team, 105
Auxiliary Gym, 61, 456
Auxiliary Gymnasium, 484
AVA, 331
Avenue, Ross, 216
Avery, 213
AVT, 105
AVT Club, 469
awards, state Democratic Women's STAR, 279
Ayomide Onadeji, 367
AYP (Adequate Yearly Progress), 169
Azalea Garden Club, 270

B

B-1 band, 226
B-1 band mates, 220, 226
B-1 Band Photographs, 327
B-1 Muster List Band, 326
B-1 Navy, 219
B1-Navy, 309
B-1 Navy Band, 219, 221–22, 224, 303, 326, 328
 Distinguished Service, 326
B-1 Navy Band Hester, 311
B-1 Navy Band Hood, 312
B-1 Navy Band in Chapel Hill, 328
B-1 Navy Band Marches in Chapel Hill, 219
B-1 Navy Band Pickett, 317
B-1 Navy Band practices, 327
B-1 Navy Band practices on campus, 327
B-1 Navy Band Sellars, 318
B-1 Preflight Navy Band, 259
B-1's bandmaster, 219–20, 326
Bably Lake, 328
Baby Boomers, 59
Baby Ruth, 431
Baccalaureate, 179
Baccalaureate sermon, 177–78
Baccalaureate Sermons and Four-Hour Graduations, 177
Baccalaureate speakers, 178–79
Bachelor of Arts degree in music, 451
Backmos, James, 318
Back-to-School Cookout for mothers and children, 376
Bacon, Michael, 262
Bailey, 473
 Claude, 26
 Sharon, 102
Baines, 108, 119–20, 456, 478
Baker, Donna, 409
Baker, Nancy, 243
Baker, Rosalyn, 377
Baldwin, 154, 419
Baldwin, 25-Cameron, 150
Baldwin, Destiny, 269
Baldwin, James, 419, 434
ballerina assoluta, 246
 prima, 247
 title prima, 247
Balliett, 30, 478
Ball State, 388
Baltimore, 235, 478
Baltimore Ravens, 373
band, jazz, 77, 125, 228, 260, 289, 396–97, 405
Band Boosters start, 408
band classes, 99, 225
Band Gilmer, 309

Bandmaster/Drum Major James Parsons, 219
Band Parent, 122
Band Practice, 125
band room, 62, 226
band uniforms, 204, 226, 412
Baptist church, 42
Baptist minister, 42, 235
Barbara Robinson Jean Ledwell, 113
Barbara Weathers, 249
Barbara Wells, 208, 493
Barber, Casey, 392
Barber, William J., 286
Barber High School, 136
Barber Shop, 439
Barbour, Anne, 111
baritone Todd Duncan, 241
BARJO Chemicals, 285
Barksdale, 43, 304
bar mitzvah, 537
Barnes, 21-Jeremiah, 150
Barnes' position, 88
Barnett, Isaac, 283
barriers, breaking, 233, 485
baseball scholarship, 281
Basic Fundamentals Program, 403
Basingstoke, 488
basketball
 attended home, 191
 coached, 37
 played, 101, 143, 385, 387, 421
 women's, 115, 359
Basketball and Golf Coach, 136
basketball coach, 133, 135, 360, 402
basketball court, 61
Basketball District, 136
basketball players, 65
basketball programs, 132
Basketball Selection Committee, 281
basketball team
 first Girls Varsity, 115
 first Lady Panthers Varsity, 110
Basketball Tournament, 375
Bass, Joan, 113
bassist Chris Carroll, 257
battle
 organized, 94
 pitched, 93
battle for integration, 303
battle of Island Mound, 301
Battle of Lake Erie, 298
Battle of New Market Heights, 302
battle of Port Hudson, 301
Battle of Road Island, 298
Beam, 304
Bearcats, 385
Beatha, 179
Beautification, 460
Beautification Committee, 473
to Become a Man, 211
Bee Cafe, 432
Beech, Harvey, 97
Belafonte, Harry, 114, 237
Belgian league championship, 385
Belgium, 385
Bell, Diane, 209
Belle, Bennett, 210, 242, 260, 473
Bell South Services, 290
Benbow Park, 479

A PLACE WHERE SUCCESS WAS EXPECTED: FINAL EDITION

Benbow Road, 40–41, 54, 61, 74
Benbow Road and Warnersville, 103
Benbow Road and Warnersville to Grimsley Senior
    High School, 103
Benbow Road good, 41
benevolent societies, 10
Ben-Israel, 294
    Ezekiel, 295
Benjamin Mittman, 230, 397
Bennett, Lyman, 21
Bennett College Alumnae Association, 107, 270
Bennett College Archives, 39
Bennett College Campus, 37, 232
Bennett College family, 360
Bennett College National Alumnae Association, 270
Bennett College Normal School, 303
Bennett College's Campus, 23
Bennett College's Songbirds, 242
Bennett College Student Association, 360
Bennett College students, 90–91, 439
Bennett Ideal Award, 270
Bennett's campuses, 166, 390
Bennett Seminary/Bennett College, 49
Bennett's High School Department, 47
Bennett Street, 226
Benson Dudley, 53
BENSON DUREN, 294
Benton, 122
    Byron L., 122
    Gwendolyn, 371
Bernice Cast, 212
Bernstein, 276, 479
Berry, Elvis, 153
Bessemer Avenue, 26, 412
Bessemer Elementary, 289
Best, Desiree, 399, 490
best basketball player Dudley, 349
Best High School Teacher in Guilford County, 399
Best-Looking Boy, 99
best schools for Negroes, 53
Best Supporting Actress, 419
Beta Club, 340–41, 397
Bethea, Bill, 382, 477
Bethea, Silvia, 494
Bethel AME Church, 125, 289
    attended, 238
Beth Helen Grier, 29
Bethune, Alvin, 210
Better Business Bureau Accredited, 443
Beverly Loraine Green, 447
BEVERLY MILLER EARLE, 290
Bible, 1, 9, 205, 536–37
Biddle University, 109
biennial Induction Program, 413
Bigelow, Misty, 210
Biggs, Benjamin, 440
Big South Conference Player, 370
Big South's top player, 370
Big Zion, 17–18, 440
Bilbro, 477
Billboard's Gospel Albums, 263
Billie Jean Mason, 29
bill Inez, 253
Billing Operations, 476
Binders, 484
Bingham, Robert, 131
Biographical Files, 488

Biographical Sketch, 478
biology teacher, 61, 129
Biomedical Technology, 170
Bird, 253
Birdcage, 260
Birmingham, 276, 475
biscuits, making, 9
Biscuitville, 255
Bishop Archie Buchanan, 338
Bishop Ithiel Clemmons, 244, 338
Bishop Larry Trotter, 243
Bishop Leroy Jackson Woolard, 244
Bishop Wells, 112
Bishop Woolard, 242
Bishop Wyoming Wells, 242, 244
Bj Felix, 153, 365–67
Black Atlanta, 445
blackboysreport.org/national-summary, 487
Black Caucus Choir, 217
Black Child Development Institute, 293
Black Codes, 465
black college North Carolina A&T State
    University, 219
Black College Workshop, 245
Black couples, 43
Black empowerment, 434
Black Entertainment Television, 420
Black Folk Played, 481
Black High Schools Classic, 143
Black History Month, 119, 341, 445
Black lady, 234
Black Lawyers Association, 284
Black Loyalists, 296–97
Black merchants, 431
Black middle class, 94
Blackmon, David, 154
Black National Anthem, 175
Black North Carolinians, 31, 33–34
Black-owned barber shops, 439
Black Pioneers, 297
Black political activism, 97
black principals, 72
black principals and teachers, 72
Black protests, 34
Black Reconstruction in America, 481
blacks, free, 297–300
Blacks for, 93
Black State Legislators, 290
Black Struggle for Freedom, 480
Black voters, 94
Blackwell, 305
    Chris, 253
    Johnny, 131
Black Women, 123, 475
    upper-class, 123
Blair, 204, 305, 390, 493
Blakney, Marsha, 68
Blanchard, 392
Blanche Taylor Grant, 58
Blaque Queens Step Team, 192
Blind Tiger, 257
Block Ashe Street, 494
Block of Ash Street in Warnersville, 27
block scheduling, 166, 211, 471
Blondean Orbert, 113
Bloomington, 484
Blue & Gold Day, 193
Blue Bell, 451

Blue Flashes, 147
Blue Gem Factory sewing darts, 466
Blue Goose, 138, 185, 395
Blue Goose-Article, 486
Blue Jays, 382
Blue Mirror Club, 238
blues artist Little Willie John, 424
Blues/soul singer, 249
Bluford, 52
Bluford Elementary, 175, 345
Bluford Elementary School, 94
Bluford Library, 40
Board of Advisors for Friends Homes, 217
Board of Commissioners, 283–84
Board of Education, 23, 46, 79–80, 89, 93
Board of Mentors Association, 289
Board of Motown Records, 424
Board of Trustees, 52, 125, 273, 285, 289
Board's change, 80
boards for Foster Friends, 285
Bob's Hatters, 282, 439, 487
    integrated, 439
Bo Diddley, 253
Boise, 291
Bolds, 479
Bolds & Lynn, 142
Bond, Julian, 484
Bonds, Asa, 152–54
BONITA GREENE HARGETT, 123
Booker, Glenn, 413, 456
Booker, Phyllis, 456
Book Published, 491
Booster Club, 204, 368, 412
Boren Brick Plant, 29
Boston Celtics, 385
Boston Conservatory of Music, 247
Boston Dance Theater, 247
BOTSO, 289, 336
Bottom Left-Right, 326
Boulevard, Franklin, 457
Bowling, 260, 280
Bowling-1957, Richard, 280
Boyers, 134–35
    Bill, 485
    named, 351
    William, 413, 493
Boykin, Craig, 212–13
Boykin, Sheree, 213
Boys & Girls Head Coach, 367
Boy Scout, largest, 277
Boy Scouts, 282, 334
Boy Scouts Troop, 125
Boy Scout troop, first, 27
Boy's Head Coach, 153
Boy Willie, 212–13
Boy Willie Cast, 212
Bradford, John, 305
Bradley, 129–30
    Chester A., 204
Bradley's players, 130
Bragg Street, 99
Brand, Elton, 375
Brandon, 91, 149, 479, 488
    Lewis, 89, 456, 467
Braswell-alto, Mike, 105
Bratcher, 134, 305
Braxton Williams, 421
Brea Evans, 471

Breast Cancer, 342
Brendan, 374–76
Brendan Haywood Single Parents Fund, 376, 489
Brendan's Fund, 376
BRENDAN TODD HAYWOOD, 374
Brentwick University, 339
Breogán, 385
Brett Claywell, 421
Brett Claywell Biography, 483
Brewington, Lins, 330
Briana Haith, 366–67
Brian Millsapp, 210–11, 230
Brian Seagraves, 402, 493
Brian Seagraves Biography, 483
Brice, Doris, 222
Brice, Dorothy, 222
bricklaying, 52
brick masonry, 135, 139, 208
Brick Masonry Program, 138
Brief History, 483, 486
Briggs, 433–34, 479
Brill Building, legendary, 253
Brinson, Christopher, 429
Brisbons, Ervin, 88, 471
Bristow, 267
Bristow portrays, 267
Bristow's film career, 267
British forces, 296
British tour, 253
Broad Avenue, 82
Broadway Costume, 241
Broadway-style selection, 114
Brock Historical Museum, 479, 488, 490
Bronze Service Stars, 336
Brooklyn, 374
Broome, Jennifer, 119
Brothers Johnson, 428
Brothers Organized, 289, 336
Browder, 467, 479
Brown, Charlie, 361
Brown, Franklin J., 157
Brown, Gloria, 91
Brown, James, 255, 428
Brown, Juanita, 222, 407
Brown's character, 157
Brown University, 421
    attended, 420
Brown vs, 93
Bru McCoy, 388
Bruner, 305
    Catherine, 209
Bruner-guitar, Evert, 105
Brunswick label, 252
Brunswick Records, 239
Buccaneers, 369
Buchanan, 12, 479
Buddha, 255, 257
Buddy Gist, 434
Buffalo Bills, 354
Building Committee, 463
Bulla, 361, 479
Burke, Solomon, 428
Burkes, 305
Burley Junior, 319
Burlington, 55, 159, 185, 443
Burwell, 213
bus, second-hand, 138
bus drivers, female, 181

A PLACE WHERE SUCCESS WAS EXPECTED: FINAL EDITION

Business Award, 287
Business Education, 123, 445
Business Partnerships, 123–24
Bus Supervisor, 398
bus transportation, 467
Butch Henry, 355
Butler, Jerry, 254
Butler Ferguson, 213
Button, Peter, 317
Buzzkillz, 493
Byers, 305
Byrd, Barbara, 113, 209
Byrd, Peter, 49

C

Cablevision, 470
Caddell, Clementine, 29
Caddell, Geraldine, 29
Caddell, Maxine, 29
Cadet Commander, 341
Cadet James, 224
Cadet Richard Williams, 330
Cadillacs, 54, 65, 256
Caesar Augustus, 205
Calculus, 75
Caldwell, David, 7
Caldwell, Lorenzo, 494
Caldwell Elementary School, attended David D., 259
Caldwell Jones Room, 478
Caldwell-Jones Room, 481
Caldwell school, segregated David D., 259
Calhoun, 146–47, 487
Calvary Baptist Church, 293
Calvary COGIC, 338
Calvert, 305
Cameo, 260
Camerata Singers, 218
Camin Randall-Peangmeth, 106
Campbell Basketball Game Picture Courtesy, 370
Campbell University, 370
Campbell University Hall of Fame, 371
Camp Carlson, 37
Camp Leatherneck, 337
Camp Lejeune, 337
    aboard, 338
campus by relocating Dudley's students, 463
campus of Shaw University, 30, 47
Canada, 296
candy, cotton, 189, 451
Cannon, 305
Canton, 487
Cao Bang, 291
CAPTAIN RAYMOND BRIAN, 340
Cardinals, 348
Cardwell, Leo, 131
Cardwell, Roland, 413
career
    college basketball, 376
    six-season pro, 369
Career & Technical Education, 123
Career Development Coordinator, 123–24
Career Expo, 123
CareySound, 260
Caribbean teaching, 265

Carlacy, 310
Carlos, 257
Carlotta Supper Club, 428
Carlson, Walter, 226, 259
Carl Well, 310
Carl Wilson Blog, 492
Carnell, Alvin, 318
Carney, William H., 302
Carolina A&T State University, 358
Carolina Hall, 24, 491
Carolina Peace Maker Award, 137
Carolinas- Claflin College, 488
Carol of the Bells, 475
CAROLYN BASKERVILLE, 404
Carolyn Walden, 475
Carolyn Walden Munchus, 217
Carpentry/Wood Working, 75
Carree, 262–63
    Angela L., 262
    Isaac, 262–63
    Kimberly, 262
Carree Children and other, 262
Carree Wilson, 243
Carroll, Chris, 257
Carter, Robert, 96
Carter's Rest Home, 412
Carter Women Veterans Historical Project, Betty H., 494
Carter Women Veterans Historical Project Oral, Betty H., 489
Carver, 464
Carver High School, 464
cases, civil disobedience, 97
Casey Foundation, Annie E., 469, 478
Cassandra, 474
Cassandra Feaster, 474
Cathey, 306, 492
    Reginald, 13
Catholic Schools, 8
Cavaliers, Cleveland, 376
Cavern Club, 253
Ceab Eleisus, 304
Cecelski, 57, 480
Cedar St, 28
Celebrating Black History/Jonathan McKee, 488
Celestine G. Bennett, 128
Celia Phelps Memorial United Methodist Church, 333
Celie, 266
census, 465
Center for Education Reform and Empower America Achievement, 481
Center of Military History, 484
Central Intercollegiate Athletic Association (CIAA), 141
Central State, 230
Central State University in Wilberforce, 230
century band member, 476
Century Magnolia House, 435
CEO, former hospital, 418
ceremonies, zoom graduation, 123
ceremony in Ketchum by Lt, 291
certificate, teacher's, 51
Certified Information Technology Professional (CITP), 370
certified nursing assistant (CNA), 444
Certified Public Accountant (CPA), 370

CGMA (Chartered Global Management Accountant), 370
Chafe, 276–77, 480
    William, 31
Chaffin's Farm, 302
Chaka Khan, 428
Challenging the Chain Stores, 489
Chambers & Anderson, 299
Champlain Brown, 322
Chancel Choir, 216
Chantal Percell, 212
Chantel Percell, 210
Chapel Hill, 97, 158, 219–20, 326–28, 375–76, 478, 480, 483–84, 488, 490, 492
Chapel Hill in Physical Education, 354
Chapelle Morgan, 473
Chapelle Morgan Davis, 227, 536
Chaplain, 270
Chappelle, 306
Chapter Alumni, 441
Chapter Twenty-One, 455
Charles, Ray, 434
Charles Alvin Sanders, 351–52
Charles Benton, 121, 493
Charles Brimmer, 314
Charles Ellis, 306
Charles Hamilton Houston, 94–95
Charles Henry Moore, 19, 488
Charles Moore School, 188
Charles Robert, 307
Charlie Foxx, 252–54
Charlie Sanders Scholarship Foundation, 353
Charlie sang, 253
Charlottee area, 449
Charlotte Hawkins, 26
Charlotte Hawkins Brown, 26, 47, 482
Charlotte-Mecklenburg, 163
Charlotte Observer, 349
Chartered Global Management Accountant (CGMA), 370
charter schools, urban, 468
charter schools outpace, urban, 468
Charter school system and voucher programs, 468
Chase McGrath, 388
Chast'ning rod, 176
Chaves Interiors, 275
Chavis, Vance, 50, 59, 65, 70, 89, 492
Chavis Library, 109, 492
Cheek, 32, 42, 75, 218, 234–36, 371–72, 480
    James, 235
    Joey, 371
    senior James E., 75
Cheek set, 371
Cheek's teammates, 372
cheerleaders, 102, 110–11, 113, 115–16, 183, 187, 189, 226, 398
cheerleaders and Pep Band, 187
Cheerleaders Help Build, 486
Cheerleading, 115
cheerleading coaches, 117
Cheers, 183
Chekov, Anton, 419
Chemistry Teacher, 133
Cherry, 306
CHERYL ROBINSON GOUL, 398
Cheryl Robinson Gould, 116
Cheshire cat, 71
Chester, 233, 324

Chester Bradley, 101, 129, 157
Chester Bradley Gymnasium, 61, 83–84, 204
Chester D., 308
Chicago, 178, 220, 235, 243, 264, 274, 281, 393, 481, 484, 488
Chicago Press, 484
Chicago School of Shoe Rebuilding, 282
Chicago Tribune, 489
Chief Dudley Safety Patrol, 473
Chief Minority Recruiting Officer, 333
Chief Musician, 220
Chief of Naval Operations in Washington, 334
Chief Williams, 228
Chief Williams Assistant Band Director, 228
child evangelist, 235
children, colored, 3, 11, 19, 23, 535
Children's Theater in Greensboro, 421
Chinese, 372
Chisolm, 306
Chocolate Funk, 257, 260
Choir, Junior, 410
Choral Music, 214
Chorus I, II, III, 75
Chowan University in Murfreesboro, 146
Christ, 32, 242, 244, 262, 277–78, 282, 473, 484, 537
Christian Services, 268
Christina McKinney, 367
Christmas, 205, 317, 475
a Christmas Blessing, 267
Christmas Concert, 205
Christmas parades, 226
Christmas Programs, 205
Christmas programs, special, 475
Christ Organization, 405
Chubbs, 179
    Reverend Howard A., 177
Chuck Cotton, 252, 255–56, 479, 493
churches, local, 177, 191
churches for Negroes, 17, 45
Church of God in Christ, 244, 537
Church of God in Christ in Greensboro, 262
Church of God in Christ's Statement of faith, 537
Church Women United, 269–70
CIAA (Central Intercollegiate Athletic Association), 141
CIAA Official Hall of Fame, 141
Cincinnati Bearcats, 385
Cincinnati Commandos, 385
Cincinnati Reds, 85
CITP (Certified Information Technology Professional), 370
city, first, 97–98
City Board, 18–19
City Champions, 142
City Co-Championship and Conference Co-Championship, 133
City Council, 24, 30, 294–95, 350, 538
city leaders, 85, 439
Citywide Championship, 358, 476
Citywide Track Championship Team, 358, 476
Civil Affairs Officer, 290
Civilities and Civil Rights, 276, 480
Civil Law, 95
civil rights, basic, 98
civil rights activists, 271, 274
Civil Rights Advocacy Training Institute, 287

A PLACE WHERE SUCCESS WAS EXPECTED: FINAL EDITION

Civil Rights Advocacy Training Institute Medgar, 287
civil rights awards, 287
civil rights cases, 95, 97, 278
Civil Rights Digital Library, 271, 480
Civil Rights Documentary, 278
civil rights lawyer Kenneth Lee, 82
civil rights marches, 277
civil rights meetings, 272
civil rights movement, 57, 95, 97, 272, 276, 479, 490
Civil War, 5–8, 10, 17, 45, 52, 299–300, 302, 465, 478, 480, 491
Civitan, 125
Clair, Bishop Matthew W., 38
Clanton, Harvey, 152
Clarence Elmer, 311
Clarence Grier, 152, 370, 493
Clarence Grier Biography, 483
Clark, Doug, 224
Clark, John, 224
Clark, Jon, 224
class, business, 116, 470
Class AAA Omaha Cardinals, 349
Class Gifts, 194, 342
Classical Ballet, 246
class reunion, 405, 476
class song, original, 194, 200
Claude Barnes, 88–89
Claude Lemuel, 320
Claudette Burroughs White, 280
Claudette Burroughs-White, 49, 279
Claudette Burroughs White-1957, 280
Clay, Henry, 316
Clayton, 305, 311
Claywell, 421–22
Cleburne, 302
Cleburne's proposal, 302
Clemson, attended, 368
Clemson Head Football Coach Debo Swinney, 369
Clemson University, 368
    attended, 341
Cleophus, 320
Clerk of Superior Court, 288
Clerks conduct proceedings, 288
Clients Come, 443
Clifton, 313, 343–44
Clifton Chenier's son C, 258
Clifton Girard Johnson, 343, 346
Clinard, 306
Clinical Pastoral Education Clinician, 339
Closing Ceremony, 372
Clover Garden Elementary School, 394
Club Mombassa, 238
Clyde, Willie, 305
CMA (Colored Merchants Association), 431, 489
CNA (certified nursing assistant), 444
Coach Bill Whites, 141
Coach Boyers, 134
Coach Davis, 146, 148–49, 380
coach Dennis Botts, 146
coaches Bob Huggins, 385
coach Furcron, 132
coaching style Davis, 146
Coach Lamb, 142
Coach Lambert, 142
Coach McKee, 136, 368
Coach of the Year and Guilford County Coach, 143

Coach Price, 402
Coach Spruill, 359
Coach Stephen Davis, 379
coach Steven Davis, 380
Coach William Furcron, 132
Coast Guard, 319, 321
Coca Cola, 143
co-chairs, 286, 406
Cochran, Terrie, 392
Coffee Yourse, 259
Co-Founded, David, 289
Co-founder Northern Virginia, 475
COGIC, 248, 338–39
Cold logic rushes, 180
Coleman, Eugene, 131
Coley, 55, 57–59, 69, 72–74, 101, 107–9, 473, 480
    Joe, 494
    Nelle, 89, 108, 119
Coley-Jenkins Extended Living Facility, 89
Coley-Jenkins Independent Living Center, 107
Coley's house, 99
Collage, 487
College, Bennett, 22–25, 27–28, 30, 37–39, 47–48, 54–55, 58, 268, 270, 273, 276, 488, 491, 535–36
College, Wiley, 37
College and University Yearbooks Online, 494
college campus, 53
college endorsements, 469
college football, played, 368, 373
College Park, 339
college scholarships, 66, 353, 412
Colley Hood, 441
Collins, 298, 314
Colon, cast member Felix F., 211
Colonel Andrew Johnson, 325
COLONEL LAZELLE E, 333
Colonel Tye, 297
Colorado Springs Alumnae Chapter, 342
colored constituency, 38
Colored Merchants Association (CMA), 431, 489
Colored People, 1, 10, 238, 430, 439, 491
colored regiments, 300
colored settlement, 15
Colored State Normal Schools, 23
Colorful Parade, 486, 488
Color Purple, 265–66, 485, 493
Color Specialist, 473
Colson, Mildred A., 58
Coltrane, John, 238
Columbia University, 35, 233, 237, 447
Columbia University School, 233
Columbia University School of Music, 214
Col Winchester, 323
Combat Infantryman's Badge, 333
Combat Logistics Regiment, 337–38, 487
comedienne Pigmeat Markham, 238
Coming Home Baby, 114
Comiskey Park, 281
commanded CLR-2, 338
commander, 70-Cedrick, 150
COMMANDER KENYATTA O, 336
Commencement, 482
commission, human rights, 276
Commissioners, 19, 281, 283–84, 293, 446, 481
Commissioner Skip Alston, 284
Commitment & Service, 412

493

Commodores, 428
common schools, 6, 8, 465, 490
　first, 8
Commonwealth, 370
Communities in Schools Awards Ceremony, 373
Communities in Schools Program, 394
community, late 1960's, 430, 432
Community, Dudley, 110, 174, 357, 380, 403, 410
community, middle class African American, 415
Community Affairs Committee, 216
Community College, 332, 469
Community Foundation of Greater Greensboro, 376
Community groups, 114, 189
Community Holiday Gathering, 404
Community House, 353
Community Justice Brotherhood/Sisterhood Citation Award, 279
Community Leadership, 411
Community Resource Specialist- Law Enforcement, 471
Community Service Award in December, 404
company
　float, 188
　major, 401
　segregated, 34
company Inward Discovery, 265
Comparative Analysis, 45
completed Nuclear Power Training, 334
Complete Poems, 481
Computer Club, 127
Concord, 185
Cone Denim, 357
Cone Elementary, 167
Cone Mills, 103, 357
Cone Mills' East White Oak Plant, 466
Confederate Armies, 490
Confederate artillery, 302
Confederate force, strong, 301
Confederate generals, 93
Conference Championships, 136, 142
Congress Location Washington, 491
Congress of Racial Equality. *See* CORE
Connie Herbin, 88–89
Conscientious Objector, 294
Conservatives, 470
Consolidated Reunion Souvenir Journal, 480
Constitution Committee, 87
Constitution Committee Chairman, 87
Construction Committee Members, 459
Construction Committee's Recommendation, 536
Construction Management Office, 535
Construction Managers, 124, 535
Consumes River College, 332
contacts, high-level, 291
Contemporary Male Vocalist, 263
contest, 229
Continental Army and Navy, 296
Continental Basketball Association's Quad City Thunder, 370
Controversial plan, 478
Cook, 306
Cooke, Sam, 434
Cookie Monster, 451
Coolidge, 320
Cooper, 306
Co-operative Society, 52
Cooper's soldiers, 301

Co-Owners, 451
Co-Owners of Scoop Zone, 451
Co-Pastor Debra Morton, 243
Copeland, 428
　Walter, 428
Corbet, 308
Cordice, 39
CORE (Congress of Racial Equality), 91, 276, 434
core subjects, 75, 347
　ninth-grade, 168
Corey Kimber, 382
Corinne-Lestch, 480
Cornelius, Eve, 238
Cornell, Edgar, 305
Corporate Citizenship Conference, 236
Corp Reserves, 310
Corps Aikens, Jessie James, 304
Corps Davis, James, 307
Corps Vincent, Thomas, 321
Cory, 382
Cosell, 105
Cosmos, 257, 260, 492
Cosmos Clubs, 257, 280
Cosmos Supper Club, 260
Co- State Championship, 136
Cotta, Terra, 11, 29–30, 490
Cotton, 255–58, 282–83, 439
　Mary, 412
Cotton and Gilyard, 439
Cotton Mill, 30
Cotton's alto skills, 255
Cotton's orbit, 257
Couch, 306
council members, 30
Counseling Psychology, 294
counselors, youth employment, 393
Countee Cullen, 74
County's Bond, 370
County Schools System, 170
County Seat of Guilford, 478
couple, 16, 99, 158, 201, 203, 251, 344, 380, 393, 459
Couple's Ministry, 339
courses
　automotive technology, 469
　doctoral, 161
　golf, 275
　industrial, 105
courses in Negro history, 66
Court, Ross, 345
Court Pleas, 8
courts, tennis, 275
Covacus, long time, 260
Covacus Band, 492
Covay, Don, 253
Covid, 258, 340, 404
COVID-19 Pandemic, 171, 404
COVID-19 Youth Crisis Hotline Counselor, 404
COVID Pandemic, 123
co-worker, former, 211
CPA (Certified Public Accountant), 370
Crawford, 134, 306
CreateSpace Independent Publishing, 479
Crescent City Studios, 428
Crews Street, 535
Criteria Consideration, 82
Croatan, 152
Crockett, 307

A PLACE WHERE SUCCESS WAS EXPECTED: FINAL EDITION

Crosby, 30, 144–45, 307, 340
   Brian, 493
   John O., 52
   Quentin C., 493
   resignation, 52
Crosby's community involvement, 340
CROSS COUNTRY HALL, 362
CROSS COUNTRY HALL of FAME, 362
Crotts' tenure, 158
Crow, Jim, 34, 48, 93
Crowder, Madison, 365–66
Crystal, 213, 473
CSK VVS Samara, 385
CTE Educator/Automotive Instructor, 106
Cultural Arts Department, 400
Culture Ambassador for United Health Group, 427
Curley, 80
Curley Neal, 78, 81
Curly Neal, 80, 132
Curriculum Development Conference, 170
Currie, 307
Curtin University, 404
Custom Sewing/Tailoring, 75
Cyber System Protection & App Development, 471
Czech-born architect husband, 237

D

Daily News, 480
Daily News Staff, 40
Dale Tonkins, 407, 457
Dallas Cowboys, 350
Dallas Mavericks, 376
Dance Recital Miss Dye, 114
dancers
   female ballet, 247
   single, 246
Daniels, Lee, 265
Dansby, 278
   David, 347, 492
Dansby's office, 278
Darden, Geraldine, 29
Darfur, 372
daughter Chapelle Morgan Davis, 227
Dave Chappelle's Block Party, 230
Davenport, 260
Davetta, 474
Davetta Florance- Bristow, 390
Davetta Florance-Bristow, 391
David Amerson, 147, 379–80, 484, 491
David Caldwell School, 20, 47
David Dallas, 313
David Dallas Jones Elementary School, 35
David Dansby Biography, 483
David Edward, 308
David Eugene, 320
David Hartmann The, 49
David Moore, 58, 79, 289, 436–38, 456, 485, 489, 536
David Moore Collection, 489
DAVID PRICE, 143
DAVID SURGEON, 398
Davie Streets, 28
Davis, 58–59, 143, 146–47, 149, 307, 368–69, 381, 473, 480, 494
   Agnes, 68, 76
   Betty, 257
   Calvin, 150

Eloise, 102
   Steven T., 146
Davis Algood, 307
Davis babysat, 147
Davis HOF, Jeffry B., 414
Davis HOF-Coach, Steven T., 414
Davis III, Lt Col William M., 330
Davis Mill Road, 12
Davis's grandparents, 147
Davis's players, 147
Davis's players value, 147
Davis Still Winning Championships, 483
Dawson Creek, 422
Day Gospel Fest, 405
Deaconess Ministry, 411
Deaf, 395
Dean's List, 404
Dear Dudley High, 194, 403
Dear Mother, 194
Debate Team, 185, 394
DEBRA L, 420
Debutante Cotillion, 201
DECA (Distributive Education Clubs of America), 104, 243, 473
DECATUR FEWELL, 324
Decca's London/American, 253
Decision Day and Communities in Schools Awards Ceremony, 373
Dedication Ceremony, 489
Deeds Jeff Thigpen, 284
Deep South, 2, 31, 34, 114
Defending Hands Foundation, 380
Defense LINK News, 490
Defense Logistics Agency, 346
Defense Video & Imagery Distribution System, 338, 480, 492
Defensive Player, named Best, 143
deficiency, tongue-tied physical, 234
degree
   doctorate, 278
   undergraduate, 128, 278, 475
Deja Robinson, 150
Dejurnette, 307
Deliverance, 255, 257, 445
Dellie Lee, 305
Delma Lee, 420
Deloatch, Lois, 238
Delta Academy, 400
Delta GEMS, 400
Delta Sigma Theta, 215, 221
Delta Sigma Theta- Decorations Chair for Community Scholarship Event, 342
Delta Sigma Theta Jabberwock competition, 405
Delta Sigma Theta's Five Point Programmatic Thrust, 400
Delta Sigma Theta Sorority, 107, 123, 215, 342, 400
Demani Bell, 231
DeMario, 377
DEMARIO LAMONTE, 378
Demario Pressley, 147
Demikia Surgeon, 392
Democrat Club, 434
Democrats, northern, 300
demolition, 440, 536
demonstrations, peaceful, 272
Denise Duffy's Music Maker foundation, 255, 258
Denorris Best, 150

DENORRIS Q, 403
Dental Corps, 315
Denver, 377
Department Chairperson, 107, 123
Department of Health Education and Welfare, 358
Department of State, 95
Deputy Director, 335
desegregating, 98
desegregation lawsuits, 274
Desert Storm, 331
Desert Storm 5years, 310
design
    costume, 167
    gymnasium's, 82
Design/Construction, 2
designed Dudley, 536
DESIREE FODRELL BEST, 399
Detroit Lions, 351, 381, 389
Detroit suburbs, 351
Deuce, 148–49, 489, 494
DHS Engineering Instructor, 106
Dick, 270, 396
Dickens, Curtis, 202
Dicks, James, 8
Dillard, 307
Dillard High School in Goldsboro, 59
Dilworth, 194, 307
    Robert, 194
director
    first African American athletic, 161
    first Women's Athletics, 359
Display Complete Honesty, 91
Distinguished Flying, 311
Distinguished Service Award, 273
Distributive Education, 69, 75, 77, 494
Distributive Education Clubs of America (DECA), 104, 243, 473
District Championships, 352
District Court Judge, 233, 292
Diva, first, 237
Diversity Club, 397
Dixon, Luther, 240
Doctor of Dental Surgery (DDS), 335
Doctor of Ministry degree, 339
Doctor of Philosophy degree, 339
Doggett, 361–62, 479
    Mary, 209
Doggett's success, 361
Dolah, 536
Dollhouse, 422
Domestic Relations Court, 279
Domingo, Santo, 298
Donald Gaines Murray, 95
Donald Wright HOF, 414
donations, 41, 291, 376, 465, 476
Donnell, Josephine, 415
Donnell, Lenora, 76–77
Donnell-1952, Ernestine, 280
Donyel Parker, 154
Donzell, 308
Dorethea Taylor, 210
Doris Mae Capps, 222
Dorothy Braswell, 364–65, 367
Dorsett, 283–84, 307
    county commissioner, 283
    Katie, 283
Dorsett and Barnett, 283
Dot Harris Furcron, 12
Dot Harris Furcron's First Grade Class, 13, 494

Dot-matrix Project, 493
Double picture- Martin Oates- Is, 127
Douglas, Patty, 318
Douglas & Amanda Johnson, 440
Douglas Johnson, 16
Douglas Powell, 186
Douglass, Frederick, 300–301, 486
Douglass, Fredrick, 129
Douglas-Shaw, 307
Douglas Walter, 308
Dow, Devin, 154
Down East, 257
down-to-Earth, 256
downtown, 28, 43, 137, 255, 439
Downtown Greensboro, 203, 250, 270, 272, 282, 439
downtown High Point, 452
Drama Critics, 419
Drama Department, 158, 167, 535
Drama I, II, III, 75
Dress-Up Day, 193
Drill Team Commander, 331
Driver Education Teachers, 181–82
Driveway Moore, 257
Drum Line, 289
Drum Major, 229, 265, 396
Drum Major for Justice Band Competition, 125
Drum Major for Justice Festival of Bands competition, 229
Dry Cleaner, 439
dual roles, played, 211
DuBois, 7, 166, 210, 465, 481
DuBois' charge, 34
Dubois High School, 464
Dubois High School in Wake County, 464
Dudley, 51–63, 72–75, 77–78, 85–90, 99–105, 114–17, 121–25, 127–47, 155–72, 183–84, 210–12, 218–19, 221, 228–30, 237–39, 280–83,
    Edward, 9
    Edward B., 51
Dudley administrators, 413
Dudley AFJROTC Cadet Corps, 330
Dudley Air Force ROTC Drill Team, 189
Dudley All-Time Baseball Team, 476
Dudley Alumni Association, 279, 281, 284, 369, 396, 412, 475, 480–81
Dudley Alumni Association- Fiftieth Anniversary Honor, James B., 410
Dudley Alumni Association President, 269
Dudley Alumni Band, 188, 396
Dudley Alumni Class, 332
Dudley Assistant Band Director, 186
Dudley athletes, 133
Dudley Baccalaureate Speaker, 179
Dudley band director, 210, 219, 326
Dudley Band Director James Morgan, 491
Dudley Begins, 536
Dudley Cheer Book, 183, 186, 474
Dudley Choral Society, 403
Dudley Christmas programs, 475
Dudley Dance Company, 123
Dudley Dance Group, 114
Dudley Divas, 237, 252
Dudley Early College Academies, James B., 403
Dudley Educational Sports Hall, James B., 489
Dudley faculty, 157, 229
Dudley Family Strong, 404
Dudley Flag Girls, 115

A PLACE WHERE SUCCESS WAS EXPECTED: FINAL EDITION

Dudley Girls, 102
Dudley Girl's Athletic Association, 101
Dudley Graduates Come, 390
Dudley graduating class, 278
Dudley Hall, James B., 124, 289, 334, 402, 407, 446
Dudley Has Historic Links, 479
Dudley High's Band, 478
Dudley High School Choir, 391, 474
Dudley High School Class, James B., 194, 482
Dudley High School Drum Line, 475
Dudley High School Gymnasium, 82
Dudley High School Hall, 362, 395
    James B., 145
Dudley High School Marching Band, 126, 229, 341, 397
    James B., 186, 188, 228, 231
Dudley High School Muster List, James B., 304
Dudley High School Names Seagraves New Head Basketball, 481
Dudley High School PTAs, James B., 204
Dudley High School seniors, James B., 177
Dudley High School's Pam Doggett, 494
Dudley High School Stage, 210
Dudley High School Thespians present, 210
Dudley High We'll, 199
Dudley Homecoming Parade, 188–89
Dudley Junior ROTC, 331
Dudley JV Basketball, coached James B., 410
Dudley Key Club, 210, 484
Dudley legacy, 412
Dudley legend, 363
Dudley Math Science, 164
Dudley Media Center, 396, 476
Dudley Mentoring Group, 289
Dudley military participation, 477
Dudley Modern Dance Company, 114, 121, 246, 398
Dudley Modern Dance Company- Coach Ms. Dye, 410
Dudley Modern Dance Group, 113–15, 474
    James B., 113
Dudley Music Department Programs, 475
Dudley music teacher Pamela Stewart, 205
Dudley National Alumni Association, 278
    James B., 270
Dudley Open Magnet School, 61–62
Dudley Open School, 192
Dudley Pantherettes, 103, 115, 247
Dudley Panthers Football Team, 380
Dudley Parent Teacher Association, 80
Dudley Pep Club, 115
    James B., 191
Dudley Powder-Puff Football Team, 410
Dudley Project Team, 62
Dudley PTA, 89, 204
Dudley PTA/PTSA, 204
Dudley PTSA, 407
Dudley PTSA Board, 204
Dudley's actors and singers, 211
Dudley's AFJROTC Unit, 409
Dudley's Airforce ROTC Unit, 343
Dudley's AP Physics, 166
Dudley's application, 166
Dudley's Athletic Director, 368
Dudley's Auditorium, 60, 205
Dudley's Band, 98, 112, 221, 224, 226, 260, 328
Dudley's band director, 214
Dudley's Choir Director and music teacher, 216

Dudley Science Club, 191
Dudley's Community and Civic Leaders, 268
Dudley Senior High School Gymnasium, James B., 81
Dudley seniors, 203
Dudley set, 151
Dudley's extracurricular AVT Team, 469
Dudley's finest, 352
Dudley's First Diva, 237
Dudley's football stadium, 85
Dudley's Girls Basketball Team- Coaches, 410
Dudley's Graduating Class, 12, 278
Dudley's Head Basketball Coach, 402
Dudley's Head Dudley AFROTC Cadets, 190
Dudley's Homecoming Parade, 187, 189, 331
Dudley's Isaiah Monroe, 152
Dudley's Joey Cheek Goes, 481
Dudley's Junior AFJROTC, 330
Dudley's Junior AFROTC, 330, 489
Dudley's Main, 204
Dudley's Main Building, 64, 204, 232, 458
Dudley's Main Gymnasium, 81, 90
Dudley's Marching Band, 219, 221, 473, 476
Dudley's Modern Dance Company, 122
Dudley's Modern Dance Company's Annual Spring Recital, 246
Dudley's Original Main Building, 536
Dudley Sports, James B., 117, 278, 360, 371, 373
Dudley's Prima Ballerina, 246
Dudley's PTSA, 205
Dudley Sr, James B., 385
Dudley's School District, 103, 535
Dudley's stadium, 130
Dudley's stage, 210
Dudley's Steven Davis II, 149, 494
Dudley's student body, 117, 130
Dudley's students, relocating, 463
Dudley staff, 110
Dudley Stage Band, 105
Dudley stakeholders, 166
Dudley's top players, 130
Dudley Street, 61, 226
Dudley Student Council, 125, 397
Dudley Student Government Association, 87, 123
Dudley Student Manifesto, 91
Dudley Style Presentation, 187
Dudley's Varsity, 474
Dudley Swim Team, 123
Dudley's Women Dominate, 364
Dudley's Women's Track and Field Team, 364
Dudley's Women's Track Team, 364
Dudley Track, James B., 361
Dudley Women's Track, 365
Dudley wrestlers, 144
Dudley Wrestling Coach Meeting New Challenges, 482
Dudley Yearbook, 166, 202, 212
Dudley Yearbook Staff, 407
Duke Ellington, 237
Duke Funds, 41
Duke Law School and NC Central School, 284
Duke University, 284, 348, 354, 475
    attended, 334
Dumfries, 340
Dunbar, 481
Durham, 24, 34, 46, 82, 94, 216, 443, 464, 474
    Oliver, 308
Durham-based residency, 255
Durham Hillside, 129–30, 223

497

Durham Hillside High School, 464
Durham's City of Medicine Academy, 474
During Past, 410
Duty Corps, 320–21
Duty/ Vietnam, 311–12
Dwayne, 322
Dwinique Peters, 210
Dye, 61, 110–11, 113–16, 410
Dye's dedication, 117
dynamics, 164
  political, 93
Dynasty Franklin, 365–67
down-to-Earth, 256
downtown, 28, 43, 137, 255, 439
Downtown Greensboro, 203, 250, 270, 272, 282, 439
downtown High Point, 452
Drama Critics, 419
Drama Department, 158, 167, 535
Drama I, II, III, 75
Dress-Up Day, 193
Drill Team Commander, 331
Driver Education Teachers, 181–82
Driveway Moore, 257
Drum Line, 289
Drum Major, 229, 265, 396
Drum Major for Justice Band Competition, 125
Drum Major for Justice Festival of Bands competition, 229
Dry Cleaner, 439
dual roles, played, 211
DuBois, 7, 166, 210, 465, 481
DuBois' charge, 34
Dubois High School, 464
Dubois High School in Wake County, 464
Dudley, 51–63, 72–75, 77–78, 85–90, 99–105, 114–17, 121–25, 127–47, 155–72, 183–84, 210–12, 218–19, 221, 228–30, 237–39, 280–83, 330–32, 390–407, 463–65, 472–77
  Edward, 9
  Edward B., 51
Dudley administrators, 413
Dudley AFJROTC Cadet Corps, 330
Dudley Air Force ROTC Drill Team, 189
Dudley All-Time Baseball Team, 476
Dudley Alumni Association, 279, 281, 284, 369, 396, 412, 475, 480–81
Dudley Alumni Association- Fiftieth Anniversary Honor, James B., 410
Dudley Alumni Association President, 269
Dudley Alumni Band, 188, 396
Dudley Alumni Class, 332
Dudley Assistant Band Director, 186
Dudley athletes, 133
Dudley Baccalaureate Speaker, 179
Dudley band director, 210, 219, 326
Dudley Band Director James Morgan, 491
Dudley Begins, 536
Dudley Cheer Book, 183, 186, 474
Dudley Choral Society, 403
Dudley Christmas programs, 475
Dudley Dance Company, 123
Dudley Dance Group, 114
Dudley Divas, 237, 252
Dudley Early College Academies, James B., 403
Dudley Educational Sports Hall, James B., 489
Dudley faculty, 157, 229
Dudley Family Strong, 404

Dudley Flag Girls, 115
Dudley Girls, 102
Dudley Girl's Athletic Association, 101
Dudley Graduates Come, 390
Dudley graduating class, 278
Dudley Hall, James B., 124, 289, 334, 402, 407, 446
Dudley Has Historic Links, 479
Dudley High's Band, 478
Dudley High School Choir, 391, 474
Dudley High School Class, James B., 194, 482
Dudley High School Drum Line, 475
Dudley High School Gymnasium, 82
Dudley High School Hall, 362, 395
  James B., 145
Dudley High School Marching Band, 126, 229, 341, 397
  James B., 186, 188, 228, 231
Dudley High School Muster List, James B., 304
Dudley High School Names Seagraves New Head Basketball, 481
Dudley High School PTAs, James B., 204
Dudley High School seniors, James B., 177
Dudley High School's Pam Doggett, 494
Dudley High School Stage, 210
Dudley High School Thespians present, 210
Dudley High We'll, 199
Dudley Homecoming Parade, 188–89
Dudley Junior ROTC, 331
Dudley JV Basketball, coached James B., 410
Dudley Key Club, 210, 484
Dudley legacy, 412
Dudley legend, 363
Dudley Math Science, 164
Dudley Media Center, 396, 476
Dudley Mentoring Group, 289
Dudley military participation, 477
Dudley Modern Dance Company, 114, 121, 246, 398
Dudley Modern Dance Company- Coach Ms. Dye 410
Dudley Modern Dance Group, 113–15, 474
  James B., 113
Dudley Music Department Programs, 475
Dudley music teacher Pamela Stewart, 205
Dudley National Alumni Association, 278
  James B., 270
Dudley Open Magnet School, 61–62
Dudley Open School, 192
Dudley Pantherettes, 103, 115, 247
Dudley Panthers Football Team, 380
Dudley Parent Teacher Association, 80
Dudley Pep Club, 115
  James B., 191
Dudley Powder-Puff Football Team, 410
Dudley Project Team, 62
Dudley PTA, 89, 204
Dudley PTA/PTSA, 204
Dudley PTSA, 407
Dudley PTSA Board, 204
Dudley's actors and singers, 211
Dudley's AFJROTC Unit, 409
Dudley's Airforce ROTC Unit, 343
Dudley's AP Physics, 166
Dudley's application, 166
Dudley's Athletic Director, 368
Dudley's Auditorium, 60, 205

A PLACE WHERE SUCCESS WAS EXPECTED: FINAL EDITION

Dudley Flag Girls, 115
Dudley Girls, 102
Dudley Girl's Athletic Association, 101
Dudley Graduates Come, 390
Dudley graduating class, 278
Dudley Hall, James B., 124, 289, 334, 402, 407, 446
Dudley Has Historic Links, 479
Dudley High's Band, 478
Dudley High School Choir, 391, 474
Dudley High School Class, James B., 194, 482
Dudley High School Drum Line, 475
Dudley High School Gymnasium, 82
Dudley High School Hall, 362, 395
   James B., 145
Dudley High School Marching Band, 126, 229, 341, 397
   James B., 186, 188, 228, 231
Dudley High School Muster List, James B., 304
Dudley High School Names Seagraves New Head Basketball, 481
Dudley High School PTAs, James B., 204
Dudley High School seniors, James B., 177
Dudley High School's Pam Doggett, 494
Dudley High School Stage, 210
Dudley High School Thespians present, 210
Dudley High We'll, 199
Dudley Homecoming Parade, 188–89
Dudley Junior ROTC, 331
Dudley JV Basketball, coached James B., 410
Dudley Key Club, 210, 484
Dudley legacy, 412
Dudley legend, 363
Dudley Math Science, 164
Dudley Media Center, 396, 476
Dudley Mentoring Group, 289
Dudley military participation, 477
Dudley Modern Dance Company, 114, 121, 246, 398
Dudley Modern Dance Company- Coach Ms. Dye 410
Dudley Modern Dance Group, 113–15, 474
   James B., 113
Dudley Music Department Programs, 475
Dudley music teacher Pamela Stewart, 205
Dudley National Alumni Association, 278
   James B., 270
Dudley Open Magnet School, 61–62
Dudley Open School, 192
Dudley Pantherettes, 103, 115, 247
Dudley Panthers Football Team, 380
Dudley Parent Teacher Association, 80
Dudley Pep Club, 115
   James B., 191
Dudley Powder-Puff Football Team, 410
Dudley Project Team, 62
Dudley PTA, 89, 204
Dudley PTA/PTSA, 204
Dudley PTSA, 407
Dudley PTSA Board, 204
Dudley's actors and singers, 211
Dudley's AFJROTC Unit, 409
Dudley's Airforce ROTC Unit, 343
Dudley's AP Physics, 166
Dudley's application, 166
Dudley's Athletic Director, 368
Dudley's Auditorium, 60, 205
Dudley's Band, 98, 112, 221, 224, 226, 260, 328

Dudley's band director, 214
Dudley's Choir Director and music teacher, 216
Dudley Science Club, 191
Dudley's Community and Civic Leaders, 268
Dudley Senior High School Gymnasium, James B., 81
Dudley seniors, 203
Dudley set, 151
Dudley's extracurricular AVT Team, 469
Dudley's finest, 352
Dudley's First Diva, 237
Dudley's football stadium, 85
Dudley's Girls Basketball Team- Coaches, 410
Dudley's Graduating Class, 12, 278
Dudley's Head Basketball Coach, 402
Dudley's Head Dudley AFROTC Cadets, 190
Dudley's Homecoming Parade, 187, 189, 331
Dudley's Isaiah Monroe, 152
Dudley's Joey Cheek Goes, 481
Dudley's Junior AFJROTC, 330
Dudley's Junior AFROTC, 330, 489
Dudley's Main, 204
Dudley's Main Building, 64, 204, 232, 458
Dudley's Main Gymnasium, 81, 90
Dudley's Marching Band, 219, 221, 473, 476
Dudley's Modern Dance Company, 122
Dudley's Modern Dance Company's Annual Spring Recital, 246
Dudley's Original Main Building, 536
Dudley Sports, James B., 117, 278, 360, 371, 373
Dudley's Prima Ballerina, 246
Dudley's PTSA, 205
Dudley Sr, James B., 385
Dudley's School District, 103, 535
Dudley's stadium, 130
Dudley's stage, 210
Dudley's Steven Davis II, 149, 494
Dudley's student body, 117, 130
Dudley's students, relocating, 463
Dudley staff, 110
Dudley Stage Band, 105
Dudley stakeholders, 166
Dudley's top players, 130
Dudley Street, 61, 226
Dudley Student Council, 125, 397
Dudley Student Government Association, 87, 123
Dudley Student Manifesto, 91
Dudley Style Presentation, 187
Dudley's Varsity, 474
Dudley Swim Team, 123
Dudley's Women Dominate, 364
Dudley's Women's Track and Field Team, 364
Dudley's Women's Track Team, 364
Dudley Track, James B., 361
Dudley Women's Track, 365
Dudley wrestlers, 144
Dudley Wrestling Coach Meeting New Challenges, 482
Dudley Yearbook, 166, 202, 212
Dudley Yearbook Staff, 407
Duke Ellington, 237
Duke Funds, 41
Duke Law School and NC Central School, 284
Duke University, 284, 348, 354, 475
   attended, 334
Dumfries, 340
Dunbar, 481
Durham, 24, 34, 46, 82, 94, 216, 443, 464, 474

499

Oliver, 308
Durham-based residency, 255
Durham Hillside, 129–30, 223
Durham Hillside High School, 464
Durham's City of Medicine Academy, 474
During Past, 410
Duty Corps, 320–21
Duty/ Vietnam, 311–12
Dwayne, 322
Dwinique Peters, 210
Dye, 61, 110–11, 113–16, 410
Dye's dedication, 117
dynamics, 164
    political, 93
Dynasty Franklin, 365–67

E

Eagles & Adams, 288
Earle, 290
Earl H. Crotts, 157
Earliest Greensboro Public High Schools, 45
Early Involvement, 492
Earth Wind, 186, 428
East Bragg Street, 181
East Carolina University, 327
Eastern Alamance High School, 394
Eastern Guilford High School, 63
Eastern High School in Washington, 89
Eastern Region, 130
East Florida Street, 94
East Gorrell Street, 40
East Greensboro, 440
Eastman Kodak Company, 420
East Market, 43
East Market Street, 28, 43, 61, 138, 432–33, 438
Eastside Community Club, 268
East Side Drive, 41
East/West All-Star, 281
East-West All-Star, 402
East White Oak, 28
East White Oak Community Center, 29
East White Oak School, 28–29, 175, 492
Eastwood Avenue, 425
Ebenezer Baptist Church, 178
Ebony, 485
Ebony magazine, 421
Echols, 307
    Bobby, 131
Economic History, 484
Economic News Release, 479
Economic Resources, 281
EC Teacher, 128
Eddie, William, 308
Eddie Favors, 130–31, 347, 536
Eddie J. U, 313
Edgecombe, 6
Edgecombe County Schools, 161
Editorial Page Editor, becoming, 425
education
    early childhood, 167
    eighth-grade, 172
    high-tech vocational, 167
Educational Outreach Program, 423
education of Negroes, 5, 7–8
Education Outcomes, 468, 480
Education Planning Committee, 371

Education Policies Commission, 36
Education Reform, 481
Education Statistics, 481
Education to subordinate-education, 481
Edward, Charlie, 316
Edward, Henry, 315
Edward, John, 305
Edward, Walter, 317
Edward G Gray, 485
Edward H. Greene, 140
Edwards, 22, 161, 305, 309, 315
    13-Savoi, 150
    14-Shannon, 150
Edwards & Broughton, 484
Edward W. U, 321
Egypt, 460
Eichelberger, 307
Eighteenth Corps, 302
Elated, 253
Elbert, 313
elderly Black workers bragging, 55
Elder Platt, 338–39
Elders & Jo Evans Lynn, 485
Elders Council, 338
electives, industrial/mechanical arts, 75
Electrical Engineering, 280
Electric Express, 428
Electronic Edition, 484
Electronic Music, 454
Elementary, Wiley, 289
Elementary, Zion, 175
Elementary Education Department, 23
Elijah, 317
Elite Warfighters, 490
Elizabeth, 43
Elizabeth City, 23, 38
Elks Club, 428
ELL (English language learner), 469
Ella, 197
Ellis, 306–8
ELL students, 469
Elmer, Albert, 311
Elmer, James, 315
Elmer Leon, 321
Elmore James, 254
Elm Street, 187, 430, 432
Eloise Logan, 214
Eloise Logan Penn, 214–15, 220–21, 237
Elon University, 476
ELPSA, 164
Elreta, 57
Elreta Alexander, 233, 485
Elreta Melton, 57, 233
El Rocco, 256
El Rocco Club, 256, 432
Elsie, 69
Elvester, 311, 324
Elvira Green, 241
Elvis Berry Abishek Pradhan, 154
Emancipation Day, 34
Emanuel, 322
Embry University- Riddle Astronautical
    University, 341
Emergency only Dental Clinic, 336
Emergency Services Personnel, 471
Emerson, 57, 481
EMMA LOU MORGAN MCADOO, 268
Emma Morgan McAdoo Scholarship, 269

A PLACE WHERE SUCCESS WAS EXPECTED: FINAL EDITION

Emma Morgan McAdoo Scholarship Fund, 269
Emmanuel Mosely, 380
Emmett, Walter, 316
employees, full-time, 466
Employer Support, 445
employment, obtaining, 393
Employment Projections, 489
Emporia Extravaganza Award, 137
Empower America Achievement, 481
endorsement, 287
Endowment Fund, 473
energy Funk, high, 260
engagements, bloody, 301
Engineering Officer, 334
Engineering Organization, 394
Engineering Physics, 284, 334, 423
Engineering Physics Degree, 334
Englewood community, 393
English Building, 62–63, 168, 456
English class assignment, 446
English Courses, 75
English teachers, 74, 170, 208
engraved pens, 187
Engraving, 173
Ennis Eugene, 316
Ensemble, 243, 429
Enterprise Unlimited, 446
Entire Dudley High School Campus, 536
Environmental Safety Office, 475
Enzlow, Carol, 13
Enzlow, Harold, 13
EOC scores, 471
Episcopal Church, 45
Epps, 308
Epsilon Upsilon Chapter, 396
Epstein, 467
Equestrianship, 124
Eric Eugene, 320
Eric Hicks, 384–85
ERIC KIMBER, 382
Eric Kimber Make It, 382
Ernest, Lee, 315
Ernest Eugene, 310
Ernestine Bennett, 445, 492
Ernestine Bennett Biography, 483
Ernest L. Sr, 312
ESPN, 379
Esquires Social Club, 331
Ethel Caffie Singers, 244
Ethel's Bake Shop, 432
Eugene, Melvin, 318
Eugene Evans, 314
Eugenia Grier Faulks, 286
Europe, 97, 237, 240, 244, 265
Eva, 238
Evacuation Hospital, 416
Eva Foster, 238, 252, 413
Evangel Fellowship COGIC, 243
Evangelical Dance, 398
Evans, 193, 259, 308, 433, 473
Evans, Benjamin A., 104
Evans, Dudley alumni Phillip R., 211
Evans, Gloria, 66, 456
Evans, Harold, 13
Evans Lynn Solution, 471
Evans sisters, 456
Eva's mentor, 238
Eva The Diva Foster, 479

Eva Turner Foster, 238
Evening School for Young Adults, 135
event- Jerome Gantt, 152
Everachievers' Retired Teachers, 268
Everett Rufel, 307
Everitt James, 413
Evers Award, 287
Excellence Choir, 243
Exceptional Children, 128
Ex-Dudley coach McKee, 482
Experimenting Colleges, 236
Expert Field Medical Badge, 336
Extraordinary Gardener & Businessman, 437
EZEKIEL BEN-ISRAEL-A, 294
Ezell, 204, 390, 493
Ezell Alexander, 305
Ezell Blair, 80, 89–90, 204
Ezikel, 210

F

Fabulous Thunderbirds, 258
façade, 60, 62, 64
Facilitator, 123
Faculty Development Committee, 360
Faculty meeting, first, 163
Faculty Senate Member and Recruitment
    Committee Chairperson, 360
Fairley, 308
Fairview Community, 11
Fairview Elementary School, 164
Falkner Elementary School in Greensboro, 400
Fame/Distinction, 145, 278, 360, 371, 373
Fame/Hall, 117
Fame/Hall of Distinction, 289, 413–14, 476, 483,
    492–93
Fame/Hall of Distinction Board, 289
Fame/Hall of Distinction Members, 413
Fame Honorary Award, 287
Fame Inductee, 354
Family Life Classes, 158
Family Practitioner, 409
fans, non COGIC Christian music, 243
fantastic Band Program, 259
Farmer's Alliance, 52
Farmers' Union, 52
Farrington, 308
Farrison, 58
father Dave Moore Sr, 475
Father's Day, 173
Father's military involvement, 259
Faye, 419
FAYE ADAMS-TAYLOR, 419
Faye Adams-Taylor Bio, 478
Fayetteville, 23, 38, 223, 464
Fayetteville State Teachers College, attended, 325
FBLA (Future Business Leaders of America), 169
FBS (Football Bowl Subdivision), 387
Features Editor, 481
Feb19, 488
FELLOW AWARD, prestigious, 281
Fellows, Dudley, 340, 396–97, 405
fellow service members, 328
Fellowship Gospel Choir, 245
female Air Force Air War College Class
    President, 342
Female Drum Major, 223
    first, 223

Female Engineer Award, 342
female executives, 420
Ferguson, 93, 308, 482
    Daniel, 212
Ferndale Middle, 403
Ferrante, 114
Ferrell, 308
Ferriera, 492
    Kenneth, 148–49
Festival, Winter, 205
Fewell, 308
Field Championships, 152, 364
Field Girls Athlete, 362
Field Hall of Fame, 362
Field Hockey Team, 102
Field Team, 152, 154, 364–65
field trips, 336, 396, 467
Fifty Years, 56
Fike High School, 133
Filene, Benjamin, 29–30
Finance Committee, 268, 449
Fine Arts, 265
finest Dudley Homecoming Parades, 193
first African American, 270, 274, 278, 280–81, 284–85, 327, 334, 346, 348, 350, 354, 356
first African American Chairman, 285
first African American Female, 445
first African American Navy Band, 226
first African American woman, 290
First All-Black Navy Band of World War II, 481
FIRST B1-NAVY BAND, 326
first Black Female, 358, 476
First Congregational Church in Birmingham, 475
first Dudley graduate, 135, 167, 247
first-grade teacher, 12
First Gym, 60–62, 70
First Gymnasium, 201
First Pantherettes, 112
first Trinity AME Zion church, 17
Fisher, 308
Fisk University, 65, 214
Flag Girl, 190, 192, 223
Flag-girls Coach, 410
Flagship, 314, 334
Fletcher James, 309
Flexible Social Club, 141
floats, bright and happy, 188
Floats, Gay, 486, 488
Florance-Bristow, 391, 474
Florence, Ann, 113, 209
Florida Street, 17, 82
Floyd Harry, 312
Football Bowl Subdivision (FBS), 387
football crowds, 224
Football State Championship, 149
Force Reserve, 319
Foreign Language, 75, 156
Forgione, 471, 481
Forgotten First B-1, 478
former college coach Bill Hayes, 146
former Dudley band members, 221
Former First Lady Michelle Obama, 426
Former Hawks All-Star Lou Hudson, 486
former Thespian Roberta Washington, 208
Forsyth County Home Guard, 35
Fort, Edward, 237
Fort, Edward B., 135
Fort Benning, 290

Fort Bragg, 332
Fort Jackson, 420
Fort Pillow, 302
Fort Ritchie, 305
Fort Wagner South Carolina, 301
Fort Worth, 339
Forty-First Quadrennial Session, 178
Foster, Denzel, 154
Foster Friends, 285
founder Sarah Herbin, 268
Founding Director, 334
Four-Hour Graduations, 177
Foushee, 308
Foust, 308
Foust Elementary, 289
Foust Elementary School in Greensboro, 161
Fowler, Bernard, 138
Fox, 239, 243, 265, 422
    David, 105
    Inez, 239, 488
Fox Shoe Repair, 439
Foxx, Charles, 254
Foxx, Inez, 239–40, 253
Foxxes, 253–54
Fragile children, 197
France's Bicentennial Celebration Parade, 229
Francine McAdoo Scott, 390, 393
Francisco, San, 373, 381
Francis Marion Foils, 482
Franklin, Dorothy, 366
Franklin, Kirk, 263
Franklin Brown, 55, 87–88, 156–57, 172, 280, 398
Frazier, attracted, 257
Frazier, Sam, 257
Freddie B. U, 320
Fred Douglas, 304
Fred William, 309
FRED YOUNG, 324
Free, 95, 211, 281, 303, 308, 333, 478, 490
    Lacy, 210
    Loretta, 222
    Margaret M., 333
    marrying Hannah R., 333
Freedman's Bureau, 465
Freedmen's Aid, 17, 21, 45
Freedmen's Bureau, 51
Freedom Drive, 434
Freedom of Choice Programs, 465
Freeman, 309
Free Military Academy, 301
French forces, 297
French III, Spanish III, 75
French National Honor Society, 394, 418
Freshman Choir, 217
Freshmen Steering Committee, 403
Fresh Prince, 202
Friday nights, 147
Front Office Assistant, 410
Front View, 83
Frye, Henry, 330
Funkhouse, 257
Furcron, William, 130
Furcron Field House, William J., 487
Future Business Leaders of America (FBLA), 169
Future Teachers-Gwendolyn Spinks Benton, 494

A PLACE WHERE SUCCESS WAS EXPECTED: FINAL EDITION

G

Gabrielle Cheek, 364–67
Gaffin, 309
Gaines, Ernest, 396
Gainesville, 415
Gaither, Jerome, 209
Galloway, 309
game field, 387
game Hendon, 388
Game- Orange Bowl, 368
Gammon Theological Seminary, 38
Gantt, Harvey, 63
Gantt Huberman Architects, 63–64, 83–84, 459
Garcia, 160
Garner Webb University in Teacher Leadership, 127
Garrett, Pearl, 58
Gary, Delores, 209
Gate City Boulevard, 94
Gatewood, 428
Gatorade North Carolina Basketball Player, 375
Gause, Marcus, 172
Gayla Kelly, 102
GCA (Greensboro Citizens Association), 97, 109
GCS Celebration Report, 471
GCS Gifted, 171
GCS School Climate Task Force, 170
GEDA (Greensboro Economic Development Alliance), 285
Gee Moore, 190
GENE KENDALL, REAR ADMIRAL, USN, 334
General Baptist State Convention, 273
General Conference, 38, 178
General Dental Practice Rotation, 335
General Douglas Cooper, 301
General George Washington, 297
General James Blunt, 301
General Patrick Cleburne, 302
General Superintendent, 490
    first, 6
generations, cross, 473
Generations Spreading, 250
Genesis, 277, 537
GENTRY GRAHAM, 324
George, Herman, 317
George Adonijah Grimsley, 25
George Allen, 204–5
George Bishop's PA, 260
George C. Simkins, Jr, 275
George E.C, 96
George Grier I, 131
George Henry, 310
George Martin Award, 356
Georgene, 61
Georgene Dye, 115, 118, 226, 398, 474, 484
    surrounded, 117
George Preston, 320
George Washington University, 445
Georgia Louise Harris Brown, 447
Georgia Tech, 354
German spies, 33
Germany & Vietnam Corps, 307
Germany & Vietnam Steele, 319
get and Take, 84
Ghana, 291
Gibbs, Richard W., 341
Gillespie, Annie, 493
Gillespie Golf, public, 274

Gillespie School, 69
Gilliard, Ebony, 212–13
Gilmer, 69, 309, 474, 482
    John S., 326
    Patricia, 494
Gilmore, 432, 436
Gilreath, 309
Gilyard, 309, 439
Girardeau, named, 233
Girl Bus Driver, 182, 478
Girls Field Hockey, 486
Girl's Gym, 62
Girls Soccer Team, 127
GLAAD award, 421
Gladney, Charles, 13
GLADYS FAULKS SHIPMAN, 286
Glasgow, 474
    Linda, 76–77
Glee Club, 215
GLEN ANDERSON, 397
Glenn Burleigh Concert Choir, 217
GLOBAL ENVIRONMENTAL SCIENTIST, 423
Global War, 340
Global War on Terrorism Service Medal, 340
Globetrotters, 81
Gloria Dean, 473
Gloria D. Evans, 201
Gloria Evans' Little Sister, 390
Glover, 47-Tayshawn, 150
GMWA (Gospel Music Workshop of America), 405
God, 1–2, 176–77, 242, 244, 262–63, 324, 343, 386, 419, 429, 537
God & Country, 328
Godette, Joe, 413
Goins, 310, 396
    Chris, 191
gold and navy, 221
Gold Bowl Team, 368
Golden Delights, 112
Golden Gophers, 349
Gold Helmet Club, 284
Goldie Frinks Wells, 456
Gold Marching Machine, 483
Goldsboro, 24, 46, 59
Goldsborough, William A., 58
Gold Star, 338
Gold Team, 171
Golf Coach, 136
Gonsavles, Edith, 105, 486
Good architecture, 447
Goode Construction Company, 470
Goodman, Richard, 291
Good Shepherd, 272
Gordon, Fannie K., 58
Gordon's flagellation scars, 299
Gorrell, Ralph, 28
Gorrell Steet, down, 440
Gorrell Street, 41, 409, 432–33
    named, 28
Gorrell Street Neighborhood Association, 475
Goshen, 11
Goshen School, 12, 30, 175, 424, 494
Gospel Expo, 243
Gospel Music Workshop, 405
Gospel Music Workshop of America (GMWA), 405
Gothic Revival Style, 60, 64

503

Gould, 116
  Cheryl, 115
Governor Jim Hunt, 284
Governor Pat McCrory, 217
Governor's Brightest Stat Award, 292
Governor William C.C, 299
Grace- Article, 486
Grace Gist, 435
Grace Lutheran Church, 345
graded schools, first, 16, 19–20, 46
Grading Scale, 75
graduation program, 471
Graduation Song, 199–200
Graduation Song's author, 200
Grady Hospital School, 415
Grammar Schools, 6
Grammy nomination, 429
Grances Raines, 29
Grand Attorney, 278
Grandison, Reverend Charles N., 22, 49
Grand Lodge, 52
grandmother's Hester James' Book, 466
grandmother Veoila Archie-Bennett, 127
Grant Award, 356, 476
Graphic Communication Systems Department, 401
Grassroots Hall of Fame, 269
Gravely, Clinton, 63
Graves, Claudette, 209
Graves, Sarah, 29
Great Atlantic, 431
Great Depression, 268, 480
Greater Greensboro, 376, 394
Greater North Carolina Jurisdiction, 244
Great Kings, 396
Great Lakes, 220
Great Sphinx, 460
Green, Calvin, 466
Green, Kevin, 144
Green, Quentin, 210
Green, Trey, 154
Greenberg, Jack, 96
Green Book, 434
Green Book-era accommodation, 432
Greenbriar Road, 216
Green Decision, 490
Greene, Agnes, 456
Greene County Training School in Snow Hill, 161
Greenfield Homes Community, 262
Greenlee, 310
  Beverly, 196
Greensboro Alumnae Chapter of Delta Sigma Theta Sorority, 400
Greensboro Alumni Chapter of Delta Sigma Theta Jabberwock competition, 405
Greensboro Area Math and Science Center Saturday Academy, 394
Greensboro Art's Council, 285
Greensboro Bar Association, 284
Greensboro Board of Education, 80
Greensboro Central Library, 473
Greensboro Chamber, 271, 273, 287
Greensboro Chapter of Gospel Music Workshop of America, 405
Greensboro Citizens Association (GCA), 97, 109
Greensboro City Council, 30, 37, 46, 58, 97, 109, 155, 285, 464, 537
Greensboro City Councilman, 70
Greensboro City Police Force, 215
Greensboro City School Board, 48, 232
Greensboro City Schools, 44, 50, 56, 59, 115, 162, 208, 215, 244, 294, 491
Greensboro City Schools/Head Start Program, 268
Greensboro City School System, 18, 58, 214, 391, 394
Greensboro Civic Ballet, 115, 247
Greensboro College, 460, 462–63, 488, 536
Greensboro Community Resource Board, 475
Greensboro Daily News, 30, 44, 144, 369, 380, 492, 536
Greensboro Day, 161
Greensboro Day School, 161, 470
Greensboro Demonstrations, 91
Greensboro Dudley Alumni Chapter President, 473
Greensboro Eagles, 378
Greensboro Economic Development Alliance (GEDA), 285
Greensboro entrepreneur and owner of Cosmos Supper Club, 260
Greensboro Galaxy, 403
Greensboro/Grimsley Senior High School, 49
Greensboro High School, 25, 135
Greensboro High School for Negroes, 155, 303
Greensboro Historical Museum, 35–36
Greensboro History, 479
Greensboro History Museum, 16
Greensboro Human Relations Commission, 273
Greensboro Kiwanis Club, 210, 484
Greensboro Mayor John Forbis, 368
Greensboro Middle College, 467
Greensboro minister Donald Trapp, 434
Greensboro NAACP, 94
Greensboro Negro Hospital Association, 39
Greensboro Negro Public Schools, 18, 156
Greensboro Negro Public School System, 221
Greensboro News & Record, 137, 145, 149, 294–95, 386, 481–83, 485, 491–92
Greensboro Pacesetters, 361
Greensboro Parks, 281, 358, 419, 476
Greensboro Police Deputy Chief James Hinson Jr, 295
Greensboro Public Schools, 18, 482
Greensboro Public School's School Board, 285
Greensboro Record's Bruce Washburn, 224
Greensboro Salvation Army Boys and Girls Club, 293
Greensboro's Black Child Development Institute, 268
Greensboro's Black Community, 56, 432
Greensboro School Board, 53, 274
Greensboro Senior High, 89–90
Greensboro Senior High School, 44, 50–51, 538
Greensboro Senior High School Gymnasium, 81
Greensboro Senior High School's Gymnasium, 80
Greensboro Senior High's Gymnasium, 81
Greensboro's Green Book listings, 433
Greensboro's mayor, 285
Greensboro's NAACP president, 485
Greensboro Spiritual Renaissance Singers, 405
Greensboro Sports Council, 284
Greensboro's schools, 274–75
  ordered, 100
Greensboro's Youth, 285
Greensboro Times, 151
Greensboro Triad area, 454

A PLACE WHERE SUCCESS WAS EXPECTED: FINAL EDITION

Greensboro Truth and Reconciliation Commission, 425
Greensboro Urban Ministries, 216, 273
Greensboro VOICES Biography, 487
Greensboro Yankees, 85
Greensboro Youth, 123
Greensboro Youth Council, 123
Greensboro YWCA, 376
Greensboro Zoning Commission, 283, 474
Green's parents, 241
Green Standard, 467
Greer, 310
Gregory, 309, 481
Gregsha, 153, 474
Gregsha Lee On Goals, 488
Grenville, 316
Griffin, Billy, 69, 494
Griggs, Cynthia, 341
Grimes, Willie, 88
Grimsley, 47, 90, 98, 101, 165, 211, 536
    Superintendent George A., 47
Grimsley application, 536
Grimsley Grit Day, 193
Grimsley High School, 141, 333
Grimsley Senior, 309
Grimsley Senior High School, 44–45, 50, 63, 70–71, 74, 103, 165–66, 211, 394, 536, 538
Grimsley Step Team, 394
groundbreaking acclaim, received, 263
group Sweet Dreams, 261
GTCC (Guilford Technical Community College), 167, 289, 410, 450, 460, 470, 472, 536
Guadalupe-Hidalgo, 487
Guam/Vietnam Charles, 307
Guard Wyche, Julius Dorman, 323
Guatemala, 291
Guildford County, 26
Guilford County Board of Education, 293
Guilford College, 228, 473
Guilford County, 7–9, 11–12, 14, 16, 30, 46–49, 275, 279, 284, 286, 292, 461–62, 465
Guilford County Board, 48, 283, 293
Guilford County Coach, 143
Guilford County Councilman Skip Alston, 287
Guilford County Health Department, 274
Guilford County High School Teacher, 490
Guilford County Negro Democratic Club, 434
Guilford County Report Cards, 469
Guilford County Saturday Enrichment Program, 330
Guilford County School Board, 63, 166, 456, 484
Guilford County Schools Construction Projects Facility, 491
Guilford County Schools Crisis Team, 404
Guilford County Schools District, 404
Guilford County School System, 48, 169, 427, 469, 475
Guilford County's High Schools, 166
Guilford County Sports Hall of Fame, 132
Guilford County Sports Hall of Fame Class, 133
Guilford Technical Community College. See GTCC
Guilford Westmoreland, 130–31, 398
Guitar Gabriel, 255
guitarist Tim Betts, 258
Gulf & Western, 424
Gumboot, 221
Gurnee Brooks, 315
Gurney, 322
Guthridge, Bill, 375
Guy, Barbara, 113
Guy, Doris, 29
Guy, John, 147
Guyrene Tyson Simkins, 274
Gwendolyn, 121
Gwendolyn Spinks, 121
Gwendolyn Spinks Benton, 121, 395
Gwen's intervention, 395
Gymnasium, Dudley, 535

H

Habitat, 341
Hairston, 272–73, 310, 449–50, 487
    Harold, 209
    Jackie, 260
    Otis, 89
    Otis L., 272, 460
    Regina, 392
Hairston Apartments, 272
Hairston book, 461
Hairston Memorial Scholarship Fund, 272
Hairston Middle, 289
Hairston Middle School, 89
Hairston's devotion, 272
Hairston Sr, Reverend Otis L., 272
Haith, Christine, 13
Haitian Revolution, 298
Half Moon, 432
Half Moon Cafeteria, 43
Hall, Antonio, 150
Hall, Bennett, 22
Hall, Dudley, 289, 294, 398
Hall, Scott, 344
Hall, Tony, 13
Halley B, 320
Hall of Distinction, 124, 135, 269, 287, 290, 407, 413, 489
Hall of Distinction on October, 334
Hall of Fame, 370, 402, 413, 487
Hall of Fame on October, 402
Hamilton, 125–26, 290, 310, 474, 482
    Esther, 125
    John, 456
Hamilton's involvement, 125
Hamilton's passion, 125
Hampton, 11, 38, 110
    Gladys, 29
    William, 97
Hampton Elementary, 175
Hampton Homes, 74
Hampton Institute, 10, 15, 25, 38, 65, 110, 418
Hampton Normal, 482
Hampton University, 38, 110, 333
Hampton Virginia, 423
Handover County, 9
Hannah, 487
Hannah Payne's daughter, 15
Hannibal Collins, 298, 479
Harbor, Pearl, 220, 326
Harcourt Brace, 481
Harden, 136, 482
Hardin, Ralph, 317
Hargett, 123–24, 310
Hargett and students, 124

Hargraves, 310
Harlem Renaissance writers, 74
Harmon Unthank, 14
Harmon Unthank House, 495
   c, 15
HAROLD ALEXANDER, 335
Harold Charles, 306
Harold Charles Cotton, 282
HAROLD CHARLES COTTON, JR, 255
Harold Cotton, Sr, 282, 439
Harold Jr, 283
Harper & Brothers, 491
Harper Collins, 487
HarperCollins Publishers, 482
Harper's New Monthly Magazine, 38, 482
harpist/singer David, 257
Harris, Elizabeth, 113
Harris, John, 26, 413
Harris-1948, John, 280
Harrisburg, 333
Harshaw, 311
Hartmann, 60, 482, 491, 536
Hartmann, Charles, 60, 63–64
Hartmann, Charles C., 50, 60
Hartmann, David, 48, 50, 535–36
Harvard Law School, 420
Harvard University, 95, 404
   attended, 420
Harvey, Steve, 263
Hastie, William, 96
Hasty, Thomas, 413
Hatchett, Harriett, 68, 76
Haulsey, 311
Hawaii, 379
Hayden, 358–59
Hayes, Josephine, 68
Hayes, Wilson, 241
Hayes Taylor YMCA, 138, 141, 226
Hayes-Taylor YMCA, 270–71, 289
Hayes Taylor YMCA Vo, 331
Hayes Taylor Y-Men's Club, 289
Hayes-Taylor Y-Men's Club, 289
Haygood, Elmer, 195
Haygood girls, 248
Haygoods, 248, 311
Haygood Sisters, 248, 484
Haywood, 311, 317, 375–76
   Barbara, 374
   Brendan, 143, 377, 421, 489
Haywood's arrival on campus, 375
HBCU-NBDC, 230
HBCUs, 360, 441
head, shaved, 81
Head Coach & Student Manager, 150
Headen, 311
   Amber, 250
   Jimmy, 13
Head Football, 133, 136
Headquarters USMC, 488
Head Wrestling Coach, 144
Health Education, 358
Health Education and Welfare (HEW), 358
Health Hero, 292
Health Science Academy, 62
Heartache, 254
Heartbeat drummettes, 202
heart of Warnersville, 15, 35, 48
Hebrew Holy Book, 537

Hebrew Literature, 536–37
Heights, Dudley, 74, 94, 103, 345
Heights, Lincoln, 74, 103, 425
Helburn Meadows, 413
helicopters, 384, 416
Henderson, Melvin, 413
Hendon Hooker, 147, 386, 389
Henry, father John D., 355
Henry, Ralph, 320
Henry, Roscoe, 317
Henry Bernard, 304
Henry Clayton, 310
heptathlon, 361–62
Herbie Mann, 114
Heritage Community, 463, 494–95
   first city, 484
HERMAN G, 338
Herman G. Platt, 244, 339
Herman's widow, 435
Herring, Kate M., 33
Herzl Junior College, 274
Hester, 311, 324
HEW (Health Education and Welfare), 358
Hicks, 311–12, 384–85, 415–17
   Derrick, 154
   quoted, 415
Hicks and other, 416
Hick's European, 385
Hicks HOF, 414
Hicks Snowball, 439
hi Diddle Diddle, 253
Higginbotham, Leon, 96
Higgins, 288
Higher Education Management Systems, 469, 489
High Growth Status, 169
High Point, 12, 48, 86, 115, 168–69, 185, 266,
   293, 384, 443, 491
High Point Andrews, 402
High Point Normal & Industrial Institute, 11, 47
High Point University, 123
High School Band, 229, 231
high school courses, 47–48
high school credits, 59, 78
high school curriculum, 471–72
High School Departments, 37, 46–47, 538
High School for Negroes in Greensboro, 44, 50,
   53–54, 464, 491, 535, 537
High Steppers, 222
Hill, Joshua, 106
Hill, Matt, 255
Hill, Oliver, 96
Hills, Clinton, 479
Hillside, 130, 464
   selected, 130
Hinnant, Shirley, 113, 209
Hinson, Catherine, 209
hired Nathan Ross Margold, 94
Historic Places, 1, 29, 82
Historic Sites, 1, 460, 463, 535–36
HIV, 374
HOD, 414
Hodge, Brenda, 218
Hodge, Tia, 157
Hodges, Johnny, 230, 461
HOF.HOD, 342
Holden Printer, 490
Holiday Inn, 435
Holiday Program, 205, 225

Holland, Chris, 213
Holland, Christopher, 212
Hollomon, Ester D., 58
Hollywood, 428
Holmes Grove United Methodist Church, 270
Holt, Roger F., 326
Homecoming, 187, 190, 193, 222
Homecoming Court, 123
Homecoming Dance, 193
Homecoming Parade, 190
Homecoming Parade, 126, 191–93, 396, 408
  annual, 193
Homecoming Parade Coordinator, 124
Homecoming Parades and Spirit Week, 187
Homecoming Queen, 239
Home Economics, 54, 75, 105, 493
Homeless Student in Transition Liaison, 404
Homeownership, 480
Homeroom Officer, 331, 473
Homeroom Secretary, 449
Hometown Hall of Famer Ceremony in November, 351
Honey Springs, 301
Honolulu, 379
Honorable Mention All-American in football, 356, 476
Honorably Discharged, 125
Honors English, 127
Honors Teacher Cadet, 127
Honors Vocal Ensemble, 218
Hood-1953, Daisy, 280
Hoodies, 442
Hooker, 386–89
Hooker's collegiate career, 388
Hooper, 312, 392
Horace, 317, 321
  Victor, 320
Horatius, 311
Horizontal Jumps Coach, 153
hospital
  first, 19
  local, 275
  private Trinity, 39–40
hostess, charismatic, 243
Hot Nuts, 224
Houghton, Israel, 263
Houston
  Sharon, 392
  visual record, 96
Houston Rockets, 370
Houston's recommendation, 95
Howard, 13, 95, 179, 309, 312, 318
HOWARD ADGER, 324
Howard Russell, 310
Howard-trained lawyers, 96
Howard University, 75, 278, 335, 373, 447, 475
Howard University Law School, 95
Howell, 395, 483
Howell, James, 101, 157
HOYES WILSON, 341
Hoyte, 314
HSTW Representative, 123
HSXtra High School Sports, 494
Hubbard, 312
Hubert, 305, 316
Hudson, 160, 349–50, 428
  Lou, 78, 89, 132, 349
Hughes, Larry, 375

Hughes, Robert, 131
Human Capital, 488
Humanitarian Award, 278, 385
Humanitarian Service Medal, 336
Humanity Volunteer, 342
Human Rights Award, 287
Human Services, 290, 445
Humble Beginnings, 489
Hummingbird, 253
Humphrey, 58
hurdles, 200-meter, 361–62
Hurman Lee, 316
Hutton, Charles, 131
Hyde County, 57, 480

I

Idaho, 290–92
  eastern, 291
Ike & Tina Turner, 428
Illinois Press, 481, 484
Illinois State Employment Service, 393
Illinois University Library, 488
Immanuel Lutheran College, attended, 282
Immanuel Lutheran School, 75
Impossible Dream, 200
Inaugural Parade, 229
India Arie, 265
Indian Territory, 301
In-door & Out-door Titles, 364
In-door State Championship, 364
In-door Women's Track & Field State Champions, 365
Inductee Dudley Hall, 475
Inductees James B. Dudley Educational, 414
Industrial Arts Departments, 25, 462
Industrial Arts teacher, former, 283
Industrial Robotics Repair, 471
Industrial Technology, 292, 294, 368
Industrial Technology Preparation, 472
Inez, 239–40, 252–53
Inez & Charlie Foxx, 240
Inez singing, 240, 253
Inez's rendition, 240
infallible written word of God, 537
Inola Leach, 68
Inola Leech, 76
In-School Suspension Personnel, 289
Inspirational Creations, 250
Instruction-Urban Education in May, 127
integration, 55, 100–101, 104–5, 107, 111, 117, 129–30, 175, 181, 478, 484
International Baccalaureate, 166
International Textile Group, 357
internships, rotating, 274
intra-racial prejudices, old, 116
Invincible Lodge, 282
Iraq, 337
Ireland, 312
Irving Park, 437
Irving Park Community, 28
Irving Reed, 316
Irving Van, 321
ISAAC CARREE, III, 262
Isaiah Monroe set, 152
Ishmael, 312
Island Mound, 301

Island Records, 253
Isley, Ernest, 13
Isley Brothers, 428
Italy, 237, 325
Ivan Cutler, 106

J

Jabberwock Bonding Co-Chair, 123
Jabberwock talent, 405
Jackson, Herbert, 413
Jackson, Jesse, 277
Jackson, Michael, 186, 424
Jackson, Roger D., 126
Jackson Junior High School, 159–60
Jackson Middle School, 159, 167, 169
Jacksonville, 340
Jack Tatum Trophy, 379
Jacobs, Wendy, 193
Jacquees, 265
Jacqueline, 312
Jacqueline Florence, 113
Jacqueline McDonald Williams, 292
Jacquelin Hall, 212
Jacquelyne, 127
Jade Meekins, 367
Jaden Lane, 150
Jahariee Paschal, 154
Jahmier Slade, 154
Jalile Elliott, 154
Jamaica, 253
James, Etta, 239
James, Eugene, 318
James, Hester, 9, 52
James, King, 537
James, Margaret, 76
James Alton, 307
James Arthur, 307, 314
James B. Dudley High School, 57–58, 83–84, 88–89, 156, 201, 222, 225–26, 241–42, 264, 268, 283–84, 332–33, 337, 364, 398, 424–25, 471, 476–77, 483–84
James B. Dudley High School Auditorium, 60
James B. Dudley High School Educational, 385, 412–13, 483, 492–93
James B. Dudley H.S, 326
James B. Dudley Undefeated, 131
James Benson Dudley High School Alma Mater, 194
James Benson Dudley High School Principal, 54
James Benson High School, 60
James Benton Parsons, 89, 219
James Brown playing, 434
James Cecil, 322
James Coffee Yourse, 261
James D. Morgan, 220, 224–25, 227, 473
James Earl, 307
James Edward, 311
James Edwin, 320
James Kelly, 314
James Odair, 304
James Odell, 304
James Parsons Carolina A, 219
James Pinnix, 153, 365–67
James Rawley, 307
James Redson, 306
James Robert Cathcart, 55
James Thelbert, 320

James Theodore, 310
Jamestown, 7, 9, 48, 144
James Weldon Johnson, 175
James Yourse, 259, 492
James Yourse I, 252
Janee, 452
Janel, 262
Janice Brewington HOD, 414
Janie Mae Harrison, 29
Janis Baines, 108, 119, 162
Janneé, 451
Janneé Jarrell, 451
Japan, 265, 338, 397, 416–17
Japan & South Kore Poole, 317
Japan Jurisdiction, 338
Jarrell's Academic Accomplishments, 332
Jarrell's Community Involvement, 331
Jarvis, David, 322
Jasper, 306
Jaybirds, 253
Jay Middle School, 168
jazz, 114, 230, 237, 260, 277
    first, 238
jazz singer, 238
Jazzy Jeff, 202
JBD, blue, 459
JBD Educational & Sports, 342
JCSU, 260
Jean, 305
JEFF, 368
Jeff Davis, 147, 369, 492
Jefferson, 328
    Johnnie, 210
Jefferson Elementary School, 468
JEFFREY, 368
Jeffries, Barbara, 68, 76
Jenkins, 24, 50–51, 54, 56, 65–66, 81–82, 267, 312–13, 483
    actor Burgess, 267
    Edward, 81
    Ida, 89
    Jim, 44, 49
Jennings, 313
Jeremiah, 154
Jerica Womack, 213
Jerome, 317
Jerry Lee, 304
Jersey City, 128
Jersey City Medical Center, 274
Jesse Louis, 309
Jesse Pratt, 168
JESSICA MARTIN-OATES, 127
Jessie, 316
Jessie James, 323
Jesus, 250
Jetson Randall-Peangmeth, 106
Jewish people, 97
Jhyheem Pittman, 150
Jibrell Khazan, 90
Jim Crow conditions, 33
Jim Crow society, 31
Jim Crow system, 34
Jirbrell Khazan, 89
Jo Ann Evans, 494
Jo Ann Evans Lynn, 394
job market, global, 471
Joebee, 211
Joe Tex signing autographs, 434

A PLACE WHERE SUCCESS WAS EXPECTED: FINAL EDITION

Jo Evans Lynn, 2–538
JOEY, 371
Johann Olav Koss, 372
John Allen, 311
John Allen Tarpley, 37, 155, 174
John A. Tarpley, Principal, 70
Johnathan Anthony McKee, 414
John Brian Heath, 210
John Carlson, 327
John Charlie, 321
John D. Henry, 355
John Emanuel, 319
John Hairston Sr, 449
John Henry, 182, 305, 313
John Lewis, 312
Johnnie Willard, 319
Johnny Evans I, 131
John O. Bigelow, 140
John Samuel, 309
Johnson, Andrew, 325, 330
Johnson, Catherine, 68
Johnson, Elliot, 13
Johnson, Howard, 435
Johnson, Inez, 252
Johnson, Lili, 325
Johnson, Nelson, 295
Johnson, Reginald H., 265
Johnson, Ron, 105
Johnson, Tommy, 87
Johnson, Walter, 209, 288, 347
Johnson, Wanda, 392
Johnson & Barbee, 292
Johnson-1940, Andrew, 280
Johnson Junior High School, 160
Johnson Music Industry Executive/Producer/Radio Personality, 484
Johnson Publishing Company, 485
Johnson's class, 325
Johnson's gifts, 265
Johnson's role, 266
Johnson-Tonkins, 288
John Thomas, 322
John Van Lindley, 30
John Vernon, 310
John Wesley, 312, 320, 323
John William, 311
John Woodrow, 323
John W. U, 309, 311
Joint Chiefs, 291
The Joint Commission (TJC), 418
Joint Professional Military Education, 340
Joint Service Achievement Medal, 338, 342
Jonathan Anthony McKee, 414
Jones, Bertha, 392
Jones, Bettye, 113
Jones, Bishop Robert E., 38
Jones, Brenda, 68, 76
Jones, James, 183
Jones, Juanita, 58
Jones, Linda, 471
Jones, Pam, 190
Jones, Quincy, 425
Jonesboro, 11, 430, 432
Jones Elementary, 175, 468
  attended David D., 477
Jones Elementary School, 348, 460
Jones Grocery, 43
Jones School, 37
Jordan, Toni, 99–100, 492
Jordan Chavis, 24, 49
Jordan Johnson, 365, 367
Jordan Sellars High School, 159
Jose Charles case, 294–95
Jose Charles Operation Transparency, 494
Joseph Charles Price School, 35–36
Joseph Charles Price School inaugural First Grade Class, 36
Joseph Daniel, 304
Joseph Taylor Stanley, 276
Journalism Institute, 467
Joyce Spruill, 348, 358–60
Joyner Elementary School and Foust Elementary School, 161
JROTC, 127
JROTC Banquet, 127
JROTC unit, 330
Juanita Tatum, 113
Jubilee Anniversary, 282
Judge Alexander, 57
Judge Elreta Alexander, 233, 492
Judge Elreta Alexander mirrors Nancy McLaughlin, 233
Judge Elreta Alexander-Ralston, 328
Judge Stanley, 274
Judicial District, 292
Judicial District Juvenile Services Division, 279
Juggy Murray, 239, 253–54
Juggy Murray Jones, 253
Julia Morrison Richmond, 391, 474
Julian Street, 228
Julia Richmond Directing, 494
JULIA RUTH MORRISON RICHMOND, 216
Julia Ruth Richmond, 218
Jump Shot Master, 491
Junior Achievement, 473
Junior Airforce ROTC, 425
Junior and Senior Class Representative, 394
Junior Championships, 362
junior class, 108, 201–2
Junior Class Advisor, 122
Junior Class of Student Practical Nurses, 68
Junior Class Practical Nurses, 68
Junior High School, 12, 159
Junior High School seniors, 77
junior Jaylee Brown setting, 364
Junior League Northern Virginia, 475
Junior Practical Nursing Class Instructor, 76
Junior Practical Nursing Class-Mary Anne Coleman, 76
Junior ROTC, 127
junior season, 379
juniors Mia Michelle Evans, 211
Junior Varsity Cheerleaders, 115
Junita Brown, 536
Juris Doctor Degree, 278, 292
Justice Band Competition, 125
Justice Board, 279
Justice Festival of Bands competition, 229
JV Cheerleading Coach, 124

K

K-12 education, 468
Kaelin Brown, 367
Kaffir Boy, 396
KAGB-FM radio station, 424

Kamala Harris, 123
Kamensky, Jane, 485
Kansas, 301, 334, 480
Kansas City Chiefs, 381
Kansas City Roster, 383
Kansas City Royals, 382
Kansas Colored, 301
Kansas Colored Volunteers, 301
Kappa Alpha Psi Fraternity, 141, 340
Kappa Kappa Psi Honorary Band Fraternity, 230
Kari Parker, 365, 367
Kathleen, 306
Kathryn Turrentine Stanley, 276
Kathy R. Hairston College, 450
KATHY ROUSON HAIRSTON, 449
Kathy Rouson Hairston HOD, 414
Katz, Jeff, 249
Kaye Frances, 320
Kee, John P., 262
Keep the faith of your fathers, 179
Kee's New Life Community Choir, John P., 262
Keianna Mims, 364, 367
Keith, Toby, 239
Kelly, Bobby, 257
Kendall, Gene, 347
Kendall Penniegraft, 367
Kennedy, Andy, 385
Kennedy
   John F., 89, 93
   President John F., 220
Kennedy School, John F., 420
Kennedy Space Center, 423
Kenneth, 252, 281, 308, 355
Kenneth Butch Henry, 355
Kenneth J. Wyrtch, 199–200, 246
Kenneth Thompson, 163
Ken Thompson, 163, 413
Kentucky Derby, 143
Kenyatta Owusu Martin HOD, 414
Kern Tips Award, 356
Kew Gardens, 374
Keyaun Dow, 154
Key Club, 127
Khalif Temple, 282
KIA, 304, 308, 310–11, 313–14, 318
Kiddy/PJ Day, 193
Kids Count Data Center, 478
Kieanna Mims, 366
King, Carole, 253
King, Chuck, 256
King, Shirley, 76
King Competition, 478
Kingfest, 419
King James Version, 205, 537
Kings Forest, 103
King V. Cheek, 41–42, 234–35
King Virgil Cheek, 42, 235
Kinston County, 443
Kirby, Marion, 146
Kiser Middle, 289
Kiser Middle School, 161
Klan meetings, open, 57
KNEELING L-R, 209
Knight, Ella, 196
Knight, Gladys, 428
Knighton Stanley, 479
Knoxville, 488
Korea, 315, 325, 416–17

Korean MASH units, 416
Korean Service Medal, 417
Korean War, 313, 416
Korean War Nurse, 486
Korean War Weaver, 321
Korean War Williams, 322
Koredell Bartley, 150, 154
Kpeglo, Jackie, 456
Ku Klux Klan, 57
Kuwait, 335

L

Laboratory Corporation, 476
labor force, primary, 30
Labor Relations, 357
Labor Statistics, 479
Lackland Air Force Base, 332
La De Dah, 253
Ladies, Dudley, 107, 122, 127, 341
Lady Panthers Field Hockey Team, 101
Lady Panthers Track Team, 110
Lady Sertoma Club, 287
Lake, Sadie, 328
Lake Brandt area, 37
Lake Erie, 298
Lakewood High School Band, 229
Lamancha, 200
Lambert, 314, 488
Lambeth-drums, Joe, 105
LAMONTE PRESSLEY, 377
Lane, Jackie, 198
Lane Drug Store, 69
Langston Hughes, 74
Langston Wood, 154
Lanier, Beverly, 197
Laquonda Oboe, 210
Larkin Streets, 18, 440
Larry F. Lewis, 162, 172
Las Amigas, 269
late Governor James Holshouser, 281
Latin I & II, 75
Laughlin, Bobby, 105
Laurean Davis, 213
Law Clerk, 292
Lawrence, Huey, 225
Lawrence Otis Graham, 201
Lawson, Brenda, 392
Lawson, Brittany, 392
lawyers, white, 234
Lazelle Free, 209, 211
Lazelle Free Army ROTC, 495
Leader Pack, 340
Lead Office Support, 404
Leaksville, 143
Learning Hub, 124
Learning Hub Champion, 124
Lee, Carl, 313
Lee, Debra, 483
Lee, Joe, 319
Lee, Kenneth, 96–97, 485
Lee, Stephen, 202
Lee, Tommy, 315
Lee, Wilton, 316
Lee Ella Williams Cheek, 42
Lee's honors, 421
Lee Street, 94, 216
Lee Woodruff, 306

A PLACE WHERE SUCCESS WAS EXPECTED: FINAL EDITION

Le'Ezra Brown, 153–54
left Atlantic Starr, 249
left Chapel Hill, 149
legacy, historical, 166
Legacy Section, 492
Legion Club, 433
Legrand, Patricia, 162
Leite Rio, 385
Lemuel Alson, 319
Lenwood Clark, 322
Leonard Medical School, 40
Lesley, George, 323
Levine Children's Hospital, 449
Lewis, David, 308
Lewis, Jonathan, 249
Lewis, Nancy, 209
Lewis, Rick, 106
Lewis, Willie, 231
Lewiston, 235
Lewis Wilson, 312
liberal arts colleges, 65
Liberal Arts/Electives, 75
liberty, 5, 175, 177, 256
Licensed Practical Nurse, 77
Licht, David, 257
Life Sciences, 397
Lillie Moore's son, 436
Lillie Morehead Moore, 436
Lilly, Michael, 13
Limuel Andrew, 306
Lin Buie-tenor, 105
Lincoln, Abraham, 52, 93
Lincoln Heights areas, 94
Lincoln Junior High, 186, 235
Lincoln Junior High School, 12, 59, 70, 77, 94, 98–99, 109, 228, 235, 345, 347
Lincoln Junior High School's Band, 188
Lincoln Middle School, 166, 186, 463
Lincoln's Junior High School students recall, 208
Lincoln Street, 109, 457
Lincoln Street View, 83
LINDA MCDOUGLE, 159
Linda Wilson, 159
Linda Wilson McDougle, 159
Lindsay Street, 433
Lindsay Street School, 19, 46–47
Lindwood J, 304
Lineberry, 100, 225, 274, 491
Lions' Assistant Director, 352
LISA JOHNSON-TONKINS, 288
Lisa Renee Richardson HOD, 414
Lisé Timmons Mclaughlin, 170
Little League, 282
Live Nation, 263
Liverpool, 253
Living Legends Foundation Award, 425
Livingston, 25
Livingston College, 15
Livingstone College, 11, 51
Livonia, 371
Lloyd Norris, 309
Local guitarist Carlos Morales, 257
local Hayes Taylor YMCA, 334
Logan, Hattie, 113
Logan Speight, 366–67
Lola Anne McAdoo, 269
Lola McAdoo, 369, 412, 492
Lola Wilson Hayes, 241

Long Hospital, 69
Long Leaf Pine, 217, 281
Lonnie Reynolds, 139, 390
Lorcey Henderson, 35, 48
Lord Dunmore, 296
Los Angeles, 428
Los Angeles Lakers, 350
Louis, John, 308
Louis Clyde Hudson, 349
Louisiana, 93, 298–99, 301
Louisiana Battalion, 303
Louisville head coach Rick Pitino, 385
Lowell Curtis Pye Sr, 262
Lowenstein-Atkinson Architects, 82
Loyal Fans, 407
Lt, Reginald R., 318
Lt Col Ronald Murphy, 330
Lt Col Thomas Clarke, 330
Lt Col Wayne Davidson, 330
Lucien Manuel, 321
Lula Belle Houpe, 216
lunches, reduced, 468–69, 478
Lunsford, 40
Luther Vandross' rendition, 200
Luvenia Turner, 29
Lyman, 213
lynching, 34
    passed resolutions condemning, 34
Lyndsay, 314
Lynn, 117, 164, 211, 262, 479, 484
Lyrics and Music, 199
Lyric Watkins, 365–67

M

MacGregor, 297, 484
Machines Clay, 309
MACK Scholar, 405
Maco, 312
Maco Beauty College, 432
Ma Coley, 107
Macomsom's classes, 138
Macomson, 138, 185
Mae, Lula, 317
Mae Sue Henry, 355, 493
Magic, Orlando, 376
Magic Johnson, 374
magistrates, 288
Magnolia House, 432–35, 479
Magnolia House Motel, 432, 475
    businesses-, 432
Main Building, 50, 60–63, 70, 83, 167, 201, 460, 463, 535, 538
    historic, 456
    original, 60, 463
    three-tiered, 50
Main Dudley Gymnasium, 61
Main Gym, 83
Main Gymnasium, 61, 82–85, 177, 187, 456, 458
    award-winning, 456
Major Contribution, 195
Majorette, Dudley, 122
majorette boots, 476
Majorette Coach, 410
majorette instructor/advisor, 117
majorettes and cheerleaders, 110
majority of students, 467–68
Major League, 281, 349

Major League Baseball, 348
Major League Baseball Amateur Draft, 382
Major League Baseball Hall of Fame, 281
Makkhar Ndiaye, 375
Malachi House, 285
Malaysia, 420
Male Athlete, 152, 340
Malois, 248
Malone, Marsha, 392
Manana Barracks, 326
man- Charles Moore, 19
Manhattan, 374
Mankind Award, 279
Manufacturing, 294
Marché Clark, 413
marches, daily, 277
Marching Band, 77, 125, 186, 190, 223, 228–30, 238, 396–97, 405, 408, 474
 high-stepping, 112
Marching Band and Dudley's AFJROTC Unit, 409
Marching Band and Pep Band, 426
Marching Band I, 75
Marching band of Thunder, 126, 230, 396, 405
marching order, 1
Marcus Gause Emagzine- High Point Discovered, 487
Mardi Gras Parade, 229
Margaret Tynes, 237
Margo, 16, 465–66, 484
Margold Report, 94, 485
Margold's report, 95
Margolin, 258
 Bob, 257
Marian Wright Edelman, 123
Marie's Grill, 432
Marine, 297, 304–7, 310–13, 315, 317–23, 337, 476, 480
Marine Commandant William Ward Burrows, 297
Marine Congressional Medal, 318
Marine Corps, 308, 312, 316, 323–24, 337, 485
Marine Corps Achievement Medal, 338
Marine Corps Jefferies, 312
Marine Corps' Magnetism Beckons Future General, 490
MARINE CORPS SP4, 324
Marine Logistics Group, 338
Marine Logistics Group II Marine Expeditionary Force, 487
Marine platoon, 297
Marine Security Guard, 312
Marion, Francis, 297
Marion's guerrillas, 297
marketplace, competitive, 432
Market Street, 187, 432, 440
Mark Fields, 409, 456, 467
Mark Lewis Fields, 409
Marques Douglas, 147
MARQUES LAMONT DOUGLAS, 373
Marriott International, 420
Marsallis Prescott, 212
Marshall, 37, 96
Marshals, Dudley's, 473
Marshals, Junior, 107–8, 121–22, 127, 167, 393, 418, 425, 474, 494

Marta, Alma, 170
MARTHA CROCKETT DICK, 396
Martin, 167, 297, 314, 336
 Frank, 385
 Jim, 229
 John, 297
 Walter, 127
Martin Luther King Blvd, 28, 99, 517
Martin Luther King Jr, 277, 517
Martin-Oates, 127, 517
Martin Robinson Delany, 301, 517
Martin Street, 434, 517
Martinsville, 225
MARVIN H, 135
MARVIN LAMBERT, 142, 517
MARY ELIZABETH, 250
Mary Evans, 473, 517
Maryland, 96, 235, 336, 339–40
Maryland case, 96
Maryland law school, 96, 517
Maryland's law school, 96, 517
Mary Lou Goins, 13, 517
Mary Louise Anderson, 111, 517
MASH, 416
MASH units, 416, 517
Mason, Bernard, 219
Masonic Mentoring Group, 125
masonry, 62, 75, 140, 158
masonry term, 55
Masons, 52, 517
Massachusetts, 22, 297, 301, 357, 517
master, young, 9
Master Achiever, 445
Master Key, 249
Master Musician, 129, 259–60, 517
Master of Education degree, 163
Master of Engineering Physics Degree, 334
master's degree, 35, 37, 156, 159, 235, 237, 339, 343, 395, 397, 447
Master Sergeant, 331, 338
Master Teacher- Mentor for new science teachers, 398
Mata, Alma, 186, 394
Mathabane, 517
 Marc, 396
Math Building, 82, 517
math instructor, 474
Math Open School, 517
Math Open School and Dudley's membership, 159
math proficiency, 169
Matkins, 517
 Tom, 105, 486
Matthew Elijah, 309, 517
Mattie Donnell Hicks, 415, 486, 489, 494, 517
Maurice D., 310
MAURICE D, 125
Maurice Drake, 113, 517
Mavericks, 376, 517
Maxwell AFB, 330, 517
Mayes, Benjamin, 235
Mayfield, 41, 517
May Friendship Day, 269, 517
Maynard, 314, 517
Mayor Bloomberg, 480
Mayor Pro-Tem, 285, 517
McAdoo, 268–69, 314–15, 335–36, 517
 Emma, 269
 married Hilton, 268
 Matt, 147
McClenton, Patricia, 392
McClure, Bobbie, 68, 76
McClurkin, Donnie, 263

McCollum, 315, 517
McConnell Road, 436, 438, 517
McCormick, Steve, 150
McCulloch Street, 15, 517
McCullough, Nicole, 213
McDonalds African American Achievement Entrepreneur Award, 287, 517
McDonald's owners/operators, 449, 517
   first black, 449
McDougle, 159–60, 487, 517
McGibbony, Billie, 29
McGriff, Jimmy, 253
McKee, 136–37, 315, 351, 368, 517
   Jonathan, 136, 413
   Loretta F., 412
McKee's football teams, 136, 517
McLaughlin, 97, 233, 287, 485, 517
   Len, 222
McLendon, Darius, 150
McLenn, Eddie, 337
McNair, 315
McNair School, 517
   Ronald E., 403
McNeil, Joseph, 90
McNeill HOF-Coach, 517
   Frank R., 414
McPherson, 193, 485
McTier, Peggy, 29
MEAC (Mid-East Athletic Conference), 141, 146, 281, 517
MEAC Commissioner Dennis Thomas, 141
MEAC institutions, 281, 517
MEAC's First Fulltime, 281, 517
Meadows, 517, 536
   Robert, 70
Meares Bible Study Circle, 517
   Essie B., 216
Mebane, Flora, 209
Mechanical College, 30, 47, 52, 201, 232, 517
Mechanical Engineering, 473, 517
Mechanized Infantryman, 125
Mecklenburg County, 16, 517
Medal of Corps, 318
Medgar, prestigious, 287
Media Center, 396
Media Company Executive, 483
Medicaid card, blue, 444
Medical Careers and Services, 471

Medicare and Medicaid Services, 418
Medicine Academy, 474
Meharry School, 274, 517
Melbourne-Palm Bay New, 342
Melvin, 304, 309, 315–16, 320, 413
Melvin C. Swann, 37, 517
Melvin Municipal Office Building, 295, 517
Member Alumni Band, 289
member Jerell Khazan, 204, 517
Memorabilia, Dudley, 187, 475, 489
Men, Dudley, 152
Mendenhall, 7, 517
   George C., 8
   Richard, 7
Mendenhall Plantation, 9, 493, 517

Mendenhall Plantation Home Place, 493, 517
mental Wellness Lead, 342
Mentors Association, 289, 517
Men-Tors Association, 289, 517
Mercy, 264
Meritorious citations, 330
Meritorious Service Awards, 335, 342
Meritorious Unit Citation, 417
Merriam-Wester English Learner's Dictionary, 409, 517
Mervyn, 475
Metcalf, George R., 95
Methodist, 45, 517
Methodist Adventures in Negro Education, 488
Methodist Church, 21, 24, 517
Methodist Church in Warnersville, 35, 517
Methodist Episcopal Church, 17, 21, 38
Methodist Women, 269, 517
Metro Boys Basketball Selection, 370
Metropolitan Opera, 241, 517
Metropolitan Opera's program, 241, 517
Mexican American War, 303, 517
Meyer's Department, 69, 91, 517
Mia Lassiter Medlock, 250, 517
Mia Michelle Evans, 210, 517
Miami Dolphins, 373, 517
Miami Heat, 385, 517
Michael Springs, 392, 517
Mickens, Chris, 213
Middle, Lincoln, 268
middle class African American families, 425
Middle College, 167–68, 173, 467, 472
Mid-East Athletic Conference. *See* MEAC
Midnite Starr, 260
Mid-Year Graduating Class, 488
Miles Davis, 257, 434
Military Action/WAR, 304
Military Hall of Fame, 292, 318
Military History, 484
Military History Quarterly, 482
Military Medicine Program, 291
Military Officer, 491
Military Outstanding Unit Award, 342
Military Outstanding Volunteer Service, 342
Military Police, 305, 313
military service, 33, 282, 284
Millennium Edition, 92, 488
Miller, Ronald, 69, 494
Miller Basketball Most Valuable Player, 477
Millsapp, 230
Millsapp's bands, 230
Millsapp's tenure, 230
Milton, Davis, 210
Minister of Music, 244
Minnesota, 348–49, 351–52
Minor League, 382
Mint Hill, 449
Miss Dudley, 70, 193, 269
Miss Dye, 102, 111, 113–15, 117, 246
Miss Dye's direction, 114
Miss Francine McAdoo, 493
Miss Georgene Dye, 493

Miss Homecoming, 488
   elected, 474
Missile Maintenance Group, 341
Missionary Department, 53
Missionary Ministry, 411

Miss Lola McAdoo, 205
Mister David Moore, 331
Mitchell, 210, 316, 321
mixture of whites, 103
mixture of whites and blacks, 103
MLB expansion team, 281
Mobile Army Surgical Hospitals Courtesy UNCG Digital Library, 416
mobile Bounce House, 452
Mockingbird, 239–40, 252–53
Mocking Jay Part II, 471
Model Academic Excellence, 91
Modern Dance, 75, 158, 208
Modern Dance Company, 77
Modern Dance Group, 102, 114–15
Modern Dance Program, 398
Modernist movement in school planning and design, 81
Modernized Disability System, 445
Modern Navy, 327, 478
Modern Style, 60, 64
Modern War Studies, 480
Moja Health, 409
Monroe, 152, 309
    Larry, 152–54
Monroe High School, 114
Monticello-Brown Summit Elementary School, 170
Mont Zion, 432
Moore, 19, 26, 289, 316, 475, 485, 492
Moore, 23-Tyler, 150
Moore, Bobby, 13
Moore, Charles, 19, 26
Moore, Charles H., 39
Moore, Charlie, 13
Moore, Lillie, 436, 438
Moore Biography, 483
Moore Gym, 359
Moorehead, 316
Moore school, 15
Moore's Gym, 61
Moore's Gymnasium on A&T State University's Campus, 80
Morehead, 150, 271, 316, 480
    David, 271
    Peter, 131
Morehead High School, 143–44
Morehead-Simkins Independent Living Center, 271
Morehouse, 409
Morehouse College, 425
Morgan, 221, 224–27, 260, 303, 326
Morgan, James, 289, 326, 474
Morgan, Leroy, 439
Morgan's strut, 225
Morgan State University, 235
Morningside Homes, 56, 74, 452
Morningside Homes Family, 248
Morningside Homes Projects, 56, 248
Morrisette, Alanis, 260
Morrow, Calvin F., 326
Moseley, 380–81
    Emanuel, 147
    Emmanuel, 380
Moses Cone Hospital, 64, 77

Moses Cone Memorial Hospital, 474
Moses James, 309
Most Outstanding Player, 402
Most Outstanding Senior Athlete, 473

Most Valuable Player for Rice football, 356
Mother Alberta Boyd, 536
Motivational Seminar, 84
Mountain Home Air Force Base, 291
MOUNT WHITNEY, 314
Mount Zion, 30
Mount Zion Baptist Church, 116, 398
movie, first Hunger Games, 471
Mozambique, 447
MSgt James Savage, 330
MSgt Nevada Jarrell, 330
MSgt Savage, replaced, 330
MS-Systems Engineering Analysis, 340
Mud Tap Johnson, 413
Mulatto, 297
Mulattoes, 297
Mulberry Bush, 253
Murfreesboro, 146
museum
    living history, 435
    received International Civil Rights, 278
museum.greensboro.edu, 479, 490
Museums Division, 488
Music/AV Cataloger, 475
Music Festival, 218
Music Liturgical Arts, 216
Musicor, 240
Musiq Soul Child, 265
MVP, 356, 362, 375, 476
    named Women's Softball, 358, 476
MVP Braxton Williams, 143
Myers, Lynn, 102
Myers Park Country Club, 260

K

K-12 education, 468
Kaelin Brown, 367
Kaffir Boy, 396
KAGB-FM radio station, 424
Kamala Harris, 123
Kamensky, Jane, 485
Kansas, 301, 334, 480
Kansas City Chiefs, 381
Kansas City Roster, 383
Kansas City Royals, 382
Kansas Colored, 301
Kansas Colored Volunteers, 301
Kappa Alpha Psi Fraternity, 141, 340
Kappa Kappa Psi Honorary Band Fraternity, 230
Kari Parker, 365, 367
Kathleen, 306
Kathryn Turrentine Stanley, 276
Kathy R. Hairston College, 450
KATHY ROUSON HAIRSTON, 449
Kathy Rouson Hairston HOD, 414
Katz, Jeff, 249
Kaye Frances, 320
Kee, John P., 262
Keep the faith of your fathers, 179
Kee's New Life Community Choir, John P., 262
Keianna Mims, 364, 367
Keith, Toby, 239
Kelly, Bobby, 257
Kendall, Gene, 347
Kendall Penniegraft, 367
Kennedy, Andy, 385
Kennedy

A PLACE WHERE SUCCESS WAS EXPECTED: FINAL EDITION

Knight, Ella, 196
Knight, Gladys, 428
Knighton Stanley, 479
Knoxville, 488
Korea, 315, 325, 416–17
Korean MASH units, 416
Korean Service Medal, 417
Korean War, 313, 416
Korean War Nurse, 486
Korean War Weaver, 321
Korean War Williams, 322
Koredell Bartley, 150, 154
Kpeglo, Jackie, 456
Ku Klux Klan, 57
Kuwait, 335

L

Laboratory Corporation, 476
labor force, primary, 30
Labor Relations, 357
Labor Statistics, 479
Lackland Air Force Base, 332
La De Dah, 253
Ladies, Dudley, 107, 122, 127, 341
Lady Panthers Field Hockey Team, 101
Lady Panthers Track Team, 110
Lady Sertoma Club, 287
Lake, Sadie, 328
Lake Brandt area, 37
Lake Erie, 298
Lakewood High School Band, 229
Lamancha, 200
Lambert, 314, 488
Lambeth-drums, Joe, 105
LAMONTE PRESSLEY, 377
Lane, Jackie, 198
Lane Drug Store, 69
Langston Hughes, 74
Langston Wood, 154
Lanier, Beverly, 197
Laquonda Oboe, 210
Larkin Streets, 18, 440
Larry F. Lewis, 162, 172
Las Amigas, 269
late Governor James Holshouser, 281
Latin I & II, 75
Laughlin, Bobby, 105
Laurean Davis, 213
Law Clerk, 292
Lawrence, Huey, 225
Lawrence Otis Graham, 201
Lawson, Brenda, 392
Lawson, Brittany, 392
lawyers, white, 234
Lazelle Free, 209, 211
Lazelle Free Army ROTC, 495
Leader Pack, 340
Lead Office Support, 404
Leaksville, 143
Learning Hub, 124
Learning Hub Champion, 124
Lee, Carl, 313
Lee, Debra, 483
Lee, Joe, 319
Lee, Kenneth, 96–97, 485
Lee, Stephen, 202
Lee, Tommy, 315

Lee, Wilton, 316
Lee Ella Williams Cheek, 42
Lee's honors, 421
Lee Street, 94, 216
Lee Woodruff, 306
Le'Ezra Brown, 153–54
left Atlantic Starr, 249
left Chapel Hill, 149
legacy, historical, 166
Legacy Section, 492
Legion Club, 433
Legrand, Patricia, 162
Leite Rio, 385
Lemuel Alson, 319
Lenwood Clark, 322
Leonard Medical School, 40
Lesley, George, 323
Levine Children's Hospital, 449
Lewis, David, 308
Lewis, Jonathan, 249
Lewis, Nancy, 209
Lewis, Rick, 106
Lewis, Willie, 231
Lewiston, 235
Lewis Wilson, 312
liberal arts colleges, 65
Liberal Arts/Electives, 75
liberty, 5, 175, 177, 256
Licensed Practical Nurse, 77
Licht, David, 257
Life Sciences, 397
Lillie Moore's son, 436
Lillie Morehead Moore, 436
Lilly, Michael, 13
Limuel Andrew, 306
Lin Buie-tenor, 105
Lincoln, Abraham, 52, 93
Lincoln Heights areas, 94
Lincoln Junior High, 186, 235
Lincoln Junior High School, 12, 59, 70, 77, 94, 98–99, 109, 228, 235, 345, 347
Lincoln Junior High School's Band, 188
Lincoln Middle School, 166, 186, 463
Lincoln's Junior High School students recall, 208
Lincoln Street, 109, 457
Lincoln Street View, 83
LINDA MCDOUGLE, 159
Linda Wilson, 159
Linda Wilson McDougle, 159
Lindsay Street, 433
Lindsay Street School, 19, 46–47
Lindwood J, 304
Lineberry, 100, 225, 274, 491
Lions' Assistant Director, 352
LISA JOHNSON-TONKINS, 288
Lisa Renee Richardson HOD, 414
Lisé Timmons Mclaughlin, 170
Little League, 282
Live Nation, 263
Liverpool, 253
Living Legends Foundation Award, 425
Livingston, 25
Livingston College, 15
Livingstone College, 11, 51
Livonia, 371
Lloyd Norris, 309
Local guitarist Carlos Morales, 257
local Hayes Taylor YMCA, 334

Logan, Hattie, 113
Logan Speight, 366–67
Lola Anne McAdoo, 269
Lola McAdoo, 369, 412, 492
Lola Wilson Hayes, 241
Long Hospital, 69
Long Leaf Pine, 217, 281
Lonnie Reynolds, 139, 390
Lorcey Henderson, 35, 48
Lord Dunmore, 296
Los Angeles, 428
Los Angeles Lakers, 350
Louis, John, 308
Louis Clyde Hudson, 349
Louisiana, 93, 298–99, 301
Louisiana Battalion, 303
Louisville head coach Rick Pitino, 385
Lowell Curtis Pye Sr, 262
Lowenstein-Atkinson Architects, 82
Loyal Fans, 407
Lt, Reginald R., 318
Lt Col Ronald Murphy, 330
Lt Col Thomas Clarke, 330
Lt Col Wayne Davidson, 330
Lucien Manuel, 321
Lula Belle Houpe, 216
lunches, reduced, 468–69, 478
Lunsford, 40
Luther Vandross' rendition, 200
Luvenia Turner, 29
Lyman, 213
lynching, 34
    passed resolutions condemning, 34
Lyndsay, 314
Lynn, 117, 164, 211, 262, 479, 484
Lyrics and Music, 199
Lyric Watkins, 365–67

M

MacGregor, 297, 484
Machines Clay, 309
MACK Scholar, 405
Maco, 312
Maco Beauty College, 432
Ma Coley, 107
Macomsom's classes, 138
Macomson, 138, 185
Mae, Lula, 317
Mae Sue Henry, 355, 493
Magic, Orlando, 376
Magic Johnson, 374
magistrates, 288
Magnolia House, 432–35, 479
Magnolia House Motel, 432, 475
    businesses-, 432
Main Building, 50, 60–63, 70, 83, 167, 201, 460, 463, 535, 538
    historic, 456
    original, 60, 463
    three-tiered, 50
Main Dudley Gymnasium, 61
Main Gym, 83
Main Gymnasium, 61, 82–85, 177, 187, 456, 458
    award-winning, 456
Major Contribution, 195
Majorette, Dudley, 122
majorette boots, 476

Majorette Coach, 410
majorette instructor/advisor, 117
majorettes and cheerleaders, 110
majority of students, 467–68
Major League, 281, 349
Major League Baseball, 348
Major League Baseball Amateur Draft, 382
Major League Baseball Hall of Fame, 281
Makkhar Ndiaye, 375
Malachi House, 285
Malaysia, 420
Male Athlete, 152, 340
Malois, 248
Malone, Marsha, 392
Manana Barracks, 326
man- Charles Moore, 19
Manhattan, 374
Mankind Award, 279
Manufacturing, 294
Marché Clark, 413
marches, daily, 277
Marching Band, 77, 125, 186, 190, 223, 228–30, 238, 396–97, 405, 408, 474
    high-stepping, 112
Marching Band and Dudley's AFJROTC Unit, 409
Marching Band and Pep Band, 426
Marching Band I, 75
Marching band of Thunder, 126, 230, 396, 405
marching order, 1
Marcus Gause Emagzine- High Point Discovered, 487
Mardi Gras Parade, 229
Margaret Tynes, 237
Margo, 16, 465–66, 484
Margold Report, 94, 485
Margold's report, 95
Margolin, 258
    Bob, 257
Marian Wright Edelman, 123
Marie's Grill, 432
Marine, 297, 304–7, 310–13, 315, 317–23, 337, 476, 480
Marine Commandant William Ward Burrows, 297
Marine Congressional Medal, 318
Marine Corps, 308, 312, 316, 323–24, 337, 485
Marine Corps Achievement Medal, 338
Marine Corps Jefferies, 312
Marine Corps' Magnetism Beckons Future General, 490
MARINE CORPS SP4, 324
Marine Logistics Group, 338
Marine Logistics Group II Marine Expeditionary Force, 487
Marine platoon, 297
Marine Security Guard, 312
Marion, Francis, 297
Marion's guerrillas, 297
marketplace, competitive, 432
Market Street, 187, 432, 440
Mark Fields, 409, 456, 467
Mark Lewis Fields, 409
Marques Douglas, 147
MARQUES LAMONT DOUGLAS, 373
Marriott International, 420
Marsallis Prescott, 212
Marshall, 37, 96
Marshals, Dudley, 473

A PLACE WHERE SUCCESS WAS EXPECTED: FINAL EDITION

Marshals, Junior, 107–8, 121–22, 127, 167, 393, 418, 425, 474, 494
Marta, Alma, 170
MARTHA CROCKETT DICK, 396
Martin, 167, 297, 314, 336
   Frank, 385
   Jim, 229
   John, 297
   Walter, 127
Martin Luther King Blvd, 28, 99, 517
Martin Luther King Jr, 277, 517
Martin-Oates, 127, 517
Martin Robinson Delany, 301, 517
Martin Street, 434, 517
Martinsville, 225
MARVIN H, 135
MARVIN LAMBERT, 142, 517
MARY ELIZABETH, 250
Mary Evans, 473, 517
Maryland, 96, 235, 336, 339–40
Maryland case, 96
Maryland law school, 96, 517
Maryland's law school, 96, 517
Mary Lou Goins, 13, 517
Mary Louise Anderson, 111, 517
MASH, 416
MASH units, 416, 517
Mason, Bernard, 219
Masonic Mentoring Group, 125
masonry, 62, 75, 140, 158
masonry term, 55
Masons, 52, 517
Massachusetts, 22, 297, 301, 357, 517
master, young, 9
Master Achiever, 445
Master Key, 249
Master Musician, 129, 259–60, 517
Master of Education degree, 163
Master of Engineering Physics Degree, 334
master's degree, 35, 37, 156, 159, 235, 237, 339, 343, 395, 397, 447
Master Sergeant, 331, 338
Master Teacher- Mentor for new science teachers, 398
Mata, Alma, 186, 394
Mathabane, 517
   Marc, 396
Math Building, 82, 517
math instructor, 474
Math Open School, 517
Math Open School and Dudley's membership, 159
math proficiency, 169
Matkins, 517
   Tom, 105, 486
Matthew Elijah, 309, 517
Mattie Donnell Hicks, 415, 486, 489, 494, 517
Maurice D., 310
MAURICE D, 125
Maurice Drake, 113, 517
Mavericks, 376, 517
Maxwell AFB, 330, 517
Mayes, Benjamin, 235
Mayfield, 41, 517
May Friendship Day, 269, 517
Maynard, 314, 517
Mayor Bloomberg, 480
Mayor Pro-Tem, 285, 517
McAdoo, 268–69, 314–15, 335–36, 517

   Emma, 269
   married Hilton, 268
McArthur, 315
McCain, 315, 517
   Franklin, 89–90
   Helen, 29
   Matt, 147
McClenton, Patricia, 392
McClure, Bobbie, 68, 76
McClurkin, Donnie, 263
McCollum, 315, 517
McConnell Road, 436, 438, 517
McCormick, Steve, 150
McCulloch Street, 15, 517
McCullough, Nicole, 213
McDonalds African American Achievement Entrepreneur Award, 287, 517
McDonald's owners/operators, 449, 517
   first black, 449
McDougle, 159–60, 487, 517
McGibbony, Billie, 29
McGriff, Jimmy, 253
McKee, 136–37, 315, 351, 368, 517
   Jonathan, 136, 413
   Loretta F., 412
McKee's football teams, 136, 517
McLaughlin, 97, 233, 287, 485, 517
   Len, 222
McLendon, Darius, 150
McLenn, Eddie, 337
McNair, 315
McNair School, 517
   Ronald E., 403
McNeil, Joseph, 90
McNeill HOF-Coach, 517
   Frank R., 414
McPherson, 193, 485
McTier, Peggy, 29
MEAC (Mid-East Athletic Conference), 141, 146, 281, 517
MEAC Commissioner Dennis Thomas, 141
MEAC institutions, 281, 517
MEAC's First Fulltime, 281, 517
Meadows, 517, 536
   Robert, 70
Meares Bible Study Circle, 517
   Essie B., 216
Mebane, Flora, 209
Mechanical College, 30, 47, 52, 201, 232, 517
Mechanical Engineering, 473, 517
Mechanized Infantryman, 125
Mecklenburg County, 16, 517
Medal of Corps, 318
Medgar, prestigious, 287
Media Center, 396
Media Company Executive, 483
Medicaid card, blue, 444
Medical Careers and Services, 471
Medicare and Medicaid Services, 418
Medicine Academy, 474
Meharry School, 274, 517
Melbourne-Palm Bay New, 342
Melvin, 304, 309, 315–16, 320, 413
Melvin C. Swann, 37, 517
Melvin Municipal Office Building, 295, 517
Member Alumni Band, 289
member Jerell Khazan, 204, 517
Memorabilia, Dudley, 187, 475, 489

Men, Dudley, 152
Mendenhall, 7, 517
   George C., 8
   Richard, 7
Mendenhall Plantation, 9, 493, 517
Mendenhall Plantation Home Place, 493, 517
mental Wellness Lead, 342
Mentors Association, 289, 517
Men-Tors Association, 289, 517
Mercy, 264
Meritorious citations, 330
Meritorious Service Awards, 335, 342
Meritorious Unit Citation, 417
Merriam-Wester English Learner's Dictionary, 409, 517
Mervyn, 475
Metcalf, George R., 95
Methodist, 45, 517
Methodist Adventures in Negro Education, 488
Methodist Church, 21, 24, 517
Methodist Church in Warnersville, 35, 517
Methodist Episcopal Church, 17, 21, 38
Methodist Women, 269, 517
Metro Boys Basketball Selection, 370
Metropolitan Opera, 241, 517
Metropolitan Opera's program, 241, 517
Mexican American War, 303, 517
Meyer's Department, 69, 91, 517
Mia Lassiter Medlock, 250, 517
Mia Michelle Evans, 210, 517
Miami Dolphins, 373, 517
Miami Heat, 385, 517
Michael Springs, 392, 517
Mickens, Chris, 213
Middle, Lincoln, 268
middle class African American families, 425
Middle College, 167–68, 173, 467, 472
Mid-East Athletic Conference. *See* MEAC
Midnite Starr, 260
Mid-Year Graduating Class, 488
Miles Davis, 257, 434
Military Action/WAR, 304
Military Hall of Fame, 292, 318
Military History, 484
Military History Quarterly, 482
Military Medicine Program, 291
Military Officer, 491
Military Outstanding Unit Award, 342
Military Outstanding Volunteer Service, 342
Military Police, 305, 313
military service, 33, 282, 284
Millennium Edition, 92, 488
Miller, Ronald, 69, 494
Miller Basketball Most Valuable Player, 477
Millsapp, 230
Millsapp's bands, 230
Millsapp's tenure, 230
Milton, Davis, 210
Minister of Music, 244
Minnesota, 348–49, 351–52
Minor League, 382
Mint Hill, 449
Miss Dudley, 70, 193, 269
Miss Dye, 102, 111, 113–15, 117, 246
Miss Dye's direction, 114
Miss Francine McAdoo, 493
Miss Georgene Dye, 493
Miss Homecoming, 488

elected, 474
Missile Maintenance Group, 341
Missionary Department, 53
Missionary Ministry, 411
Miss Lola McAdoo, 205
Mister David Moore, 331
Mitchell, 210, 316, 321
mixture of whites, 103
mixture of whites and blacks, 103
MLB expansion team, 281
Mobile Army Surgical Hospitals Courtesy UNCG Digital Library, 416
mobile Bounce House, 452
Mockingbird, 239–40, 252–53
Mocking Jay Part II, 471
Model Academic Excellence, 91
Modern Dance, 75, 158, 208
Modern Dance Company, 77
Modern Dance Group, 102, 114–15
Modern Dance Program, 398
Modernist movement in school planning and design, 81
Modernized Disability System, 445
Modern Navy, 327, 478
Modern Style, 60, 64
Modern War Studies, 480
Moja Health, 409
Monroe, 152, 309
   Larry, 152–54
Monroe High School, 114
Monticello-Brown Summit Elementary School, 170
Mont Zion, 432
Moore, 19, 26, 289, 316, 475, 485, 492
Moore, 23-Tyler, 150
Moore, Bobby, 13
Moore, Charles, 19, 26
Moore, Charles H., 39
Moore, Charlie, 13
Moore, Lillie, 436, 438
Moore Biography, 483
Moore Gym, 359
Moorehead, 316
Moore school, 15
Moore's Gym, 61
Moore's Gymnasium on A&T State University's Campus, 80
Morehead, 150, 271, 316, 480
   David, 271
   Peter, 131
Morehead High School, 143–44
Morehead-Simkins Independent Living Center, 271
Morehouse, 409
Morehouse College, 425
Morgan, 221, 224–27, 260, 303, 326
Morgan, James, 289, 326, 474
Morgan, Leroy, 439
Morgan's strut, 225
Morgan State University, 235
Morningside Homes, 56, 74, 452
Morningside Homes Family, 248
Morningside Homes Projects, 56, 248
Morrisette, Alanis, 260
Morrow, Calvin F., 326
Moseley, 380–81
   Emanuel, 147
   Emmanuel, 380

A PLACE WHERE SUCCESS WAS EXPECTED: FINAL EDITION

Moses Cone Hospital, 64, 77
Moses Cone Memorial Hospital, 474
Moses James, 309
Most Outstanding Player, 402
Most Outstanding Senior Athlete, 473
Most Valuable Player for Rice football, 356
Mother Alberta Boyd, 536
Motivational Seminar, 84
Mountain Home Air Force Base, 291
MOUNT WHITNEY, 314
Mount Zion, 30
Mount Zion Baptist Church, 116, 398
movie, first Hunger Games, 471
Mozambique, 447
MSgt James Savage, 330
MSgt Nevada Jarrell, 330
MSgt Savage, replaced, 330
MS-Systems Engineering Analysis, 340
Mud Tap Johnson, 413
Mulatto, 297
Mulattoes, 297
Mulberry Bush, 253
Murfreesboro, 146
museum
    living history, 435
    received International Civil Rights, 278
museum.greensboro.edu, 479, 490
Museums Division, 488
Music/AV Cataloger, 475
Music Festival, 218
Music Liturgical Arts, 216
Musicor, 240
Musiq Soul Child, 265
MVP, 356, 362, 375, 476
    named Women's Softball, 358, 476
MVP Braxton Williams, 143
Myers, Lynn, 102
Myers Park Country Club, 260

N

NAACP (National Association for the Advancement of Colored People), 94–96, 107, 109, 273–74, 278, 282, 286–87, 482, 485
NAACP Hall of Fame, 425
NAACP membership and voter registration, 97
NAACP's Legal Defense Fund, 96
NAACP's plan, 274
Nabrit, James, 96
named Bennett Hall, 22
named James Benson Dudley High, 49
named James Benson Dudley High School, 5, 232, 537
naming of A&T's College of Health and Sciences, 450
NANCY BAKER CARREE WILSON, 243
Nancy Wilson-Designed, 243
NANNIE MCADOO-DICK, 270
Nannie McAdoo-Dick Media Center, 270
NASA, 423
NASA Langley Research Center, 423
NASA SPACE, 423
Nash, 296, 485
Nashville, 65
Nat Greene Award for community contributions, 271
Nathalya Daniels, 364–67

National Alumni Association, 205, 368, 412
National Alumni Service Award, 289
National Association for the Advancement of Colored People. *See* NAACP
National Association of School Architects, 82
National Band Director's' Consortium, 230
National Black Music Collegiate Gospel Choir Competition, 245
National Board-Certified Teacher, 399
National Board of Directors for National Symphony Orchestra, 421
National Call for Moral Revival, 286
National Caucus of Black State Legislators, 290
National Center, 469, 481, 489
National Championship, 369
National Conference for Community Justice Brotherhood/Sisterhood Citation Award, 279
National Defense Medal, 340
National Defense Service Medals, 331, 333, 336, 417
National Education Association, 36
National Football League, 373
National Geographic Learning, 486
National Historic Site, 26
National Honor Society, 107, 127–28, 340–41, 347, 356, 393, 397, 418, 425, 473–74, 476
National Honor Society Induction Fall, 126
National Human Services Honor Society, 404
National Military Command Center, 335
National Museum of American History, 282
National Negro Business League, 431, 493
National Park Service, 478
National Peach Bowl Parade in Atlanta, 229
National Political Congress of Black Women, 475
National Postal Mail Handlers Union, 289
National Prominence-Bennett College, 489
National Register, 1, 29, 82, 463, 536
National Register Criterion, 81
National Register of Historic Places criteria, 2
National Scholar-Athlete, 356, 476
National Semifinals, 375
National Social Work Honor Society and Omicron, 404
National Symphony Orchestra, 421
National Theaters, 43
National Women's Law Center, 421
nationwide, science teachers, 423
Native American populations, 46–47, 465
Native Americans, 8
Native American students, 47
Native name Library of Congress Location Washington, 491
Nat Turner insurrection, 7
Naval Academy, 314, 334, 336
Naval Academy Minority Association, 340
Naval Enlisted Scientific Education Program, 334
Naval Operations, 334
Naval Operation's Strategic Studies Group, 335
Naval War College in Newport RI, 335
Navy Achievement Medal, 340
Navy B-1 Band, 328
Navy Band, 219, 224, 226, 475
    first all-African American, 328
Navy Band B-1, 481
Navy Chaplains, 317
Navy Commendation Medal, 340
Navy forms, 220

Navy hospital ships, 416
Navy Hyman, 312
Navy in November, 220
Navy shipyard, 325
Navy's School of Music, 220, 327
NBA career, 350
NBA career average, 350
NBA championship, 376
NBA Draft, 350, 370, 376
NBA Hall of Fame, 350
NBA Summer League, 385
NCAA, 375
NCAA Division, 281, 354, 387
NCAA Division I-A Player Defense Statistics-2011, 486
NCAA ranks, 354
NC Arts Council, 261
NCA&T, 282
NC A&T, attended, 433
NCA&T Alumni Association, 284
NC A&T Employer, 473
NCA&T Joint School, 393
NC A&T Sports Hall of Fame, 473
NC A&T State University, 40, 358, 364
NCA&T students, 393
NCA&T Women's Basketball Program, 359
NC Central School of Law, 284
NC Coaches Association, 137
NCCU music instructor and daughter, 241
NC Democratic Party, 261
NC education spending on decades-long slide, 479
NCHSAA, 137, 149, 364
    crowned, 403
NCHSAA boys state titles, 143
NCHSAA Centennial Celebration, 362
NCHSAA championship, 151
NCHSAA Female Athlete, 361–63
NCHSAA Pictures, 153
NCHSAA Regional Award, 143
NCHSAA state championship game record, 151
NCHSAC, 130, 133, 136–37
NCHSSA Class, 149
NC NAACP, 286
NC Preps' All-State Player, received, 386
NC Retired Governmental Employees Association, 216
NCSAA Black History, 488
NC schools re-emerges, low-performing, 478
NCSHAA, 152
NCTA, 421
Neal, Jimmy, 131
Neal, Johnathan, 150
Neal, Pat, 150
Neal, Robin, 102
Neal, Whitney, 392
Nebraska, 368
Negro Bishops, 38
Negro Business, 123
Negro City Schools, 214
Negro Education, 488
Negroes, 5, 7–8, 15, 17, 23–24, 26, 38–40, 44–46, 48, 50–51, 53–55, 155, 301, 303, 462
    bellum, 5
    intelligent, 5
Negroes of Rhode Island Genealogy Trails, 479
Negro graded school, 19
Negro High School, 37, 232, 482
Negro High School Division, 37

Negro hospital, 39–40
Negro leadership, 95
Negro League, 281
Negro National Anthem, 484
Negro Race, 484
Negro Regiments, 301
Negro soldier, 302
Negro Women, 107, 269
Nehemiah, 320
neighborhoods
    affluent, 28
    black, 18, 103, 375, 431, 440
    earliest planned, 27
    exclusive, 41
Nelle Artis, 58–59, 473
Nelle Artis Coley, 73, 107
Nellis Air Force Base, 343, 346
Nelson, 316
NELSON MACOMSOM, 138
Nelson Macomson, 139
Nepal, 291
Nettles, 316
Neuse Mental Health Clinic, 418
Nevada Jarrell, 331, 399, 493
Nevada Jarrell HOD & Robert, 414
New Age Beverages, 424
Newark, 128
New Artist, 263
New Beginnings Christian Fellowship, 243
New Breed, 485
Newburgh, 284
new Field House, 487
New Hanover County, 51
New Jersey, 128, 424
New Jersey City University, 128
New Kent County, 466
New Life Community Choir, 262
New Light Missionary Baptist Church, 293–94
New Market Heights, 302
New Orleans Saints, 373, 377–78
Newport, 334
Newport RI, 335
News & Record, 137, 428, 479, 487, 492
Newton, 316
New Year's Day, 155
New York, 22, 94, 237, 241, 253, 296, 374, 480–83, 485, 487, 490–91
New York City, 239, 245, 264
New York City- Harlem, 238
New York City Landmarks Preservation Commission, 446
New York City Opera, 237
New York College, 236
New York Daily News, 480
New York Jets, 373
New York Public Library, 485
New York Public Library Digital Gallery, 493
New Zion Missionary Baptist Church, 28, 205, 410–11
NFL and College Football Hall of Fame, 354
NFL Draft, 369, 377, 379, 381, 389
NFL Enshrinement Speech, 132, 487
NFL Europe team, 373
NFL Hall, 134
NFL Pro Football Hall of Fame, 353
NFL Rookie, 352
NFL's Special Teams Coach, 354
Nicholson, 252, 264

A PLACE WHERE SUCCESS WAS EXPECTED: FINAL EDITION

Nicknamed Sweet Lou, 350
Nilijah Darden, 364–67
Ninth Grade Academy, 63, 167
Ninth-Grade Program Coordinator, 164
Nishel Alphonso, 319
Nocho, 41
    Jacob R., 41
Nocho Community, 41–42, 50
Nocho Park, 37, 41, 103, 479
Nocho Park Community, 54, 409
Noelle Millner, 364, 366–67
Nolan, Francis, 157
Non-Commissioned Officer (NCO), 331
Non-Commissioned Officer Leadership Academy, 332
Non-commissioned Officers Leadership School, 332
non-profit United Way Agency, 285
non-profit United Way Agency in Greensboro, 285
nontraditional roles, 390, 415
Norfolk, 326
Norfolk New Journal, 58
North America, 296
North Annex, 62–64, 456
North Carlina, 143
North Carolina, 1–3, 5–10, 17–20, 23, 25–26, 30–31, 33–38, 51–52, 54–57, 96–98, 168–69, 216–17, 278–81, 292–94, 463–65, 467–70, 478–80, 482–84, 490–92, 494–95
North Carolina Association, 396
North Carolina A&T, 146, 224
North Carolina A&T College, 55
North Carolina A&T College students, 219, 326
North Carolina A&T State University, 93–94, 141–43, 230, 232, 237–38, 268, 276–77, 292, 294, 343, 394–96, 400–401, 403, 449–51, 473–75
North Carolina A&T State University Board, 271
North Carolina A&T State University Dallas/Ft, 441
North Carolina A&T State University Gate City Alumni, 268
North Carolina A&T State University Marching Band, 481
North Carolina A&T State University School, 393, 473
North Carolina A&T State University's Sports Hall, 360
North Carolina Auto Mechanics State Competition, 138
North Carolina Central University, 109, 159, 216, 270, 288, 335
North Carolina-Chapel Hill, 278
North Carolina Coaches Association, 129
North Carolina Democratic Party, 290
North Carolina Department, 281, 283, 335
North Carolina Drama Competition, 208
North Carolina Gatorade Track, 362
North Carolina High School Athletic Association, 133
North Carolina High School Athletic Conference, 132–33
North Carolina High School Track, 362
North Carolina Home Schools, 485
North Carolina Nursing History, 486
North Carolina Policy Watch, 470, 490
North Carolina Press, 480, 490
North Carolina Recreation, 281

North Carolina-Rocky Point, 225
North Carolina School, 395
North Carolina School System, 478
North Carolina's Common Schools, 6
North Carolina's Pearsall Plan for school desegregation, 98
North Carolina Sports Hall, 350, 353
North Carolina Standard, 6, 486
North Carolina state exam, 51
North Carolina State House, 290
North Carolina State University, 123, 280, 348, 404, 421
North Carolina Teachers Association, 107
North Carolina Teaching Fellow, 403
North Carolina War Savings Committee, 33
North Charleston, 479
North Church Street, 17
North Cincinnati, 45
Northeast Greensboro, 285
Northern District of Illinois, 220
Northern Lutherans, 17
Northern Presbyterian Board, 18
Northern Soul, 240
Northern Virginia, 475
North Forbis Street, 25
Northwest High School, 166
Nosco Wright, 131
noted gospel singer Isaac Carree, 243
NPS-2007, 340
Nuclear Deterrence Service Medal, 342
Nurse Corps, 317
Nursing Service, 68
Nxumalo, 23, 51–53, 486
Nyenwance Johnson, 210

O

Oakey Springs Baptist Church Cemetery, 466
Oakland County, 353
Oakland Raiders, 354, 379, 484
Oakley, 130
    Lloyd, 131
    Mike, 105
Oak Ridge, 293
Obituary Charlie Foxx, 486
Occupational Safety, 475
Occupational Statistics, 470, 489
off-Broadway, 237
Officer Sam Penn, 215
Ogburn, 317
Ogden Air Logistics Complex, 341
Ohio Players, 260, 428
Ohio's Capitol, 298
Okinawa, 338
Okoro, Kenny, 147
Old Ashe Street School, 35
Old Dixie Conference, 141
Old Dominion University, 423
Old-Fashioned Hamburgers Franchisee, 445
Old Lace, 208
old Lincoln Junior High School, 460
Old Media Center, 459
Old Negro Spirituals, 205
Old North State Council, 282
Old North State Council Boy Scouts of America, 125
old time Dudley Pride, 170
Ole Dudley High Spirit, 441

Ole time Dudley Spirit, 172
Oliver Hazard Perry, 298
Olympian, 371
Olympic size pool, 395
Omega Psi Phi, 284
Omega Psi Phi Fraternity, 222, 333, 475
Omeshia Bowens, 213
Omicron, 404
One-On-One Personal Care, 443
On-site Construction Manager, 459
opened Phillip Weaver Education Center, 158
Open House, 459
Operation Desert Shield, 331
Operation Enduring Freedom, 337
Operation Enduring Lt, 322
operations of Scoop Zone, 452
Operation Transparency's Protection Brigade, 294–95
Oprah Winfrey, 266
Oral Roberts University, 294, 474
Orange Bowl Game, 368
Orange County, 173, 278, 370
Orchestra I, II, III, 75
Orchestra's Christmas Recital, 77
Organizational Excellence Award, 342
organized Trinity AME Zion Church, 17
Original Architectural Drawing, 50, 491
original Charles Hartmann design, 63
Original Script, 489
Original Shiloh Baptist Church, 440
original Trinity AME Zion, 440
Orlando, 170, 229
Orlando Music Festival, 218
Orrell, 317
Osbey Smith, 43
Oscar Robertson Awards, 385
Otis Hairston Jr, 272
Otis Redding, 255
Out-door State Track, 364
Out-door Track, 152
Out-door Women's Track & Field State, 366
Outstanding Instructor, 332
Outstanding Public Service Award, 291
Overseas Short Tour Ribbon, 331
Owens, Cedric, 92
Owens, Nancy, 13
owners, wealthy slave, 8
Oxford, 480
Oxford Companion, 480
Oxford Handbook, 485
Oxford University Press, 480
Ozan Korea, 338

P

Pacesetter's coach Charlie Brown, 361
Pacific Coast League, 348
Pacific Tea Company, 431
Padres, 348
Pageant, Dudley, 405
Page High School, 146, 161, 166, 170–71, 468, 473
Page Senior High School, 157, 391
Paige McKinney, 367
Palace Theater, 18, 43, 432, 440
Palace Theatre, 43

Palgrave Macmillan, 488
Palmer, 317
Palmer Building, 25
Palmer Memorial Institute, 24–26, 47, 54, 59, 201, 232, 398
Pam Doggett, 361, 363
PAM DOGGETT, DUDLEY HIGH SCHOOL, 362
Pamela Fruster Stewart, 194
Pamela Fruster Stewart HOD, 414
Pamela M. Truesdale, 426, 493
Pamela Stewart, 218, 400
Pamela Truesdale profiles, 493
Pan American Junior Championships, 362
Pankey, Larry, 13
Pantherette Coach, 410
Pantherettes, 111–13, 115, 117, 190, 192–93, 223, 226, 399, 401, 473, 478
    high-kicking, 112
Pantherettes-Article, 486
Pantherettes Squad, 401
Panther Kids Wrestling, 144
PANTHER mascot, 397
Panther Pride, 91, 128
Panthers, 143, 146, 149, 151–52, 156, 183, 185, 361, 364, 478–79, 482, 485–86, 493–94
    former, 402
    mighty, 183
Panthers, Carolina, 377, 381
Panthers, Dudley, 149, 152, 364
Panthers Basketball Team, 402
Panther's claim, 152
Panther's Claw, 159, 181, 204, 395, 478–81, 485, 487–89, 491, 536
PANTHER'S CLAW, 474
Panther's Claw Newspaper, 89, 187, 394, 396, 425, 486
Panther's Claw News Paper, 483
Panther's Claw Staff, 473
Panther's Claw Yearbook, 218
Panthers football team, 379
Panthers for Christ Organization, 405
Panthers in Nontraditional Roles, 415
Panther Spirit-Article, 486
Panthers senior QB Jahmier Slade, 151
Panthers to state titles, 146
Panthers' winning, 152
Panther Yearbook, 92, 119, 396, 479, 488, 490
parade routes, 189, 407
Paragon Restaurant, 26
Parent Advisory Council, 293
Parental support, 361, 408
parents in Warnersville, 11
Paris, 201, 229, 299, 392
Park City, 350
Parker, 21, 45, 317
Parks, Rosa, 26
Parks & Rec Department, 225
Parks Society, 281
Parliament-Funkadelic, 428
Parochial schools, 17, 19, 45
Parsons, 220–22, 303, 326
    James B., 326, 489
Parsons' Induction, 220
Partnership Village, 216
Pass-Miller, Natalie, 435
Past Chairman, 289
Past Master, 278

A PLACE WHERE SUCCESS WAS EXPECTED: FINAL EDITION

Patrol Coastal Squadron, 307, 340
Patterson, Veda, 536
Pattillo High School of Tarboro, 161
Paula, Melba, 395
Paul Charles, 305
Paul Laurence Dunbar, 31, 74, 481
Paul Laurence Dunbar High School, 57
Paul Maurice, 313
Paylor, 267
    Kathryn, 70, 412
Payne, 488
P-Diddy, 265
Peabody Graded School in Wilmington, 51
Peacemaker, Carolina, 22–23, 29, 486–87, 489, 492
Peacemaker Award, 273
Pearl Garrett Bradley, 238
Pearlie, 304
Pearsall Plan, 98
Pearson, 96
Peay, 317
Peck Elementary, 289
Peeler, 35, 37, 462
    Abraham H., 35
    principal, 36
    Reverend Silas A., 49
Penn, 214–15, 221, 475
Pennix, 317
Pennsylvania, 14, 51, 325, 333, 417, 481
Pentagon, 335
People's Church, 277
Peoples Congregational United Church of Christ in Washington, 277
Pep Band, 187, 426
Pep Club, 115
PepsiCo, 424
Percussionist & Actor, 264
Percy Street, 19, 24
Percy Street School, 16, 19–20, 46
Performing Arts, 454
Performing Nursing Duties, 494
Perkins Jimmy Rogers, 258
Perry, William, 317
Perry Group Publishers, 478
Perry's African American, 298
Perry's death, 298
Perry Windell, 321
Persian Gulf, 320
Peru, 127
Peter's Auto Mall on South Main Street, 384
Pete W. U, 314
Petition, 80, 487
Pettiford, Raymond, 326
Pettiford-1961, Harvey, 280
Phi Delta Theta, 422
Phi Kappa Mu, 404
Philander Priestley Claxton, 53
Philanthropy, 449
Philathea Missionary Circle, 108
Phillips, Joseph, 249
Phillips University, 332
Phi Mu Alpha Sinfonia Music Fraternity, 230
Phoenix, Pam, 102
photographer André Adolphe Eugéne Disdéri, 299
Phyllis Martin, 167
physical education, 75, 116, 134, 142, 161, 354, 398, 449, 493
physical education teachers, 115–17

pianist Clark Stern, 255
piano, 105, 213, 245, 248, 259, 264, 406, 454, 475
Piano Lesson, 212–13, 259
Pickard, Nathaniel, 210
Pickens, Gloria, 76–77
Pickett, Wilson, 428
Picture Courtesy Panther Yearbook, 139–40
pictured Howard Stewart, 280
Pictures Courtesy of B-1 Navy Band, 326, 328
Piedmont area, 8, 229
Piedmont Natural Gas, 434
Piedmont Press, 478
Pierce, Bryan, 262
Pinehurst, 336
Pinetop, 258
Pi Omicron Omega Chapter, 427
Pioneers, Dudley, 348
pioneers, young, 347
Pips, 265, 428
Pitt, Edward, 91
Pittsburg, 382
Pittsburgh Courier, 434
Pittsburgh Steelers, 354, 356–57
Pittsburg Steelers, 379
Place Best Band, 125
plans, freedom of choice, 100
Plaque Ceremony, 164
Platt, 317, 338–39
    Gwen, 102
played opposite Omari Hardwick, 267
player Fred Neal, 80
Players, Harrison, 419
Plaza Manor Hotel, 434
Pleasant Garden, 30, 48
Pleasant Garden School, 48
Pledge, 175, 177
Pless Edward Morrison, 216
Plessy, 96
Plessy decision, 93, 95
Plessy vs, 93
Plymouth Congregational United Church of Christ in Detroit, 277
Point Guard on Dudley's Girls Basketball Team-Coaches, 410
Policy Watch, 478
Polish league All-Star Game, 385
Political Mojo, 485
political newcomer Bill Knight, 285
Polpak Swiecie, 385
Pomona, 30
Pomona Nursery, 30
Pomona Terra Cotta Company, 30, 271
Pomp, 394
Pone Jones Billiards, 432
Poole-1939, 280
Poor, Salem, 297
Poor People's Campaign, 286
Poplar Grove, 11
Poplar Grove School, 175
popularity, international, 254
Pop Warner, 380
Port Hudson, 301
Posed Forms- Pictorial, 494
position
    city council, 285
    first head coaching, 402
    first teaching, 51
    fortified Confederate, 301

Postal Retirement Club, 289
Postal Service in Greensboro, 337
Post-Civil War, 45
Post Civil War Education, 10
Post-Squadron Command Resiliency, 341
post-World War II period, 94
Powell, 186, 476
    Richard, 150
    Teddy, 424
Powell's compilation, 186
Power Five, 387
Power Five Colleges and universities, 387
Powers Boothe, 422
Practical Nursing, 75
Presbyterian Church, 17, 45
Presbyterian Church on Church Street, 41
Presbyterian Women mission communicator, 216
Preservation Greensboro, 433, 440, 479
preservationgreensboro.org/the- secrets-of-nocho-park- clinton-hills-and Benbow-park, 479
Preservation North Carolina Conference, 463
Preservation Society, 536
president, national, 281
President, Samet, 124
President Abraham Lincoln, 300
President- Black Child Development, 70
President Davis, 303
President Senior Year, 125
President Truman, 56
Presley, 317
Pressley, 317, 340, 377–78
Preston, Billy, 254
Pre-Veterinarian Medicine, 395
Price, 35–37, 59, 67, 77, 143, 188, 228, 460–62, 536
Price building, 462
Price in Rowan County, 463
Price Junior High School, 242
Price Lyceum, 463
Price Middle School, 477
Price Oral History Project, 488
Price School, 12, 20, 36, 48, 77, 175, 228, 461–63, 479, 488, 490
Price School Scrapbook, 20–21
Price's teams, 143
Price Teacher, 490
Prieto, Jorge, 106
Prince Hall Grand Lodge, 278
Prince Hall Masonic Family, 125
Princeton, attended, 372
Principal Franklin Brown, 101
principal Larry Lewis, 162
principal Tony Watlington, 399
Prison Ministries, 28, 339
private Trinity Hospital for Negroes, 39–40
private Trinity Hospital for Negroes in Detroit, 39
Pro Bowl, 352
produced Inez, 240
producer Luther Dixon, 240
Professional Theater, 265
Professional Women, 123
Pro Football Focus, 379
Progressive National Baptist Convention, 273
Project Analyst, 476
Project Homestead, 107
Project Team, 170, 270
Prom, Dudley, 122
Prom Jennifer, 202

Prom Queen, 202
Protection Specialist, 475
Proud Tradition, 489
Providence Baptist Church, 17, 107, 179, 215, 225, 237, 285
Providence Service Guild, 108
Provisional Chair, 427
Proximity, 28
PSAT, 133
PTA Board, 204
PTA leader, 204
PTSA Executive Board, 123
PTSA President, 205
Public Domain, 491
Public Education of Black Boys, 487
Public graded school for African American students, 47
Puckett, 355, 487
Punk Rock Day, 193
Purcell, 322
Purple Heart, 333
Put-In-Bay, 478
P-Valley, 264
Pythagoras, 125

Q

Quadra soul, 236
Quaker Friend, 14
Quaker pacifist Richard Mendenhall, 9
Quakers, 7, 9, 11, 17, 45, 47
Quaker-style home, 9
qualified teachers, 22
quarterback Jahmier Slade, 149
Quarter Sessions, 8
Quentin Crosby, 144–45
questioned Cousin Reather Belle Tyler, 466
Quick, Amos, 483, 492
quoted Winston Churchill, 292

R

race groups, 18
race relations, local, 35
Rachael Leigh Coo, 422
Racial tension, 81, 90
Radio Operator Avery, 304
Ragsdale High School in Jamestown, 144
Raiders, 379–80
Raiford, Ernest L., 58
Railway Express Agency, 42
Raleigh-Durham, 397
Ralph Lee, 323
Rambert, 318
Ramel Keyton, 388
Ramert, Reggie, 382
Ramseth, 291, 487
Rankin Elementary School, 405
Raphael, 296, 487
Ravens, 373
Ray, Hannah, 172
Ray Crosby, 407, 413
Ray Leo, 313
Raymond Brian Crosby HOD, 414
Rayshawn, 318–19
Ray Warren Homes, 74
RB (Robert Bingham), 131, 150

A PLACE WHERE SUCCESS WAS EXPECTED: FINAL EDITION

Rear Admiral Gene Kendall, 478
Rear Admiral Kendall, 334–35
Received Jack Gibson Trophy, 473
Reconciliation Commission, 425
Reconstruct Democracy, 481
Recreation Department, 281, 358, 476
Recruiting Colored Regiments, 301
Recruitment Committee Chairperson, 360
Red Cross, 291–92
Red Cross Club, 331
Redistricting, 133
Red Scare, 34
Reeder's Family, 404
Reese, Mary F., 113
Reeves, 290–92, 318, 487
    hospital equipment, 291
    legal work, 291
    Reginald, 290
Regan's Street, 17
Regency Room, 203
Regent University in Virginia Beach, 339
Reginald, Johnson, 493
Reginald N. Johnson, 265, 484
REGINALD R, 290
Regional Command, 337
Regional Commissioner's Citation, 445
Registered Nurses, 77, 473
Rehoboth Methodist Church, 185
Reid, Governor David S., 490
Reidsville, 57, 258, 443
Rena Bullock Reunion, 13, 494
Rena Bullock School, 12, 59, 77, 175, 494
Rena Bullock School's First Grade Class, 12
Reprisal, 297
Republican National Convention, 52
Republican Party, 52, 93
Republicans, 93, 285, 472
    northern, 300
Republic of Vietnam, 333
Research Triangle, 397, 401
restaurants, first McDonald's, 449
Returning home, 95
Reunion Yearbook, 477
Reverend Amos Quick, 489
Reverend Cecil Bishop, 177–79
Reverend Frank Tigg, 49
Reverend Hairston, 272
Reverend Joseph Oscar Foster, 238
Reverend Otis Hairston, 177
Revolutionary War, 296, 298
Revolution's Black Soldiers, 487
Rhode Island, 297
Rhode Island Genealogy Trails, 479
Ricardo, 318
Rice College, 356
Rice University, 134, 348, 356, 476
Richard, Gayle, 76
Richard Alan Fields, 418
RICHARD ALAN FIELDS, 418
Richard Bowling, 260, 280
Richard Fields, 494
Richard Harold, 323
Richard Henry, 313
Richardson, Christopher, 212
Richardson Hospital, 68, 77, 259, 415, 424, 470, 535
Richardson Memorial, 19

Richardson Memorial Hospital, 40, 68, 75, 201, 409, 432, 473–74
Richardson's family, 41
Richmond, 4-Jaylan, 150
Richmond, David, 89–90
Richmond County and Reidsville, 443
Richmond Senior, 143
Richmond's tenure, 218
Rick Redwine, 319
rides, underprivileged women, 427
Rings, Heaven, 214
Rivera, 316
Road Island, 298
Roberson, 318
Roberta, 320, 490
Roberta Clarke, 113
Roberta Washington, 446, 490
Robert Benson, 307
Robert Bingham. *See* RB
Robert Butler, 365–67
ROBERT CARL JARRELL, 405
Robert Jarrell, 451, 454, 493
Robert Jarrell Jr, 454
Robert Lee, 304, 311
Robert Lynn, 311
Robinson, Jackie, 232, 348, 434
Robinson, Ursula, 414
Robinson, Wayne, 161
ROBINSON BURWELL, 242
Robinson Burwell, Thelma S., 414
Robinson Street, 224
Rochester, 353
Rocket ball, signature, 451
Rockies, 341
Rockingham County, 8, 57, 536
Rocky Mount, 257, 409
RODNEY DOWE WESTMORELAND, 402
Rodney Wilds, 169, 390
Rodriguez, 294–95, 494
    Joseph, 12
Roebuck, 431
Roethlisberger, 379
Roger Charles, 313
Roger F. U, 312
Roger H. Lake, 328
Rogers, Gladys F., 58
ROGER WADDELL, 324
role models, 116, 129, 147, 248, 259, 270, 368
Rolling Stones, 253, 258
Romero, Daniel, 106
Romie Russell, 314
Ronald McDonald House, 376, 449
Ronald Stewart, 319
Rookie Year, 389
Roosevelt, 309, 311
Roper, Ella, 51
Rosa Jeffries, 113
Rosa T. Yourse, 74, 493
Roselyn Roberson, 111
ROTC, 284, 318, 331, 333, 341, 343, 346, 482
    state university, 333
ROTC instructor, 211, 325
ROTC Instructor N, 308
ROTC Program, 290, 332
ROTC uniforms, 167
Rowan County, 463
Royal Governor, 296
Roy H. Lake, 326, 328, 475

Ruff, Sylvia P., 15
Rufus C. U, 306
Russell, Ruby, 113
Russia, 385
Ruth, Julia, 492
Rylee Jackson, 367

S

Sable Arm, 480
Sacramento City College, 332
Sacred Dance, 116
SACS (Southern Association of Colleges and Schools), 164
Safety Patrols, 474
Sain-bass, Wayne, 105
Saint Matthews United Methodist Church, 495
Saints, 243, 267
Saints and Sinners, 267
Salem, Peter, 297
Salmasek, 487
Salomé, 237
Salt Lake City, 372
Salutatorian, 166
Salvation Army, 342
Samet Corporation, 124
Sam Pass, 435
Sam Pass time, 434
Sampson County, 51
Samson's Drug, 432
Samuel Benjamin Jones, 40
Samuel Junius, 308
Samuel Martin, 305
Samuel Penn, 214, 317, 475
Samuel Penn Pass, 215, 435
Samuel Stuart, 321
Samuel Wilson, 305
Sanai Wells-Scott, 367
Sanders, Charles A., 483
Sanders, Charlie, 78, 132, 134, 147, 351, 353, 485
San Diego Padres, 348, 382
Sandifer, 318
Sandra & Daisy, 248
San Francisco Opera, 241
sang senior Tanya Williamson, 211
Santiago California Cooper, 306
Sapp, Marvin, 263
Sarasota, 355
SASI, next, 330
Saslow's Jewelry, 69
Satchell Paige, 281
Saunders, 160
Save Dudley, 289, 407, 409, 425, 456, 460, 462, 473, 535–36
Scales' Pool Room, 439
Scholar recognition, 404
Scholarship Board, 332
scholarship endowments, 450
scholarships, athletic, 355, 473
School Administration, 123, 161, 169, 400
School Board Member, 70
school for Negro children, 20, 47
SCHOOL for NEGROES, 45
School Merger, 162
School's Gymnasium, 90
School Spirit Committee, 115
School Supply Give-a-Way, 384

School Support Administrator and AIG Director for GCS Gifted, 171
School Treasurer, 404
Schott Foundation for Public Education, 487
science, physical, 54, 395, 397
Science and Math Open School and Dudley's membership, 159
Science Building, 62–63, 456
Science Center Saturday Academy, 394
Science Club Secretary, 449
Science Department, 398
Science Department Chairperson and Master Teacher- Mentor, 398
Scoop Mobile, 452–53
Scoop Zone, 451–53
Scoop Zone's success, 452
Scott, James B., 326
Scott Manring, 257
Seagraves, 154, 402
    Shawn, 150
Seaman, 307, 312, 317
seamstresses, 42, 58, 116, 433
    local, 201
Searcy, Jarvis, 311
Sears, 431
seasons Denorris, 403
Seasons Mall, 452
seating, balcony, 43
Seattle Washington, 382
Sea World performance, 229
Sebastain, Carl, 308
Sebastian, 39–40
SECJ (Student Executive Committee for Justice), 91
Secondary Principal, 169
Secondary School Study News Bulletin, 72, 489
Second Class, 310
Second Confiscation Act, 300
Second Edition, 195–207, 536
Second Fleet, 314, 334
Second-team all-NBA, 350
Second Ward, 163
Second Ward Consolidated High School, 164
Second Ward School, 164
Secret Lovers, 249
Security Team, 125, 289
Sedaka, Neil, 253
Segall, 57, 490
segregation
    laws legalizing, 93
    legal, 31, 34
    occupational, 33
    outlawed public school, 98
Seifert, Heather, 456
Self-Motivation, 91
self-reliant, 432
Selig, 296–97, 299, 487
Semi-conductor, 329
Seminary, Bennett, 11, 21–22, 24, 28, 30, 37, 45–46, 48, 155, 158, 232, 296, 303
Seminary and High/Normal school, 39
Seminary/College, Bennett, 22, 38, 172, 303
Senadzi Rankin, 365–67
Senior Citizens, 412
senior class activities, 123
Senior Class President, 356, 418, 476
Senior Class Representative, 394
Senior High School, 49

A PLACE WHERE SUCCESS WAS EXPECTED: FINAL EDITION

Senior High School for whites, 55
Senior Modern Dancers, 118
Senior Practical Nursing Class, 76
Senior Professional, 357
Senior Professional in Human Resources (SPHR), 357
Senior Safety Patrols, 54, 393–94
Senior Statistics, 486
Sentinel Boys, 257
Serenitie Johnson, 365–67
Service Army Reserves Burnett, 305
Service Force/National Guard, 312
Service Johnson, 313
Service Querida-Quinn/Hoyes, 323
SGA Advisor, 123
Shabazz, Betty, 123
Shabbat Service, 489
Shamalia Carpenter, 365
Shamilia Carpenter, 367
Shannon Stewart Minor, 218, 473
Sharonda Breeden, 210
Shatarra, 121
Shaw, 134, 297, 302, 488
   Mia, 150
   Michael, 152, 154
   Micheal, 153
Shaw & Donnelley, 297
Shaw & Donnelly, 297
Shaw Air Force Base, 332
Shaw University, 30, 40, 47, 75, 196, 235, 273, 394
   attended, 51, 272
Sheik Johnson, 345
Shell Competition, 106
Shell's Eco-marathon, 487
Shelton Williams, 226, 228, 473, 490
Sherman's invasion, 302
Shevon Sanders, 213
Shiloh Baptist, 273
Shiloh Baptist Church, 28, 273, 495
Shipman, 286–87, 443–44
   Gladys, 286, 485
   Gladys L., 443
Shipman Family, 443
Shipman Family Home Care, 286, 443–44, 490, 493
Shipman's office, 287
Shoe Project, 114
Shoe Rebuilding, 282
Shoffner, Jackie, 13
Shoffner, Ted, 196
Shop Steward, 289
Shrine Bowl, 146, 379
Siera, Joe, 488
Sierra Leone, 296
Siger, Johnny, 124
Sigma Pi Phi Fraternity, 284
Signing Day, 377
Siler, Natalie, 213
Silver Streak Taxi, 432
Simkins, 274–75, 482
   George, 89
   George C., 274, 482, 492
   honor George C., 275
Simkins Elementary School, George C., 482
Simkins Sr, George C., 274
Simon, Carly, 239
Simone, Nina, 238

Simon Powell Sebastian, 40
Simpson, Brad, 105
Simpson, Chuck, 105
Simpson, Thelma, 222
Sims, Patty, 102
Singapore & Hong Kong, 378
singer, hundred noted jazz, 238
singer/guitarist David Lewis, 249
singer Michel'le Toussaint, 267
singer Roland Hayes, 241
sing for Atlantic Star, 260
single parent families, underprivileged, 376
Single Season Shot Block Record, 385
Single's Ministry, 339
Sirera, 149, 488
Sir Henry Clinton, 296
Sirley Craven, 113
Sister Haygood, 248
sister Helen Cheek Dean, 42
sister Inez, 252
sisters Beula, 536
Site-Based Leadership Committee, 123
Site Coordinator, 393
Sit-in Movement, 89, 204, 286
Skateland, 371
skating, speed, 371
Skylight Restaurant, 432
Slackson label, 429
slaves, escaped, 299
SLICK SLACK, 428
Slick Slack Johnson, 494
SlickSlackShowGram, 494
Smith, 19, 80, 98–99, 134, 170–71, 223, 230, 318–19, 465–66, 488
   57-Braxton, 150
   Jonathan, 153–54
   Sandra, 76
Smith-1966, Daryl, 280
Smith administrators, 101
Smith College in New England, 65
Smithfield, 233
Smith Funeral Home, 439
Smith High School, 98–99, 230, 391, 457, 464, 468, 471
Smith High School Classmates, 492
Smith Magazine, 143
Smith Senior High School, 100
Smithsonian, 282
Smith University, Johnson C., 109, 161, 259–60
Smith University's Alumni Centennial Award, Johnson C., 109
Snake River Valley, 291
SNCAE (Student Association of Educators), 360
Snow Hill, 161
Social Action, 400
Social Club, 114, 201, 393
Social Security Administration, 445
Social Studies Department Co-Chairperson, 164
Soft Case Dad Hats, 441
Sondra Kathryn Wilson, 484
Sonja Gail Westmoreland Cobb, 410
Sonja Gail Westmoreland Cobb HOD, 414
Son Tong City, 338
Sophomore Choir, 494
Sophomore Class, 187
Sophomore/Freshman Orientation, 186
Sophomore Orientation, 187
sophomore Pam Doggett, 361

sophomore season, 375, 379
Soul Stepping, 481
Sound, Carey, 255
South Africa, 221, 424
South Africans, 424
South Annexes, 62–64, 456, 536
South Ashe Street, 16
South Carolina, 138, 146, 233, 297, 328, 340, 388, 433, 479, 481, 488
South Carolina State, 359
South Central Idaho District Health Department, 292
Southeast Asia in Thailand, 420
Southeastern Region AME Church, 445
Southeast Greensboro, 28, 273, 409
Southeast Guilford County, 12, 479
Southeast Middle School, 168
South Elm-Eugene Street, 28
Southern aristocracy, 7, 465
Southern Association, 55, 164
Southern Association Accreditation, 56
Southern Association of Colleges and Schools (SACS), 164
Southern Baptist Theological Seminary, 338
Southern Bell, 470
Southern Christian Leadership Conference, 229
Southern Democrats, 93
Southern Durham High School, 474
Southern Educational Society, 17
Southern Education Society, 21, 45
Southern elementary schools, 483
Southern Historical Collection, 97, 492
Southern Negro, 483
Southern Post-Civil War Educational Society, 45
Southern Republican Party, 93
Southern school districts, 468
Southern singer/songwriter, 349
Southern states, 10, 45, 296, 466, 468
Southern whites, 66, 465–66, 468
South Main Street in High Point, 384
South Stairwell, 54
southwest, 30, 337
Southwest Asia Service Medal, 336
Space Discharge Systems, 329
Space Shuttle, 423
Spanish Club, 121, 169
Spartan accommodations, 417
Spartanburg, 146, 433
Spaulding, 319
Spears, Aaron, 154
Special Assistant, 334
Special Collections, 40, 327
Special Dudley Black History Edition, 479, 489
Special Education Teacher, 128, 165
Special Programs Coordinator, 164
Special Teams Coordinator, 354
Spencer, Joseph, 308
Spencer Davis Group, 253
SPHINX, 313
SPHR (Senior Professional in Human Resources), 357
Spinks, Gwendolyn, 494
Spinks' husband, 121
Spirit Committee-Member, 331
Spirit week, 193
Spoleto Festival, 237
sponsored local unions, 52
sponsoring Little League Teams, 449

Spoon, Tracy, 105
Spoon River Anthology, 208
sports, played, 368
Sports and Educational Hall of Fame/Distinction, 278, 360, 371, 373
Sports and Educational Hall of Fame/Hall of Distinction, 117
Sports Development Director, 378
Sports Dreams, 285
Sports Hall of Fame/Hall of Distinction, 413–14, 476, 483, 492–93
Sports Hall of Fame on October, 385
Sports Medicine, 161
spot, head coaching, 146
Springfield, Dusty, 239
Springfield College, 161
Sprinkle, 319
Spruill, 319, 358–59, 476
SSA's Modernized Disability System, 446
staff, first teaching, 155
Stage Band and Orchestra, 486
St. Agnes Catholic, 46
St. Agnes Catholic Church, 538
St. Agnes Catholic Church building, 25
St. Agnes Catholic Church School, 47
Stahle Vincent, 134, 147, 356–57, 413
Stalmasek, Scott, 159
standards, high academic, 347–48
Standford, 443
Standing-Reginald Whitsitt, 412
Stanley Frank Lifetime Achievement Award, 285
Stanley Johnson, 121, 166, 395
Star Basketball Game, 143
Star Game, 143
starred Vincent Whitt, 421
Star-Spangled Banner, 175
Starting Halfback, 473
Starz, 264
State & Psychiatric Hospital Compliance Collaborative, 418
State Baseball Champions, 137
STATE CHAMPIONS 3A MEN'S, 154
State Championship Basketball Team, 421
State championship game, 143
State Championships, 66, 130, 136, 143, 152, 347, 364, 386, 441
    back-to-back, 143
    first, 476
State Championship Team, 131–32, 398
State Champions Women's Indoor & Outdoor State Track, 367
State Democratic Party, 273
State Houses, 93
State Indoor & Outdoor Track & Field, 364
State Legislator, 89, 277, 465
State Normal Schools for Coloreds in other, 23
State Playoff, 130, 133
State Softball Team Tournament, 360
state Supreme Court, 233
Statesville, 149, 216, 364, 494
State University, attended Winston-Salem, 267, 400
State University Army ROTC division, 290
State University Marching Band, 188
St. Augustine, 229
Stax Records, 424
Steel Construction, 82
Steele, Reverend Wilbur F., 49

A PLACE WHERE SUCCESS WAS EXPECTED: FINAL EDITION

Steering Committee, 123, 280
St. Elizabeth College, 128
STEPHANIE QUERIDA QUINN, 341
Steptoe & Johnson, 420
Sternberger, Emanuel, 41
Sterne Library, 475
Steven Davis, 146, 148, 150, 380, 487, 492
Steven Davis II, 148, 152–54, 492
Stewart, Charles, 218
Stewart Air Force base, 284
St. James Baptist Church, 405
St. James Presbyterian Church, 19, 216
St. James's Presbyterian Church, 41
St. Louis, 52, 333, 348, 350
St. Louis Cardinals, 348–49
St. Louis Hawks, 350
St. Mary, 537
St. Mary's Catholic School, 42
St. Mary's Parish School, 49
St. Mathews Methodist Church, 82
St. Matthews, 27
St. Matthews United Methodist Church, 21, 27, 35
Stockard, 7–8, 10, 488
Stoneville High School, 143
St. Petersburg, 229
Strachan, Calvin, 117
strategist, 70
Stratford, 319
Strayhorn, Billy, 238
Strong Leadership, 155, 204
Struthers Tap, 114
St. Stephen, 282
St. Stephens Church, Pastor Paul Morton's Greater, 262
St. Stephen United Church, 282
Stubblefield, 319
Student Association of Educators (SNCAE), 360
student-athletes, 123, 474
Student-Athletes, Dudley, 347
student body, assembled, 87
student body president, first elected, 87
Student Bus Drivers, 181–82, 494
student conductor, 405
student drivers, 181
Student Election, 157
Student Executive Committee for Justice (SECJ), 91
Student-Faculty game, 105
Student Government Association, 92, 123, 488
  elected, 91
Student Government Organization, 396
Student Government President, 91
Student Manifesto, 488
Student Practical Nurses, 68
students, first UNC-CH, 278
students David Alaya, 106
Students Recall Beloved School/Rena Bullock School Served Black, 479
Student Support Plans, 393
style
  crowd-pleasing, 223
  unique, 221
success of Dudley's extracurricular AVT Team, 469
successor Lori Bolds, 119
Success Personified, 232
Sue R&B, 253
Sue Records, 239
Summer Band Camp, 408
Summerfield Elementary, 169
Summerfield Elementary School in Summerfield, 169
Summers, Lenora, 76
Sunday, established College Church, 216
Sunday best, 201
Sunday Company, 2
Sunday school classes, 17
Sun Valley Charitable Foundation, 291
Super Bowl Champion, first, 378
Super Bowl LIV, 381
  watched, 380
Super Bowl XLIV, 378
superintendent, first Guilford County, 46
Superintendent Advisory Representative, 123
Superintendent Fred Archer, 48
Superintendent Phillip Weaver, 135
Superior Court, 288
Supreme Court Case, 93
Supreme Court decision, 93
Surface Navy Association, 340
Surface Warfare Officer School in Newport, 334
Surviving Compton, 267
Survivor's Remorse, 267
Sussex Records, 424
Sustained Outstanding Contributions, 445
Swahili, 409
Swamp Fox, 297
Swann, 37, 320
  Barbara, 101–2
Swanson, 311
SWC all-time record, 356
Sweeney, 320
Sweet Dreams, 261
Sweetheart Song, 215, 221
Sweet Holy Spirit, 243
Sweet Holy Spirit Church, 243
Sweet Little Jesus Child, 205
Sweet Lou, 350
Sweet Lou Hudson, 491
Sweet Shoppe, 439
Swift Meat Packing Plant, 466
Swinson, 320
Sylvania Rogers, 13
Symphonic Band, 397
Symphonic Orchestra, 396

T

Tabu Productions, 424
Tactical Air Command NCO Leadership School, 332
Taj Mahal, 239, 460
Take Home Carry, 439
talented Barbara Weathers, 249
Talented Program, 171
Taliferro, 316
Talladega College, 274, 475
Talmadge, 316, 318
Tampa Bay Buccaneers, 368–69, 373
Tampa Florida, 125
Tank Platoon Leader, 333
Tanya Legette Lassiter, 250
Tanzania Washington, 364–67
Tap Dance Kid, 283

Tarboro, 161
Tarheel Junior Historian, 480
Tar Heel Junior Historian, 489
Tar Heel Junior Historian Association, 480
Tar Heels, 34, 375–76
Tar Heel Triad Girl Scout Council, 279
Tarpley, John, 44, 395
Tarpley, John A., 48, 54–55, 58, 66, 70, 172, 280
Tarpley and other, 155
Tarpley's duties, 56
Tarpley's focus on nontraditional roles, 390
Tarpley's graduation, 390
Tarpley's leadership, 156
Tarpley's strategizing, 70
Tarpley Stadium, 226, 489
    John A., 86
Tarpley's tenure, 390
Tashawn Neal, 154
Tate, 134, 320
    Blanche, 196
Tau Beta Sigma National Band Sorority, 230
Tau Omega Chapter, 475
Taylor, James, 239
Taylor, Malcolm, 212
Teacher Leadership, 127
teaching Radio, 156
teaching Radio and electronics, 156
TeachMeHowToPlayPiano@gmail.com, 455
teach music, 214, 391
Teague, Jane, 165
Team All-America, 376
Team Darfur, 372
Team Douglas Properties, 373
teammates, 101, 363
T-E-A-M Yea Team, 184
Tea Room, 91
Technical College, 23, 48, 50, 53, 61, 81, 284
Technical State University, 19, 30, 52, 125, 244, 337, 403
Technologies, 471
Technology Academy, 164
Technology Department, 401
Teddy P Lounge, 424
Teen Singers, 216
Telindus BC Oostende, 385
Temple Emanuel, 293, 489
Temptations' rendition, 200
Tennessee, 14, 65, 302, 381, 388, 488
Tennessee Sports; Titans; Volunteers, 373, 379, 388
Tequilla Jackson, 367
Tequille Jackson, 153, 365–66
Terra Cotta Company, 30
Terra Cotta Heritage Foundation, 490
Terrance Oates Kameron, 154
Terrence Jr, 127
Terror Expeditionary Medal, 340
Terrorism Service Medal, 340
Texas, 37, 294, 356, 376, 476, 490
Thadford, 322
Thailand, 420
Thayer, 22
    Edward O., 49
Thayer Administration, 22
Theater, Carolina, 43, 238
THELMA LIVONIA SPRUILL, 242
Thelma Livonia Spruill Robinson Burwell, 487

Thelonious Monk, 238
Theodore C. U, 313
Theolis Edward, 305
Theria Glover, 392
Thespians, 167, 208, 210–11
Thespians, Dudley, 77, 185, 208, 210–11, 239, 247, 394, 419, 474, 476, 484
Thespians' advisor, 211
at the Wells, 248
Thigpen, 284
Thomas, James, 131
Thomas, Michael, 392
THOMAS EDISON ALSTON, 348
Thomas Franklin, 313, 318
Thomas Gavin, 327
Thomas Jefferson, 314
Thomasville, 12
Thompson, Andrew, 412
Thompson, Christine, 59
Thornton, 489
Thui Romah, 106
Thurgood Marshall Lifetime Achievement Award, 425
THURMAN, 324
Thurston, 319
Tigernet.com, 483
Tigers, Raleigh, 281
Tilden Foundations, 485
Tillery Deroy, 320
Timmons McLaughlin, 170–71
Timmons Mclaughlin's leadership, 171
Title IX enforcement procedures, 358
Tiyette Neal, 222
TJC (The Joint Commission), 418
TOC & Medica National Guard Pettiford, 317
Tolbert, 430–31, 489
TOMKINS, 288
Tommie Abner, 314
Toni Cameron, 246–47
Toni Cameron Vincent, 246
Tonkins, Ashley, 213
Tonkins HOF, Tiffany V., 414
Tony Watlington, 162, 164, 413
Torah, 537
Torino gold medal, 372
Torino Winter Olympics, 372
Toronto Canada, 418
Torpey, 470, 489
Toshumba, 320
Totton, 320
Tour of Duty Evans, 308
Tour of Duty/Vietnam, 311–12, 316–19, 321
Townes, Doris M., 194
Townsend, 320
Toyin Afeila, 212
Track Director & Vertical Jumps, 153
track teams, 142, 364, 370, 403, 441
Trademark Office, 329
Transfer Portal, 388
Transition Liaison, 404
Transportation Services, 287, 334
Treasury Department, 173
Trevon Humphrey, 150
Triads favorite mobile ice cream parlor, 451
Trial Lawyers, 284
Trinidad, 298
Trinity, 18, 440
Trinity AME Zion, 18
Trinity AME Zion Church, 17, 178–79, 294

A PLACE WHERE SUCCESS WAS EXPECTED: FINAL EDITION

Trojanowski, 415–16, 489
troops, black, 297, 302, 480
Trophy, Cheyenne, 342
Troxler, 320
Troy, 22
Troy State University, 343
Truesdale, 426, 476, 489
Trulove-trumpets, Fred, 105
Trumpet Co-Section Leader, 125
Trumpet Section- Dudley High School Marching Band, 125
Trustee Emeritus, named, 421
Trustees, former Greensboro College, 100
Tuckahoe, 224
Tulsa, 439
Turkey, 294
Turner, Tina, 253, 434
Tuskegee Airmen, 325
Tuskegee Experiment, 325
Tuskegee Institute, 325, 431
Tuskegee Vietnam, 313
Tyla Gamble, 365, 367
Tylei Woolard, 154
Tynes, 179, 237, 320
    Baccalaureate speaker Reverend Morris H., 178
    Reverend Morris H., 178–79
    Victor, 99
Tyson, 321

U

UGA Library Retrieved, 480
Uhuru Bookstore, 268
Ulysses, 321, 323
UMOJA Male Step Team, 265, 397
UMOJA Male Step Team Advisor, 396
Unborn, 176
UNC Chapel Hill, 328, 425
UNC-Chapel Hill, 348
UNC-Chapel Hill School of Medicine, 409
UNC-Charlotte, 170
UNC-CH Branch, 278
UNCG, 30
UNCG and NCA&T Joint School of Social Work, 393
UNCG Board, 284
UNCG Digital Collection, 494
UNC-Greensboro, 348
uncle Prentiss Bennett, 127
UNC Press, 478
UNC record, 375
UNC's law school, 97
undefeated teams- Dudley, 130
Underground Railroad, 9, 287
unincorporated community of Pomona in Guilford County, 30
Union Army, 299–300, 480
Union Flag, 302
Union forces, 299
Union for Experimenting Colleges and Universities, 236
Union Memorial Church, 412
Union Memorial United Methodist Church, 268–69
Union Memorial United Methodist Church Kindergarten Service Award, 269
Union Navy, 300
Union pickets, 302

Union war effort, 301
United Black Christians, 282
United Church, 278, 282
United Daycare Services Project Independence, 268
United Health Group, 427
United Indoor Football League, 385
United Institutional Baptist Church, 137, 251
United Kingdom, 240, 339
United Methodist Women, 268, 270
United Nations Service Medal, 417
United State Marine Corp, 141
United States Air Force, 142, 294, 343–44, 441
United States Air Force Wilson, 341
United States Army, 125, 298, 333
United States Army in Vietnam, 477
United States Colored Troops (USCT), 299–301
United States Congress, 299
United States Department of Labor, 479
United States Department of State, 490
United States District Court, 220
United States History and Art Museum, 298
United States Marine Corps (USMC), 297
United States Military Academy, 95
United States Naval Academy, 336, 340
United States Navy, 328, 335, 339–40, 475
United States Navy B-1 Band, 328
United States Navy Chaplains' Corp, 339
United States Senate on August, 220
United States War Department, 300, 490
United Way, 273, 279, 353
University, Stanford, 355, 480
University of Alabama, 260, 475
University of Chapel Hill, 488
University of Chicago, 235
University of Chicago Press, 484
University of Cincinnati, 385, 475
University of Idaho, 292
University of Illinois Press, 481, 484
University of Iowa, 475
University of Kansas, 334
University of Kentucky, 354
University of Madrid in Spain, 95
University of Maryland, 339
University of Maryland law school, 96
University of Massachusetts, 357
University of Miami on December, 375
University of Michigan, 37
University of Minnesota, 348–49, 352
University of Minnesota and All-Pro, 351
University of North Carolina-Chapel Hill, 278
University of North-Chapel Hill, 278
University of Oklahoma, 339
University of Phoenix, 473
University of Tennessee, 388
University of Texas, 490
University of Wisconsin, 35, 109
University Press of Kansas, 480
University Women, 107
University Yearbooks Online, 494
Unsung Hero Award, 278
Unthank, 14–15
upper class, black, 41, 201
Upper Room Church in Son Tong City, 338
Urban Charter School Study Report, 480
Urban Ministry Five Year Service Award, 268
Urgent Care, 409
Ursula Robinson Brown's Funeral, 242

531

US Air Force, 331
USATF Juniors, 362
USATF National Junior Olympic Champion, 362
USATF National Junior Olympic Champion Heptathlon, 362
US charts, 240
USCT (United States Colored Troops), 299–301
USCT regiments, 301
US Department of Education study, 471
US flag, 372
Usher Board, 410
USJAG Corp, 284, 313
USMC (United States Marine Corps), 297
US Patent Office, 474
USS FLETCHER, 313, 334
USS MOUNT WHITNEY, 334
USS SPHINX, 334
USS TYHOON, 340
Utah, 89, 341, 350

V

Vacation Bible School, 216
Valued segregated schools for African American, 490
Vample, Ronald, 494
Vance Chavis- Greensboro City Council, 89
Vance Chavis Library, 89
Vance Gregory Hines, 238
Vance H. Chavis, 58, 109
Vandalia, 453, 455
Vanguard Sports Group, 354
Van Perry Quintet, 238
Varsity Baseball, 477
varsity basketball team, 352, 385, 418
    played, 370
    three-sport athlete playing, 477
Vaughan, 491
Vaughn Walls, 201
Veda, 475–76
Veda Malia, 475
Vegetable Song, 196
Venita Burwell, 212
Venture Records, 424
Verdie Wilkes, 113
Verdi's Macbeth, 237
verse, new Bible, 537
VICA (Vocational Industrial Clubs of America), 104
vice president, 113, 235–36, 286, 405, 475
Vice-President, 331, 449
vice president of academic affairs, 236
Vice President of Pro Personnel and Pro Personnel Director, 354
Vick Chemical, 271
Victor, 99–100, 306, 314
Vietnam, 65, 291, 304, 308, 310–14, 318–19, 325, 333, 477
Vietnam Adger, 304
Vietnam Airforce, 308
Vietnam Barksdale, 304
Vietnam- Bronze Star, 304
Vietnam Cheek, 306
Vietnam Corps, 305, 311, 315, 317
Vietnam Davis, 307
Vietnamese Honor Medal, 333
Vincent, 136, 321, 356–57, 476

Deborah, 106, 469
Vines, 439
Virgil Calvin, 319
Virginia, 7, 11, 15, 38, 110, 136, 225, 230, 296, 302, 466
Virginia Beach, 339
Virginia Historical Society, 466, 490
Virginia Mark, 13
Virginia Tech Hooker, 387
Virginia Tech Sports, 387
Virginia Weathers, 392
Vocational Education, 204, 493
VOCATIONAL EDUCATION classes, 139–40
Vocational Education Department, 138
Vocational Industrial Clubs, 104
Volt Records, 240
volunteer youth sports coach, 357
Vonii Bristow, 267, 492
vote, direct popular, 87
voted Best Dressed, 99
voucher programs, 467–68, 470
vouchers, 470–71, 490

W

Waddell, 313, 321, 490
    Dennis L., 30
Wadesboro, 109
Wadlington, Marlene, 68, 76
wages, high, 470, 489
Wake County, 464
Wake Forest, 355
Wake Forest University, 348, 355
Waldo, 306
Waldrum, 321
Walgreen Drug, 91
Walker, Lewis, 150
Walk/Run, 342
Wallace, George, 93
Wallace, James E., 49
Wallace Lee, 309
Walter, Robert, 315
Walter, Thomas, 317
Walter Camp Football Foundation, 379
Walter Filmore, 310
Walter Henry, 312
Walter Lee, 313
Walter Mac, 309
Walter P. U, 314
WALTER THANIEL JOHNSON, 284
War Babies, 59
Ware, James, 316
War James McHenry, 297
War Memorial Stadium, 86, 129–30, 185, 187, 226
Warmoth Thomas, Jr, 309
Warmouth, 221, 326, 475
Warmouth Gibbs, 220–21, 226
Warmouth T, 327
Warnersville, 11, 15–18, 20, 27, 35, 47–48, 430, 432, 439–40, 460–63, 480, 484
    paint, 15
Warnersville and Jonesboro, 11, 430
Warnersville and other, 16
Warnersville Community, 14, 21, 27, 45, 181, 228, 244, 273, 460–62, 477, 494–95
    old, 461

A PLACE WHERE SUCCESS WAS EXPECTED: FINAL EDITION

Warnersville Community and attended Jones Elementary School, 242
Warnersville Community Center, 189
Warnersville Community Coalition, 15, 27–28, 494–95
Warnersville Heritage & Music Festival, 462
Warnersville Methodist Episcopal, 45
Warnersville Methodist Episcopal Church, 495
Warnersville Methodist Episcopal Church North, 21
Warnersville on May, 35
Warnersville resident, 16
War of Rebellion, 490
Warren, Mildred, 13
Warren County's Randy Jordan, 152
Warren Dorsett, 140, 283, 390
Warren Dorsett-Guilford County Commissioner, 89
War Savings Stamps, 33
Washington, 89, 95, 235–36, 238, 241, 255, 277, 282, 334–35, 446–47, 479–80, 488, 490
   Booker T., 1, 431
   Dewayne, 379
   inspire, 447
Washington Elementary, 268
Washington Post, 479
Washington Redskins, 379
Washington Street Elementary, 289
Washington Street School, 3, 23, 42, 44, 48, 55, 59, 94, 107, 155, 214
   attended, 238
Washington Street site, 55
Washington Wizards, 376
Watkins Named Associate Vice Chancellor, 482
Watkins School, attended George W., 466
Watlington, 165–67, 400, 490
Watlington's tenure, 166
Watson, Christopher, 210–11
Watson Eugene, 308
Wayman, 313
Wayman Bernard, 484
WAYMAN BERNARD JOHNSON, 428
WBIG Greensboro, 238
WCP Consulting, 443
WCP Consulting & Communications, 443, 493
WCP Consulting &Communications, 490
WEAL, 428
   local radio station, 255
Wealthy Place, 339
Weathers, 249
   Barbra, 260
WEATHERS LEGETTE, 250
Weathers sang, 249
Weaver Center, 208, 457
Weaver Education Center, 275
Weeks, Kenneth J., 198
Well, Bonnie, 308
Wellness Ministry, 28
Wells, 26, 101, 212, 321, 339, 473, 482, 484
   Barbara J., 474
Wells Memorial, 248
Wells Memorial Church of God in Christ, 242, 473, 484
Wells Memorial COGIC, 26, 338–39
Wells Temple, attended, 248

Wells Temple Church of God in Christ, 244
Wells Temple Family, 248
Wells Temple/Memorial Church, attended, 262
Wells Temple/Memorial COGIC, 262
Wendell, 313, 321, 343, 345–46
Wendell Johnson, 343
Wendy's system, 445
we owe it all to Charlie, 96
Wesley, 69, 134, 307, 321–23
Wesley Long Community Hospital, 473
Westbow Press, 484
Westbrook, 322
West Charlotte, 464
Western Carolina League, 281
Western North Carolina Conference, 27
West Market Street, 255
West McCulloch Street, 15
Westmoreland, 130, 322, 402–3
   Julia, 412
   Rodney, 402
WESTMORELAND COBB, 410
West Point, 95
West Virginia State University, 333
WFMY, 286, 482
WGIV-FM, 428
Wharton, Elsie, 494
Wharton, Jesse R., 46
Whipped Peter, 299
Whirligig, 333, 495
White, Alma P., 58
White, Claudette B., 347
White, Edwin, 456
White, Erwin, 456
White, Maurice, 249
white editorialists, 33
Whitehead, Dwayne, 492
white mob, 35
White Oak Mills, 28
white parents, 8, 464
White Quakers, 93
White Rock Baptist Church, 82
Whites, Bill, 70–71
White schools, 24, 46, 56, 65
Whites Downtown, 43
Whiteside, 131, 322, 337–38
Whiteside Commanding Officer, Col Dwayne A., 487
Whiteside Courtesy Defense Video, 338
White Street Landfill, 279
Whitsett-1962, Reginald, 280
Whitt, Vincent, 143
Whitted High School, 464
Widdie, 250–51
Widdie's ministry, 250
wife Brenda Hodges, 461
Wiggins, 322
Wilberforce, 230
Wilberforce University, 51
Wild n, 265
Wilds' leadership, 169
Will, Dudley, 196
Willeena U, 307
William, Ernest, 316
William, Percy, 312
William C. U, 305
William D. U, 306
William Henry Powell, 298
William J. Furcron, 132, 486

533

WILLIAM JOSEPH N, 371
William Penn High School, 11, 47, 86, 100
William R. U, 307
Williams, Angela, 262
Williams, Herman, 131
Williams, Joseph, 292
Williams, Larry, 254
Williams, Rufus, 536
Williams, Wendy, 265
WILLIAM SLADE, 324
Williamson, Tonya, 210
William Thomas, 323
Willie Benjamin, 306
Willie Henry, 305
Willie Howard, 304
Willie James, 312
Willie Lee, 308, 310, 316
Willie Lee Harrison, 29
Willie Lobo, 419
Willie Odell, 309
Willing Workers, 537
Willow Road, 536
Wilson, Miranda, 102
Wilson, Stephanie, 493
Wilson, Stephanie Q., 341
Wilson, Susan, 102
Wilson Dale Tonkins, 413
Wilson HOD, Stephanie Q., 414
Winchester, Kathleen, 223
Wind Ensemble, 405
Windsor Community, 115
Windsor Community Center, 41, 141, 281
Windsor Publications, 481
Wingate Andrews High School in High Point, 169
Wingate University, 170
Wing's F-15E Division, 343, 346
Winsor Center Pool, 395
Winsor Community Center, 409
Winsor Community Center and Warnersville Community Center, 189
Winsor Community Center Cheerleaders, 189
Winston, Lonnie, 129, 131
Winston-Salem, 23, 34, 94, 135, 185, 464
Winston-Salem Carver, 223
Winston Salem/Forsyth County, 443
Winston-Salem Forsyth County School System, 142
Winston Salem State University, 399
Winston-Salem State University, 143
Winterhalter, Hugo, 114
Winton-Salem District, 339
Winton-Salem Forsyth County School System, 168
Wisconsin, 35, 109
Wise, Arthur, 228
woeful inequality, 467
    documented, 96
woman of the year, 445
Woman's College, 279
Woman's Indoor Track State Championship, 364
Women, Dudley, 364
Women Builders, 25, 480
Women in Cable and Telecommunications, 421
Women's Athletic Program, 360
Women's Basketball Teams, 403
Women's Caucus, 447

Women's Gym, 61
Women's Home Missionary Society, 23
Women's Office, 62
Women's Resource Center, 285
Women's Society of Christian Services, 268
Women's Sports Department, 359
Women's Step Team, 401
women's teams, 359
Wonder, Stevie, 428
Wooden, 323
Woodland Hills, 481
Woods, Carolina, 271
Woods, innovative laminated, 81
Woods, Maurice F., 49
Woods-1930, Maurice, 280
Woodson, 5, 7, 9, 11, 150, 491
    53-Soti, 150
    Charles, 380
Wood's research, 423
woodworking, 67, 104
Woody, Joel, 105
WOODY MARSHALL, 152
Woolworth, 91, 276, 279, 431, 435
Woolworth lunch, 439
Woolworth sit-ins, 97
Wooten, 433
World Geography, 164
World History, 164
World Junior Championships, 371
World Sprint Championships, 371–72
world stage, 266
World University Games, 350
World War I, 31, 33–35, 433–34
World War II, 54, 56, 59, 214, 220–21, 226, 325, 328, 415, 475, 481
World War II Victory Medal, 417
Worley, Dennis, 257
Worthington, Nicole, 213
WRAL News, 468
Wray Herring Collection, 327
Wray Rapheal, 311
Wray Rapheal Herring, 326
wrestling coach, contact Dudley's, 145
Wrestling Program, 145
wrestling team, 144, 397
Wright, 147, 183, 205, 320, 323, 491
    Jesse, 40
Wright Toshumba, 323
Writing Process, 481
WSB TV, 445
WWII, 226, 304–23
WWII Augustus, 314
WWII- B1 Navy Band, 311
WWII Briggs, 305
WWII Clarence, 315
WWII Evan Gelist, 320
WWII Franklin, 321
WWII Henry, Jr, 307
WWII James, Cpl, 307
WWII Jr, 321
WWII Lawrence, 309
WWII Martin, 314
WWII Matthew, 314
WWII Murdock, 316
WWII Staff Sgt, 319
Wynn, Margaret, 209
Wynn household, 477
Wyrtch, Kenneth, 252

A PLACE WHERE SUCCESS WAS EXPECTED: FINAL EDITION

Wyrtch's song, 200

Y

Y'all, 198
Yancey, 6
Yanceyville, 225
Yard-Dash, 361
Yardley, 350, 491
Yardley Warner, 14, 16
Yasten Burton, 269
Year Award, 136, 269, 332, 354, 375, 421
Yearbook Advisor, 119
Yearbook Committee, 405
Yearbook Dedication, 478
Yearbook Staff, 119, 401
yearly NAACP Martin Luther King Jr, 405
yellow fever, 297
YMCA, 29, 271, 375
Yost, 491
Young, Whitney M., 334
Young, Willie, 413
Young Adults, 135
Young Jabari, 267
young protégé Thurgood Marshall, 96
Yourse
    Elliot, 231
    hired, 260
Yvonne, 244–45, 248, 285
YVONNE HAYGOOD SMITH, 244
YVONNE JOHNSON, 285
Yvonne Johnson-Greensboro City
    Councilwoman, 89
YWCA Advisory Board, 279

Z

Zachariah, 312
Zack Alven, 305
Zariah Jones, 367
Zaruba, Richard, 211
Zenobia, 248
Zenobia Goldston-1949, 280
Zenobia Haygood, 69
Ziegler, Joanna, 106
Zimmerman, 67
Zimmerman Price, 494
Zion Church, 449
Zion Wesley Institute, 11

Dr. Jo Evans Lynn, Ed.D.

Author's Notes

A Place Where Success Was Expected; Final Edition is "our book." It was written to preserve and elevate our history. One of my most embarrassing moments as a teacher involved my lack of knowledge about "us." When the Committee to Save Dudley disbanded, I assigned myself to the Construction Committee. I went to the construction trailer frequently, put on a hard hat and toured the construction site during all its phases. Although I overheard the construction manager referring to me as a "pain in the @#*", he was always pleasant and patient with his explanations. When it was time to put the finishing touches on the interior design for the Drama Department, he asked me to come to the Construction Management Office in High Point and present a proposal for the "ideal drama department". While I was there to make that presentation, the Construction Manager brought out a set of Architectural Plans. He said, "Since the Drama Department will be directly behind the stage area. These original design plans might be helpful."

I looked at the name under the drawing of what was supposed to be the Main Building of Dudley High School. It said, **The High School for Negroes in Greensboro** and it was signed by David Hartmann. I thought that man was messing with me. I said, "That looks like Dudley, but the name is all wrong."

He said, "No ma'am, this is the original design. That's how all the drawings are labeled. It wasn't named James B. Dudley Senior High School until sometime after it was built. Before the high school was built on its current site, there were just a handful of Colored children going to High School at Bennett College. This was long before it was named for Mr. Dudley."

I didn't believe him. I was born in L. Richardson Hospital. My early years were spent on Crews Street, a dirt road which was right next to Bennett College. I never lived anywhere that was outside of Dudley's school district. I started first grade at Washington Street School when it was still two stories high; then I went to Lincoln Junior High School when they were adding the first Annexes to it, and I graduated from Dudley in 1967 when the Dudley Gymnasium was still considered an architectural marvel. I could not believe that something like that was true about our school, and no one had ever told me about it.

I didn't fuss with him about it. I just did my presentation and drove home and started to do some additional research. I wasn't in a hurry until something else happened. During the fight to save Dudley, I wrote the first draft for Dudley to become a historic site. I focused on the dozens of famous people who had attended Dudley, but the Preservation Society decided that the fact that David Hartmann had designed Dudley was enough to qualify it as an historic site.

Not too long after that Greensboro College purchased J.C. Price School from Guilford Technical Community College (GTCC). They planned to build a football stadium on the site. One of the members of the Committee to Save Dudley gave Mr. Meadows my phone number. He called and asked me to work on getting J. C. Price on the Register of Historic Sites. However, before I could complete the application, Greensboro College reversed course and promised to preserve J. C. Price. Four years later they reversed course again and I was asked to complete the process. Unfortunately, I was told that I could not save the school by having it placed on the Register because another school named for J. C. Price, designed by the same architect, had already been placed on the Register.

I told the man I was talking to, "That's a lie. Grimsley Senior High School which was designed by David Hartmann was placed on the National Register in 2006, three years after James B. Dudley High School which was also designed by Hartmann was placed on the Register."

A PLACE WHERE SUCCESS WAS EXPECTED: FINAL EDITION

He said, "Ma'am I hate to be the one to tell you this, but that school was totally demolished."

I said, "That's not true. Dudley's Original Main Building, Gym, and all but three of the other original buildings are still standing."

He responded, "The Application and the declaration are still online. Grimsley offered definitive proof that the other high school designed by Hartmann in Greensboro was totally demolished."

He wasn't lying. On the Grimsley application there was a copy of the article that was published in the Greensboro Daily News the morning after the School Board first voted, with the headline, "**Board Accepts Construction Committee's Recommendation to Demolish the Entire Dudley High School Campus.**" Then there were pictures of the North and South Annexes, and Cafeteria being demolished and the headline, "**Demolition of Dudley Begins**. The final picture was of the back of Dudley High School from Willow Road, looking all brand new.

In one sweep, a part of our history had been wiped out and a vital link to our past was mis formed in the minds of some people. I decided then and there that there needed to be a book with as much of our history as I could find so that no one could ever again tell our story in a way that diminished us. During my research, I found dozens of facts that were unknown to me. I was fortunate. Many of the people who lived or had relatives who had lived in earlier parts of our history were still alive. Mother Alberta Boyd gave me information about the high school at Bennett College that her sisters Beula, Lula, and Dolah were fortunate enough to attend because they were the first set of living triplets born in Rockingham County. Junita Brown not only gave me a picture of some of the earliest Dudley Majorettes, but she also practically wrote the selection about band director Warmouth T. Gibbs, Jr. David Moore lent me a scrapbook that belonged to his mother who was one of the first graduates from the school at its current site. That scrapbook contained a wealth of articles from The Panther's Claw, Dudley's first school newspaper. Numerous others like Virginia Griffin, Rufus Williams, Chapelle Morgan Davis, Eddie Favors, and Veda Patterson contributed to this Edition and to both of the previous Editions of <u>A Place Where Success Was Expected.</u> In the Second Edition and in this Final Edition, I tried to correct and further explain any areas that I was told that I had fallen short.

I know it is hard to accept information as factual when it seems to contradict long held beliefs. One year when I was teaching 10th grade World Literature at Grimsley Senior High School. I introduced the next unit of Hebrew Literature and made the first homework assignment "The Creation." The next morning a young man wearing a kippah and carrying a Bible was waiting for me outside my classroom. He said very respectfully, "Ma'am may I talk to you about last night's assignment?"

I unlocked my door. Turned on the lights and said, "Come in."

He explained, "I read the assignment, but the first selection you assigned is not Hebrew Literature. It is Christian Literature. Look here. It says that Eve was the first woman God created. That is not so. Lilith was the first woman according to the Hebrew Holy Book. Even this version of your Bible seems to acknowledge this. Then he read from Chapter 1 in Genesis from the King James Version,

> [26] And God said, let us make man in our image, after our likeness: and let **them** have dominion over the fish of the sea, and over the fowl of the air, and over the cattle, and over all the earth, and over every creeping thing that creepeth upon the earth.

27 So God created man in his own image, in the image of God created he him; male **and female created he them**.

28 And God blessed **them**, and God said unto **them**, be fruitful, and multiply, and replenish the earth, and subdue it: and have dominion over the fish of the sea, and over the fowl of the air, and over every living thing that moveth upon the earth.

When he finished reading, he said, "Do you see, the first woman Lilith was created in the first Chapter of Genesis and your Eve was not created until the second chapter of Genesis. The full story of Lilith is told in my people's holy book the Torah, but King James did not like Lilith because she would not obey Adam. King James commanded the scribes whom he had commissioned to translate the Torah into his version of the Bible not to include Lilith. I know all this because learning the Torah is the most important part of preparing for Bar mitzvah…" He went on and on until the first bell rang, but I didn't hear anything else.

I was in shock. Like most black children who grew up during the fifties, I was raised in Church-Methodist then Holiness in the Church of God in Christ. Sunday School was not an option. Sunday morning and evening services were mandatory. Tuesday Night Bible Study and YPWW (Young People are Willing Workers) were required. We also attended Summer Bible School which was sponsored by the sisters at St. Mary's. My mother was strict about each of us learning a new Bible verse to say each evening before dinner. Part of The Church of God in Christ's Statement of faith says, "We believe the Bible to be the only infallible written word of God." The very foundation of my faith was shaken- somethings you just know that you know. After I confirmed that what the young man said was true, I convinced myself that I would focus only on the New Testament of the Bible. It wasn't until I was going through a particularly difficult time in my life that God put the 121: Psalm before me:

1 I will lift up mine eyes unto the hills, from whence cometh my help.2 My help cometh from the LORD, which made heaven and earth. 3 He will not suffer thy foot to be moved: he that keepeth thee will not slumber. 4 Behold, he that keepeth Israel shall neither slumber nor sleep. 5 The LORD is thy keeper: the LORD is thy shade upon thy right hand. 6 The sun shall not smite thee by day, nor the moon by night. 7 The LORD shall preserve thee from all evil: he shall preserve thy soul. 8 The LORD shall preserve thy going out and thy coming in from this time forth, and even for evermore. This song bathed my spirit and lifted me up through one of the hardest times of my life.

I know that asking you to read <u>A Place Where Success Was Expected: Final Edition</u> with an open mind and heart is asking a lot. I have been told that plans are already under way to celebrate Dudley's so-called 100th Anniversary. You can still celebrate the 100th Year since the school was named James Benson Dudley High School but remember that we must acknowledge the 44 years before that when **The High School for Negroes in Greensboro** existed as the first public high school with Negro students whose tuition was paid for by the Greensboro City Council. It is fully documented that in 1879 the Greensboro City Council agreed to pay for Negro students who lived inside the city limits to attend school beyond the 8th grade at the new High School Department at Bennett Seminary.

The sign in front of Grimsley Senior High School says that the school was founded in 1899 when the City Council agreed to buy the High School Department from St. Agnes Catholic Church; although the current Main Building was built in 1928 and completed in 1929 just like Dudley. Greensboro Senior High School was not named Grimsley Senior High School until 1963. The sign in front of James Benson Dudley High School should read, Founded in 1879.

Made in the USA
Middletown, DE
28 June 2024